D1737082

The Political Writings
of John Adams

CONSERVATIVE LEADERSHIP SERIES

EAGLE PUBLISHING, INC.

EAGLE BOOK CLUBS, INC.

REGNERY PUBLISHING, INC.

The Conservative Leadership Series is a joint project of Regnery Publishing, Inc. and Eagle Book Clubs, Inc., divisions of Eagle Publishing, Inc., to make the classics of conservative thought available in hardcover collectors' editions.

The Political Writings
of John Adams

Edited with an Introduction by George W. Carey

REGNERY
PUBLISHING, INC.

An Eagle Publishing Company • Washington D.C.

ISBN 0-89526-292-4

Published in the United States by
Regnery Publishing, Inc.
An Eagle Publishing Company
One Massachusetts Avenue, NW
Washington, DC 20001

Distributed to the trade by
National Book Network
4720-A Boston Way
Lanham, MD 20706

Printed on acid-free paper
Manufactured in the United States of America

10 9 8 7 6 5 4 3 2 1

Books are available in quantity for promotional or premium use. Write to Director of Special Sales, Regnery Publishing, Inc., One Massachusetts Avenue, NW, Washington, DC 20001, for information on discounts and terms or call (202) 216-0600.

Contents

Introduction

GEORGE W. CAREY

Two centuries after he retired from public life, John Adams's place in our history still seems unsettled. He stands, in this regard, in sharp contrast to acknowledged giants of the founding era. George Washington, the "father" of our country, the most respected and revered individual of that era, now enjoys legendary status for his exploits and sacrifices on behalf of his country; Thomas Jefferson, despite the controversies that have surrounded his beliefs and way of life, occupies a very special place in our hearts as the author of the Declaration of Independence; James Madison, at best a mediocre president, is honored as "father" of the Constitution and the Bill of Rights; and Alexander Hamilton, despite a bad press over the decades, is nevertheless held in high regard for his efforts to secure a stronger union.

Adams, by contrast, suffers to a considerable extent the fate of important but lesser known individuals of the founding era; namely, there is no single contribution, episode, or position with which he can be readily identified that captures the public mind, one that would distinguish him and secure him an undisputed place among the front ranks of the founders. While an important figure during virtually the entire founding period, he never occupied center stage. For instance, no one can deny that he did as much, if not more, than any other individual through his persistent efforts in the Continental Congresses from 1774 through 1776 to bring about the separation of the colonies from Great Britain. He was, as more than one delegate dubbed him, the "Atlas" of independence, having served as a member of some ninety Congressional committees and chairman of twenty-five during his tenure. Yet he was not the principal author of the Declaration of Independence, a document, many claim, that expresses the sentiments of the Revolutionary era and also provides the core principles of our "civil theology." In fact, as a member of the drafting committee, Adams urged that Jefferson be its principal author, not realizing the enormous significance that would later be attached to it. Likewise, at one point, Adams was appointed the sole Commissioner to negotiate the terms of peace with Great Britain. As Fate would have it, however, he ended up having to share credit for the Treaty of Paris (1783) with Benjamin Franklin and John Jay. Again, although Adams had set forth his views on the nature and ends of government, as well as its proper institutions and functions, far more extensively than any American up to that point in our history—in fact, he was the principal drafter of the widely admired Massachusetts Constitution of 1780—he could not attend the Constitutional Convention, where he might well have become a dominant voice. At the time, he was attending to American interests as Minister to the Court of St. James. Or again, he was not our first president, but our second. Worse still, his Presidency stands in the shadows of the giants who preceded and followed him.

Adams would not be surprised at the murkiness that surrounds his place in our tradition. On more than one occasion he contemplated how future generations might look upon him, especially how they would compare him with his contemporaries, principally Washington and Franklin. And he was invariably pessimistic. He writes to Benjamin Rush that he agrees with the assessment of William Cabbott, "There never was a greater difference between two men than between Washington and Adams in one point, the desire of fame. Washington had an enormous, an insatiable thirst for it; but Adams was as excessively careless of it." Noting that this assessment was not intended as a "compliment," Adams continues, "I am very sensible that I have been negligent of it to a fault, and a very great fault, too." He acknowledges that there were "very many times" when he was "so agitated" that he gave "no consideration at all" to how his "words, actions, and even writings would be considered by others." "Indeed," he continues, "I never could bring myself seriously to consider that I was a great man or of much importance or consideration in the world. The few traces that remain of me must, I believe, go down to posterity in much confusion and distraction, as my life has been passed."[1]

This should not be taken to mean that Adams did not seek or desire fame. On the contrary, his concern over his reputation and how he would be regarded by posterity is evident from his letters at virtually every stage of his adult life. In 1759, for instance, at the outset of his legal career, he writes in his diary: "Reputation ought to be the perpetual subject of my thoughts, and aim of my behavior." He wonders how he should go about gaining "a reputation" and spreading "an opinion of myself as a lawyer of distinguished genius, learning, and virtue." He might cultivate friendships, "make frequent visits in the neighborhood, and converse familiarly with men, women, and children, in their own style, on the common tittle-tattle of the town and the ordinary concerns of a family." But this he felt would be a "lingering method" that would "require more art, and address, and patience, too, than I am master of." Or "Shall I," he asks, "by making remarks and proposing questions to the lawyers at the bar, endeavor to get a great character for understanding and learning with them?" This approach he deems "slow and tedious" and most probably "ineffectual," if only because "envy, jealousy, and self-interest, will not suffer them to give a young fellow a free, generous character, especially me." Still another alternative he envisions is seeking "a cause to speak to," to "take one bold determined leap into the midst of fame, case, and business." In his mind, the choice came down to "a bold push, a resolute attempt, a determined enterprise, or a slow, silent, imperceptible creeping." In other words, he asks, "shall I creep or fly?"[2]

In another letter to Rush in 1811, more than a decade after losing the presidency to Jefferson, Adams presents a gloomy view of how future generations will look upon his contributions and place in the American

[1] Letter to Benjamin Rush, July 26, 1806, John A. Shutz and Douglass Adair, *The Spur of Fame: Dialogues of John Adams and Benjamin Rush, 1805-1813* (San Marino, California: The Huntington Library, 1966), 60-1.

[2] *Diary, Works,* II, March 14, 1759, 63.

tradition. On this occasion, he took exception with Rush's opinion that "The sensibility of the public mind" would produce a highly favorable assessment of his career and service. To this Adams responds: "By the treatment I have received and continue to receive I should expect that a large majority of all parties would cordially rejoice to hear that my head was laid low." He remarks that "Washington and Franklin could never do anything but what was imputed to pure disinterested patriotism. I never could do anything but what was ascribed to sinister motives." In a humorous vein, he writes, "If I should inculcate fidelity to the marriage bed, it would be said that it proceeded from resentment to General Hamilton and a malicious desire to hold up to posterity his libertinism." "Others," he continues, "would say that it is only a vainglorious ostentation of my own continence."[3]

Adams's pessimism on this score is somewhat exaggerated, but not entirely without foundation. To understand the grounds for his pessimism, however, requires some explanation because so much of what he did and wrote, particularly his writings prior to independence, only redounded to his credit.

It would seem, to recur to his youthful thoughts on reputation, that he chose to "fly" by taking up the cause of independence. In this endeavor, there can be no question that he expressed views that were either controversial when they first appeared or often out of step with the prevailing opinions. Nevertheless, it is now clear, he was leading a cause whose time had come, and so, within a relatively short period, his views became less and less controversial and more mainstream. As a consequence his status as a leader in the struggle for independence grew enormously.

Consider his "Dissertation on the Canon and Feudal Law" (1765), his first substantial venture into political writing. In this work, Adams endeavors to provide a unique overview of America's place in history and the ideals that inspired its settlers. He portrays an America uncontaminated by the canon and feudal laws, in his view the two major sources of tyranny that had perpetuated ignorance and supported tyranny during the Middle Ages.

[3] Letter to Benjamin Rush, August 28, 1811, *Spur of Fame,* 192.

A notable aspect of this work is its implicit call for Americans to think again about the sources of their liberties. Rather than being grants from the crown or parliament, as commonly believed, these liberties, he insists, derived "from remote antiquity" so that even "the foundations of British laws and government" are to be discovered "in the frame of human nature, in the constitution of the intellectual and moral world."[4] In these terms, Britain, which had advanced far in overcoming the legacy of the feudal and canon laws, was still less pure, so to speak, than America, whose early settlers, totally liberated from the pernicious influences of these laws, understood the true foundations of these cherished liberties. Thus, he holds Americans are being called upon to defend the traditional rights and liberties that are part of the uniquely American heritage, a theme that he emphasizes during the struggle for independence. In his "Dissertation," he also took the opportunity to place contemporary events into his broader perspective and framework. The Stamp Act, for instance, he viewed as part of a grander effort to impose feudalism on America by depriving the American people "in a great measure of the means of knowledge, by loading the press, the colleges, and even an almanack and a newspaper, with restraints and duties...by taking from the poorer sort of people all their little subsistence, and conferring it on a set of stamp officers, distributors, and their deputies."[5]

In many ways, the "Dissertation" made the case for independence well before most colonists were willing to embrace the cause. Yet, while the validity of Adams's thesis has been seriously questioned on a variety of grounds over the decades, his reputation hardly suffered from its publication. On the contrary, it served to establish his credentials as a spokesman for the colonists and later for the cause of separation from Great Britain. In fact, under the title "True Sentiments of America," it was republished in the *London Chronicle* in 1768.

His other major work written before independence was formally declared, *Novanglus*, also advances a bold thesis. *Novanglus* was originally a

---

[4] "Dissertation," *Works,* III, 463.
[5] "Dissertation," 464.

series of articles that appeared between December 1774 and April 1775 in
the *Boston Gazette* answering "Massachusettensis" (Daniel Leonard) who,
in another series of articles, set forth the argument for Parliamentary
supremacy over the colonies. For his part, Adams advanced the position
that "our provincial legislatures are the only supreme authorities in our
colonies." Whereas "Parliament," for its part, "may be allowed an authority supreme and sovereign over the ocean," this authority may be "limited by the banks of the ocean, or the bounds of our charters."[6] Adams
did acknowledge that the colonies owed an allegiance to the King and
that "the colonies ever have been, and will be, ready and willing to concede" to Parliament the authority to regulate trade. But he was unwilling
to make any further concessions: "What religious, moral, or political obligations... are we under," he asks, "to submit to parliament as a supreme
legislative?" His answer: "None at all."[7]

A key element in Adams's argument centers on a theme that echoed
throughout the colonies: Parliament cannot exercise supremacy over the
colonial legislatures consistent with "reason, justice, policy, morality, or
humanity, without the consent of the colonies on some new plan of connection." Consent of the people through representation plays a crucial role
in this line of argument. "There are," he insists, "but two sorts of men in
the world, freemen and slaves." Freemen, he points out, are not bound by
laws to which they have not given their consent. Consequently, he reasons,
lacking the means of "giving or withholding their consent to the acts
of... parliament," Americans are but slaves. On his showing, the "unlimited subjugation of three millions of people... at three thousand miles distance" to Parliament—no matter how wise, "virtuous" and "pure" the
members of that Parliament might be—constitutes "real slavery."[8]

The formidable arguments advanced by Adams were not entirely new
or unheard of prior to their publication. In fact, James Wilson in August
1774 had published "Considerations on the Nature and Extent of the
Legislative Authority of the British Parliament." Though Wilson's pre-

---

[6] *Novanglus, Works,* IV, 105.

[7] *Novanglus,* 38.

[8] *Novanglus,* 28.

sentation differed from Adams's in many ways, it still covered much the same ground as *Novanglus* and came to essentially the same conclusion regarding the status of the colonies which anticipated the relationships that would later characterize the British Commonwealth. This conclusion—though perhaps a bit daring at the time of its airing—far from detracting from Adams's stature, eventually came to be widely accepted as an essential part of the colonists' case for independence.

Nor, can it be said, that Adams's reputation suffered from his authorship of the "Instructions of the Town of Braintree to Their Representative" (1765) that sets forth the reasons for the constituents' opposition to the Stamp Act and thoroughly condemns "the alarming extension of the powers of courts of admiralty" that it authorizes. Taking a position somewhat different from that articulated toward the end of his "Dissertation," the "Instructions" declare the Stamp Act to be "unconstitutional," "inconsistent with the common law" and contrary to the "grand and fundamental principle of the constitution, that no freeman should be subject to any tax to which he has not given his own consent." They reject the notion that the colonists are "subject to any tax imposed by the British Parliament" on grounds that they "are not represented in that assembly in any sense, unless it be by a fiction of law," a proposition fully developed in *Novanglus*. In turn, they assail the powers granted to the Admiralty Courts because only one judge presides, without jury and without regard to the "laws of the land" or the "due process" provided by the "Great Charter."[9]

Perhaps the one episode that provides Adams with a special niche among our founders was his defense of Captain Preston and the British soldiers involved in the "Boston Massacre" (1770). These soldiers, fearing for their safety, had fired on an rioting mob protesting the Townshend Acts, mortally wounding five. As he records in his *Autobiography*, Adams (with Josiah Quincy) took on their defense in part because he believed that the incident might have been "intentionally wrought up by designing men, who knew that they were aiming at better than the instruments employed." The

---

[9] "Instructions," *Works*, III, 466-67.

soldiers, he believed, should be punished for the illegal conduct, but if they acted in "self-defense," they "must be acquitted." "To depend upon the perversion of law," he wrote, "and the corruption or partiality of juries, would insensibly disgrace the jurisprudence of the country and corrupt the morals of the people." At another level, Adams readily accepted their defense because he felt "that counsel ought to be the very last thing that an accused person should want in a free country; the bar ought... to be independent and impartial, at all times and in every circumstance, and that persons whose lives were at stake ought to have the counsel they preferred." But, he added, the accused "must... expect from me no art or address, no sophistry or prevarication, in such a cause, nor any thing more than fact, evidence, and law would justify."[10] Captain Preston and six of his men were acquitted; two were found guilty of manslaughter and dismissed after their thumbs were branded.

Throughout his life Adams maintained that his reputation suffered because of his role in this trial. Typical is a letter to James Lloyd in 1815, where, in touching upon the "trial of Captain Preston and his soldiers," he writes, "To this hour my conduct in it is remembered, and is alleged against me to prove that I am an enemy to my country, and always have been."[11] But the facts belie his assessment. Shortly after the trial, he was elected by a large majority at a Boston town hall meeting as a representative to the General Court. This election was the more remarkable in light of Adams's observation in his *Autobiography*, "I had never been at a Boston town meeting, and was not at this, until messengers were sent to me to inform me that I was elected."[12] In any event, there is scant evidence to confirm his opinion of the consequences of his role in this affairs and a good deal to suggest otherwise, e.g., his subsequent election to the First and Second Continental Congresses, where he was named chairman of its "Board war and ordnances," the most important and active committee within the Congress. It is safe to say that, far from diminishing Adams's stature with future generations, his defending Captain Preston and his men

[10] *Diary, Works,* II, 230-31.
[11] Letter to James Lloyd, April 24, 1815, *Works,* X, 162.
[12] *Diary, Works,* II, 232.

is universally regarded as exemplary, as championing the rule of law in the most trying circumstances for principled reasons.

Perhaps less heralded by subsequent generations is Adams's service on behalf of the United States in the diplomatic arena been 1778 and 1788. This service was undertaken at great personal sacrifice, not the least being separation from his wife, Abigail, during the better part of this decade.

His first assignment was commissioner to France in 1778, where he would join Benjamin Franklin and Arthur Lee. This brief undertaking involved a good deal of unpleasantness. Soon after he settled in, Adams noted in his *Diary* that the "public business had never been methodically conducted. There never was, before I came, a minute-book, a letter-book, or an account-book.... It was utterly impossible to acquire any clear idea of our affairs." He also discovered financial irregularities. Then, as if to provide some explanation for this state of affairs, he remarks, "Invitations were sent to Dr. Franklin and me, every day in the week, to dine in some great or small company. I determined on my part, to decline as many as I could... and attend to my studies of French, and the examination and execution of that public business which suffered for want of attention."[13] Adams, perhaps because he was almost completely overshadowed by Franklin, wrote to Samuel Adams that the system of diplomatic representation should be overhauled; that there was no need for three commissioners when one minister plenipotentiary would suffice. But when the Congress in September 1778, actually followed his advice by naming Franklin minister plenipotentiary, it failed to specify what Adams's new position would be. Feeling slighted, and without waiting for further instructions, he booked passage on the first America-bound vessel. He arrived in Massachusetts in time to play the major role in drafting its Constitution of 1780.

Adams's second diplomatic tour begins with his appointment as minister plenipotentiary for peace treaty negotiations with Great Britain in 1779, a mission which required that he return to Paris. Initially, he had little to do in this capacity, since the British were unwilling to enter into peace negotiations at this point. He did undertake, however, to defend

[13] *Diary,* April 21, 1778, *Works,* III, 143.

American positions and interests in a manner to cause such serious friction between him and Count de Vergennes, the French minister of state for foreign affairs, that he was in danger of being recalled. As it was, his discretionary authority in the peace negotiations was severely circumscribed by the Congress. As a further rebuke, Congress appointed four additional peace commissioners to serve with Adams, though only two of those appointed, Jay and Franklin, actually participated in the negotiations. Adams's actions, which led to this state of affairs, stemmed from his belief that the interests of the United States and France were not identical; that too often French interests were given priority for fear of losing French support, while forgetting that even more important French priorities were being advanced through its support of the American cause. In any event, both in his exchanges with Vergennes and in his capacity as commissioner in negotiating the peace treaty, Adams gained a grudging respect for his efforts to protect and advance American interests.

With the peace process in limbo and to avoid further troubles in Paris, Adams turned his attention to Holland in order to secure both recognition and much needed loans for the American war effort. He soon realized that he had undertaken a difficult mission largely because Holland wanted to maintain neutrality between England and France. But when England declared war on Holland, his prospects improved markedly. Moreover, his strategy of appealing over the heads of the officialdom at The Hague to the people and to the constituencies of the central legislative body, the States-General, worked well. Recognition of the United States came in 1782. Soon thereafter Holland's major financial centers extended loans to the United States and a treaty of commerce was concluded. Charles Francis Adams puts the mission of his grandfather into the following perspective: "although this event, if measured by its consequences, may not claim in itself so important a place in history as some others in which he took a decisive part, yet, as being the most exclusively the result of his own labors, it well merits to be ranking, in the way he ranked it, as *the greatest triumph of his life.*"[14]

---

[14] *The Life of John Adams, Works,* I, 353.

In late 1782 Adams returned to Paris to take his place on the commission to negotiate a treaty of peace with Great Britain. Negotiations were already far along when he joined Franklin and Jay in this undertaking, and the issues separating the two sides had come down to three: fixing the northern boundary of the United States, indemnity for the Tories whose properties had been confiscated during the war, and fishing rights. The boundary differences were settled without difficulty. Adams's position on indemnity is presented in his diary in his forceful response to the British contention that their "national honor" was at stake on this issue. "If a nation thought itself bound in honor to compensate these people," he contended, "it might easily do it, for it cost the nation more money to carry on the war one month, than it would cost to compensate them all." Moreover, he "could not comprehend this doctrine of national honor; those people, by their misrepresentations, had deceived the nation who had followed the impulsion of their devouring ambition until it had brought an indelible stain on the British name."[15] Because the fishery rights was an issue of particular interest to New England, Adams took the lead in successfully removing restrictions that the British had initially insisted upon.

Soon after negotiations on the peace treaty were successfully concluded, Adams, Jay, and Franklin were all commissioned to negotiate a commercial treaty with Great Britain. Given Great Britain's unwillingness even to enter into negotiations on this matter, this appointment provided Adams with free time. He took this opportunity to visit England for the first time and to renew his contacts at The Hague. He was soon joined by his wife Abigail. They settled down in a country house near Paris where he continued his work as a member of a new commission, this time with Franklin and Jefferson, empowered to negotiate commercial treaties with all the European powers. On 5 May 1785, he received word that he had been appointed minister to the Court of St. James.

His tour at the Court of St. James passed without any progress on key matters, the most notable of these being movement toward a commercial

[15] *Diary,* November 10, 1782, *Works,* III, 309.

treaty. His major accomplishment during this period was the completion of *Defence of the Constitutions of Government of the United States*, a massive and far ranging three-volume work originally undertaken to answer M. Turgot's advocacy of unicameralism and his attacks on the institutions and processes of the state governments in the United States. This work and *Discourses on Davila*—published originally in 1791 as a series of essays when he was vice president and which he considered to be the fourth volume of *Defence*—comprise Adams's major writings in political theory. Although both works consist mainly of extensive quotations from a variety of authors and works in history and political science, his views on many of the most critical and perennial issues of political philosophy are clear from his selection of materials and sporadic commentary.

Not long after his return from England in 1788, Adams was elected as Washington's vice-president under the new Constitution. At this point he became an active participant in the political process and his writings, principally the *Defence* and *Discourses*, constituted a "paper trail" that would provide his political opponents with the ammunition for damaging attacks on his conduct and motivations. His early efforts as president of the Senate to prescribe titles for office holders and his view that the president of the United States should have trappings not unlike those of a monarch, only served to confirm the suspicions of his political opponents that he was no friend of republican government; that he harbored a secret desire to change the constitutional system to conform as closely as possible to the British, which he was known to admire for its "balance." His essays on Davila appeared in John Fenno's *Gazette of the United States* and only confirmed these suspicions for those inclined to believe. In these essays, Adams argues that the French Revolution is doomed to fail if only because its underlying egalitarianism precludes "balanced" government. Toward the end of the *Discourses*, he counsels: "Instead of throwing false imputation on republican governments; instead of exciting or fomenting a vulgar malignity against the most respectable men and families, let us draw the proper inferences from history and experience; let us lay it down for a certain fact, first, that emulation between individuals, and rivalries among families never can be prevented. Second, let us adopt it as a certain principle, that they ought not to be prevented, but directed to virtue, and then stimulated and encouraged by generous applause and honorable rewards.""And from these premises," he continues, "let the conclusion be, that an effectual control be provided in the constitution, to check their excesses and balance their weights."[16] Passages such as this, universal in their scope, were not unreasonably read as an endorsement of the British government and as pointing to deficiencies in the existing Constitution. In the final essay of the series, an essay not reproduced in the collected volume of the *Discourses*, Adams maintains that the only reason men opt to live under hereditary monarchs is because "they had almost unanimously been convinced that hereditary succession was attended with fewer evils that frequent elections."[17] This statement then was taken by his political opposition to reveal his preference for an hereditary monarchy over a republic; not an unreasonable supposition given other passages in *Discourses* that point to the unsettling effects of elections. In writing of "elective governments," for example, he points to their progressive deterioration when "there are rivals for the first place": first come "slanders and libels," followed by "mobs and seditions," culminating in "civil war, with all her hissing snakes, burning torches, and haggard horrors at last."[18]

Adams's views on human motivation, the main principles of which are set forth in the first part of the *Discourses*, provide the background for understanding these conclusions. The most "essential and remarkable" among men's passions, he believed, was the "*passion for distinction*," which he defines as "a desire to be observed, considered, esteemed, praised, beloved, and admired by his fellows."[19] This passion, "furnished" by "nature" and inherent to men, he points out, may take many paths, e.g., "properly called *Emulation*" when "it is a desire to excel another, by fair industry in the search of truth, and the practice of virtue," or "*Ambition*" when "power" is sought "as a means of distinction."[20] Indeed, he main-

[16] *Discourses, Works,* VI, 398.
[17] *Gazette of the United States* (Philadelphia), April 27, 1791, 829.
[18] *Discourses, Works,* VI, 455-56.
[19] *Discourses,* 232.
[20] *Discourses,* 233.

tains that this passion for distinction, in all its ramifications, "is a principal source of the virtues and vice, the happiness and misery of human life; and the history of mankind is little more than a simple narration of its operations and effects." Borrowing from Adam Smith, he sees this rather egoistic passion as vital to the life and preservation of society; as a force actually holding society together. "Nature has ordained it," he contends, "as a constant incentive to activity and industry, that, to acquire the attention and complacency, the approbation and admiration of their fellows, men might be urged to constant exertions of beneficence." Even those, he continues, "who have the least of reason, virtue, or benevolence, are chained down to an incessant servitude to their follow creatures; laboring... to produce something which shall contribute to the comfort, convenience, pleasure, profit, or utility of some or other of the species." Thus, he concludes, men "are really thus constituted by their own vanity, slaves to mankind."[21]

He was acutely aware of the fact that it is the passion for distinction that motivates the vast majority of men, not the pursuit of a higher or virtuous end for its own rewards. For instance, he remarks that "A sense of duty; a love of truth; a desire to alleviate the anxieties of ignorance, may, no doubt, have an influence on some minds. But the universal object and idol of men of letters is *reputation*. It is the *notoriety*, the *celebration*, which constitute the charm that is to compensate the loss of appetite and sleep, and sometimes of riches and honors."[22] In this context, then, it is important that worthy goals are served by those seeking distinction in various fields of endeavor; that their passions "should be gratified, encouraged, and arranged on the side of virtue."[23] The essence of "the theory of education" and "the science of government," he goes so far to say, is "comprehended in the knowledge of the means of actively conducting, controlling, and regulating the emulation and ambition of the citizens."[24] And this, to return to his specific proposals, would embrace conferring titles that would serve as incentives and rewards to attract qualified individuals, and

[21] *Discourses*, 245.
[22] *Discourses*, 240.
[23] *Discourses*, 246.
[24] *Discourses*, 248.

avoiding electoral competition that would arouse and even encourage recourse to the base passions.

Discourses can perhaps best be viewed as one of the initial salvos in a political war marked by an unusually high degree of intensity that divided the political elite into two camps each holding fundamentally different views of the French Revolution and, most importantly, the assumptions and values it embodied. This division grew in intensity and aspects of it, particularly in the foreign policy area (e.g., over Washington's Proclamation of Neutrality), dominated the political landscape during the better part of Washington's tenure. Moreover, this division and the complex of issues surrounding it, which also embraced our relationship with Great Britain, hasten the growth of political parties.

By all accounts, our relationship to France was the central issue during Adams's term as president. After the French revolutionary government refused to accept General Pinckney as minister plenipotentiary, this relationship was strained. But when the full details of the "X,Y, Z affair" were revealed—i.e., the extortionist demands placed upon the newly appointed American ministers to France as a precondition for negotiations between the two countries—war between the two countries seemed imminent. Adams, however, refused to yield to those elements of the Federalist party that favored hostilities, and through his persistence finally succeeded in restoring diplomatic relations between the two nations. Adams's posture on this matter, his desire to avoid a war with France, even to the extent of enduring humiliation, was clearly a major factor in causing further divisions in the ranks of the Federalists. At the same time, this policy of accommodation toward France did belie the picture painted of him by his Republican antagonists.

In 1798, at the height of the difficulties with France, which was also accompanied by domestic unrest largely fomented by French agents and their Republican sympathizers, Congress passed the Alien and Sedition Acts. There were two Alien Acts, one which extended the period of residency for citizenship; the other, never employed, authorizing the president to deport aliens who might endanger the safety of the country. The most controversial measure was the Sedition Act, which applied to both aliens and citizens. Specifically, section two of the act made it unlawful for individuals to "defame the government" or bring the Congress or the president into "contempt or disrepute, or to excite against them" through "false, scandalous and malicious writing" or utterances. The act provided for its own expiration on March 3, 1801.[25]

The passage of the Sedition Act is considered by many modern historians to be an indelible black mark on the Adams administration primarily because, in their view, it constituted an unconstitutional abridgment of the first amendment free speech and press provisions and represented a calculated effort on the part of the Adams administration to silence its political opposition. The arguments set forth by Jefferson and his Republican allies likewise asserted the unconstitutionality of the act on grounds that it violated the tenth amendment; that the national government, in attempting to regulate speech and press, had encroached on the exclusive domain of the States. Curiously, in this controversy, criticism of Jefferson for setting forth a doctrine of nullification in the Kentucky Resolution protesting the Alien and Sedition Acts—a doctrine which, if sanctioned, would soon lead to the disintegration of the Union—is muted, at least when compared with the condemnations of Adams.

It is true, as some sympathetic biographers have pointed out (in an apparent effort to distance Adams from this measure) that he did not initiate it. But it is also true that he signed the measure into law and that it enjoyed his support. In light of this, and given as well Adams's concern about liberty over the decades, the summary and excessively harsh judgment of Adams by modern historians on this issue reveals an ideological bias that has contributed mightily to the ambiguous image we have of him today. What is seldom pointed out is that neither Adams nor the Federalists, including John Marshall, believed the Sedition Act unconstitutional. And they had good reason for their position: the Act liberalized the existing common law procedures relating to seditious speech or writing that prevailed all of the States. Specifically, section three of the act, unlike the common law, allowed the defendant "upon the trial of the cause, to give in

[25] The Sedition Act, July 14, 1798, *U.S. Statutes at Large,* Volume I, 596–97.

evidence in his defense, the truth of the matter contained in the publication charged as a libel." It also provided, again in contrast to the common
law, that "the jury who shall try the cause, shall have a right to determine
the law and the fact, under the direction of the court, as in other cases."[26]

Equally important, Adams and the Federalists did have legitimate concerns about the stability of the new republic, not even ten years old. For all
intents and purposes, the nation was in a *de facto* war with France, inflamed
by thousands of French agents in the country agitating against the policies
of the government. Moreover, Adams had come to believe that these
agents and their followers were preparing to offer armed resistance to the
government. In May 1798, two months prior to the passage of the Sedition Act, he publicly reveals this concern: "I take freedom to say that this
country never appeared to me to be in greater danger than at this
moment, from within and without."[27] Some years later, in an exchange
of views on "the terrorism of a former day," he takes the opportunity to
upbraid Jefferson. "I believe," he wrote, "you never felt the terrorism of
Mr. Gallatin's insurrection in Pennsylvania....You certainly never felt the
terrorism excited by Mr. Genet, in 1793, when ten thousand people in the
streets of Philadelphia, day after day, threatened to drag Washington out
of his house, and effect a revolution in the government, or compel it to
declare war in favor of the French Revolution and against England." He
remarks that even "[t]he coolest and firmest minds, even among the
Quakers in Philadelphia, have given their opinions to me, that nothing but
the yellow fever... could have saved the United States from a fatal revolution of government." Beginning on a satirical note, he recounts his personal experiences with terrorism: "I have no doubt you were fast asleep, in
philosophical tranquillity, when ten thousand people, and, perhaps, many
more, were parading the streets of Philadelphia on the evening of my
Fast Day; when even Governor Mifflin himself thought it his duty to
order a patrol of horse and foot to preserve the peace; when Market Street
was as full as men could stand by one another, and, even before my door;

[26] The Sedition Act, 597.
[27] "To the Young Men of Boston, Massachusetts," May 22, 1798, *Works*, IX, 194.

when some of my domestics, in frenzy, determined to sacrifice their lives in my defense, when all were ready to make a desperate sally among the multitude, and others were, without difficulty and danger, dragged back by the rest; when I, myself, judged it prudent and necessary to order chests of arms from the war-office to be brought through by-lanes and back-doors, determined to defend my house at the expense of my life and the lives of the few, very few domestics and friends within it. What think you of terrorism, Mr. Jefferson?"[28]

Finally, it would be difficult to argue that the Sedition Act was used to silence opposition to the administration. During its life twenty-five individuals were indicted; fifteen were convicted.

The summary negative judgment of most historians toward Adams's connection with the Alien and Sedition Acts is noteworthy because the ideological biases that inform this judgment are overt, obvious to those with some familiarity of the era and the constitutional issues in question. What is not so obvious is that these same biases also preclude an even-handed assessment of Adams's place in the American tradition. In an important sense, Adams was aware of this. Writing to Jefferson in 1813, he remarks: "In Truth my 'defense of the Constitutions' and 'Discourses on Davila' laid the foundation of that immense Unpopula[ri]ty, which fell like the Tower of Siloam upon me." And he attributes Jefferson's "Unbounded Popularity" to his "steady defense of democratical Principles" and "invariable favourable Opinion of the french Revolution."[29] Adams, to put this matter otherwise, was never a friend of the French Revolution, and he was well aware that his hostility toward it, as well as towards its goals and underlying assumptions, put him on the "wrong" side of public opinion during his political career. By the same token, for historians of modern times, Adams is an interesting "reactionary" or "eccentric" who fought a valiant, but losing, battle against the Enlightenment postulates and ideals that are the essence of progressivism or modern-day liberalism.

---

[28] Letter to Thomas Jefferson, June 20, 1813, *Works*, X, 47-8.

[29] Letter to Thomas Jefferson, July 13, 1813, Lester J. Cappon (ed.), *The Adams-Jefferson Letters* (Chapel Hill: University of North Carolina Press, 1959), II, 356.

Yet, Adams was right about the French Revolution. And, after his retirement, he is not at all reluctant to crow, so to speak, by pointing out that his estimate of the Revolution and its outcome was essentially correct, that history had vindicated his judgment. He writes to Rush in 1811 that he and Jefferson "differed in opinion about the French Revolution"; Jefferson regarding it as "wise and good, and that it would end in the establishment of a free republic." But, he continues, "I saw through it, to the end of it, before it broke out, and was sure it could end only in a restoration of the Bourbons, or a military despotism, after deluging France and Europe in blood." Then, noting that Rush also supported the French Revolution, he adds, "I might suspect you both [Rush and Jefferson] to sacrifice a little to the infernal gods, and perhaps unconsciously to suffer your judgments to be a little swayed by a love of popularity and possibly by a little spice of ambition."[30] Once he resumes correspondence with Jefferson, he continues in this vein. He notes that while Jefferson was "well persuaded" that the French would end up with "a free Republican Government," his firm view was "that a project of such a Government, over five and twenty millions people, when four and twenty millions and five hundred thousand of them could neither write nor read: was as unnatural irrational and impracticable; as it would be over the Elephants Lions Tigers Panthers Wolves and Bears in the Royal Menagerie, at Versailles. Napoleon has lately invented a Word, which perfectly expresses my Opinion at that time and ever since. He calls the Project Ideology." In his next letter to Jefferson, he asks, "very seriously," "Where are now in 1813, the Perfection and perfectability of human Nature? Where is now, the progress of the human Mind? Where is the Amelioration of Society? Where the Augmentations of human Comforts? Where the diminution of human Pains and Miseries?"[31]

The basic reason, though, that Adams has been judged somewhat harshly by modern historians is not due primarily to his prescience with regard to the outcome of the French Revolution, but rather that his polit-

[30] Letter to Benjamin Rush, December 25, 1811, *Spur of Fame,* 201.
[31] Letter to Thomas Jefferson, July 13, 1813, *Adams-Jefferson Letters,* 358.

ical theory, the main outlines of which were evident well before the
French Revolution, thoroughly rejects the major assumptions, principles,
and goals that fueled that revolution. To begin with, throughout his life
he maintained the same understanding of equality that he conveyed to
John Taylor: "That all men are born to equal rights is true. Every being has
a right to his own, as clear, as moral, as sacred, as any other being has. This
is as indubitable as a moral government in the universe. But to teach that
all men are born with equal powers and faculties, to equal influence in
society, to equal property and advantages through life, is as gross a fraud,
as glaring an imposition on the credulity of the people, as ever was prac-
ticed by monks, by Druids, by Brahmins, by priests of the immortal Lama,
or by the self-styled philosophers of the French revolution."[32]

Again, in answering M. Turgot's contention that "republics are 'founded
on the equality of all citizens, and, therefore, "orders" and "equilibriums"
are unnecessary, and occasion disputes,'" Adams asks: "what are we to
understand here by equality." He goes on to inquire further, "Are the citizens to be all of the same age, sex, size, strength, stature, activity, courage,
hardiness, industry, patience, ingenuity, wealth, knowledge, fame, wit,
temperance, constancy, and wisdom?" He concludes that there never was
or will be a society of equals "in natural and acquired qualities."[33] In fact,
Adams held that every society possessed a hierarchy, "superiors and inferiors, because God has laid in the constitution and course of nature the
foundations of the distinction."[34]

Nor did he entertain notions of perfectibility. "I really wish," he wrote
to Rush, "you would tell me what you understand by this mighty discovery of Price, Priestley, or Condorcet. Perfectibility I should suppose
to mean capability of perfection, or susceptibility of perfection. But what
is perfection? It is self-evident there cannot be more than one perfect
being in the universe.... These great philosophers... cannot be supposed
to mean that every man, woman, and child is capable of becoming a

[32] Letter III to John Taylor, *Works,* VI, 453-54.
[33] *Defence, Works,* IV, 393.
[34] *Defence, Works,* IV, 426.

supreme and all-perfect being. What then do they mean? Do they mean perfection in this world or in a future state?" "Price and Priestly," he concedes, "were honest enthusiasts carried away by the popular contagion of the times," but consistent with the assumptions and approach of both the *Defence* and *Discourses*, he feels constrained to add that "the greater part of political and philosophers who prated about the perfectibility of man mean nothing but to seize, occupy, and confound the attention of the public, while they were amusing and cheating the populace with promises of equality and levelism, which they know impracticable and never intended to promote any further than for the purposes of present plunder."[35]

Likewise Adams consistently subscribed to the proposition that "Though we allow benevolence and generous affections to exist in the human breast, yet every moral theorist will admit the selfish passions in the generality of men to be the strongest."[36] He never scrupled to flatter the people or to believe that the human nature can be rendered so benevolent that precautions against despotism would be unnecessary. "Human appetites, passions, prejudices, and self-love," he writes to Samuel Adams, "will never be conquered by benevolence and knowledge alone, introduced by human means. The millennium itself neither supposes nor implies it. All civil government is then to cease, and the Messiah is to reign. That happy and holy state is therefore wholly out of the question." He is highly skeptical of Samuel Adams's assertion that "'the Love of liberty... is interwoven in the soul of man'." "So it is, according to La Fontaine," he responds, "in that of a wolf; and I doubt whether it be much more rational, generous, or social, in one than in the other, until in man it is enlightened by experience, reflection, education, and civil and political institutions, which are at first produced, and constantly supported and improved by a few; that is, by nobility." In this vein, he continues, "The numbers of men in all ages have preferred ease, slumber, and good cheer to liberty, when they have been in

[35] Letter to Benjamin Rush, November 11, 1806, *Spur of Fame,* 68.
[36] *Defence, Works,* IV, 57.

competition. We must not then depend alone upon the love of liberty in the soul of man for its preservation. Some political institutions must be prepared, to assist this love against its enemies."[37]

He also rejects the Enlightenment view that "the increase and dissemination of knowledge" will obviate the need for checks and balances. On the contrary, he contends, such a development increases the need for controls. "Bad men," he remarks, "increase in knowledge as fast as good men; and science, arts, taste, sense, and letters, are employed for the purposes of injustice and tyranny, as well as those of law and liberty; for corruption, as well as for virtue."[38]

These views, to go no further, are typical of his adversely critical attitude towards the key elements of the ideology that guided the French Revolution. They indicate as well the extent to which he was out of step with his times.

The basic elements of Adams's political thought are plain and largely consistent with his view of man, human motivation, and the sources of conflict within society. At bottom is the proposition that "[s]elf-interest, private avidity, ambition, and avarice, will exist in every state of society, and under every form of government. A succession of powers and persons, by frequent elections, will not lessen these passions in any case, in a governor, senator, or representative, nor will the apprehension of an approaching election restrain them from indulgence if they have the power."[39] Given this state of affairs, how is despotism to be avoided in republican regimes? Adams is consistent throughout in insisting upon a legislature with three parts, each capable of exercising a veto power over the other. He advances this idea first in his *Thoughts on Government* (1776) where he maintains that a bicameral legislature should "unite and by joint ballot choose a governor, who after being stripped of most of those badges of domination called prerogatives, should have a free and independent exercise of his judgment and be made also an integral part of the legislature."[40] In this

[37] Letter to Samuel Adams, October 14, 1790, *Works,* VI, 417–18.

[38] *Discourses, Works,* VI, 276.

[39] *Defence, Works,* VI, 57.

[40] "Thoughts on Government," *Works,* IV, 196.

connection, it should be noted, his principal objection to the Philadelphia Constitution was that the executive was not given an absolute veto and that the Senate was allowed a share of executive powers.

He is consistent throughout, as well, in maintaining that if any groups or component of society—the royalty (the one), the aristocracy (the few), or the people (the many)—is unchecked despotism or tyranny will ensue because the controlling power will rule for its own benefit, often at the expense of the other elements of society. Adams often praised aristocracy—including in his understanding a "natural," as opposed to hereditary, aristocracy—for its many fine qualities, but he was as fearful of an unchecked aristocracy since it, too, would rule despotically to further its own interests. An aristocracy sufficiently checked by "two masters"—i.e., another legislative chamber and the executive—however, was another matter: "It is agreed that patricians, nobles, senators, the aristocratical part of the community, call it by what name you please, are noble patriots when they are kept under; they are really then the best men and the best citizens." They are, he adds, "the guardians, ornaments, and glory of the community." [41]

In his scheme, as he finally developed it, the "third" house of the legislature, i.e., the executive, would moderate the conflicts and differences between the lower house, representing the people, and the upper chamber, representing the aristocracy. Thus, he envisioned a "balanced" government resulting from his institutional arrangement; one which would be marked by moderation, compromise, and give and take, with the interests of the basic components of society not only protected, but also having a substantial say in the final legislative outcome. Leaving to one side institutional differences, in many important particulars his theory resembles the "concurrent majority" system set forth by John C. Calhoun in his *Disquisition*.

In these terms, his genuine alarm over placing sovereignty in the hands of a single, elective legislative chamber is readily understandable. There would be no checks, no balance, no moderation, only an inevitable despotism. He regarded rule by the many through such a chamber, i.e., a simple democracy, "the most ignoble, unjust, and

[41] *Defence, Works,* VI, 73.

detestable form of government; worse than even a well digested simple monarchy or aristocracy."[42] For views such as these, Adams was branded an enemy of popular government. Yet, for Adams, controlling the aristocracy provided the greatest challenge. The sources of aristocracy, he realized, could be many: wealth, reputation, birth, strength, intelligence, or even good looks. In functional terms, he defined an aristocrat in a republican regime to be "every man who can command or influence TWO VOTES; ONE BESIDES HIS OWN." But, no matter what its source, aristocrats had somehow to be confined to one legislative chamber so that they might be checked. If thrown into a single assembly with the commoners, they would soon control: the union of representatives possessed of "fortune," "eloquence," and "learning," combined with those adept at "cunning" and "intrigue," though a minority, would control a majority of votes.[43]

Perhaps, in the last analysis, Adams's place in our tradition will always remain unsettled because his views, controversial in his own time, are so much at odds with principles and precepts of liberal democracy that have gained almost universal acceptance in the West today. Added to this is the fact that by contemporary standards, he seems to have come from another world. For over a quarter of a century he served his country at great personal sacrifice. Well educated, widely read, highly intelligent, introspective, inquisitive, he was a man of honor and principle, who led an exemplary life. For intellectual and moral rectitude Adams stands at or near the top of American presidents. To be sure, by all accounts he had his faults. Even friendly biographers point out he could be stubborn, impetuous, at times paranoic, and overly concerned about his image. As his writings reveal, he was not a soft-headed observer of human behavior and politics, but in the political arena of the real world, he was no match for Hamilton or Jefferson. While he abhorred factionalism and party politics, it was his lot to serve as president when political divisions threatened the very survival of the new republic. Under the conditions

---

[42] *Defence, Works,* VI, 70.
[43] Letter IV to John Taylor, *Works,* VI, 456.

that prevailed when he was president, that he was able to leave the political arena with the country united, at peace, and his integrity intact, is a
tribute to his sagacity and forbearance.

While there is no gainsaying Adams's contributions to the cause of
independence, his major writings in political theory, the *Defence* and *Discourses*, are viewed as a liability, as detracting from his stature. To be sure,
these works are far from polished efforts, containing little in the way of
original thought. His views on balanced government and its virtues are
derived largely from others, among them Aristotle, Polybius, Harrington,
and Montesquieu. Then, too, at times his theory is too narrow and rigid,
focusing almost exclusively on institutions and structures as the only way
to achieve balance. He seems unaware, for instance, of Madison's extended
republic theory that relies upon a multiplicity and diversity of interests
over an extensive territory to achieve essentially the same results.

The enduring value of his political theory, however, is not to be found
in its substance, but in directing attention to the problems and difficulties
associated with establishing a political order that will simultaneously provide for the rule of law, ensure ordered liberty, and cultivate civility and
virtue, while providing for consensual decision making. His thoughts
take on added relevance as the United States endeavors to make the
"world safe for democracy" or, as is more and more frequently the case,
even tries to export its principles of self-government. Adams's teachings
inform us that establishing lasting republics involves far more than holding
periodic elections that comply with the principle "one person, one vote."
His realism, his hard-headed look at history, his understanding of the
nature of man, his search for the causes of conflict, as also his understanding of what can be and what cannot be changed or altered, provide a
much needed antidote to prevailing views and practices that derive largely
from the ideology that propelled the French Revolution. Adams, to say
the least, would have taken vigorous exception to the notion that a lasting self-government could be built on by preaching toleration of all views,
by proclaiming the brotherhood of all mankind, by promulgating decla-
rations of human rights, by guaranteeing unlimited free speech and press,
or, *inter alia*, by embarking upon egalitarian projects of one sort or another.

Be that as it may, one contribution resulting from the union of John and Abigail Adams, about which there should be no controversy, is the so-called "Adams Dynasty." Starting with John and Abigail, it includes their son, John Quincy Adams (our sixth president), his son, Charles Francis, and Charles Francis's three sons, Charles, Brooks, and Henry. This is a remarkable, unparalleled "dynasty" which assures the Adams family an esteemed and lasting place in our tradition.

Note on the Text

All of the writings in this volume were taken from *The Works of John Adams* compiled by Charles Francis Adams, John Adams's grandson. *The Works* consist of ten volumes published by Little, Brown and Company between 1850 and 1856. They contain all of John Adams's major political writings but only a small portion of his voluminous correspondence.

At an early stage of this project, it was decided for a number of reasons to include only materials from *The Works.* To begin with, these volumes contain materials highly pertinent to Adams's political thought that are not widely or readily available. In this category would fall his letters to John Taylor wherein Adams spells out at great length his major political principles, particularly those that impelled him to write his *Defence of the Constitutions of the Government of the United States of America.* In this category also may be placed the *Report of a Constitution or form of Government for the Commonwealth of Massachusetts, 1789,* which shows the enormity of his input into the Massachusetts Constitution of 1780. These are but two items among many that are reproduced here that seldom see the light of day, despite the fact that they provide keen insights into Adams's political thinking.

It is true that his correspondence, particularly with Thomas Jefferson and Benjamin Rush, also reveals a good deal about Adams's most deeply held values. This much is remarked upon in the Introduction to this volume. But none of this correspondence is included in this volume, because these letters can be easily obtained in carefully annotated collections. Moreover, much of this correspondence is unrelated to his political thought or simply reflects positions found in his major works.

Finally, decisions concerning the selection and editing of the materials included were guided by a concern to present as fully as possible in one volume the depth and breadth of Adams's political thought. Although editing was held to a minimum, some selections, particularly *Defence,* did require heavy editing. The guiding rule, however, was to preserve as far as possible the integrity of the original work and, when necessary, to eliminate only those portions that were redundant or added little to understanding Adams's political philosophy.

Some remarks on the scholarly apparatus of this volume are in order. Throughout *The Political Writings of John Adams,* the reader will find several sets of footnotes. Numbered footnotes represent Charles Francis Adams's annotations to the works of his grandfather. Numbered footnotes in square brackets represent the annotations of the volume editor of this book. Footnotes bearing symbols are John Adams's own annotations to his works. Square brackets in the footnotes of Charles Francis Adams and John Adams represent further annotations by the volume editor. Square-bracketed annotations in the text are those of the volume editor. In addition, the series and volume editors would like to thank Dr. Michael Hendry of Bowling Green State University for identifying and translating Adams's Latin and Greek quotations and Prof. Warren Johnson of Arkansas State University at Jonesboro for identifying and translating Adams's French.

Chronology
of
John Adams's
Life

1735—Born at Braintree (now Quincy) to John Adams and Susanna Boylston Adams.

1751—Enters Harvard University.

1755—Graduates from Harvard and accepts teaching position in Worcester, Massachusetts.

1756—Begins study of law.

1758—Admitted to the bar and begins practice of law in Braintree.

1764—Marries Abigail Smith, daughter of the Reverend William and Elizabeth Smith of Weymouth, Massachusetts, after three year courtship.

1765—Publishes *Dissertation on the Canon and Feudal Law.*

1770—Defends Captain Preston and British soldiers implicated in the "Boston Massacre."

1774—Chosen delegate from Massachusetts to the First Continental Congress in Philadelphia.

1774-75—Authors the *Novanglus* letters.

1775—Chosen delegate from Massachusetts to Second Continental Congress; nominates George Washington as Commander of Continental Army. Accepts appointment as Chief Justice of the Superior Court of Massachusetts; never assumes office and resigns in 1777.

1776—Writes "Thoughts on Government."

1778—Named Commissioner to France.

1779—Returns from France. Serves as principal drafter of the Massachusetts Constitution of 1780. Leaves for France as minister to negotiate peace with Great Britain.

1782—Secures loan, commercial treaty, and recognition from Holland; serves with Jay and Franklin in peace negotiations with Great Britain.

1783—Signs peace treaty (Treaty of Paris).

1785—Appointed Minister to Court of St. James.

1788—Returns to Massachusetts.

1789—Elected vice president to serve with George Washington.

1791—Authors *Discourses on Davila*.

1792—Re-elected vice president.

1796—Elected president.

1800—Ends naval war with France; defeated for presidency by Thomas Jefferson in re-election bid.

1801—Retires to home in Quincy, Massachusetts.

1812—Renews correspondence with Thomas Jefferson.

1818—Suffers loss of wife, Abigail.

1820—Serves as delegate to Massachusetts Constitutional Convention.

1826—Dies July 4, at home in Quincy.

I

Major Political Works

A
Dissertation
on the
Canon and Feudal Law
(1765)

T he "Dissertation" represents Adams's first serious venture into the
realm of political thought. It appeared in four installments in the
Boston Gazette in August 1765, at the height of the protests over
the Stamp Act. That same year it was published in the London Chronicle
and, in 1768, was republished in England as a volume entitled "The True
Sentiments of America."

The essay constitutes the refinement and expansion of an essay originally written by Adams for the "Solidarity Club," a group of four lawyers,
including Adams, brought together by Jeremiah Gridley, who was Adams's
legal mentor and a prominent member of the Boston Bar. In the original
essay, but missing from the "Dissertation," is the following view of America's destiny: "I always consider the settlement of America with reverence
and wonder, as the opening of a grand scene and design in Providence
for the illumination of the ignorant, and the emancipation of the slavish
part mankind all over the earth." (*Works*, I, 66)

Although later in life Adams sought to distance himself from this work,
he touches upon concerns that preoccupied him throughout his entire
life. The "Dissertation" is taken from *Works*, III, 447-64.

A
DISSERTATION
ON THE
CANON AND FEUDAL LAW.

"IGNORANCE and inconsideration are the two great causes of the ruin of mankind." This is an observation of Dr. Tillotson, with relation to the interest of his fellow men in a future and immortal state. But it is of equal truth and importance if applied to the happiness of men in society, on this side the grave. In the earliest ages of the world, absolute monarchy seems to have been the universal form of government. Kings, and a few of their great counsellors and captains, exercised a cruel tyranny over the people, who held a rank in the scale of intelligence, in those days, but little higher than the camels and elephants that carried them and their engines to war.

By what causes it was brought to pass, that the people in the middle ages became more intelligent in general, would not, perhaps, be possible in these days to discover. But the fact is certain; and wherever a general knowledge and sensibility have prevailed among the people, arbitrary government and every kind of oppression have lessened and disappeared in proportion. Man has certainly an exalted soul; and the same principle in human nature,—that aspiring, noble principle founded in benevolence, and cherished by knowledge; I mean the love of power, which has been so often the cause of slavery,—has, whenever freedom has existed, been the cause of freedom. If it is this principle that has always prompted the princess and nobles of the earth, by every species of fraud and violence to shake off all the limitations of their power, it is the same that has always stimulated the common people to aspire at independency, and to endeavor at confining the power of the great within the limits of equity and reason.

The poor people, it is true, have been much less successful than the great. They have seldom found either leisure or opportunity to form a union and exert their strength; ignorant as they were of arts and letters, they have seldom been able to frame and support a regular opposition.

This, however, has been known by the great to be the temper of mankind; and they have accordingly labored, in all ages, to wrest from the populace, as they are contemptuously called, the knowledge of their rights and wrongs, and the power to assert the former or redress the latter. I say RIGHTS, for such they have, undoubtedly, antecedent to all earthly government,—*Rights,* that cannot be repealed or restrained by human laws—*Rights,* derived from the great Legislator of the universe.

Since the promulgation of Christianity, the two greatest systems of tyranny that have sprung from this original, are the canon and the feudal law. The desire of dominion, that great principle by which we have attempted to account for so much good and so much evil, is, when properly restrained, a very useful and noble movement in the human mind. But when such restraints are taken off, it becomes an encroaching, grasping, restless, and ungovernable power. Numberless have been the systems of iniquity contrived by the great for the gratification of this passion in themselves; but in none of them were they ever more successful than in the invention and establishment of the canon and the feudal law.

By the former of these, the most refined, sublime, extensive, and astonishing constitution of policy that ever was conceived by the mind of man was framed by the Romish clergy for the aggrandisement of their own order.* All the epithets I have here given to the Romish policy are just, and will be allowed to be so when it is considered, that they even persuaded mankind to believe, faithfully and undoubtingly, that God Almighty had entrusted them with the keys of heaven, whose gates they might open and close at pleasure; with a power of dispensation over all the rules and obligations of morality; with authority to license all sorts of sins and crimes; with a power of deposing princes and absolving subjects from allegiance; with a power of procuring or withholding the rain of heaven and the beams of the sun; with the management of earthquakes, pestilence, and famine; nay, with the mysterious, awful, incomprehensible power of creating out of bread and wine the flesh and blood of God him-

---

* Robertson's History of Charles V. ch. v. pp. 54, 141, 315.

This work did not appear until the year after the publication of this Dissertation in England. The two references are in the handwriting of Mr. Adams, in the margin of his printed copy.

self. All these opinions they were enabled to spread and rivet among the people by reducing their minds to a state of sordid ignorance and staring timidity, and by infusing into them a religious horror of letters and knowledge. Thus was human nature chained fast for ages in a cruel, shameful, and deplorable servitude to him, and his subordinate tyrants, who, it was foretold, would exalt himself above all that was called God, and that was worshipped.

In the latter we find another system, similar in many respects to the former;[1] which, although it was originally formed, perhaps, for the necessary defence of a barbarous people against the inroads and invasions of her neighboring nations, yet for the same purposes of tyranny, cruelty, and lust, which had dictated the canon law, it was soon adopted by almost all the princes of Europe, and wrought into the constitutions of their government. It was originally a code of laws for a vast army in a perpetual encampment. The general was invested with the sovereign propriety of all the lands within the territory. Of him, as his servants and vassals, the first rank of his great officers held the lands; and in the same manner the other subordinate officers held of them; and all ranks and degrees held their lands by a variety of duties and services, all tending to bind the chains the faster on every order of mankind. In this manner the common people were held together in herds and clans in a state of servile dependence on their lords, bound, even by the tenure of their lands, to follow them, whenever they commanded, to their wars, and in a state of total ignorance of every thing divine and human, excepting the use of arms and the culture of their lands.

But another event still more calamitous to human liberty, was a wicked confederacy between the two systems of tyranny above described. It seems to have been even stipulated between them, that the temporal grandees should contribute every thing in their power to maintain the ascendency of the priesthood, and that the spiritual grandees in their turn, should employ their ascendency over the consciences of the people, in impressing on their minds a blind, implicit obedience to civil magistracy.

[1] Rob. Hist. ch. v. pp. 178–9, &c.

Thus, as long as this confederacy lasted, and the people were held in ignorance, liberty, and with her, knowledge and virtue too, seem to have deserted the earth, and one age of darkness succeeded another, till God in his benign providence raised up the champions who began and conducted the Reformation. From the time of the Reformation to the first settlement of America, knowledge gradually spread in Europe, but especially in England; and in proportion as that increased and spread among the people, ecclesiastical and civil tyranny, which I use as synonymous expressions for the canon and feudal laws, seem to have lost their strength and weight. The people grew more and more sensible of the wrong that was done them by these systems, more and more impatient under it, and determined at all hazards to rid themselves of it; till at last, under the execrable race of the Stuarts, the struggle between the people and the confederacy aforesaid of temporal and spiritual tyranny, became formidable, violent, and bloody.

It was this great struggle that peopled America. It was not religion alone, as is commonly supposed; but it was a love of universal liberty, and a hatred, a dread, a horror, of the infernal confederacy before described, that projected, conducted, and accomplished the settlement of America.

It was a resolution formed by a sensible people,—I mean the Puritans,—almost in despair. They had become intelligent in general, and many of them learned. For this fact, I have the testimony of Archbishop King himself, who observed of that people, that they were more intelligent and better read than even the members of the church, whom he censures warmly for that reason. This people had been so vexed and tortured by the powers of those days, for no other crime than their knowledge and their freedom of inquiry and examination, and they had so much reason to despair of deliverance from those miseries on that side the ocean, that they at last resolved to fly to the wilderness for refuge from the temporal and spiritual principalities and powers, and plagues and scourges of their native country.

After their arrival here, they began their settlement, and formed their plan, both of ecclesiastical and civil government, in direct opposition to the canon and the feudal systems. The leading men among them, both of the clergy and the laity, were men of sense and learning. To many of them the historians, orators, poets, and philosophers of Greece and Rome were quite familiar; and some of them have left libraries that are still in being, consisting chiefly of volumes in which the wisdom of the most enlightened ages and nations is deposited,—written, however, in languages which their great-grandsons, though educated in European universities, can scarcely read.[2]

Thus accomplished were many of the first planters in these colonies. It may be thought polite and fashionable by many modern fine gentlemen, perhaps, to deride the characters of these persons, as enthusiastical, superstitious, and republican. But such ridicule is founded in nothing but foppery and affectation, and is grossly injurious and false. Religious to some degree of enthusiasm it may be admitted they were; but this can be no peculiar derogation from their character; because it was at that time almost the universal character not only of England, but of Christendom. Had this, however, been otherwise, their enthusiasm, considering the principles on which it was founded and the ends to which it was directed, far from being a reproach to them, was greatly to their honor; for I believe it will be found universally true, that no great enterprise for the honor or happiness of mankind was ever achieved without a large mixture of that noble infirmity. Whatever imperfections may be justly ascribed to them, which, however, are as few as any mortals have discovered, their judgment in framing their policy was founded in wise, humane, and benevolent principles. It was founded in revelation and in reason too. It was consistent with the principles of the best and greatest and wisest legislators of antiquity. Tyranny in every form, shape, and appearance was their disdain and abhorrence; no fear of punishment, nor even of death itself in exquisite tortures, had been sufficient to conquer that steady, manly, pertinacious spirit with which they had opposed the tyrants of those days in church and state. They were very far from being enemies to monarchy; and

[2] "I always consider the settlement of America with reverence and wonder, as the opening of a grand scene and design in Providence for the illumination of the ignorant, and the emancipation of the slavish part of mankind all over the earth."

they knew as well as any men, the just regard and honor that is due to the character of a dispenser of the mysteries of the gospel of grace. But they saw clearly, that popular powers must be placed as a guard, a control, a balance, to the powers of the monarch and the priest, in every government, or else it would soon become the man of sin, the whore of Babylon, the mystery of iniquity, a great and detestable system of fraud, violence, and usurpation. Their greatest concern seems to have been to establish a government of the church more consistent with the Scriptures, and a government of the state more agreeable to the dignity of human nature, than any they had seen in Europe, and to transmit such a government down to their posterity, with the means of securing and preserving it forever. To render the popular power in their new government as great and wise as their principles of theory, that is, as human nature and the Christian religion require it should be, they endeavored to remove from it as many of the feudal inequalities and dependencies as could be spared, consistently with the preservation of a mild limited monarchy. And in this they discovered the depth of their wisdom and the warmth of their friendship to human nature. But the first place is due to religion. They saw clearly, that of all the nonsense and delusion which had ever passed through the mind of man, none had ever been more extravagant than the notions of absolutions, indelible characters, uninterrupted successions, and the rest of those fantastical ideas, derived from the canon law, which had thrown such a glare of mystery, sanctity, reverence, and right reverend eminence and holiness, around the idea of a priest, as no mortal could deserve, and as always must, from the constitution of human nature, be dangerous in society. For this reason, they demolished the whole system of diocesan episcopacy; and, deriding, as all reasonable and impartial men must do, the ridiculous fancies of sanctified effluvia from episcopal fingers, they established sacerdotal ordination on the foundation of the Bible and common sense. This conduct at once imposed an obligation on the whole body of the clergy to industry, virtue, piety, and learning, and rendered that whole body infinitely more independent on the civil powers, in all respects, than they could be where they were formed into a scale of subordination, from a pope down to priests and friars and confessors,—

necessarily and essentially a sordid, stupid, and wretched herd,—or than they could be in any other country, where an archbishop held the place of a universal bishop, and the vicars and curates that of the ignorant, dependent, miserable rabble aforesaid,—and infinitely more sensible and learned than they could be in either. This subject has been seen in the same light by many illustrious patriots, who have lived in America since the days of our forefathers, and who have adored their memory for the same reason. And methinks there has not appeared in New England a stronger veneration for their memory, a more penetrating insight into the grounds and principles and spirit of their policy, nor a more earnest desire of perpetuating the blessings of it to posterity, than that fine institution of the late Chief Justice Dudley, of a lecture against popery, and on the validity of presbyterian ordination. This was certainly intended by that wise and excellent man, as an eternal memento of the wisdom and goodness of the very principles that settled America. But I must again return to the feudal law. The adventurers so often mentioned, had an utter contempt of all that dark ribaldry of hereditary, indefeasible right,— the Lord's anointed,—and the divine, miraculous original of government, with which the priesthood had enveloped the feudal monarch in clouds and mysteries, and from whence they had deduced the most mischievous of all doctrines, that of passive obedience and non-resistance. They knew that government was a plain, simple, intelligible thing, founded in nature and reason, and quite comprehensible by common sense. They detested all the base services and servile dependencies of the feudal system. They knew that no such unworthy dependencies took place in the ancient seats of liberty, the republics of Greece and Rome; and they thought all such slavish subordinations were equally inconsistent with the constitution of human nature and that religious liberty with which Jesus had made them free. This was certainly the opinion they had formed; and they were far from being singular or extravagant in thinking so. Many celebrated modern writers in Europe have espoused the same sentiments. Lord Kames, a Scottish writer of great reputation, whose authority in this case ought to have the more weight as his countrymen have not the most worthy ideas of liberty, speaking of the feudal law, says,—"A constitution so contradictory to all the principles which govern mankind can never be brought about, one should imagine, but by foreign conquest or native usurpations."* Rousseau, speaking of the same system, calls it,—"That most iniquitous and absurd form of government by which human nature was so shamefully degraded."† It would be easy to multiply authorities, but it must be needless; because, as the original of this form of government was among savages, as the spirit of it is military and despotic, every writer who would allow the people to have any right to life or property or freedom more than the beasts of the field, and who was not hired or enlisted under arbitrary, lawless power, has been always willing to admit the feudal system to be inconsistent with liberty and the rights of mankind.

To have holden their lands allodially, or for every man to have been the sovereign lord and proprietor of the ground he occupied, would have constituted a government too nearly like a commonwealth. They were contented, therefore, to hold their lands of their king, as their sovereign lord; and to him they were willing to render homage, but to no mesne or subordinate lords; nor were they willing to submit to any of the baser services. In all this they were so strenuous, that they have even transmitted to their posterity a very general contempt and detestation of holdings by quitrents, as they have also a hereditary ardor for liberty and thirst for knowledge.

They were convinced, by their knowledge of human nature, derived from history and their own experience, that nothing could preserve their posterity from the encroachments of the two systems of tyranny, in opposition to which, as has been observed already, they erected their government in church and state, but knowledge diffused generally through the whole body of the people. Their civil and religious principles, therefore, conspired to prompt them to use every measure and take every precaution in their power to propagate and perpetuate knowledge. For this purpose they laid very early the foundations of colleges, and invested them with

* Brit. Ant, p. 2.
† Social Compact, page 164.

ample privileges and emoluments; and it is remarkable that they have left among their posterity so universal an affection and veneration for those seminaries, and for liberal education, that the meanest of the people contribute cheerfully to the support and maintenance of them every year, and that nothing is more generally popular than projections for the honor, reputation, and advantage of those seats of learning. But the wisdom and benevolence of our fathers rested not here. They made an early provision by law, that every town consisting of so many families, should be always furnished with a grammar school. They made it a crime for such a town to be destitute of a grammar schoolmaster for a few months, and subjected it to a heavy penalty. So that the education of all ranks of people was made the care and expense of the public, in a manner that I believe has been unknown to any other people ancient or modern.

The consequences of these establishments we see and feel every day. A native of America who cannot read and write is as rare an appearance as a Jacobite or a Roman Catholic, that is, as rare as a comet or an earthquake. It has been observed, that we are all of us lawyers, divines, politicians, and philosophers. And I have good authorities to say, that all candid foreigners who have passed through this country, and conversed freely with all sorts of people here, will allow, that they have never seen so much knowledge and civility among the common people in any part of the world. It is true, there has been among us a party for some years, consisting chiefly not of the descendants of the first settlers of this country, but of high churchmen and high statesmen imported since, who affect to censure this provision for the education of our youth as a needless expense, and an imposition upon the rich in favor of the poor, and as an institution productive of idleness and vain speculation among the people, whose time and attention, it is said, ought to be devoted to labor, and not to public affairs, or to examination into the conduct of their superiors. And certain officers of the crown, and certain other missionaries of ignorance, foppery, servility, and slavery, have been most inclined to countenance and increase the same party. Be it remembered, however, that liberty must at all hazards be supported. We have a right to it, derived from our Maker. But if we had not, our fathers have earned and bought it for us, at the expense of their ease, their estates, their pleasure, and their blood. And liberty cannot be preserved without a general knowledge among the people, who have a right, from the frame of their nature, to knowledge, as their great Creator, who does nothing in vain, has given them understandings, and a desire to know; but besides this, they have a right, an indisputable, unalienable, indefeasible, divine right to that most dreaded and envied kind of knowledge, I mean, of the characters and conduct of their rulers. Rulers are no more than attorneys, agents, and trustees, for the people; and if the cause, the interest and trust, is insidiously betrayed, or wantonly trifled away, the people have a right to revoke the authority that they themselves have deputed, and to constitute abler and better agents, attorneys, and trustees. And the preservation of the means of knowledge among the lowest ranks, is of more importance to the public than all the property of all the rich men in the country. It is even of more consequence to the rich themselves, and to their posterity. The only question is, whether it is a public emolument; and if it is, the rich ought undoubtedly to contribute, in the same proportion as to all other public burdens,—that is, in proportion to their wealth, which is secured by public expenses. But none of the means of information are more sacred, or have been cherished with more tenderness and care by the settlers of America, than the press. Care has been taken that the art of printing should be encouraged, and that it should be easy and cheap and safe for any person to communicate his thoughts to the public. And you, Messieurs printers,[3] whatever the tyrants of the earth may say of your paper, have done important service to your country by your readiness and freedom in publishing the speculations of the curious. The stale, impudent insinuations of slander and sedition, with which the gormandizers of power have endeavored to discredit your paper, are so much the more to your honor; for the jaws of power are always opened to devour, and her arm is always stretched out, if possible, to destroy the freedom of thinking, speaking, and writing. And if the public interest, liberty, and happiness have been in danger from the ambition

---

[3] Edes and Gill, printers of the Boston Gazette.

or avarice of any great man, whatever may be his politeness, address, learning, ingenuity, and, in other respects, integrity and humanity, you have done yourselves honor and your country service by publishing and pointing out that avarice and ambition. These vices are so much the more dangerous and pernicious for the virtues with which they may be accompanied in the same character, and with so much the more watchful jealousy to be guarded against.

"Curse on such virtues, they've undone their country."

Be not intimidated, therefore, by any terrors, from publishing with the utmost freedom, whatever can be warranted by the laws of your country; nor suffer yourselves to be wheedled out of your liberty by any pretences of politeness, delicacy, or decency. These, as they are often used, are but three different names for hypocrisy, chicanery, and cowardice. Much less, I presume, will you be discouraged by any pretences that malignants on this side the water will represent your paper as factious and seditious, or that the great on the other side the water will take offence at them. This dread of representation has had for a long time, in this province, effects very similar to what the physicians call a hydropho, or dread of water. It has made us delirious; and we have rushed headlong into the water, till we are almost drowned, out of simple or phrensical fear of it. Believe me, the character of this country has suffered more in Britain by the pusillanimity with which we have borne many insults and indignities from the creatures of power at home and the creatures of those creatures here, than it ever did or ever will by the freedom and spirit that has been or will be discovered in writing or action. Believe me, my countrymen, they have imbibed an opinion on the other side the water, that we are an ignorant, a timid, and a stupid people; nay, their tools on this side have often the impudence to dispute your bravery. But I hope in God the time is near at hand when they will be fully convinced of your understanding, integrity, and courage. But can any thing be more ridiculous, were it not too provoking to be laughed at, than to pretend that offence should be taken at home for writings here? Pray, let them look at home. Is not the human understanding exhausted there? Are not reason, imagination, wit, passion, senses, and all, tortured to find out satire and invective against the characters of the vile and futile fellows who sometimes get into place and power? The most exceptionable paper that ever I saw here is perfect prudence and modesty in comparison of multitudes of their applauded writings. Yet the high regard they have for the freedom of the press, indulges all. I must and will repeat it, your paper deserves the patronage of every friend to his country. And whether the defamers of it are arrayed in robes of scarlet or sable, whether they lurk and skulk in an insurance office, whether they assume the venerable character of a priest, the sly one of a scrivener, or the dirty, infamous, abandoned one of an informer, they are all the creatures and tools of the lust of domination.

The true source of our sufferings has been our timidity.

We have been afraid to think. We have felt a reluctance to examining into the grounds of our privileges, and the extent in which we have an indisputable right to demand them, against all the power and authority on earth. And many who have not scrupled to examine for themselves, have yet for certain prudent reasons been cautious and diffident of declaring the result of their inquiries.

The cause of this timidity is perhaps hereditary, and to be traced back in history as far as the cruel treatment the first settlers of this country received, before their embarkation for America, from the government at home. Everybody knows how dangerous it was to speak or write in favor of any thing, in those days, but the triumphant system of religion and politics. And our fathers were particularly the objects of the persecutions and proscriptions of the times. It is not unlikely, therefore, that although they were inflexibly steady in refusing their positive assent to any thing against their principles, they might have contracted habits of reserve, and a cautious diffidence of asserting their opinions publicly. These habits they probably brought with them to America, and have transmitted down to us. Or we may possibly account for this appearance by the great affection and veneration Americans have always entertained for the country from whence they sprang; or by the quiet temper for which they have been remarkable, no country having been less disposed to discontent than this; or by a sense they have that it is their duty to acquiesce under the

administration of government, even when in many smaller matters grievous to them, and until the essentials of the great compact are destroyed
or invaded. These peculiar causes might operate upon them; but without
these, we all know that human nature itself, from indolence, modesty,
humanity, or fear, has always too much reluctance to a manly assertion of
its rights. Hence, perhaps, it has happened, that nine tenths of the species
are groaning and gasping in misery and servitude.

But whatever the cause has been, the fact is certain, we have been
excessively cautious of giving offence by complaining of grievances. And
it is as certain, that American governors, and their friends, and all the
crown officers, have availed themselves of this disposition in the people.
They have prevailed on us to consent to many things which were grossly
injurious to us, and to surrender many others, with voluntary tameness,
to which we had the clearest right. Have we not been treated, formerly,
with abominable insolence, by officers of the navy? I mean no insinuation against any gentleman now on this station, having heard no complaint
of any one of them to his dishonor. Have not some generals from England
treated us like servants, nay, more like slaves than like Britons? Have we not
been under the most ignominious contribution, the most abject submission, the most supercilious insults, of some custom-house officers? Have
we not been trifled with, brow-beaten, and trampled on, by former governors, in a manner which no king of England since James the Second has
dared to indulge towards his subjects? Have we not raised up one family,
in them placed an unlimited confidence, and been soothed and flattered
and intimidated by their influence, into a great part of this infamous tameness and submission? "These are serious and alarming questions, and
deserve a dispassionate consideration."

This disposition has been the great wheel and the mainspring in the
American machine of court politics. We have been told that "the word
rights is an offensive expression;" "that the king, his ministry, and parliament, will not endure to hear Americans talk of their *rights;*" "that Britain
is the mother and we the children, that a filial duty and submission is due
from us to her," and that "we ought to doubt our own judgment, and
presume that she is right, even when she seems to us to shake the foun-

dation of government;" that "Britain is immensely rich and great and powerful, has fleets and armies at her command which have been the dread and terror of the universe, and that she will force her own judgment into execution, right or wrong." But let me entreat you, sir, to pause. Do you consider yourself as a missionary of loyalty or of rebellion? Are you not representing your king, his ministry, and parliament, as tyrants,— imperious, unrelenting tyrants,—by such reasoning as this? Is not this representing your most gracious sovereign as endeavoring to destroy the foundations of his own throne? Are you not representing every member of parliament as renouncing the transactions at Runing Mede, (the meadow, near Windsor, where Magna Charta was signed;) and as repealing in effect the bill of rights, when the Lords and Commons asserted and vindicated the rights of the people and their own rights, and insisted on the king's assent to that assertion and vindication? Do you not represent them as forgetting that the prince of Orange was created King William, by the people, on purpose that their rights might be eternal and inviolable? Is there not something extremely fallacious in the commonplace images of mother country and children colonies? Are we the children of Great Britain any more than the cities of London, Exeter, and Bath? Are we not brethren and fellow subjects with those in Britain, only under a somewhat different method of legislation, and a totally different method of taxation? But admitting we are children, have not children a right to complain when their parents are attempting to break their limbs, to administer poison, or to sell them to enemies for slaves? Let me entreat you to consider, will the mother be pleased when you represent her as deaf to the cries of her children,—when you compare her to the infamous miscreant who lately stood on the gallows for starving her child,—when you resemble her to Lady Macbeth in Shakespeare, (I cannot think of it without horror,) who

> "Had given suck, and knew
> How tender 't was to love the babe that milked her,"

but yet, who could

> "Even while 't was smiling in her face,
> Have plucked her nipple from the boneless gums,
> And dashed the brains out."

Let us banish for ever from our minds, my countrymen, all such unworthy ideas of the king, his ministry, and parliament. Let us not suppose that all are become luxurious, effeminate, and unreasonable, on the other side the water, as many designing persons would insinuate. Let us presume, what is in fact true, that the spirit of liberty is as ardent as ever among the body of the nation, though a few individuals may be corrupted. Let us take it for granted, that the same great spirit which once gave Cæsar so warm a reception, which denounced hostilities against John till Magna Charta was signed, which severed the head of Charles the First from his body, and drove James the Second from his kingdom, the same great spirit (may heaven preserve it till the earth shall be no more) which first seated the great grandfather of his present most gracious majesty on the throne of Britain,—is still alive and active and warm in England; and that the same spirit in America, instead of provoking the inhabitants of that country, will endear us to them for ever, and secure their good-will.

This spirit, however, without knowledge, would be little better than a brutal rage. Let us tenderly and kindly cherish, therefore, the means of knowledge. Let us dare to read, think, speak, and write. Let every order and degree among the people rouse their attention and animate their resolution. Let them all become attentive to the grounds and principles of government, ecclesiastical and civil. Let us study the law of nature; search into the spirit of the British constitution; read the histories of ancient ages; contemplate the great examples of Greece and Rome; set before us the conduct of our own British ancestors, who have defended for us the inherent rights of mankind against foreign and domestic tyrants and usurpers, against arbitrary kings and cruel priests, in short, against the gates of earth and hell. Let us read and recollect and impress upon our souls the views and ends of our own more immediate forefathers, in exchanging their native country for a dreary, inhospitable wilderness. Let us examine into the nature of that power, and the cruelty of that oppression, which drove them from their homes. Recollect their amazing fortitude, their bitter sufferings,—the hunger, the nakedness, the cold, which they patiently endured,—the severe labors of clearing their grounds, building their houses, raising their provisions, amidst dangers from wild beasts and savage men, before they had time or money or materials for commerce. Recollect the civil and religious principles and hopes and expectations which constantly supported and carried them through all hardships with patience and resignation. Let us recollect it was liberty, the hope of liberty for themselves and us and ours, which conquered all discouragements, dangers, and trials. In such researches as these, let us all in our several departments cheerfully engage,—but especially the proper patrons and supporters of law, learning, and religion!

Let the pulpit resound with the doctrines and sentiments of religious liberty. Let us hear the danger of thraldom to our consciences from ignorance, extreme poverty, and dependence, in short, from civil and political slavery. Let us see delineated before us the true map of man. Let us hear the dignity of his nature, and the noble rank he holds among the works of God,—that consenting to slavery is a sacrilegious breach of trust, as offensive in the sight of God as it is derogatory from our own honor or interest or happiness,—and that God Almighty has promulgated from heaven, liberty, peace, and good-will to man!

Let the bar proclaim, "the laws, the rights, the generous plan of power" delivered down from remote antiquity,—inform the world of the mighty struggles and numberless sacrifices made by our ancestors in defence of freedom. Let it be known, that British liberties are not the grants of princes or parliaments, but original rights, conditions of original contracts, coequal with prerogative, and coeval with government; that many of our rights are inherent and essential, agreed on as maxims, and established as preliminaries, even before a parliament existed. Let them search for the foundations of British laws and government in the frame of human nature, in the constitution of the intellectual and moral world. There let us see that truth, liberty, justice, and benevolence, are its everlasting basis; and if these could be removed, the superstructure is overthrown of course.

Let the colleges join their harmony in the same delightful concert. Let every declamation turn upon the beauty of liberty and virtue, and the deformity, turpitude, and malignity, of slavery and vice. Let the public disputations become researches into the grounds and nature and ends of government, and the means of preserving the good and demolishing the evil. Let the dialogues, and all the exercises, become the instruments of impressing on the tender mind, and of spreading and distributing far and wide, the ideas of right and the sensations of freedom.

In a word, let every sluice of knowledge be opened and set a-flowing. The encroachments upon liberty in the reigns of the first James and the first Charles, by turning the general attention of learned men to government, are said to have produced the greatest number of consummate statesmen which has ever been seen in any age or nation. The Brookes, Hampdens, Vanes, Seldens, Miltons, Nedhams, Harringtons, Nevilles, Sidneys, Lockes, are all said to have owed their eminence in political knowledge to the tyrannies of those reigns. The prospect now before us in America, ought in the same manner to engage the attention of every man of learning, to matters of power and of right, that we may be neither led nor driven blindfolded to irretrievable destruction. Nothing less than this seems to have been meditated for us, by somebody or other in Great Britain. There seems to be a direct and formal design on foot, to enslave all America. This, however, must be done by degrees. The first step that is intended, seems to be an entire subversion of the whole system of our fathers, by the introduction of the canon and feudal law into America. The canon and feudal systems, though greatly mutilated in England, are not yet destroyed. Like the temples and palaces in which the great contrivers of them once worshipped and inhabited, they exist in ruins; and much of the domineering spirit of them still remains. The designs and labors of a certain society, to introduce the former of them into America, have been well exposed to the public by a writer of great abilities;★ and the further attempts to the same purpose, that may be made by that society, or by the ministry or parliament, I leave to the conjectures of the thoughtful. But it seems very manifest from the Stamp Act itself, that a design is formed to strip us in a great measure of the means of knowledge, by loading the press, the colleges, and even an almanack and a newspaper, with restraints and duties; and to introduce the inequalities and dependencies of the

★ The late Rev. Dr. Mayhew.

feudal system, by taking from the poorer sort of people all their little sub-sistence, and conferring it on a set of stamp officers, distributors, and their deputies. But I must proceed no further at present. The sequel, whenever I shall find health and leisure to pursue it, will be a "disquisition of the pol-icy of the stamp act." In the mean time, however, let me add,—These are not the vapors of a melancholy mind, nor the effusions of envy, disap-pointed ambition, nor of a spirit of opposition to government, but the emanations of a heart that burns for its country's welfare. No one of any feeling, born and educated in this once happy country, can consider the numerous distresses, the gross indignities, the barbarous ignorance, the haughty usurpations, that we have reason to fear are meditating for our-selves, our children, our neighbors, in short, for all our countrymen and all their posterity, without the utmost agonies of heart and many tears.

Novanglus
(1774–1775)

Upon his return from the Continental Congress in 1774, Adams encountered a series of articles in *Post Boy* ably setting forth the Tory position that the Colonies were totally subject to the authority of Parliament. These articles were signed with the pen name "Massachusettensis" and addressed "To the Inhabitants of the Province of the Massachusetts Bay." Adams was quick to respond. In a series of twelve lengthy articles in the *Boston Gazette* between December 1774 and April 1775, signed "Novanglus" (New England), he offered a point-by-point rebuttal of the Tory position.

Until very late in his life, Adams believed that Massachusettensis was his old friend Jonathan Sewall. It is now known that these articles were written by Daniel Leonard. The following selections from *Novanglus* are taken from *Works*, IV: 11–28; 36–39; 45–57; 99–134; 146–151; 175–177.

NOVANGLUS.
ADDRESSED TO THE
INHABITANTS OF THE
COLONY OF MASSACHUSETTS BAY.

No. I

MY FRIENDS,—A writer, under the signature of *Massachusettensis,* has addressed you, in a series of papers, on the great national subject of the present quarrel between the British administration and the Colonies. As I have not in my possession more than one of his essays, and that is in the

Gazette of December 26, I will take the liberty, in the spirit of candor and decency, to bespeak your attention upon the same subject.

There may be occasion to say very severe things, before I shall have finished what I propose, in opposition to this writer, but there ought to be no reviling. *Rem ipsam dic, mitte male loqui,* which may be justly translated, speak out the whole truth boldly, but use no bad language.

It is not very material to inquire, as others have done, who is the author of the speculations in question. If he is a disinterested writer, and has nothing to gain or to lose, to hope or to fear, for himself more than other individuals of your community; but engages in this controversy from the purest principles, the noblest motives of benevolence to men, and of love to his country, he ought to have no influence with you, further than truth and justice will support his argument. On the other hand, if he hopes to acquire or preserve a lucrative employment, to screen himself from the just detestation of his countrymen, or whatever other sinister inducement he may have, so far as the truth of facts and the weight of argument are in his favor, he ought to be duly regarded.

He tells you, "that the temporal salvation of this province depends upon an entire and speedy change of measures, which must depend upon a change of sentiment respecting our own conduct and the justice of the British nation."[1]

The task of effecting these great changes, this courageous writer has undertaken in a course of publications in a newspaper. *Nil desperandum* is a good motto, and *nil admirari* is another. He is welcome to the first, and I hope will be willing that I should assume the last. The public, if they are not mistaken in their conjecture, have been so long acquainted with this

---

[1] Were I not fully convinced, upon the most mature deliberation that I am capable of, that the temporal salvation of this province depends upon an entire and speedy change of measures, which must depend upon a change of sentiment respecting our own conduct and the justice of the British nation, I never should have obtruded myself on the public. I repeat my promise, to avoid personal reflection, as much as the nature of the task will admit of; but will continue faithfully to expose the wretched policy of the whigs, though I may be obliged to penetrate the arcana, and discover such things as, were there not a necessity for it, I should be infinitely happier in drawing a veil over, or covering with a mantle." *Massachusettensis.*

gentleman, and have seen him so often disappointed, that if they were not habituated to strange things, they would wonder at his hopes, at this time, to accomplish the most unpromising project of his whole life. In the character of *Philanthrop,* he attempted to reconcile you to Mr. Bernard. But the only fruit of his labor was, to expose his client to more general examination, and consequently to more general resentment and aversion. In the character of *Philalethes,* he essayed to prove Mr. Hutchinson a patriot, and his letters not only innocent but meritorious. But the more you read and considered, the more you were convinced of the ambition and avarice, the simulation and dissimulation, the hypocrisy and perfidy of that destroying angel.

This ill-fated and unsuccessful, though persevering writer, still hopes to change your sentiments and conduct, by which it is supposed that he means to convince you, that the system of colony administration which has been pursued for these ten or twelve years past is a wise, righteous, and humane plan; that Sir Francis Bernard and Mr. Hutchinson, with their connections, who have been the principal instruments of it, are your best friends; and that those gentlemen, in this province, and in all the other colonies, who have been in opposition to it, are, from ignorance, error, or from worse and baser causes, your worst enemies.

This is certainly an inquiry that is worthy of you; and I promise to accompany this writer in his ingenious labors to assist you in it. And I earnestly entreat you, as the result of all shall be, to change your sentiments or persevere in them, as the evidence shall appear to you, upon the most dispassionate and impartial consideration, without regard to his opinion or mine.

He promises to avoid personal reflections, but to "penetrate the arcana" and "expose the wretched policy of the whigs." The cause of the whigs is not conducted by intrigues at a distant court, but by constant appeals to a sensible and virtuous people; it depends entirely on their good-will, and cannot be pursued a single step without their concurrence, to obtain which, all their designs, measures, and means, are constantly published to the collective body. The whigs, therefore, can have no arcana; but if they had, I dare say they were never so left, as to communicate them to this writer; you will therefore be disappointed, if you expect from him any thing which is true, but what has been as public as records and newspapers could make it.

I, on my part, may, perhaps, in a course of papers, penetrate arcana too; show the wicked policy of the tories; trace their plan from its first rude sketches to its present complete draught; show that it has been much longer in contemplation than is generally known,—who were the first in it—their views, motives, and secret springs of action, and the means they have employed. This will necessarily bring before your eyes many characters, living and dead. From such a research and detail of facts, it will clearly appear, who were the aggressors, and who have acted on the defensive from first to last; who are still struggling, at the expense of their ease, health, peace, wealth, and preferment, against the encroachments of the tories on their country, and who are determined to continue struggling, at much greater hazards still, and, like the Prince of Orange, are resolved never to see its entire subjection to arbitrary power, but rather to die fighting against it in the last ditch.

It is true, as this writer observes, "that the bulk of the people are generally but little versed in the affairs of state;" that they "rest the affairs of government in the hands where accident has placed them." If this had not been true, the designs of the tories had been many years ago entirely defeated. It was clearly seen by a few, more than ten years since, that they were planning and pursuing the very measures we now see executing. The people were informed of it, and warned of their danger; but they had been accustomed to confide in certain persons, and could never be persuaded to believe, until prophecy became history. Now, they see and feel that the horrible calamities are come upon them, which were foretold so many years ago, and they now sufficiently execrate the men who have brought these things upon them. Now, alas! when perhaps it is too late. If they had withdrawn their confidence from them in season, they would have wholly disarmed them.

"The same game, with the same success, has been played in all ages and countries," as Massachusettensis observes. When a favorable conjuncture has presented, some of the most intriguing and powerful citizens have conceived the design of enslaving their country, and building their own greatness on its ruins. Philip and Alexander are examples of this in Greece; Cæsar in Rome; Charles V. in Spain; Louis XII. in France; and ten thousand others.

"There is a latent spark in the breasts of the people, capable of being kindled into a flame, and to do this has always been the employment of the disaffected." What is this latent spark? The love of liberty. *A Deo hominis est indita naturæ.*[2] Human nature itself is evermore an advocate for liberty. There is also in human nature a resentment of injury and indignation against wrong; a love of truth, and a veneration for virtue. These amiable passions are the "latent spark" to which those whom this writer calls the "disaffected" apply. If the people are capable of understanding, seeing, and feeling the difference between true and false, right and wrong, virtue and vice, to what better principle can the friends of mankind apply, than to the sense of this difference? Is it better to apply, as this writer and his friends do, to the basest passions in the human breast—to their fear, their vanity, their avarice, ambition, and every kind of corruption? I appeal to all experience, and to universal history, if it has ever been in the power of popular leaders, uninvested with other authority than what is conferred by the popular suffrage, to persuade a large people, for any length of time together, to think themselves wronged, injured, and oppressed, unless they really were, and saw and felt it to be so.

"They," the popular leaders, "begin by reminding the people of the elevated rank they hold in the universe, as men; that all men by nature are equal; that kings are but the ministers of the people; that their authority is delegated to them by the people, for their good, and they have a right to resume it, and place it in other hands, or keep it themselves, whenever it is made use of to oppress them. Doubtless, there have been instances when these principles have been inculcated to obtain a redress of real grievances; but they have been much oftener perverted to the worst of purposes."

These are what are called revolution principles. They are the principles of Aristotle and Plato, of Livy and Cicero, and Sidney, Harrington, and

[1][Literally, "It (= liberty) has been placed in the nature of man by God." Ed.]

Locke; the principles of nature and eternal reason; the principles on which the whole government over us now stands. It is therefore astonishing, if any thing can be so, that writers, who call themselves friends of government, should in this age and country be so inconsistent with themselves, so indiscreet, so immodest, as to insinuate a doubt concerning them.

Yet we find that these principles stand in the way of Massachusettensis and all the writers of his class. The Veteran, in his letter to the officers of the army, allows them to be noble and true; but says the application of them to particular cases is wild and utopian.[3] How they can be in general true, and not applicable to particular cases, I cannot comprehend. I thought their being true in general, was because they were applicable in most particular cases.

Gravity is a principle in nature. Why? Because all particular bodies are found to gravitate. How would it sound to say, that bodies in general are heavy; yet to apply this to particular bodies, and say, that a guinea or a ball is heavy, is wild? "Adopted in private life," says the honest amiable veteran, "they would introduce perpetual discord." This I deny; and I think it plain, that there never was a happy private family where they were not adopted. "In the state, perpetual discord." This I deny; and affirm, that order, concord, and stability in this state, never was nor can be preserved without them. "The least failure in the reciprocal duties of worship and obedience in the matrimonial contract would justify a divorce." This is no consequence from these principles. A total departure from the ends and designs of the contract, it is true, as elopement and adultery, would by these principles justify a divorce; but not the least failure, or many smaller failures in the reciprocal duties, &c. "In the political compact, the smallest defect in the prince, a revolution." By no means; but a manifest design in the prince, to annul the contract on his part, will annul it on

---

[3] This refers to a well-written pamphlet, entitled "A Letter from a Veteran to the Officers of the Army, encamped at Boston," and printed without date of place, in 1774. The purport of it is to deprecate excessive harshness in the punishment about to be inflicted on the rebellious colonists.

To a thorough understanding of the American Revolution by future generations, a general history of the mass of pamphlets which it occasioned is becoming very essential.

the part of the people. A settled plan to deprive the people of all the benefits, blessings, and ends of the contract, to subvert the fundamentals of the constitution, to deprive them of all share in making and executing laws, will justify a revolution.

The author of a "Friendly Address to all reasonable Americans"[4] discovers his rancor against these principles in a more explicit manner; and makes no scruples to advance the principles of Hobbes and Filmer boldly, and to pronounce damnation, *ore rotundo*,[5] on all who do not practise implicit, passive obedience to an established government, of whatever character it may be. It is not reviling, it is not bad language, it is strictly decent to say, that this angry bigot, this ignorant dogmatist, this foulmouthed scold, deserves no other answer than silent contempt. Massachusettensis and the Veteran—I admire the first for his art, the last for his honesty.

Massachusettensis is more discreet than any of the others; sensible that these principles would be very troublesome to him, yet conscious of their truth, he has neither admitted nor denied them. But we have a right to his opinion of them, before we dispute with him. He finds fault with the application of them. They have been invariably applied, in support of the revolution and the present establishment, against the Stuarts, the Charleses, and the Jameses, in support of the Reformation and the Protestant religion; and against the worst tyranny that the genius of toryism has ever yet invented; I mean the Roman superstition. Does this writer rank the revolution and present establishment, the Reformation and Protestant religion, among his worst of purposes? What "worse purpose" is there than established tyranny? Were these principles ever inculcated in favor of such tyranny? Have they not always been used against such tyrannies, when

---

[4] This is the title of a pamphlet published anonymously, and without date of place, in the year 1774. It is supposed to have been the work of Dr. Myles Cooper, President of King's College, New York, a gentleman who came from the mother country to fill that post, and whose political principles inclined towards the absolute school. The drift of the pamphlet seems to be to rouse the jealousy of the English church against the puritan republicanism of New England.

[5] [Literally, "with a round mouth," meaning either "loudly" or "eloquently." Horace, *Art of Poetry* 323. Ed.]

the people have had knowledge enough to be apprized of them, and courage to assert them? Do not those who aim at depriving the people of their liberties, always inculcate opposite principles, or discredit these?

"A small mistake in point of policy," says he, "often furnishes a pretence to libel government, and persuade the people that their rulers are tyrants, and the whole government a system of oppression." This is not only untrue, but inconsistent with what he said before. The people are in their nature so gentle, that there never was a government yet in which thousands of mistakes were not overlooked. The most sensible and jealous people are so little attentive to government, that there are no instances of resistance, until repeated, multiplied oppressions have placed it beyond a doubt, that their rulers had formed settled plans to deprive them of their liberties; not to oppress an individual or a few, but to break down the fences of a free constitution, and deprive the people at large of all share in the government, and all the checks by which it is limited. Even Machiavel himself allows, that, not ingratitude to their rulers, but much love, is the constant fault of the people.

This writer is equally mistaken, when he says, the people are sure to be losers in the end. They can hardly be losers if unsuccessful; because, if they live, they can but be slaves, after an unfortunate effort, and slaves they would have been, if they had not resisted. So that nothing is lost. If they die, they cannot be said to lose, for death is better than slavery. If they succeed, their gains are immense. They preserve their liberties. The instances in antiquity which this writer alludes to are not mentioned, and therefore cannot be answered; but that in the country from whence we are derived, is the most unfortunate for his purpose that could have been chosen. No doubt he means, the resistance to Charles I. and the case of Cromwell. But the people of England, and the cause of liberty, truth, virtue, and humanity, gained infinite advantages by that resistance. In all human probability, liberty, civil and religious, not only in England, but in all Europe, would have been lost. Charles would undoubtedly have established the Romish religion, and a despotism as wild as any in the world. And as England has been a principal bulwark, from that period to this, of civil liberty and the Protestant religion in all Europe, if Charles's schemes had succeeded, there is great reason to apprehend that the light of science would have been extinguished, and mankind drawn back to a state of darkness and misery like that which prevailed from the fourth to the fourteenth century. It is true, and to be lamented, that Cromwell did not establish a government as free as he might and ought; but his government was infinitely more glorious and happy to the people than Charles's. Did not the people gain by the resistance to James II.? Did not the Romans gain by the resistance to Tarquin? Without that resistance, and the liberty that was restored by it, would the great Roman orators, poets, and historians, the great teachers of humanity and politeness, the pride of human nature, and the delight and glory of mankind for seventeen hundred years, ever have existed? Did not the Romans gain by resistance to the Decemvirs? Did not the English gain by resistance to John, when *Magna Charta* was obtained? Did not the Seven United Provinces gain by resistance to Philip, Alva, and Granvelle? Did not the Swiss Cantons, the Genevans, and Grisons gain by resistance to Albert and Gessler?

No. II

I HAVE heretofore intimated my intention of pursuing the tories through all their dark intrigues and wicked machinations, and to show the rise and progress of their schemes for enslaving this country. The honor of inventing and contriving these measures is not their due. They have been but servile copiers of the designs of Andros, Randolph, Dudley, and other champions of their cause towards the close of the last century. These latter worthies accomplished but little; and their plans had been buried with them for a long course of years, until, in the administration of the late Governor Shirley, they were revived by the persons who are now principally concerned in carrying them into execution. Shirley was a crafty, busy, ambitious, intriguing, enterprising man; and, having mounted, no matter by what means, to the chair of this province, he saw, in a young, growing country, vast prospects of ambition opening before his eyes, and conceived great designs of aggrandizing himself, his family, and his friends. Mr. Hutchinson and Mr. Oliver, the two famous letter-writers, were his principal ministers of state; Russell, Paxton, Ruggles, and a few others, were *subordinate* instruments. Among other schemes of this junto, one was to have a revenue in America, by authority of parliament.

In order to effect their purpose, it was necessary to concert measures with the other colonies. Dr. Franklin, who was known to be an active and very able man, and to have great influence in the province of Pennsylvania, was in Boston in the year 1754, and Mr. Shirley communicated to him the profound secret,—the great design of taxing the colonies by act of parliament. This sagacious gentleman, this eminent philosopher and distinguished patriot, to his lasting honor, sent the Governor an answer in writing, with the following remarks upon his scheme, remarks which would have discouraged any honest man from the pursuit. The remarks are these:—

"That the people always bear the burden best, when they have, or think they have, some *share* in the direction.

"That when public measures are generally distasteful to the people, the wheels of government must move more heavily.

"That excluding the people of America from all share in the choice of a grand council for their own defence, and taxing them in parliament, where they have no representative, would probably give extreme dissatisfaction.

"That there was no reason to doubt the willingness of the colonists to contribute for their own defence. That the people themselves, whose all was at stake, could better judge of the force necessary for their defence, and of the means for raising money for the purpose, than a British parliament at so great distance.

"That natives of America would be as likely to consult wisely and faithfully for the safety of their native country, as the governors sent from Britain, whose object is generally to make fortunes, and then return home, and who might therefore be expected to carry on the war against France, rather in a way by which themselves were likely to be gainers, than for the greatest advantage of the cause.

"That compelling the colonies to pay money for their own defence, without their consent, would show a suspicion of their loyalty, or of their regard for their country, or of their common sense, and would be treating them as conquered enemies, and not as free Britons, who hold it for their undoubted right, not to be taxed but by their own consent, given through their representatives.

"That parliamentary taxes, once laid on, are often continued, after the necessity for laying them on ceases; but that if the colonists were trusted to tax themselves, they would remove the burden from the people as soon as it should become unnecessary for them to bear it any longer.

"That if parliament is to tax the colonies, their assemblies of representatives may be dismissed as useless.

"That taxing the colonies in parliament for their own defence against the French, is not more just, than it would be to oblige the cinque-ports, and other parts of Britain, to maintain a force against France, and tax them for this purpose, without allowing them representatives in parliament.

"That the colonists have always been indirectly taxed by the mother country, (besides paying the taxes necessarily laid on by their own assemblies); inasmuch as they are obliged to purchase the manufactures of Britain, charged with innumerable heavy taxes, some of which manufactures they could make, and others could purchase cheaper at markets.

"That the colonists are besides taxed by the mother country, by being obliged to carry great part of their produce to Britain, and accept a lower price than they might have at other markets. The difference is a tax paid to Britain.

"That the whole wealth of the colonists centres at last in the mother country, which enables her to pay her taxes.

"That the colonies have, at the hazard of their lives and fortunes, extended the dominions and increased the commerce and riches of the mother country; that therefore the colonists do not deserve to be deprived of the native right of Britons, the right of being taxed only by representatives chosen by themselves.

"That an adequate representation in parliament would probably be acceptable to the colonists, and would best raise the views and interests of the whole empire."[6]

---

[6] See the letters to Governor Shirley. Sparks's *Works of B. Franklin,* vol. iii. pp. 56–68.

The last of these propositions seems not to have been well considered; because an adequate representation in parliament is totally impracticable; but the others have exhausted the subject.★

Whether the ministry at home, or the junto here, were discouraged by these masterly remarks, or by any other cause, the project of taxing the colonies was laid aside; Mr. Shirley was removed from this government, and Mr. Pownall was placed in his stead.

Mr. Pownall seems to have been a friend to liberty and to our constitution, and to have had an aversion to all plots against either; and, consequently, to have given his confidence to other persons than Hutchinson and Oliver, who, stung with envy against Mr. Pratt and others, who had the lead in affairs, set themselves, by propagating slanders against the Governor among the people, and especially among the clergy, to raise discontents, and make him uneasy in his seat. Pownall, averse to wrangling, and fond of the delights of England, solicited to be recalled, and after some time Mr. Bernard was removed from New Jersey to the chair of this province.

Bernard was the man for the purpose of the junto. Educated in the highest principles of monarchy; naturally daring and courageous; skilled enough in law and policy to do mischief, and avaricious to a most infamous degree; needy, at the same time, and having a numerous family to provide for, he was an instrument suitable in every respect, excepting one, for this junto to employ. The exception I mean was blunt frankness, very opposite to that cautious cunning, that deep dissimulation, to which they had, by long practice, disciplined themselves. However, they did not despair of teaching him this necessary artful quality by degrees, and the event showed that they were not wholly unsuccessful in their endeavors to do it.

While the war lasted, these simple provinces were of too much importance in the conduct of it, to be disgusted by any open attempt against their liberties. The junto, therefore, contented themselves with preparing

★ If any one should ask what authority or evidence I have of this anecdote, I refer to the second volume of the Political Disquisitions, pp. 276–9. A book which ought to be in the hands of every American who has learned to read.

their ground, by extending their connection and correspondencies in England, and by conciliating the friendship of the crown-officers occasionally here, and insinuating their designs as necessary to be undertaken in some future favorable opportunity, for the good of the empire, as well as of the colonies.

The designs of Providence are inscrutable. It affords conjunctures, favorable for their designs, to bad men, as well as to good. The conclusion of the peace was the most critical opportunity for our junto that could have presented. A peace, founded on the destruction of that system of policy, the most glorious for the nation that ever was formed, and which was never equalled in the conduct of the English government, except in the interregnum, and perhaps in the reign of Elizabeth; which system, however, by its being abruptly broken off, and its chief conductor discarded before it was completed, proved unfortunate to the nation, by leaving it sinking in a bottomless gulf of debt, oppressed and borne down with taxes.

At this lucky time, when the British financier was driven out of his wits, for ways and means to supply the demands upon him, Bernard is employed by the junto, to suggest to him the project of taxing the colonies by act of parliament.

I do not advance this without evidence. I appeal to a publication made by Sir Francis Bernard himself, the last year, of his own Select Letters on the Trade and Government of America; and the Principles of Law and Polity applied to the American Colonies. I shall make use of this pamphlet[7] before I have done.

In the year 1764, Mr. Bernard transmitted home to different noblemen and gentlemen, four copies of his Principles of Law and Polity, with a preface, which proves incontestably, that the project of new-regulating the American Colonies was not first suggested to him by the ministry, but by him to them. The words of this preface are these: "The present expectation, that a new regulation of the American governments will soon take place, probably arises more from the opinion the public has of the abilities of the present ministry, than from any thing that has transpired

---

[7] Printed in London, in 1774.

from the cabinet. It cannot be supposed that their penetration can over-look the necessity of such a regulation, nor their public spirit fail to carry it into execution. But it may be a question, whether the present is a proper time for this work; more urgent business may stand before it; some preparatory steps may be required to precede it; but these will only serve to postpone. As we may expect that this reformation, like all others, will be opposed by powerful prejudices, it may not be amiss to reason with them at leisure, and endeavor to take off their force before they become opposed to government."

These are the words of that arch-enemy of North America, written in 1764, and then transmitted to four persons, with a desire that they might be communicated to others.

Upon these words, it is impossible not to observe: First, that the min-istry had never signified to him any intention of new-regulating the colonies, and therefore, that it was he who most officiously and imperti-nently put them upon the pursuit of this *will-with-a-wisp,* which has led him and them into so much mire; secondly, the artful flattery with which he insinuates these projects into the minds of the ministry, as matters of absolute necessity, which their great penetration could not fail to discover, nor their great regard to the public omit; thirdly, the importunity with which he urges a speedy accomplishment of his pretended reformation of the governments; and, fourthly, his consciousness that these schemes would be opposed, although he affects to expect from powerful prejudices only, that opposition, which all Americans say, has been dictated by sound reason, true policy, and eternal justice. The last thing I shall take notice of is, the artful, yet most false and wicked insinuation, that such new regula-tions were then generally expected. This is so absolutely false, that, except-ing Bernard himself, and his junto, scarcely anybody on this side the water had any suspicion of it,—insomuch that, if Bernard had made public, at that time, his preface and principles, as he sent them to the ministry, it is much to be doubted whether he could have lived in this country; certain it is, he would have had no friends in this province out of the junto.

The intention of the junto was, to procure a revenue to be raised in America by act of parliament. Nothing was further from their designs and wishes, than the drawing or sending this revenue into the exchequer in England, to be spent there in discharging the national debt, and lessening the burdens of the poor people there. They were more selfish. They chose to have the fingering of the money themselves. Their design was, that the money should be applied, first, in a large salary to the governor. This would gratify Bernard's avarice; and then, it would render him and all other governors, not only independent of the people, but still more absolutely a slave to the will of the minister. They intended likewise a salary for the lieutenant-governor. This would appease in some degree the gnawings of Hutchinson's avidity, in which he was not a whit behind Bernard himself. In the next place, they intended a salary to the judges of the common law, as well as admiralty. And thus, the whole government, executive and judicial, was to be rendered wholly independent of the people, (and their representatives rendered useless, insignificant, and even burthensome,) and absolutely dependent upon, and under the direction of the will of the minister of state. They intended, further, to new-model the whole continent of North America; make an entire new division of it into distinct, though more extensive and less numerous colonies; to sweep away all the charters upon the continent with the destroying besom of an act of parliament; and reduce all the governments to the plan of the royal governments, with a nobility in each colony, not hereditary indeed at first, but for life. They did indeed flatter the ministry and people in England with distant hopes of a revenue from America, at some future period, to be appropriated to national uses there. But this was not to happen, in their minds, for some time. The governments must be new-modelled, new-regulated, reformed, first, and then the governments here would be able and willing to carry into execution any acts of parliament, or measures of the ministry, for fleecing the people here, to pay debts, or support pensioners on the American establishment, or bribe electors or members of parliament, or any other purpose that a virtuous ministry could desire.

But, as ill luck would have it, the British financier was as selfish as themselves, and, instead of raising money for them, chose to raise it for himself. He put the cart before the horse. He chose to get the revenue into the exchequer, because he had hungry cormorants enough about him in England, whose cawings were more troublesome to his ears than the croaking of the ravens in America. And he thought, if America could afford any revenue at all, and he could get it by authority of parliament, he might have it himself, to give to his friends, as well as raise it for the junto here, to spend themselves, or give to theirs. This unfortunate, preposterous improvement, of Mr. Grenville, upon the plan of the junto, had wellnigh ruined the whole.

I will proceed no further without producing my evidence. Indeed, to a man who was acquainted with this junto, and had any opportunity to watch their motions, observe their language, and remark their countenances, for these last twelve years, no other evidence is necessary; it was plain to such persons what this junto were about. But we have evidence enough now, under their own hands, of the whole of what was said of them by their opposers through the whole period.

Governor Bernard, in his letter of July 11, 1764, says, "that a general reformation of the American governments would become not only a desirable but a necessary measure." What his idea was, of a general reformation of the American governments, is to be learned from his Principles of Law and Polity, which he sent to the ministry in 1764. I shall select a few of them in his own words; but I wish the whole of them could be printed in the newspapers, that America might know more generally the principles, and designs, and exertions of our junto.

His 29th proposition is: "The rule that a British subject shall not be bound by laws, or liable to taxes, but what he has consented to by his representatives, must be confined to the inhabitants of Great Britain only; and is not strictly true even there.

"30. The Parliament of Great Britain, as well from its rights of sovereignty, as from occasional exigencies, has a right to make laws for, and impose taxes upon, its subjects in its external dominions, although they are not represented in such Parliament. But,

"31. Taxes imposed upon the external dominions ought to be applied to the use of the people from whom they are raised.

"32. The Parliament of Great Britain has a right and a duty to take care to provide for the defence of the American colonies; especially as such colonies are unable to defend themselves.

"33. The Parliament of Great Britain has a right and a duty to take care that provision be made for a sufficient support of the American governments." Because,

"34. The support of the government is one of the principal conditions upon which a colony is allowed the power of legislation." Also, because,

"35. Some of the American colonies have shown themselves deficient in the support of their several governments, both as to sufficiency and independency."

His 75th proposition is: "Every American government is capable of having its constitution altered for the better.

"76. The grants of the powers of government to the American colonies, by charters, cannot be understood to be intended for other than their infant or growing states.

"77. They cannot be intended for their mature state, that is, for perpetuity; because they are in many things unconstitutional, and contrary to the very nature of a British government. Therefore,

"78. They must be considered as designed only as temporary means, for settling and bringing forward the peopling the colonies; which being effected, the cause of the peculiarity of their constitution ceases.

"79. If the charters can be pleaded against the authority of parliament, they amount to an alienation of the dominions of Great Britain, and are, in effect, acts of dismembering the British empire, and will operate as such, if care is not taken to prevent it.

"83. The notion which has heretofore prevailed, that the dividing America into many governments, and different modes of government, will be the means to prevent their uniting to revolt, is ill-founded; since, if the governments were ever so much consolidated, it will be necessary to have so many distinct states, as to make a union to revolt impracticable." Whereas,

"84. The splitting America into many small governments, weakens the governing power and strengthens that of the people; and thereby makes revolting more probable and more practicable.

"85. To prevent revolts in future times, (for there is no room to fear them in the present,) the most effectual means would be, to make the governments large and respectable, and balance the powers of them.

"86. There is no government in America at present, whose powers are properly balanced; there not being in any of them a real and distinct third legislative power mediating between the king and the people, which is the peculiar excellence of the British constitution.

"87. The want of such a third legislative power adds weight to the popular, and lightens the royal scale, so as to destroy the balance between the royal and popular powers.

"88. Although America is not now, (and probably will not be for many years to come) ripe enough for a hereditary nobility, yet it is now capable of a nobility for life.

"89. A nobility appointed by the king for life, and made independent, would probably give strength and stability to the American governments as effectually as a hereditary nobility does to that of Great Britain.

"90. The reformation of the American governments should not be controlled by the present boundaries of the colonies, as they were mostly settled upon partial, occasional, and accidental considerations, without any regard to the whole.

"91. To settle the American governments to the greatest possible advantage, it will be necessary to reduce the number of them; in some places to unite and consolidate; in others to separate and transfer; and in general to divide by natural boundaries instead of imaginary lines.

"92. If there should be but one form of government established for all the North American provinces, it would greatly facilitate the reformation of them; since, if the mode of government was everywhere the same, people would be more indifferent under what division they were ranged.

"93. No objections ought to arise to the alteration of the boundaries of provinces from proprietors, on account of their property only; since there is no occasion that it should in the least affect the boundaries of properties.

"94. The present distinctions of one government being more free or more popular than another, tends to embarrass and to weaken the whole, and should not be allowed to subsist among people subject to one king and one law, and all equally fit for one form of government.

"95. The American colonies, in general, are at this time arrived at that state, which qualifies them to receive the most perfect form of government which their situation and relation to Great Britain make them capable of.

"96. The people of North America, at this time, expect a revisal and reformation of the American governments, and are better disposed to submit to it than ever they were, or perhaps ever will be again.

"97. This is, therefore, the proper and critical time to reform the American governments, upon a general, constitutional, firm, and durable plan; and if it is not done now, it will probably every day grow more difficult, till at last it becomes impracticable."

My friends, these are the words, the plans, principles, and endeavors of Governor Bernard, in the year 1764. That Hutchinson and Oliver, notwithstanding all their disguises, which you well remember, were in unison with him in the whole of his measures, can be doubted by no man. It appeared sufficiently in the part they all along acted, notwithstanding their professions. And it appears incontestably from their detected letters; of which more hereafter.

Now, let me ask you, if the Parliament of Great Britain had all the natural foundations of authority, wisdom, goodness, justice, power, in as great perfection as they ever existed in any body of men since Adam's fall; and if the English nation was the most virtuous, pure, and free that ever was; would not such an unlimited subjection of three millions of people to that parliament, at three thousand miles distance, be real slavery? There are but two sorts of men in the world, freemen and slaves. The very definition of a freeman is one who is bound by no law to which he has not consented. Americans would have no way of giving or withholding their consent to the acts of this parliament, therefore they would not be freemen. But when luxury, effeminacy, and venality are arrived at such a shocking pitch in England; when both electors and elected are become one mass of corruption; when the nation is oppressed to death with debts and taxes, owing to their own extravagance and want of wisdom, what would be your condition under such an absolute subjection to parliament? You would not only be slaves, but the most abject sort of slaves, to the worst sort of masters! at least this is my opinion.

Judge you for yourselves between Massachusettensis and Novanglus.

No. III

...

The grand aphorism of the policy of the whigs has been to unite the people of America, and divide those of Great Britain. The reverse of this has been the maxim of the tories, namely,—to unite the people of Great Britain, and divide those of America. All the movements, marches, and countermarches of both parties, on both sides of the Atlantic, may be reduced to one or the other of these rules. I have shown, in opposition to Massachusettensis, that the people of America are united more perfectly than the most sanguine whig could ever have hoped, or than the most timid tory could have feared. Let us now examine whether the people of Great Britain are equally united against us. For, if the contending countries were equally united, the prospect of success in the quarrel would depend upon the comparative wisdom, firmness, strength, and other advantages of each. And if such a comparison was made, it would not appear to a demonstration that Great Britain could so easily subdue and conquer. It is not so easy a thing for the most powerful state to conquer a country a thousand leagues off. How many years time, how many millions of money, did it take, with five-and-thirty thousand men, to conquer the poor province of Canada? And, after all the battles and victories, it never would have submitted, without a capitulation which secured to them their religion and properties.

But we know that the people of Great Britain are not united against us. We distinguish between the ministry, the house of commons, the officers of the army, navy, excise, customs, &c., who are dependent on the ministry, and tempted, if not obliged, to echo their voices, and the body of the people. We are assured, by thousands of letters from persons of good intelligence, by the general strain of publications in public papers, pamphlets, and magazines, and by some larger works written for posterity, that the body of the people are friends to America, and wish us success in our struggles against the claims of parliament and administration. We know, that millions in England and Scotland will think it unrighteous, impolitic, and ruinous to make war upon us; and a minister, though he may have a marble heart, will proceed with a diffident, desponding spirit. We know that London and Bristol, the two greatest commercial cities in the empire, have declared themselves, in the most decisive manner, in favor of our cause,—so explicitly, that the former has bound her members under their hands to assist us; and the latter has chosen two known friends of America, one attached to us by principle, birth, and the most ardent affection,[8] the other an able advocate for us on several great occasions.[9] We know that many of the most virtuous and independent of the nobility and gentry are for us, and among them, the best bishop that adorns the bench,[10] as great a judge as the nation can boast,[11] and the greatest statesman it ever saw.[12] We know that the nation is loaded with debts and taxes, by the folly and iniquity of its ministers, and that, without the trade of America, it can neither long support its fleet and army, nor pay the interest of its debt.

But we are told that the nation is now united against us; that they hold they have a right to tax us and legislate for us, as firmly as we deny it; that we are a part of the British empire; that every state must have an uncontrollable power coextensive with the empire; that there is little probability of serving ourselves by ingenious distinctions between external andinternal taxes; that if we are not a part of the state, and subject to the supreme authority of parliament, Great Britain will make us so; that if this opportunity of reclaiming the colonies is lost, they will be dismembered from the empire; and, although they may continue their allegiance to the king, they will own none to the imperial crown.

[8] Mr. Cruger, a native of New York, better known as he who said "ditto" to Mr. Burke.
[9] Edmund Burke.
[10] Dr. Shipley, Bishop of St. Asaph.
[11] Lord Camden.
[12] Lord Chatham.

To all this I answer, that the nation is not so united; that they do not so universally hold they have such a right. And my reasons I have given before; that the terms "British Empire" are not the language of the common law, but the language of newspapers and political pamphlets; that the dominions of the king of Great Britain have no power coextensive with them. I would ask, by what law the parliament has authority over America? By the law of God, in the Old and New Testament, it has none; by the law of nature and nations, it has none; by the common law of England, it has none, for the common law, and the authority of parliament founded on it, never extended beyond the four seas; by statute law it has none, for no statute was made before the settlement of the colonies for this purpose; and the declaratory act, made in 1766, was made without our consent, by a parliament which had no authority beyond the four seas. What religious, moral, or political obligations then are we under to submit to parliament as a supreme legislative? None at all. When it is said, that if we are not subject to the supreme authority of parliament, Great Britain will make us so, all other laws and obligations are given up, and recourse is had to the *ratio ultima* of Louis XIV, and the *suprema lex* of the king of Sardinia,—to the law of brickbats and cannon balls, which can be answered only by brickbats and balls.

This language, "the imperial crown of Great Britain," is not the style of the common law, but of court sycophants. It was introduced in allusion to the Roman empire, and intended to insinuate that the prerogative of the imperial crown of England was like that of the Roman emperor, after the maxim was established, *quod principi placuit legis habet vigorem;*[13] and, so far from including the two houses of parliament in the idea of this imperial crown, it was intended to insinuate that the crown was absolute, and had no need of lords or commons to make or dispense with laws. Yet even these court sycophants, when driven to an explanation, never dared to put any other sense upon the words *imperial crown* than this, that the crown of England was independent of France, Spain, and all other kings and states in the world.

---

[1]["What the prince has decided has the force of law." Ed.]

When he says, that the king's dominions must have an uncontrollable power coextensive with them, I ask whether they have such a power or not? and utterly deny that they have, by any law but that of Louis XIV, and the king of Sardinia. If they have not, and it is necessary that they should have, it then follows that there is a defect in what he calls the British empire; and how shall this defect be supplied? It cannot be supplied consistently with reason, justice, policy, morality, or humanity, without the consent of the colonies and some new plan of connection. But if Great Britain will set all these at defiance, and resort to the *ratio ultima,* all Europe will pronounce her a tyrant, and America never will submit to her, be the danger of disobedience as great as it will.

But there is no need of any other power than that of regulating trade, and this the colonies ever have been, and will be, ready and willing to concede to her. But she will never obtain from America any further concession while she exists. We are then asked, "for what she protected and defended the colonies against the maritime powers of Europe, from their first settlement to this day?" I answer, for her own interest; because all the profits of our trade centred in her lap. But it ought to be remembered, that her name, not her purse, nor her fleets and armies ever protected us, until the last war, and then the minister who conducted that war informed us that the annual millions from America enabled her to do it.

We are then asked, for what she purchased New York of the Dutch? I answer, she never did. The Dutch never owned it, were never more than trespassers and intruders there, and were finally expelled by conquest. It was ceded, it is true, by the treaty of Breda, and it is said in some authors, that some other territory in India was ceded to the Dutch in lieu of it. But this was the transaction of the king, not of parliament, and therefore makes nothing to the argument.

But admitting, for argument sake, (since the cautious Massachusettensis will urge us into the discussion of such questions,) what is not a supposable case, that the nation should be so sunk in sloth, luxury, and corruption, as to suffer their minister to persevere in his mad blunders, and send fire and sword against us, how shall we defend ourselves? The colonies south of Pennsylvania have no men to spare, we are told. But we know better; we know that all those colonies have a back country, which is inhabited by a hardy, robust people, many of whom are emigrants from New England, and habituated, like multitudes of New England men, to carry their fuzees or rifles upon one shoulder, to defend themselves against the Indians, while they carry their axes, scythes, and hoes upon the other, to till the ground. Did not those colonies furnish men the last war, excepting Maryland? Did not Virginia furnish men, one regiment particularly, equal to any regular regiment in the service? Does the soft Massachusettensis imagine, that in the unnatural, horrid war he is now supposing, their exertions would be less? If he does, he is very ill informed of their principles, their present sentiments and temper.

...

No. IV

...

Massachusettensis and his friends the tories are startled at the calamities they have brought upon their country; and their conscious guilt, their smarting, wounded mind, will not suffer them to confess, even to themselves, what they have done. Their silly denials of their own share in it, before a people who, they know, have abundant evidence against them, never fail to remind me of an ancient *fugitive,* whose conscience could not bear the recollection of what he had done. "I know not; am I my brother's keeper?" he replies, with all the apparent simplicity of truth and innocence, to one from whom he was very sensible his guilt could not be hid. The still more absurd and ridiculous attempts of the tories, to throw off the blame of these calamities from themselves to the whigs, remind me of another story, which I have read in the Old Testament. When Joseph's brethren had sold him to the Ishmaelites for twenty pieces of silver, in order to conceal their own avarice, malice, and envy, they dip the coat of many colors in the blood of a kid, and say that an evil beast had rent him in pieces and devoured him. However, what the sons of Israel intended for ruin to Joseph, proved the salvation of the family; and I hope and believe that the whigs will have the magnanimity, like him, to suppress their resentment, and the felicity of saving their ungrateful brothers.

This writer has a faculty of insinuating errors into the mind almost imperceptibly, he dresses them so in the guise of truth. He says, that "the revenue to the crown from America amounted to but little more than the charges of collecting it," at the close of the last war. I believe it did not to so much. The truth is, there never was a pretence of raising a revenue in America before that time, and when the claim was first set up, it gave an alarm like a warlike expedition against us. True it is, that some duties had been laid before by parliament, under pretence of regulating our trade, and, by a collusion and combination between the West India planters and the North American governors, some years before, duties had been laid upon molasses, &c. under the same pretence; but, in reality, merely to advance the value of the estates of the planters in the West India Islands, and to put some plunder, under the name of thirds of seizures, into the pockets of the governors. But these duties, though more had been collected in this province than in any other, in proportion, were never regularly collected in any of the colonies. So that the idea of an American revenue, for one purpose or another, had never, at this time, been formed in American minds.

Our writer goes on: "She (Great Britain) thought it as reasonable that the colonies should bear a part of the national burden, as that they should share in the national benefit."

Upon this subject Americans have a great deal to say. The national debt, before the last war, was near a hundred millions. Surely America had no share in running into that debt. What is the reason, then, that she should pay it? But a small part of the sixty millions spent in the last war was for her benefit. Did she not bear her full share of the burden of the last war in America? Did not the province pay twelve shillings in the pound in taxes for the support of it; and send a sixth or seventh part of her sons into actual service? And, at the conclusion of the war, was she not left half a million sterling in debt? Did not all the rest of New England exert itself in proportion? What is the reason that the Massachusetts has paid its debt, and the British minister, in thirteen years of peace, has paid none of his? Much of it might have been paid in this time, had not such extravagance and speculation prevailed, as ought to be an eternal warning to

America, never to trust such a minister with her money. What is the reason that the great and necessary virtues of simplicity, frugality, and economy cannot live in England, Scotland, and Ireland, as well as America?

We have much more to say still. Great Britain has confined all our trade to herself. We are willing she should, so far as it can be for the good of the empire. But we say, that we ought to be allowed as credit, in the account of public burdens and expenses, so much, paid in taxes, as we are obliged to sell our commodities to her cheaper than we could get for them at foreign markets. The difference is really a tax upon us for the good of the empire. We are obliged to take from Great Britain commodities that we could purchase cheaper elsewhere. This difference is a tax upon us for the good of the empire. We submit to this cheerfully; but insist that we ought to have credit for it in the account of the expenses of the empire, because it is really a tax upon us.

Another thing; I will venture a bold assertion,—let Massachusettensis or any other friend of the minister confute me,—the three million Americans, by the tax aforesaid, upon what they are obliged to export to Great Britain only, what they are obliged to import from Great Britain only, and the quantities of British manufactures which, in these climates, they are obliged to consume more than the like number of people in any part of the three kingdoms, ultimately pay more of the taxes and duties that are apparently paid in Great Britain, than any three million subjects in the three kingdoms. All this may be computed and reduced to stubborn figures by the minister, if he pleases. We cannot do it; we have not the accounts, records, &c. Now let this account be fairly stated, and I will engage for America, upon any penalty, that she will pay the overplus, if any, in her own constitutional way, provided it is to be applied for national purposes, as paying off the national debt, maintaining the fleet, &c., not to the support of a standing army in time of peace, placemen, pensioners, &c.

Besides, every farthing of expense which has been incurred, on pretence of protecting, defending, and securing America, since the last war, has been worse than thrown away; it has been applied to do mischief. Keeping an army in America has been nothing but a public nuisance.

Furthermore, we see that all the public money that is raised here, and have reason to believe all that will or can be raised, will be applied, not for public purposes, national or provincial, but merely to corrupt the sons of America, and create a faction to destroy its interest and happiness.

There are scarcely three sentences together, in all the voluminous productions of this plausible writer, which do not convey some error in fact or principle, tinged with a coloring to make it pass for truth. He says, "the idea that the stamps were a tax, not only exceeding our proportion, but beyond our utmost ability to pay, united the colonies generally in opposing it." That we thought it beyond our proportion and ability is true; but it was not this thought which united the colonies in opposing it. When he says that at first, we did not dream of denying the authority of parliament to tax us, much less to legislate for us, he discovers plainly either a total inattention to the sentiments of America, at that time, or a disregard of what he affirms.

The truth is, the authority of parliament was never generally acknowledged in America. More than a century since, Massachusetts and Virginia both protested against even the act of navigation, and refused obedience, for this very reason, because they were not represented in parliament and were therefore not bound; and afterwards confirmed it by their own provincial authority. And from that time to this, the general sense of the colonies has been, that the authority of parliament was confined to the regulation of trade, and did not extend to taxation or internal legislation.

In the year 1764, your house of representatives sent home a petition to the king against the plan of taxing them. Mr. Hutchinson, Oliver, and their relations and connections were then in the legislature, and had great influence there. It was by their influence that the two houses were induced to wave the word *rights* and an express denial of the right of parliament to tax us, to the great grief and distress of the friends of liberty in both houses. Mr. Otis and Mr. Thacher labored in the committee to obtain an express denial. Mr. Hutchinson expressly said, he agreed with them in opinion, that parliament had no right, but thought it ill policy to express this opinion in the petition. In truth, I will be bold to say, there was not any member of either house who thought that parliament had such a right at that time.

The house of representatives, at that time, gave their approbation to Mr. Otis's Rights of the Colonies, in which it was shown to be inconsistent with the right of British subjects to be taxed but by their own representatives.

In 1765, our house expressly resolved against the right of parliament to tax us. The congress at New York resolved:

"3. That it is inseparably essential to the freedom of a people, and the undoubted right of Englishmen, that no tax be imposed on them, but with their own consent, given personally, or by their representatives.

"4. That the people of the colonies are not, and from their local circumstances cannot, be represented in the house of commons of Great Britain.

"5. That the only representatives of the people of the colonies are the persons chosen therein by themselves; and that no taxes ever have been, or can be constitutionally imposed on them, but by their respective legislatures."

Is it not a striking disregard to truth, in the artful Massachusettensis, to say, that, at first, we did not dream of denying the right of parliament to tax us? It was the principle that united the colonies to oppose it, not the *quantum* of the tax. Did not Dr. Franklin deny the right in 1754, in his remarks upon Governor Shirley's scheme, and suppose that all America would deny it? We had considered ourselves as connected with Great Britain, but we never thought parliament the supreme legislature over us. We never generally supposed it to have any authority over us, but from necessity, and that necessity we thought confined to the regulation of trade, and to such matters as concerned all the colonies together. We never allowed them any authority in our internal concerns.

This writer says, "acts of parliament for regulating our internal polity were familiar."[14] This I deny. So far otherwise, that the Hatter's Act was

---

[14] "We had paid postage, agreeable to act of parliament, for establishing a post-office, duties imposed for regulating trade, and even for raising a revenue to the crown, without questioning the right, though we closely adverted to the rate or *quantum*. We knew that in all those acts of government the good of the whole had been consulted; and whenever, through want of information, any thing grievous had been ordained, we were sure of obtaining redress by a proper representation of it." *Massachusettensis*.

never regarded; the act to destroy the Land Bank scheme raised a greater ferment in this province than the Stamp Act did, which was appeased only by passing province laws directly in opposition to it. The act against slitting-mills and tilt-hammers never was executed here. As to the postage, it was so useful a regulation, so few persons paid it, and they found such a benefit by it, that little opposition was made to it. Yet every man who thought about it, called it a usurpation. Duties for regulating trade we paid, because we thought it just and necessary that they should regulate the trade which their power protected. As for duties for a revenue, none were ever laid by parliament for that purpose, until 1764, when, and ever since, its authority to do it has been constantly denied. Nor is this complaisant writer near the truth when he says, "We knew that in all those acts of government, the good of the whole had been consulted." On the contrary, we know that the private interest of provincial governors and West India planters had been consulted in the duties on foreign molasses, &c., and the private interest of a few Portugal merchants, in obliging us to touch at Falmouth with fruit, &c., in opposition to the good of the whole, and in many other instances.

The resolves of the house of burgesses of Virginia upon the Stamp Act did great honor to that province, and to the eminent patriot, Patrick Henry, who composed them.[15] But these resolves made no alteration in the opinion of the colonies, concerning the right of parliament to make that act. They expressed the universal opinion of the continent at that time; and the alacrity with which every other colony, and the congress at New York, adopted the same sentiment in similar resolves, proves the entire union of

[15] "Some few months after it was known that the Stamp Act was passed, some resolves of the house of burgesses in Virginia, denying the right of parliament to tax the colonies, made their appearance. We read them with wonder; they savored of independence; they flattered the human passions; the reasoning was specious; we wished it conclusive. The transition to believing it so was easy; and we, almost all America, followed their example, in resolving that the parliament had no such right. It now became unpopular to suggest the contrary. His life would be in danger that asserted it. The newspapers were open to but one side of the question; and the inflammatory pieces that issued weekly from the press, worked up the populace to a fit temper to commit the outrages that ensued." *Massachusettensis*.

the colonies in it, and their universal determination to avow and support it. What follows here,—that it became so popular, that his life was in danger who suggested the contrary, and that the press was "open to one side only,"—are direct misrepresentations and wicked calumnies.

Then we are told by this sincere writer, that when we obtained a partial repeal of the statute imposing duties on glass, paper, and teas, "this was the lucky moment when to have closed the dispute." What? with a board of commissioners remaining, the sole end of whose creation was to form and conduct a revenue? With an act of parliament remaining, the professed design of which, expressed in the preamble, was to raise a revenue, and appropriate it to the payment of governors' and judges' salaries; the duty remaining, too, upon an article which must raise a large sum, the consumption of which would constantly increase? Was this a time to retreat? Let me ask this sincere writer a simple question,—does he seriously believe that the designs of imposing other taxes, and of new-modelling our governments, would have been laid aside by the ministry or by the servants of the crown here? Does he think that Mr. Bernard, Mr. Hutchinson, the commissioners, and others would have been content then to have desisted? If he really thinks so, he knows little of the human heart, and still less of those gentlemen's hearts. It was at this very time that the salary was given to the governor, and an order solicited for that to the judges.

Then we are entertained with a great deal of ingenious talk about whigs and tories, and at last are told, that some of the whigs owed all their importance to popularity.[16] And what then? Did not as many of the tories owe their importance to popularity? And did not many more owe all their importance to unpopularity? If it had not been for their taking

---

[16] "There were two parties in this province of pretty long standing, known by the name of whig and tory, which at this time were not a little embittered against each other. Men of abilities and acknowledged probity were on both sides. If the tories were suspected of pursuing their private interest through the medium of court favor, there was equal reason to suspect the whigs of pursuing their private interest by the means of popularity. Indeed, some of them owed all their importance to it, and must in a little time have sunk into obscurity, had these turbulent commotions then subsided." *Massachusettensis*.

an active part on the side of the ministry, would not some of the most
conspicuous and eminent of them have been unimportant enough?
Indeed, through the two last administrations, to despise and hate the people, and to be despised and hated by them, were the principal recommendations to the favors of government, and all the qualification that
was required.

"The tories," says he, "were for closing the controversy." That is, they
were for contending no more; and it was equally true, that they never were
for contending at all, but lying at mercy. It was the very end they had
aimed at from the beginning. They had now got the governor's salary
out of the revenue, a number of pensions and places; they knew they could
at any time get the judges' salaries from the same fountain; and they
wanted to get the people reconciled and familiarized to this, before they
went upon any new projects.

"The whigs were averse to restoring government; they even refused to
revive a temporary Riot Act which expired about this time." Government
had as much vigor then as ever, excepting only in those cases which
affected this dispute. The Riot Act expired in 1770, immediately after the
massacre in King Street. It was not revived, and never will be in this
colony; nor will any one ever be made in any other, while a standing army
is illegally posted here to butcher the people, whenever a governor or a
magistrate, who may be a tool, shall order it. "Perhaps the whigs thought
that mobs were a necessary ingredient in their system of opposition."
Whether they did or not, it is certain that mobs have been thought a
necessary ingredient by the tories in their system of administration, mobs
of the worst sort, with red coats, fuzees, and bayonets; and the lives and
limbs of the whigs have been in greater danger from these, than ever the
tories were from others.

"The scheme of the whigs flattered the people with the idea of independence; the tories' plan supposed a degree of subordination." This is artful enough, as usual, not to say jesuitical. The word independence is one of
those which this writer uses, as he does treason and rebellion, to impose
upon the undistinguishing on both sides of the Atlantic. But let us take
him to pieces. What does he mean by independence? Does he mean inde-

pendent of the crown of Great Britain, and an independent republic in America, or a confederation of independent republics? No doubt he intended the undistinguishing should understand him so. If he did, nothing can be more wicked, or a greater slander on the whigs; because he knows there is not a man in the province among the whigs, nor ever was, who harbors a wish of that sort. Does he mean that the people were flattered with the idea of total independence on parliament? If he does, this is equally malicious and injurious; because he knows that the equity and necessity of parliament's regulating trade has always been acknowledged; our determination to consent and submit to such regulations constantly expressed; and all the acts of trade, in fact, to this very day, much more submitted to and strictly executed in this province than any other in America.

There is equal ambiguity in the words "degree of subordination." The whigs acknowledge a subordination to the king, in as strict and strong a sense as the tories. The whigs acknowledge a voluntary subordination to parliament, as far as the regulation of trade. What degree of subordination, then, do the tories acknowledge? An absolute dependence upon parliament as their supreme legislative, in all cases whatever, in their internal polity, as well as taxation? This would be too gross, and would lose Massachusettensis all his readers; for there is nobody here who will expose his understanding so much, as explicitly to adopt such a sentiment. Yet it is such an absolute dependence and submission that these writers would persuade us to, or else there is no need of changing our sentiments and conduct. Why will not these gentlemen speak out, show us plainly their opinion, that the new government they have fabricated for this province is better than the old, and that all the other measures we complain of are for our and the public good, and exhort us directly to submit to them? The reason is, because they know they should lose their readers.

"The whigs were sensible that there was no oppression that could be seen or felt." The tories have so often said and wrote this to one another, that I sometimes suspect they believe it to be true. But it is quite otherwise. The castle of the province was taken out of their hands and garrisoned by regular soldiers. This they could see, and they thought it indicated a hostile intention and disposition towards them. They continually paid their money to collectors of duties; this they could both see and feel. A host of placemen, whose whole business it was to collect a revenue, were continually rolling before them in their chariots. These they saw. Their governor was no longer paid by themselves, according to their charter, but out of the new revenue, in order to render their assemblies useless, and indeed contemptible. The judges' salaries were threatened every day to be paid in the same unconstitutional manner. The dullest eyesight could not but see to what all this tended, namely,—to prepare the way for greater innovations and oppressions. They knew a minister would never spend his money in this way, if he had not some end to answer by it. Another thing they both saw and felt. Every man, of every character, who, by voting, writing, speaking, or otherwise, had favored the Stamp Act, the Tea Act, and every other measure of a minister or governor, who they knew was aiming at the destruction of their form of government, and introducing parliamentary taxation, was uniformly, in some department or other, promoted to some place of honor or profit for ten years together; and, on the other hand, every man who favored the people in their opposition to those innovations, was depressed, degraded, and persecuted, so far as it was in the power of the government to do it.

This they considered as a systematical means of encouraging every man of abilities to espouse the cause of parliamentary taxation and the plan of destroying their charter privilege, and to discourage all from exerting themselves in opposition to them. This they thought a plan to enslave them; for they uniformly think that the destruction of their charter, making the council and judges wholly dependent on the crown, and the people subject to the unlimited power of parliament as their supreme legislative, is slavery. They were certainly rightly told, then, that the ministry and their governors together had formed a design to enslave them, and that when once this was done, they had the highest reason to expect window-taxes, heart-taxes, land-taxes, and all others; and that these were only paving the way for reducing the country to lordships. Were the people mistaken in these suspicions? Is it not now certain, that Governor Bernard, in 1764, had formed a design of this sort? Read his Principles of Polity. And that Lieutenant-Governor Oliver, as late as 1768, or 9, enforced the same plan? Read his letters. Now, if Massachusettensis will be ingenuous, avow this design, show the people its utility, and that it ought to be done by parliament, he will act the part of an honest man. But to insinuate that there was no such plan, when he knows there was, is acting the part of one of the junto.

It is true, that the people of this country in general, and of this province in special, have a hereditary apprehension of and aversion to lordships, temporal and spiritual. Their ancestors fled to this wilderness to avoid them; they suffered sufficiently under them in England. And there are few of the present generation who have not been warned of the danger of them by their fathers or grandfathers, and enjoined to oppose them. And neither Bernard nor Oliver ever dared to avow before them, the designs which they had certainly formed to introduce them. Nor does Massachusettensis dare to avow his opinion in their favor. I do not mean that such avowal would expose their persons to danger, but it would their character and writings to universal contempt.

When you were told that the people of England were depraved, the parliament venal, and the ministry corrupt, were you not told most melancholy truths? Will Massachusettensis deny any of them? Does not every man who comes from England, whig or tory, tell you the same thing? Do they make any secret of it, or use any delicacy about it? Do they not most of them avow that corruption is so established there as to be incurable, and a necessary instrument of government? Is not the British constitution arrived nearly to that point where the Roman republic was when Jugurtha left it, and pronounced it, "a venal city, ripe for destruction, if it can only find a purchaser?" If Massachusettensis can prove that it is not, he will remove from my mind one of the heaviest loads which lie upon it.

Who has censured the tories for remissness, I know not. Whoever it was, he did them great injustice. Every one that I know of that character has been, through the whole tempestuous period, as indefatigable as human nature will admit, going about seeking whom he might devour, making use of art, flattery, terror, temptation, and allurements, in every shape in which human wit could dress it up, in public and private; but all to no purpose. The people have grown more and more weary of them every day, until now the land mourns under them.

Massachusettensis is then seized with a violent fit of anger at the clergy.[17] It is curious to observe the conduct of the tories towards this sacred body. If a clergyman, of whatever character, preaches against the principles of the revolution, and tells the people that, upon pain of damnation, they must submit to an established government, the tories cry him up as an excellent man and a wonderful preacher, invite him to their tables, procure him missions from the society and chaplainships to the navy, and flatter him with the hopes of lawn sleeves. But if a clergyman preaches Christianity, and tells the magistrates that they were not distinguished from their brethren for their private emolument, but for the good of the people; that the people are bound in conscience to obey a good government, but are not bound to submit to one that aims at destroying all the ends of government,—oh sedition! treason!

The clergy in all ages and countries, and in this in particular, are disposed enough to be on the side of government as long as it is tolerable. If they have not been generally in the late administration on that side, it is a demonstration that the late administration has been universally odious. The clergy of this province are a virtuous, sensible, and learned set of men, and they do not take their sermons from newspapers, but the Bible; unless it be a few, who preach passive obedience. These are not generally curious enough to read Hobbes. It is the duty of the clergy to accommodate their discourses to the times, to preach against such sins as are most prevalent, and recommend such virtues as are most wanted. For example,—if exorbitant ambition and venality are predominant, ought they not to warn their hearers against those vices? If public spirit is much wanted, should

[17] "All our dissenting ministers were not inactive on this occasion. When the clergy engage in a political warfare, religion becomes a most powerful engine, either to support or overthrow the state. What effect must it have had upon the audience, to hear the same sentiments and principles, which they had before read in a newspaper, delivered on Sundays from the sacred desk, with a religious awe, and the most solemn appeals to Heaven, from lips, which they had been taught from their cradles to believe could utter nothing but eternal truths!" *Massachusettensis.*

they not inculcate this great virtue? If the rights and duties of Christian magistrates and subjects are disputed, should they not explain them, show their nature, ends, limitations, and restrictions, how much soever it may move the gall of Massachusettensis?

Let me put a supposition. Justice is a great Christian, as well as moral, duty and virtue, which the clergy ought to inculcate and explain. Suppose a great man of a parish should, for seven years together, receive six hundred pounds sterling a year, for discharging the duties of an important office, but, during the whole time, should never do one act or take one step about it. Would not this be great injustice to the public? And ought not the parson of that parish to cry aloud and spare not, and show such a bold transgressor his sin; show that justice was due to the public as well as to an individual; and that cheating the public of four thousand two hundred pounds sterling is at least as great a sin as taking a chicken from a private hen-roost, or perhaps a watch from a fob?

Then we are told that newspapers and preachers have excited "outrages disgraceful to humanity." Upon this subject, I will venture to say, that there have been outrages in this province which I neither justify, excuse, nor extenuate; but these were not excited, that I know of, by newspapers or sermons; that, however, if we run through the last ten years, and consider all the tumults and outrages that have happened, and at the same time recollect the insults, provocations, and oppressions which this people have endured, we shall find the two characteristics of this people, religion and humanity, strongly marked on all their proceedings. Not a life, nor, that I have ever heard, a single limb, has been lost through the whole. I will take upon me to say, there is not another province on this continent, nor in his majesty's dominions, where the people, under the same indignities, would not have gone greater lengths. Consider the tumults in the three kingdoms; consider the tumults in ancient Rome, in the most virtuous of her periods; and compare them with ours. It is a saying of Machiavel no wise man ever contradicted, which has been literally verified in this province, that "while the mass of the people is not corrupted, tumults do no hurt." By which he means, that they leave no lasting ill effects behind.

But let us consider the outrages committed by the tories; half a dozen men shot dead in an instant in King Street; frequent resistance and affronts to civil officers and magistrates; officers, watchmen, citizens, cut and mangled in a most inhuman manner; not to mention the shootings for desertion, and the frequent cruel whippings for other faults, cutting and mangling men's bodies before the eyes of citizens, spectacles which ought never to be introduced into populous places. The worst sort of tumults and outrages ever committed in this province were excited by the tories. But more of this hereafter.

We are then told, that the whigs erected a provincial democracy, or republic, in the province. I wish Massachusettensis knew what a democracy or a republic is. But this subject must be considered another time.

No. VII

OUR rhetorical magician, in his paper of January the 9th, continues to *wheedle:* You want nothing but "to know the true state of facts, to rectify whatever is amiss." He becomes an advocate for the poor of Boston! is for making great allowance for the whigs. "The whigs are too valuable a part of the community to lose. He would not draw down the vengeance of Great Britain. He shall become an advocate for the leading whigs," &c. It is in vain for us to inquire after the *sincerity* or *consistency* of all this. It is agreeable to the precept of Horace:

Irritat, mulcet, falsis terroribus implet,

Ut magus,[18]

And that is all he desires.

After a long discourse, which has nothing in it but what has been answered already, he comes to a great subject indeed, the British constitution; and undertakes to prove, that "the authority of parliament extends to the colonies."

Why will not this writer state the question fairly? The whigs allow that, from the necessity of a case not provided for by common law, and to

---

[18][On a skilled poet: "Like a magician, he stirs up, he soothes, he fills with false fears." Horace, *Epistles* II, 1, 212-13 Ed.]

supply a defect in the British dominions, which there undoubtedly is, if they are to be governed only by that law, America has all along consented, still consents, and ever will consent, that parliament, being the most powerful legislature in the dominions, should regulate the trade of the dominions. This is founding the authority of parliament to regulate our trade, upon *compact* and *consent* of the colonies, not upon any principle of common or statute law; not upon any original principle of the English constitution; not upon the principle that parliament is the supreme and sovereign legislature over them in all cases whatsover. The question is not, therefore, whether the authority of parliament extends to the colonies in any case, for it is admitted by the whigs, that it does in that of commerce; but whether it extends in all cases.

We are then detained with a long account of the three simple forms of government; and are told, that "the British constitution, consisting of king, lords, and commons, is formed upon the principles of monarchy, aristocracy, and democracy, in due proportion; that it includes the principal excellences, and excludes the principal defects of the other kinds of government,—the most perfect system that the wisdom of ages has produced, and Englishmen glory in being subject to, and protected by it."

Then we are told, "that the colonies are a part of the British empire." But what are we to understand by this? Some of the colonies, most of them, indeed, were settled before the kingdom of Great Britain was brought into existence. The union of England and Scotland was made and established by act of parliament in the reign of Queen Anne, and it was this union and statute which erected the kingdom of Great Britain. The colonies were settled long before, in the reigns of the Jameses and Charleses. What authority over them had Scotland? Scotland, England, and the colonies were all under one king before that; the two crowns of England and Scotland united on the head of James I., and continued united on that of Charles I., when our first charter was granted. Our charter, being granted by him, who was king of both nations, to our ancestors, most of whom were *post nati,* born after the union of the two crowns, and consequently, as was adjudged in Calvin's case, free, natural subjects of Scotland, as well as England,—had not the king as good a right to have governed the colonies by his Scottish, as by his English parliament, and to have granted our charters under the seal of Scotland, as well as that of England?

But to wave this. If the English parliament were to govern us, where did they get the right, without our consent, to take the Scottish parliament into a participation of the government over us? When this was done, was the American share of the democracy of the constitution consulted? If not, were not the Americans deprived of the benefit of the democratical part of the constitution? And is not the democracy as essential to the English constitution as the monarchy or aristocracy? Should we have been more effectually deprived of the benefit of the British or English constitution, if one or both houses of parliament, or if our house and council, had made this union with the two houses of parliament in Scotland, without the king?

If a new constitution was to be formed for the whole British dominions, and a supreme legislature coextensive with it, upon the general principles of the English constitution, an equal mixture of monarchy, aristocracy, and democracy, let us see what would be necessary. England has six millions of people, we will say; America had three. England has five hundred members in the house of commons, we will say; America must have two hundred and fifty. Is it possible she should maintain them there, or could they at such a distance know the state, the sense, or exigencies of their constituents? Ireland, too, must be incorporated, and send another hundred or two of members. The territory in the East Indies and West India Islands must send members. And after all this, every navigation act, every act of trade must be repealed. America, and the East and West Indies, and Africa too, must have equal liberty to trade with all the world, that the favored inhabitants of Great Britain have now. Will the ministry thank Massachusettensis for becoming an advocate for such a union, and incorporation of all the dominions of the King of Great Britain? Yet, without such a union, a legislature which shall be sovereign and supreme in all cases whatsoever, and coextensive with the empire, can never be established upon the general principles of the English constitution which Massachusettensis lays down, namely,—an equal mixture of monarchy, aristocracy, and democracy. Nay, further, in order to comply with this principle, this new government, this mighty colossus, which is to bestride the narrow world, must have a house of lords, consisting of Irish, East and West Indian, African, American, as well as English and Scottish noblemen; for the nobility ought to be scattered about all the dominions, as well as the representatives of the commons. If in twenty years more America should have six millions of inhabitants, as there is a boundless territory to fill up, she must have five hundred representatives. Upon these principles, if in forty years she should have twelve millions, a thousand; and if the inhabitants of the three kingdoms remain as they are, being already full of inhabitants, what will become of your supreme legislative? It will be translated, crown and all, to America. This is a sublime system for America. It will flatter those ideas of independency which the tories impute to them, if they have any such, more than any other plan of independency that I have ever heard projected.

"The best writers upon the law of nations tell us, that when a nation takes possession of a distant country, and settles there, that country, though separated from the principal establishment, or mother country, naturally becomes a part of the state, equal with its ancient possessions." We are not told who these "best writers" are. I think we ought to be introduced to them. But their meaning may be no more, than that it is best they should be incorporated with the ancient establishment by contract, or by some new law and institution, by which the new country shall have equal right, powers, and privileges, as well as equal protection, and be under equal obligations of obedience, with the old. Has there been any such contract between Britain and the colonies? Is America incorporated into the realm? Is it a part of the realm? Is it a part of the kingdom? Has it any share in the legislative of the realm? The constitution requires that every foot of land should be represented in the third estate, the democratical branch of the constitution. How many millions of acres in America, how many thousands of wealthy landholders, have no representatives there?

But let these "best writers" say what they will, there is nothing in the law of nations, which is only the law of right reason applied to the conduct of nations, that requires that emigrants from a state should continue, or be made, a part of the state.

The practice of nations has been different. The Greeks planted colonies, and neither demanded nor pretended any authority over them; but they became distinct, independent commonwealths. The Romans continued their colonies under the jurisdiction of the mother commonwealth; but, nevertheless, they allowed them the privileges of cities. Indeed, that sagacious city seems to have been aware of difficulties similar to those under which Great Britain is now laboring. She seems to have been sensible of the impossibility of keeping colonies planted at great distances, under the absolute control of her *senatus-consulta*.[19] Harrington tells us, that "the commonwealth of Rome, by planting colonies of its citizens within the bounds of Italy, took the best way of propagating itself and naturalizing the country; whereas, if it had planted such colonies without the bounds of Italy, it would have alienated the citizens, and given a root to liberty abroad, that might have sprung up foreign, or savage, and hostile to her; *wherefore it never made any such dispersion of itself and its strength* till it was under the yoke of the emperors, who, disburdening themselves of the people, as having less apprehension of what they could do abroad than at home, took a contrary course."* But these Italian cities, although established by decrees of the senate of Rome, to which the colonist was always party, either as a Roman citizen about to emigrate, or as a conquered enemy treating upon terms, were always allowed all the rights of Roman citizens, and were governed by senates of their own. It was the policy of Rome to conciliate her colonies by allowing them equal liberties with her citizens. Witness the example of the Privernates. This people had been conquered, and, complaining of oppressions, revolted. At last they sent ambassadors to Rome to treat of peace. The senate was divided in opinion. Some were for violent, others for lenient measures. In the course of the debate, a senator, whose opinion was for *bringing them to his feet,* proudly asked one of the ambassadors what punishment he thought his countrymen deserved. *"Eam,*

[19] ["decrees of the senate" Ed.]
* Oceana, p. 43.

inquit, quam merentur, qui se libertate dignos censent. "[20] That punishment which those deserve who think themselves worthy of liberty. Another senator, seeing that the *ministerial members* were exasperated with the honest answer, in order to divert their anger, asks another question:—What if we remit all punishment? What kind of a peace may we hope for with you? *"Si bonam dederitis, inquit, et fidam et perpetuam; si malam, haud diuturnam."* If you give us a just peace, it will be faithfully observed, and perpetually; but if a bad one, it will not last long. The *ministerial* senators all on fire at this answer, cried out sedition and rebellion; but the wiser majority decreed,— *"Viri et liberi, vocem auditam; an credi posse ullum populum, aut hominem denique, in ea conditione, cujus eum pœniteat, diutius quam necesse sit mansurum? Ibi pacem esse fidam, ubi voluntarii pacati sint; neque eo loco, ubi servitutem esse velint, fidem sperandam esse."* That they had heard the voice of a man, and a son of liberty; that it was not natural or credible that any people, or any man, would continue longer than necessity should compel him in a condition that grieved and displeased him. A faithful peace was to be expected from men whose affections were conciliated; nor was any kind of fidelity to be expected from slaves. The consul exclaimed,—*"Eos demum, qui nihil præterquam de libertate cogitent, dignos esse qui Romani fiant."* That they who regarded nothing so much as their liberty, deserved to be Romans. *"Itaque et in senatu causam obtinuere; et ex auctoritate patrum, latum ad populum est, ut Privernatibus civitas daretur."* Therefore the Privernates obtained their cause in the senate; and it was, by the authority of those fathers, recommended to the people, that the privileges of a city should be granted them. The practice of free nations only can be adduced, as precedents of what the law of nature has been thought to dictate upon this subject of colonies. Their practice is different. The senate and people of Rome did not interfere commonly by making laws for their colonies, but left them to be ruled by governors and senates. Can Massachusettensis produce from the whole history of Rome, or from the Digest, one example of a *senatus-consultum*,[21] or a *plebiscitum*,[22] laying taxes on the colony?

[20][The next five quotations are from Livy VIII, xxi. Ed.]
[21]["decree of the senate" Ed.]
[22]["plebiscite" Ed.]

Having mentioned the wisdom of the Romans, for not planting colonies out of Italy, and their reasons for it, I cannot help recollecting an observation of Harrington:—"For the colonies in the Indies," says he, "they are yet babes, that cannot live without sucking the breasts of their mother cities, but such as I mistake, if, when they come of age, they do not wean themselves, which causes me to wonder at princes that delight to be exhausted in that way." This was written one hundred and twenty years ago; the colonies are now nearer manhood than ever Harrington foresaw they would arrive in such a period of time. Is it not astonishing, then, that any British minister should ever have considered this subject so little as to believe it possible for him to new-model all our governments, to tax us by an authority that never taxed us before, and subdue us to an implicit obedience to a legislature that millions of us scarcely ever thought any thing about?

I have said, that the practice of free governments alone can be quoted with propriety to show the sense of nations. But the sense and practice of nations is not enough. Their practice must be reasonable, just, and right, or it will not govern Americans.

Absolute monarchies, whatever their practice may be, are nothing to us; for, as Harrington observes, "Absolute monarchy, as that of the Turks, neither plants its people at home nor abroad, otherwise than as tenants for life or at will; wherefore, its national and provincial government is all one."

I deny, therefore, that the practice of free nations, or the opinions of the best writers upon the law of nations, will warrant the position of Massachusettensis,[23] that, "when a nation takes possession of a distant ter-

---

[23] "The colonies are a part of the British empire. The best writers upon the law of nations tell us, that when a nation takes possession of a distant country, and settles there, that country, though separated from the principal establishment, or mother country, naturally becomes a part of the state, equal with its ancient possessions. Two supreme or independent authorities cannot exist in the same state. It would be what is called *imperium in imperio* ["a sovereign power within a sovereign power" Ed.], the height of political absurdity. The analogy between the political and human body is great. Two independent authorities in a state would be like two distinct principles of volition and action in the human body, dissenting, opposing, and destroying each other. If, then, we are a part of the British

ritory, that becomes a part of the state equally with its ancient possessions."
The practice of free nations and the opinions of the best writers are in
general on the contrary.

I agree, that "two supreme and independent authorities cannot exist in
the same state," any more than two supreme beings in one universe; and,
therefore, I contend, that our provincial legislatures are the only supreme
authorities in our colonies. Parliament, notwithstanding this, may be
allowed an authority supreme and sovereign over the ocean, which may be
limited by the banks of the ocean, or the bounds of our charters; our charters give us no authority over the high seas. Parliament has our consent
to assume a jurisdiction over them. And here is a line fairly drawn between
the rights of Britain and the rights of the colonies, namely, the banks of the
ocean, or low-water mark; the line of division between common law,
and civil or maritime law. If this is not sufficient,—if parliament are at a
loss for any principle of natural, civil, maritime, moral, or common law,
on which to ground any authority over the high seas, the Atlantic especially, let the colonies be treated like reasonable creatures, and they will discover great ingenuity and modesty. The acts of trade and navigation might
be confirmed by provincial laws, and carried into execution by our own
courts and juries, and in this case, illicit trade would be cut up by the
roots forever. I knew the smuggling tories in New York and Boston would
cry out against this, because it would not only destroy their profitable
game of smuggling, but their whole place and pension system. But the
whigs, that is, a vast majority of the whole continent, would not regard the
smuggling tories. In one word, if public principles, and motives, and arguments were alone to determine this dispute between the two countries,
it might be settled forever in a few hours; but the everlasting clamors of
prejudice, passion, and private interest drown every consideration of that
sort, and are precipitating us into a civil war.

empire, we must be subject to the supreme power of the state, which is vested in the estates
of parliament, notwithstanding each of the colonies have legislative and executive powers
of their own, delegated or granted to them, for the purposes of regulating their own
internal police, which are subordinate to, and must necessarily be subject to the checks,
control, and regulation of the supreme authority." *Massachusettensis.*

"If, then, we are a part of the British empire, we must be subject to the supreme power of the state, which is vested in the estates in parliament."

Here, again, we are to be conjured out of our senses by the magic in the words "British empire," and "supreme power of the state." But, however it may sound, I say we are not a part of the British empire; because the British government is not an empire. The governments of France, Spain, &c. are not empires, but monarchies, supposed to be governed by fixed fundamental laws, though not really. The British government is still less entitled to the style of *an empire*. It is a limited monarchy. If Aristotle, Livy, and Harrington knew what a republic was, the British constitution is much more like a republic than an empire. They define a republic to be a *government of laws, and not of men*. If this definition be just, the British constitution is nothing more nor less than a republic, in which the king is first magistrate. This office being hereditary, and being possessed of such ample and splendid prerogatives, is no objection to the government's being a republic, as long as it is bound by fixed laws, which the people have a voice in making, and a right to defend. An empire is a despotism, and an emperor a despot, bound by no law or limitation but his own will; it is a stretch of tyranny beyond absolute monarchy. For, although the will of an absolute monarch is law, yet his edicts must be registered by parliaments. Even this formality is not necessary in an empire. There the maxim is *quod principi placuit legis habet vigorem,* even without having that will and pleasure recorded. There are but three empires now in Europe, the German or Holy Roman, the Russian, and the Ottoman.

There is another sense, indeed, in which the word *empire* is used, in which it may be applied to the government of Geneva, or any other republic, as well as to monarchy or despotism. In this sense it is synonymous with *government, rule,* or *dominion.* In this sense we are within the dominion, rule, or government of the King of Great Britain.

The question should be, whether we are a part of the kingdom of Great Britain. This is the only language known in English laws. We are not then a part of the British kingdom, realm, or state; and therefore the supreme power of the kingdom, realm, or state is not, upon these principles, the supreme power of us. That "supreme power over America is vested in the estates in parliament," is an affront to us; for there is not an acre of American land represented there; there are no American estates in parliament.

To say, that we "must be" subject, seems to betray a consciousness that we are not by any law, or upon any principles but those of mere power; and an opinion that we ought to be, or that it is necessary that we should be. But if this should be admitted for argument's sake only, what is the consequence? The consequences that may fairly be drawn are these; that Britain has been imprudent enough to let colonies be planted, until they are become numerous and important, without ever having wisdom enough to concert a plan for their government, consistent with her own welfare; that now it is necessary to make them submit to the authority of parliament; and, because there is no principle of law, or justice, or reason, by which she can effect it, therefore she will resort to war and conquest— to the maxim, *delenda est Carthago*.[24] These are the consequences, according to this writer's idea. We think the consequences are, that she has, after one hundred and fifty years, discovered a defect in her government, which ought to be supplied by some just and reasonable means, that is, by the consent of the colonies; for metaphysicians and politicians may dispute forever, but they will never find any other moral principle or foundation of rule or obedience, than the consent of governors and governed. She has found out that the great machine will not go any longer without a new wheel. She will make this herself. We think she is making it of such materials and workmanship as will tear the whole machine to pieces. We are willing, if she can convince us of the necessity of such a wheel, to assist with artists and materials in making it, so that it may answer the end. But she says, we shall have no share in it; and if we will not let her patch it up as she pleases, her Massachusettensis and other advocates tell us, she will tear it to pieces herself, by cutting our throats. To this kind of reasoning, we can only answer, that we will not stand still to be butchered. We will defend our lives as long as Providence shall enable us.

[24]["Carthage must be destroyed." The elder Cato always ended his speeches with these words. Ed.]

"It is beyond doubt, that it was the sense both of the *parent country* and *our ancestors,* that they were to remain subject to parliament."[25]

This has been often asserted, and as often contradicted and fully confuted. The confutation may not, however, have come to every eye which has read this newspaper.

The public acts of kings and ministers of state, in that age when our ancestors emigrated, which were not complained of, remonstrated and protested against by the commons, are looked upon as sufficient proof of the "sense" of the parent country.

The charter to the treasurer and company of Virginia, 23 May, 1609, grants ample powers of government, legislative, executive, and judicial, and then contains an express covenant, "to and with the said treasurer and company, their successors, factors, and assigns, that they, and every of them, shall be free from all taxes and impositions forever, upon any goods or merchandises, at any time or times hereafter, either upon importation thither, or exportation from thence, into our realm of England, or into any other of our realms or dominions."

I agree with this writer, that the authority of a supreme legislature includes the right of taxation. Is not this quotation, then, an irresistible proof, that it was not "the sense of King James or his ministers, or of the ancestors of the Virginians, that they were to remain subject to parliament as a supreme legislature?"

After this, James issued a proclamation recalling the patent, but this was never regarded. Then Charles issued another proclamation, which produced a remonstrance from Virginia, which was answered by a letter from the lords of the privy council, 22 July, 1634, containing the royal assurance, that "all their estates, trade, freedom, and privileges should be enjoyed by them in as extensive a manner as they enjoyed them before those proclamations."

[25] "It is beyond a doubt, that it was the sense both of the parent country, and our ancestors, that they were to remain subject to parliament. It is evident, from the charter itself; and this authority has been exercised by parliament from time to time, almost ever since the first settlement of the country, and has been expressly acknowledged by our provincial legislatures. It is not less our interest than our duty, to continue subject to the authority of parliament, which will be more fully considered hereafter." *Massachusettensis.*

Here is another evidence of the sense of the king and his ministers.

Afterwards, parliament sent a squadron of ships to Virginia; the colony rose in open resistance, until the parliamentary commissioners granted them conditions, that they should enjoy the privileges of Englishmen; that their assembly should transact the affairs of the colonies; that they should have a free trade to all places and nations, as the people of England; and fourthly, that "Virginia shall be free from all *taxes,* customs, and impositions whatever, and none to be imposed on them without consent of the grand assembly; and so that neither forts nor castles be erected, or garrisons maintained, without their consent."

One would think this was evidence enough of the sense both of the parent country and our ancestors.

After the acts of navigation were passed, Virginia sent agents to England, and a remonstrance against those acts. Charles, in answer, sent a declaration under the privy seal, 19 April, 1676, affirming "that taxes ought not to be laid upon the inhabitants and proprietors of the colony, but by the common consent of the general assembly; except such impositions as the parliament should lay on the commodities imported into England from the colony." And he ordered a charter under the great seal, to secure this right to the Virginians.

What becomes of the "sense of the parent country and our ancestors"? for the ancestors of the Virginians are our ancestors, when we speak of ourselves as Americans.

From Virginia let us pass to Maryland. Charles I., in 1633, gave a charter to the Baron of Baltimore, containing ample powers of government, and this express covenant: "to and with the said Lord Baltimore, his heirs and assigns, that we, our heirs and successors, shall at no time hereafter, set or make, or cause to be set, any imposition, custom, or other taxation, rate, or contribution whatsoever, in and upon the dwellings and inhabitants of the aforesaid province, for their lands, tenements, goods, or chattels within the said province; or to be laden or unladen, within the ports or harbors of the said province."

What, then, was the "sense of the parent country and the ancestors" of Maryland? But if, by "our ancestors," he confines his idea to New

England, or this province, let us consider. The first planters of Plymouth were "our ancestors" in the strictest sense. They had no charter or patent for the land they took possession of; and derived no authority from the English parliament or crown to set up their government. They purchased land of the Indians, and set up a government of their own, on the simple principle of nature; and afterwards purchased a patent for the land of the council at Plymouth; but never purchased any charter for government, of the crown or the king, and continued to exercise all the powers of government, legislative, executive, and judicial, upon the plain ground of an original contract among independent individuals for sixty-eight years, that is, until their incorporation with Massachusetts by our present charter. The same may be said of the colonies which emigrated to Say-Brook, New Haven, and other parts of Connecticut. They seem to have had no idea of dependence on parliament, any more than on the conclave. The Secretary of Connecticut has now in his possession an original letter from Charles II. to that colony, in which he considers them rather as friendly allies, than as subjects to his English parliament; and even requests them to pass a law in their assembly relative to piracy.

The sentiments of your ancestors in the Massachusetts, may be learned from almost every ancient paper and record. It would be endless to recite all the passages, in which it appears that they thought themselves exempt from the authority of parliament, not only in the point of taxation, but in all cases whatsoever. Let me mention one. Randolph, one of the predecessors of Massachusettensis, in a representation to Charles II., dated 20 September, 1676, says, "I went to visit the governor at his house, and, among other discourse, I told him, I took notice of several ships that were arrived at Boston, some since my being there, from Spain, France, Straits, Canaries, and other parts of Europe, contrary to your majesty's laws for encouraging navigation and regulating the trade of the plantations. He freely declared to me, that the law made by your majesty and your parliament, obligeth them in nothing but what consists with the interest of that colony; that the legislative power is and abides in them solely to act and make laws by virtue of a charter from your majesty's royal father."

Here is a positive assertion of an exemption from the authority of parliament, even in the case of the regulation of trade.

Afterwards, in 1677, the general court passed a law which shows the sense of our ancestors in a very strong light. It is in these words:—

"This court being informed, by letters received this day from our messengers, of his majesty's expectation, that the acts of trade and navigation be exactly and punctually observed by this his majesty's colony, his pleasure therein not having before now been signified unto us, either by express from his majesty or any of his ministers of state:

"It is therefore hereby ordered, and by the authority of this court enacted, that henceforth, all masters of ships, ketches, or other vessels, of greater or lesser burthen, arriving in, or sailing from any of the ports in this jurisdiction, do, without coven or fraud, yield faithful and constant obedience unto, and observation of, all the said acts of navigation and trade, on penalty of suffering such forfeitures, loss, and damage, as in the said acts are particularly expressed. And the governor and council, and all officers commissionated and authorized by them, are hereby ordered and required to see to the strict observation of the said acts."

As soon as they had passed this law, they wrote a letter to their agent, in which they acknowledge they had not conformed to the acts of trade; and they say, they "apprehended them to be an invasion of the rights, liberties, and properties of the subjects of his majesty in the colony, they not being represented in parliament; and, according to the usual sayings of the learned in the law, *the laws of England were bounded within the four seas, and did not reach America.* However, as his majesty had signified his pleasure that these acts should be observed in the Massachusetts, they had made provision, by a law of the colony, that they should be strictly attended to from time to time, although it greatly discouraged trade, and was a great damage to his majesty's plantation."

Thus, it appears, that the ancient Massachusettensians and Virginians had precisely the same sense of the authority of parliament, namely,— that it had none at all; and the same sense of the necessity that, by the voluntary act of the colonies—their free, cheerful consent—it should be allowed the power of regulating trade; and this is precisely the idea of the late congress at Philadelphia, expressed in the fourth proposition in their Bill of Rights.

But this was the sense of the parent country, too, at that time; for King Charles II., in a letter to the Massachusetts, after this law had been laid before him, has these words: "We are informed that you have lately made *some good provision* for observing the acts of trade and navigation, which is well pleasing unto us." Had he or his ministers an idea that parliament was the sovereign legislative over the colony? If he had, would he not have censured this law, as an insult to that legislative?

I sincerely hope we shall see no more such round affirmations, that "it was the sense of the parent country and our ancestors, that they were to remain subject to parliament." So far from thinking themselves subject to parliament, it is clear that, during the interregnum, it was their desire and design to have been a free commonwealth, an independent republic; and after the restoration, it was with the utmost reluctance that, in the course of sixteen or seventeen years, they were brought to take the oaths of allegiance; and for some time after this, they insisted upon taking an oath of fidelity to the country, before that of allegiance to the king.

That "it is evident, from the charter itself, that they were to remain subject to parliament," is very unaccountable, when there is not one word in either charter concerning parliament.

That the authority of parliament "has been exercised almost ever since the first settlement of the country," is a mistake; for there is no instance, until the first Navigation Act, which was in 1660, more than forty years after the first settlement. This act was never executed nor regarded until seventeen years afterwards, and then it was not executed as an act of parliament, but as a law of the colony, to which the king agreed.

This "has been expressly acknowledged by our provincial legislatures." There is too much truth in this. It has been twice acknowledged by our house of representatives, that parliament was the supreme legislative; but this was directly repugnant to a multitude of other votes, by which it was denied. This was in conformity to the distinction between taxation and legislation, which has since been found to be a distinction without a difference.

When a great question is first started, there are very few, even of the greatest minds, which suddenly and intuitively comprehend it, in all its consequences.

It is both "our interest and our duty to continue subject to the authority of parliament," as far as the regulation of our trade, if it will be content with that, but no longer.

"If the colonies are not subject to the authority of parliament, Great Britain and the colonies must be distinct states, as completely so as England and Scotland were before the union, or as Great Britain and Hanover are now."[26] There is no need of being startled at this consequence. It is very harmless. There is no absurdity at all in it. Distinct states may be united under one king. And those states may be further cemented and united together by a treaty of commerce. This is the case. We have, by our own express consent, contracted to observe the Navigation Act, and by our implied consent, by long usage and uninterrupted acquiescence, have submitted to the other acts of trade, however grievous some of them may be. This may be compared to a treaty of commerce, by which those distinct states are cemented together, in perpetual league and amity. And if any further ratifications of this pact or treaty are necessary, the colonies would readily enter into them, provided their other liberties were inviolate.

That "the colonies owe no allegiance to any imperial crown," provided such a crown involves in it a house of lords and a house of commons, is certain. Indeed, we owe no allegiance to any crown at all. We owe allegiance to the person of his majesty, King George III., whom God preserve. But allegiance is due universally, both from Britons and

[26] "The principal argument against the authority of parliament is this: the Americans are entitled to all the privileges of an Englishman; it is the privilege of an Englishman to be exempt from all laws, that he does not consent to in person, or by representative; the Americans are not represented in parliament, and therefore are exempt from acts of parliament, or in other words, not subject to its authority. This appears specious, but leads to such absurdities as demonstrate its fallacy. If the colonies are not subject to the authority of parliament, Great Britain and the colonies must be distinct states, as completely so as England and Scotland were before the union, or as Great Britain and Hanover are now." *Massachusettensis.*

Americans to the person of the king, not to his crown; to his natural, not his politic capacity, as I will undertake to prove hereafter, from the highest authorities, and the most solemn adjudications, which were ever made within any part of the British dominions.

If his majesty's title to the crown is "derived from an act of parliament, made since the settlement of these colonies," it was not made since the date of our charter. Our charter was granted by King William and Queen Mary, three years after the revolution; and the oaths of allegiance are established by a law of the province. So that our allegiance to his majesty is not due by virtue of any act of a British parliament, but by our own charter and province laws. It ought to be remembered that there was a revolution here, as well as in England, and that we, as well as the people of England, made an original, express contract with King William.

If it follows from thence, that he appears "King of Massachusetts, King of Rhode Island, King of Connecticut, &c."[27] this is no absurdity at all. He will appear in this light, and does appear so, whether parliament has authority over us or not. He is King of Ireland, I suppose, although parliament is allowed to have authority there. As to giving his majesty those titles, I have no objection at all; I wish he would be graciously pleased to assume them.

The only proposition in all this writer's long string of pretended absurdities, which he says follows from the position that we are distinct states,

---

[27] "Let us wave this difficulty, and suppose allegiance due from the colonies to the person of the King of Great Britain. He then appears in a new capacity, of King of America, or rather in several new capacities, of King of Massachusetts, King of Rhode Island, King of Connecticut, &c. &c. For if our connection with Great Britain by the parliament be dissolved, we shall have none among ourselves, but each colony become as distinct from the others, as England was from Scotland before the union. Some have supposed that each state, having one and the same person for its king, is a sufficient connection. Were he an absolute monarch, it might be; but in a mixed government it is no union at all. For as the king must govern each state, by its parliament, those several parliaments would pursue the particular interest of its own state; and however well disposed the king might be to pursue a line of interest, that was common to all, the checks and control that he would meet with, would render it impossible. If the King of Great Britain has really these new capacities, they ought to be added to his titles; and another difficulty will arise; the prerogatives of these new crowns have never been defined or limited." *Massachusettensis.*

is this:—That "as the king must govern each state by its parliament, those several parliaments would pursue the particular interest of its own state; and however well disposed the king might be to pursue a line of interest that was common to all, the checks and control that he would meet with would render it impossible." Every argument ought to be allowed its full weight; and therefore candor obliges me to acknowledge, that here lies all the difficulty that there is in this whole controversy. There has been, from first to last, on both sides of the Atlantic, an idea, an apprehension, that it was necessary there should be some superintending power, to draw together all the wills, and unite all the strength of the subjects in all the dominions, in case of war, and in the case of trade. The necessity of this, in case of trade, has been so apparent, that, as has often been said, we have consented that parliament should exercise such a power. In case of war, it has by some been thought necessary. But in fact and experience, it has not been found so. What though the proprietary colonies, on account of disputes with the proprietors, did not come in so early to the assistance of the general cause in the last war as they ought, and perhaps one of them not at all? The inconveniences of this were small, in comparison of the absolute ruin to the liberties of all which must follow the submission to parliament, in all cases, which would be giving up all the popular limitations upon the government. These inconveniences fell chiefly upon New England. She was necessitated to greater exertions; but she had rather suffer these again and again than others infinitely greater. However, this subject has been so long in contemplation, that it is fully understood now in all the colonies; so that there is no danger, in case of another war, of any colony's failing of its duty.

But, admitting the proposition in its full force, that it is absolutely necessary there should be a supreme power, coextensive with all the dominions, will it follow that parliament, as now constituted, has a right to assume this supreme jurisdiction? By no means.

A union of the colonies might be projected, and an American legislature; for, if America has three millions of people, and the whole dominions, twelve millions, she ought to send a quarter part of all the members to the house of commons; and, instead of holding parliaments always at

Westminster, the haughty members for Great Britain must humble themselves, one session in four, to cross the Atlantic, and hold the parliament in America.

There is no avoiding all inconveniences in human affairs. The greatest possible, or conceivable, would arise from ceding to parliament power over us without a representation in it. The next greatest would accrue from any plan that can be devised for a representation there. The least of all would arise from going on as we began, and fared well for one hundred and fifty years, by letting parliament regulate trade, and our own assemblies all other matters.

As to "the prerogatives not being defined, or limited," it is as much so in the colonies as in Great Britain, and as well understood, and as cheerfully submitted to in the former as the latter.

But "where is the British constitution, that we all agree we are entitled to?"[28] I answer, if we enjoy, and are entitled to more liberty than the British constitution allows, where is the harm? Or if we enjoy the British constitution in greater purity and perfection than they do in England, as is really the case, whose fault is this? Not ours.

We may find all the blessings of this constitution "in our provincial assemblies." Our houses of representatives have, and ought to exercise every power of the house of commons. The first charter to this colony is nothing to the present argument; but it did grant a power of taxing the

[28] "But let us suppose the same prerogatives inherent in the several American crowns as are in the imperial crown of Great Britain, where shall we find the British constitution, that we all agree we are entitled to? We shall seek for it in vain in our provincial assemblies. They are but faint sketches of the estates of parliament. The houses of representatives, or burgesses, have not all the powers of the house of commons; in the charter governments, they have no more than what is expressly granted by their several charters. The first charters granted to this province, did not empower the assembly to tax the people at all. Our council boards are as destitute of the constitutional authority of the house of lords, as their several members are of the noble independence and splendid appendages of peerage. The house of peers is the bulwark of the British constitution, and through successive ages has withstood the shocks of monarchy, and the sappings of democracy; and the constitution gained strength by the conflict. Thus, the supposition of our being independent states, or exempt from the authority of parliament, destroys the very idea of our having a British constitution." *Massachusettensis.*

people, implicitly, though not in express terms. It granted all the rights and liberties of Englishmen, which include the power of taxing the people.

"Our council boards" in the royal governments, "are destitute of the noble independence and splendid appendages of peerage." Most certainly, they are the meanest creatures and tools in the political creation, dependent every moment for their existence on the tainted breath of a prime minister. But they have the authority of the house of lords, in our little models of the English constitution; and it is this which makes them so great a grievance. The crown has really two branches of our legislature in its power. Let an act of parliament pass at home, putting it in the power of the king to remove any peer from the house of lords at his pleasure, and what will become of the British constitution? It will be overturned from the foundation. Yet we are perpetually insulted by being told, that making our council by mandamus brings us nearer to the British constitution. In this province, by charter, the council certainly hold their seats for the year, after being chosen and approved, independent of both the other branches. For their creation, they are equally obliged to both the other branches; so that there is little or no bias in favor of either; if any, it is in favor of the prerogative. In short, it is not easy, without an hereditary nobility, to constitute a council more independent, more nearly resembling the house of lords, than the council of this province has ever been by charter.

But perhaps it will be said, that we are to enjoy the British constitution in our supreme legislature, the parliament, not in our provincial legislatures. To this I answer, if parliament is to be our supreme legislature, we shall be under a complete oligarchy or aristocracy, not the British constitution, which this writer himself defines a mixture of monarchy, aristocracy, and democracy. For king, lords, and commons, will constitute one great oligarchy, as they will stand related to America, as much as the decemvirs did in Rome; with this difference for the worse, that our rulers are to be three thousand miles off. The definition of an oligarchy is a government by a number of grandees, over whom the people have no control. The States of Holland were once chosen by the people frequently, then chosen for life; now they are not chosen by the people at all. When a member dies, his place is filled up, not by the people he is to represent, but by the States. Is not this depriving the Hollanders of a free constitution, and subjecting them to an aristocracy, or oligarchy? Will not the government of America be like it? Will not representatives be chosen for them by others, whom they never saw nor heard of? If our provincial constitutions are in any respect imperfect, and want alteration, they have capacity enough to discern it, and power enough to effect it, without the interposition of parliament. There never was an American constitution attempted by parliament before the Quebec bill, and Massachusetts bill. These are such *samples* of what they may, and probably will be, that few Americans are in love with them. However, America will never allow that parliament has any authority to alter their constitution at all. She is wholly penetrated with a sense of the necessity of resisting it at all hazards. And she would resist it, if the constitution of the Massachusetts had been altered as much for *the better* as it is for the worse. The question we insist on most is, not whether the alteration is for the better or not, but whether parliament has any right to make any alteration at all. And it is the universal sense of America, that it has none.

We are told, that "the provincial constitutions have no principle of stability within themselves."[29] This is so great a mistake, that there is not more order or stability in any government upon the globe, than there ever has been in that of Connecticut. The same may be said of the Massachusetts and Pennsylvania; and, indeed, of the others very nearly. "That these constitutions, in turbulent times, would become wholly monarchical, or wholly republican," they must be such times as would have a similar effect upon the constitution at home. But in order to avoid the danger of this, what is to be done? Not give us an English constitution, it seems, but make sure of us at once, by giving us constitutions wholly monarchical, annihilating our houses of representatives first, by taking from them the

---

[29] "The provincial constitutions, considered as subordinate, are generally well adapted to those purposes of government for which they were intended; that is, to regulate the internal police of the several colonies; but have no principle of stability within themselves; they may support themselves in moderate times, but would be merged by the violence of turbulent ones, and the several colonies become wholly monarchical or wholly republican, were it not for the checks, controls, regulations, and supports, of the supreme authority of the empire." *Massachusettensis.*

support of government, &c., and then making the council and judges wholly dependent on the crown.

That a representation in parliament is impracticable, we all agree; but the consequence is, that we must have a representation in our supreme legislatures here. This was the consequence that was drawn by kings, ministers, our ancestors, and the whole nation, more than a century ago, when the colonies were first settled, and continued to be the general sense until the last peace; and it must be the general sense again soon, or Great Britain will lose her colonies.

"This is apparently the meaning of that celebrated passage in Governor Hutchinson's letter, that rung through the continent, namely,—'There must be an abridgment of what is called English liberties.' " [30] But all the art and subtlety of Massachusettensis will never vindicate or excuse that expression. According to this writer, it should have been, "there is an abridgment of English liberties, and it cannot be otherwise." But every candid reader must see that the letter-writer had more than that in his *view* and in his *wishes.* In the same letter, a little before, he says, "what marks of resentment the parliament will show, whether they will be upon the province in general, or particular persons, is extremely uncertain; but that they will be placed somewhere is most certain; and I add, *because I think it ought to be so.*"[31] Is it possible to read this, without thinking of the Port Bill, the Charter Bill, and the resolves for sending persons to England, by the statute of Henry VIII., to be tried? But this is not all: "This is most certainly a crisis," says he, &c. "If no measure shall have been taken to secure this dependence, (that is, the dependence which a colony ought to have upon the parent state,) it is all over with us." "The friends of government will be utterly disheartened; and the friends of anarchy will be afraid of

[30] "If that be the case, the right or privilege that we complain of being deprived of, is not withheld by Britain; but the first principles of government, and the immutable laws of nature, render it impossible for us to enjoy it. This is apparently the meaning of that celebrated passage in Governor Hutchinson's letter, that rung through the continent, namely,— There must be an abridgment of what is called English liberties." *Massachusettensis.*

[31] These extracts are taken from the most significant of the letters obtained in England, and sent out by Dr. Franklin, which betrayed the real policy of Governor Hutchinson. See the *Diary,* vol. ii. pp. 318, 319.

nothing, be it ever so extravagant." But this is not all: "I never think of the measures necessary for the peace and good order of the colonies without pain." "There must be an abridgment of what are called English liberties." What could he mean? Any thing less than depriving us of trial by jury? Perhaps he wanted an act of parliament to try persons here for treason, by a court of admiralty. Perhaps an act, that the province should be governed by a governor and a mandamus council, without a house of representatives. But to put it out of all doubt, that his meaning was much worse than Massachusettensis endeavors to make it, he explains himself in a subsequent part of the letter: "I wish," says he, "the good of the colony, *when I wish to see some further restraint of liberty.*" Here it is rendered certain, that he is pleading for a further restraint of liberty, not explaining the restraint he apprehended the constitution had already laid us under.

My indignation at this letter has sometimes been softened by compassion. It carries on the face of it evident marks of *madness.* It was written in such a transport of passions, *ambition* and *revenge* chiefly, that his reason was manifestly overpowered. The vessel was tost in such a hurricane, that she could not feel her helm. Indeed, he seems to have had a confused consciousness of this himself. "Pardon me this excursion," says he; "it really proceeds from the state of mind into which our perplexed affairs often throw me."

"It is our highest interest to continue a part of the British empire; and equally our duty to remain subject to the authority of parliament," says Massachusettensis.

We are a part of the British dominions, that is, of the King of Great Britain, and it is our interest and duty to continue so. It is equally our interest and duty to continue subject to the authority of parliament, in the regulation of our trade, as long as she shall leave us to govern our internal policy, and to give and grant our own money, and no longer.

This letter concludes with an agreeable flight of fancy.[32] The time may not be so far off, however, as this writer imagines, when the colonies may

---

[32] The passage is one of some beauty, and deserves to be inserted:—"After many more centuries shall have rolled away, long after we, who are now bustling upon the stage of life, shall have been received to the bosom of mother earth, and our names are forgotten,

have the balance of numbers and wealth in their favor. But when that shall happen, if we should attempt to rule her by an American parliament, without an adequate representation in it, she will infallibly resist us by her arms.

No. VIII

IT has often been observed by me, and it cannot be too often repeated, that *colonization* is *casus omissus*[33] at common law. There is no such title known in that law. By common law, I mean that system of customs written and unwritten, which was known and in force in England in the time of King Richard I. This continued to be the case down to the reign of Elizabeth and King James I. In all that time, the laws of England were confined to the realm, and within the four seas. There was no provision made in this law for governing colonies beyond the Atlantic, or beyond the four seas, by authority of parliament; no, nor for the king to grant charters to subjects to settle in foreign countries. It was the king's prerogative to prohibit the emigration of any of his subjects, by issuing his writ *ne exeat regno.*[34] And, therefore, it was in the king's power to permit his subjects to leave the kingdom. "It is a high crime to disobey the king's lawful commands or prohibitions, as not returning from beyond sea upon the king's letters to that purpose; for which the offender's lands shall be seized until he return; and when he does return, he shall be fined, &c.; or going beyond sea against the king's will, expressly signified, either by the writ *ne exeat regno,* or under the great or privy seal, or signet, or by proclamation."[35] When a subject left the kingdom by the king's permission, and if the nation did not remonstrate against it, by the nation's permission too, at least connivance, he carried with him, as a man, all the rights of nature.

---

the colonies may be so far increased as to have the balance of wealth, numbers, and power in their favor; the good of the empire may make it necessary to fix the seat of government here; and some future George, equally the friend of mankind with him that now sways the British sceptre, may cross the Atlantic, and rule Great Britain by an American parliament."

[33] ["[an] omitted case" Ed.]

[34] ["that he should not go out of the kingdom" Ed.]

[35] Hawkins' *Pleas of the Crown,* c. xxii. § 4.

His allegiance bound him to the king, and entitled him to protection. But how? Not in France; the King of England was not bound to protect him in France. Nor in America. Nor in the dominions of Louis. Nor of Sassacus, or Massachusetts. He had a right to protection and the liberties of England, upon his return there, not otherwise. How, then, do we New Englandmen derive our laws? I say, not from parliament, not from common law, but from the law of nature, and the compact made with the king in our charters. Our ancestors were entitled to the common law of England when they emigrated, that is, to just so much of it as they pleased to adopt, and no more. They were not bound or obliged to submit to it, unless they chose it. By a positive principle of the common law they were bound, let them be in what part of the world they would, to do nothing against the allegiance of the king. But no kind of provision was ever made by common law for punishing or trying any man, even for treason committed out of the realm. He must be tried in some county of the realm by that law, the county where the overt act was done, or he could not be tried at all. Nor was any provision ever made, until the reign of Henry VIII., for trying treasons committed abroad, and the acts of that reign were made on purpose to catch Cardinal Pole.

So that our ancestors, when they emigrated, having obtained permission of the king to come here, and being never commanded to return into the realm, had a clear right to have erected in this wilderness a British constitution, or a perfect democracy, or any other form of government they saw fit. They, indeed, while they lived, could not have taken arms against the King of England, without violating their allegiance; but their children would not have been born within the king's allegiance, would not have been natural subjects, and consequently not entitled to protection, or bound to the king.

Massachusettensis seems possessed of these ideas, and attempts in the most awkward manner to get rid of them. He is conscious that America must be a part of the realm, before it can be bound by the authority of parliament; and, therefore, is obliged to suggest that we are annexed to the realm, and to endeavor to confuse himself and his readers, by confounding the realm with the empire and dominions.

But will any man soberly contend, that America was ever annexed to the realm? to what realm? When New England was settled, there was a realm of England, a realm of Scotland, and a realm of Ireland. To which of these three realms was New England annexed? To the realm of England, it will be said. But by what law? No territory could be annexed to the realm of England but by an act of parliament. Acts of parliament have been passed to annex Wales, &c. &c. to the realm; but none ever passed to annex America. But if New England was annexed to the realm of England, how came she annexed to the realm of, or kingdom of Great Britain? The two realms of England and Scotland were, by the act of union, incorporated into one kingdom, by the name of Great Britain; but there is not one word about America in that act.

Besides, if America was annexed to the realm, or a part of the kingdom, every act of parliament that is made would extend to it, named or not named. But everybody knows, that every act of parliament, and every other record, constantly distinguishes between this kingdom and his majesty's other dominions. Will it be said that Ireland is annexed to the realm, or a part of the kingdom of Great Britain? Ireland is a distinct kingdom, or realm, by itself, notwithstanding British parliament claims a right of binding it in all cases, and exercises it in some. And even so, the Massachusetts is a realm, New York is a realm, Pennsylvania another realm, to all intents and purposes, as much as Ireland is, or England or Scotland ever were. The King of Great Britain is the sovereign of all these realms.

This writer says, "that in denying that the colonies are annexed to the realm, and subject to the authority of parliament, individuals and bodies of men subvert the fundamentals of government, deprive us of British liberties, and build up absolute monarchy in the colonies."

This is the first time that I ever heard or read that the colonies are annexed to the realm. It is utterly denied that they are, and that it is possible they should be, without an act of parliament and acts of the colonies. Such an act of parliament cannot be produced, nor any such law of any one colony. Therefore, as this writer builds the whole authority of parliament upon this fact, namely,—that the colonies are annexed to the realm, and as it is certain they never were so annexed, the consequence is, that his whole superstructure falls.

When he says, that they subvert the fundamentals of government, he begs the question. We say, that the contrary doctrines subvert the fundamentals of government. When he says, that they deprive us of British liberties, he begs the question again. We say, that the contrary doctrine deprives us of English liberties; as to British liberties, we scarcely know what they are, as the liberties of England and Scotland are not precisely the same to this day. English liberties are but certain rights of nature, reserved to the citizen by the English constitution, which rights cleaved to our ancestors when they crossed the Atlantic, and would have inhered in them if, instead of coming to New England, they had gone to Otaheite or Patagonia, even although they had taken no patent or charter from the king at all. These rights did not adhere to them the less, for their purchasing patents and charters, in which the king expressly stipulates with them, that they and their posterity should forever enjoy all those rights and liberties.

The human mind is not naturally the clearest atmosphere; but the clouds and vapors which have been raised in it by the artifices of temporal and spiritual tyrants, have made it impossible to see objects in it distinctly. Scarcely any thing is involved in more systematical obscurity than the rights of our ancestors, when they arrived in America. How, in common sense, came the dominions of King Philip, King Massachusetts, and twenty other sovereigns, independent princes here, to be within the allegiance of the Kings of England, James and Charles? America was no more within the allegiance of those princes, by the common law of England, or by the law of nature, than France and Spain were. Discovery, if that was incontestable, could give no title to the English king, by common law, or by the law of nature, to the lands, tenements, and hereditaments of the native Indians here. Our ancestors were sensible of this, and, therefore, honestly purchased their lands of the natives. They might have bought them to hold allodially, if they would.

But there were two ideas, which confused them, and have continued to confuse their posterity; one derived from the feudal, the other from the canon law. By the former of these systems, the prince, the general, was supposed to be sovereign lord of all the lands conquered by the soldiers in his army; and upon this principle, the King of England was considered in law as sovereign lord of all the land within the realm. If he had sent an army here to conquer King Massachusetts, and it had succeeded, he would have been sovereign lord of the land here upon these principles; but there was no rule of the common law that made the discovery of the country by a subject a title to that country in the prince. But conquest would not have annexed the country to the realm, nor have given any authority to the parliament. But there was another mist cast before the eyes of the English nation from another source. The pope claimed a sovereign propriety in, as well as authority over, the whole earth. As head of the Christian church, and vicar of God, he claimed this authority over all Christendom; and, in the same character, he claimed a right to all the countries and possessions of heathens and infidels; a right divine to exterminate and destroy them at his discretion, in order to propagate the Catholic faith. When King Henry VIII. and his parliament threw off the authority of the pope, stripped his holiness of his supremacy, and invested it in himself by an act of parliament, he and his courtiers seemed to think that all the rights of the holy see were transferred to him; and it was a union of these two, (the most impertinent and fantastical ideas that ever got into a human pericranium, namely,—that, as feudal sovereign and supreme head of the church together, a king of England had a right to all the land his subjects could find, not possessed by any Christian state or prince, though possessed by heathen or infidel nations,) which seems to have deluded the nation about the time of the settlement of the colonies. But none of these ideas gave or inferred any right in parliament, over the new countries conquered or discovered; and, therefore, denying that the colonies are a part of the realm, and that as such they are subject to parliament, by no means deprives us of English liberties. Nor does it "build up absolute monarchy in the colonies." For, admitting these notions of the common and feudal law to have been in full force, and that the king was absolute in America, when it was settled; yet he had a right to enter into a contract with his subjects, and stipulate that they should enjoy all the rights and liberties of Englishmen forever, in consideration of their under-taking to clear the wilderness, propagate Christianity, pay a fifth part of ore, &c. Such a contract as this has been made with all the colonies, royal governments, as well as charter ones. For the commissions to the gover-nors contain the plan of the government, and the contract between the king and subject in the former, as much as the charters in the latter.

Indeed, this was the reasoning, and upon these feudal and *catholic* prin-ciples, in the time of some of the predecessors of Massachusettensis. This was the meaning of Dudley, when he asked, "Do you think that English liberties will follow you to the ends of the earth?" His meaning was, that English liberties were confined to the realm, and, out of that, the king was absolute. But this was not true; for an English king had no right to be absolute over Englishmen out of the realm, any more than in it; and they were released from their allegiance, as soon as he deprived them of their liberties.

But "our charters suppose regal authority in the grantor." True, they suppose it, whether there was any or not. "If that authority be derived from the British (he should have said English) crown, it presupposes this territory to have been a part of the British (he should have said English) dominion, and as such subject to the imperial sovereign." How can this writer show this authority to be derived from the English crown, includ-ing in the idea of it lords and commons? Is there the least color for such an authority, but in the popish and feudal ideas before mentioned? And do these popish and feudal ideas include parliament? Was parliament, were lords and commons, parts of the head of the church; or was parliament, that is, lords and commons, part of the sovereign feudatory? Never. But why was this authority derived from the English, any more than the Scot-tish or Irish crown? It is true, the land was to be held in socage, like the manor of East Greenwich; but this was compact, and it might have been as well to hold, as they held in Glasgow or Dublin.

But, says this writer, "if that authority was vested in the person of the king in a different capacity, the British constitution and laws are out of the question, and the king must be absolute as to us, as his prerogatives have never been limited." Not the prerogatives limited in our charters, when in every one of them all the rights of Englishmen are secured to us? Are not the rights of Englishmen sufficiently known? and are not the prerogatives of the king among those rights?

As to those colonies which are destitute of charters, the commissions to their governors have ever been considered as equivalent securities, both for property, jurisdiction, and privileges, with charters; and as to the power of the crown being absolute in those colonies, it is absolute nowhere. There is no fundamental or other law that makes a king of England absolute anywhere, except in conquered countries; and an attempt to assume such a power, by the fundamental laws, forfeits the prince's right even to the limited crown.

As to "the charter governments reverting to absolute monarchy, as their charters may happen to be forfeited by the grantees not fulfilling the conditions of them," I answer, if they could be forfeited, and were actually forfeited, the only consequence would be, that the king would have no power over them at all. He would not be bound to protect the people, nor, that I can see, would the people here, who were born here, be, by any principle of common law, bound even to allegiance to the king. The connection would be broken between the crown and the natives of the country.

It has been a great dispute, whether charters granted within the realm can be forfeited at all. It was a question debated with infinite learning, in the case of the charter of London. It was adjudged forfeited in an arbitrary reign; but afterwards, after the revolution, it was declared in parliament not forfeited, and by an act of parliament made incapable of forfeiture. The charter of Massachusetts was declared forfeited too. So were other American charters. The Massachusetts alone were tame enough to give it up. But no American charter will ever be decreed forfeited again; or if any should, the decree will be regarded no more than a vote of the lower house of the Robinhood society. The court of chancery has no authority without the realm; by common law, surely it has none in America. What! the privileges of millions of Americans depend on the discretion of a lord chancellor? God forbid! The passivity of this colony in receiving the present charter in lieu of the first, is, in the opinion of some, the deepest stain upon its character. There is less to be said in excuse for it than the witchcraft, or hanging the Quakers. A vast party in the province were against it at the time, and thought themselves betrayed by their agent. It has been a warning to their posterity, and one principal motive with the people never to trust any agent with power to concede away their privileges again. It may as well be pretended that the people of Great Britain can forfeit their privileges, as the people of this province. If the contract of state is broken, the people and king of England must recur to nature. It is the same in this province. We shall never more submit to decrees in chancery, or acts of parliament, annihilating charters, or abridging English liberties.

Whether Massachusettensis was born, as a politician, in the year 1764, I know not; but he often writes as if he knew nothing of that period. In his attempt to trace the denial of the supreme authority of the parliament, he commits such mistakes as a man of age at that time ought to blush at.[36] He says, that "when the Stamp Act was made, the authority of parliament to impose external taxes, or, in other words, to lay duties upon goods and merchandise, was admitted," and that when the Tea Act was made, "a new distinction was set up, that parliament had a right to lay duties upon merchandise for the purpose of regulating trade, but not for the purpose of raising a revenue." This is a total misapprehension of the declared opinions of people at those times. The authority of parliament to lay taxes for a revenue has been always generally denied. And their right

[36] "It is curious, indeed, to trace the denial and oppugnation to the supreme authority of the state. When the Stamp Act was made, the authority of parliament to impose internal taxes was denied; but their right to impose external ones, or, in other words, to lay duties upon goods and merchandise, was admitted. When the act was made, imposing duties upon tea, &c., a new distinction was set up, that the parliament had a right to lay duties upon merchandise for the purpose of regulating trade, but not for the purpose of raising a revenue; that is, the parliament had good right, and lawful authority, to lay the former duty of a shilling on the pound, but had none to lay the present duty of threepence. Having got thus far safe, it was only taking one step more to extricate ourselves entirely from their fangs, and become independent states; that our patriots most heroically resolved upon, and flatly denied that parliament had a right to make any laws whatever, that should be binding upon the colonies." *Massachusettensis.*

to lay duties to regulate trade has been denied by many, who have ever contended that trade should be regulated only by prohibitions.

The act of parliament of the 4th George III., passed in the year 1764, was the first act of the British parliament that ever was passed, in which the design of raising a revenue was expressed. Let Massachusettensis name any statute, before that, in which the word revenue is used, or the thought of raising a revenue is expressed. This act is entitled "an act for granting certain duties in the British colonies and plantations in America," &c. The word revenue, in the preamble of this act, instantly ran through the colonies, and rang an alarm, almost as much as if the design of forging chains for the colonists had been expressed in words. I have now before me a pamphlet, written and printed in the year 1764, entitled "The Sentiments of a British American," upon this act. How the idea of a revenue, though from an acknowledged external tax, was relished in that time, may be read in the frontispiece of that pamphlet.

Ergo quid refert mea
Cui serviam? clitellas dum portem meas.—PHÆDRUS.[37]

The first objection to this act, which was made in that pamphlet, by its worthy author, OXENBRIDGE THACHER, who died a martyr to that anxiety for his country which the conduct of the junto gave him, is this:—
"that a tax is thereby laid on several commodities, to be raised and levied in the plantations, and to be remitted home to England. This is esteemed a grievance, inasmuch as the same are laid without the consent of the representatives of the colonists. It is esteemed an essential British right, that no person shall be subject to any tax, but what in person, or by his representative, he hath a voice in laying." Here is a tax, unquestionably external,

---

[37]["So what difference does it make to me whom I serve, as long as I still carry my baggage-packs?" Phaedrus, *Fables* I, 15, lines 9-10. Phaedrus was an ex-slave who put Aesop's fables into Latin verse in the early first century A.D. Phaedrus was a stylistically unsophisticated writer of proletarian literature, and was imprisoned under Tiberius. The speaker of this particular fable is an ass, who tells his master why he has no intention of fleeing when their town is attacked by human enemies. In the previous lines, he asks his owner whether the enemy will make him carry a double load, and the old man says no. So, the ass concludes, why should he care if he changes masters. Ed.]

in the sense in which that word is used in the distinction that is made by some between external and internal taxes, and unquestionably laid in part for the regulation of trade, yet called a grievance, and a violation of an essential British right, in the year 1764, by one who was then at the head of the popular branch of our constitution, and as well acquainted with the sense of his constituents as any man living. And it is indisputable, that in those words he wrote the almost universal sense of this colony.

There are so many egregious errors in point of fact, and respecting the opinions of the people, in this writer, which it is difficult to impute to wilful misrepresentation, that I sometimes think he is some smart young gentleman, come up into life since this great controversy was opened; if not, he must have conversed wholly with the junto, and they must have deceived him respecting their own sentiments.

This writer sneers at the distinction between a right to lay the former duty of a shilling on the pound of tea, and the right to lay the three-pence. But is there not a real difference between laying a duty to be paid in England upon exportation, and to be paid in America upon importation? Is there not a difference between parliament's laying on duties within their own realm, where they have undoubted jurisdiction, and laying them out of their realm, nay, laying them on in our realm, where we say they have no jurisdiction? Let them lay on what duties they please in England, we have nothing to say against that.

"Our patriots most heroically resolved to become independent states, and flatly denied that parliament had a right to make any laws whatever, that should be binding upon the colonies."

Our scribbler, more heroically still, is determined to show the world, that he has courage superior to all regard to modesty, justice, or truth. Our patriots have never determined or desired to be independent states, if a voluntary cession of a right to regulate their trade can make them dependent even on parliament; though they are clear in theory that, by the common law and the English constitution, parliament has no authority over them. None of the patriots of this province, of the present age, have ever denied that parliament has a right, from our voluntary cession, to make laws which shall bind the colonies, so far as their commerce extends.

"There is no possible medium between absolute independence and subjection to the authority of parliament." If this is true, it may be depended upon, that all North America are as fully convinced of their independence, their absolute independence, as they are of their own existence; and as fully determined to defend it at all hazards, as Great Britain is to defend her independence against foreign nations. But it is not true. An absolute independence on parliament, in all internal concerns and cases of taxation, is very compatible with an absolute dependence on it, in all cases of external commerce.

"He must be blind indeed, that cannot see our dearest interest in the latter, (that is, in an absolute subjection to the authority of parliament,) notwithstanding many pant after the former," (that is, absolute independence.) The man who is capable of writing, in cool blood, that our interest lies in an absolute subjection to parliament, is capable of writing or saying any thing for the sake of his pension. A legislature that has so often discovered a want of information concerning us and our country; a legislature interested to lay burdens upon us; a legislature, two branches of which, I mean the lords and commons, neither love nor fear us! Every American of fortune and common sense, must look upon his property to be sunk downright one half of its value, the moment such an absolute subjection to parliament is established.

That there are any who pant after "independence," (meaning by this word a new plan of government over all America, unconnected with the crown of England, or meaning by it an exemption from the power of parliament to regulate trade,) is as great a slander upon the province as ever was committed to writing. The patriots of this province desire nothing new; they wish only to keep their old privileges. They were, for one hundred and fifty years, allowed to tax themselves, and govern their internal concerns as they thought best. Parliament governed their trade as they thought fit. This plan they wish may continue forever. But it is honestly confessed, rather than become subject to the absolute authority of parliament in all cases of taxation and internal polity, they will be driven to throw off that of regulating trade.

"To deny the supreme authority of the state, is a high misdemeanor; to oppose it by force, an overt act of treason." True; and therefore, Massachusettensis, who denies the king represented by his governor, his majesty's council by charter, and house of representatives, to be the supreme authority of this province, has been guilty of a high misdemeanor; and those ministers, governors, and their instruments, who have brought a military force here, and employed it against that supreme authority, are guilty of ____, and ought to be punished with ____. I will be more mannerly than Massachusettensis.

"The realm of England is an appropriate term for the ancient realm of England, in contradistinction to Wales and other territories that have been annexed to it."

There are so many particulars in the case of Wales analogous to the case of America, that I must beg leave to enlarge upon it.

Wales was a little portion of the island of Great Britain, which the Saxons were never able to conquer. The Britons had reserved this tract of land to themselves, and subsisted wholly by pasturage among their mountains. Their princes, however, during the Norman period, and until the reign of King Edward I., did homage to the crown of England, as their feudal sovereign, in the same manner as the prince of one independent state in Europe frequently did to the sovereign of another. This little principality of shepherds and cowherds had, however, maintained its independence through long and bloody wars against the omnipotence of England, for eight hundred years. It is needless to enumerate the causes of the war between Lewellyn and Edward I. It is sufficient to say, that the Welsh prince refused to go to England to do homage, and Edward obtained a new aid of a fifteenth from his parliament, to march with a strong force into Wales. Edward was joined by David and Roderic, two brothers of Lewellyn, who made a strong party among the Welsh themselves, to assist and second the attempts to enslave their native country. The English monarch, however, with all these advantages, was afraid to put the valor of his enemies to a trial, and trusted to the *slow effects of famine* to subdue them. Their pasturage, with such an enemy in their country, could not subsist them, and Lewellyn at last submitted, and bound himself to pay a reparation of damages, to do homage to the crown of England, and almost to surrender his independence as a prince, by permitting all the other barons of Wales, excepting four, to swear fealty to the same crown. But fresh complaints soon arose. The English grew insolent on their bloodless victory, and oppressed the inhabitants; many insults were offered, which at last raised the indignation of the Welsh, so that they determined again to take arms, rather than bear any longer the oppression of the haughty victors. The war raged some time, until Edward summoned all his military tenants, and advanced with an army too powerful for the Welsh to resist. Lewellyn was at last surprised by Edward's General, Mortimer, and fighting at a great disadvantage, was slain, with two thousand of his men. David, who succeeded in the principality, maintained the war for some time, but at last was betrayed to the enemy, sent in chains to Shrewsbury, brought to a formal trial before the peers of England, and, although a sovereign prince, ordered by Edward to be hanged, drawn, and quartered, as a traitor, for defending by arms the liberties of his native country! All the Welsh nobility submitted to the conqueror. The laws of England, sheriffs, and other ministers of justice were established in that principality.

Now Wales was always part of the dominions of England. "Wales was always feudatory to the kingdom of England." It was always held of the crown of England, or the kingdom of England; that is, whoever was King of England had a right to homage, &c. from the Prince of Wales. But yet Wales was not parcel of the realm or kingdom, nor bound by the laws of England. I mention and insist upon this, because it shows that, although the colonies are bound to the crown of England; or, in other words, owe allegiance to whosoever is King of England; yet it does not follow that the colonies are a parcel of the realm or kingdom, and bound by its laws. As this is a point of great importance, I must beg pardon, however unentertaining it may be, to produce my authorities.

"Wales was always feudatory to the kingdom of England."★

Held of the crown, but not parcel;† and, therefore, the Kings of Wales did homage and swore fealty to Henry II. and John and Henry III.

★Comyn's Digest, vol. v. p. 626.
†Per Cook. 1 Roll. 247; 2 Roll. 29.

And 11 Edward I. Upon the conquest of Lewellyn, Prince or King of Wales, that principality became a part of the dominion of the realm of England. And by the statute Walliae, 12 Edward I., it was annexed and united to the crown of England, *tanquam partem corporis ejusdem,* &c.[38] Yet, if the statute Walliae, made at Rutland, 12 Edward I., was not an act of parliament, (as it seems that it was not,) the incorporation made thereby was only a union *jure feudali, et non jure proprietatis.*"[39]

"Wales, before the union with England, was governed by its proper laws," &c.

By these authorities it appears, that Wales was subject, by the feudal law, to the crown of England before the conquest of Lewellyn, but not subject to the laws of England; and indeed, after this conquest, Edward and his nobles did not seem to think it subject to the English parliament, but to the will of the king, as a conqueror of it in war. Accordingly, that instrument which is called *Statutum Walliae,* and to be found in the appendix to the statutes, although it was made by the advice of the peers, or officers of the army more properly, yet it never was passed as an act of parliament, but as an edict of the king. It begins, not in the style of an act of parliament: *"Edwardus Dei gratia Rex Angliæ, Dominus Hyberniæ, et Dux Aquitaniæ, omnibus fidelibus suis, &c. in Wallia. Divina Providentia, quæ in sui dispositione,* says he, *non fallitur, inter alia dispensationis suæ munera, quibus nos et Regnum nostrum Angliæ decorare dignata est, terram Walliae, cum incolis suis prius nobis* jure feudali *subjectam, jam sui gratia,* in proprietatis nostræ dominium, *obstaculis quibuscumque cessantibus, totaliter et cum integritate convertit,* et coronæ regni prædicti, tanquam partem corporis ejusdem annexuit et univit."[40]

---

[38] ["as a part of the same body" Ed.]

[39] ["by feudal right, and not by right of possession" Ed.]

[40] ["Edward by grace of God king of England, Lord of Scotland, and Duke of Aquitaine, to all his faithful subjects, etc., in Wales. Divine Providence, which makes no mistakes in its dispensation, among the other gifts of its dispensation, with which it has seen fit to adorn our Kingdom of England, has now, after the cessation of whatsoever obstacles existed, wholly and entirely transferred the land of Wales, previously subject to us by feudal right, along with its inhabitants, into the dominion of our possession, and has annexed and unified it, as a part of the same body, to the crown of the aforementioned kingdom." Ed.]

Here is the most certain evidence,—1. That Wales was subject to the kings of England by the feudal law before the conquest, though not bound by any laws but their own. 2. That the conquest was considered, in that day, as conferring the property, as well as jurisdiction of Wales, to the English crown. 3. The conquest was considered as annexing and uniting Wales to the English crown, both in point of property and jurisdiction, as a part of one body. Yet, notwithstanding all this, parliament was not considered as acquiring any share in the government of Wales by this conquest. If, then, it should be admitted that the colonies are all annexed and united to the crown of England, it will not follow that lords and commons have any authority over them.

. . .

No. IX

. . .

"With us, in England," says Blackstone, "it becoming a settled principle of tenure, that all lands in the kingdom are holden of the king, as their sovereign and lord paramount, &c. the oath of allegiance was necessarily confined to the person of the king alone. By an easy analogy, the term of allegiance was soon brought to signify all other engagements which are due from subjects, as well as those duties which were simply and merely territorial. And the oath of allegiance, as administered for upwards of six hundred years, contained a promise 'to be true and faithful to the king and his heirs, and truth and faith to bear of life and limb and terrene honor, and not to know or hear of any ill or damage intended him, without defending him therefrom.' But at the revolution, the terms of this oath being thought, perhaps, to favor too much the notion of non-resistance, the present form was introduced by the convention parliament, which is more general and indeterminate than the former, the subject only promising 'that he will be faithful, and bear true allegiance to the king,' without mentioning 'his heirs,' or specifying in the least wherein that allegiance consists."

Thus, I think that all the authorities in law coincide exactly with the observation which I have heretofore made upon the case of Wales, and show that subjection to a king of England does not necessarily imply subjection to the crown of England; and that subjection to the crown of England does not imply subjection to the parliament of England; for allegiance is due to the person of the king, and to that alone, in all three cases; that is, whether we are subject to his parliament and crown, as well as his person, as the people in England are; whether we are subject to his crown and person, without parliament, as the Welsh were after the conquest of Lewellyn and before the union; or as the Irish were after the conquest and before Poyning's law; or whether we are subject to his person alone, as the Scots were to the King of England, after the accession of James I., being not at all subject to the parliament or crown of England.

We do not admit any binding authority in the decisions and adjudications of the court of king's bench or common pleas, or the court of chancery, over America; but we quote them as the opinions of learned men. In these we find a distinction between a country conquered and a country discovered. Conquest, they say, gives the crown an absolute power; discovery only gives the subject a right to all the laws of England. They add, that all the laws of England are in force there. I confess I do not see the reason of this. There are several cases in books of law which may be properly thrown before the public. I am no more of a lawyer than Massachusettensis, but have taken his advice, and conversed with many lawyers upon our subject, some honest, some dishonest, some living, some dead, and am willing to lay before you what I have learned from all of them. In Salkeld, 411, the case of Blankard and Galdy: "In debt on a bond, the defendant prayed oyer of the condition, and pleaded the statute E. 6, against buying offices concerning the administration of justice; and averred, that this bond was given for the purchase of the office of provost-marshal in Jamaica, and that it concerned the administration of justice, and *that Jamaica is part of the revenue and possessions of the crown of England.* The plaintiff replied, that Jamaica is an island *beyond the seas,* which was conquered from the Indians and Spaniards in Queen Elizabeth's time, and the inhabitants are governed by their own laws, and not by the laws of England. The defendant rejoined, that, before such conquest, they were governed by their own laws; but since that, by the laws of England. Shower argued for the plaintiff, that, on a judgment in Jamaica, no writ of error lies here, but only an appeal to the council; *and as they are not represented in our parliament, so they are not bound by our statutes,* unless specially named.★ Pemberton, contra, argued that, *by the conquest of a nation, its liberties, rights, and properties are quite lost;* that by consequence, their laws are lost too, for the law is but the rule and guard of the other; those that conquer cannot, by their victory, lose their laws and become subject to others.† That error lies here upon a judgment in Jamaica, which could not be, if they were not under the same law. Et per Holt, C. J. and Cur. 1st. In case of an uninhabited country, newly found out by English subjects, all laws in force in England are in force there; so it seemed to be agreed. 2. Jamaica being conquered, and not pleaded to be parcel of the kingdom of England, but part of the possessions and revenue of the crown of England, the laws of England did not take place there, until declared so by the conqueror or his successors. The Isle of Man and Ireland are part of the *possessions* of the crown of England, yet retain their ancient laws; that, in Davis, 36, it is not pretended that the custom of tanistry was determined by the conquest of Ireland, but by the new settlement made there after the conquest; that it was impossible the laws of this nation, by mere conquest, without more, should take place in a conquered country; because, for a time, there must want officers, without which our laws can have no force; that if our law did take place, yet they, in Jamaica, having power to make new laws, our general laws may be altered by theirs in particulars; also, they held that in case of an infidel country, their laws, by conquest, do not entirely cease, but only such as are against the law of God; and that in such cases, where the laws are rejected or silent, the conquered country shall be governed according to the rule of natural equity. Judgment *pro quer'.*"[41]

Upon this case I beg leave to make a few observations:—

1. That Shower's reasoning, that we are not bound by statutes, because not represented in parliament, is universal, and, therefore, his exception,

★And. 115.
†Vaugh. 405.
[41] ["for the plaintiff" Ed.]

"unless specially named," although it is taken from analogy to the case of Ireland, by Lord Coke and others, yet is not taken from the common law, but is merely arbitrary and groundless, as applied to us; because, if the want of representation could be supplied by "expressly naming" a country, the right of representation might be rendered null and nugatory. But of this, more another time.

2. That, by the opinion of Holt and the whole court, the laws of England, common and statute, are in force in a vacant country, discovered by Englishmen. But America was not a vacant country; it was full of inhabitants; our ancestors purchased the land; but, if it had been vacant, his lordship has not shown us any authority at common law, that the laws of England would have been in force there. On the contrary, by that law, it is clear they did not extend beyond seas, and therefore could not be binding there, any further than the free will of the discoverers should make them. The discoverers had a right by nature to set up those laws if they liked them, or any others that pleased them better, provided they were not inconsistent with their allegiance to the king.

3. The court held, that a country must be parcel of the kingdom of England, before the laws of England could take place there; which seems to be inconsistent with what is said before, because discovery of a vacant country does not make it parcel of the kingdom of England, which shows that the court, when they said, that all laws in *force* in England are in *force* in the discovered country, meant no more than that the discoverers had a right to all such laws, if they chose to adopt them.

4. The idea of the court, in this case, is exactly conformable to, if not taken from, the case of Wales. They consider a conquered country as Edward I. and his successors did Wales, as by the conquest annexed to the crown, as an absolute property, possession, or revenue, and, therefore, to be disposed of at its will; not entitled to the laws of England, although bound to be governed by the king's will, in parliament or out of it, as he pleased.

5. The Isle of Man and Ireland are considered, like Wales, as conquered countries, and part of the possessions (by which they mean property or revenue) of the crown of England, yet have been allowed by the king's will to retain their ancient laws.

6. That the case of America differs totally from the case of Wales, Ireland, Man, or any other case which is known at common law or in English history. There is no one precedent in point in any English records, and, therefore, it can be determined only by eternal reason and the law of nature. But yet that the analogy of all these cases of Ireland, Wales, Man, Chester, Durham, Lancaster, &c. clearly concur with the dictates of reason and nature, that Americans are entitled to all the liberties of Englishmen, and that they are not bound by any acts of parliament whatever, by any law known in English records or history, excepting those for the regulation of trade, which they have consented to and acquiesced in.

7. To these let me add, that, as the laws of England and the authority of parliament were by common law confined to the realm and within the four seas, so was the force of the great seal of England. "The great seal of England is appropriated to England, and what is done under it has relation to England, and to no other place."* So that the king, by common law, had no authority to create peers or governments, or any thing out of the realm, by his great seal; and, therefore, our charters and commissions to governors, being under the great seal, gives us no more authority, nor binds us to any other duties, than if they had been given under the privy seal, or without any seal at all. Their binding force, both upon the crown and us, is wholly from compact and the law of nature.

There is another case in which the same sentiments are preserved.† "It was said by the master of the rolls to have been determined by the lords of the privy council, upon an appeal to the king in council from the foreign plantations; 1st. That if there be a new and uninhabited country, found out by English subjects, as the law is the birthright of every subject, so, wherever they go, they carry their laws with them, and, therefore, such new found country is to be governed by the laws of England; though after such country is inhabited by the English, acts of parliament made in England, without naming the foreign plantations, will not bind them; for which reason it has been determined, that the statute of frauds and

---

*Salkeld, 510.
†It is in 2 P. Williams, 75, Memorandum, 9th August, 1722.

perjuries, which requires three witnesses, and that these should subscribe in the testator's presence in the case of a devise of land, does not bind Barbadoes; but that, 2dly. Where the King of England conquers a country, it is a different consideration; for there the conqueror, by saving the lives of the people conquered, gains a right and property in such people! In consequence of which, he may impose upon them what laws he pleases; but, 3dly. Until such laws, given by the conquering prince, the laws and customs of the conquered country shall hold place; unless where these are contrary to our religion, or enact any thing that is *malum in se,* or are silent; for in all such cases the laws of the conquering country shall prevail."

No. X

GIVE me leave, now, to descend from these general matters to Massachusettensis. He says, "Ireland, who has perhaps the greatest possible subordinate legislature, and sends no members to the British parliament, is bound by its acts when expressly named." But if we are to consider what ought to be, as well as what is, why should Ireland have the greatest possible subordinate legislature? Is Ireland more numerous and more important to what is called the British empire than America? Subordinate as the Irish legislature is said to be, and a conquered country, as undoubtedly it is, the parliament of Great Britain, although they claim a power to bind Ireland by statutes, have never laid one farthing of tax upon it. They knew it would occasion resistance if they should. But the authority of parliament to bind Ireland at all, if it has any, is founded upon entirely a different principle from any that takes place in the case of America. It is founded on the consent and compact of the Irish by Poyning's law to be so governed, if it have any foundation at all; and this consent was given, and compact made, in consequence of a conquest.

...

The principle upon which Ireland is bound by English statutes, in which it is named, is this, that being a conquered country, and subject to the mere will of the king, it voluntarily consented to be so bound. This appears in part already, and more fully in Blackstone, who tells us "that

Ireland is a distinct, though a dependent, subordinate kingdom." But how came it dependent and subordinate? He tells us, that "King John, in the twelfth year of his reign, after the conquest, went into Ireland, carried over with him many able sages of the law; and there by his letters-patent, in right of the dominion of conquest, is said to have ordained and established that Ireland should be governed by the laws of England; which letters-patent Sir Edward Coke apprehends to have been there confirmed in parliament. ... By the same rule, that no laws made in England between King John's time and Poyning's law were then binding in Ireland, it follows, that no acts of the English parliament, made since the tenth of Henry VII., do now bind the people of Ireland, unless specially named, or included under general words. And on the other hand, it is equally clear, that where Ireland is particularly named, or is included under general words, they are bound by such acts of parliament. For this follows from the very nature and constitution of a dependent state; dependence being very little else but an obligation to conform to the will or law of that superior person or state upon which the inferior depends. The original and true ground of this superiority in the present case, is what we usually call, though somewhat improperly, the right of conquest; a right allowed by the law of nations, if not by that of nature; but which in reason and civil policy can mean nothing more than that, in order to put an end to hostilities, a compact is either expressly or tacitly made between the conqueror and the conquered, that if they will acknowledge the victor for their master, he will treat them for the future as subjects, and not as enemies."

These are the principles upon which the dependence and subordination of Ireland are founded. Whether they are just or not is not necessary for us to inquire. The Irish nation have never been entirely convinced of their justice, have been ever discontented with them, and ripe and ready to dispute them. Their reasonings have been ever answered by the *ratio ultima* and *penultima* of the tories; and it requires, to this hour, no less than a standing army of twelve thousand men to confute them, as little as the British parliament exercises the right, which it claims, of binding them by statutes, and although it never once attempted or presumed to tax them, and although they are so greatly inferior to Britain in power, and so near in situation.

But thus much is certain, that none of these principles take place in the case of America. She never was conquered by Britain. She never consented to be a state dependent upon, or subordinate to the British parliament, excepting only in the regulation of her commerce; and therefore the reasonings of British writers upon the case of Ireland are not applicable to the case of the colonies, any more than those upon the case of Wales.

Thus have I rambled after Massachusettensis through Wales and Ireland, but have not reached my journey's end. I have yet to travel through Jersey, Guernsey, and I know not where. At present, I shall conclude with one observation. In the history of Ireland and Wales, though undoubtedly conquered countries, and under the very eye and arm of England, the extreme difficulty, the utter impracticability of governing a people who have any sense, spirit, or love of liberty, without incorporating them into the state, or allowing them in some other way equal privileges, may be clearly seen. Wales was forever revolting, for a thousand years, until it obtained that mighty blessing. Ireland has been frequently revolting, although the most essential power of a supreme legislature, that of imposing taxes, has never been exercised over them; and it cannot now be kept under but by force. And it would revolt forever if parliament should tax them. What kind of an opinion, then, must the ministry entertain of America,—when her distance is so great, her territory so extensive, her commerce so important; not a conquered country, but dearly purchased and defended; when her trade is so essential to the navy, the commerce, the revenue, the very existence of Great Britain as an independent state? They must think America inhabited by three millions of fools and cowards.

No. XII

...

Heirs and successors of the king are supposed to be the same persons, and are used as synonymous words in the English law. There is no positive artificial provision made by our laws, or the British constitution, for revolutions. All our positive laws suppose that the royal office will descend to the eldest branch of the male line, or, in default of that, to the eldest female, &c., forever, and that the succession will not be broken. It is true that nature, necessity, and the great principles of self-preservation, have often overruled the succession. But this was done without any positive instruction of law. Therefore, the grants being by the king, for his heirs and successors, and the tenures being of the king, his heirs and successors, and the reservation being to the king, his heirs and successors, are so far from proving that we were to be part of an empire, as one state, subject to the supreme authority of the English or British state, and subject to its protection, that they do not so much as prove that we are annexed to the English crown. And all the subtilty of the writers on the side of the ministry, has never yet proved that America is so much as annexed to the crown, much less to the realm. "It is apparent the king acted in his royal capacity, as king of England." This I deny. The laws of England gave him no authority to grant any territory out of the realm. Besides, there is no color for his thinking that he acted in that capacity, but his using the great seal of England; but if the king is absolute in the affair of the seal, and may make or use any seal that he pleases, his using that seal which had been commonly used in England is no certain proof that he acted as king of England; for it is plain he might have used the English seal in the government of Scotland, and in that case it will not be pretended that he would have acted in his royal capacity as king of England. But his acting as king of England "necessarily supposes the territory granted to be a part of the English dominions, and holden of the crown of England." Here is the word "dominions" systematically introduced instead of the word "realm." There was no English dominions but the realm. And I say, that America was not any part of the English realm or dominions. And therefore, when the king granted it, he could not act as king of England, by the laws of England. As to the "territory being holden of the crown, there is no such thing in nature or art." Lands are holden according to the original notices of feuds, of the natural person of the lord. Holding lands, in feudal language, means no more than the relation between lord and tenant. The reciprocal duties of these are all personal. Homage, fealty, &c., and all other services, are personal to the lord; protection, &c. is personal to the tenant. And therefore no homage, fealty, or other services, can ever be rendered to the body politic, the political capacity, which is not corporated, but only a frame in the mind, an idea. No lands here, or in England, are held of the crown, meaning by it the political capacity; they are all held of the royal person, the natural person of the king. Holding lands, &c. of the crown, is an impropriety of expression; but it is often used; and when it is, it can have no other sensible meaning than this, that we hold lands of that person, whoever he is, who wears the crown; the law supposes he will be a right, natural heir of the present king forever.

Massachusettensis then produces a quotation from the first charter, to prove several points. It is needless to repeat the whole; but the parts chiefly relied on are italicized. It makes the company a body politic in fact and name, &c., and enables it "to sue and be sued." Then the writer asks, "whether this looks like a distinct state or independent empire?" I answer, no. And that it is plain and uncontroverted, that the first charter was intended only to erect a corporation within the realm; and the governor and company were to reside within the realm; and their general courts were to be held there. Their agents, deputies, and servants only were to come to America. And if this had taken place, nobody ever doubted but they would have been subject to parliament. But this intention was not regarded on either side; and the company came over to America, and brought their charter with them. And as soon as they arrived here, they got out of the English realm, dominions, state, empire, call it by what name you will, and out of the legal jurisdiction of parliament. The king might, by his writ or proclamation, have commanded them to return; but he did not.

A Defence of the Constitutions
of the
United States of America
(1786-87)

A s the subtitle indicates, the proximate cause for these volumes was Adams's overriding concern to defend the American State Constitutions against the charges leveled at them by Turgot in a 1778 letter to Dr. Price. The letter came to Adams's attention when it appeared as an appendage to Price's work entitled "Observations on the Importance of the American Revolution and the Means of making it a Benefit to the World." As Adams put it in a letter to John Trumbull (January 23, 1791, *Works*, IX, 572-3), "My three volumes are a defence of the American Constitutions on that side on which they are attacked. Mr. Turgot attacked them for aiming at three orders and a balance. I defended them on this point only."

Later correspondence reveals other motives. In his letter to Samuel Perley of 19 June 1809 (*Works*, IX, 623), he writes: "I never thought of writing till the Assembly of Notables in France had commenced a revolution, with the Duke de la Rouchefoucauld [M. Turgot] and Mr. Condorcet at their head, who I knew would establish a government in one assembly, and that I knew would involve France and all Europe in all the horrors we have seen; carnage and desolation, for fifty, perhaps for a hundred years." "At the same time," he continues, "every western wind brought us news of town and county meetings in Massachusetts, adopting Mr. Turgot's ideas, condemning my Constitution, reprobating the office of governor and the assembly of the Senate as expensive, and pernicious, and not only proposing to toss them off, but rising in rebellion against them. In this situation," he adds, "I was determined to wash my hands of the blood that was about to be shed in France, Europe, and America, and show to the world that neither my sentiments nor actions should have any share in countenancing or encouraging any such pernicious, destructive, and fatal schemes." At still another level, he remarks that Turgot's "intention was to celebrate Franklin's [the Pennsylvania Constitution marked by unicameralism] and condemn mine [the Massachusetts Constitution of 1780]."

Whatever his motives, Adams clearly saw an urgency in putting out these volumes. While serving as the United States' first Minister to the Court of St. James, he began work at a feverish pace in October 1786 and finished in December 1787. The first volume was reprinted in the United States and available to the members of the Philadelphia Convention, though any estimate of its impact on them is purely conjectural.

The bulk of these volumes consists of extensive quotations from the writings of others, principally historians and political theorists, designed to show the advantages and security inherent in mixed and balanced governments, as well as the dangers of centralized, unchecked power. Its scope is extremely broad. The first volume consists of ten chapters and covers "Modern Democratic Republics" (San Marino, Biscay, Switzerland—with a survey of seven of its Cantons), "Aristocratic Republics" (nine of the Cantons of Switzerland, Lucca, Genoa, and Venice), "Monarchical or Regal Republics" (England, Poland, Nenchatel); "Opinions of Philosophers" (Swift, Franklin, Price), "Writers on Government" (Machiavelli, Sidney, Montesquieu, Harrington), "Opinions of Historians" (Polybius, Dionysius of Halicarnassus, Plato, Locke, Milton, Hume), "Ancient Democratical Republics" (Carthage, Athens, Achaia, Crete, Corinth, Argos, Elis, Thebes, Sybaris, Locris, Rome), "Ancient Aristocratical Republics" (Rome, Lacedemonia, Crotona), and "Ancient Monarchical Republics" (Ancient Germans, Phonecia, Ithica). The second volume is devoted to "Italian Republics of the Middle Age." The bulk of this volume treats with Florence and Siena, though chapters are devoted to Bologna, Pistoia, Cremona, Padua. and Mantua. The final volume consists of three chapters and a conclusion all of which deal with aspects of Marchamont Nedham's writings.

The work, taken as a whole, lacks cohesion and, save for a few notable places, it is short on analysis. Adams was well aware of its many shortcomings, all of which were outweighed by his belief that, as noted above, its message might forestall an impending crisis.

In his editorial "Preface" to *Defence*, Charles Francis Adams writes that he "had not advanced many pages in his work of revision of the many and glaring errors of the press, before he became impressed with the necessity of deciding a question deeper than these. The choice was before him, on the one hand, of implicitly following the text and the order of arrangement of the former editions, however obvious the disadvantage to a work of too much learning and profound reflection not to deserve placing in a better permanent form, or, on the other, of exercising within certain limits the liberty of revision and of correction." He chose the course of "thorough revision"; reorganizing, correcting errors "in dates and name ... as well as translations." Where these errors were minor, they were corrected "tacitly"; where important, they are "pointed out in the notes."

He also remarks that two of John Adams's English friends, Granville Sharp and Brand Hollis, found "a few notes to the first volume." These are included in the text "with the initial of the writer attached" (*Works,* IV, 274-75.)

The following selections from the *Defence* are taken from *Works,* IV: 283-302, 379-415, 469-92, 542-56, 570-78, 579-88; VI: 3-15, 56-70, 113-18, 140-44, 185-211, 217-20.

———————

A Defence of the
Constitutions of Government
of the United States of America,
Against the Attack of
M. Turgot, in His Letter to
Dr. Price, Dated the
Twenty-Second Day of March, 1778.
By John Adams.
"All Nature's difference keeps all Nature's peace." Pope

VOLUME I

Preface

THE arts and sciences, in general, during the three or four last centuries, have had a regular course of progressive improvement. The inventions in mechanic arts, the discoveries in natural philosophy, navigation, and commerce, and the advancement of civilization and humanity, have occasioned changes in the condition of the world, and the human character, which would have astonished the most refined nations of antiquity. A continuation of similar exertions is every day rendering Europe more and more like one community, or single family. Even in the theory and practice of government, in all the simple monarchies, considerable improvements have been made. The checks and balances of republican governments have been in some degree adopted at the courts of princes. By the erection of various tribunals, to register the laws, and exercise the judicial power— by indulging the petitions and remonstrances of subjects, until by habit they are regarded as rights—a control has been established over ministers of state, and the royal councils, which, in some degree, approaches the spirit of republics. Property is generally secure, and personal liberty seldom invaded. The press has great influence, even where it is not expressly tolerated; and the public opinion must be respected by a minister, or his place becomes insecure. Commerce begins to thrive; and if religious toleration were established, personal liberty a little more protected, by giving an absolute right to demand a public trial in a certain reasonable time, and the states were invested with a few more privileges, or rather restored to some that have been taken away, these governments would be brought to as great a degree of perfection, they would approach as near to the character of governments of laws and not of men, as their nature will probably admit of. In so general a refinement, or more properly a reformation of manners and improvement in science, is it not unaccountable that the knowledge of the principles and construction of free governments, in which the happiness of life, and even the further progress of improvement in education and society, in knowledge and virtue, are so deeply interested, should have remained at a full stand for two or three thousand years?

According to a story in Herodotus, the nature of monarchy, aristocracy, and democracy, and the advantages and inconveniences of each, were as well understood at the time of the neighing of the horse of Darius, as they are at this hour. A variety of mixtures of these simple species were conceived and attempted, with various success, by the Greeks and Romans. Representations, instead of collections, of the people; a total separation of the executive from the legislative power, and of the judicial from both; and a balance in the legislature, by three independent, equal branches, are perhaps the only three discoveries in the constitution of a free government, since the institution of Lycurgus. Even these have been so unfortunate, that they have never spread: the first has been given up by all the nations, excepting one, which had once adopted it; and the other two, reduced to practice, if not invented, by the English nation, have never been imitated by any other, except their own descendants in America.

While it would be rash to say, that nothing further can be done to bring a free government, in all its parts, still nearer to perfection, the representations of the people are most obviously susceptible of improvement. The end to be aimed at, in the formation of a representative assembly, seems to be the sense of the people, the public voice. The perfection of the portrait consists in its likeness. Numbers, or property, or both, should be the rule; and the proportions of electors and members an affair of calculation.

The duration should not be so long that the deputy should have time to forget the opinions of his constituents. Corruption in elections is the great enemy of freedom. Among the provisions to prevent it, more frequent elections, and a more general privilege of voting, are not all that might be devised. Dividing the districts, diminishing the distance of travel, and confining the choice to residents, would be great advances towards the annihilation of corruption. The modern aristocracies of Holland, Venice, Bern, &c., have tempered themselves with innumerable checks, by which they have given a great degree of stability to that form of government; and though liberty and life can never be there enjoyed so well as in a free republic, none is perhaps more capable of profound sagacity. We shall learn to prize the checks and balances of a free government, and even those of the modern aristocracies, if we recollect the miseries of Greece, which arose from its ignorance of them. The only balance attempted against the ancient kings was a body of nobles; and the consequences were perpetual alternations of rebellion and tyranny, and the butchery of thousands upon every revolution from one to the other. When kings were abolished, aristocracies tyrannized; and then no balance was attempted but between aristocracy and democracy. This, in the nature of things, could be no balance at all, and therefore the pendulum was forever on the swing.

It is impossible to read in Thucydides,★ his account of the factions and confusions throughout all Greece, which were introduced by this want of an equilibrium, without horror. "During the few days that Eurymedon, with his troops, continued at Corcyra, the people of that city extended the massacre to all whom they judged their enemies. The crime alleged was, their attempt to overturn the democracy. Some perished merely through private enmity; some, by the hands of the borrower, on account of the money they had lent. Every kind of death, every dreadful act, was perpetrated. Fathers slew their children; some were dragged from altars, some were butchered at them; numbers, immured in temples, were starved. The contagion spread through the whole extent of Greece; factions raged in every city; the licentious many contending for the Athenians, and the

★ Lib. iii. 81, 82.

aspiring few for the Lacedæmonians. The consequence was, seditions in cities, with all their numerous and tragical incidents."

"Such things ever will be," says Thucydides, "so long as human nature continues the same." But if this nervous historian had known a balance of three powers, he would not have pronounced the distemper so incurable, but would have added—*so long as parties in cities remain unbalanced.* He adds,—"Words lost their signification; brutal rashness was fortitude; prudence, cowardice; modesty, effeminacy; and being wise in every thing, to be good for nothing: the hot temper was manly valor; calm deliberation, plausible knavery; he who boiled with indignation, was trustworthy; and he who presumed to contradict, was ever suspected. Connection of blood was less regarded than transient acquaintance; associations were not formed for mutual advantage, consistent with law, but for rapine against all law; trust was only communication of guilt; revenge was more valued, than never to have suffered an injury; perjuries were master-pieces of cunning; the dupes only blushed, the villains most impudently triumphed."

"The source of all these evils was a thirst of power, from rapacious and ambitious passions. The men of large influence, some contending for the just equality of the democratical, and others for the fair decorum of aristocratical government, by artful sounds, embarrassed those communities, for their own private lucre, by the keenest spirit, the most daring projects, and most dreadful machinations. Revenge, not limited by justice or the public welfare, was measured only by such retaliation as was judged the sweetest; by capital condemnations, by iniquitous sentences, and by glutting the present rancor of their hearts with their own hands. The pious and upright conduct was on both sides disregarded; the moderate citizens fell victims to both. Seditions introduced every species of outrageous wickedness into the Grecian manners. Sincerity was laughed out of countenance; the whole order of human life was confounded; the human temper, too apt to transgress in spite of laws, now having gained the ascendant over law, seemed to glory that it was too strong for justice, and an enemy to all superiority."

Mr. Hume has collected, from Diodorus Siculus alone, a few massacres which happened in only sixty of the most polished years of Greece:—

"From Sybaris, 500 nobles banished; of Chians, 600 citizens; at Ephesus, 340 killed, 1000 banished; of Cyrenians, 500 nobles killed, all the rest banished; the Corinthians killed 120, banished 500; Phæbidas banished 300 Bœotians. Upon the fall of the Lacedæmonians, democracies were restored in many cities, and severe vengeance taken of the nobles; the banished nobles returning, butchered their adversaries at Phialæ, in Corinth, in Megara, in Phliasia, where they killed 300 of the people; but these again revolting, killed above 600 of the nobles, and banished the rest. In Arcadia, 1400 banished, besides many killed; the banished retired to Sparta and Pallantium; the latter were delivered up to their countrymen, and all killed. Of the banished from Argos and Thebes, there were 500 in the Spartan army. The people, before the usurpation of Agathocles, had banished 600 nobles; afterwards that tyrant, in concurrence with the people, killed 4000 nobles, and banished 6000; and killed 4000 people at Gela; his brother banished 8000 from Syracuse. The inhabitants of Ægesta, to the number of 40,000, were killed, man, woman, and child, for the sake of their money; all the relations of the Libyan army, fathers, brothers, children, killed; 7000 exiles killed after capitulation. These numbers, compared with the population of those cities, are prodigious; yet Agathocles was a man of character, and not to be suspected of wanton cruelty, contrary to the maxims of his age."[1]

Such were the fashionable outrages of unbalanced parties. In the name of human and divine benevolence, is such a system as this to be recommended to Americans, in this age of the world? Human nature is as incapable now of going through revolutions with temper and sobriety, with patience and prudence, or without fury and madness, as it was among the Greeks so long ago. The latest revolution that we read of was conducted, at least on one side, in the Grecian style, with laconic energy; and with a little Attic salt, at least, without too much patience, foresight, and prudence, on the other. Without three orders, and an effectual balance between them, in every American constitution, it must be destined to frequent unavoidable revolutions; though they are delayed a few years, they

---

[1] On the Populousness of Ancient Nations. Hurne's *Essays*, vol. i. p. 477, note BB.

must come in time. The United States are large and populous nations, in comparison with the Grecian commonwealths, or even the Swiss cantons; and they are growing every day more disproportionate, and therefore less capable of being held together by simple governments. Countries that increase in population so rapidly as the States of America did, even during such an impoverishing and destructive war as the last was, are not to be long bound with silken threads; lions, young or old, will not be bound by cobwebs. It would be better for America, it is nevertheless agreed, to ring all the changes with the whole set of bells, and go through all the revolutions of the Grecian States, rather than establish an absolute monarchy among them, notwithstanding all the great and real improvements which have been made in that kind of government.

The objection to it is not because it is supported by nobles, and a subordination of ranks; for all governments, even the most democratical, are supported by a subordination of offices, and of ranks too. None ever existed without it but in a state of anarchy and outrage, in a contempt of law and justice, no better than no government. But the nobles, in the European monarchies, support them more by opposing than promoting their ordinary views. The kings are supported by their armies; the nobles support the crown, as it is in full possession of the gift of all employments; but they support it still more by checking its ministers, and preventing them from running into abuses of power and wanton despotism; otherwise the people would be pushed to extremities and insurrections. It is thus that the nobles reconcile the monarchical authority to the obedience of the subjects; but take away the standing armies, and leave the nobles to themselves, and in a few years, they would overturn every monarchy in Europe, and erect aristocracies.

It is become a kind of fashion among writers, to admit, as a maxim, that if you could be always sure of a wise, active, and virtuous prince, monarchy would be the best of governments. But this is so far from being admissible, that it will forever remain true, that a free government has a great advantage over a simple monarchy. The best and wisest prince, by means of a freer communication with his people, and the greater opportunities to collect the best advice from the best of his subjects, would have an immense advantage in a free state over a monarchy. A senate consisting of all that is most noble, wealthy, and able in the nation, with a right to counsel the crown at all times, is a check to ministers, and a security against abuses, such as a body of nobles who never meet, and have no such right, can never supply. Another assembly, composed of representatives chosen by the people in all parts, gives free access to the whole nation, and communicates all its wants, knowledge, projects, and wishes to government; it excites emulation among all classes, removes complaints, redresses grievances, affords opportunities of exertion to genius, though in obscurity, and gives full scope to all the faculties of man; it opens a passage for every speculation to the legislature, to administration, and to the public; it gives a universal energy to the human character, in every part of the state, such as never can be obtained in a monarchy.

There is a third particular which deserves attention both from governments and people. In a simple monarchy, the ministers of state can never know their friends from their enemies; secret cabals undermine their influence, and blast their reputation. This occasions a jealousy ever anxious and irritated, which never thinks the government safe without an encouragement of informers and spies, throughout every part of the state, who interrupt the tranquility of private life, destroy the confidence of families in their own domestics and in one another, and poison freedom in its sweetest retirements. In a free government, on the contrary, the ministers can have no enemies of consequence but among the members of the great or little council, where every man is obliged to take his side, and declare his opinion, upon every question. This circumstance alone, to every manly mind, would be sufficient to decide the preference in favor of a free government. Even secrecy, where the executive is entire in one hand, is as easily and surely preserved in a free government, as in a simple monarchy; and as to despatch, all the simple monarchies of the whole universe may be defied to produce greater or more numerous examples of it than are to be found in English history. An Alexander, or a Frederic, possessed of the prerogatives only of a king of England, and leading his own armies, would never find himself embarrassed or delayed in any honest enterprise. He might be restrained, indeed, from running mad, and from making conquests to the ruin of his nation, merely for his own glory; but this is no argument against a free government.

There can be no free government without a democratical branch in the constitution. Monarchies and aristocracies are in possession of the voice and influence of every university and academy in Europe. Democracy, simple democracy, never had a patron among men of letters. Democratical mixtures in government have lost almost all the advocates they ever had out of England and America. Men of letters must have a great deal of praise, and some of the necessaries, conveniences, and ornaments of life. Monarchies and aristocracies pay well and applaud liberally. The people have almost always expected to be served gratis, and to be paid for the honor of serving them; and their applauses and adorations are bestowed too often on artifices and tricks, on hypocrisy and superstition, on flattery, bribes, and largesses. It is no wonder then that democracies and democratical mixtures are annihilated all over Europe, except on a barren rock, a paltry fen, an inaccessible mountain, or an impenetrable forest. The people of England, to their immortal honor, are hitherto an exception; but, to the humiliation of human nature, they show very often that they are like other men. The people in America have now the best opportunity and the greatest trust in their hands, that Providence ever committed to so small a number, since the transgression of the first pair; if they betray their trust, their guilt will merit even greater punishment than other nations have suffered, and the indignation of Heaven. If there is one certain truth to be collected from the history of all ages, it is this; that the people's rights and liberties, and the democratical mixture in a constitution, can never be preserved without a strong executive, or, in other words, without separating the executive from the legislative power. If the executive power, or any considerable part of it, is left in the hands either of an aristocratical or a democratical assembly, it will corrupt the legislature as necessarily as rust corrupts iron, or as arsenic poisons the human body; and when the legislature is corrupted, the people are undone.

The rich, the well-born, and the able, acquire an influence among the people that will soon be too much for simple honesty and plain sense, in a house of representatives. The most illustrious of them must, therefore, be separated from the mass, and placed by themselves in a senate; this is, to all honest and useful intents, an ostracism.* A member of a senate, of immense wealth, the most respected birth, and transcendent abilities, has no influence in the nation, in comparison of what he would have in a single representative assembly. When a senate exists, the most powerful man in the state may be safely admitted into the house of representatives, because the people have it in their power to remove him into the senate as soon as his influence becomes dangerous. The senate becomes the great object of ambition; and the richest and the most sagacious wish to merit an advancement to it by services to the public in the house. When he has obtained the object of his wishes, you may still hope for the benefits of his exertions, without dreading his passions; for the executive power being in other hands, he has lost much of his influence with the people, and can govern very few votes more than his own among the senators.

It was the general opinion of ancient nations, that the Divinity alone was adequate to the important office of giving laws to men. The Greeks entertained this prejudice throughout all their dispersions; the Romans cultivated the same popular delusion; and modern nations, in the conse-cration of kings, and in several superstitious chimeras of divine right in princes and nobles, are nearly unanimous in preserving remnants of it. Even the venerable magistrates of Amersfort devoutly believe themselves God's vicegerents. Is it that obedience to the laws can be obtained from mankind in no other manner? Are the jealousy of power, and the envy of superiority, so strong in all men, that no considerations of public or private utility are sufficient to engage their submission to rules for their own

* "Mr. Pulteney and Mr. Pitt were ostracized, but the intent of their being so was neither honest nor useful. They lost, however, their popular influence, by their removal into the house of lords, which proves the use of a senate, as contended for. Unluckily, indeed, these examples go somewhat further. They show how the ostracism of a senate may be abused." S. No such abuse as is here pointed out is likely to happen through any form of popular election. The working of the present constitution of the United States, in the particular noticed in the text, appears thus far to have excited little obser-vation. It would be a curious, and not unprofitable subject of speculation, to consider what might have been the effect upon the government, had several leading members of the senate been, for an equally long period, in the house of representatives.

happiness? Or is the disposition to imposture so prevalent in men of experience, that their private views of ambition and avarice can be accomplished only by artifice? It was a tradition in antiquity that the laws of Crete were dictated to Minos by the inspiration of Jupiter. This legislator and his brother Rhadamanthus were both his sons; once in nine years they went to converse with their father, to propose questions concerning the wants of the people; and his answers were recorded as laws for their government. The laws of Lacedæmon were communicated by Apollo to Lycurgus; and, lest the meaning of the deity should not have been perfectly comprehended, or correctly expressed, they were afterwards confirmed by his oracle at Delphos. Among the Romans, Numa was indebted for those laws which procured the prosperity of his country to his conversations with Egeria. The Greeks imported these mysteries from Egypt and the East, whose despotisms, from the remotest antiquity to this day, have been founded in the same solemn empiricism; their emperors and nobles being all descended from their gods. Woden and Thor were divinities too; and their posterity ruled a thousand years in the north by the strength of a like credulity. Manco Capac was the child of the sun, the visible deity of the Peruvians; and transmitted his divinity, as well as his earthly dignity and authority, through a line of incas. And the rudest tribes of savages in North America have certain families from which their leaders are always chosen, under the immediate protection of the god War. There is nothing in which mankind have been more unanimous; yet nothing can be inferred from it more than this, that the multitude have always been credulous, and the few are always artful.

The United States of America have exhibited, perhaps, the first example of governments erected on the simple principles of nature;★ and if

★ *"Query,* whether the principles of the American governments are not rather the result of reason and judgment, than the dictates of simple nature?

"But be this as it may, it is perhaps saying rather too much, to affirm that the United States have exhibited the first example, &c., especially after the great and just encomiums on the English constitution to be found throughout this work. A constitution which the American legislator and politician professedly drew his system from." S.

It would seem as if the question of the commentator should be answered affirmatively. But this answer will impair the force of his subsequent remark. The author, in his men are now sufficiently enlightened to disabuse themselves of artifice, imposture, hypocrisy, and superstition, they will consider this event as an era in their history. Although the detail of the formation of the American governments is at present little known or regarded either in Europe or in America, it may hereafter become an object of curiosity. It will never be pretended that any persons employed in that service had interviews with the gods, or were in any degree under the inspiration of Heaven, more than those at work upon ships or houses, or laboring in merchandise or agriculture; it will forever be acknowledged that these governments were contrived merely by the use of reason and the senses, as Copley painted Chatham; West, Wolf; and Trumbull, Warren and Montgomery; as Dwight, Barlow, Trumbull, and Humphries composed their verse, and Belknap and Ramsay history; as Godfrey invented his quadrant, and Rittenhouse his planetarium; as Boylston practised inoculation, and Franklin electricity; as Paine exposed the mistakes of Raynal, and Jefferson those of Buffon, so unphilosophically borrowed from the* despicable dreams of De Pan. Neither the people, nor their conventions, committees, or sub-committees, considered legislation in any other light than as ordinary arts and sciences, only more important. Called without expectation, and compelled without previous inclination, though undoubtedly at the best period of time, both for England and America, suddenly to erect new systems of laws for their future government, they adopted the method of a wise architect, in erecting a new palace for the residence of his sovereign. They determined to consult Vitruvius, Palladio, and all other writers of reputation in the art; to examine the most celebrated buildings, whether they remain entire or in ruins; to compare these with the principles of writers; and to inquire how far both the theories and models were founded in nature, or created by fancy; and when this was done, so far as their circumstances would allow, to adopt the advantages and reject the inconveniences of all. Unembarrassed by attachments to noble families, hereditary

reasoning, obviously has reference only to the *intent* of the lawgiver, which is not so clearly discernible in the slow and unequal progress of formation of the English constitution, as in the models adopted in America.

* *Recherches Philosophiques sur les Americains.*

lines and successions, or any considerations of royal blood, even the pious mystery of holy oil had no more influence than that other one of holy water. The people were universally too enlightened to be imposed on by artifice; and their leaders, or more properly followers, were men of too much honor to attempt it. Thirteen governments thus founded on the natural authority of the people alone, without a pretence of miracle or mystery, and which are destined to spread over the northern part of that whole quarter of the globe, are a great point gained in favor of the rights of mankind. The experiment is made, and has completely succeeded; it can no longer be called in question, whether authority in magistrates and obedience of citizens can be grounded on reason, morality, and the Christian religion, without the monkery of priests, or the knavery of politicians. As the writer was personally acquainted with most of the gentlemen in each of the states, who had the principal share in the first draughts, the following work was really written to lay before the public a specimen of that kind of reading and reasoning which produced the American constitutions.

It is not a little surprising that all this kind of learning should have been unknown to any illustrious philosopher and statesman, and especially one who really was, what he has been often called, "a well of science." But if he could be unacquainted with it, or it could have escaped his memory, we may suppose millions in America have occasion to be reminded of it. The writer has long seen with anxiety the facility with which philosophers of greatest name have undertaken to write of American affairs, without knowing any thing of them, and have echoed and reëchoed each other's visionary language. Having neither talents, leisure, nor inclination to meet such champions in the field of literary controversy, he little thought of venturing to propose to them any questions. Circumstances, however, have lately occurred which seem to require that some notice should be taken of one of them. If the publication of these papers should contribute any thing to turn the attention of the younger gentlemen of letters in America to this kind of inquiry, it will produce an effect of some importance to their country. The subject is the most interesting that can engage the understanding or the heart; for whether the end of man, in this stage of his existence, be enjoyment, or improvement, or both, it can never be attained so well in a bad government as a good one.

The practicability or the duration of a republic, in which there is a governor, a senate, and a house of representatives, is doubted by Tacitus, though he admits the theory to be laudable: "Cunctas nationes et urbes, populus, aut priores, aut singuli, regunt. Delecta ex his et constituta reipublicæ forma, laudari facilius quam inveniri; vel, si evenit, haud diuturna esse potest."[2] Cicero asserts, "Statuo esse optime constitutam rempublicam, quæ ex tribus generibus illis, regali, optimo, et populari, modice confusa," in such peremptory terms the superiority of such a government to all other forms, that the loss of his book upon republics is much to be regretted. From a few passages that have been preserved, it is very probable he entered more largely into an examination of the composition of monarchical republics than any other ancient writer.[3] He was so far from apprehending "disputes" from a variety of orders, that he affirms it to be the firmest bond of justice, and the strongest anchor of safety to the community. As the treble, the tenor, and the bass exist in nature, they will be heard in the concert. If they are arranged by Handel, in a skilful composition, they produce rapture the most exquisite that harmony can excite; but if they are confused together, without order, they will

"Rend with tremendous sound your ears asunder."

"Ut in fidibus aut tibiis, atque in cantu ipso, ac vocibus, concentus est quidam tenendus ex distinctis sonis, quem immutatum aut discrepantem aures eruditæ ferre non possunt; isque concentus, *ex dissimillimarum vocum moderatione, concors tamen efficitur et congruens;* sic *ex summis et infimis et inter-*

---

[2] *Annales,* liber iv. c. 33. ["For all nations and cities are ruled either by the people, or by nobles, or by individuals. A form of republic selected and combined from these is easier to praise than to find, or if it does come about, it cannot be long-lasting." Tacitus, *Annals* IV, 33. Ed.]

[3] Since this was written, a considerable addition to the former fragments has been made, through the industry of Angelo Mai; but, so far as it goes, it does not fulfil the conjecture here made. ["I consider the best constituted commonwealth to be the one made from these three kinds, regal, aristocratic, and democratic, suitably blended." Cicero, *On the Commonwealth* II, xxiii, 41. Ed.]

jectis ordinibus, ut sonis, moderata ratione, civitas consensu dissimillimo-
rum concinit; et quæ harmonia a musicis dicitur in cantu, ea est in civitate concordia arctissimum atque optimum omni in republica vinculum
incolumitatis; eaque sine justitia nullo pacto esse potest."[4] As all the ages
of the world have not produced a greater statesman and philosopher
united than Cicero, his authority should have great weight. His decided
opinion in favor of three branches is founded on a reason that is
unchangeable; the laws, which are the only possible rule, measure, and
security of justice, can be sure of protection, for any course of time, in no
other form of government; and the very name of a republic implies, that
the property of the people should be represented in the legislature, and
decide the rule of justice. "Respublica est res populi. Populus autem non
omnis hominum cœtus quoquo modo congregatus, sed cœtus multitudinis juris consensu, et utilitatis communione sociatus."[5]

"Respublica res est populi, cum bene ac juste geritur, sive ab uno rege,
sive a paucis optimatibus, sive ab universo populo. Cum vero injustus est
rex, quem tyrannum more græco voco; aut injusti optimates, quorum
consensus factio est; aut injustus ipse populus, cui nomen usitatum nullum
reperio, nisi ut etiam ipsum tyrannum appellem; non jam vitiosa, sed
omnino nulla respublica est; quoniam non est res populi, cum tyrannus
eam factiove capessat; nec ipse populus jam populus est si sit injustus,
quoniam non est multitudo juris consensu, et utilitatis communione soci-
ata sicut populus fuerat definitus."[6]

---

[4]["As in the case of lyres and flutes, and in the singing of voices, a certain harmony
of diverse tones must be preserved, which educated ears cannot bear when it is changed
or disagrees; and ." Cicero, *On the Commonwealth* II, xlii, 69. Ed.]

[5] [Scipio Africanus, quoted by Cicero, explains the etymology of *res publica*: "The
republic (= 'public thing') is the people's affair. But 'the people' is not just any collection
of human beings gathered together in any sort of way, but the gathering of a large number of people associated by their agreement on the laws for the common good." Cicero,
On the Commonwealth I, xxv, 39. Ed.]

[6] ["A republic is 'the people's thing' only when it is well and justly governed, whether
by a single king, or by a few nobles, or by the whole people. But when there is an unjust
king, one whom I call, in the Greek manner, a tyrant; or unjust aristocrats, whose agreement is a faction; or the people themselves are unjust, a matter for which I find no word
in common use, unless I should call them 'tyrant' too; then there is not a defective

"Ubi justitia vera non est, nec jus potest esse. Quod enim jure fit, profecto juste fit. Quod autem fit injuste, nec jure fieri potest. Non enim jura dicenda sunt, vel putanda, iniqua hominum constituta; cum illud etiam ipsi jus esse dicant quod de justitiæ fonte manaverit; falsumque sit, quod a quibusdam non recte sentientibus dici solet, id jus esse, quod ei, qui plus potest, utile est."[7] According to this, a simple monarchy, if it could in reality be what it pretends to be, a government of laws, might be justly denominated a republic. A limited monarchy, therefore, especially when limited by two independent branches, an aristocratical and a democratical power in the constitution, may with strict propriety be called by that name.

If Cicero and Tacitus could revisit the earth, and learn that the English nation had reduced the great idea[8] to practice, and brought it nearly to perfection, by giving each division a power to defend itself by a negative; had found it the most solid and durable government, as well as the most free; had obtained by means of it a prosperity among civilized nations, in an enlightened age, like that of the Romans among barbarians; and that

republic but no republic at all. Since it is not 'the people's thing' when a tyrant or a faction takes control, nor is the people still the people if it is unjust, since it is not an assemblage associated by a common acknowledgment of law, and by a community of interests." Augustine, *The City of God* II, xxii, paraphrasing Cicero's *On the Commonwealth*. The latter survives only in fragments, so in many cases, as here, we have only Augustine to tell us what Cicero said. Ed.]

[7] ["Where there is no true justice there can be no right. For that which is done by right is justly done, and what is unjustly done cannot be done by right. For the unjust establishments of humans should neither be thought of nor spoken of as rights, since even they themselves say that right is that which flows from the fountain of justice, denying the definition commonly given by those who misconceive the matter, that right is what is useful to the stronger." Augustine, *The City of God* XIX, xxi, paraphrasing Cicero's *On the Commonwealth*. See note on previous passage. Ed.]

[8] "Id enim tenetote, quod initio dixi, nisi æquabilis hæc in civitate compensatio sit et juris et officii et muneris, ut et potestatis satis in magistratibus, et auctoritatis in principum consilio, et libertatis in populo sit, non posse hunc incommutabilem rei publicæ conservari statum." *De Republica*. ["For you must keep in mind what I said before, that unless there is a balance of rights and duties and offices in the state, so that there is enough power in the public officials, enough authority in the council of nobles (i.e. the senate), and enough liberty in the people, it is not possible for this state of the republic to be preserved unchanged." Cicero, *On the Commonwealth* II, xxxiii, 57. Ed.]

the Americans, after having enjoyed the benefits of such a constitution a century and a half, were advised by some of the greatest philosophers and politicians of the age to renounce it, and set up the governments of ancient Goths and modern Indians,—what would they say? That the Americans would be more reprehensible than the Cappadocians, if they should listen to such advice.

It would have been much to the purpose, to have inserted a more accurate investigation of the form of government of the ancient Germans and modern Indians; in both, the existence of the three divisions of power is marked with a precision that excludes all controversy. The democratical branch, especially, is so determined, that the real sovereignty resided in the body of the people, and was exercised in the assembly of king, nobles, and commons together. These institutions really collected all authority into one centre of kings, nobles, and people. But, small as their numbers and narrow as their territories were, the consequence was confusion; each part believed it governed the whole; the chiefs thought they were sovereigns; the nobles believed the power to be in their hands; and the people flattered themselves that all depended upon them. Their purposes were well enough answered, without coming to an explanation, so long as they were few in number, and had no property; but when spread over large provinces of the Roman empire, now the great kingdoms of Europe, and grown populous and rich, they found the inconvenience of each not knowing its place. Kings, nobles, and people claimed the government in turn; and after all the turbulence, wars, and revolutions, which compose the history of Europe for so many ages, we find simple monarchies established everywhere. Whether the system will now become stationary, and last forever, by means of a few further improvements in monarchical government, we know not; or whether still further revolutions are to come. The most probable, or rather the only probable change, is the introduction of democratical branches into those governments. If the people should ever aim at more, they will defeat themselves; as they will, indeed, if they aim at this by any other than gentle means and by gradual a dvances, by improvements in general education, and by informing the public mind.

The systems of legislators are experiments made on human life and manners, society and government. Zoroaster, Confucius, Mithras, Odin, Thor, Mahomet, Lycurgus, Solon, Romulus, and a thousand others, may be compared to philosophers making experiments on the elements. Unhappily, political experiments cannot be made in a laboratory, nor determined in a few hours. The operation once begun, runs over whole quarters of the globe, and is not finished in many thousands of years. The experiment of Lycurgus lasted seven hundred years, but never spread beyond the limits of Laconia. The process of Solon expired in one century; that of Romulus lasted but two centuries and a half; but the Teutonic institutions, described by Cæsar and Tacitus, are the most memorable experiment, merely political, ever yet made in human affairs. They have spread all over Europe, and have lasted eighteen hundred years. They afford the strongest argument that can be imagined in support of the position assumed in these volumes. Nothing ought to have more weight with America, to determine her judgment against mixing the authority of the one, the few, and the many, confusedly in one assembly, than the widespread miseries and final slavery of almost all mankind, in consequence of such an ignorant policy in the ancient Germans. What is the ingredient which in England has preserved the democratical authority? The balance, and that only. The English have, in reality, blended together the feudal institutions with those of the Greeks and Romans, and out of all have made that noble composition, which avoids the inconveniences, and retains the advantages of both.

The institutions now made in America will not wholly wear out for thousands of years. It is of the last importance, then, that they should begin right. If they set out wrong, they will never be able to return, unless it be by accident, to the right path. After having known the history of Europe, and of England in particular, it would be the height of folly to go back to the institutions of Woden and of Thor, as the Americans are advised to do. If they had been counselled to adopt a single monarchy at once, it would have been less mysterious.

Robertson, Hume, and Gibbon have given such admirable accounts of the feudal institutions and their consequences, that it would have been, perhaps, more discreet to have referred to them, without saying any thing more upon the subject. To collect together the legislation of the Indians would take up much room, but would be well worth the pains. The sovereignty is in the nation, it is true, but the three powers are strong in every tribe; and their royal and aristocratical dignities are much more generally hereditary, from the popular partiality to particular families, and the superstitious opinion that such are favorites of the God of War, than late writers upon this subject have allowed.

GROSVENOR SQUARE, January 1, 1787.

Preliminary Observations.

THREE writers in Europe of great abilities, reputation, and learning, M. Turgot, the Abbé de Mably, and Dr. Price, have turned their attention to the constitutions of government in the United States of America, and have written and published their criticisms and advice. They all had the most amiable characters, and unquestionably the purest intentions. They all had experience in public affairs, and ample information respecting the nature of man, the necessities of society, and the science of government.

There are in the productions of all of them, among many excellent things, some sentiments, however, that it will be difficult to reconcile to reason, experience, the constitution of human nature, or to the uniform testimony of the greatest statesmen, legislators, and philosophers of all enlightened nations, ancient and modern.

M. Turgot, in his letter to Dr. Price, confesses, "that he is not satisfied with the constitutions which have hitherto been formed for the different states of America." He observes, "that by most of them the customs of England are imitated, without any particular motive. Instead of collecting all authority into one centre, that of the nation, they have established different bodies, a body of representatives, a council, and a governor, because there is in England a house of commons, a house of lords, and a king. They endeavor to balance these different powers, as if this equilibrium, which in England may be a necessary check to the enormous influence of royalty, could be of any use in republics founded upon the equality of all the citizens, and as if establishing different orders of men was not a source of divisions and disputes."

There has been, from the beginning of the revolution in America, a party in every state, who have entertained sentiments similar to these of M. Turgot. Two or three of them have established governments upon his principle; and, by advices from Boston, certain committees of counties have been held, and other conventions proposed in the Massachusetts, with the express purpose of deposing the governor and senate as useless and expensive branches of the constitution;* and as it is probable that the publication of M. Turgot's opinion has contributed to excite such discontents among the people, it becomes necessary to examine it, and, if it can be shown to be an error, whatever veneration the Americans very justly entertain for his memory, it is to be hoped they will not be misled by his authority.

M. Turgot is offended, because the customs of England are imitated in most of the new constitutions in America, without any particular motive. But, if we suppose English customs to be neither good nor evil in themselves, and merely indifferent; and the people, by their birth, education, and habits, were familiarly attached to them; would not this be a motive particular enough for their preservation, rather than to endanger the public tranquility, or unanimity, by renouncing them? If those customs were wise, just, and good, and calculated to secure the liberty, property, and safety of the people, as well, or better, than any other institutions, ancient or modern, would M. Turgot have advised the nation to reject them, merely because it was at that time justly incensed against the English government? What English customs has it retained which may with any propriety be called evil? M. Turgot has instanced only one, namely,—"that a body of representatives, a council, and a governor, have been established, because there is in England a house of commons, a house of lords, and a king." It

★ "Should it appear that the real object of the committees and conventions in endeavoring to depose the governor and senate is the passing of pernicious laws by the representative body, such as the abolishing or postponing the payment of debts, or the emission of an unfunded paper currency, the necessity of supporting the governor and senate will be more obvious." S.

was not so much because the legislature in England consisted of three branches, that such a division of power was adopted by the states, as because their own assemblies had ever been so constituted. It was not so much from attachment by habit to such a plan of power that it was continued, as from conviction that it was founded in nature and reason.

M. Turgot seems to be of a different opinion, and is for "collecting all authority into one centre, the nation." It is easily understood how all authority may be collected into "one centre" in a despot or monarch; but how it can be done when the centre is to be the nation, is more difficult to comprehend. Before we attempt to discuss the notions of an author, we should be careful to ascertain his meaning. It will not be easy, after the most anxious research, to discover the true sense of this extraordinary passage. If, after the pains of "collecting all authority into one centre," that centre is to be the nation, we shall remain exactly where we began, and no collection of authority at all will be made. The nation will be the authority, and the authority the nation. The centre will be the circle, and the circle the centre. When a number of men, women, and children, are simply congregated together, there is no political authority among them; nor any natural authority, but that of parents over their children. To leave the women and children out of the question for the present, the men will all be equal, free, and independent of each other. Not one will have any authority over any other. The first "collection" of authority must be an unanimous agreement to form themselves into a *nation, people, community,* or *body politic,* and to be governed by the majority of suffrages or voices. But even in this case, although the authority is collected into one centre, that centre is no longer the nation, but the majority of the nation. Did M. Turgot mean that the people of Virginia, for example, half a million of souls scattered over a territory of two hundred leagues square, should stop here, and have no other authority by which to make or execute a law, or judge a cause, but by a vote of the whole people, and the decision of a majority! Where is the plain large enough to hold them; and what are the means, and how long would be the time, necessary to assemble them together?

A simple and perfect democracy never yet existed among men. If a village of half a mile square, and one hundred families, is capable of exercising all the legislative, executive, and judicial powers, in public assemblies of the whole, by unanimous votes, or by majorities, it is more than has ever yet been proved in theory or experience. In such a democracy, for the most part, the moderator would be king, the town-clerk legislator and judge, and the constable sheriff; and, upon more important occasions, committees would be only the counsellors of both the former, and commanders of the latter.

Shall we suppose, then, that M. Turgot intended that an assembly of representatives should be chosen by the nation, and vested with all the powers of government; and that this assembly should be the centre in which all the authority was to be collected, and should be virtually deemed the nation? After long reflection, I have not been able to discover any other sense in his words, and this was probably his real meaning. To examine this system in detail may be thought as trifling an occupation as the labored reasonings of Sidney and Locke, to show the absurdity of Filmer's superstitious notions, appeared to Mr. Hume to be in his enlightened day. Yet the mistakes of great men, and even the absurdities of fools, when they countenance the prejudices of numbers of people, especially in a young country and under new governments, cannot be too fully confuted. I shall not then esteem my time misspent, in placing this idea of M. Turgot in all its lights; in considering the consequences of it; and in collecting a variety of authorities against it.

...

CHAPTER III.

Recapitulation.

As we have taken a cursory view of those countries in Europe where the government may be called, in any reasonable construction of the word, republican, let us now pause a few moments, and reflect upon what we have seen.

Among every people, and in every species of republics, we have constantly found *a first magistrate, a head, a chief,* under various denominations, indeed, and with different degrees of authority, with the title of stadtholder, burgomaster, avoyer, doge, gonfaloniero, president, syndic, mayor, alcalde, capitaneo, governor, or king; in every nation we have met with a distinguished officer. If there is no example, then, in any free government, any more than in those which are not free, of a society without a principal personage, we may fairly conclude that the body politic cannot subsist, any more than the animal body, without a head. If M. Turgot had made any discovery which had escaped the penetration of all the legislators and philosophers who have lived before him, he ought at least to have communicated it to the world for their improvement; but as he has never hinted at any such invention, we may safely conclude that he had none; and, therefore, that the Americans are not justly liable to censure for instituting *governors.*

In every form of government we have seen a *senate,* or *little council,* a composition, generally, of those officers of state who have the most experience and power, and of a few other members selected from the highest ranks and most illustrious reputations. On these lesser councils, with the first magistrate at their head, generally rests the principal burden of administration, a share in the legislative, as well as executive and judicial authority of government. The admission of such senates to a participation of these three kinds of power, has been generally observed to produce in the minds of their members an ardent aristocratical ambition, grasping equally at the prerogatives of the first magistrate, and the privileges of the people, and ending in the nobility of a few families, and a tyrannical oligarchy. But in those states, where the senates have been debarred from all executive power, and confined to the legislative, they have been observed to be firm barriers against the encroachments of the crown, and often great supporters of the liberties of the people. The Americans, then, who have carefully confined their senates to the legislative power, have done wisely in adopting them.

We have seen, in every instance, another and a larger assembly, composed of the body of the people, in some little states; of representatives chosen by the people, in others; of members appointed by the senate, and supposed to represent the people, in a third sort; and of persons appointed by themselves or the senate, in certain aristocracies; to prevent them from becoming oligarchies. The Americans, then, whose assemblies are the most adequate, proportional, and equitable representations of the people, that are known in the world, will not be thought mistaken in appointing houses of representatives.

In every republic,—in the smallest and most popular, in the larger and more aristocratical, as well as in the largest and most monarchical,—we have observed a multitude of curious and ingenious inventions to balance, in their turn, all those powers, to check the passions peculiar to them, and to control them from rushing into those exorbitancies to which they are most addicted. The Americans will then be no longer censured for endeavoring to introduce an equilibrium, which is much more profoundly meditated, and much more effectual for the protection of the laws, than any we have seen, except in England. We may even question whether that is an exception.

In every country we have found a variety of *orders,* with very great distinctions. In America, there are different orders of *offices,* but none of *men.* Out of office, all men are of the same species, and of one blood; there is neither a greater nor a lesser nobility. Why, then, are the Americans accused of establishing different orders of men? To our inexpressible mortification, we must have observed, that the people have preserved a share of power, or an existence in the government, in no country out of England, except upon the tops of a few inaccessible mountains, among rocks and precipices, in territories so narrow that you may span them with a hand's breadth, where, living unenvied, in extreme poverty, chiefly upon pasturage, destitute of manufactures and commerce, they still exhibit the most charming picture of life, and the most dignified character of human nature.

Wherever we have seen a territory somewhat larger, arts and sciences more cultivated, commerce flourishing, or even agriculture improved to any great degree, an aristocracy has risen up in a course of time, consisting of a few rich and honorable families, who have united with each other against both the people and the first magistrate; who have wrested from the former, by art and by force, all their participation in the government; and have even inspired them with so mean an esteem of themselves, and so deep a veneration and strong attachment to their rulers, as to believe and confess them a superior order of beings.

We have seen these noble families, although necessitated to have a head, extremely jealous of his influence, anxious to reduce his power, and to constrain him to as near a level as possible with themselves; always endeavoring to establish a rotation, by which they may all equally be entitled in turn to the preëminence, and likewise anxious to preserve to themselves as large a share as possible of power in the executive and judicial, as well as the legislative departments of the state.

These patrician families have also appeared in every instance to be equally jealous of each other, and to have contrived, by blending lot and choice, by mixing various bodies in the elections to the same offices, and even by a resort to the horrors of an inquisition, to guard against the sin that so easily besets them, of being wholly influenced and governed by a junto or oligarchy of a few among themselves.

We have seen no one government in which is a distinct separation of the legislative from the executive power, and of the judicial from both, or in which any attempt has been made to balance these powers with one another, or to form an equilibrium between the one, the few, and the many, for the purpose of enacting and executing equal laws, by common consent, for the general interest, excepting in England.

Shall we conclude, from these melancholy observations, that human nature is incapable of liberty, that no honest equality can be preserved in society, and that such forcible causes are always at work as must reduce all men to a submission to despotism, monarchy, oligarchy, or aristocracy?

By no means. We have seen one of the first nations in Europe, possessed of ample and fertile territories at home and extensive dominions abroad, of a commerce with the whole world, immense wealth, and the greatest naval power which ever belonged to any nation, which has still preserved the power of the people by the equilibrium we are contending for, by the trial by jury, and by constantly refusing a standing army.[9] The people of England alone, by preserving their share in the legislature, at the expense of the blood of heroes and patriots, have enabled their king to curb the nobility, without giving him a standing army.

---

[9] "Would that it had constantly been refused! A standing army is dangerous in any hands! Even if the people had preserved their share in the legislature, a standing army in their pay would be inexpedient and dangerous." S.

After all, let us compare every constitution we have seen with those of the United States of America, and we shall have no reason to blush for our country. On the contrary, we shall feel the strongest motives to fall upon our knees, in gratitude to heaven for having been graciously pleased to give us birth and education in that country, and for having destined us to live under her laws! We shall have reason to exult, if we make our comparison with England and the English constitution. Our people are undoubtedly sovereign; all the landed and other property is in the hands of the citizens; not only their representatives, but their senators and governors, are annually chosen; there are no hereditary titles, honors, offices, or distinctions; the legislative, executive, and judicial powers are carefully separated from each other; the powers of the one, the few, and the many are nicely balanced in the legislatures; trials by jury are preserved in all their glory, and there is no standing army; the *habeas corpus* is in full force; the press is the most free in the world. Where all these circumstances take place, it is unnecessary to add that the laws alone can govern.

CHAPTER IV.

Opinions of Philosophers.

DR. SWIFT.

THE authority of legislators and philosophers, in support of the system we contend for, is not difficult to find. The greatest lights of humanity, ancient and modern, have approved it, which renders it difficult to explain how it comes, in this enlightened age, to be called in question, as it certainly has been, by others as well as M. Turgot. I shall begin with one, who, though seldom quoted as a legislator, appears to have considered this subject, and to have furnished arguments enough forever to determine the question. Dr. Swift observes,★ "that the best legislators of all ages agree in this, that

★ *"A Discourse of the Contests and Dissensions between the Nobles and Commons of Athens and Rome, with the Consequences they had upon both those States."*
  Much of the substance of this, the best of all the political tracts of Dean Swift, is given in the text.

the absolute power, which originally is in the whole body, is 'a trust too great to be committed to any one man or assembly;' and, therefore, in their several institutions of government, power, in the last resort, was always placed by them in balance among the one, the few, and the many; 'and it will be an eternal rule in politics among every free people, that there is a balance of power to be carefully held by every state within itself.'

"A mixed government, partaking of the known forms received in the schools, is by no means of Gothic invention, but hath place in nature and reason, and seems very well to agree with the sentiments of most legislators.... For, not to mention the several republics of this composition in Gaul and Germany, described by Cæsar and Tacitus, Polybius tells us, the best government is that which consists of three forms, *regis, optimatium, et populi imperio.*★ Such was that of Sparta in its primitive institution by Lycurgus, who, observing the corruptions and depravations to which every one of these was subject, compounded his scheme out of all; so that it was made up of *reges, seniores, et populus.* Such also was the state of Rome under its consuls; and such, at Carthage, was the power in the last resort; they had their kings, senate, and people." A limited and divided power seems to have been the most ancient and inherent principle, both of the Greeks and Italians, in matters of government. "The difference between the Grecian monarchies and Italian republics was not very great. The power of those Grecian princes, who came to the siege of Troy, was much of a size with that of the kings of Sparta, the archon of Athens, the suffetes at Carthage, and the consuls at Rome." Theseus established at Athens rather a mixed monarchy than a popular state, assigning to himself the guardianship of the laws and the chief command in war. This institution continued during the series of kings to the death of Codrus, from whom Solon was descended,

"Who, finding the people engaged in two violent factions, of the poor and the rich, and in great confusion, refusing the monarchy which was offered him, chose rather to cast the government after another model,

---

★ *Fragm.* lib. vi. [(made from) "the sovereign power of the king, the nobles, and the people." Ed.]

wherein he made due provision for *settling the balance of power,* choosing a
senate of four hundred, and disposing the magistracies and offices according to men's estates; leaving to the multitude their votes in electing, and
the power of judging certain processes by appeal. This council of four
hundred was chosen, one hundred out of each tribe, and seems to have
been a body representative of the people, though the people collective
reserved a share of power to themselves."

"In all free states, the evil to be avoided is tyranny; that is to say, the
summa imperii, or unlimited power, solely in the hands of the one, the
few, or the many."

"Though we cannot prolong the period of a commonwealth beyond
the decree of heaven or the date of its nature, any more than human life
beyond the strength of the seminal virtue, yet we may manage a sickly
constitution, and preserve a strong one; we may watch, and prevent accidents; we may turn off a great blow from without, and purge away an ill
humor that is lurking within; and, by these and other such methods, render a state long-lived, though not immortal. Yet some physicians have
thought, that if it were practicable to keep the several humors of the body
in an exact *balance* of each with its opposite, it might be immortal; and so
perhaps would a political body, if the *balance of power* could be always held
exactly even."

All independent bodies of men seem naturally to divide the three
powers, of the one, the few, and the many. A free people met together, as
soon as they fall into any acts of civil society, do of themselves divide into
three ranks. "The first is that of some one eminent spirit, who, having
signalized his valor and fortune in defence of his country, or, by the practice of popular arts at home, comes to have great influence on the people, to grow their leader in warlike expeditions, and to preside, after a
sort, in their civil assemblies. And this is grounded upon the principles of
nature and common reason, which, in all difficulties or dangers, where
prudence or courage is required, do rather incite us to fly for counsel or
assistance to a single person, than a multitude. The second is, of such men,
who have acquired large possessions, and, consequently, dependencies, or
descend from ancestors who have left them great inheritances, together

with an hereditary authority; these, easily uniting in opinions, and acting in concert, begin to enter upon measures for securing their properties, which are best upheld by preparing against invasions from abroad and maintaining peace at home; this commences a great council or senate for the weighty affairs of the nation. The last division is of the mass of the people, whose part of power is great and indisputable, whenever they can unite, either collectively or by deputation, to exert it."

"The true meaning of a balance of power is best conceived by considering what the nature of a balance is. It supposes three things,—first, the part which is held, together with the hand that holds it; and then the two scales, with whatever is weighed therein.... In a state within itself, the balance must be held by a third hand, who is to deal the remaining power with the utmost exactness into the several scales.... The balance may be held by the weakest, who, by his address and conduct, removing from either scale and adding of his own, may keep the scales duly poised.

"When the balance is broken by mighty weights fallen into either scale, the power will never continue long, in equal division, between the two remaining parties; but, till the balance is fixed anew, will run entirely into one." This is made to appear by the examples of the Decemviri in Rome, the Ephori in Sparta, the four hundred in Athens, the thirty in Athens, and the Dominatio Plebis in Carthage and Argos.

"In Rome, from the time of Romulus to Julius Cæsar, the commons were growing by degrees into power, gaining ground upon the patricians, as it were, inch by inch, till at last they quite overturned the balance, leaving all doors open to popular and ambitious men, who destroyed the wisest republic, and enslaved the noblest people that ever entered on the stage of the world.

"Polybius tells us, that in the second Punic war, the Carthaginians were declining, because the balance was got too much on the side of the people; whereas the Romans were in their greatest vigor, by the power remaining in the senate."

"The ambition of private men did by no means begin or occasion the war between Pompey and Cæsar, though civil dissensions never fail of introducing and spiriting the ambition of private men; ... for, while the

balance of power is equally held, the ambition of private men, whether
orators or commanders, gives neither danger nor fear, nor can possibly
enslave their country; but that once broken, the divided parties are forced
to unite each to its head, under whose conduct or fortune one side is at
first victorious, and at last both are slaves. And to put it past dispute, that
the entire subversion of Roman liberty was altogether owing to those
measures which had broken the balance between the patricians and plebeians, whereof the ambition of private men was but an effect and consequence, we need only consider, that when the uncorrupted part of the
senate, by the death of Cæsar, made one great effort to restore the former
liberty, the success did not answer their hopes; but that whole assembly was
so sunk in its authority, that those patriots were forced to fly, and give
way to the madness of the people, who by their own dispositions, stirred
up with the harangues of their orators, were now wholly bent upon single
and despotic slavery. Else how could such a profligate as Antony, or a boy
of eighteen, like Octavius, ever dare to dream of giving the law to such
an empire and people? Wherein the latter succeeded, and entailed the
vilest tyranny that Heaven, in its anger, ever inflicted on a corrupt and poi-
soned people."[10]

It is "an error to think it an uncontrollable maxim, that power is always
safer lodged in many hands than in one; for if these many hands be made
up only from one of those three divisions, it is plain, from the examples
produced, and easy to be paralleled in other ages and countries, that they
are as capable of enslaving the nation, and of acting all manner of tyranny
and oppression, as it is possible for a single person to be, though we should
suppose their number not only to be of four or five hundred, but above
three thousand.

"In order to preserve a balance in a mixed state, the limits of power
deposited with each party ought to be ascertained and generally known.
The defect of this is the cause that introduces those strugglings in a state
about prerogative and liberty; about encroachments of the few upon the

---

[10] "It was the throne of the dragon, that is, of the devil and his angels, whose dominion was permitted by the Almighty, and foretold by his prophets." S.

rights of the many, and of the many upon the privileges of the few; which
ever did, and ever will, conclude in a tyranny; first, either of the few or
the many, but at last, infallibly, of a *single person;* for, whichever of the
three divisions in a state is upon the scramble for more power than its
own, (as one or other of them generally is,) unless due care be taken by the
other two, upon every new question that arises, they will be sure to decide
in favor of themselves, talk much of inherent right; they will nourish up
a dormant power, and reserve privileges *in petto,* to exert upon occasions,
to serve expedients, and to urge upon necessities; they will make large
demands and scanty concessions, ever coming off considerable gainers.
Thus, at length, the balance is broken, and tyranny let in; from which door
of the three it matters not.

"The desires of men are not only exorbitant, but endless; they grasp at
all, and can form no scheme of perfect happiness with less. Ever since men
have been united into governments, the hopes and endeavors after universal monarchy have been bandied among them.... The Athenians, the
Spartans, the Thebans, and the Achaians, several times aimed at the universal monarchy of Greece; the commonwealths of Carthage and Rome
affected the universal monarchy of the then known world. In like manner has absolute power been pursued by the several parties of each
particular state; wherein single persons have met with most success,
though the endeavors of the few and the many have been frequent
enough; yet, being neither so uniform in their designs, nor so direct in
their views, they neither could manage nor maintain the power they had
got, but were deceived by the popularity and ambition of some single person. So that it will be always a wrong step in policy, for the nobles and
commons to carry their endeavors after power so far as to overthrow the
balance.

"With all respect for popular assemblies be it spoken, it is hard to recollect one folly, infirmity, or vice, to which a single man is subject, and
from which a body of commons, either collective or represented, can be
wholly exempt.... Whence it comes to pass, that in their results have
sometimes been found the same spirit of cruelty and revenge, of malice
and pride; the same blindness, and obstinacy, and unsteadiness; the same

ungovernable rage and anger; the same injustice, sophistry, and fraud, that ever lodged in the breast of any individual.

"When a child grows easy and content, by being humored; and when a lover becomes satisfied by small compliances, without farther pursuits; then expect to find popular assemblies content with small concessions. If there could one single example be brought from the whole compass of history, of any one popular assembly who, after beginning to contend for power, ever sat down quietly with a certain share; or of one that ever knew, or proposed, or declared, what share of power was their due; then might there be some hopes that it were a matter to be adjusted by reasonings, conferences, or debates.

"A usurping populace is its own dupe, a mere under-worker, and a purchaser in trust for some single tyrant, whose state and power they advance to their own ruin, with as blind an instinct as those worms that die with weaving magnificent habits for beings of a superior order to their own.

"The people are much more dexterous at pulling down and setting up, than at preserving what is fixed; and they are not fonder of seizing more than their own, than they are of delivering it up again to the *worst bidder,* with their own into the bargain. For although, in their corrupt notions of divine worship, they are apt to multiply their gods; yet their earthly devotion is seldom paid to above one idol at a time, of their own creation, whose oar they pull with less murmuring, and much more skill, than when they *share the leading,* or even *hold the helm.*"

It will be perceived by the style, that it is Dr. Swift that has been speaking; otherwise the reader might have been deceived, and imagined that I was entertaining him with further reflections upon the short account previously given, in these letters, of the modern republics. There is not an observation here that is not justified by the history of every government we have considered. How much more maturely had this writer weighed the subject than M. Turgot! Perhaps there are not to be found in any library so many accurate ideas of government, expressed with so much perspicuity, brevity, and precision.

DR. FRANKLIN.

As it is impossible to suppose that M. Turgot intended to recommend to the Americans a simple monarchy or aristocracy, we have admitted, as a supposition the most favorable to him, that, by collecting all authority into one centre, he meant a single assembly of representatives of the people, without a governor, and without a senate; and, although he has not explained, whether he would have the assembly chosen for life or years, we will again admit, as the most benign construction, that he meant the representatives should be annually chosen.

Here we shall be obliged to consider the reputed opinion of another philosopher, I mean Dr. Franklin. I say reputed, because I am not able to affirm that it is really his. It is, however, so generally understood and reported, both in Europe and America, that his judgment was in opposition to two assemblies, and in favor of a single one, that in a disquisition like this it ought not to be omitted. Shortly before the date of M. Turgot's letter, Dr. Franklin had arrived in Paris with the American constitutions, and among the rest that of Pennsylvania, in which there was but one assembly. It was reported, too, that the doctor had presided in the convention when it was made, and there approved it. M. Turgot, reading over the constitutions, and admiring that of Pennsylvania, was led to censure the rest, which were so different from it. I know of no other evidence that the Doctor ever gave his voice for a single assembly, but the common anecdote which is known to everybody. It is said, that in 1776, in the convention of Pennsylvania, of which the Doctor was president, a project of a form of government by one assembly was before them in debate; a motion was made to add another assembly, under the name of a senate or council. This motion was argued by several members, some for the affirmative, and some for the negative; and before the question was put, the opinion of the president was requested. The president rose, and said, that "two assemblies appeared to him like a practice he had somewhere seen, of certain wagoners, who, when about to descend a steep hill with a heavy load, if they had four cattle, took off one pair from before, and chaining them to the hinder part of the wagon drove them up hill; while the pair before and the weight of the load, overbalancing the strength of those behind, drew them slowly and moderately down the hill."[11]

The president of Pennsylvania might, upon such an occasion, have recollected one of Sir Isaac Newton's laws of motion, namely,—"that reaction must always be equal and contrary to action," or there can never be any *rest*. He might have alluded to those angry assemblies in the heavens, which so often overspread the city of Philadelphia, fill the citizens with apprehension and terror, threatening to set the world on fire, merely because the powers within them are not sufficiently balanced. He might have recollected, that a pointed rod, a machine as simple as a wagoner, or a monarch, or a governor, would be sufficient at any time, silently and innocently, to disarm those assemblies of all their terrors, by restoring between them the balance of the powerful fluid, and thus prevent the danger and destruction to the properties and lives of men, which often happen for the want of it.

However, allusions and illustrations drawn from pastoral and rural life are never disagreeable, and, in this case, might be as apposite as if they had been taken from the sciences and the skies. Harrington, if he had been present in convention, would have exclaimed, as he did when he mentioned his two girls dividing and choosing a cake, "O! the depth of the wisdom of God, which, in the simple invention of a carter, has revealed to mankind the whole mystery of a commonwealth; which consists as much in dividing and equalizing forces; in controlling the weight of the load and the activity of one part by the strength of another, as it does in dividing and choosing." Harrington, too, instead of his children dividing and choosing their cake, might have alluded to those attractions and repulsions by which the balance of nature is preserved; or to those centripetal

[11] "The answer of Dr. Franklin is oracular; that is to say, is ambiguous. It may be taken both ways, like the oracles of old." S.

Dr. Franklin's marked characteristic was caution. The only inference that can be drawn from this declaration is to be obtained from the decision of the assembly. Since the publication of his Writings, however, there can be no doubt of his opinion. See Sparks's *Franklin*, vol. i. p. 409, vol. v. p. 165, vol. x pp. 345, 361.

and centrifugal forces by which the heavenly bodies are continued in their orbits, instead of rushing to the sun, or flying off in tangents among comets and fixed stars; impelled or drawn by different forces in different directions, they are blessings to their own inhabitants and the neighboring systems; but if they were drawn only by one, they would introduce anarchy wherever they should go. There is no objection to such allusions, whether simple or sublime, so far as they may amuse the fancy and illustrate an argument; all that is insisted on is, that whatever there is in them of wit or argument, is all in favor of a complication of forces, of more powers than one; of three powers indeed, because a balance can never be established between two orders in society, without a third to aid the weakest.

All that is surprising here is, that the real force of the simile should have been misunderstood; if there is any similitude, or any argument in it, it is clearly in favor of two assemblies. The weight of the load itself would roll the wagon on the oxen and the cattle on one another, in one scene of destruction, if the forces were not divided and the balance formed; whereas, by checking one power by another, all descend the hill in safety, and avoid the danger. It should be remembered, too, that it is only in descending uncommon declivities that this division of strength becomes necessary. In travelling in ordinary plains, and always in ascending mountains, the whole team draws together, and advances faster as well as easier on its journey; it is also certain, there are oftener arduous steeps to mount, which require the united strength of all, with all the skill of the director, than there are precipices to descend, which demand a division of it.

Let us now return to M. Turgot's idea of a government consisting in a single assembly. He tells us our republics are "founded on the equality of all the citizens, and, therefore, 'orders' and 'equilibriums' are unnecessary, and occasion disputes." But what are we to understand here by equality? Are the citizens to be all of the same age, sex size, strength, stature, activity, courage, hardiness, industry, patience, ingenuity, wealth, knowledge, fame, wit, temperance, constancy, and wisdom? Was there, or will there ever be, a nation, whose individuals were all equal, in natural and acquired qualities, in virtues, talents, and riches? The answer of all mankind must be in the negative. It must then be acknowledged, that in every state, in the Massachusetts, for example, there are inequalities which God and nature have planted there, and which no human legislator ever can eradicate. I should have chosen to have mentioned Virginia, as the most ancient state, or indeed any other in the union, rather than the one that gave me birth, if I were not afraid of putting suppositions which may give offence, a liberty which my neighbors will pardon. Yet I shall say nothing that is not applicable to all the other twelve.

In this society of Massachusettensians then, there is, it is true, a moral and political equality of rights and duties among all the individuals, and as yet no appearance of artificial inequalities of condition, such as hereditary dignities, titles, magistracies, or legal distinctions; and no established marks, as stars, garters, crosses, or ribbons; there are, nevertheless, inequalities of great moment in the consideration of a legislator, because they have a natural and inevitable influence in society. Let us enumerate some of them:—1. There is an inequality of wealth; some individuals, whether by descent from their ancestors, or from greater skill, industry, and success in business, have estates both in lands and goods of great value; others have no property at all; and of all the rest of society, much the greater number are possessed of wealth, in all the variety of degrees between these extremes; it will easily be conceived that all the rich men will have many of the poor, in the various trades, manufactures, and other occupations in life, dependent upon them for their daily bread; many of smaller fortunes will be in their debt, and in many ways under obligations to them; others, in better circumstances, neither dependent nor in debt, men of letters, men of the learned professions, and others, from acquaintance, conversation, and civilities, will be connected with them and attached to them. Nay, farther, it will not be denied, that among the wisest people that live, there is a degree of admiration, abstracted from all dependence, obligation, expectation, or even acquaintance, which accompanies splendid wealth, insures some respect, and bestows some influence. 2. Birth. Let no man be surprised that this species of inequality is introduced here. Let the page in history be quoted, where any nation, ancient or modern, civilized or savage, is mentioned, among whom no difference was made between the citizens, on account of their extraction. The truth is, that more influence is allowed to this advantage in free republics than in despotic governments, or than would be allowed to it in simple monarchies, if severe laws had not been made from age to age to secure it. The children of illustrious families have generally greater advantages of education, and earlier opportunities to be acquainted with public characters, and informed of public affairs, than those of meaner ones, or even than those in middle life; and what is more than all, an habitual national veneration for their names, and the characters of their ancestors described in history, or coming down by tradition, removes them farther from vulgar jealousy and popular envy, and secures them in some degree the favor, the affection, and respect of the public. Will any man pretend that the name of Andros, and that of Winthrop, are heard with the same sensations in any village of New England? Is not gratitude the sentiment that attends the latter, and disgust the feeling excited by the former? In the Massachusetts, then, there are persons descended from some of their ancient governors, counsellors, judges, whose fathers, grandfathers, and great-grandfathers, are remembered with esteem by many living, and who are mentioned in history with applause, as benefactors to the country, while there are others who have no such advantage. May we go a step farther,—Know thyself, is as useful a precept to nations as to men. Go into every village in New England, and you will find that the office of justice of the peace, and even the place of representative, which has ever depended only on the freest election of the people, have generally descended from generation to generation, in three or four families at most. The present subject is one of those which all men respect, and all men deride. It may be said of this part of our nature, as Pope said of the whole:—

"Of human nature, wit her worst may write,

We all revere it in our own despite."

If, as Harrington says, the ten commandments were voted by the people of Israel, and have been enacted as laws by all other nations; and if we should presume to say, that nations had a civil right to repeal them, no nation would think proper to repeal the fifth, which enjoins honor to parents. If there is a difference between right and wrong; if any thing can be sacred; if there is one idea of moral obligation; the decree of nature must force upon every thinking being and upon every feeling heart the conviction that honor, affection, and gratitude are due from children to those who gave them birth, nurture, and education. The sentiments and affections which naturally arise from reflecting on the love, the cares, and the blessings of parents, abstracted from the consideration of duty, are some of the most forcible and most universal. When religion, law, morals, affection, and even fashion, thus conspire to fill every mind with attachment to parents, and to stamp deep upon the heart their impressions, is it to be expected that men should reverence their parents while they live, and begin to despise or neglect their memories as soon as they are dead? This is in nature impossible. On the contrary, every little unkindness and severity is forgotten, and nothing but endearments remembered with pleasure.

The son of a wise and virtuous father finds the world about him sometimes as much disposed as he himself is, to honor the memory of his father; to congratulate him as the successor to his estate; and frequently to compliment him with elections to the offices he held. A sense of duty, his passions and his interest, thus conspiring to prevail upon him to avail himself of this advantage, he finds a few others in similar circumstances with himself; they naturally associate together, and aid each other. This is a faint sketch of the source and rise of the family spirit; very often the disposition to favor the family is as strong in the town, county, province, or kingdom, as it is in the house itself. The enthusiasm is indeed sometimes wilder, and carries away, like a torrent, all before it.[12]

These observations are not peculiar to any age; we have seen the effects of them in San Marino, Biscay, and the Grisons, as well as in Poland and all other countries. Not to mention any notable examples which have lately happened near us, it is not many months since I was witness to a conver-

[12] The late election of a president in France, by the popular vote, will occur as a striking illustration of the force of these observations.

sation between some citizens of Massachusetts. One was haranguing on the jealousy which a free people ought to entertain of their liberties, and was heard by all the company with pleasure. In less than ten minutes, the conversation turned upon their governor; and the jealous republican was very angry at the opposition to him. "The present governor," says he, "has done us such services, that he ought to rule us, he and his posterity after him, for ever and ever." "Where is your jealousy of liberty?" demanded the other. "Upon my honor," replies the orator, "I had forgot that; you have caught me in an inconsistency; for I cannot know whether a child of five years old will be a son of liberty or a tyrant." His jealousy was the dictate of his understanding. His confidence and enthusiasm the impulse of his heart.

The pompous trumpery of ensigns, armorials, and escutcheons are not, indeed, far advanced in America. Yet there is a more general anxiety to know their originals, in proportion to their numbers, than in any nation of Europe; arising from the easier circumstances and higher spirit of the common people. And there are certain families in every state equally attentive to all the proud frivolities of heraldry. That kind of pride, which looks down on commerce and manufactures as degrading, may, indeed, in many countries of Europe, be a useful and necessary quality in the nobility. It may prevent, in some degree, the whole nation from being entirely delivered up to the spirit of avarice. It may be the cause why honor is preferred by some to money. It may prevent the nobility from becoming too rich, and acquiring too large a proportion of the landed property. In America, it would not only be mischievous, but would expose the highest pretensions of the kind to universal ridicule and contempt. Those other hauteurs, of keeping the commons at a distance, and disdaining to converse with any but a few of a certain race, may in Europe be a favor to the people, by relieving them from a multitude of assiduous attentions and humiliating compliances, which would be troublesome. It may prevent the nobles from caballing with the people, and gaining too much influence with them in elections and otherwise. In America, it would justly excite universal indignation; the vainest of all must be of the people, or be nothing. While every office is equally open to every competitor, and the people must decide upon every pretension to a place in the legislature, that of governor and senator, as well as representative, no such airs will ever be endured. At the same time, it must be acknowledged, that some men must take more pains to deserve and acquire an office than others, and must behave better in it, or they will not hold it.

We cannot presume that a man is good or bad, merely because his father was one or the other; and we should always inform ourselves first, whether the virtues and talents are inherited, before we yield our confidence. Wise men beget fools, and honest men knaves; but these instances, although they may be frequent, are not general. If there is often a likeness in feature and figure, there is generally more in mind and heart, because education contributes to the formation of these as well as nature. The influence of example is very great, and almost universal, especially that of parents over their children. In all countries it has been observed, that vices, as well as virtues, very often run down in families from age to age. Any man may go over in his thoughts the circle of his acquaintance, and he will probably recollect instances of a disposition to mischief, malice, and revenge, descending in certain breeds from grandfather to father and son. A young woman was lately convicted at Paris of a trifling theft, barely within the law which decreed a capital punishment. There were circumstances, too, which greatly alleviated her fault; some things in her behavior that seemed innocent and modest; every spectator, as well as the judges, was affected at the scene, and she was advised to petition for a pardon, as there was no doubt it would be granted. "No," says she; "my grandfather, father, and brother were all hanged for stealing; it runs in the blood of our family to steal, and be hanged. If I am pardoned now, I shall steal again in a few months more inexcusably; and, therefore, I will be hanged now." An hereditary passion for the halter is a strong instance, to be sure, and cannot be very common; but something like it too often descends, in certain breeds, from generation to generation.

If vice and infamy are thus rendered less odious, by being familiar in a family, by the example of parents and by education, it would be as unhappy as unaccountable, if virtue and honor were not recommended and rendered more amiable to children by the same means.

There are, and always have been, in every state, numbers possessed of some degree of family pride, who have been invariably encouraged, if not flattered in it, by the people. These have most acquaintance, esteem, and friendship with each other, and mutually aid each other's schemes of interest, convenience, and ambition. Fortune, it is true, has more influence than birth. A rich man, of an ordinary family and common decorum of conduct, may have greater weight than any family merit commonly confers without it.

It will be readily admitted, there are great inequalities of merit, or talents, virtues, services, and what is of more moment, very often of reputation. Some, in a long course of service in an army, have devoted their time, health, and fortunes, signalized their courage and address, exposed themselves to hardships and dangers, lost their limbs, and shed their blood, for the people. Others have displayed their wisdom, learning, and eloquence in council, and in various other ways acquired the confidence and affection of their fellow-citizens to such a degree, that the public have settled into a kind of habit of following their example and taking their advice.

There are a few, in whom all these advantages of birth, fortune, and fame are united.

These sources of inequality, which are common to every people, and can never be altered by any, because they are founded in the constitution of nature; this natural aristocracy among mankind, has been dilated on, because it is a fact essential to be considered in the institution of a government. It forms a body of men which contains the greatest collection of virtues and abilities in a free government, is the brightest ornament and glory of the nation, and may always be made the greatest blessing of society, if it be judiciously managed in the constitution. But if this be not done, it is always the most dangerous; nay, it may be added, it never fails to be the destruction of the commonwealth.

What shall be done to guard against it? Shall they be all massacred? This experiment has been more than once attempted, and once at least executed. Guy Faux attempted it in England; and a king of Denmark,[13]

[13] This is an allusion to the massacre of Stockholm, committed by Christian II, denominated the Nero of the North.

aided by a popular party, affected it once in Sweden; but it answered no good end. The moment they were dead another aristocracy instantly arose, with equal art and influence, with less delicacy and discretion, if not principle, and behaved more intolerably than the former. The country, for centuries, never recovered from the ruinous consequences of a deed so horrible, that one would think it only to be met with in the history of the kingdom of darkness.

There is but one expedient yet discovered, to avail the society of all the benefits from this body of men, which they are capable of affording, and at the same time, to prevent them from undermining or invading the public liberty; and that is, to throw them all, or at least the most remarkable of them, into one assembly together, in the legislature; to keep all the executive power entirely out of their hands as a body; to erect a first magistrate over them, invested with the whole executive authority; to make them dependent on that executive magistrate for all public executive employments;[14] to give that first magistrate a negative on the legislature, by which he may defend both himself and the people from all their enterprises in the legislature; and to erect on the other side an impregnable barrier against them, in a house of commons, fairly, fully, and adequately representing the people, who shall have the power both of negativing all their attempts at encroachment in the legislature, and of withholding from them and from the crown all supplies, by which they may be paid for their services in executive offices, or even the public service may be carried on to the detriment of the nation.

We have seen, both by reasoning and in experience, what kind of equality is to be found or expected in the simplest people in the world. There is not a city nor a village, any more than a kingdom or a commonwealth, in Europe or America; not a horde, clan, or tribe, among the negroes of Africa, or the savages of North or South America; nor a private club in the world, in which inequalities are not more or less visible. There is, then, a certain degree of weight, which property, family, and merit, will have in

---

[14] "If this means the appointment to offices, it is not advisable any more than the negative." S.

the public opinion and deliberations. If M. Turgot had discovered a mode of ascertaining the quantity which they ought to have, and had revealed it to mankind, so that it might be known to every citizen, he would have deserved more of gratitude than is due to all the inventions of philosophers. But, as long as human nature shall have passions and imagination, there is too much reason to fear that these advantages, in many instances, will have more influence than reason and equity can justify.

Let us then reflect, how the single assembly in the Massachusetts, in which our great statesman wishes all authority concentrated, will be composed. There being no senate nor council, all the rich, the honorable, and meritorious will stand candidates for seats in the house of representatives, and nineteen in twenty of them will obtain elections. The house will be found to have all the inequalities in it that prevailed among the people at large. Such an assembly will be naturally divided into three parts. The first is, some great genius,—some one masterly spirit, who unites in himself all the qualities which constitute the natural foundations of authority, such as benevolence, wisdom, and power; and all the adventitious attractions of respect, such as riches, ancestry, and personal merit. All eyes are turned upon him for president or speaker. The second division comprehends a third, or a quarter, or, if you will, a sixth or an eighth of the whole; and consists of those who have the most to boast of resembling their head. In the third class are all the rest, who are nearly on a level in understanding and in all things. Such an assembly has in it, not only all the persons of the nation, who are most eminent for parts and virtues, but all those who are most inflamed with ambition and avarice, and who are most vain of their descent. These latter will, of course, constantly endeavor to increase their own influence, by exaggerating all the attributes they possess, and by augmenting them in every way they can think of; and will have friends, whose only chance of rising into public view will be under their protection, who will be even more active and zealous in their service than themselves. Notwithstanding all the equality that can ever be hoped for among men, it is easy to see that the third class will, in general be but humble imitators and followers of the second. Every man in the second class will have constantly about him a circle of members of the third, who will be his admirers, perhaps afraid of his influence in the districts they represent, or related to him by blood, or connected with him in trade, or dependent upon him for favors. There will be much envy, too, among individuals of the second class, against the speaker, although a sincere veneration is shown him by the majority, and great external respect by all. I said there would be envy; because there will be among the second class several whose fortunes, families, and merits, in the acknowledged judgment of all, approach near to the first; and, from the ordinary illusions of self-love and self-interest, they and their friends will be much disposed to claim the first place as their own right. This will introduce controversy and debate, as well as emulation; and those who wish for the first place, and cannot obtain it, will of course endeavor to keep down the speaker as near upon a level with themselves as possible, by paring away the dignity and importance of his office, as we saw was the case in Venice, Poland, and, indeed, everywhere else.

A single assembly thus constituted, without any counterpoise, balance, or equilibrium, is to have all authority, legislative, executive, and judicial, concentrated in it. It is to make a constitution and laws by its own will, execute those laws at its own pleasure, and adjudge all controversies that arise concerning the meaning and application of them, at its own discretion. What is there to restrain it from making tyrannical laws, in order to execute them in a tyrannical manner? Will it be pretended, that the jealousy and vigilance of the people, and their power to discard them at the next election, will restrain them? Even this idea supposes a balance, an equilibrium, which M. Turgot holds in so much contempt; it supposes the people at large to be a check and control over the representative assembly. But this would be found a mere delusion. A jealousy between the electors and the elected neither ought to exist, nor is it possible to exist. It is a contradiction to suppose that a body of electors should have at one moment a warm affection and entire confidence in a man, so as to intrust him with authority, limited or unlimited, over their lives and fortunes; and the next moment after his election, to commence a suspicion of him, that shall prompt them to watch all his words, actions, and motions,[15] and dispose them to renounce and punish him. They choose him, indeed, because they think he knows more, and is better disposed than the generality, and very often even than themselves. Indeed, the best use of a representative assembly, arises from the cordial affection and unreserved confidence which subsists between it and the collective body of the people. It is by such kind and candid intercourse alone, that the wants and desires of the people can be made known, on the one hand, or the necessities of the public communicated or reconciled to them, on the other. In what did such a confidence in one assembly end, in Venice, Geneva, Biscay, Poland, but in an aristocracy and an oligarchy? There is no special providence for Americans, and their nature is the same with that of others.

DR. PRICE.

To demonstrate the necessity of two assemblies in the legislature, as well as of a third branch in it, to defend the executive authority, it may be laid down as a first principle, that neither liberty nor justice can be secured to the individuals of a nation, nor its prosperity promoted, but by a fixed constitution of government, and stated laws, known and obeyed by all. M. Turgot, indeed, censures the "falsity of the notion, so frequently repeated by almost all republican writers, 'that liberty consists in being subject only to the laws;' as if a man could be free while oppressed by an unjust law. This would not be true, even if we could suppose that all laws were the work of an assembly of the whole nation; for certainly every individual has his rights, of which the nation cannot deprive him, except by violence and an unlawful use of the general power."

We often hear and read of free states, a free people, a free nation, a free country, a free kingdom, and even of free republics; and we understand,

---

[15] "But future conduct may give just cause of suspicion; and, therefore, the representative, (according to the English constitution in its purity,) was elected only for a single session, the cause of which, if novel, was expressed in the election writs; and the representative had no right to determine in any new device, without consulting his constituents. These are the proper checks to aristocracy." S.

in general, what is intended, although every man may not be qualified to enter into philosophical disquisitions concerning the meaning, or to give a logical definition of the word liberty.

Our friend Dr. Price has distinguished very well, concerning physical, moral, religious, and civil liberty; and has defined the last to be "the power of a civil society to govern itself, by its own discretion, or by laws of its own making, by the majority, in a collective body, or by fair representation. In every free state every man in his own legislator. Legitimate government consists only in the dominion of *equal laws* made with *common consent,* and not in the dominion of any men over other men."

M. Turgot, however, makes the doctor too great a compliment at the expense of former English writers, when he represents him as "the first of his countrymen who has given a just idea of liberty, and shown the falsity, so often repeated by almost all republican writers, that liberty consists in being subject only to the laws."

I shall cheerfully agree with M. Turgot, that it is very possible that laws, and even equal laws, made by common consent, may deprive the minority of the citizens of their rights. A society, by a majority, may govern itself, even by equal laws, that is by laws to which all, majority and minority, are *equally* subject, so as to oppress the minority. It may establish a uniformity in religion; it may restrain trade; it may confine the personal liberty of all equally, and against the judgment of many, even of the best and wisest, without reasonable motives, use, or benefit. We may go farther, and say that a nation may be unanimous in consenting to a law restraining its natural liberty, property, and commerce, and its moral and religious liberties too, to a degree that may be prejudicial to the nation and to every individual in it. A nation of catholics might unanimously consent to prohibit labor upon one half the days in the year, as feast days. The whole American nation might unanimously consent to a Sunday law and a warden act, which should deprive them of the use of their limbs one day in seven. A nation may unanimously agree to a navigation act, which should shackle the commerce of all. Yet Dr. Price's definition of civil liberty is as liable to this objection as any other. These would be all *equal laws* made with *common consent;* these would all be acts of legitimate government. To take in M. Turgot's idea, then, we must add to Dr. Price's ideas of *equal laws* by *common consent,* this other—for the *general interest* or the *public good.* But it is generally supposed that nations understand their own interest better than another; and, therefore, they may be trusted to judge of the public good; and in all the cases above supposed, they will be as free as they desire to be; and, therefore, they may with great propriety be called free nations, and their constitutions free republics. There can be no way of compelling nations to be more free than they choose to be.

But M. Turgot has mistaken the sense of republican writers, especially of the English ones. What republican writers he had in view, I know not. There is none that I remember, of any name, who has given so absurd a definition of liberty. His countryman, Montesquieu, who will scarcely be denominated a republican writer, has said something the most like it; but it is manifest that his meaning was confined to equal laws, made by common consent. Although there may be unjust and unequal laws, obedience to which would be incompatible with liberty; yet no man will contend that a nation can be free that is not governed by fixed laws. All other government than that of permanent known laws, is the government of mere will and pleasure, whether it be exercised by one, a few, or many. Republican writers in general, and those of England in particular, have maintained the same principle with Dr. Price, and have said that legitimate governments, or well ordered commonwealths, or well constituted governments, were those where the laws prevailed; they have always explained their meaning to be *equal laws* made by *common consent* or the *general will*—that is to say, made by the majority, and equally binding upon majority and minority. As it is of importance to rescue the good old republican writers from such an imputation, let me beg your patience while we look into some of them.

Aristotle says, that "a government where the *laws alone* should prevail, would be the kingdom of God." This indeed shows that this great philosopher had much admiration of such a government. But it is not the assertion that M. Turgot condemns, namely,—that liberty consists in being subject to the laws only.

Aristotle says too, in another place, "Order is law, and it is more proper that law should govern, than any one of the citizens; upon the same principle, if it is advantageous to place the supreme power in some particular persons, they should be appointed to be only guardians and the servants of the laws." These too are very just sentiments, but not a formal definition of liberty.

Livy, too, speaks of happy, prosperous, and glorious times, when "Imperia legum potentiora fuerunt quam hominum."[16] But he nowhere says that liberty consists in being subject only to the *legum imperio.*

Sidney says, "No sedition was hurtful to Rome, until, through their prosperity, some men gained a power above the laws."

In another place he tells us too, from Livy, that some, whose ambition and avarice were impatient of restraint, complained that "leges rem surdam esse, inexorabilem, salubriorem inopi quam potenti."[17]

And, in another, that "no government was thought to be well constituted, unless the laws prevailed against the commands of men." But he has nowhere defined liberty to be subjection to the laws only.

Harrington says, "Government *de jure,* or, according to ancient prudence, is an art, whereby a civil society of men is instituted and preserved upon the foundation of *common interest;* or, to follow Aristotle and Livy, it is an empire of laws and not of men. And government, to define it according to modern prudence, or *de facto,* is an art by which some man, or some few men, subject a city or a nation, and rule it according to his or their private interest; which, because the laws in such cases are made according to the interest of a man, or a few families, may be said to be the empire of men and not of laws."

Harrington[18] agrees, that law proceeds from the will of man, whether a monarch or people; and that this will must have a mover; and that this mover is interest. But the interest of the people is one thing—it is the public interest; and where the public interest governs, it is a government of

---

[16] ["The powers of the laws were stronger than those of men." Livy, II, 1, 1 Ed.]

[17] ["Laws are a deaf thing, not to be argued with, healthier for the poor man than the powerful man." Livy II, 3, 4. Ed.]

[18] *Politicaster,* scene 2.

laws, and not of men. The interest of a king, or of a party, is another thing—it is a private interest; and where private interest governs, it is a government of men, and not of laws. If in England there has ever been any such thing as a government of laws, was it not *magna charta?* and have not our kings broken *magna charta* thirty times? Did the law govern when the law was broken? or was that a government of men? On the contrary, hath not *magna charta* been as often repaired by the people? and, the law being so restored, was it not a government of laws, and not of men? Why have our kings, in so many statutes and oaths engaged themselves to govern by law, if there were not in kings a capacity of governing otherwise? It is true, that laws are neither made by angels, nor by horses, but by men. The voice of the people is as much the voice of men as the voice of a prince is the voice of a man; and yet the voice of the people is the voice of God, which the voice of a prince is not. The government of laws, said Aristotle, is the government of God. In a monarchy, the laws, being made according to the interest of one man, or a few men, must needs be more private and partial than suits with the nature of justice; but in a commonwealth, the laws, being made by the whole people, must come up to the public interest, which is common right and justice; and if a man know not what is his own interest, who should know it? and that which is the interest of the most or greatest number of particular men, being summed up in the common vote, is the public interest.

Sidney says, "Liberty consists solely in an independency on the will of another; and, by a slave, we understand a man who can neither dispose of his person or goods, but enjoys all at the will of his master." And again, "As liberty consists only in being subject to no man's will, and nothing denotes a slave but a dependence upon the will of another; if there be no other law in a kingdom but the will of a prince, there is no such thing as liberty."

M. Turgot might have perceived in these writers that a government of laws and not of men was intended by them as a description of a commonwealth, not a definition of liberty. There may be various degrees of liberty established by the laws, and enjoyed by the citizens, in different commonwealths; but still the general will, as well as the general interest, as far as it is understood by the people, prevails in all that can be denominated free. As the society governs itself, it is free, according to the definition of Dr. Price. The inquiry of these writers, in such passages, was not into the highest point of liberty, or greatest degree of it, which might be established by the general will and the common sense of interest, in their results or laws. They have taken it for granted that human nature is so fond of liberty, that, if the whole society were consulted, a majority would never be found to put chains upon themselves by their own act and voluntary consent.

But all men, as well as republican writers, must agree, that there can be no uninterrupted enjoyment of liberty, nor any good government in society, without laws, or where standing laws do not govern. In despotic states, in simple monarchies, in aristocracies, in democracies, in all possible mixtures of these, the individual continually enjoys the benefit of law, as he does that of light and air, although, in most of those governments, he has no security for the continuance of it. If the laws were all repealed at once, in any great kingdom, and the event made known suddenly to all, scarcely a house in the great cities would remain in possession of its present inhabitants.

The great question therefore is, What combination of powers in society, or what form of government, will compel the formation, impartial execution, and faithful interpretation of good and equal laws, so that the citizens may constantly enjoy the benefit of them, and may be sure of their continuance? The controversy between M. Turgot and me is, whether a single assembly of representatives be this form? He maintains the affirmative. I am for the negative. Because such an assembly will, upon the first day of its existence, be an aristocracy; in a few days, or at least years, an oligarchy; and then it will divide into two or three parties, who will soon have as many armies; after which, when the battle is decided, the victorious general will govern without or with the advice of any council or assembly, as he pleases; or else, if the assembly continues united, it will in time exclude the people from all share even in elections, and make the government hereditary in a few families.

In order to be fully convinced of this, we must take an extensive view of the subject; and the first inquiry should be, what kind of beings men are? You and I admire the fable of Tristram Shandy more than the fable of the Bees, and agree with Butler rather than Hobbes. It is weakness rather than wickedness, which renders men unfit to be trusted with unlimited power. The passions are all unlimited; nature has left them so; if they could be bounded, they would be extinct; and there is no doubt they are of indispensable importance in the present system. They certainly increase too, by exercise, like the body. The love of gold grows faster than the heap of acquisition; the love of praise increases by every gratification, till it stings like an adder, and bites like a serpent; till the man is miserable every moment when he does not snuff the incense. Ambition strengthens at every advance, and at last takes possession of the whole soul so absolutely, that a man sees nothing in the world of importance to others or himself, but in his object. The subtlety of these three passions, which have been selected from all the others because they are aristocratical passions, in subduing all others, and even the understanding itself, if not the conscience too, until they become absolute and imperious masters of the whole mind, is a curious subject of speculation. The cunning with which they hide themselves from others, and from a man himself too; the patience with which they wait for opportunities; the torments they voluntarily suffer for a time, to secure a full enjoyment at length; the inventions, the discoveries, the contrivances they suggest to the understanding, sometimes in the dullest dunces in the world, if they could be described in writing, would pass for great genius.

We are not enough acquainted with the physical or metaphysical effects produced on our bodies or minds, to be able to explain the particular reason why every instance of indulgence strengthens and confirms the subsequent emotions of desire. The cause has hitherto been too deep, remote, and subtle, for the search of corporeal or intellectual microscopes; but the fact is too decided to deceive or escape our observation. Men should endeavor at a *balance* of affections and appetites, under the monarchy of reason and conscience, within, as well as at a balance of power without. If they surrender the guidance for any course of time to any one passion, they may depend upon finding it, in the end, a usurping, domineering, cruel tyrant. They were intended by nature to live together in

society, and in this way to restrain one another, and in general they are a
very good kind of creatures; but they know each other's imbecility so well,
that they ought never to lead one another into temptation.★ The passion
that is long indulged and continually gratified becomes mad; it is a species
of delirium; it should not be called guilt, but insanity. But who would trust
his life, liberty, and property to a madman or an assembly of them? It
would be safer to confide in knaves. Five hundred or five thousand
together, in an assembly, are not less liable to this extravagance than one.
The nation that commits its affairs to a single assembly, will assuredly
find that its passions and desires augment as fast as those of a king.
And, therefore, a constitution with a single assembly must be essentially
defective.

Others have seen this quality in human nature through a more gloomy
medium.

Machiavel says, "those who have written on civil government lay it
down as a first principle, and all historians demonstrate the same, that
whoever would found a state, and make proper laws for the government
of it, must presume that all men are bad by nature; that they will not fail
to show that natural depravity of heart whenever they have a fair opportunity;† and that though it may possibly lie for a while concealed, on
account of some secret reason, which does not then appear to men of
small experience, yet time, which is therefore justly called the father of
truth, commonly brings it to light in the end." Machiavel's translator
remarks, that although this seems a harsh supposition, does not every

---

★ Οἱ πλεῖστοι χαχόι. The majority are wicked. Bias (J. A.)

The notes marked with the author's initials have been found written in the margin
of his copy.

† *Hooker's Ecc. Pol.* lib. i. ss. 1; *Ibid.* ss. 10.

"Laws politic, ordained for external order and regiment amongst men, are never
framed as they should be, unless presuming the will of man to be inwardly obstinate,
rebellious, and averse from all obedience unto the sacred laws of his nature; in a word,
unless presuming man to be, in regard of his depraved mind, little better than a wild beast,
they do accordingly provide, notwithstanding, so to frame his outward actions that they
be no hindrance unto the common good for which societies are instituted; unless they do
this, they are not perfect."

Christian daily justify the truth of it, by confessing it before God and the world? and are we not expressly told the same in several passages of the Holy Scriptures, and in all systems of human philosophy?

Montesquieu says, "Constant experience shows us that every man invested with power is apt to abuse it. He pushes on till he comes to something that limits him. Is it not strange, though true, to say that virtue itself has need of limits? To prevent the abuse of power, it is necessary, that, by the very disposition of things, power should be a check to power. A government may be so constituted, as that no man shall be compelled to do things to which the law does not oblige him, nor forced to abstain from things which the law permits."

"So endless and exorbitant are the desires of men, that they will grasp at all, and can form no scheme of perfect happiness with less. It is hard to recollect one folly, infirmity, or vice, to which a single man is subjected, and from which a body of commons, collective or representative," (and he might have added a body of nobles,) "can be wholly exempt." *Swift.*

"Laws are intended not to trust to what men will do, but to guard against what they may do." *Junius.*

"Ogni uomo si fa centro di tutte le combinazioni del globo."
Beccaria.[19]

"The ambitious deceive themselves, when they propose an end to their ambition; for that end, when attained, becomes a means." *Rochefoucauld.*

"Experience evinces that the happiest dispositions are not proof against the allurements of power, which has no charms but as it leads on to new advances. Authority endures not the very idea of restraint; nor does it cease to struggle, till it has beaten down every boundary." *De Lolme.*

Hobbes, Mandeville, Rochefoucauld, have drawn still more detestable pictures; and Rousseau, in his *Inequalities among Mankind,* gives a description of a civilized heart, too black and horrible to be transcribed.*

[19] ["Every man makes himself the center of his whole world." Cesare Beccaria, *De Delitti e delle Pene (On Crimes and Punishments),* 1763, chapter 2. Ed.]
* "Heaven's Sovereign saves all beings but himself
That hideous sight, a naked human heart."
Night Thoughts. Narcissa. (J. A.)

Even our amiable friends, those benevolent Christian philosophers, Dr. Price and Dr. Priestley, acquaint us that they are constrained to believe human nature no better than it should be. The latter says, there is no power on earth but has grown exorbitant when it has met with no control.

The former: "Such are the principles that govern human nature; such the weakness and folly of men; such their love of domination, selfishness, and depravity, that none of them can be raised to an elevation above others, without the utmost danger. The constant experience of the world has verified this, and proved that nothing intoxicates the human mind so much as power. In the establishment, therefore, of civil government, it would be preposterous to rely on the discretion of any men. A people will never oppress themselves or invade their own rights; but if they trust the arbitrary will of a body or succession of men, they trust enemies."

Shall we say that all these philosophers were ignorant of human nature? With all my soul, I wish it were in my power to quote any passages in history or philosophy, which might demonstrate all these satires on our species to be false. But the phenomena are all in their favor; and the only question to be raised with them is, whether the cause is wickedness, weakness, or insanity?

In all events, we must agree, that human nature is not fit to be trusted with M. Turgot's system, of all authority in a single assembly.

A single assembly will never be a steady guardian of the laws, if Machiavel is right when he says: "Men are never good but through necessity. On the contrary, when good and evil are left to their choice, and they can practise the latter with impunity, they will not fail to throw every thing into disorder and confusion.[20] Hunger and poverty may make men industrious, but laws only can make them good; for, if men were so of themselves, there would be no occasion for laws; but, as the case is far otherwise, they are absolutely necessary. After the Tarquins were dead, who had been such a check upon the nobility, some other expedient was wanting that might have the same effect; so that, after much confusion and

[20] So great is the depravity of the human heart, that ministers, who only can know it, are in charity to mankind bound to keep it a secret, &c. (J. A.)

disorder, and many dangerous contests between the patricians and plebeians, certain officers, called *tribunes,* were created for the security of the latter; who, being vested with such privileges and authority as enabled them to become arbiters betwixt those two estates, effectually curbed the insolence of the former." Or, in the language of Dr. Franklin, the people insisted upon hitching a yoke of cattle behind the wagon, to draw up hill, when the patricians before should attempt to go too fast; or, in the style of Harrington, the commons, finding the patricians disposed to divide the cake unequally, demanded the privilege of choosing.

If Harrington's authority is not of great weight with some men, the reasons he assigns in support of his judgment are often eternal and unanswerable by any man. In his Oceana, he says: "Be the interest of popular government right reason, a man does not look upon reason as it is right or wrong in itself, but as it makes for him or against him. Wherefore, unless you can show such *orders* of a government as, like those of God in nature, shall be able to constrain this or that creature to shake off that inclination which is more peculiar to it, and take up that which regards the common good or interest; all this is to no more end, than to persuade every man in a popular government not to carve for himself of that which he desires most, but to be mannerly at the public table, and give the best from himself to decency and the *common interest.* But that such *orders* may be established, as may, nay must, give the upper hand in all cases to common right or interest, notwithstanding the nearness of that which sticks to every man in private, and this in a way of equal certainty and facility, is known even to girls; being no other than those which are of common practice with them in divers cases. For example,—two of them have a cake yet undivided, which was given between them. That each of them, therefore, might have that which is due, 'divide,' says one, 'and I will choose; or let me divide, and you shall choose.' If this be but once agreed upon, it is enough; for the divident, dividing unequally loses, in regard that the other takes the better half; wherefore, she divides equally, and so both have right. And thus, what great philosophers are disputing upon in vain, is brought to light by two harmless girls; even the whole mystery of a commonwealth, which lies only in dividing and choosing."

Now, if all authority is to be collected into one central assembly, it will have the whole power of division and choice; and we may easily conjecture what division and choice it will be. It will soon have possession of all the cakes, loaves, and fishes.

Harrington proceeds: "Nor has God, if his works in nature be understood, left so much to mankind to dispute upon, as who shall divide and who choose, but distributed them forever into two orders; whereof the one has the natural right of dividing, and the other of choosing. For example,—a commonwealth is but a civil society of men. Let us take any number of men, as twenty, and immediately make a commonwealth. Twenty men, if they be not all idiots, perhaps if they be, can never come so together but there will be such a difference in them, that about a third will be wiser, or at least less foolish, than all the rest. These, upon acquaintance, though it be but small, will be discovered, and (as stags that have the largest heads) lead the herd. For, while the six, discoursing and arguing one with another, show the eminence of their parts, the fourteen discover things that they never thought on, or are cleared in divers truths which had formerly perplexed them. Wherefore, in matter of common concernment, difficulty, or danger, they hang upon their lips as children upon their fathers; and the influence thus acquired by the six, the eminence of whose parts are found to be a stay and comfort to the fourteen, is the authority of the fathers—*auctoritas patrum*. Wherefore, this can be no other than a *natural aristocracy,* diffused by God throughout the whole body of mankind, to this end and purpose; and, therefore, such as the people have not only a natural, but a positive obligation to make use of as their guides; as where the people of Israel are commanded to take wise men, and understanding, and known among their tribes, to be made rulers over them. The six then approved of, as in the present case, are the senate; not by hereditary right, or in regard to the greatness of their estates only, which would tend to such power as might force or draw the people; but by election for their excellent parts, which tends to the advancement of the influence of their virtue or authority, that leads the people. Wherefore, the office of the senate is not to be commanders, but counsellors of the people; and that which is proper to counsellors, is first to debate, and afterwards to give advice in the business whereon they have debated; whence the decrees of the senate are never laws, nor so called—*senatus consulta;* and these, being maturely framed, it is their duty to propose to the people. Wherefore, the senate is no more than the debate of the commonwealth. But to debate is to discern, or put a difference between things, that, being alike, are not the same; or it is separating and weighing this reason against that, and that reason against this; which is *dividing.*

"The senate, then, having divided, who shall choose? Ask the girls; for, if she that divided must have chosen also, it had been little worse for the other, in case she had not divided at all, but kept the whole cake to herself; in regard that, being to choose too, she divided accordingly.

"Wherefore, if the senate have any further power than to divide, the commonwealth can never be equal. But, *in a commonwealth consisting of a single council, there is no other to choose than that which divided.* Whence it is, that such a council fails not to *scramble,* that is, to be factious; there being no other dividing of the cake, in that case, but among themselves; *nor is there any other remedy, but to have another council to choose.* The wisdom of the few may be the light of mankind; but the interest of the few is not the profit of mankind, nor of a commonwealth. Wherefore, seeing we have granted interest to be reason, they must not choose, lest it put out their light. But as the council dividing consists of the wisdom of the commonwealth, so the assembly or council choosing should consist of the interest of the commonwealth; as the wisdom of the commonwealth is in the aristocracy, so the interest of the commonwealth is in the whole body of the people. And whereas this, in case the commonwealth consist of a whole nation, is too unwieldy a body to be assembled, this council is to consist of such a representative as may be equal, and so constituted as it can never contract any other interest than that of the whole people. But, in the present case, the six dividing, and the fourteen choosing, must of necessity take in the whole interest of the twenty. Dividing and choosing, in the language of a commonwealth, is debating and resolving; and whatsoever, upon debate of the senate, is proposed to the people, and resolved by them, is enacted by the authority of the fathers, and by the power of the people—*auctoritate patrum et jussu populi;* which concurring make a law."

Upon these principles, and to establish a method of enacting laws that must of necessity be wise and equal, the people of most of the United States of America agreed upon that division of the legislative power into two houses, the house of representatives and the senate, which have given so much disgust to M. Turgot. Harrington will show us equally well the propriety and necessity of the other branch, the governor. But, before we proceed to that, it may be worth while to observe the similitude between this passage and some of those sentiments and expressions of Swift, which were quoted in a former letter; and there is in the *Idea of a Patriot King*, written by his friend, Lord Bolingbroke, a passage to the same purpose, so nobly expressed, that I cannot forbear the pleasure of transcribing it. "It seems to me that, in order to maintain the moral system of the universe at a certain point, far below that of ideal perfection, (for we are made capable of conceiving what we are not capable of attaining,) it has pleased the Author of Nature to mingle, from time to time, among the societies of men a few, and but a few of those on whom he has been graciously pleased to confer a larger proportion of the ethereal spirit, than in the ordinary course of his providence he bestows on the sons of men. These are they who engross almost the whole reason of the species. Born to direct, to guide, and to preserve, if they retire from the world their splendor accompanies them, and enlightens even the darkness of their retreat. If they take a part in public life, the effect is never indifferent. They either appear the instruments of Divine vengeance, and their course through the world is marked by desolation and oppression, by poverty and servitude; or they are the guardian angels of the country they inhabit, studious to avert the most distant evil, and to procure peace, plenty, and the greatest of human blessings, liberty."

If there is, then, in society such a natural aristocracy as these great writers pretend, and as all history and experience demonstrate, formed partly by genius, partly by birth, and partly by riches, how shall the legislator avail himself of their influence for the equal benefit of the public? and how, on the other hand, shall he prevent them from disturbing the public happiness? I answer, by arranging them all, or at least the most conspicuous of them, together in one assembly, by the name of a senate; by separating them from all pretensions to the executive power, and by controlling in the legislative their ambition and avarice, by an assembly of representatives on one side, and by the executive authority on the other. Thus you will have the benefit of their wisdom, without fear of their passions. If among them there are some of Lord Bolingbroke's guardian angels, there will be some of his instruments of Divine vengeance too. The latter will be here restrained by a threefold tie,—by the executive power, by the representative assembly, and by their peers in the senate. But if these were all admitted into a single popular assembly, the worst of them might in time obtain the ascendency of all the rest. In such a single assembly, as has been observed before, almost the whole of this aristocracy will make its appearance, being returned members of it by the election of the people. These will be one class. There will be another set of members, of middling rank and circumstances, who will justly value themselves upon their independence, their integrity, and unbiased affection to their country, and will pique themselves upon being under no obligation. But there will be a third class, every one of whom will have his leader among the members of the first class, whose character he will celebrate, and whose voice he will follow; and this party, after a course of time, will be the most numerous. The question then will be, whether this aristocracy in the house will unite or divide? and it is too obvious, that destruction to freedom must be the consequence equally of their union or of their division. If they unite generally in all things, as much as they certainly will in respecting each other's wealth, birth, and parts, and conduct themselves with prudence, they will strengthen themselves by insensible degrees, by playing into each other's hands more wealth and popularity, until they become able to govern elections as they please, and rule the people at discretion. An independent member will be their aversion; all their artifices will be employed to destroy his popularity among his constituents, and bring in a disciple of their own in his place.

But if they divide, each party will, in a course of time, have the whole house, and consequently the whole state, divided into two factions, which will struggle in words, in writing, and at last in arms, until Cæsar or Pompey must be emperor, and entail an endless line of tyrants on the nation.

But long before this catastrophe, and indeed through every scene of the drama, the laws, instead of being permanent, and affording constant protection to the lives, liberties, and properties of the citizens, will be alternately the sport of contending factions, and the mere vibrations of a pendulum. From the beginning to the end it will be a government of men, now of one set, and then of another; but never a government of laws.
…

CHAPTER VII.

Ancient Democratical Republics.

CARTHAGE.

IN order to show the theory of Socrates, as reported by Plato, in a clearer light, and to be convinced that he has not exaggerated in his description of the mutability in the characters of men and the forms of government, we should look into the history of those ancient republics from whence he drew his observations and reasonings. Although it is probable that Greece was his principal theatre, yet we may reasonably suppose that Carthage and a multitude of other republics in Italy, besides that of Rome, were not unknown to him.

The history of Greece should be to our countrymen what is called in many families on the continent a *boudoir,* an octagonal apartment in a house, with a full-length mirror on every side, and another in the ceiling. The use of it is, when any of the young ladies, or young gentlemen if you will, are at any time a little out of humor, they may retire to a place where, in whatever direction they turn their eyes, they see their own faces and figures multiplied without end. By thus beholing their own beautiful persons, and seeing, at the same time, the deformity brought upon them by their anger, they may recover their tempers and their charms together. A few short sketches of the ancient republics will serve to show, not only that the *orders* we defend were common to all of them; but that the prosperity and duration of each was in proportion to the care taken to *balance* them; and that they all were indebted, for their frequent seditions, the rise and progress of corruption, and their decline and fall, to the imperfection of their orders, and their defects in the balance.

As there are extant no writings of any Carthaginian philosopher, statesman, or historian, we have no exact information concerning the form of their commonwealth, but what appears in a few hints of Greek and Roman authors. Their commerce and riches, their empire of the sea, and extensive dominion of two thousand miles on the sea coast, their obstinate military contests with Rome, and the long duration of their government, prove both that their population and power were very great, and their constitution good; especially as, for the space of five hundred years, their tranquility was never interrupted by sedition, nor their liberties attempted by the ambition of any of their citizens.

The national character was military, as well as commercial; and, although they were avaricious, they were not effeminate.

The monarchical power was in two suffetes, the aristocratical in the senate, and the democratical was held by the people in a body. These are said to have been nicely balanced, but we know not in what manner. The chief magistrates were annually elected by the people. The senators were elected too, and, although it is not certain, it is most probable, by the people; but it appears that three qualifications were indispensable in every senator,—birth, merit, and wealth. This last requisite rendered commerce honorable, even in the first of the patricians and senators themselves, and animated the commercial genius of the nation. This government, thus far, resembles those of the States of America, more than any other of the ancient republics, perhaps more than any of the modern; but when we inquire for the balance, it is not to be found. The suffetes had not more authority than Roman consuls; they had but a part of the executive, and none of the legislative power. Much of the executive and all the legislative was in the senate and people. The balance, then, could only be between these two. Now, it is impossible to balance two assemblies without introducing a third power; one or other will be most powerful, and, whichever it is, will continually scramble till it gets the whole. In fact, the people here had the whole as much as in any of our states; so that, while the citizens were uncorrupted and gave their votes honestly for suffetes and senators, all went well. And it is extremely remarkable that, with all their acknowledged eagerness for money, this people were so many centuries untainted with luxury and venality, and preserved their primitive frugality of manners and integrity in elections. As to the Roman accusations of insincerity, there is no more reason to believe them, than there would be to believe a Carthaginian who should retort the reproach. This, as well as other instances, may lead us to doubt the universality of the doctrine, that commerce corrupts manners. There was another remarkable institution, that the senate should always be unanimous; and if any one senator insisted upon his own opinion against all the rest, there could be no decision, but by an appeal to the people. This, again, gave a strong democratical cast to the constitution. Such a tendency could only be balanced by the laws, which, requiring a large fortune for every senator and public officer, in order to support his dignity, and secure him against the temptations to corruption, confined the choice to the first families and abilities united. This was liable to great objection; because great abilities might often be possessed by men of obscure original and smaller property, who were thereby excluded. To this law, nevertheless, may be ascribed the duration of the republic.

Another remarkable check, which was, perhaps, the model from whence the Venetian inquisition was copied, was a committee of one hundred and four members of the senate appointed to watch the ambition of the great families. To this body all their admirals and generals were required to render an account of their conduct at the end of every year.

Out of this body were elected a sub-committee of five, who had very great power. Their office was for life; and they filled up their own vacancies out of the one hundred and four, and all the vacancies, even in the one hundred and four, out of the senate; they had the supreme tribunal of criminal jurisdiction. This power must have been terrible to all,—to the people, senate, and suffetes; yet it was the check which preserved the state from sedition and convulsions. It grew unpopular; and the law which at last made it annual and elective, probably laid the foundation of the ruin of the commonwealth, by changing the balance, and introducing the *dominatio plebis.*[21] The balances in this, the most democratical republic of antiquity, contrived by the people themselves to temper their own power, are extremely remarkable. The suffetes represented, like the consuls at Rome, the majesty of the commonwealth, and had a share of executive authority; the council of five had criminal jurisdiction and inquisitorial power; the one hundred and four were a body chosen out of the senate, by the five, for their support; then comes the senate at large; and, last of all, the people at large. Here are five orders completely distinct, besides the necessary legal qualification of great wealth; yet all these checks, although they preserved the state five hundred years, could not prolong its period above seven hundred; because, after all, the balance was not natural nor effectual. The executive power was not separated from the legislative; nor the different parts of the legislature properly divided or balanced. Both the executive and judicial power were chiefly in legislative hands.

The noble families, thus secured in possession both of legislative and executive power, could not be restrained by all the ligaments which had been contrived to preserve the equipoise between them and the people. They divided into two factions, with the family of Hanno at the head of one, and that of Barcas of the other. They first attacked the council of five, whose power was unpopular, as well as odious to the nobles; then easily procured a law to make it annually elective, or, in other words, an instrument always in the hands of the prevailing faction, as such a small body, so changeable, must ever be; and, lastly, overturned the constitution. The Romans had all the advantage of these dissensions in the war, by which they finally destroyed their rival power so effectually, that scarce a trace of it remains to be seen, even in ruins. Their virtues were not extinguished to the last; and some of the greatest examples of patriotism and heroism were exhibited even in their expiring agonies.

ATHENS

CECROPS, an Egyptian, conducted a colony that settled in Athens, and first engaged the wandering shepherds and hunters of Attica to unite in villages

---

[21] ["the domination of the common people," i.e. the plebeians or lower classes, not just 'the people' as opposed to the elected officials. Ed.]

of husbandmen. Although the government of Egypt was an absolute monarchy, he found it necessary to establish his own upon a more limited plan.

The two rival families of Perseus and Pelops, anciently contended for the dominion of the Grecian peninsula. The fortune of the descendants of the latter prevailed, and their superior prosperity led them to persecute their enemies. The descendants of Hercules, who was a son of Jupiter by Alcmena, of the line of Perseus, were stripped of all their possessions, and driven into exile. After a series of misfortunes, Temenus, Cresphontes, and Aristodemus, descendants in the fifth degree from Hercules, conducted an expedition into Greece and conquered the whole country.

The governments of the little states of Greece in the first ages, though of no very regular and certain constitution, were all limited monarchies. When, therefore, the Heraclides possessed themselves of Peloponnesus, they established everywhere that hereditary limited monarchy, which was the only government assimilated to the ideas and temper of the age, and an equality among themselves. Those vigorous principles of aristocracy, and some traces of the spirit of democracy, which had always existed in the Grecian governments, began to ferment; and, in the course of a few ages, monarchy was everywhere abolished. The very name of king was proscribed; a republic was thought the only government to which it became men to submit; and the term *tyrant* was introduced to denote those who, in opposition to these new political principles, acquired monarchical authority. Absolute monarchy was unknown as a legal constitution. The title of king implied a superiority of lawful dignity and authority in one person, above all others, for their benefit, not a right of absolute power. Legislation was never within their prerogative.

A distinction of families into those of higher and lower rank obtained very early throughout Greece, and nowhere more than at Athens, where, by the constitution of Theseus, the Eupatridæ, or nobly born, formed a distinct order of the state with great privileges. Afterwards wealth became the principal criterion of rank, which amounted probably to the same thing, as the nobly born were generally most wealthy. Every citizen in every Grecian state was bound to military service, as in modern times, among the feudal kingdoms. It was natural that the rich should serve on horseback; and this was the origin of knighthood both in ancient and modern nations. Where the noble or the rich held all the power, they called their own government *aristocracy,* or government of the better sort, or *optimacy,* government of the best sort. The people allowed the appellation of aristocracy only to those governments where persons, elected by themselves for their merit, held the principal power. Democracy signified a government by all the freemen of the state or the people at large, forming in assembly the legal, absolute sovereign. But as this, above all others, was subject to irregularity, confusion, and absurdity, when unchecked by some balancing power lodged in fewer hands, it was called *ochlocracy,* or mob rule. Most of the Grecian states had some mixture of two or more of these forms. The mixture of oligarchy and democracy, in which the former was superior, yet the latter sufficed to secure liberty and equal right to the people, might, according to Aristotle, be called aristocracy. That mixture where the democratic power prevailed, yet was in some degree balanced by authority lodged in steadier hands, is distinguished by that great author by the name of *polity.* An equal mixture of all three was never known in Greece, and, therefore, never obtained a distinct name in that language.

A war happened between the Athenians and Peloponnesians; the armies were encamped near each other, and the Delphian oracle was consulted. The answer of the Pythoness implied, that the Peloponnesians would be victorious, provided they did not kill the Athenian king. Codrus, disguising himself like a clown, with a fagot on his shoulder and a fork in his hand, determined to devote his life, entered the enemy's camp, and was killed. The Peloponnesian chiefs finding the body to be Codrus, and fearing the prophecy, withdrew their forces, and a peace ensued. Medon, the eldest son of Codrus, was lame; and bodily ability was held in so high rank in popular esteem, that his younger brother disputed the succession. Each had a powerful party; but the dispute brought forward a third, which was for abolishing the royalty, and having no king but Jupiter. Fatal dissensions were apprehended, when a declaration of the oracle was procured in favor of Medon; and it was amicably accommodated that Medon

should be first magistrate, with the title of archon, but not king. Although
the honor was to be hereditary, and the archon to be accountable to the
assembly of the people for his administration, it was agreed that a colony
should be sent to Asia Minor, under Nelius and Androclus, younger sons
of Codrus. The most restless spirits joined in the migration, and no further
materials for history remain for several generations.

From the period where Homer's history ceases, to that in which the
first prose historians lived, a space of two hundred and fifty years, there is
little light to be obtained. Twelve archons are named, who followed
Medon by hereditary succession, and filled up three hundred years. On the
death of Alcmæon, Charops was raised to the archonship, upon condition of holding it for ten years only. Six archons followed Charops, by
appointment, for ten years; but on the expiration of the archonship of
Eryxias, it was resolved that the office should be annual, and that there
should be nine persons to execute it. They had not all equal dignity, nor
the same functions; one represented the majesty of the state, and was usually called the *archon;* the second had the title of king, and was head of
the church; the polemarch was third, and chief of military affairs. The other
six had the title of thesmothetes; they presided as judges in ordinary courts
of justice. The nine together formed the council of state. Here methinks
I see the Polish nobles running down the king, or those of Venice the
doge, and dividing the spoils of his prerogative among themselves. Legislation was in the assembly of the people; but the whole administration,
civil, military, religious, and judiciary, was with the archons, who were
commonly appointed by lot; but sometimes the assembly of the people
interfered, and exercised the power of naming them. From the appointment of annual archons there was nothing but intestine troubles. That
weight which, from earliest times, a few principal families possessed
among the Attic people, and which was in a great degree confirmed to
them by the constitution of Theseus, remained, amid all the turbulence
of democracy, to a late period. Among those families the Alcmæonides,
claiming some connection by blood with the perpetual archons and kings
of the ancient Neleid line, were of great fame. Megacles, head of this
family, was archon when Cylon, a man of a very ancient and powerful

family, attempted to acquire the sovereignty of his country. He seized the citadel of Athens, with some troops he received from Theagenes, tyrant of Megara, whose daughter he had married. His vanity was excited not only by his birth and marriage, but his personal merit, having been victor in a chariot race at the Olympic games. The people ran to arms under their archons, and laid siege to the citadel. Cylon fled, and his party fled to the altars. They were promised pardon, but condemned and executed. This was an atrocious infidelity, and made the actors in it as odious, as it rendered Cylon and his party again popular and powerful.

The miseries of a fluctuating jurisprudence became insufferable, and all parties united at last in the resolution to appoint a lawgiver. Draco was raised to this important office; a man whose morals and integrity recommended him to the people, but whose capacity was equal to no improvement in the political constitution, and to no greater invention for reforming the judicatures, than that of inflicting capital punishments in all offences; and the knowing ones had no other remedy than to get the oracle to pronounce that the laws of Draco were written in blood; an expression which struck the imagination and touched the heart, and, therefore, soon rendered this system unpopular.[22]

Salamis, perceiving the divisions at Athens, revolted, and allied itself to Megara. Several attempts to recover it having failed, the lower people, in opposition to their chiefs, carried a law, making it capital to propose a renewal of the enterprise. Solon, of an ancient royal family, who had hitherto pursued nothing but literature and poetry, perceiving that this rash act of the populace began to give general disgust and repentance, especially to the young Athenians, ventured to lead the people to repeal it. He caused it to be reported that he was mad, and for some time kept his house; in this retirement he composed a poem, such as he thought would excite the multi-

---

[22] Yet it seems clear that he discriminated in the moral nature of offences.

"The few fragments of the Draconian tables which have reached us, far from exhibiting indiscriminate cruelty, introduce, for the first time, into the Athenian law, mitigating distinctions in respect to homicide; founded on the variety of concomitant circumstances." Grote, *Hist. of Greece,* vol. iii, p. 102.

It is difficult also to account for the popularity the author of so unpopular a system is reputed to have enjoyed till his death.

tude; then watching his opportunity, during an assembly of the people, he ran into the Agora like one frantic, mounted on a rock, and read his poem to the people. Some of his friends, who were in the secret, were present, and ready to wonder and appland. The enthusiasm spread, the law was repealed, and an expedition sent under Solon's friends, which, being skilfully conducted, recovered the island. But the party of Cylon were still clamorous against the partisans of Megacles, for their breach of faith. Solon persuaded the accused to submit to a trial. They were condemned to banishment; but this punishment not being sufficient to appease the deity, the bones of those who had been executed were removed beyond the mountains.

During these troubles Salamis was retaken. Superstition now gained the ascendant; phantoms and omens were seen, and expiations and purifica-tions were necessary. Epimenides, a Cretan philosopher, of great reputation for religious knowledge, and an intimate friend of Solon, was invited to superintend the religion of Athens. Epimenides was the ostensible direc-tor, but Solon concerted with him the various improvements in jurispru-dence. By means of religious pomp, ceremony, sacrifices, and processions, he amused the people into some degree of order and suspension of their factions; but the tranquillity was not likely to be lasting. Three political parties existed,—one for democracy, composed of the landholders of the mountains; another for an aristocracy of the rich, consisting of the pos-sessors of the plain; a third preferred a mixture of oligarchy and democracy, consisting of the inhabitants of the coast, and the most disinterested men. There was another division of the people, into the parties of the rich and the poor. Dangerous convulsions were so apprehended, that many sober men thought the establishment of a tyranny, in one, necessary to prevent greater evils. Solon's reputation for wisdom and integrity was universal; and, as he had friends in all parties, they procured the place of archon, with power to reform the constitution. His first object was to reconcile the rich with the poor; this he accomplished by lowering the interest without annulling the debt,[23] and by taking from the creditor the exorbitant pow-

---

[23] The extent to which he went in his interference between the debtor and creditor, is a subject which, like almost every other connected with these times, has been much

ers over the person and family of the debtor. He found such a predilection for democracy in the minds of the citizens, that he preserved to every free Athenian his equal vote in the assembly of the people, which he made supreme in all cases, legislative, executive, and judicial. He had not, probably, tried the experiment of a democracy in his own family, before he attempted it in the city, according to the advice of Lycurgus; but was obliged to establish such a government as the people would bear, not that which he thought the best, as he said himself.

As the laws of Solon were derived from Crete and Egypt, were afterwards adopted by the Romans as their model, and have by them been transmitted to all Europe, they are a most interesting subject of inquiry; but it is not possible to ascertain exactly which were his, which were those of Epimenides or Theseus, or what was, in fact, the constitution of Athens. The first inquiry is, who were citizens? By a poll that was taken in the time of Pericles, they were found to be fourteen thousand persons. By another, in the time of Demetrius Phalereus, they were twenty-one thousand. At the same time, there were ten thousand freemen, consisting of foreigners and freed slaves, and four hundred thousand souls in actual bondage, who had no vote in the assembly of the people. The persons, therefore, who shared the power being not a tenth part of the nation,[24] were excused from labor, in agriculture as well as manufactures, and had time for education; they were paid, too, for attendance on public affairs, which enabled the poorer citizens to attend their duty. This is one circumstance which rendered a government so popular practicable for a time. Another was, the division of Attica into tribes and boroughs, or districts, like the

disputed. But the better opinion is, that the statement in the text is below the truth. He diminished the weight of the money of account more than a quarter part, and probably annulled, directly or indirectly, the mortgages on all lands. It may be doubted whether any more radical measure was ever adopted in legislation.

[24] This subject has been since very carefully examined by Boeckh, in his work on *The Public Economy of Athens,* and he makes the number of citizens of Attica twenty thousand, in a population of half a million. Clinton comes to the same result. *Fast. Hell.* vol. ii. appendix, p. 477.

There are about the same number of citizens at this time, 1851, in Boston, with a population of one hundred and forty thousand; and the proportion is smaller there than in other parts of Massachusetts, and the free States generally.

American counties, towns, and parishes, or the shires, hundreds, and tithings of England. The tribes, at first, were four, afterwards ten. Each tribe had its presiding magistrate, called *phylarchus,* analogous to the English Sheriff; and each borough, of which there were one hundred and seventy-four, its demarchus, like a constable or headborough. As the title of king was preserved to the high-priest, so the person presiding over the religion of each tribe was called *philobasileus,* king's friend, and was always appointed from among the nobly born, *eupatridæ.* Thus, religion was always in the hands of the aristocratical part of the community. As the oracles and priests were held by the people in so much sacred veneration, the placing them, with all their splendid shows and rites, always in the power of the aristocratical families, or persons of best education, was as great a check to the democracy as can well be imagined. It should be here recollected, too, that almost all these *eupatridæ,* or nobles, among the Greeks, were believed to be descended from the gods, nearly or remotely. Nobility, as well as royalty, was believed of divine right, because the gods and goddesses had condescended to familiar intercourse with women and men, on purpose to beget persons of a superior order to rule among nations. The superiority of priests and nobles was assumed and conceded with more consistency than it is in Poland, Switzerland, and Venice; and they must have had a proportional influence with the people.

Another check to this "authority in one centre," the nation, established by Solon, was countenanced by precedent introduced by Theseus, who divided the Attic people into three ranks. All magistrates were taken exclusively out of the first. Solon, by a new division, made four ranks, determined by property, and confined all magistracies to the first three. By this regulation, he excluded all those who had no will of their own, and were dependent on others; but by still allowing to the fourth, who were more numerous than all the others, their equal votes in the assembly of the people, he put all power into hands the least capable of properly using it; and, accordingly, these, by uniting, altered the constitution at their pleasure, and brought on the ruin of the nation. By these precautions, however, we see the anxiety of Solon to avail himself of every advantage of birth, property, and religion, which the people would respect, to balance the sovereign democracy. With the same view, he instituted a senate of one hundred persons out of each of the four tribes;[25] and this great council, to which he committed many of the powers of the archons, he hoped would have a weight which all the archons together had not been able to preserve. It was afterwards increased to five hundred, when the tribes were increased to ten, fifty out of each, and was then called the council of five hundred. They were appointed annually by lot; but certain legal qualifications were required, as well as a blameless life. The members of each tribe, in turn, for thirty-five days, had superior dignity and additional powers, with the title of *prytanes,* from whence the hall was called *Prytaneium.* The prytanes were by turns presidents, had the custody of the seal, and the keys of the treasury and citadel, for one day. The whole assembly formed the council of state of the commonwealth, and had the constant charge of its political affairs; the most important of which was the preparation of business for the assembly of the people, in which nothing was to be proposed which had not first been approved here. This was Solon's law; and, if it had been observed, would have formed a balance of such importance, that the commonwealth would have lasted longer and been more steady. But factious demagogues were often found to remind the people, that all authority was collected into one centre, and that the sovereign assembly was that centre; and a popular assembly being in all ages as much disposed, when unchecked by an absolute negative, to overleap the bounds of law and constitution as the nobles or a king, the laws of Solon

---

[25] The precise manner in which this body was formed is not clearly understood, and it has therefore given rise to much discussion. Niebuhr and some later writers maintain that the four Ionic tribes were exclusively of the class of Eupatridæ, in which ease, the senate must have been purely aristocratic, and made still more so by the property qualifications superinduced by Solon. The weight of authority must be conceded to be against this construction. But, whether this be correct or not, the effect of an exclusive distinction granted to a well-defined portion of the community was very certainly in the end to create, if it did not merely confirm, an aristocracy. To form an idea of the effect of it, we have only to imagine what would now be the case had a similar exception been made in favor of the first Puritan families of Massachusetts, or of the Dutch race in New York, or of the Quakers in Pennsylvania. That this must have been a consequence at Athens is clear, from the fact, that one of the first steps taken by Cleisthenes, the real founder of the democracy, was to do away with the confined division of the Ionic tribes, and to form the more extended one mentioned in the text, by which the nature of the senate was completely altered, and it was subjected to popular influences.

were often spurned, and the people demanded and took all power, whenever they thought proper.

Sensible that the business of approving and rejecting magistrates, receiving accusations, catalogues of fines, enacting laws, giving audience to ambassadors, and discussions of religion, would very often be uninteresting to many even of the most judicious and virtuous citizens; that every man's business is no man's; Solon[26] ordained it criminal in any one not to take a side in civil disturbances. Certain times were stated for the meeting of the general assembly; all gates were shut but that which led to it; fines were imposed for non-attendance; and a small pay allowed by the public to those who attended punctually at the hour. Nine *proedri* were appointed from the council; from whom the moderator, *epistates,* was appointed, too, by lot, with whom sat eleven *nomophylaces,* whose duty it was to explain the tendency of any motions contrary to the spirit of the constitution. The prytanes, too, had distinct and considerable powers in the assembly. When any change in the law was judged necessary by the people, another court, consisting of a thousand persons, called *nomothetæ,*[27] were directed to consider of the best mode of alteration, and prepare a bill; after all, five syndics were appointed to defend the old law before the new one could be enacted. A law, passed without, having been previously published, conceived in ambiguous terms, or contrary to any former law, subjected the proposer to penalties. It was usual to repeal the old law before a new one was proposed, and this delay was an additional security to the constitution.

The regular manner of enacting a law was this: a bill was prepared by the council; any citizen might, by petition or memorial, make a proposition to the *prytanes,* whose duty it was to present it to the council; if

[26] Mr. Grote, in his late work on Greece, assigns a different cause for this regulation,—the necessity of bringing such disturbances to an end as soon as possible, by the active interposition of the whole community.

[27] Many writers consider this court as one of the conservative checks upon the popular will devised by Solon. In fact, it became the lever by which to shake the whole system. It is scarcely possibly that a sagacious lawgiver could have made so great a mistake. The probability would seem to favor the idea, founded on the language of Aristotle, that Cleisthanes made some changes in the formation of the court which let in the democratic influence.

approved by them, it became a *proboulema;* and, being written on a tablet, was exposed for several days for public consideration, and at the next assembly read to the people; then proclamation was made by a crier: "Who of those above fifty years of age chooses to speak?" When these had made their orations, any other citizen, not disqualified by law, for having fled from his colors in battle, being deeply indebted to the public, or convicted of any crime, had an opportunity to speak. But the *prytanes* had a general power to enjoin silence on any man, subject, no doubt, to the judgment of the assembly. Without this, debates might be endless. When the debate was finished, the crier, at the command of the *proedri,* proclaimed that the question waited the determination of the people, which was given by holding up the hand. In some uncommon cases, particularly of impeachments, the votes were given privately, by casting pebbles into urns. The *proedri* examined the votes and declared the majority. The *prytanes* dismissed the assembly. Every one of these precautions demonstrated Solon's conviction of the necessity of balances to such an assembly, though they were found by experience to be all ineffectual.

From the same solicitude for balances against the turbulence of democracy, he restored the court of Areopagus, improved its constitution, and increased its power. He composed it of those who had held with reputation the office of archon and admitted them into this dignity and authority for life. The experience, the reputation, and permanency of these Areopagites must have been a very powerful check. From the Areopagus alone, no appeal lay to the people; yet if they chose to interfere, no balancing power existed to resist their despotic will. The constitution authorized the Areopagus to stop the judicial decrees of the assembly of the people; annul an acquittal, or grant a pardon; to direct all draughts on the public treasury; to punish impiety, immorality, and disorderly conduct; to superintend the education of youth; punish idleness; to inquire by what means men of no property or employment maintained themselves. The court sat in the night, without light,[28] that the members might be less

---

[28] This statement depends upon authority comparatively modern, and somewhat questionable.

liable to prejudice. Pleaders were confined to simple narration of facts and application of laws, without ornaments of speech or address to the passions. Its reputation for wisdom and justice was so high, that Cicero said, the commonwealth of Athens could no more be governed without the court of Areopagus, than the world without the providence of God.

The urgent necessity for balance to a sovereign assembly, in which all authority, legislative, executive, and judicial, was collected into one centre, induced Solon, though in so small a state, to make his constitution extremely complicated. No less than ten courts of judicature, four for criminal causes, and six for civil, besides the Areopagus and general assembly, were established at Athens. In conformity to his own saying, celebrated among those of the seven wise men, that "the most perfect government is that where an injury to any one is the concern of all," he directed that, in all the ten courts, causes should be decided by a body of men, like our juries, taken from among the people; the archons only presiding like our judges. As the archons were appointed by lot, they were often but indifferent lawyers, and chose two persons of experience to assist them. These, in time, became regular constitutional officers, by the name of *Paredri,* assessors. The jurors were paid for their service, and appointed by lot. This is the glory of Solon's laws. It is that department which ought to belong to the people at large; they are most competent for this; and the property, liberty, equality, and security of the citizens, all require that they alone should possess it. Itinerant judges, called *the Forty,* were appointed to go through the counties, to determine assaults, and civil actions under a certain sum.

Every freeman was bound to military service. The multitude of slaves made this necessary, as well as practicable. Rank and property gave no other distinction than that of serving on horseback.

The fundamental principle of Solon's government was the most like M. Turgot's idea of any we have seen. Did this prevent him from establishing different orders and balances? Did it not render necessary a greater variety of orders, and more complicated checks, than any in America? Yet all were insufficient, for want of the three checks, absolute and independent. Unless three powers have an absolute *veto,* or negative, to every law, the

constitution can never be long preserved; and this principle we find verified in the subsequent history of Athens, notwithstanding the oath he
had the address and influence to persuade all the people to take, that they
would change none of his institutions for ten years. Soon after his departure, the three parties of the highlands, lowlands, and coasts began to
show themselves afresh. These were, in fact, the party of the rich, who
wanted all power in their own hands, and to keep the people in absolute
subjection, like the nobles in Poland, Venice, Genoa, Bern, Soleure, &c.; the
democratical party, who wanted to abolish the council of five hundred, the
Areopagus, the ten courts of judicature, and every other check, and who,
with furious zeal for equality, were the readiest instruments of despotism;
and the party of judicious and moderate men, who, though weaker than
either of the others, were the only balance between them. This last party,
at this time, was supported by the powerful family of the Alcmæonides,
of whom Megacles, the chief, had greatly increased the wealth and splendor of his house, by marrying the daughter of the tyrant of Sicyon, and
had acquired fame by victories in the Olympian, Pythian, and Isthmian
games. The head of the oligarchic party was Lycurgus, not the Spartan
lawgiver. The democratical party was led by Pisistratus, claiming descent
from Codrus and Nestor, with great abilities, courage, address, and reputation for military conduct in several enterprises. Upon Solon's return,
after an absence of ten years, he found prejudices deeply rooted; attachment to their three leaders dividing the whole people. He was too old to
direct the storm. The factions continued their manœuvres; and at length
Pisistratus, by an artifice, became master of the commonwealth. Wounding
himself and his horses, he drove his chariot violently into the Agora, where
the assembly of the people was held, and, in a pathetic speech, declared
"that he had been waylaid as he was going into the country; that it was for
being the man of the people that he had thus suffered; that it was no
longer safe for any man to be a friend of the poor; it was not safe for him
to live in Attica, unless they would take him under their protection." Aris-
ton, one of his partisans, moved for a guard of fifty men, to defend the person of the friend of the people, the martyr for their cause. In spite of the
utmost opposition of Solon, though Pisistratus was his friend, this point

was carried. Pisistratus, with his guards, seized the citadel; and, his opponents forced into submission or exile, he became the first man, and from this time is called the Tyrant of Athens; a term which meant a citizen of a republic, who by any means obtained a sovereignty over his fellow-citizens. Many of them were men of virtue, and governed by law, after being raised to the dignity by the consent of the people; so that the term tyrant was arbitrarily used by the ancients, sometimes to signify a lawful ruler, and sometimes an usurper.

Pisistratus, of whom Solon said, "Take away his ambition, cure him of his lust of reigning, and there is not a man of more virtue, or a better citizen," changed nothing in the constitution. The laws, assembly, council, courts of justice, and magistrates, all remained; he himself obeyed the summons of the Areopagus, upon the charge of murder. Solon trusted to his old age against the vengeance of the tyrant, and treated him in all companies with very imprudent freedoms of speech. But Pisistratus carried all his points with the people; and had too much sense to regard the venerable legislator, or to alter his system. He returned his reproaches with the highest respect; and gained upon him, according to some authors, to condescend to live with him in great familiarity, and assist him in his administration. Others say that Solon, after having long braved the tyrant's resentment, and finding the people lost to all sense of their danger, left Athens and never returned.

Solon died at the age of eighty, two years after the usurpation. The usurper soon fell. The depressed rival chiefs, Megacles and Lycurgus, uniting their parties, expelled him; but the confederated rivals could not agree. Megacles proposed a coalition with Pisistratus, and offered him his daughter in marriage. The condition was accepted; but the people in assembly must be gained. To this end they dressed a fine girl with all the ornaments and armor of Minerva, and drove into the city, heralds proclaiming before them, "O Athenians, receive Pisistratus, whom Minerva honoring above all men, herself conducts into your citadel." The people believed the maid to be a goddess, worshipped her, and received Pisistratus again into the tyranny.

Is this government, or the waves of the sea?

But Pisistratus was soon obliged to retire to Eretria, and leave the party of Megacles masters of Athens. He strengthened his connections; and in the eleventh year of this his second banishment, he returned to Attica with an army, and was joined by his friends. The party of Megacles met him with another army, ill disciplined and commanded, from the city, were attacked by surprise and defeated. Pisistratus proclaimed that none need fear who would return peaceably home. The known honor, humanity, and clemency of his character, procured him confidence; his enemies fled, and he entered the city without opposition. He made no fundamental change in the constitution, though, as head of a party, he had the principal influence. He depended upon a large fortune of his own and a good understanding with Thebes and Argos to support him in it. He died in peace, and left his son successor to his influence. Both his sons, Hippias and Hipparchus, were excellent characters; and arts, agriculture, gardening, and literature, as well as wisdom and virtue, were singularly cultivated by the whole race of these tyrants. Harmodius and Aristogiton, however, conspired the death both of Hippias and Hipparchus; the latter was killed, and Hippias was led to severities. Many Athenians were put to death. Hippias, to strengthen his interest with foreign powers, married his only daughter to the son of the Tyrant of Lampsacus. Her epitaph shows that the title of tyrant was not then a term of reproach,—"This dust covers Archedice, daughter of Hippias, in his time the first of the Greeks. Daughter, sister, wife, and mother of tyrants, her mind was never elated to arrogance."

The opposite party were watchful to recover Athens, and to increase their interest with the other Grecian states for that end. The temple of Delphi was burnt. The Alcmæonides, to ingratiate themselves with the oracle, the Amphictyons, and all Greece, rebuilt it with Parian marble, instead of Porine stone, as they had contracted to do, without asking any additional price. The consequence was, that whenever the Lacedæmonians consulted the oracle, the answer always concluded with an admonition to give liberty to Athens. At length the oracle was obeyed; and, after some variety of fortune, the Alcmæonides, aided by Cleomenes the Spartan, prevailed, and Hippias retired to Sigeium.

It was one maxim of the Spartans, constantly to favor aristocratical power; or rather, wherever they could, to establish an oligarchy. For in every Grecian city there were always an aristocratical, oligarchical, and democratical faction. Whenever the Grecian states had a war with one another, or a sedition within themselves, the Lacedæmonians were ready to interfere as mediators. They conducted the business generally with great caution, moderation, and sagacity; but never lost sight of their view to extend the influence of their state; nor of their favorite measure for that end, the encouragement of aristocratical power, or rather oligarchical; for a few principal families, indebted to Lacedæmon for their preëminence, and unable to retain it without her assistance, were the best instruments for holding the state in alliance. This policy they now proposed to follow at Athens. Cleisthenes, son of Megacles, head of the Alcmæonides, was the first person of the commonwealth. Having no great abilities,[29] a party was formed against him under Isagoras, with whom most of the principal people joined. The party of Cleisthenes was among the lower sort, who being all powerful in the general assembly, he made by their means some alterations in the constitution favoring his own influence. Cleisthenes was now Tyrant of Athens, as much as Pisistratus had been. In the contests of Grecian factions, the alternative was generally victory, exile, or death; the inferior party, therefore, resorted sometimes to harsh expedients. Isagoras and his adherents applied to Lacedæmon. Cleomenes, violent in his temper, entered with zeal into the cause of Isagoras, and sent a herald to Athens, by whom he imperiously denounced banishment against Cleisthenes and his party, on the old pretence of criminality for the execution of the partisans of Cylon. Cleisthenes obeyed. Exalted by this proof of a dread of Spartan power, Cleomenes went to Athens with a small military force, and banished seven hundred families at once.

Such was Athenian liberty.

---

[29] The tendency among modern scholars who have pursued their investigations into the nature of the institutions of Greece with extraordinary industry, is to consider Cleisthenes as the real author of the democratic system of ancient Athens. He scarcely could have been a man of "no great abilities."

Grote, *Hist. of Greece,* vol. iv. p. 186.

He was then proceeding to change the constitution to suit the views of Spartan ambition, by dissolving the council of five hundred, and committing the whole power to a new council of three hundred, all partisans of Isagoras. Athens was not so far humbled. The five hundred resisted, and excited the people, who flew to arms, and besieged Cleomenes and Isagoras in the citadel; who the third day surrendered, upon condition that the Lacedæmonians might depart in safety. Isagoras went with them. Many of his party were executed, and Cleisthenes and the exiled families returned; but conscious of their danger from their hostile fellow-citizens in concert with Lacedæmon, they sent to solicit an alliance with Artaphernes, the satrap of Persia. The answer was, If they would give earth and water to Darius they might be received, otherwise they must depart. The ambassadors, considering the imminent danger of their country and party, consented to these humiliating terms. Although Athens was distracted with domestic factions, and pressed with the fear of an attack from Cleomenes, the conduct of her ambassadors, in acknowledging subjection to the Persian king, in hopes of his protection, was highly reprobated upon their return; and it does not appear that Persian assistance was further desired. Yet the danger which hung over Athens was very great. Cleomenes, bent on revenge, formed a confederacy against them, of the Thebans, Corinthians, and Chalcidians. These could not agree, and the Athenians gained some advantages of two of them.

Cleomenes then pretended that Sparta had acted irreligiously in expelling Hippias, who ought to be restored; because, when he was besieged in the citadel at Athens, he had discovered in collusion between the Delphic priests and the Alcmæonides. Sparta was willing to restore Hippias; but Corinth, their ally; was not. Hippias, despairing of other means, now in his turn applied to Persia, and brought upon his country the Persian war; from which it was delivered by Miltiades, at the battle of Marathon. Miltiades became the envy of the Alcmæonid family. Xanthippus, one of the principal men of Athens, who had married a daughter of Megacles, the great opponent of Pisistratus, conducted a capital accusation against him. He was condemned in a fine of fifty talents, more than he was worth. His wound, which prevented him from attending the trial, mortified, and he died in prison. In order to brand the family of Pisistratus, the fame of Harmodius and Aristogiton was now cried up. They had assassinated Hipparchus from mere private revenge; but they were now called asserters of public liberty. The tyrannicides, as it was called, was celebrated by songs, statues, ceremonies, and religious festivals.

It must be acknowledged that every example of a government, which has a large mixture of democratical power, exhibits something to our view which is amiable, noble, and I had almost said, divine. In every state hitherto mentioned, this observation is verified. What is contended for, is, that the people in a body cannot manage the executive power, and, therefore, that a simple democracy is impracticable; and that their share of the legislative power must be always tempered with two others, in order to enable them to preserve it, as well as to correct its rapid tendency to abuse. Without this, they are but a transient glare of glory, which passes away like a flash of lightning, or like a momentary appearance of a goddess to an ancient hero, which, by revealing but a glimpse of celestial beauties, only excited regret that he had ever seen them.

The republic of Athens, the schoolmistress of the whole civilized world for more than three thousand years, in arts, eloquence, and philosophy, as well as in politeness and wit, was, for a short period of her duration, the most democratical commonwealth of Greece. Unfortunately her history, between the abolition of her kings and the time of Solon, has not been circumstantially preserved. During this period, the people seem to have endeavored to collect all authority into one centre, and to have avoided a composition of orders and balances as carefully as M. Turgot. But that centre was a group of nobles, not the nation. Their government consisted in a single assembly of nine archons chosen annually by the people. But even here was a check; for by law the archons must all be chosen out of the nobility. But this form of government had its usual effects, in introducing anarchy, and such a general profligacy of manners, that the people could at length be restrained from even the most ordinary crimes by nothing short of the last punishment. Draco accordingly proposed a law; by which death should be inflicted on every violation of the law. Humanity shuddered at so shocking a severity! and the people chose rather that all offences should go unpunished, than that a law thus written in blood, as they termed it both in horror and contempt, should be executed.

Confusions increased, and divided the nation into three factions; and their miseries became so extreme, that they offered Solon an absolute monarchy. He had too much sense, as well as virtue, to accept it; but employed his talents in new-modelling the government. Sensible, from experience, of the fatal effects of a government too popular, he wished to introduce an aristocracy, moderated like that of Sparta; but thought the habits and prejudices of the people too strong to bear it. The archons he continued; but, to balance their authority, he erected a senate of four hundred, to be chosen by ballot of the people.[30] He also revived the court of Areopagus, which had jurisdiction in criminal cases, and the care of religion. He excluded from the executive or the magistracy all the citizens who were not possessed of a certain fortune; but vested the sovereignty in a legislative assembly of the people, in which all had a right to vote. In this manner Solon attempted a double balance. The Areopagus was to check the executive in the hands of the archons; and the senate of four hundred, the fickleness and fire of the people. Every one must see that these devices would have been no effectual control in either case; yet they were better than none. It was very right that the people should have all elections; but democratical prejudices were so inveterate, that he was obliged not only to make them, assembled in a body, an essential branch of the legislature, but to give them cognizance of appeals from all the superior courts. Solon himself, in his heart, must have agreed with Anacharsis, that this constitution was but a cobweb to bind the poor, while the rich would easily break through it. Pisistratus soon proved it, by bribing a party, procuring himself a guard, demolishing Solon's whole system before his eyes, and establishing a single tyranny. The tyrant was expelled several times by the opposition, but as often brought back, and he finally transmitted his

---

[30] This is declared by Wachsmuth not to be sustained by any authority, as it certainly conflicts with the statement made a few pages back, that they were chosen by lot. Dr. Thirlwall, on the other hand, maintains that they were elected. The truth is, that very little is known of the constitution of Solon's senate. Wachsmuth, *Historical Antiquities of the Greeks,* translated by E. Woolrych, vol. i. p. 378; Thirlwall, *History of Greece,* vol. ii. p. 42.

monarchy to his sons. One of these was assassinated by Harmodius and Aristogiton; and the other was driven into banishment by the opposition, aided by the neighboring state, Sparta. He fled to the Persians, excited Darius against his country, and was killed at Marathon.

These calamities inspired the people with such terrors of a single tyrant, that, instead of thinking to balance effectually their "orders," they established the ostracism, to prevent any man from becoming too popular. A check indeed, but a very injudicious one; for it only banished their best men. History nowhere furnishes so frank a confession of the people themselves, of their own infirmities and unfitness for managing the executive branch of government, or an unbalanced share of the legislature, as this institution. The language of it is, "We know ourselves so well, that we dare not trust our own confidence and affections, our own admiration and gratitude for the greatest talents and sublimest virtues. We know our heads will be turned, if we suffer such characters to live among us, and we shall always make them kings." What more melancholy spectacle can be conceived even in imagination, than that inconstancy which erects statues to a patriot or a hero one year, banishes him the next, and the third erects fresh statues to his memory?[31]

Such a constitution of government, and the education of youth which follows necessarily from it, always produce such characters as Cleon and Alcibiades; mixtures of good qualities enough to acquire the confidence of a party, and bad ones enough to lead them to destruction; whose lives show the miseries and final catastrophe of such imperfect polity.

From the example of Athens, it is clear that the government of a single assembly of archons, chosen by the people, was found intolerable; that, to remedy the evils of it, Solon established four several orders,—an assembly of the people, an assembly of four hundred, an assembly of archons, and the Areopagus; that he endeavored to balance one singly by another, instead of forming his balance out of three branches. Thus, these attempts

[31] Mr. Grote's defence of the ostracism as a conservative feature of the government, on the grounds recited in the text, in deserving of consideration on account of its ingenuity, even if it do not create entire conviction of its soundness. *History of Greece,* vol. iii. pp. 200–215.

at an equilibrium were ineffectual; produced a never-ending fluctuation in the national councils; continual factions, massacres, proscriptions, banishment, and death of the best citizens. And the history of the Peloponnesian war, by Thucydides, informs us how the raging flames at last burnt out.

The people in each of the United States, have, after all, more real authority than they had in Athens.[32] Planted, as they are, over large dominions, they cannot meet in one assembly, and, therefore, are not exposed to those tumultuous commotions, like the raging waves of the sea, which always agitated the ecclesia at Athens. They have all elections of governor and senators, as well as representatives, so prudently guarded, that there is scarce a possibility of intrigue. The property required in a representative, senator, or even a governor, is so small, that multitudes have equal pretensions to be chosen. No election is confined to any order of nobility, or to any great wealth; yet the legislature is so divided into three branches, that no law can be passed in a passion, nor any inconsistent with the constitution. The executive is excluded from the two legislative assemblies; and the judiciary power is independent, as well as separate from all. This will be a fair trial, whether a government so popular can preserve itself. If it can, there is reason to hope for all the equality, all the liberty, and every other good fruit of an Athenian democracy, without any of its ingratitude, levity, convulsions, or factions.

[32] "There was no want, at Athens, of well-conceived and strict regulations; but what is the use of provident measures, where the spirit of the administration is bad? Men have at all times been unjust, and covetous, and unprincipled, and above all, the Greeks distinguished themselves for the uncontrolled gratification of their own desires, and their contempt for the happiness of others. If any competent judge of moral actions will contemplate their character without prejudice, and unbiased by their high intellectual endowments, he will find that their private life was unstable, and devoid of virtue; that their public life was a tissue of restless intrigues and passions; and, what was the worst of all, that there existed, to a far greater degree than in the Christian world, a want of moral principle, and a harshness and cruelty in the popular mind. The display of noble actions, it is true, has ceased, and will never re-appear with the same brilliancy; but the principles of the majority of mankind have been elevated, even if we allow that some distinguished individuals in ancient times were as pure as the most exalted characters in modern days; and in this general elevation consists the progress of mankind." Boeckh's *Public Economy of Athens,* translated by Lewis, p. 194.

...

CHAPTER VIII.

Ancient Aristocratical Republics.

ROME.

DIONYSIUS HALICARNASSENSIS, in the speech which he puts into the mouth of Valerius, has not only given us his own judgment, that the most perfect form of government is that which consists of an equal mixture of monarchy, aristocracy, and democracy, but he has repeated the same sentiment, in his own name, in other parts of his work. In the seventh section of his second book of the Roman Antiquities, he says of Romulus, that he was extremely capable of instituting the most perfect form of government. And, again; "I shall first speak of the form of government he instituted, which I look upon, of all others, to be the most self-sufficient to answer all the ends both of peace and war." This is a mixture of monarchy, aristocracy, and democracy, extolled by Polybius; and is nearly the same with that of Lycurgus, instituted at Sparta about a hundred years before. As the constitutions of Rome and Sparta lasted so many centuries longer than others of Greece and Italy, and produced effects so amazing upon the human character, we may rationally ascribe that duration and those effects to this composition, although the balance was very imperfect in both. The legal power, both of the kings and people, in both, was unequal to that of the senate, and, therefore, the predominant character in both was aristocracy. In Sparta, the influence of the monarchy and democracy was derived chiefly from the oath taken by the kings and ephori to support each other. An authority founded thus, in opinion, in religion, or rather in superstition, and not in legal power, would keep the senate in some awe, but not in any certain restraint.

Romulus divided all the people into three parts, and appointed a person of the first rank to be the chief of each of them. Then he subdivided each of these into ten others, and appointed as many of the bravest men to be the leaders of these. The greater divisions he called *tribes*, and the lesser *curiæ*. The commanders of the tribes were called *tribuni;* and those of the curiæ, *curiones.* He then divided the land into thirty portions, and gave one of them to each curia. He distinguished those who were eminent for their birth, virtues, and riches; and to these he gave the name of *fathers.* The obscure, the mean, and the poor, he called *plebeians,* in imitation of the government at Athens, where, at that time, those who were distinguished by their birth and fortune, were called "well-born," to whom the administration of government was committed; and the rest of the people, who had no share in it, "husbandmen." Romulus appointed the patricians to be priests, magistrates, and judges. The institution by which every plebeian was allowed to choose any patrician for his patron,[33] introduced an intercourse of good offices between these orders, made the patricians emulate each other in acts of civility and humanity to their clients, and contributed to preserve the peace and harmony of Rome in so remarkable a manner, that, in all the contests which happened for six hundred and twenty years, they never proceeded to bloodshed.

The king, according to the institution of Romulus, had several important functions, namely,—1. Supremacy in religion, ceremonies, sacrifices, and worship. 2. The guardianship of the laws, and administration of justice, in all cases, whether founded on the law of nature, or the civil law; he was to take cognizance of the greatest crimes in person, leaving the lesser to the senate; and to observe that no errors were committed in their judgments; he was to assemble both the senate and the people; to deliver his opinion first, and pursue the resolutions of the majority. Romulus, however, wisely avoided that remarkable Spartan absurdity of two kings.

The senate were to deliberate and determine, by a majority of votes, all questions which the king should propose to them. This institution, also, Romulus took from the constitution of the Lacedæmonians. The kings, in both constitutions, were so far from being absolute, that they had not the whole executive power, nor any negative upon the legislature; in short, the whole power of the government was vested in the senate.

---

[33] Upon this relation, as well as the story of the early kings, much has been written of late years, calculated to throw doubt upon former impressions, but not to substitute entirely clear ideas.

The people had three privileges,—to choose magistrates (yet all the great employments must be confined to patricians); to enact laws; and to determine concerning war, when proposed by the king. But the concurrence of the senate being necessary to give a sanction to their decisions, their power was not without control.

To separate the executive from the legislative power, and the judicial from both, and to give the king, the senate, and people, each a negative in the legislature, is so simple, and to us appears so obvious an improvement of this plan, that it is surprising it did not occur to Romulus as well as to Lycurgus; but, in those early times, perhaps neither kings nor nobles, nor people were willing to have their prerogatives and privileges so exactly ascertained. The nobles in both nations had almost all the influence, and were no doubt as jealous of royal as they were of popular power. It is certain that, although the government was called monarchical, it was in reality aristocratical in a high degree. There is a remarkable example of aristocratical art in the manner of obtaining the determination of the people. They were not permitted to vote in one common assembly; they were called in their curiæ; the majority of votes in a curia decided its voice; and a majority of curiæ was the resolve of the whole people.

Had Romulus died in peace, and left a son, his monarchy would probably have descended in his family. But a contest arose immediately here (as it has done in all other nations where the people had not a negative, and where the executive power has been partly in the hands of a king, and partly in a senate,) between the king and the nobles; and Romulus was put to death by the patricians for aiming, as they pretended, at more power than his share. This enabled the patricians to carry their first point; for it was always the first point of the aristocracy to make the first magistrate elective; in this they are always at first joined by the people; but, after seeing the use which the nobles make of these elections a few times, the people themselves have always made it hereditary.

Numa was chosen; a man of peace, piety, and humanity, who had address enough to make the nobles and people believe that he was married to the goddess Egeria, and received from his celestial consort all his laws and measures.

Tullus Hostilius, a man of great merit, was chosen in his stead; but after a glorious, at least a victorious, reign of thirty-two years, was murdered by the patricians, headed by Ancus Marcius, grandson of Numa by his only daughter, who thought his family right prior to that of Tullius.

Ancus was elected king, and died a natural death.

Lucius Tarquinius, after a reign of thirty-eight years, in which he had enlarged the territory, beautified the city, and shown himself worthy of the crown, was assassinated in his palace by the two sons of Ancus Marcius, who had learned the family policy. But their project was unfortunate; the people loved Lucius, execrated the instruments of the murder, banished the two sons of Ancus, and confiscated their estates.

Servius Tullius, who had married the daughter of Lucius, was now elevated to the throne by the people, much against the will of the senate and patricians, because Lucius was not one of them, but of Greek extraction. Tullius was chiefly supported by the people, always disagreeable to the patricians, who held his advancement to the throne to be illegal. The administration of Tullius is an artful system of duplicity, to preserve his character of the man of the people, and, at the same time, appease the fury of the patricians, by really undermining the authority of the people, and throwing the whole power into their hands.[34] In pursuance of his principle, to please both sides, he made excellent equitable regulations for registering the people, establishing a militia, and proportioning the burdens of war according to the property and abilities of all ranks; but he subdivided the six classes into one hundred and ninety-three centuries. The first class was composed wholly of the rich, and contained ninety-

---

[34] "Deinde equitum magno numero ex omni populi summa separato, reliquum populum distribuit in quinque classes, senioresque a junioribus divisit; eosque ita disparavit, ut suffragia non in multitudinis sed in locupletium potestate essent; curavitque, quod semper in republica tenendum est, ne plurimum valeant plurimi." Cicero, *De Rep.* ii. 22. [King Servius reorganizes the Roman state: "Then after a large number of knights had been selected from the whole number of the people, he distributed the rest of the people into five classes, and divided the old men from the young; and he fixed it so that votes would not be in the power of the multitude but in that of the wealthy; and he took care—something that should always be preserved in a republic—that the many not have too much power." Cicero, *On the Republic* II, xxii, 39. Ed.]

eight of the centuries. If the centuries of the first class were unanimous, as they generally were, they carried every point by a majority of three; if they disagreed, the centuries of the second class were called; if they disagreed, the third came forward; and so on, till ninety-seven centuries agreed. If the numbers continued equal, ninety-six to ninety-six, the sixth class was called, which was composed wholly of the poorest people, and contained but one century; but even the votes of the fourth class were rarely called for, and the votes of the fifth and sixth were generally useless. When the people voted by curiæ, the vote of every citizen was given, and, as the poor were most numerous, they were always sure of a large majority; but, when thus taken by centuries, that numerous body of the poor, which composed the sixth century, were wholly insignificant, and those of the fifth and fourth very nearly so. By changing the votes from curiæ to centuries, Tullius wholly changed the fundamental constitution, and threw the elections of magistrates, civil and military, the power of enacting and repealing laws, declaring war, and making peace, all into the power of the rich patricians. The people had not sense enough to see this; nor to see another thing of more importance, namely,—that the king had been driven to the necessity of this artful flattery of the patricians, by his not being independent of them, and by their sharing with him in the executive power. Tullius had two daughters, married to the grandsons of his predecessor, Aruns and Tarquinius. The patricians were still caballing against Tullius, and set up Tarquin, one of his sons-in-law, against him; but as a majority were not for his deposition, Tarquin and his impious and incestuous wife joined the cabal in the murder of her first husband and her father. Tarquin, in time, murdered on all hands, patricians and plebeians. He was expelled by Brutus.

This whole history, from Romulus to Tarquin, is one continued struggle of the noble families for the first place; and another unanswerable proof of the necessity of having three orders, and each order independent, in order to form an effectual equilibrium. The people were very little regarded by the senate or patricians; the kings only now and then courted the people for support against their rivals among the patrician families. The tyranny of Tarquin made the name of *king* odious and unpopular.

The patricians, who were the principal conductors of the revolution, took advantage of this—for what? To restore and improve Romulus's plan of a mixed government? No; but to establish their favorite aristocracy upon the ruins of monarchy. Two consuls, in imitation of the two Spartan kings, were to be elected annually, by the votes of the people, which carried the name of a democratical power; but the votes were taken by centuries, not by tribes, which made the patricians masters of the elections, and constituted an aristocracy in reality. From this moment a haughty faction of selfish patricians appears, who affected to despise the people, to reduce them to servitude, and establish a despotic oligarchy. The people had suffered their prejudices to blind them so far as to be tricked out of their king, who was at least a better friend to them than the patricians were; and now, the contests were wholly between patricians and plebeians. The former had got the consuls, and consequently the executive power, as much in their hands as ever the nobles in Venice had their doge, or as the nobles in Poland have their king.

The plebeians were now in a most wretched situation. They were obliged to serve in the wars, to keep out the Tarquins and their allies, at their own expense, which frequently obliged them to borrow money at exorbitant interest of the patricians, who had engrossed the greater part of the wealth; and, as the country was often ravaged by the enemy, many lost all their effects. Unable to pay the principal, with loads of interest accumulated upon interest, they were frequently confined in chains by their creditors, and scourged with whips; for the law, to which they had foolishly consented, had made the debtor a slave to the creditor. The people began to demand an abolition of debts; the senate appointed a dictator. A confusion of foreign wars and domestic dissensions ensues, till we come to the story so beautifully told by Livy and Dionysius, of the man who had been in twenty-eight battles, who appeared before the people, and showed on his back the bleeding scars inflicted by a merciless creditor. At this time, the patricians had plunged into their usual difficulty, a violent contest among themselves, between a furious headlong party, which always appears for an oligarchy, and the moderate men, who desire to continue the aristocracy; the young patricians generally follow the haughty Claudius, and the mild Valerius courts the people. The oligarchy prevails, and the decemvirate is established; their tyranny drives the people to the sacred mountain; and, at last, the tribunate was established.

Here is the first symptom of any system pursued by the people. This was a balance; but what kind of a balance? Nobody thought of another council, a house of representatives, who should have a negative; and, if they had, it would not have availed without a king; for such a new assembly would soon have been either wholly subjected to the senate, or would have voted it useless. In truth, the monarchical power being suppressed, and the executive authority, as well as legislative, being now only in the senate and people, a struggle commenced between these two.

The people were on the scramble for more power; and first obtained a law, that all laws passed in their assemblies by tribes, should have equal force with those made in the assembly by centuries; then, that all posts and dignities should be enjoyed by the plebeians equally with the patricians; and that the decrees of the people should have the same force, and affect the patricians in the same manner, as those passed by the senate. All this was very just, and only brought the democracy to an equality with the aristocracy; but whenever these two are equal in legal power, numbers will soon turn the balance in favor of the democracy, unless there is a third power to intervene. Accordingly it so happened here, and the people went on from step to step, increasing their own importance, and diminishing that of the senate, until it was found shut up in Utica; but, before this, the people were divided into parties, and Cæsar, at the head of one, passed the Rubicon, that is, set the most sacred law of his country at open defiance. From this time the government became a government of men, and the worst of men.

From this example, as from all others, it appears that there can be no government of laws without a balance, and that there can be no balance without three orders; and that even three orders can never balance each other, unless each in its department is independent and absolute. For want of this the struggle was first between the king and senate; in which case the king must always give way, unless supported by the people. Before the creation of tribunes, the people were in no sense independent, and, therefore, could not support the kings. After the abolition of kings, the senate had no balance either way, and accordingly became at once a tyrannical oligarchy. When the people demanded their right, and obtained a check, they were not satisfied; and grasped at more and more power, until they obtained all, there being no monarchical power to aid the senate. But the moment the power became collected into this one centre, it was found in reality split into three; and as Cæsar had the largest of the three shares, he instantly usurped the whole.

LACEDÆMON.

FROM the days of Homer to those of Lycurgus, the governments in Greece were monarchical in name and pretension, but aristocratical in reality. The archons were impatient of regal government, constantly struggling against their kings; and they had prevailed in every other city, except Sparta, to abolish the royal authority and substitute an aristocracy of archons in its place. In Lacedæmon, too, where there were eight-and-twenty archons contending against two kings, they had brought the whole country into the utmost confusion. The circumstance of two kings, which perhaps prolonged the regal power longer in Sparta than in any other city, originated in the fondness of a mother. Aristodemus, one of the descendants of Hercules, to whose share Laconia fell, upon the division of the Peloponnesus, after the return of that family from banishment, died leaving twin sons, Eurysthenes and Procles; their mother refusing to determine which had the right of primogeniture, it was agreed that both should succeed to the crown with equal authority, and that the posterity of each should inherit. The nobles took advantage of all the jealousies which arose between the two families, obliged each to court them, and from time to time to make them concessions, until the royal authority was lost; and as the archons could not agree, each party now began to court the people, and universal anarchy prevailed.

Lycurgus, of the family of Procles, and only in the tenth descent from Hercules, succeeded his brother Polydectes; but being told his brother's widow was with child, he declared himself protector only, and resigned the crown. Such a disinterested indifference to a crown in any one of royal or noble blood, was so unexampled in that age, that no wonder it was much admired and very popular. The ambitious princess, his sister, offered to marry him and remove out of his way the only competitor, by procuring an abortion. He deceived her by counterfeited tenderness; and diverted her from the thoughts of an abortion, by promising to take the disposition of the child upon himself when it should be born. The infant was sent to him, when at supper with the principal magistrates. He took it in his arms, and cried, "A king, Spartans, is born to you," and placed it in his own seat. The company were touched at the tenderness of the scene, and fell into a transport of enthusiasm, both of piety to the blood of Hercules, and admiration of the disinterested integrity of Lycurgus, who, like an able statesman, perpetuates the memory of the event, and the joy at it, by the name with which, upon the spot, he christens the boy Charilaus, *the people's joy.* But all this exalted merit, added to his acknowledged divine descent, and the undoubted possession of royal power, were not sufficient to overawe the jealousy of the nobles, a strong party of whom joined the irritated queen and her brother, and raised continual factions against him. Weary of cabals, and stimulated with a thirst for knowledge, he determined to travel; visited Crete and Egypt, the two sources of the theology and policy of Greece; and brought home with him, on his return to his own country, Thales, the poet, and the writings of Homer, with the resolution to adopt the martial discipline and political liberty which he read in the poet, and had seen exemplified in Crete. Nothing could be better calculated than his two poets, to inspire the nation with that enthusiasm which he wanted, and confirm the belief, that kings were from Jupiter, and beloved by him, excepting the response of the oracle, which he took care to procure. "Welcome, Lycurgus, to this happy place, thou favorite of heaven! I stand in doubt whether I shall pronounce thee god or man; inclining still to think thou art a god!"*

The disorders in Sparta were now become insupportable; the kings had as little authority as the laws. All parties, except the two kings, in despair of their private schemes, applied to the great legislator, pointed out

* Herodotus.

to all, by his divine original, the inspiration of Homer and Thales, his own integrity, wisdom, knowledge, and commanding authority over the minds of men, as well as his special divine mission pronounced by the oracle, to be the only man capable of new-modelling the constitution.

In Crete he had acquired a deep insight into human nature, at least he had informed himself fully of the length and breadth, the height and depth, of the passion of ambition in the human heart. That complication of affections, which is called by so many names, the love of esteem, of praise, of fame, of glory; that sense of honor in which Montesquieu tells us monarchies are founded; which Tacitus tells us made the ancient Teutons submit quietly to be sold by their inferiors, when they had gambled away their liberty; which at this day enforces so punctual a payment of debts of honor contracted at play; which supports against all laws throughout Europe the custom of duelling, and produces more suicides than any other cause; which is commonly known by the denomination of *the point of honor,* and may with as much propriety be called ambition, Lycurgus appears to have understood better than any other legislator, and to have made the foundation of his institution. For this reason, Plato with great propriety calls it "The ambitious republic."

Lycurgus in secret consulted the nobles, but not the kings; formed a powerful party, and called an assembly of the people, before whom his friends appeared in arms. Charilaus and Archelaus were not in the secret, but found themselves obliged to submit. What is all this but a body of nobles completing, by the aid of Lycurgus, that abolition of monarchy which they had been pursuing for ages, unrestrained by any legal check in the people, and unresisted by any adequate power in the crown? But what was his new institution?

In compliance with old prejudices, and from attachment to his family, he confirmed the two families on the throne, established the hereditary descent of the crown, but limited its authority. The kings were to continue high priests, to be commanders-in-chief of the armies, and presidents of the senate. Charilaus and Archelaus, terrified by the fate of all the other kings of Greece, agreed to accept of a certain, though limited authority, in lieu of pretensions more absolute and more precarious.

The ancient dignities of the nobles were confirmed and enlarged. A senate of eight-and-twenty of their chiefs was formed, at the head of whom the two kings were placed. To the people he committed the election of future senators. But as the present twenty-eight were for life, and the influence of kings and senators would be commonly used with great unanimity, in favor of the eldest son, to fill up a vacancy made by the death of his father; and as the people were not permitted to debate, their choice was perhaps★ little more than a consent by acclamation to a nomination made by the king, and amounted to the same thing with a hereditary house of peers. To this senate the whole executive power was committed, and the most important part of the legislative; for as all laws were to originate there only, they had a negative before debate. Here is indeed all authority nearly collected into one centre, and that centre the nobility; for the king was but the first among equals, having no negative upon the senate.

If the legislator had rested here, his institution would have been in effect a simple hereditary oligarchy, possessed of the whole legislative, executive, and judicial power, and probably as restless as ever, to reduce the kings to elections for life or years, then to take from them the power of religion, the command of armies, and lastly to change the title from king to archon, or from the family of Hercules to other houses. With a view to counterbalance this dangerous authority, he instituted assemblies of the people, but intrusted them only with the power of confirming or rejecting what the senate proposed, and expressly forbade them all debate. The citizens were to give their simple ayes or noes, without being allowed to speak, even so far as to give a reason for their vote. He instituted, moreover, as a farther check upon the senate, five magistrates to inspect the administration and maintain the constitution; to convoke, prorogue, and dissolve both the greater assembly of the people, composed of nine thousand inhabitants of the city, and the lesser, consisting of thirty thousand inhabitants of the country or inferior villages. These magistrates were called the *ephori,* and were to be annually appointed. But the lawgiver saw that the king and people were both too weak, and the senate would

★ "No authority for this 'perhaps.'"

still have power to scramble after both; he therefore contrived a kind of solemn alliance to be perpetually renewed between the monarchical and democratical branches, by which the senate might be awed into moderation. He ordered an oath to be taken every month, by the kings and the ephori. The former swore to observe the laws, and the latter swore, for themselves and the people whom they represented, to maintain the hereditary honors of the race of Hercules, to revere them as ministers of religion, to obey them as judges, and follow them as leaders. This was indeed a balance founded in opinion and in religion, though not a legal and independent check; as it was not a negative in either.

In this constitution, then, were three orders, and a balance, not indeed equal to that of England, for want of a negative in each branch; but the nearest resembling it of any we have yet seen. The kings, the nobles, the senate, and the people, in two assemblies, are surely more orders than a governor, senate, and house. The balance here attempted was as strong as religion operating on human nature could make it, though not equivalent to a negative in each of three branches. Another balance was attempted, in the rigorous separation of the city from the country, in two assemblies. It avoided the danger of jealousies between town and country in the deliberations of the people, and doubled the chances both of the monarchy and democracy, for preserving their importance in case of encroachments by the senate. If the senate and nobles should prevail in one assembly of the people, so far as to carry any unconstitutional point, the kings and ephori would find a resource in the other to lead them back. The Lacedæmonian republic may then, with propriety, be called monarchical, and had the three essential parts of the best possible government; it was a mixture of monarchy, aristocracy, and democracy. It failed, however, in that essential particular, the balance. The aristocracy had a legal power so eminent above that of king or people, that it would soon have annihilated both, if other precautions had not been taken, which destroyed all the real merit of this celebrated institution.

That the glory of the descendants of Hercules and of their republic might be the pride of every citizen, and that a superstitious attachment to both might be perpetuated, it was necessary to extinguish every other appetite, passion, and affection in human nature. The equal division of property; the banishment of gold and silver; the prohibition of travel and intercourse with strangers; the prohibition of arts, trades, and agriculture; the discouragement of literature; the public meals; the incessant warlike exercises; the doctrine that every citizen was the property of the state, and that parents should not educate their own children; although they served to keep up the constant belief of the divine mission of Lycurgus, and an enthusiastic passion for the glory of the republic, and the race of Hercules; and although they are celebrated by the aristocratical philosophers, historians, and statesmen of antiquity; must be considered as calculated to gratify his own family pride rather than promote the happiness of his people. Four hundred thousand slaves must be devoted to forty thousand citizens; weak and deformed children must be exposed; morality and humanity, as well as all the comforts, elegancies, and pleasures of life must be sacrificed to this glaring phantom of vanity, superstition, and ambition. Separated from the rest of mankind, they lived together, destitute of all business, pleasure, and amusement, but war and politics, pride and ambition; and these occupations and passions they transmitted from generation to generation, for seven hundred years; as if fighting and intriguing, and not life and happiness, were the end of man and society; as if the love of one's country and of glory were amiable passions, when not limited by justice and general benevolence; and as if nations were to be chained together forever, merely that one family might reign among them. Whether Lycurgus believed the descent of his ancestor from Jupiter, the divine inspiration of Homer and Thales, or the divinity of the Oracle, any more than Mahomet believed his divine mission, may well be doubted. Whether he did or not, he shackled the Spartans to the ambitious views of his family for fourteen successions of Herculean kings, at the expense of the continual disturbance of all Greece, and the constant misery of his own people. Amidst the contradictions of ancient and modern writers, that account has been followed concerning the institution of the ephori, which appears most favorable to Lycurgus.[35] The Roman

[35] "That opinion is continually gaining ground, which in the main regards Lycurgus as the regulator of existing institutions, and in particular instances only, as the author of original laws." Wachsmuth, *Historical Antiq. of the Greeks,* vol. i. p. 322.

tribunes, and perhaps the Venetian inquisitors, were borrowed from this institution.

Human nature perished under this frigid system of national and family pride. Population, the surest indication of national happiness, decreased so fast, that not more than one thousand old Spartan families remained, while nine thousand strangers had intruded, in spite of all their prohibitory laws. The conquest of Athens gave them a taste of wealth, and even the fear of the penalty of death could not restrain them from travelling. Intercourse with strangers brought in foreign manners. The ephori were sometimes bribed. Divisions arose between the two kings, Agis and Leonidas; one joined with the people, the other with the nobles, and the sedition proceeded to blood. Kings became so fond of subsidies from foreign powers, that Agesilaus received them from a King of Egypt, and his enemy at the same time. Agis was murdered by the order of the ephori, who, instead of honoring the blood of Hercules, according to their oath, took the sovereign power into their own hands. Here the balance broke; Cleomenes, who endeavored, like Agis, to restore the old laws and maxims, fell a sacrifice; and nothing appears afterwards in the history of Sparta but profligacy, tyranny, and cruelty, like that in Rome under the worst of the Cæsars.

The institution of Lycurgus was well calculated to preserve the independence of his country, but had no regard to its happiness, and very little to its liberty. As the people's consent was necessary to every law, it had so far the appearance of political liberty; but the civil liberty of it was little better than that of a man chained in a dungeon—a liberty to rest as he is. The influence of this boasted legislation on the human character was to produce warriors and politicians, and nothing else. To say that this people were happy, is to contradict every quality in human nature except ambition. They had no other gratification. Science and letters were sacrificed, as well as commerce, to the ruling passion; and Milton had no reason to "wonder how museless and unbookish they were, minding nought but the feats of war;" since it was not so much because Lycurgus was "addicted to elegant learning, or to mollify the Spartan surliness with smooth songs and odes, the better to plant among them law and civility," that he brought the scattered works of Homer from Ionia, and Thales from Crete; but merely to propagate his own and his family imposture. The plan was profound, and means were with great ability fitted to the end; but, as a system of legislation, which should never have any other end than the greatest happiness of the greatest number, *saving to all their rights,* it was not only the least respectable, but the most detestable in all Greece. To do it justice, however, it is much to be desired, that exercises like those established by Lycurgus, running, wrestling, riding, swimming, skating, fencing, dancing, should be introduced into public and private education in America, which would fortify the bodies and invigorate the minds of youth; instead of those sedentary amusements which debilitate, and are taking entire possession of society all over the world. The ladies, too, might honor some of these entertainments, though not all, with their presence and participation, to the great advantage of their own health, and that of posterity, without injury to their charms or their reputations. But, above all, the existence of an all-perfect Intelligence, the parent of nature, the wise and moral ruler of it; the responsibility of every subordinate intellectual and moral agent; a future state of rewards and punishments; and the sacred obligation of oaths, as well as of the relative duties of social life, cannot be too clearly fixed by rational arguments in the minds of all the citizens. In this respect Lycurgus merits praise.

But, as a civil and political constitution, taken all together, it is infinitely inferior to another, which Americans have taken for their model. The English constitution is the result of the most mature deliberation on universal history and philosophy. If Harrington's council of legislators had read over the history, and studied the constitution of every nation, ancient and modern, remarked the inconveniences and defects of each, and bent the whole force of their invention to discover a remedy for it, they would have produced no other regulations than those of the English constitution, in its theory, unless they had found a people so circumstanced as to be able to bear annual elections of the king and senate. This improvement, the Americans, in the present stage of society among them, have ventured on; sensible, however, of the danger, and knowing perfectly well a remedy, in case their elections should become turbulent. Of this, at present, there is no appearance.

...

CHAPTER IX

...

ITHACA.

THE court of Ithaca, in the absence of Ulysses, is an admirable example of the intrigues of the archons, and their insatiable ambition. The throne of Ithaca, and the sceptre of Laertes and former kings, were the objects which had so many charms in the eyes of the suitors; and Penelope's hand was chiefly courted, because that would reconcile the archon who should possess her to the superstition of the people, and enable him to wield the sceptre. The suitors deny the sceptre to be hereditary; and Telemachus himself is doubtful. He threatens, indeed, to call a council or assembly of the people; but is afraid to trust them, for fear they should set up some other Grecian prince, whose blood might be nearer that of their ancient kings.

> "To tempt the spouseless queen with am'rous wiles,
> Resort the nobles from the neighb'ring isles;
> From Samos, circled with th' Jonian main,
> Dulichium, and Zacynthus' aylvan reign.
> Ev'n with presumptuous hope her bed t' ascend,
> The lords of Ithaca their right pretend.
> . . . .
> My sentence hear; with stern distaste avow'd,
> To their own districts drive the suitor crowd.
> . . . .
> I, to the peers assembled, shall propose
> The firm resolve, I here in few disclose.
> No longer live the cankers of my court;
> All to your *several states* with speed resort;
> Waste in wild riot what *your land* allows,
> There ply the early feast and late carouse.
> Elect by Jove, his delegate of sway,
> With joyous pride the summons I'd obey.

. . . .

Should factious power dispute my lineal right,
Some *other Greeks* a fairer claim may plead,
To your pretence their title would precede.
At least, the sceptre lost, I still should reign
Sole o'er my vassals, and domestic train."★

. . . .

"If ruin to our royal race ye doom,
Be you the spoilers, and our wealth consume.
Then might we hope redress from juster laws,
And raise all Ithaca to aid our cause;
But while your sons commit th' unpunished wrong,
You make the arm of violence too strong."†
"To heaven, alone,
Refer the choice to fill the vacant throne.
Your patrimonial stores in peace possess,
Undoubted, all your filial claim confess.
Your private right should impious pow'r invade,
The peers of Ithaca would arm in aid."‡

It is thus agreed, on all hands, that, as one of the archons, his hereditary
title to his estates, vassals, and government, was indisputable. This was the
common cause of all the archons, and they would arm in support of the
claim of any one. But the throne and sceptre of Ithaca were to be disposed of by augury, by the will of Jove, signified by some omen. To this
Telemachus pays some respect; but still insists on his right of blood, and
says, that if the omen should be unfavorable to him, it would not promote the hopes of any of the archons of Ithaca; but some other Greeks,
nearer of kin to the royal blood, would set up their claims. The archons,
not likely to succeed in their scheme of getting the sceptre by the marriage of Penelope, nor by persuading Telemachus to submit the question
to Jupiter and his omens, and afraid to appeal to the people, or to call them

★ *Od.* i. 315–508.
† *Od.* ii. 83–88.
‡ *Od.* i. 509–514.

out in arms to dispute the succession, knowing the family of Laertes and Ulysses to be more popular than themselves, take the resolution to assassinate the young prince:—

> "But die he shall, and thus condemn'd to bleed,
> Be now the scene of instant death decreed.
>
> . . . .
>
> Wait ye, till he to arms in council draws
> The Greeks, averse too justly to our cause?
> Strike, ere, the states conven'd, the foe betray,
> Our murd'rous ambush on the wat'ry way.
> Or choose ye vagrant from their rage to fly,
> Outcasts of earth, to breathe an unknown sky?
>
> . . . .
>
> But if, submissive, you resign the sway,
> Slaves to a boy; go, flatter and obey;
> Retire we instant to our native reign,
> Nor be the wealth of kings consum'd in vain."★

Telemachus had before declared, that, if any archon of Ithaca, or any other Greek, obtained the sceptre, he would no longer remain in the confederation, but would reign separately over his paternal domain. Now, Antinous declares, that, if the rest of the archons submit to the boy, he will not, but will retire to his native archonship.

> "Amphinomus ascends,
> Who o'er Dulichium stretch'd his spacious reign,
> A land of plenty, bless'd with every grain.
>
> . . . .
>
> O friends, forbear, and be the thought withstood!
> 'Tis horrible to shed imperial blood;
> Consult we, first, th' all-seeing powers above,
> And the sure oracles of righteous Jove."†

★ *Od.* xvi. 386–405.
† *Od.* xvi. 409–419.

Neither in Poland nor in Venice was the aristocratical rage to render weak, unsteady, and uncertain the royal authority, more conspicuous than it was here. They were afraid of the people and the auguries; but neither was a legal check; and we shall see, hereafter, that these struggles of the archons very soon abolished every monarchy in Greece, even that of Sparta, until it was renewed, upon another plan, by Lycurgus. And the same progress of passions, through seditions, rebellions, and massacres, must forever take place in a body of nobles against the crown, where they are not effectually restrained by an independent people, known and established in the legislature, collectively or by representation.

That the Grecian kings, claiming from Jupiter, and supported by their anguries and bards, thought themselves absolute, and often punished the crimes of the archons very tyrannically, is true. Ulysses is an example of it. Instead of bringing the suitors to trial before the nation, or their peers, he shoots them all, without judge or jury, with his own bow. A more remarkable assertion of a claim to absolute monarchy cannot be imagined.

Antinous would retire to his native district, and spend his revenues among his own people, not consume his royal wealth by attendance at a court of a confederation which would be no longer to his taste. This was a popular sentiment in his own dominions; his people wished to have their king reside among them, and were very willing to have the confederacy broken. This principle it was that afterwards crumbled all the Greek confederations to dust.

The similitude between the ancient Greek monarchies, as they are generally called, though the predominance of aristocracy in all of them is very manifest, and the feudal aristocracies described by Tacitus, is very obvious. The democratical power is nevertheless much more regular, though not independent, in the latter; for, in addition to what is before quoted, it appears that the judicial authority was commonly exercised in national assemblies:—"Licet apud concilium accusare quoque, et discrimen capitis intendere. Distinctio pœnarum ex delicto; proditores et transfugas arboribus suspendunt; ignavos, et imbelles, et corpore infames, cœno ac palude, injectâ insuper crate, mergunt. Diversitas supplicii illuc respicit, tanquam scelera ostendi opporteat dum puniuntur, flagitia abscondi. Sed et levioribus delictis, pro modo, pœna; equorum pecorumque numero convicti multantur; pars multæ regi, vel civitati, pars ipsi qui vindicatur, vel propinquis ejus exsolvitur."[36]

Although the mixture of monarchy, aristocracy, and democracy, is visible in the republic of Phæacia, yet the king appears little more among the archons than the first among equals, and the authority of the people is still more faint and feeble. In Ithaca, there appears a strong claim of sovereignty in the king, and as strong a pretension to it in the archons; and, although the people are dreaded by both, and their claim to interfere in the disposition of the crown is implicitly acknowledged, yet it seems to be as judges of certain religious ceremonies, by which the will of Jupiter was to be collected, rather than as any regular civil authority.

> Homer was a royalist, at least as much as Plato and Aristotle.
> "Jove loves our chief, from Jove his honor springs.
> Beware! for dreadful is the wrath of kings.
> . . . .
> Be silent, wretch! and think not here allowed
> That worst of tyrants, a usurping crowd.
> To one sole monarch Jove commits the sway;
> His are the laws, and him let all obey."[†]

The name of a republic is not found in any of his writings. Yet, in every Grecian government described by him, we find a mixture, not only of an aristocracy, consisting in a council of princes; but of a democracy, in an assembly of the people.

---

[36] *Germania,* c. xii. [Among the Germans of Tacitus' time, "It is also permitted to make accusations and bring capital charges before the assembly. There is a division of penalties according to the crime; they hang traitors and deserters from trees; cowards, and the unwarlike, and sexual perverts they plunge in the mud of marshes with a wicker frame over their heads. The difference of punishment looks to the principle that crimes should be put on display as they are punished, but disgraceful acts concealed. There is also a proportional penalty for lighter offenses; those convicted are fined a number of horses and cattle; part of the fine is paid to the king or the state; part to the person himself who wins his case, or to his relatives." Tacitus, Germania xii. Ed.]

[†] *Il.* ii. 233–244.

Agamemnon, in the second *Iliad,* calls together the whole body.
"The king despatched his heralds with commands
To range the camp, and summon all the bands.
The gathering hosts the monarch's word obey,
While to the fleet Atrides bends his way.
In his black ship the Pylian prince he found,
There calls a senate of the peers around.
Th' assembly plac'd, the king of men exprest
The counsels lab'ring in his artful breast.
Friends and confed'rates! with attentive ear
Receive my words, and credit what you hear;

. . . .

Ill fits a chief who mighty nations guides,
Directs in council, and in war presides,
To whom its safety a whole people owes;
To waste long nights in indolent repose.

. . . .

Now, valiant chiefs! since heaven itself alarms,
Unite, and rouse the sons of Greece to arms.
But first, with caution, try what yet they dare,
Worn with nine years of unsuccessful war.
To move the troops to measure back the main
Be mine; and yours the province to detain.
————The kings without delay
Dissolve the council, and their chief obey.
The sceptr'd rulers lead; the following host,
Pour'd forth by thousands, darkens all the coast.

. . . .

Nine sacred heralds now, proclaiming loud
The monarch's will, suspend the list'ning crowd.

. . . .

The king of kings his awful figure raised,
High in his hand the golden sceptre blazed—

. . . .

Ye sons of Mars! partake your leader's care,
Heroes of Greece, and brothers of the war!

. . . .

Fly, Grecians, fly! your sails and oars employ,
And dream no more of heaven-defended Troy.
His deep design unknown, the hosts approve
Atrides' speech;—the mighty numbers move."★

It appears from the whole narration, that the great body of the people were discontented and desirous of raising the siege. The king alarmed, was obliged to call them together, with an artful design to obtain their consent to persevere. He feigns an intention to return home; the people were rejoiced at it. Then Ulysses, in concert with Agamemnon, receives the sceptre of command, and endeavors to persuade the people to make another effort. To this end Ulysses harangues them.

"He runs, he flies through all the Grecian train,
Each prince of name, or chief in arms approved,
He fired with praise, or with persuasion moved.

. . . .

But if a clam'rous, vile plebeian rose,
Him with reproof he checked, or tamed with blows.
Be still, thou slave, and to thy betters yield,
Unknown alike in council or in field!
Ye gods! what dastards would our host command!
Swept to the war, the lumber of a land.
Be silent, wretch! and think not here allow'd
That worst of tyrants, an usurping crowd.

. . . .

With words like these the troops Ulysses rul'd,
The loudest silenc'd, and the fiercest cool'd.
Back to th' assembly roll the thronging train,

★ *Il.* ii. 61–174.

Desert the ships, and pour upon the plain.
. . . .
Thersites only clamor'd in the thrung,
Loquacious, loud, and turbulent of tongue.
Aw'd by no shame, by no respect control'd,
In scandal busy, in reproaches bold,
With witty malice studious to defame,
Scorn all his joy, and laughter all his aim.
But chief he gloried, with licentious style
To lash the great, and monarchs to revile.
. . . .
Spleen to mankind his envious heart possest,
And much he hated all, but most the best;
Ulysses or Achilles still his theme;
But royal scandal his delight supreme.
Long had he liv'd, the scorn of ev'ry Greek,
Vext when he spoke, yet still they heard him speak."*

If from this only, and the subsequent harangue of Thersites, we were to form a judgment, we should conclude that popular assemblies were very frequent, and that the freedom of speech in them was far advanced and well established; but the furious answer of Ulysses, and the unmerciful flogging he gives him for his boldness, in the face of the whole assembly, which is applauded universally, shows that the demagogues had yet but very little influence, very little courage, and that popular assemblies had as yet very little constitutional power.

The principles of government were very little understood, and all the political institutions extremely confused, in the time of the Trojan war, and from thence to Homer's time. Nothing was precisely defined; no laws were written. The most distinct rules, which are now to be traced, were a supremacy of kings, in religion and war. Sometimes they exercised judicial power. Monarchies were generally hereditary; yet a right of the nation to

---

* Il. ii. 224–272.

interfere and alter the succession is admitted. The right of the sons of the archons, to succeed to their estates and districts, was an agreed point among them; but these very archons chose to keep open to competition the succession to the throne, so that there might always be room for the pretensions of the most powerful, who would easily make themselves thought the most worthy. The most celebrated kings, when advanced in years and unable to sustain the fatigues of war and cares of government, were obliged to resign their power. The anxiety of Achilles, expressed to Ulysses in the Shades, is a proof of this.

> "Say if my sire, the reverend Peleus, reigns
> Great in his Pthia, and his throne maintains;
> Or, weak and old, my youthful arm demands
> To fix the sceptre steadfast in his hands?
> O might the lamp of life rekindled burn,
> And death release me from the silent urn!
> This arm, that thunder'd o'er the Phrygian plain
> And swell'd the ground with mountains of the slain,
> Should vindicate my injur'd father's fame,
> Crush the proud rebel, and assert his claim.★

Kings and their families, claiming their descent and power from Jupiter, contended very naturally and consistently that the one was hereditary and the other absolute; and, accordingly, when the prince who swayed the sceptre was active, brave, and able, he kept the archons in awe, and governed as he pleased. But when he was feeble, the archons grew ambitious, disputed the succession, and limited the royal power. To this end, both they and the kings, or heirs of kings, sometimes looked to the people, and seemed to admit in them a right to be present at the religious ceremonies, by which the will of Jupiter was to be declared; for all parties agree, that the will of Jupiter confers the sceptre, not the mere election of the people.

★ *Od.* xi. 605.

The right of primogeniture was favored by popular opinion, as well as hereditary descent, because the family was the family of Jupiter, related to him, and descended from him by blood; and it was natural to suppose that Jupiter's inclinations for descent and primogeniture resembled those of other fathers of families.

The chiefs, who are all called kings, as well as the head of them, or archons, were like the Teutonic counts or feudal barons, who exercised royal rights within their own districts, states, or separate territories. This principle preserved the real and legal power chiefly in their hands, and constituted the whole government more properly an aristocracy than a royalty. This gave an uncontrollable pride to these nobles, which could not willingly submit to the pretensions of the kings, (as representatives of Jupiter,) to omnipotence, at least to unlimited power. Hence the continual struggle between the kings and archons; from Homer's time to that great and memorable revolution throughout Greece, from monarchy to aristocracy; that is, from kings to archons. The people not yet possessing nor claiming an authority sufficiently regular and independent to be a check to monarchy or aristocracy, the latter at last prevailed over the former, as it ever did and ever will, where the contest is merely between these two.

The people, only in extraordinary cases, in the most essential matters, and when the chiefs were greatly divided, were at all consulted; yet, in the course of the struggle between the kings and archons, the multitude were so often called upon, and so much courted, that they came by degrees to claim the whole power, and prepared the way in many of the Grecian states for another subsequent revolution from aristocracy to democracy.

Through the whole of Tacitus and Homer, the three orders are visible both in Germany and Greece; and the continual fluctuations of law, the uncertainty of life, liberty, and property, and the contradictory claims and continual revolutions, arose entirely from the want of having the prerogatives and privileges of those orders defined, from the want of independence in each of them, and a balance between them.

CHAPTER X.

Conclusion.

BY the authorities and examples already recited, you will be convinced that three branches of power have an unalterable foundation in nature; that they exist in every society natural and artificial; and that if all of them are not acknowledged in any constitution of government, it will be found to be imperfect, unstable, and soon enslaved; that the legislative and executive authorities are naturally distinct; and that liberty and the laws depend entirely on a separation of them in the frame of government; that the legislative power is naturally and necessarily sovereign and supreme over the executive; and, therefore, that the latter must be made an essential branch of the former, even with a negative, or it will not be able to defend itself, but will be soon invaded, undermined, attacked, or in some way or other totally ruined and annihilated by the former. This is applicable to every state in America, in its individual capacity; but is it equally applicable to the United States in their federal capacity?

The people of America and their delegates in congress were of opinion, that a single assembly was every way adequate to the management of all their federal concerns; and with very good reason, because congress is not a legislative assembly, nor a representative assembly, but only a diplomatic assembly.[36] A single council has been found to answer the purposes

---

[36] This sentence drew from Mr. Jefferson a remonstrating comment. In a letter dated Paris, 23 February, 1787, hitherto unpublished, occurs the following passage, which, in view of the subsequent history of both the parties, is worthy of record.

"I have read your book with infinite satisfaction and improvement. It will do great good in America. Its learning and its good sense will, I hope, make it an institute for our politicians, old as well as young. There is one opinion in it, however, which I will ask you to reconsider, because it appears to me not entirely accurate, and not likely to do good. 'Congress is not a legislative, but a diplomatic assembly.' Separating into parts the whole sovereignty of our states, some of these parts are yielded to congress. Upon these I should them both legislative and executive, and that they could have been judiciary also, had not the confederation required them for certain purposes to appoint a judiciary. It has accordingly been the decision of our courts, that the confederation is a part of the law of the land, and superior in authority to the ordinary laws, because it cannot be altered by the legislature of any one state. I doubt whether they are at all a diplomatic assembly."

of confederacies very well. But in all such cases the deputies are responsible to the states; their authority is clearly ascertained; and the states, in their separate capacities, are the checks. These are able to form an effectual balance, and at all times to control their delegates. The security against the dangers of this kind of government will depend upon the accuracy and decision with which the governments of the separate states have their own orders arranged and balanced.

The necessity we are under of submitting to a federal government, is an additional and a very powerful argument for three branches, and a balance by an equal negative, in all the separate governments. Congress will always be composed of members from the natural and artificial aristocratical body in every state, even in the northern, as well as in the middle and southern states. Their natural dispositions, then, in general will be, (whether they shall be sensible of it or not, and whatever integrity or abilities they may be possessed of,) to diminish the prerogatives of the governors and the privileges of the people, and to augment the influence of the aristocratical parties. There have been causes enough to prevent the appearance of this inclination hitherto; but a calm course of prosperity would very soon bring it forth, if effectual provision against it be not made in season. It will be found absolutely necessary, therefore, to give negatives to the governors, to defend the executive against the influence of this body, as well as the senate and representatives in their several states. The necessity of a negative in the house of representatives will be called in question by nobody.

Dr. Price and the Abbé de Mably are zealous for additional powers to congress. Full power in all foreign affairs and over foreign commerce, and, perhaps, some authority over the commerce of the states with one another, may be necessary; and it is hard to say that more authority in other things is not wanted. Yet the subject is of such extreme delicacy and difficulty, that the people are much to be applauded for their caution. To collect together the ancient and modern leagues,—the Amphictyonic, the Olynthian, the Argive, the Arcadian, and the Achæan confederacies, among the Greeks; the general diet of the Swiss cantons, and the states-general of the United Netherlands; the union of the Hansetowns, &c., which have been found to answer the purposes both of government and liberty; to compare them all with the circumstances, the situation, the geography, the commerce, the population, and the forms of government, as well as the climate, the soil, and manners of the people, and consider what further federal powers are wanted, and may be safely given, would be a useful work.

According to M. Turgot's idea of a perfect commonwealth, a single assembly is to be possessed of all authority, legislative, executive, and judicial. It will be a proper conclusion of all our speculations upon this, the most interesting subject which can employ the thoughts of men, to consider in what manner such an assembly will conduct its deliberations and exert its power. The executive power is properly the government; the laws are a dead letter until an administration begins to carry them into execution. Let us begin, then, with this. If there is an army to raise, this single assembly is to appoint all its officers. The man of the most ample fortune, the most honorable descent, the greatest abilities, especially if there is any one among them who has had experience, rendered important services, and acquired fame in war, will be chosen general. This event is a great point gained by the aristocracy; and a great advance towards the selection of one, in case of convulsions and confusions, for monarchy. The general has vast influence, of course, with the whole nation, and especially with the officers of his army; whose articles of war, and whose habits, both of obedience and command, establish a system of subordination of which he is the centre, and produce an attachment that never wears out. The general, even without being sensible of it, will naturally fall in with the views of the aristocratical body, in promoting men of family, property, and abilities; and indeed, in general, it will be his duty to do this, as such are, undoubtedly, in general, the fittest for the service. His whole corps of officers will grow habitually to respect such only, or at least chiefly, and, it must be added, because experience proves it, and the truth requires it to be mentioned, to entertain some degree of contempt for the rest of the people, as "rank and file." The general's recommendation will have great weight in the assembly, and will in time be given chiefly, if not wholly, to men who are either of the aristocratical body them-

selves, or at least recommended by such as are so. All the other officers of
the army are to be appointed by this assembly; and we must suppose that
all the general officers and field officers will be of patrician families,
because each candidate will be unknown to nine tenths of the assembly.
He comes from a part of the state which a vast majority of the members
of the assembly do not particularly represent and are unacquainted with;
they must, therefore, take his character upon trust from his patron in the
house, some member who is his neighbor, and who, perhaps, owes his
election to him or his particular friends. Here is an endless source of
debate and delay. When there are two or more candidates for a commission, and there will generally be several, how shall an assembly of five hundred or one hundred men, collected from all the most distant parts of a
large state, become informed of the merits and pretensions of each candidate? It can only be done in public or in private. If in public, it exposes
the characters of the candidates to a public discussion, which few men can
bear; it consumes time without end; and it will frequently happen that
the time of the whole assembly shall be wasted, and all the public affairs
delayed, for days and weeks, in deliberating and debating, affirming and
denying, contradicting and proving, in the appointment of a single officer;
and, after all, he who has friends of the most influence in the house, who
will be generally of the aristocratical complexion, will be preferred. It is
moderate to say, that the loss of time and delay of business will be a greater
burthen to the state than the whole support of a governor and council.

If there is a navy, the same process must be gone through respecting
admirals, captains, and all other officers. All the officers of revenue, police,
justice, must be appointed in the same way. Ambassadors, consuls, agents
to foreign countries, must be appointed, too, by vote of assembly. This
branch of business alone would fill up the whole year, and be more than
could be done. An assembly must be informed before it can act. The
understanding and conscience of every member should be clearly satisfied
before he can vote. Information is to be had only by debate and examination of evidence. Any man may see that this must be attended with
difficulty; but no man who has not seen the inside of such an assembly, can
conceive the confusion, uncertainty, and procrastination of such proceed-

ings. The American provincial congresses had experience enough of this; and gentlemen were more convinced, by what they there saw, heard, and felt, of the necessity of three branches, than they would have been by reasoning or reading; it was generally agreed that the appointment of officers by lot would have been a more rational method.

But this is not all. The army, the navy, revenue, excise, customs, police, justice, and all foreign ministers, must be gentlemen, that is to say, friends and connections of the rich, well-born and well-educated members of the house; or, if they are not, the community will be filled with slander, suspicion, and ridicule against them, as ill-bred, ignorant, and in all respects unqualified for their trusts; and the plebeians themselves will be as ready as any to join in the cry, and run down their characters. In the second place, there never was yet a people who must not have somebody or something to represent the dignity of the state, the majesty of the people, call it what you will,—a doge, an avoyer, an archon, a president, a consul, a syndic; this becomes at once an object of ambition and dispute, and, in time, of division, faction, sedition, and rebellion.

The next inquiry is, concerning the administration of justice. Shall every criminal be brought before this assembly and tried? shall he be there accused before five hundred men? witnesses introduced, counsel heard? This again would take up more than the whole year; and no man, after all, would consider his life, liberty, or property, safe in such a tribunal. These all depend upon the disquisitions of the counsel, the knowledge of the law in the judges, the confrontation of parties and witnesses, the forms of proceedings, by which the facts and the law are fairly stated before the jury for their decision, the rules of evidence, by which the attention of the jury is confined to proper points, and the artifices of parties and counsel avoided. An assembly of five hundred men are totally incapable of this order, as well as knowledge; for, as the vote of the majority must determine, every member must be capable, or all is uncertain. Besides, it is the unanimity of the jury that preserves the rights of mankind. Must the whole five hundred be unanimous?

Will it be said that the assembly shall appoint committees to try causes? But who are to make these appointments? Will not a few haughty palatines in the assembly have influence enough to determine the election in favor of their friends? and will not this make the judges the tools of a party? If the leaders are divided into parties, will not one prevail at one year, and another the next? and will not this introduce the most wretched of servitudes, an uncertain jurisprudence?

Will it be said that the assembly shall appoint committees for the nomination of officers? The same intrigues and greater struggles would be introduced for the place of a committee-man; and there would be frequent appeals from those committees to the body that appointed them.

Shall the assembly appoint a governor or president, and give him all the executive power? Why should not the people at large appoint him? Giving this power to the assembly will open a wider door to intrigue for the place; and the aristocratical families will be sure, nine times in ten, to carry their choice in this way; and, what is much worse, the first magistrate will be considered as dependent on every obscure member of the house, but in reality he will be dependent only on a dozen or a score, perhaps on two or three, of the whole. He will be liable to daily motions, debates, and votes of censure. Instead of thinking of his duty to the people at large, he will confine his attention chiefly to the assembly, and believe, that if he can satisfy them, or a majority of them, he has done his duty.

After all, any of these devices are only changing words; they are, in reality, erecting different orders of men, and aiming at balances, as much as the system which so much displeases M. Turgot; they are introducing, in effect, all the inequalities and disputes that he so greatly apprehends, without any of that security to the laws, which ought to be the principal object; they render the executive power, which is in truth the government, the instrument of a few grandees. If these are capable of a combination with each other, they will seldom disagree in their opinion, which is the richest man and of the first family; and, as these will be all their inquiries, they will generally carry their election. If they are divided, in constant wrangles with each other, and perpetual attacks upon the president about the discharge of his functions, they will keep the nation anxious and irritated, with controversies which can never be decided nor ended. If they agree, and the plebeians still carry the vote against them, the choice will nevertheless probably fall upon one of their number, who will be disposed to favor them too much; but if it falls upon a plebeian, there commences at once a series of contests between the rich and the poor, which will never end but in the ruin of the popular power and the national liberty; or at least in a revolution and a new constitution. As the executive power, the essence of government, is ever odious to popular envy and jealousy, it will ever be in the power of a few illustrious and wealthy citizens to excite clamors and uneasiness, if not commotions and seditions, against it. Although it is the natural friend of the people, and the only defence which they or their representatives can have against the avarice and ambition of the rich and distinguished citizens, yet, such is their thoughtless simplicity, they are ever ready to believe that the evils they feel are brought upon them by the executive power. How easy is it, then, for a few artful men among the aristocratical body to make a president, thus appointed and supported, unpopular, though he conducts himself with all the integrity and ability which his office requires?

But we have not yet considered how the legislative power is to be exercised in this single assembly. Is there to be a constitution? Who are to compose it? The assembly itself, or a convention called for that purpose? In either case, whatever rules are agreed on for the preservation of the lives, liberties, properties, and characters of the citizens, what is to hinder this assembly from transgressing the bounds which they have prescribed to themselves, or which the convention has ordained for them? The convention has published its code and is no more. Shall a new convention be called, to determine every question which arises concerning a violation of the constitution? This would require that the convention should sit whenever the assembly sits, and consider and determine every question which is agitated in it. This is the very thing we contend for, namely,—that there may be two assemblies; one to divide, and the other to choose. Grant me this, and I am satisfied; provided you will confine both the convention and assembly to legislation, and give the whole executive power to another body. I had almost ventured to propose a third assembly for the executive power; but the unity, the secrecy, the dispatch of one man has no equal; and the executive power should be watched by all men; the attention of the whole nation should be fixed upon one point, and the blame and censure, as well as the impeachments and vengeance for abuses of this power, should be directed solely to the ministers of one man. But to pursue our single assembly. The first year, or the first seven years, they may be moderate; especially in dangerous times, and while an exiled royal family, or exiled patricians or nobles, are living, and may return; or while the people's passions are alive, and their attention awake, from the fresh remembrance of danger and distress. But when these transitory causes pass away, as there is an affection and confidence between the people and their representatives, suppose the latter begin to make distinctions, by making exceptions of themselves in the laws. They may frank letters; they are exempted from arrests; they can privilege servants; one little distinction after another, in time makes up a large sum. Some few of the people will complain; but the majority, loving their representatives, will acquiesce. Presently they are exempted from taxes. Then their duration is too short; from annual they become biennial, triennial, septennial, for life; and at length, instead of applying to constituents to fill up vacancies, the assembly takes it upon itself, or gives it to their president. In the mean time, wars are conducted by heroes to triumph and conquest, negotiations are carried on with success, commerce flourishes, the nation is prosperous; the citizens are flattered, vain, proud of their felicity, envied by others. It would be the basest, the most odious ingratitude, at least it would be so represented, to find fault with their rulers. In a word, as long as half a score of capital characters agree, they will gradually form the house and the nation into a system of subordination and dependence to themselves, and govern all at their discretion—a simple aristocracy or oligarchy in effect, though a simple democracy in name. But, as every one of these is emulous of others, and more than one of them is constantly tormented with a desire to be the first, they will soon disagree; and then the house and the nation gradually divides itself into four parties, one of which, at least, will wish for monarchy, another for aristocracy, a third for democracy, and a fourth for various mixtures of them; and these parties can never come to a decision but by a struggle, or by the sword. There is no remedy for this, but in a convention of deputies from all parts of the state; but an equal convention can hardly be obtained, except in times like those we have lately seen, when the danger could only be warded off by the aid and exertions of the whole body of the people. When no such danger from without shall press, those who are proud of their wealth, blood, or wit, will never give way to fair and equal establishments. All parties will be afraid of calling a convention; but if it must be agreed to, the aristocratical party will push their influence, and obtain elections even into the conventions, for themselves and their friends, so as to carry points there which perhaps they could not have carried in the assembly.

But shall the people at large elect a governor and council annually to manage the executive power, and a single assembly to have the whole legislative? In this case, the executive power, instead of being independent, will be the instrument of a few leading members of the house; because the executive power, being an object of jealousy and envy to the people, and the legislative an object of their confidence and affection, the latter will always be able to render the former unpopular, and undermine its influence. But if the people for a time support an executive disagreeable to the leaders in the legislative, the constitution will be disregarded, and the nation will be divided between the two bodies, and each must at last have an army to decide the question. A constitution consisting of an executive in one single assembly, and a legislative in another, is already composed of two armies in battle array; and nothing is wanting but the word of command to begin the combat.

In the present state of society and manners in America, with a people living chiefly by agriculture, in small numbers, sprinkled over large tracts of land, they are not subject to those panics and transports, those contagions of madness and folly, which are seen in countries where large numbers live in small places, in daily fear of perishing for want. We know, therefore, that the people can live and increase under almost any kind of government, or without any government at all. But it is of great importance to begin well; misarrangements now made, will have great, extensive, and distant consequences; and we are now employed, how little soever we may think of it, in making establishments which will affect the happiness of a hundred millions of inhabitants at a time, in a period not very distant. All nations, under all governments, must have parties; the great secret is to control them. There are but two ways, either by a monarchy and standing army, or by a balance in the constitution. Where the people have a voice, and there is no balance, there will be everlasting fluctuations, revolutions, and horrors, until a standing army, with a general at its head, commands the peace, or the necessity of an equilibrium is made appear to all, and is adopted by all.

VOLUME III.

CHAPTER I.

The Right Constitution of a Commonwealth Examined.

MARCHAMONT NEDHAM.

THE English nation, for their improvements in the theory of government, has, at least, more merit with the human race than any other among the moderns. The late most beautiful and liberal speculations of many writers, in various parts of Europe, are manifestly derived from English sources. Americans, too, ought for ever to acknowledge their obligations to English writers, or rather have as good a right to indulge a pride in the recollection of them as the inhabitants of the three kingdoms. The original plantation of our country was occasioned, her continual growth has been promoted, and her present liberties have been established by these generous theories.

There have been three periods in the history of England, in which the principles of government have been anxiously studied, and very valuable productions published, which, at this day, if they are not wholly forgotten in their native country, are perhaps more frequently read abroad than at home.

The first of these periods was that of the Reformation, as early as the writings of Machiavel himself, who is called the great restorer of the true politics. The "Shorte Treatise of Politicke Power, and of the True Obedience which Subjects owe to Kyngs and other Civile Governors, with an

Exhortation to all True Natural Englishemen, compyled by John Poynet, D. D.," was printed in 1556, and contains all the essential principles of liberty, which were afterwards dilated on by Sidney and Locke. This writer is clearly for a mixed government, in three equiponderant branches, as appears by these words:—

"In some countreyes they were content to be governed and have the laws executed by one king or judge; in some places by many of the best sorte; in some places by the people of the lowest sorte; and in some places also by the king, nobilitie, and the people all together. And these diverse kyndes of states, or policies, had their distincte names; as where one ruled, a monarchie; where many of the best, aristocratie; and where the multitude, democratie; and where all together, that is a king, the nobilitie, and commons, a mixte state; and which men by long continuance have judged to be the best sort of all. For where that mixte state was exercised, there did the commonwealthe longest continue."

The second period was the Interregnum, and indeed the whole interval between 1640 and 1660. In the course of those twenty years, not only Ponnet and others were reprinted, but Harrington, Milton, the *Vindiciæ contra Tyrannos,*[37] and a multitude of others, came upon the stage.

The third period was the Revolution in 1688, which produced Sidney, Locke, Hoadley, Trenchard, Gordon, Plato Redivivus, who is also clear for three equipollent branches in the mixture, and others without number. The discourses of Sidney were indeed written before, but the same causes produced his writings and the Revolution.

Americans should make collections of all these speculations, to be preserved as the most precious relics of antiquity, both for curiosity and use. There is one indispensable rule to be observed in the perusal of all of them; and that is, to consider the period in which they were written, the circumstances of the times, and the personal character as well as the political situation of the writer. Such a precaution as this deserves particular attention in examining a work, printed first in the Mercurius Politicus, a

[37] ["defense (or 'Vindication') against Tyrants." This is the title of a book by an author calling himself Junius Brutus, subtitled "or Concerning the Legitimate Power of a Prince over the People, and of the People over a Prince." Ed.]

periodical paper published in defence of the commonwealth, and reprinted in 1656, by Marchamont Nedham, under the title of "The Excellency of a Free State, or the Right Constitution of a Commonwealth."[38] The nation had not only a numerous nobility and clergy at that time disgusted, and a vast body of the other gentlemen, as well as of the common people, desirous of the restoration of the exiled royal family, but many writers explicitly espoused the cause of simple monarchy and absolute power. Among whom was Hobbes, a man, however unhappy in his temper, or detestable for his principles, equal in genius and learning to any of his contemporaries. Others were employed in ridiculing the doctrine, that laws, and not men, should govern. It was contended, that to say "that laws do or can govern, is to amuse ourselves with a form of speech, as when we say time, or age, or death, does such a thing. That the government is not in the law, but in the person whose will gives a being to that law. That the perfection of monarchy consists in governing by a nobility, weighty enough to keep the people under, yet not tall enough, in any particular person, to measure with the prince; and by a moderate army, kept up under the notion of guards and garrisons, which may be sufficient to strangle all seditions in the cradle; by councils, not such as are coördinate with the prince, but purely of advice and despatch, with power only to persuade, not limit, the prince's will."* In such a situation, writers on the side of liberty thought themselves obliged to consider what was then practicable, not abstractedly what was the best. They felt the necessity of leaving the monarchical and aristocratical orders out of their schemes of

---

* See the political pamphlets of that day, written on the side of monarchy.

[38] This work was reprinted in London, in 1767, under the direction of Thomas Hollis, in a thin octavo, containing one hundred and seventy-six pages. The copy found in the author's library bears the following inscription:—

"Mr. Brand Hollis requests the favor of his friend, Mr. Adams, to accept benevolently this book, to be deposited among his republican tracts, which, after the pomp and pageantry of monarchy, 'the trappings of which would maintain a moderate republic,' will relish well.

"*Chesterfield Street,* 19 January, 1787."

It is not improbable that it was the presentation of the work at this time that occasioned the elaborate review of it, which constitutes the most vigorous part of the present work.

government, because all the friends of those orders were their enemies, and of addressing themselves wholly to the democratical party, because they alone were their friends; at least there appears no other hypothesis on which to account for the crude conceptions of Milton and Nedham. The latter, in his preface, discovers his apprehensions and feelings, too clearly to be mistaken, in these words:—"I believe none will be offended with this following discourse, but those that are enemies to public welfare. Let such be offended still; it is not for their sake that I publish this ensuing treatise, but for your sakes that have been *noble patriots, fellow soldiers;* and *sufferers* for the liberties and freedoms of your country." As M. Turgot's idea of a commonwealth, in which "all authority is to be collected into one centre," and that centre the nation, is supposed to be precisely the project of Marchamont Nedham, and probably derived from his book, and as "The Excellency of a Free State" is a valuable morsel of antiquity well known in America, where it has many partisans, it may be worth while to examine it, especially as it contains every semblance of argument which can possibly be urged in favor of the system, as it is not only the popular idea of a republic both in France and England, but is generally intended by the words *republic, commonwealth,* and *popular state,* when used by English writers, even those of the most sense, taste, and learning.

Marchamont Nedham lays it down as a fundamental principle and an undeniable rule, "that the people, (that is, such as shall be successively chosen to represent the people,) are the best keepers of their own liberties, and that for many reasons. First, because they never think of usurping over other men's rights, but mind which way to preserve their own."

Our first attention should be turned to the proposition itself,—"The people are the best keepers of their own liberties."

But who are the people?

"Such as shall be successively chosen to represent them."

Here is a confusion both of words and ideas, which, though it may pass with the generality of readers in a fugitive pamphlet, or with a majority of auditors in a popular harangue, ought, for that very reason, to be as carefully avoided in politics as it is in philosophy or mathematics. If by *the people* is meant the whole body of a great nation, it should never be forgotten, that they can never act, consult, or reason together, because they cannot march five hundred miles, nor spare the time, nor find a space to meet; and, therefore, the proposition, that they are the best keepers of their own liberties, is not true. They are the worst conceivable; they are no keepers at all. They can neither act, judge, think, or will, as a body politic or corporation. If by *the people* is meant all the inhabitants of a single city, they are not in a general assembly, at all times, the best keepers of their own liberties, nor perhaps at any time, unless you separate from them the executive and judicial power, and temper their authority in legislation with the maturer counsels of the one and the few. If it is meant by *the people,* as our author explains himself, a representative assembly, "such as shall be successively chosen to represent the people," still they are not the best keepers of the people's liberties or their own, if you give them all the power, legislative, executive, and judicial. They would invade the liberties of the people, at least the majority of them would invade the liberties of the minority, sooner and oftener than an absolute monarchy, such as that of France, Spain, or Russia, or than a well-checked aristocracy, like Venice, Bern, or Holland.

An excellent writer has said, somewhat incautiously, that "a people will never oppress themselves, or invade their own rights." This compliment, if applied to human nature, or to mankind, or to any nation or people in being or in memory, is more than has been merited. If it should be admitted that a people will not unanimously agree to oppress themselves, it is as much as is ever, and more than is always, true. All kinds of experience show, that great numbers of individuals do oppress great numbers of other individuals; that parties often, if not always, oppress other parties; and majorities almost universally minorities. All that this observation can mean then, consistently with any color of fact, is, that the people will never unanimously agree to oppress themselves. But if one party agrees to oppress another, or the majority the minority, the people still oppress themselves, for one part of them oppress another.

"The people never think of usurping over other men's rights."

What can this mean? Does it mean that the people never *unanimously* think of usurping over other men's rights? This would be trifling; for there would, by the supposition, be no other men's rights to usurp. But if the people never, jointly nor severally, think of usurping the rights of others, what occasion can there be for any government at all? Are there no robberies, burglaries, murders, adulteries, thefts, nor cheats? Is not every crime a usurpation over other men's rights? Is not a great part, I will not say the greatest part, of men detected every day in some disposition or other, stronger or weaker, more or less, to usurp over other men's rights? There are some few, indeed, whose whole lives and conversations show that, in every thought, word, and action, they conscientiously respect the rights of others. There is a larger body still, who, in the general tenor of their thoughts and actions, discover similar principles and feelings, yet frequently err. If we should extend our candor so far as to own, that the majority of men are generally under the dominion of benevolence and good intentions, yet, it must be confessed, that a vast majority frequently transgress; and, what is more directly to the point, not only a majority, but almost all, confine their benevolence to their families, relations, personal friends, parish, village, city, county, province, and that very few, indeed, extend it impartially to the whole community. Now, grant but this truth, and the question is decided. If a majority are capable of preferring their own private interest, or that of their families, counties, and party, to that of the nation collectively, some provision must be made in the constitution, in favor of justice, to compel all to respect the common right, the public good, the universal law, in preference to all private and partial considerations.

The proposition of our author, then, should be reversed, and it should have been said, that they mind so much their own, that they never think enough of others. Suppose a nation, rich and poor, high and low, ten millions in number, all assembled together; not more than one or two millions will have lands, houses, or any personal property; if we take into the account the women and children, or even if we leave them out of the question, a great majority of every nation is wholly destitute of property, except a small quantity of clothes, and a few trifles of other movables. Would Mr. Nedham be responsible that, if all were to be decided by a vote of the majority, the eight or nine millions who have no property, would not think of usurping over the rights of the one or two millions who have? Property is surely a right of mankind as really as liberty. Perhaps, at first, prejudice, habit, shame or fear, principle or religion, would restrain the poor from attacking the rich, and the idle from usurping on the industrious; but the time would not be long before courage and enterprise would come, and pretexts be invented by degrees, to countenance the majority in dividing all the property among them, or at least, in sharing it equally with its present possessors. Debts would be abolished first; taxes laid heavy on the rich, and not at all on the others; and at last a downright equal division of every thing be demanded, and voted. What would be the consequence of this? The idle, the vicious, the intemperate, would rush into the utmost extravagance of debauchery, sell and spend all their share, and then demand a new division of those who purchased from them. The moment the idea is admitted into society, that property is not as sacred as the laws of God, and that there is not a force of law and public justice to protect it, anarchy and tyranny commence. If "THOU SHALT NOT COVET," and "THOU SHALT NOT STEAL," were not commandments of Heaven, they must be made inviolable precepts in every society, before it can be civilized or made free.

If the first part of the proposition, namely, that "the people never think of usurping over other men's rights," cannot be admitted, is the second, namely, "they mind which way to preserve their own," better founded?

There is in every nation and people under heaven a large proportion of persons who take no rational and prudent precautions to preserve what they have, much less to acquire more. Indolence is the natural character of man, to such a degree that nothing but the necessities of hunger, thirst, and other wants equally pressing, can stimulate him to action, until education is introduced in civilized societies, and the strongest motives of ambition to excel in arts, trades, and professions, are established in the minds of all men. Until this emulation is introduced, the lazy savage holds property in too little estimation to give himself trouble for the preservation or acquisition of it. In societies the most cultivated and polished, vanity, fashion, and folly prevail over every thought of ways to preserve their own. They seem rather to study what means of luxury, dissipation, and extravagance they can invent to get rid of it.

"The case is far otherwise among kings and grandees," says our author, "as all nations in the world have felt to some purpose."

That is, in other words, kings and grandees think of usurping over other men's rights, but do not mind which way to preserve their own. It is very easy to flatter the democratical portion of society, by making such distinctions between them and the monarchical and aristocratical; but flattery is as base an artifice, and as pernicious a vice, when offered to the people, as when given to the others. There is no reason to believe the one much honester or wiser than the other; they are all of the same clay; their minds and bodies are alike. The two latter have more knowledge and sagacity, derived from education, and more advantages for acquiring wisdom and virtue. As to usurping others' rights, they are all three equally guilty when unlimited in power. No wise man will trust either with an opportunity; and every judicious legislator will set all three to watch and control each other. We may appeal to every page of history we have hitherto turned over, for proofs irrefragable, that the people, when they have been unchecked, have been as unjust, tyrannical, brutal, barbarous, and cruel, as any king or senate possessed of uncontrollable power. The majority has eternally, and without one exception, usurped over the rights of the minority.

"They naturally move," says Nedham, "within the circle of domination, as in their proper centre."

When writers on legislation have recourse to poetry, their images may be beautiful, but they prove nothing. This, however, has neither the merit of a brilliant figure, nor of a convincing argument. The populace, the rabble, the *canaille,* move as naturally in the circle of domination, whenever they dare, as the nobles or a king; nay, although it may give pain, truth and experience force us to add, that even the middling people, when uncontrolled, have moved in the same circle; and have not only tyrannized over all above and all below, but the majority among themselves has tyrannized over the minority.

"And count it no less security, than wisdom and policy, to brave it over the people."

Declamatory flourishes, although they may furnish a mob with watch-words, afford no reasonable conviction to the understanding. What is meant by braving it? In the history of Holland you will see the people braving it over the De Witts; and in that of Florence, Siena, Bologna, Pistoia, and the rest, over many others.★

"Cæsar, Crassus, and another, made a contract with each other, that nothing should be done without the concurrence of all three: Societatem iniere, ne quid ageretur in republica, quod displicuisset ulli e tribus."

Nedham could not have selected a less fortunate example for his purpose, since there never was a more arrant creature of the people than Cæsar; no, not even Catiline, Wat Tyler, Massaniello, or Shays: The people created Cæsar on the ruins of the senate, and on purpose to usurp over the rights of others. But this example, among innumerable others, is very apposite to our purpose. It happens universally, when the people in a body, or by a single representative assembly, attempt to exercise all the powers of government, they always create three or four idols, who make a bargain with each other first, to do nothing which shall displease any one; these hold this agreement, until one thinks himself able to disembarrass himself of the other two; then they quarrel, and the strongest becomes single tyrant. But why is the name of Pompey omitted, who was the third of this triumvirate? Because it would have been too unpopular; it would have too easily confuted his argument, and have turned it against himself, to have said that this association was between Pompey, Cæsar, and Crassus, against Cato, the senate, the constitution, and liberty, which was the fact.

Can you find a people who will never be divided in opinion? who will be always unanimous? The people of Rome were divided, as all other people ever have been, and will be, into a variety of parties and factions. Pompey, Crassus, and Cæsar, at the head of different parties, were jealous of each other. Their divisions strengthened the senate and its friends, and furnished means and opportunities of defeating many of their ambitious designs. Cæsar perceived it, and paid his court both to Pompey and Crassus, in order to hinder them from joining the senate against him. He

★ Read the *Harangue*, vol. ii. p. 67. In this work vol. v. p. 55.

separately represented the advantage which their enemies derived from their misunderstandings, and the ease with which, if united, they might concert among themselves all affairs of the republic, gratify every friend, and disappoint every enemy.★ The other example, of Augustus, Lepidus, and Antony, is equally unfortunate. Both are demonstrations that the people did think of usurping others' rights, and that they did not mind any way to preserve their own. The senate was now annihilated, many of them murdered. Augustus, Lepidus, and Antony were popular demagogues, who agreed together to fleece the flock between them, until the most cunning of the three destroyed the other two, fleeced the sheep alone, and transmitted the shears to a line of tyrants.

How can this writer say, then, that, "while the government remained untouched in the people's hands, every particular man lived safe?" The direct contrary is true. Every man lived safe, only while the senate remained as a check and balance to the people; the moment that control was destroyed, no man was safe. While the government remained untouched in the various orders, the consuls, senate, and people, mutually balancing each other, it might be said, with some truth, that no man could be undone, unless a true and satisfactory reason was rendered to the world for his destruction. But as soon as the senate was destroyed, and the government came untouched into the people's hands, no man lived safe but the triumvirs and their tools; any man might be, and multitudes of the best men were, undone, without rendering any reason to the world for their destruction, but the will, the fear, or the revenge of some tyrant. These popular leaders, in our author's own language, "saved and destroyed, depressed and advanced whom they pleased, with a wet finger."

The second argument to prove that the people, in their successive single assemblies, are the best keepers of their own liberties, is,—

"Because it is ever the people's care to see that authority be so constituted, that it shall be rather a burden than benefit to those that undertake it; and be qualified with such slender advantages of profit or pleasure, that men shall reap little by the enjoyment. The happy consequence whereof is

---

★ Dio. Cass. lib. xxxvii. c. 54, 55. Plutarch in Pomp. Cæsar, and Crassus.

this, that none but honest, generous, and public spirits will then desire to be in authority, and that only for the common good. Hence it was that, in the infancy of the Roman liberty, there was no canvassing of voices; but single and plain-hearted men were called, entreated, and, in a manner, forced with importunity to the helm of government, in regard of that great trouble and pains that followed the employment. Thus Cincinnatus was fetched out of the field from his plough, and placed (much against his will) in the sublime dignity of dictator. So the noble Camillus, and Fabius, and Curius, were, with much ado, drawn from the recreation of gardening to the trouble of governing; and, the consul-year being over, they returned with much gladness again to their private employment."

The first question which would arise in the mind of an intelligent and attentive reader would be, whether this were burlesque, and a republic travesty? But as the principle of this second reason is very pleasing to a large body of narrow spirits in every society, and as it has been adopted by some respectable authorities, without sufficient consideration, it may be proper to give it a serious investigation.

The people have, in some countries and seasons, made their services irksome, and it is popular with some to make authority a burden. But what has been the consequence to the people? Their service has been deserted, and they have been betrayed. Those very persons who have flattered the meanness of the stingy, by offering to serve them gratis, and by purchasing their suffrages, have carried the liberties and properties of their constituents to market, and sold them for very handsome private profit to the monarchical and aristocratical portions of society. And so long as the rule of making their service a burthen is persisted in, so long will the people be served with the same kind of address and fidelity, by hypocritical pretences to disinterested benevolence and patriotism, until their confidence is gained, their affections secured, and their enthusiasm excited, and by knavish bargain and sale of their cause and interest afterwards. But, although there is always among the people a party who are justly chargeable with meanness and avarice, envy and ingratitude, and this party has sometimes been a majority, who have literally made their service burdensome, yet this is not the general character of the people. A more universal fault is too much affection, confidence, and gratitude; not to such as really serve them, whether with or against their inclinations, but to those who flatter their inclinations, and gain their hearts. Honest and generous spirits will disdain to deceive the people; and if the public service is wilfully rendered burdensome, they will really be averse to be in it; but hypocrites enough will be found, who will pretend to be also loth to serve, and feign a reluctant consent for the public good, while they mean to plunder in every way they can conceal.

There are conjunctures when it is the duty of a good citizen to hazard and sacrifice all for his country. But, in ordinary times, it is equally the duty and interest of the community not to suffer it. Every wise and free people, like the Romans, will establish the maxim, to suffer no generous action for the public to go unrewarded. Can our author be supposed to be sincere, in recommending it as a principle of policy to any nation to render her service in the army, navy, or in council, a burden, an unpleasant employment, to all her citizens? Would he depend upon finding human spirits enough to fill public offices, who would be sufficiently elevated in patriotism and general benevolence to sacrifice their ease, health, time, parents, wives, children, and every comfort, convenience, and elegance of life, for the public good? Is there any religion or morality that requires this? which permits the many to live in affluence and ease, while it obliges a few to live in misery for their sakes? The people are fond of calling public men their servants, and some are not able to conceive them to be servants, without making them slaves, and treating them as planters treat their negroes. But, good masters, have a care how you use your power; you may be tyrants as well as public officers. It seems, according to our author himself, that honesty and generosity of spirit, and the passion for the public good, were not motives strong enough to induce his heroes to desire to be in public life. They must be called, entreated, and forced. By single and plain-hearted men, he means the same, no doubt, with those described by the other expressions, honest, generous, and public spirits. Cincinnatus, Camillus, Fabius, and Curius, were men as simple and as generous as any; and these all, by his own account, had a strong aversion to the public service. Either these great characters must be supposed to have practised the *Nolo Episcopari,* to have held up a fictitious aversion for what they really desired, or we must allow their reluctance to have been sincere. If counterfeit, these examples do not deserve our imitation; if sincere, they will never be followed by men enough to carry on the business of the world.

...

If "the life of liberty, and the only remedy against self-interest lies in succession of powers and persons," the United States of America have taken the most effectual measures to secure that life and that remedy, in establishing annual elections of their governors, senators, and representatives. This will probably be allowed to be as perfect an establishment of a succession of powers and persons as human laws can make; but in what manner annual elections of governors and senators will operate, remains to be ascertained. It should always be remembered, that this is not the first experiment that was ever made in the world of elections to great offices of state; how they have hitherto operated in every great nation, and what has been their end, is very well known. Mankind have universally discovered that chance was preferable to a corrupt choice, and have trusted Providence rather than themselves. First magistrates and senators had better be made hereditary at once, than that the people should be universally debauched and bribed, go to loggerheads, and fly to arms regularly every year. Thank Heaven! Americans understand calling conventions; and if the time should come, as it is very possible it may, when hereditary descent shall become a less evil than annual fraud and violence, such a convention may still prevent the first magistrate from becoming absolute as well as hereditary. But if this argument of our author is considered as he intended it, as a proof that a succession of powers and persons in one assembly is the most perfect commonwealth, it is totally fallacious.

Though we allow benevolence and generous affections to exist in the human breast, yet every moral theorist will admit the selfish passions in the generality of men to be the strongest. There are few who love the public better than themselves, though all may have some affection for the public. We are not, indeed, commanded to love our neighbor better than ourselves. Self-interest, private avidity, ambition, and avarice, will exist in every state of society, and under every form of government. A succession of powers and persons, by frequent elections, will not lessen these passions in any case, in a governor, senator, or representative; nor will the apprehension of an approaching election restrain them from indulgence if they have the power. The only remedy is to take away the power, by controlling the selfish avidity of the governor, by the senate and house; of the senate, by the governor and house; and of the house, by the governor and senate. Of all possible forms of government, a sovereignty in one assembly, successively chosen by the people, is perhaps the best calculated to facilitate the gratification of self-love, and the pursuit of the private interest of a few individuals; a few eminent conspicuous characters will be continued in their seats in the sovereign assembly, from one election to another, whatever changes are made in the seats around them; by superior art, address, and opulence, by more splendid birth, reputations, and connections, they will be able to intrigue with the people and their leaders, out of doors, until they worm out most of their opposers, and introduce their friends; to this end, they will bestow all offices, contracts, privileges in commerce, and other emoluments, on the latter and their connections, and throw every vexation and disappointment in the way of the former, until they establish such a system of hopes and fears throughout the state, as shall enable them to carry a majority in every fresh election of the house. The judges will be appointed by them and their party, and of consequence, will be obsequious enough to their inclinations. The whole judicial authority, as well as the executive, will be employed, perverted and prostituted to the purposes of electioneering. No justice will be attainable, nor will innocence or virtue be safe, in the judicial courts, but for the friends of the prevailing leaders; legal prosecutions will be instituted and carried on against opposers, to their vexation and ruin; and as they have the public purse at command, as well as the executive and judicial power, the public money will be expended in the same way. No favors will be attainable but by those who will court the ruling demagogues in the house, by voting for their friends and instruments; and pensions and pecuniary rewards and gratifications, as well as honors and offices of every kind, will be voted to friends and partisans. The leading minds and most influential characters among the clergy will be courted, and the views of the youth in this department will be turned upon those men, and the road to promotion and employment in the church will be obstructed against such as will not worship the general idol. Capital characters among the physicians will not be forgotten, and the means of acquiring reputation and practice in the healing art will be to get the state trumpeters on the side of youth. The bar, too, will be made so subservient, that a young gentleman will have no chance to obtain a character or clients, but by falling in with the views of the judges and their creators. Even the theatres, and actors and actresses, must become politicians, and convert the public pleasures into engines of popularity for the governing members of the house. The press, that great barrier and bulwark of the rights of mankind, when it is protected in its freedom by law, can now no longer be free; if the authors, writers, and printers, will not accept of the hire that will be offered them, they must submit to the ruin that will be denounced against them. The presses, with much secrecy and concealment, will be made the vehicles of calumny against the minority, and of panegyric and empirical applauses of the leaders of the majority, and no remedy can possibly be obtained. In one word, the whole system of affairs, and every conceivable motive of hope and fear, will be employed to promote the private interests of a few, and their obsequious majority; and there is no remedy but in arms. Accordingly we find in all the Italian republics the minority always were driven to arms in despair.

"The attaining of particular ends requires length of time; designs must lie long in fermentation to gain the opportunity to bring matters to perfection." It is true; but less time will be necessary in this case, in general, than even in a simple hereditary monarchy or aristocracy.

An aristocracy, like the Roman senate, between the abolition of royalty and the institution of the tribunate, is of itself a faction, a private partial interest. Yet it was less so than an assembly annually chosen by the people, and vested with all authority, would be; for such an assembly runs faster and easier into an oligarchy than an hereditary aristocratical assembly. The leading members having, as has been before shown in detail, the appointment of judges, and the nomination to all lucrative and honorable offices, they have thus the power to bend the whole executive and judicial authority to their own private interest, and by these means to increase their own reputations, wealth, and influence, and those of their party, at every new election; whereas, in a simple hereditary aristocracy, it is the interest of the members in general to preserve an equality among themselves as long as they can; and as they are smaller in number, and have more knowledge, they can more easily unite for that purpose, and there is no opportunity for any one to increase his power by any annual elections. An aspiring aristocrat, therefore, must take more time, and use more address, to augment his influence; yet we find in experience, that even hereditary aristocracies have never been able to prevent oligarchies rising up among them, but by the most rigorous, severe, and tyrannical regulations, such as the institution of inquisitions, &c.

It may sound oddly to say that the majority is a faction; but it is, nevertheless, literally just. If the majority are partial in their own favor, if they refuse or deny a perfect equality to every member of the minority, they are a faction; and as a popular assembly, collective or representative, cannot act, or will, but by a vote, the first step they take, if they are not unanimous, occasions a division into majority and minority, that is, into two parties, and the moment the former is unjust it is a faction. The Roman decemvirs themselves, were set up by the people, not by the senate; much longer time would have been required for an oligarchy to have grown up among the patricians and in the senate, if the people had not interposed and demanded a body of laws, that is, a constitution. The senate opposed the requisition as long as they could, but at last appointed the decemvirs, much against their own inclinations, and merely in compliance with the urgent clamors of the people. Nedham thinks, that "as the first founders of the Roman liberty did well in driving out their kings; so, on the other side, they did very ill in settling a standing authority within themselves." It is really very injudicious, and very ridiculous, to call those Roman nobles, who expelled their kings, founders of the Roman liberty; nothing was farther from their heads or their hearts than national liberty; it was merely a struggle for power between a king and a body of haughty envious nobles;

240 THE POLITICAL WRITINGS OF JOHN ADAMS

the interests of the people and of liberty had no share in it. The Romans might do well in driving out their king; he might be a bad and incorrigible character; and in such a case any people may do well in expelling or deposing a king. But they did not well in demolishing the single executive magistracy; they should have then demanded a body of laws, a definite constitution, and an integral share in the legislature for the people, with a precise delineation of the powers of the first magistrate and senate. In this case they would have been entitled to the praise of founders of Roman liberty; but as it was, they only substituted one system of tyranny for another, and the new one was worse than the old.

They certainly "did very ill in settling a standing 'sovereign' supreme authority within themselves." Thus far our author is perfectly in the right, and the reason he gives for this opinion is very well founded; it is the same that was given thousands of years before him, by Plato, Socrates, and others, and has been constantly given by all succeeding writers in favor of mixed governments, and against simple ones, "because, lying open to the temptations of honor and profit," or, in other words, having their ambition and vanity, avarice and lust, hatred and resentment, malice and revenge, in short, their self-love, and all their passions ("which are sails too big for any human bulk") unrestrained by any controlling power, they were at once transported by them, and made use of their public power not for the good of the commonwealth, but for the gratification of their private passions, whereby they put the commonwealth into frequent flames of discontent and sedition.

Thus far is very well; but when our author goes on to say, "which might all have been prevented, could they have settled the state free, indeed, by placing an orderly succession of supreme authority in the hands of the people," he can be followed by no one who knows what is in man, and in society; because that supreme authority falls out of the whole body into a majority at the first vote. To expect self-denial from men, when they have a majority in their favor, and consequently power to gratify themselves, is to disbelieve all history and universal experience; it is to disbelieve Revelation and the Word of God, which informs us, the heart is deceitful above all things, and desperately wicked. There have been examples of self-denial, and will be again; but such exalted virtue never yet existed in any large body of men, and lasted long; and our author's argument requires it to be proved, not only that individuals, but that nations and majorities of nations, are capable, not only of a single act, or a few acts, of disinterested justice and exalted self-denial, but of a course of such heroic virtue for ages and generations; and not only that they are capable of this, but that it is probable they will practise it. There is no man so blind as not to see, that to talk of founding a government upon a supposition that nations and great bodies of men, left to themselves, will practise a course of self-denial, is either to babble like a new-born infant, or to deceive like an unprincipled impostor.

Nedham has himself acknowledged, in several parts of this work, the depravity of men in very strong terms. In this fifth reason he avers "temptations of honor and profit" to be "sails too big for any human bulk." Why then does he build a system on a foundation which he owns to be so unstable? If his mind had been at liberty to follow his own ideas and principles, he must have seen that a succession of supreme authority in the hands of the people, by their house of representatives, is at first an aristocracy as despotical as a Roman senate, and becomes an oligarchy even sooner than that assembly fell into the decemvirate. There is this infallible disadvantage in such a government, even in comparison with an hereditary aristocracy, that it lets in vice, profligacy, and corruption, like a torrent, with tyranny; whereas the latter often guards the morals of the people with the utmost severity. Even the despotism of aristocracy preserves the morals of the people.

It is pretended by some, that a sovereignty in a single assembly, annually elected, is the only one in which there is any responsibility for the exercise of power. In the mixed government we contend for, the ministers, at least of the executive power, are responsible for every instance of the exercise of it; and if they dispose of a single commission by corruption, they are responsible to a house of representatives, who may, by impeachment, make them responsible before a senate, where they may be accused, tried, condemned, and punished by independent judges. But in a single sovereign assembly, each member, at the end of his year, is only responsible to his constituents; and the majority of members who have been of one

party, and carried all before them, are to be responsible only to their constituents, not to the constituents of the minority who have been overborne, injured, and plundered. And who are these constituents to whom
the majority are accountable? Those very persons, to gratify whom they
have prostituted the honors, rewards, wealth, and justice of the state. These,
instead of punishing, will applaud; instead of discarding, will reëlect, with
still greater eclat, and a more numerous majority; for the losing cause will
be deserted by numbers. And this will be done in hopes of having still
more injustice done, still more honors and profits divided among themselves, to the exclusion and mortification of the minority. It is then astonishing that such a simple government should be preferred to a mixed
one, by any rational creature, on the score of responsibility.

There is, in short, no possible way of defending the minority, in such a
government, from the tyranny of the majority, but by giving the former
a negative on the latter,—the most absurd institution that ever took place
among men. As the major may bear all possible relations of proportion to
the minor part, it may be fifty-one against forty-nine in an assembly of a
hundred, or it may be ninety-nine against one only. It becomes therefore
necessary to give the negative to the minority, in all cases, though it be
ever so small. Every member must possess it, or he can never be secure that
himself and his constituents shall not be sacrificed by all the rest. This is the
true ground and original of the *liberum veto*[39] in Poland; but the consequence has been ruin to that noble but ill-constituted republic. One fool,
or one knave, one member of the diet, which is a single sovereign assembly, bribed by an intriguing ambassador of some foreign power, has prevented measures the most essential to the defence, safety, and existence of
the nation. Hence humiliations and partitions! This also is the reason on
which is founded the law of the United Netherlands, that all the seven
provinces must be unanimous in the assembly of the states-general; and
all the cities and other voting bodies in the assemblies of the separate
states. Having no sufficient checks in their uncouth constitution, nor any

---

[39] ["free veto," in other words the right of any minority, even a minority of one, to prevent something from being done. Ed.]

mediating power possessed of the whole executive, they have been driven to demand unanimity instead of a balance. And this must be done in every government of a single assembly, or the majority will instantly oppress the minority. But what kind of government would that be in the United States of America, or any one of them, that should require unanimity, or allow of the *liberum veto?* It is sufficient to ask the question, for every man will answer it alike.

No controversy will be maintained with our author, that "a free state is more excellent than simple monarchy or simple aristocracy." But the question is, What is a free state? It is plain our author means a single assembly of representatives of the people, periodically elected, and vested with the supreme power. This is denied to be a free state. It is at first a government of grandees, and will soon degenerate into a government of a junto or oligarchy of a few of the most eminent of them, or into an absolute monarchy of one of them. The government of these grandees, while they are numerous, as well as when they become few, will be so oppressive to the people, that the people, from hatred or fear of the gentlemen, will set up one of them to rule the rest, and make him absolute.

Will it be asked how this can be proved? It is proved, as has been often already said, by the constitution of human nature, by the experience of the world, and the concurrent testimony of all history. The passions and desires of the majority of the representatives in an assembly being in their nature insatiable and unlimited by any thing within their own breasts, and having nothing to control them without, will crave more and more indulgence, and, as they have the power, they will have the gratification; and Nedham's government will have no security for continuing free, but the presumption of self-denial and self-government in the members of the assembly, virtues and qualities that never existed in great bodies of men, by the acknowledgment of all the greatest judges of human nature, as well as by his own, when he says that "temptations of honor and profit are sails too big for any human bulk." It would be as reasonable to say, that all government is altogether unnecessary, because it is the duty of all men to deny themselves, and obey the laws of nature and the laws of God. However clear the duty, we know it will not be performed; and, therefore, it is our duty to enter into associations, and compel one another to do some of it.

It is agreed that the people are the best keepers of their own liberties, and the only keepers who can be always trusted; and, therefore, the people's fair, full, and honest consent, to every law, by their representatives, must be made an essential part of the constitution; but it is denied that they are the best keepers, or any keepers at all, of their own liberties, when they hold collectively, or by representation, the executive and judicial power, or the whole and uncontrolled legislative; on the contrary, the experience of all ages has proved, that they instantly give away their liberties into the hand of grandees, or kings, idols of their own creation. The management of the executive and judicial powers together always corrupts them, and throws the whole power into the hands of the most profligate and abandoned among themselves. The honest men are generally nearly equally divided in sentiment, and, therefore, the vicious and unprincipled, by joining one party, carry the majority; and the vicious and unprincipled always follow the most profligate leader, him who brides the highest, and sets all decency and shame at defiance. It becomes more profitable, and reputable too, except with a very few, to be a party man than a public-spirited one.

It is agreed that "the end of all government is the good and ease of the people, in a secure enjoyment of their rights, without oppression;" but it must be remembered, that the rich are *people* as well as the poor; that they have rights as well as others; that they have as clear and as *sacred* a right to their large property as others have to theirs which is smaller; that oppression to them is as possible and as wicked as to others; that stealing, robbing, cheating, are the same crimes and sins, whether committed against them or others. The rich, therefore, ought to have an effectual barrier in the constitution against being robbed, plundered, and murdered, as well as the poor; and this can never be without an independent senate. The poor should have a bulwark against the same dangers and oppressions; and this can never be without a house of representatives of the people. But neither the rich nor the poor can be defended by their respective guardians in the constitution, without an executive power, vested with a negative, equal to either, to hold the balance even between them, and decide when they cannot agree. If it is asked, When will this negative be used? it may be answered, Perhaps never. The known existence of it will prevent all occasion to exercise it; but if it has not a being, the want of it will be felt every day. If it has not been used in England for a long time past, it by no means follows that there have not been occasions when it might have been employed with propriety. But one thing is very certain, that there have been many occasions since the Revolution, when the constitution would have been overturned if the negative had not been an indubitable prerogative of the crown.

It is agreed that the people are "most sensible of their own burdens; and being once put into a capacity and freedom of acting, are the most likely to provide remedies for their own relief." For this reason they are an essential branch of the legislature, and have a negative on all laws, an absolute control over every grant of money, and an unlimited right to accuse their enemies before an impartial tribunal. Thus far they are most sensible of their burdens, and are most likely to provide remedies. But it is affirmed that they are not only incapable of managing the executive power, but would be instantly corrupted by it in such numbers, as would destroy the integrity of all elections. It is denied that the legislative power can be wholly intrusted in their hands with a moment's safety. The poor and the vicious would instantly rob the rich and virtuous, spend their plunder in debauchery, or confer it upon some idol, who would become the despot; or, to speak more intelligibly, if not more accurately, some of the rich, by debauching the vicious to their corrupt interest, would plunder the virtuous, and become more rich, until they acquired all the property, or a balance of property and of power, in their own hands, and domineered as despots in an oligarchy.

It is agreed that the "people know where the shoe wrings, what grievances are most heavy," and, therefore, they should always hold an independent and essential part in the legislature, and be always able to prevent the shoe from wringing more, and the grievances from being made more heavy; they should have a full hearing of all their arguments, and a full share of all consultations, for easing the foot where it is in pain, and for lessening the weight of grievances or annihilating them. But it is denied that they have right, or that they should have power to take from one man his property to make another easy, and that they *only* know "what fences they stand in need of to shelter them from the injurious assaults of those powers that are above them;" meaning, by the powers above them, senators and magistrates, though, properly speaking, there are no powers above them but the law, which is above all men, governors and senators, kings, and nobles, as well as commons.

The Americans have agreed with this writer in the sentiment, that "it is but reason that the people should see that none be interested in the supreme authority but persons of their own election, and such as must, in a short time, return again into the same condition with themselves." This hazardous experiment they have tried, and, if elections are soberly made, it may answer very well; but if parties, factions, drunkenness, bribes, armies, and delirium come in, as they always have done sooner or later, to embroil and decide every thing, the people must again have recourse to conventions and find a remedy. Neither philosophy nor policy has yet discovered any other cure, than by prolonging the duration of the first magistrate and senators. The evil may be lessened and postponed, by elections for longer periods of years, till they become for life; and if this is not found an adequate remedy, there will remain no other but to make them hereditary. The delicacy or the dread of unpopularity that should induce any man to conccal this important truth from the full view and contemplation of the people, would be a weakness, if not a vice. As to "reaping the same benefit or burden, by the laws enacted, that befalls the rest of the people," this will be secured, whether the first magistrate and senate be elective or hereditary, so long as the people are an integral branch of the legislature, can be bound by no laws to which they have not consented, and can be subjected to no tax which they have not agreed to lay. It is agreed that the "issue of such a constitution," whether the governor and senate be hereditary or elective, must be this, "that no load be laid upon any, but what is common to all, and that always by common consent; not to serve the lusts of any, but only to supply the necessities of their country."

The next paragraph is a figurative flourish, calculated to amuse a populace without informing their understandings. Poetry and mystics will answer no good end in discussing questions of this nature. The simplest style, the most mathematical precision of words and ideas, is best adapted to discover truth, and to convey it to others, in reasoning on this subject. There is here a confusion that is more than accidental—it is artful. The author purposely states the question, and makes the comparison only between simple forms of government, and carefully keeps out of sight the idea of a judicious mixture of them all. He seems to suppose, that the supreme power must be wholly in the hands of a simple monarch, or of a single senate, or of the people, and studiously avoids considering the sovereignty lodged in a composition of all three. "When a supreme power long continues in the hands of any person or persons, they, by greatness of place, being seated above the middle region of the people, sit secure from all winds and weathers, and from those storms of violence that nip and terrify the inferior part of the world." If this is popular poetry, it is not philosophical reasoning. It may be made a question, whether it is true in fact, that persons in the higher ranks of life are more exempted from dangers and evils that threaten the commonwealth than those in the middle or lower rank? But if it were true, the United States of America have established their governments upon a principle to guard against it; and, "by a successive revolution of authority, they come to be degraded of their earthly godheads, and return into the same condition with other mortals;" and, therefore, "they must needs be the more sensible and tender of what is laid upon them."

Our author is not explicit. If he meant that a fundamental law should be made, that no man should be chosen more than one year, he has nowhere said so. He knew the nation would not have borne it. Cromwell and his creatures would all have detested it; nor would the members of the Long Parliament, or their constituents, have approved it. The idea would have been universally unpopular. No people in the world will bear to be deprived, at the end of one year, of the service of their best men, and be obliged to confer their suffrages, from year to year, on the next best, until the rotation brings them to the worst. The men of greatest interest and influence, moreover, will govern; and if they cannot be chosen themselves, they will generally influence the choice of others so decidedly, that they may be said to have the appointment. If it is true that "the strongest obligation that can be laid upon a man in public matters, is to see that he engage in nothing but what must either offensively or beneficially reflect upon himself," it is equally true at least in a mixed government as in a simple democracy. It is, indeed, more clearly and universally true, because in the first the representatives of the people being the special guardians of equality, equity, and liberty, for the people, will not consent to unequal laws; but in the second, where the great and rich will have the greatest influence in the public councils, they will continually make unequal laws in their own favor, unless the poorer majority unite, which they rarely do, set up an opposition to them, and run them down by making unequal laws against them. In every society where property exists, there will ever be a struggle between rich and poor. Mixed in one assembly, equal laws can never be expected. They will either be made by numbers, to plunder the few who are rich, or by influence, to fleece the many who are poor. Both rich and poor, then, must be made independent, that equal justice may be done, and equal liberty enjoyed by all. To expect that in a single sovereign assembly no load shall be laid upon any but what is common to all, nor to gratify the passions of any, but only to supply the necessities of their country, is altogether chimerical. Such an assembly, under an awkward, unwieldly form, becomes at once a simple monarchy in effect. Some one overgrown genius, fortune, or reputation, becomes a despot, who rules the state at his pleasure, while the deluded nation, or rather a deluded majority, thinks itself free; and in every resolve, law, and act of government, you see the interest, fame, and power of that single individual attended to more than the general good.

It is agreed, that "if any be never so good a patriot," (whether his power be prolonged or not,) "he will find it hard to keep self from creeping in upon him, and prompting him to some extravagances for his own private benefit." But it is asserted, that power will be prolonged in the hands of the same patriot, the same rich, able, powerful, and well-descended citizen, &c.

as much as if he had a seat for life, or a hereditary seat in a senate, and, what is more destructive, his power and influence is constantly increasing, so that self is more certainly and rapidly growing upon him; whereas, in the other case, it is defined, limited, and never materially varies. If, in the first case, "he be shortly to return to a condition common with the rest of his brethren," it is only for a moment, or a day, or a week, in order to be reëlected with fresh eclat, redoubled popularity, increased reputation, influence, and power. Self-interest, therefore, binds him to propagate a false report and opinion, that he "does nothing but what is just and equal," while, in fact, he is every day doing what is unjust and unequal; while he is applying all the offices of the state, great and small, the revenues of the public, and even the judicial power, to the augmentation of his own wealth and honors, and those of his friends, and to the punishment, depression, and destruction of his enemies, with the acclamations and hosannas of the majority of the people.

"This, without controversy, must needs be the most noble, the most just, and the most excellent way of government in free states," provided our author meant only a mixed state, in which the people have an essential share, and the command of the public purse, with the judgment of causes and accusations as jurors, while their power is tempered and controlled by the aristocratical part of the community in another house, and the executive in a distinct branch. But as it is plain his meaning was to jumble all these powers in one centre, a single assembly of representatives, it must be pronounced the most ignoble, unjust, and detestable form of government; worse than even a well-digested simple monarchy or aristocracy. The greatest excellency of it is, that it cannot last, but hastens rapidly to a revolution

...

The question between us and our author, is not whether the people shall be excluded from all interest in government or not. In this point we are perfectly agreed, namely,—that there can be no constitutional liberty, no free state, no right constitution of a commonwealth, where the people are excluded from the government; where, indeed, the people have not an independent equal share with the two other orders of the state, and an absolute control over all laws and grants of money. We agree, therefore, in his next example, the commonwealth of Venice, "where the people being excluded from all interest in government, the power of making and executing of laws, and bearing offices, with all other immunities, lies only in the hands of a standing senate and their kindred, which they call the patrician or noble order. Their duke is indeed restrained." But far from being "made just such another officer as were the Lacedæmonian kings," he is reduced in dignity and authority much below them," differing from the rest of the senate only in a corner of his cap, besides a little outward ceremony and splendor. The senators themselves have, indeed, liberty at random arbitrarily to ramble and do what they please with the people, who, excepting the city itself, are so extremely oppressed in all their territories, living by no law but the arbitrary dictates of the senate, that it seems rather a junta than a commonwealth; and the subjects take so little content in it, that seeing more to be enjoyed under the Turk, they that are his borderers take all opportunities to revolt, and submit rather to the mercy of a Pagan tyranny. Which disposition if you consider, together with the little courage in their subjects, by reason they press them so hard, and how that they are forced for this cause to rely upon foreign mercenaries in all warlike expeditions, you might wonder how this state hath held up so long, but that we know the interest of Christendom being concerned in her security, she hath been chiefly supported by the supplies and arms of others."

All this is readily allowed. We concur also most sincerely in our author's conclusion, in part, namely,—"That since kings and all standing powers are so inclinable to act according to their own wills and interests, in making, expounding, and executing of laws, to the prejudice of the people's liberty and security, no laws whatsoever should be made but by the people's consent, as the only means to prevent arbitrariness." But we must carry the conclusion farther, namely,—that since all men are so inclinable to act according to their own wills and interests, in making, expounding, and executing laws, to the prejudice of the people's liberty and security, the sovereign authority, the legislative, executive, and judicial power, can never be safely lodged in one assembly, though chosen annually by the people; because the majority and their leaders, the *principes populi,* will as certainly oppress the minority, and make, expound, and execute laws for their own wealth, power, grandeur, and glory, to the prejudice of the liberty and security of the minority, as hereditary kings or standing senates.

The conclusion, therefore, that "the people, in a succession of their supreme single assemblies, are the best keepers of their liberties," must be wholly reprobated.

The twelfth reason is, "because this form is most suitable to the nature and reason of mankind."

If Socrates and Plato, Cicero and Seneca, Hutcheson and Butler are to be credited, reason is rightfully supreme in man, and, therefore, it would be most suitable to the reason of mankind to have no civil or political government at all. The moral government of God, and his vicegerent, Conscience, ought to be sufficient to restrain men to obedience, to justice, and benevolence, at all times and in all places; we must therefore descend from the dignity of our nature, when we think of civil government at all. But the nature of mankind is one thing, and the reason of mankind another; and the first has the same relation to the last as the whole to a part. The passions and appetites are parts of human nature, as well as reason and the moral sense. In the institution of government, it must be remembered that, although reason ought always to govern individuals, it certainly never did since the Fall, and never will, till the Millennium; and human nature must be taken as it is, as it has been, and will be. If, as Cicero says, "man is a noble creature, born with affections to rule rather than obey, there being in every man a natural desire of principality," it is yet certain that every man ought to obey as well as to rule, ἄρχειν χαι ἄρχεσθαι, and that every man cannot rule alone. Each man must be content with his share of empire; and if the nature and reason of mankind, the nobleness of his qualities and affections, and his natural desires, prove his right to a share in the government, they cannot surely prove more than the constitutions of the United States have allowed,—an annual election of the whole legislative and executive, the governor, senate, and house. If we admit them to prove more, they would prove that every man has every year a right to be governor, senator, and representative; which, being impossible, is absurd.

Even in our author's "Right Constitution," every man would have an equal right to be representative, chosen or not. The reason why one man is content to submit to the government of another, as assigned by our author, namely,—"not because he conceives himself to have less right than another to govern, but either because he finds himself less able, or else because he judgeth it will be more convenient for himself and the community, if he submits to another's government," is a proof of this; because, the moment it is allowed that some are more able than others, and that the community are judges who the most able are, you take away the right to rule, derived from the nobleness of each man's individual nature, from his affections to rule rather than obey, or from his natural appetite or desire of principality, and give the right of conferring the power to rule to the community. As a share in the appointment of deputies is all that our author can with any color infer from this noble nature of man, his nature will be gratified and his dignity supported as well, if you divide his deputies into three orders,—of governor for the executive and an integral share in the legislative, of senators for another independent part of the legislative, and of representatives for a third;—and if you introduce a judicious balance between them, as if you huddle them into one assembly, where they will soon disgrace their own nature and that of their constituents, by ambition, avarice, jealousy, envy, faction, division, sedition, and rebellion. Nay, if it should be found that annual elections of governors and senators cannot be supported without introducing venality and convulsions, as is very possible, the people will consult the dignity of their nature better by appointing a standing executive and senate, than by insisting on elections, or at least by prolonging the duration of those high trusts, and making elections less frequent.

It is indeed a "most excellent maxim, that the original and fountain of all just power and government is in the people;" and if ever this maxim was fully demonstrated and exemplified among men, it was in the late American Revolution, where thirteen governments were taken down from the foundation, and new ones elected wholly by the people, as an architect would pull down an old building and erect a new one. There will be no dispute, then, with Cicero, when he says, "A mind well instructed by the light of nature, will pay obedience," willingly "to none but such as command, direct, or govern for its good or benefit;" nor will our author's inferences from these passages from that oracle of human wisdom be denied:

"1. That by the light of nature people are taught to be their own carvers and contrivers in the framing of that government under which they mean to live.

"2. That none are to preside in government, or sit at the helm, but such as shall be judged fit, and chosen by the people.

"3. That the people are the only proper judges of the convenience or inconvenience of a government when it is erected, and of the behavior of governors after they are chosen."

But then it is insisted, that rational and regular means shall be used that the whole people may be their own carvers, that they may judge and choose who shall preside, and that they may determine on the convenience or inconvenience of government, and the behavior of governors. But then it is insisted, that the town of Berwick upon Tweed shall not carve, judge, choose, and determine for the whole kingdom of Great Britain, nor the county of Berkshire for the Massachusetts; much less that a lawless tyrannical rabble shall do all this for the state, or even for the county of Berkshire.

It may be, and is admitted, that a free government is most natural, and only suitable to the reason of mankind; but it by no means follows "that the other forms, as of a standing power in the hands of a particular person, as a king; or of a set number of great ones, as in a senate," much less that a mixture of the three simple forms "are beside the dictates of nature, and mere artificial devices of great men, squared out only to serve the ends and interests of avarice, pride, and ambition of a few, to a vassalizing of the community." If the original and fountain of all power and government is in the people, as undoubtedly it is, the people have as clear a right to erect a simple monarchy, aristocracy, or democracy, or an equal mixture, or any other mixture of all three, if they judge it for their liberty, happiness, and prosperity, as they have to erect a democracy; and infinitely greater and better men

254 THE POLITICAL WRITINGS OF JOHN ADAMS

than Marchamont Nedham, and the wisest nations that ever lived, have preferred such mixtures, and even with such standing powers as ingredients in their compositions. But even those nations who choose to reserve in their own hands the periodical choice of the first magistrate, senate, and assembly, at certain stated periods, have as clear a right to appoint a first magistrate for life as for years, and for perpetuity in his descendants as for life.

When I say for perpetuity or for life, it is always meant to imply, that the same people have at all times a right to interpose, and to depose for maladministration—to appoint anew. No appointment of a king or senate, or any standing power, can be, in the nature of things, for a longer period than *quam diu se bene gesserit,*[40] the whole nation being judge. An appointment for life or perpetuity can be no more than an appointment until further order; but further order can only be given by the nation. And, until the nation shall have given the order, an estate for life or in fee is held in the office. It must be a great occasion which can induce a nation to take such a subject into consideration, and make a change. Until a change is made, an hereditary limited monarch is the representative of the whole nation, for the management of the executive power, as much as a house of representatives is, as one branch of the legislature, and as guardian of the public purse; and a house of lords, too, or a standing senate, represents the nation for other purposes, namely, as a watch set upon both the representative and the executive power. The people are the fountain and original of the power of kings and lords, governors and senates, as well as the house of commons, or assembly of representatives. And if the people are sufficiently enlightened to see all the dangers that surround them, they will always be represented by a distinct personage to manage the whole executive power; a distinct senate, to be guardians of property against levellers for the purposes of plunder, to be a repository of the national tradition of public maxims, customs, and manners, and to be controllers, in turn, both of kings and their ministers on one side, and the

---

[40] ["as long as he has acted (= behaved) well," i.e. on condition of good behavior. Ed.]

representatives of the people on the other, when either discover a disposition to do wrong; and a distinct house of representatives, to be the guardians of the public purse, and to protect the people, in their turn, against both kings and nobles.

A science certainly comprehends all the principles in nature which belong to the subject. The principles in nature which relate to government cannot all be known, without a knowledge of the history of mankind. The English constitution is the only one which has considered and provided for all cases that are known to have generally, indeed to have always, happened in the progress of every nation; it is, therefore, the only scientifical government. To say, then, that standing powers have been erected, as "mere artificial devices of great men, to serve the ends of avarice, pride, and ambition of a few, to the vassalizing of the community," is to declaim and abuse. Standing powers have been instituted to avoid greater evils,—corruption, sedition, war, and bloodshed, in elections; it is the people's business, therefore, to find out some method of avoiding them, without standing powers. The Americans flatter themselves they have hit upon it; and no doubt they have for a time, perhaps a long one; but this remains to be proved by experience.

. . .

CHAPTER II.

Objections Answered.

MARCHAMONT NEDHAM.

. . .

Our author's conscience was always uppermost. He always betrays something which shows that he knew very well what the truth was. He judges very rightly here.

"And though it may be objected," says he, "that afterwards they fell into many divisions and miseries, even in that form, yet whoever observes the story shall find, it was not the fault of the government, but of themselves, in swerving from the rules of a free state, by permitting the continuance of power in particular hands; who having an opportunity thereby to create parties of their own among the people, did for their own ends inveigle, engage, and entangle them in popular tumults and divisions. This was the true reason of their miscarriages; and, if ever any government of the people did miscarry, it was upon that account."

It is plain, from this passage, that our author was well read, and judged very well upon these subjects. He knew how it was; but he has not candidly told us what he knew. That they fell into divisions and miseries he owns; but denies that it was the fault of the government—it was the fault of themselves. Is it not the fault of themselves under all governments, despotisms, monarchies, aristocracies, oligarchies, as well as democracies? Was it not the fault of themselves under their kings, their perpetual archons, their archons for life, their ten archons, as well as under the Pisistratidæ, that they were tormented with divisions and miseries? The law of nature would be sufficient for the government of men, if they would consult their reason, and obey their consciences. It is not the fault of the law of nature, but of themselves, that it is not obeyed; it is not the fault of the law of nature that men are obliged to have recourse to civil government at all, but of themselves; it is not the fault of the ten commandments, but of themselves, that Jews or Christians are ever known to steal, murder, covet, or blaspheme. But the legislator who should say the law of nature is enough, if you do not obey it, it will be your own fault, therefore no other government is necessary, would be thought to trifle.

We certainly know, from the known constitution of the human mind and heart and from uniform experience, that the law of nature, the decalogue, and all the civil laws, will be violated, if men's passions are not restrained; and, therefore, to presume that an unmixed democratical government will preserve the laws, is as mad as to presume that a king or senate will do it. If a king or senate do not observe the laws, we may say it is not the fault of the government, but of themselves. What then? We know that themselves will commit the fault, and so will a simple democracy, and, therefore, it is in all these cases the fault of the government as well as of themselves. The government should be so constituted, that themselves cannot commit the fault. Swerving from rules is no more the fault of standing kings and senates, than it is of standing or successive popular assemblies. Of the three, the last have the strongest disposition to swerve, and always do swerve the soonest when unbalanced. But the fault of permitting the continuance of power in particular hands, is incurable in the people, when they have the power. The people think you a fool, when you advise them to reject the man you acknowledge to be the ablest, wisest, and best, and whom you and they know they love best, and appoint another, who is but second in their confidence. They ever did, and ever will continue him, nay, and augment his power; for their love of him, like all their other passions, never stands still; it constantly grows, until it exceeds all bounds. These continual reëlections, this continuance of power in particular men, gives them "an opportunity to create parties of their own among the people, and for their own ends to inveigle, engage, and entangle them in popular tumults and divisions."

Let me now ask Marchamont Nedham, or any advocate for his system: Do you believe that the people, unbalanced, ever will avoid to confer a continuance of power on their favorites? Do you believe they ever did in any age or country? The answer must be in the negative. Do you believe it possible, from the constitution of human nature, that they ever will, any more than that they will universally obey the law of nature and the ten commandments? The answer must be in the negative. Why then is the world any longer amused with a speculative phantom, that all enlightened men know never did, and never can exist? My hand is impatient of the pen, and longs to throw it down, while I am laboring through a series of popular sophisms, which disgraces a work that abounds with sense and learning, with excellent principles, maxims, and rules of government, miserably perverted to answer a present purpose, to run down one party, and support another.[41] But as this book is known in America, and ought to be perused by Englishmen, in whatever part of the globe, as a valuable monument of the early period in which the true principles of liberty began to be adopted and avowed in the nation, I shall pursue the subject to the end.

---

[41] The personal history of Nedham sufficiently proves that his work was written for no other reason. He was one of that numerous class of writers, bred in the contests of all free countries, who are ever ready to defend the strongest side for pay.

Lacedæmon is next introduced as an instance of levelism.

"After they had tried the government of one king, then of two, afterwards came in the Ephori, as supervisors of their kings. After they had tried themselves through all the forms of a standing power, and found them all to be levellers of the people's interest and property, then necessity taught them to seek shelter in *a free state, under which they lived happily,* till, by the error of the Athenians, they were drawn into parties by powerful persons, and so made the instruments of division among themselves, for the bringing of new *lèvellers* into play, such as were Machanidas and Nabis."

The Ephori were supervisors of the senate, rather than of kings. They swore, both for themselves and the people, to support the kings forever against the enterprises of the senate. But when did the Lacedæmonians take shelter in a free state? Never, according to our author's definition of a free state, until the Ephori murdered the king, instead of supporting him, according to their oath, and until the people set up Machanidas and Nabis. And it is always thus. The first thing a people broke loose from all restraints of their power do, is to look out for a chief, whom they instantly make a despot in substance, and very soon in form. The government of Sparta was as different from a free state, during the six or seven centuries that Lycurgus's institution lasted, as the English constitution is, and much more. The people had not half the weight in it. Standing powers, both of king and senate, stood like Mount Atlas while the republic existed, and when the free state succeeded, it was the tyranny of Machanidas and Nabis, not better than that of Nero. It is droll enough to call the Spartans levellers, to be sure; they who supported a haughty aristocracy at home, and in every other city of Greece where they could negotiate. When the institution of Lycurgus was worn out, and the people began to gain in power, they used it as the Athenians and all others have done when unbalanced; they set up idols, continued and increased their power, were drawn into parties and divisions, and made themselves instruments of division, until despotism became inevitable.

Rome, in her turn, comes round.

"After the standing form of kings was extinct, and a new one established, the people found as little safety and property as ever."

Here the fact is truly stated, and the expressions are very just, "for the
standing senate and the decemviri proved as great levellers as kings." It is
burlesque again to call the senate and decemviri *levellers*. They were the
very antithesis. But if by *levellers* he means arbitrary men, it is very true.

"So that they were forced to settle the government of the people by a
due and orderly succession of their supreme assemblies."

I wonder when. To quote Athens, Sparta, and Rome, as examples of a
government of one sovereign representative assembly, is dishonest; nothing
can be further from the purpose. The standing power of the senate existed
from Romulus to Cæsar, as our author very well knew, and the people
never obtained even an effectual check. So far from settling the government of the people by a due and orderly succession of their supreme
assemblies, if "they ever recovered their property, in having somewhat they
might call their own," they owed the blessing to the senate's wisdom and
equity; for the people were so far from being sovereign in their successive assemblies, that they had not an equal share of power with the senate, allowing for all the assistance they derived from the tribunes. But as
soon as they began to arrogate a superior power, or even an equal share,
they began to run into "the error of Lacedæmonians, Athenians," and all
other people that ever lived; "swerving from the rules of a free state;" or, in
other words, trampling on the laws, "lengthening of power in particular
hands, they were drawn and divided into parties, to serve the lusts of such
powerful men as by craft became their leaders; so that by this means,
through their own default, they were deprived of their liberty long before
the days of imperial tyranny. Thus Cinna, Sylla, Marius, and the rest of
that succeeding gang, down to Cæsar, used the people's favor to obtain a
continuation of power in their own hands; and then, having saddled the
people with a new standing form of their own, they immediately rooted
up the people's liberty and property by arbitrary sentences of death, proscriptions, fines, and confiscations; which strain of *levelling,* (more intolerable than the former) was maintained by the same arts of devilish policy
down to Cæsar, who, striking in a favorite of the people, and, making use

of their affections to lengthen power in his own hands, at length, by this error of the people, gained opportunity to introduce a new levelling form of standing power in himself, to an utter and irrecoverable ruin of the Roman liberty and property."

Thus it is that our author accumulates examples from history, which are demonstrations against his own system, and in favor of the English and American constitutions. A good Englishman, or a good American, with the most diligent search, could not find facts more precisely in vindication of those balances to the power of the people, a senate, and an executive first magistrate. Nothing else can ever prevent the people from running into the same error, and departing from the rules of a free state, and even the fundamental laws.

...

The fourth objection is, "that such a government brings great damage to the public, by their frequent discontents, divisions, and tumults."

In answer to this, he considers several cases:—1. When any citizens arrogate privileges to themselves or their families, beyond the ordinary standard of the people, then discontents, divisions, and tumults arise. In Rome, the senate retaining the power of the old government in the hands of themselves and their families, upon the expulsion of the Tarquins, occasioned the subsequent discontents and tumults. "Had Brutus made them free when he declared them so, or had the senate followed the advice and example of Publicola, all occasion of discontent had been taken away."

2. "When the people felt themselves not fairly dealt withal" by their leaders and generals. In Syracuse, Dionysius being made general, under pretence of defending the people's liberties, and then using his power to other purposes, became the firebrand of the state, and put the people all into flames for his expulsion.

"In Sparta, the people were peaceable until they found themselves overreached, and their credulity abused, for converting liberty into tyranny under Machanidas and Nabis. In old Rome, under the people's government, it was a sad sight to see the people swarming in tumults, their shops shut up, all trade given over, and the city forsaken, as also in Athens; the occasion was the same; for though the people naturally love ease and peace, yet finding themselves outwitted by slights, and abused by feats of the senate, they grew out of all patience. When any one of their senators or of themselves arrived to any height of power, by insinuating into the people's favor upon specious and popular pretences, and then made a forfeiture of those pretences, as Sylla and Marius, they were the causes of those tumults and slaughters among the Romans, the infamy whereof has been cast most injuriously upon the people's government by the profane pens of court pensioners. Cæsar, too, was the cause of all those civil broils and tragedies among the people."

An impartial writer would have brought every one of these examples in proof of the direct contrary; for they all show, that in proportion as the people gained an authority uncontrolled, or more than a balance for the senate, they grew more discontented, divided, and tumultuous, the more inclined to stir up factious leaders, as Pericles, Alcibiades, Cleon, the Gracchi, Marius, Sylla, and Catiline and Cæsar. The people were certainly peaceable under the kings, though the archons and nobles were not. The people were peaceable under the Grecian archons and Roman senate, so peaceable as to bear extreme oppression; but their turbulence began with their aspiring at power, and increased as it grew, and grew intolerable the moment they obtained the exercise of that authority which our author contends they ought always to exercise. These examples, therefore, all show the necessity of a balance to the people's exercise of power in a mixed government.

3. The people are tumultuous when sensible of oppression, although naturally of a peaceable temper, minding nothing but a free enjoyment; but if circumvented, misled, or squeezed by such as they have trusted, they swell like the sea, overrun the bounds of justice and honesty, ruining all before them; but unhappily they very often mistake and swell against the most honest and faithful men, and insist upon being misled by the most artful and knavish. A great majority of the people, and those as honest as any, are too fond of ease and peace to trouble themselves with public affairs, which leaves an opportunity to the profligate and dissolute to have more influence than they ought, to set up such idols as will flatter and seduce them, by gifts, by offices, and by partial-

ity in judgments; which shows, that although they are very competent to the choice of one branch of the legislative, they are altogether incapable of well managing the executive power. It is really unaccountable, but by that party spirit which destroys the understanding as well as the heart, that our author should conclude, "there is not one precedent of tumults or sedition, which can be cited out of all stories, where the people were in fault." It was even their fault to be drawn in or provoked; it was their fault to set up idols, whose craft or injustice, and whose fair pretences had designs upon the public liberty. They ought to know that such pretenders will always arise, and that they never are to be trusted uncontrolled.

But he seems to be aware that all this would not be quite satisfactory. In order to extenuate the evil, he admits, for argument sake, that the people were tumultuous in their own nature; and he ought to have admitted, from regard to truth, that without laws, government, and force to restrain them, they really are so.

"Tumults, when they happen, are more easily to be borne than those inconveniences that arise from the tyranny of monarchs and great ones."

It is a great question, whether anarchy or tyranny be the greater evil? No man who reads the third book of Thucydides, or Plato's description of a democratical city, or who considers the nature of mankind, will hesitate to say that anarchy, while it lasts, is a greater evil than simple monarchy, even exercised by tyrants. But as anarchy can never last long, and tyranny may be perpetual, no man who loves his country, and is willing to submit to a present evil for a future public good, would hesitate to prefer anarchy, provided there was any hope that the fair order of liberty and a free constitution would arise out of it. A chance of this would be preferred by a patriot to the certainty in the other case. Some men too would prefer anarchy, conscious of more address with the people than with a monarch. But if anarchy and tyranny were to be alike permanent and durable, the generality of mankind would and ought to prefer tyranny; at least monarchy, upon the principle that a thousand tyrants are worse than one.

But our author extenuates the evils of tumults:—

1. "The injury of them never extends further than some few persons, and those for the most part guilty enough, as the thirty grandees in Athens, the ten in Rome, &c." Such tumults, however, have often proceeded to greater lengths, and have had innocent and excellent men for their objects. Examples enough have been cited from Greece and Italy, as well as Holland.

2. "Tumults are not lasting. An eloquent oration of a grave man, as Menenius Agrippa, Virginius, or Cato, may pacify them." True sometimes, but much oftener the grave man will fall a sacrifice to their fury.

3. "Tumults usually turn to the good of the public; the great are kept in awe, the spirits of the people kept warm with high thoughts of liberty." This has some weight in monarchies and aristocracies, where they may be quelled; but in simple democracy, where they cannot, they would be fatal.

4. "In Rome they obtained the law of the twelve tables, procured the tribunes and supreme assemblies and frequent confirmation of them." The supreme assemblies they obtained are very unluckily quoted, because these, having no control, destroyed the commonwealth.

All this "is far otherwise under the standing power of the great ones. They, in their counsels, projects, and designs, are fast and tenacious."

As this is an acknowledgment that the people are not fast and tenacious, that is, steady, it should seem an argument in favor of a standing senate, at least of some senate appointed from the persons of most experience, best education, most respectable families and considerable property, who may be supposed thoroughly to understand the constitution, to have the largest views, and be "fast and tenacious" of the maxims, customs, and laws of the nation, to temper the unsteadiness of the people, and even of their representatives.

"The evils under these forms are more remediless and universal." Not at all in mixed governments. They are, on the contrary, more easily "remedied," for the house of commons is the grand inquest of the nation.

"Those tumults and quarrels that arise among them, never end but in further oppression of the people." Quarrels among them have commonly given more weight to the people, and must always end in relieving the people, where the people have a full share.

Upon the whole, tumults arise in all governments; but they are certainly most remediless and certainly fatal in a simple democracy. Cheats and tricks of great men will as certainly take place in simple democracy as in simple aristocracy or monarchy, and will be less easily resisted or remedied; and, therefore, our author has not vindicated his project from the objection of its danger from tumults. A mixed government, of all others, is best calculated to prevent, to manage, and to remedy tumults, by doing justice to all men on all occasions, to the minority as well as majority; and by forcing all men, majority as well as minority, to be contented with it.

...

CHAPTER THIRD.

Errors of Government and Rules of Policy.

MARCHAMONT NEDHAM.

"THE first error in ancient Christian policy, which hath indeed been a main foundation of tyranny, is that corrupt division of a state into ecclesiastical and civil."

Our author enlarges upon this error, and his speculations are worth reading; but as this is not likely to be the error of America, I shall leave it to be read when such danger approaches.

"The second error is very frequent under all forms of government. It is this,—that care hath not been taken, upon all occasions of alteration, to prevent the passage of tyranny out of one form into another, in all the nations of the world. The interest of absolute monarchy and its inconveniences have been visible and fatal under the other forms, and given undeniable proof of this maxim by experience, in all times, *that the interest of monarchy may reside in the hands of many as well as of a single person.*"

The interest of absolute monarchy he defines to be,—

"An unlimited, uncontrollable, unaccountable station of power and authority in the hands of a particular person, who governs only according to the dictates of his own will and pleasure; and though it hath often been disguised by sophisters in policy, so as it hath lost its own name by shifting forms, yet the thing in itself hath been discovered under the artificial covers of every form, in the various revolutions of government. In Athens, when they had laid aside their king, the kingly power was retained still in all the after turns of government; for their decimal governors and their thirty tyrants were but a multiplied monarchy, the people being in a worse condition than before; for their kings had supervisors and senatic assemblies that did restrain and correct them; but the new governors having none, ran into all the heats and fits and wild extravagancies of an unbounded prerogative. Necessity and extremity opening the people's eyes, they at length saw all the inconveniences of kingship wrapt up in new forms, and rather increased than diminished; so that (as the only remedy) they dislodged the power out of those hands, putting it into their own, and placing it in a constant, orderly revolution of persons elective by the community. And now, one would have thought there was no shelter for a monarchal interest, under a popular form too. But alas! they found the contrary; for *the people not keeping a strict watch over themselves, according to the rules of a free state,* but being *won by specious pretences,* and *deluded by created necessities* to intrust the management of affairs into some particular hands, such an occasion was given thereby to those men to frame parties of their own, that by this means they in a short time became able to do what they list without the people's consent; and, in the end, not only discontinued, but utterly extirpated their successive assemblies."

I have given this at length, in our author's own words, because it is an exact compendium of the whole history of Athens, and shows that he had read it attentively, and understood it perfectly well; and because it is a complete refutation of his own system, his Right Constitution of a Commonwealth. Absolute monarchy, unlimited power in a particular person, who governed by his own will, run through all the history and changes in Athens, according to his own account, even when the people had placed the supreme power in an orderly revolution of persons elective by themselves. Why? "Because the people did not keep a watch over themselves." Did any other people keep a strict watch over themselves? Will any people ever keep a strict watch over themselves? No, surely. Is not this, then, a sufficient reason for instituting a senate to keep a strict watch over them? Is not this a sufficient reason for separating the whole executive power from them, which they know will, and must corrupt them, throw them off their guard, and render it impossible to keep a strict watch over themselves?"

"They did not observe the rules of a free state."

Did any people, that ever attempted to exercise unlimited power, observe the rules of a free state? Is it possible they should, any more than obey, without sin, the law of nature and nature's God? When we find one of these sorts of obedience, we may expect the other. If this writer had been one of the enthusiasts of that day, and told the people they must pray to God for his omnipotent grace to be poured out upon them, to distinguish them from all the rest of mankind as his favorite people, more even than the Jews were, that they might be enabled to observe the rules of a free state, though all history and experience, even that of the Hebrews themselves, and the constitution of human nature, proved it impossible without a miracle; or if he had told them that they were a chosen people, different from all other men, numbers would have believed him, and been disappointed; for it is impious presumption to suppose that Providence will thus distinguish any nation; but it would have been more sensible than thus to acknowledge in effect, as he does repeatedly, the impracticability of his scheme, and still insist upon it.

"The people were won by specious pretences, and deluded by created necessities, to intrust the management of affairs into some particular hands."

And will not the people always be won by specious pretences, when they are unchecked? Is any people more sagacious or sensible than the Athenians, those ten thousand citizens, who had four hundred thousand slaves to maintain them at leisure to study? Will not a few capital characters in a single assembly always have the power to excite a war, and thus create a necessity of commanders? Has not a general a party of course? Are not all his officers and men at his devotion so long as to acquire habits of it? When a general saves a nation from destruction, as the people think, and brings home triumph, peace, glory, and prosperity to his country, is there not an affection, veneration, gratitude, admiration, and adoration of him, that no people can resist? It is want of patriotism not to adore him; it is enmity to liberty; it is treason. His judgment, which is his will, becomes the only law; reason will allay a hurricane as soon; and if the executive and judicial power are in the people, they at once give him both, in substance at first, and not long afterwards in form. The representatives lose all authority before him. If they disoblige him, they are left out by their constituents at the next election, and one of his idolaters is chosen.

"In Rome, also, the case was the same, under every alteration; and all occasioned by the crafty contrivances of grandizing parties, and the people's own facility and negligence in suffering themselves to be deluded; for with the Tarquins (as it is observed by Livy and others) only the name *king* was expelled, but not the thing; the power and interest of kingship was still retained in the senate, and engrossed by the consuls; for besides the rape of Lucretia, among the other faults objected against Tarquin, this was most considerable, that he had acted all things after his own head, and discontinued consultations with the senate, which was the very height of arbitrary power; but yet as soon as the senate was in the saddle, they forgot what was charged by themselves upon Tarquin, and ran into the same error, by establishing an arbitrary, hereditary, unaccountable, power in themselves and their posterity, not admitting the people (whose interest and liberty they had pleaded) into any share in consultation or government, as they ought to have done, by a present erecting of their successive assemblies; so that you see the same kingly interest, which was in one before, resided then in the hands of many. Nor is it my observation only, but pointed out by Livy, in his second book, and in many other places, 'Cum a patribus non consulem sed carnificem, &c.' when the senators strove to create, not consuls, but executioners and tormentors, to vex and tear the people, &c. And in another place of the same book, 'Consules, immoderatâ infinitaque potestate, omnes metus legum, &c.' the consuls, having an immoderate and unlimited power, turned the terror of laws and punishments only upon the people, themselves (in the mean while) being accountable to none but themselves, and their confederates in the senate.[42] Then, the consular government being cashiered, came on the decemviri: 'Cum consulari imperio ac regio, sine provocatione,' saith my author; being invested with a consular and kingly power, without appeal to any other. And in his third book he saith, 'Decem regum species erat,' it was a form of ten kings; the miseries of the people being increased ten times more than they were under kings and consuls.[43] For remedy, therefore, the ten were cashiered also; and consuls being restored, it was thought fit, for the bridling of their power, to revive also the dictatorship (which was a temporary kingship, used only now and then upon occasion of necessity) and also those deputies of the people, called tribunes, which one would have thought had been sufficient bars against monarchic interest, especially being assisted by the people's successive assemblies; but yet, for all this, the people were cheated through their own neglect, and bestowing too much confidence and trust upon such as they thought their friends; for when they swerved from the rules of a free state, by lengthening the dictatorship in any hand, then monarchic interest stept in there, as it did under Sylla, Cæsar, and others, long before it returned to a declared monarchal form; and when they lengthened commands in their armies, then it crept in there, as it did under the aforenamed persons, as well as Marius, Cinna, and others also; and even Pompey himself, not forgetting the pranks of the two triumvirates, who all made a shift under every form, being sometimes called consuls, sometimes dictators, and sometimes tribunes of the people, to outact all the flagitious enormities of an absolute monarchy."

This valuable passage, so remarkable as an abridgment of the Roman history, as containing the essence of the whole that relates to the constitution, as a profound judgment of what passes in all societies, has been transcribed in the author's own words; and, it may be truly said, it contains a full confutation of his own system, and a complete proof of the

[42] [Livy II, lvi, 7; Livy III, ix, 4. Ed.]
[43] [Livy III, xxxvi, 5. Ed.]

necessity of the composition of three branches. It is strictly true, that there is a strong and continual effort in every society of men, arising from the constitution of their minds, towards a kingly power; it is as true in a simple democracy, or a democracy by representation, as it is in simple aristocracy, oligarchy, or monarchy, and in all possible combinations and mixtures of them. This tendency can never be eradicated; it can only be watched and controlled; and the whole art of government consists in combining the powers of society in such a manner, that it shall not prevail over the laws. The excellence of the Spartan and Roman constitutions lay in this; that they were mixtures which did restrain it, in some measure, for a long period, but never perfectly. Why? Because the mixture was not equal. The balance of three branches is alone adequate to this end; and one great reason is, because it gives way to human nature so far, as to determine who is the first man. Such is the constitution of men's minds, that this question, if undecided, will forever disorder the state. It is a question that must be decided, whatever blood or wounds it may occasion, in every species of gregarious animals, as well as men. This point, in the triple division of power, is always determined; and this alone is a powerful argument in favor of such a form.

Our author's Right Constitution is the worst of all possible forms in this respect. There are more pretenders; the choice of means is multiplied; the worst men have too much influence in the decision, more, indeed, than the best; and the whole executive and judicial powers, and the public treasure too, will be prostituted to the decision of this point. In the state of nature, when savage, brutal man ranged the forests with all his fellow-creatures, this mighty contest was decided with nails and teeth, fists, stones, and clubs, in single combats, between all that dared to pretend. Amidst all the refinements of humanity, and all the improvements of civil life, the same nature remains, and war, with more serious and dreadful preparations, and rencounters of greater numbers, must prevail, until the decision takes place.

"The people," says our author, "were cheated through their own neglect, and bestowing too much confidence and trust upon such as they thought their friends." And could he quote an instance from all history of a people who have not been cheated; who have not been negligent; who have not bestowed too much confidence and trust upon such as they thought their friends; who have not swerved from the rules of a free state, by lengthening power in hands that hold it? Can he give a plausible reason to hope that such a people will ever appear? On the contrary, is it not demonstrable that such a people is impossible, without a miracle and a renovation of the species? Why, then, should the people be bribed to betray themselves? Putting the executive power into their hands is bribing them to their own destruction; putting it into the hands of their representatives is the same thing, with this difference for the worse, that it gives more opportunity to conceal the knavery. Giving the executive power to the senate is nearly the same, for it will be in that case used in bribes, to elevate certain senatorial families.

All projects of government, formed upon a supposition of continual vigilance, sagacity, and virtue, firmness of the people, when possessed of the exercise of supreme power, are cheats and delusions. The people are the fountain of power; they must, in their constitution, appoint different orders to watch one another, and give them the alarm in time of danger. When a first magistrate, possessed of the executive, can appeal to the people in time of danger; when a senate can appeal to the people; and when a house of commons can appeal to the people; when it is the interest of each, in its turn, to appeal to the people; when self-preservation causes such appeal; then, and then only, can the people hope to be warned of every danger, and be put constantly on their guard, kept constantly vigilant, penetrating, virtuous, and steady. When their attention, too, is fixed only upon the preservation of the laws, and they cannot be diverted like apes, by throwing the nuts of the executive power among them, to divide them. When they have any thing to do with the executive power, they think of nothing else but scrambling for offices, and neglect altogether the legislature and the laws, which are their proper department. All the flagitious enormities of absolute monarchy will be practised by the democratical despot, triumvirs, decemvirs, who get possession of the confidence of the majority.

Florence testifies the same truth.

"Even when it seemed most free, it was ever the business of one upstart or other, either in the senate or among the people, to make way to their own ambitious ends, and hoist themselves into a kingly posture through the people's favor; as Savonarola, Soderini, and the Medici, whose family fixed itself in a dukedom. Nor can it be forgotten how much of monarchy, of late, crept into the United Provinces."

The conclusion is that, "since the interest of monarchy" (that is, arbitrary power, or the government of men) "may reside in a consul as well as in a king; in a dictator as well as in a consul; in the hands of many as well as of a single person; and that its custom hath been to lurk under every form, in the various turns of government; therefore it concerns every people in a state of freedom, to keep close to the rules of a free state for the turning out of monarchy, whether simple or compound, both name and thing, in one or many; so they ought ever to have a *reverend and noble respect* of such founders of free states and commonwealths, as shall block up the way against monarchic tyranny, by declaring for the liberty of the people, as it consists in a due and orderly succession of authority in their supreme assemblies;" that is, for himself, Oliver Cromwell, and their party, for no other such founders of commonwealth had then ever existed.

The true conclusion from all the reasoning and all the examples, under this second head of Error in Policy, ought to have been, that arbitrary power, or the interest of monarchy, or the government of men, cannot be prevented, nor the government of laws supported, but by mixing the powers of the one, the few, and the many, in equal proportions, in the legislature; by separating the executive from the legislative power, and the judicial department from both.

. . .

I am not without apprehensions that I have not made myself fully understood. The people, in all nations, are naturally divided into two sorts, the gentlemen and the simplemen, a word which is here chosen to signify the common people. By gentlemen are not meant the rich or the poor, the high-born or the low-born, the industrious or the idle; but all those who have received a liberal education, an ordinary degree of erudition in liberal arts and sciences, whether by birth they be descended from magistrates and officers of government, or from husbandmen, merchants, mechanics, or laborers; or whether they be rich or poor. We must, nevertheless, remember, that *generally* those who are rich, and descended from families in public life, will have the best education in arts and sciences, and therefore the gentlemen will ordinarily, notwithstanding some exceptions to the rule, be the richer, and born of more noted families. By the common people we mean laborers, husbandmen, mechanics, and merchants in general, who pursue their occupations and industry without any knowledge in liberal arts or sciences, or in any thing but their own trades or pursuits; though there may be exceptions to this rule, and individuals may be found in each of these classes who may really be gentlemen.

Now it seems to be clear, that the gentlemen in every country are, and ever must be, few in number, in comparison of the simplemen. If you please, then, by the democratical portion of society we will understand the common people, as before explained; by the aristocratical part of the community we will understand the gentlemen. The distinctions which have been introduced among the gentlemen, into nobility greater or lesser, are perfectly immaterial to our present purpose; knights, barons, earls, viscounts, marquises, dukes, and even princes and kings, are still but gentlemen, and the word noble signifies no more than knowable, or conspicuous. But the gentlemen are more intelligent and skilful, as well as generally richer and better connected, and therefore have more influence and power than an equal number of the common people. There is a constant energy and effort in the minds of the former to increase the advantages they possess over the latter, and to augment their wealth and influence at their expense. This effort produces resentments and jealousies, contempt, hatred, and fear, between the one sort and the other. Individuals among the common people endeavor to make friends, patrons, and protectors among the gentlemen. This produces parties, divisions, tumults, and war. But as the former have most address and capacity, they gain more and more continually, until they become exorbitantly rich, and the others miserably poor. In this progress, the common people are continually looking up for a protector among the gentlemen, and he who is most able and willing to protect them acquires their confidence. They unite together by their feelings, more than their reflections, in augmenting his power, because the more power he has, and the less the gentlemen have, the safer they are. This is a short sketch of the history of that progress of passions and feelings which has produced every simple monarchy in the world; and, if nature and its feelings have their course without reflection, they will produce a simple monarchy forever. It has been the common people, then, and not the gentlemen, who have established simple monarchies all over the world. The common people, against the gentlemen, established a simple monarchy in Cæsar at Rome, in the Medici at Florence, &c., and are now in danger of doing the same thing in Holland; and if the British constitution should have its euthanasia in simple monarchy, according to the prophecy of Mr. Hume, it will be effected by the common people, to avoid the increasing oppressions of the gentlemen.

If this is the progress and course of things (and who does not know that it is?) it follows, that it is the true interest and best policy of the common people to take away from the body of the gentlemen all share in the distribution of offices and management of the executive power. Why? Because if any body of gentlemen have the gift of offices, they will dispose of them among their own families, friends, and connections; they will also make use of their votes in disposing of offices, to procure themselves votes in popular elections to the senate or other council, or to procure themselves appointments in the executive department. It is the true policy of the common people to place the whole executive power in one man, to make him a distinct order in the state, from whence arises an inevitable jealousy between him and the gentlemen; this forces him to become a father and protector of the common people, and to endeavor always to humble every proud, aspiring senator, or other officer in the state, who is in danger of acquiring an influence too great for the law or the spirit of the constitution. This influences him to look for merit among the common people, and to promote from among them such as are capable of public employments; so that the road to preferment is open to the common people much more generally and equitably in such a government than in an aristocracy, or one in which the gentlemen have any share in appointments to office.

From this deduction it follows, that the precept of our author, "to educate children (of the common people) in principles of dislike and enmity against kingly government, and enter into an oath of abjuration to abjure a toleration of kings and kingly powers," is a most iniquitous and infamous aristocratical artifice, a most formal conspiracy against the rights of mankind, and against that equality between the gentlemen and the common people which nature has established as a moral right, and law should ordain as a political right, for the preservation of liberty.

By kings and kingly power is meant, both by our author and me, the executive power in a single person. American common people are too enlightened, it is hoped, ever to fall into such a hypocritical snare; the gentlemen, too, it is hoped, are too enlightened, as well as too equitable, ever to attempt such a measure; because they must know that the consequence will be, that, after suffering all the evils of contests and dissensions, cruelty and oppression, from the aristocratics, the common people will perjure themselves, and set up an unlimited monarchy instead of a regal republic.

The second rule of policy is, "not to suffer particular persons to grandize or greaten themselves more than ordinary; for that by the Romans was called '*affectatio regni,*' an aspiring to kingship." Mælius and Manlius are again cited. "The name of the latter was ever after disowned by his whole family, that famous family of the Manlii, and both the name and memory of him and of his consulship were razed out of all public records by decree of the senate."

It is certainly an essential rule in a free government, to suffer no man to greaten himself above the law. But it is impossible it should ever be observed in a simple democracy or aristocracy. What might not Manlius have done, if Rome had been governed by a single sovereign assembly of representatives? It was the aristocracy that murdered Manlius, much against the will of the democracy, so that the instance is against the author. The Orange family in Holland are mentioned too; but it is the common people who have supported that family for their protection against the aristocracy. It is agreed, however, by many respectable writers, that the family of Orange have been dangerous in that state, because the people have no constitutional share in the government, and the authority exercised by the stadtholder is not legally defined. If the people, therefore, in their anger, should augment the power of that house too much above the aristocracy, it would be absolute; but if the people should expel that house, they must set up another, as well as demand a share in the legislature for themselves, or become slaves and a prey to the aristocracy. It is a good rule for Holland to beware of too great a man; but it is equally necessary to beware of five thousand men, who may easily become too great. But in our author's Right Constitution the observance of the rule is impossible. The people, if unrestrained by a senate or a king, will set up some one man, and advance him to a greatness of dignity and authority inconsistent with liberty. As soon as any one in such a government gets the command-in-chief of an army, he has the state in his power. The common people in Holland would assist the army in making the prince absolute (if, indeed, the prince would accept of a gift that would ruin his country as well as his house) if they were not restrained by a standing aristocratical power, which our author abhors.

"*Third Rule. Non diurnare imperia;* not to permit a continuation of command and authority in the hands of particular persons or families."[44]

This rule is undoubtedly necessary to preserve a simple aristocracy or democracy; but it is impracticable in both, and, therefore, it is impracticable to preserve an aristocracy or democracy. But this is by no means a necessary or proper rule in a well constituted free government. Command and authority may be continued for any number of years, or for life, in the same person, without the least danger; because, upon the smallest symptom of an inclination to abuse his power, he may be displaced by the executive, without danger or inconvenience. But in a simple aristocracy or democracy he cannot be removed at all; the majority will support him at all events; or, if they do not, the majority that removes him will be so small, that the minority who are his friends may often raise convulsions.

---

[44] [Literally "not to make sovereign powers long-lasting." Ed.]

It is a necessary rule, too, in such a mixed government as that of Rome, where, in the best of times, the people had an authority nearly equal to that of the senate. Where the mixture is of two powers only, and the executive is wholly in one of them, or partly in one and partly in another, they are in continual danger of the tyranny of a single person, on account of the frequent disputes between the two branches about the exercise of the executive and judicial power; but where the executive is in one hand, the legislative in three, and the judicial in hands different from both, there is rarely, if ever, any danger from a continuance of command in any one. Livy had good reason in the Roman state to say, "*Libertatis magna custodia est, si magna imperia esse non sinas, et temporis modus imponatur;* it is a grand preservative of liberty, if you do not permit great powers and commands to continue long, and if you limit in point of time."[45] And to this purpose the Æmilian law, if it could have been observed, would have been a good one. The noble Roman, in the ninth book, spoke in character, when he said, "*Hoc quidem regno simile est,*" and this indeed is like a kingship, that I alone should bear this great office of censorship *triennium et sex menses* three years and six months, contrary to the Æmilian law."[46] Livy, too, speaks in character, as a good citizen of an aristocratical government, when "in his third book he speaks of a monstrous business, that the ides of May were come (which was the time of their year's choice) and yet no new election appointed. *Id vero regnum haud dubie videri; deploratur in perpetuum libertas;* it without doubt seems no other than a kingdom, and liberty is lost for ever.[47] It was treason for any man to hold that high office of the dictatorship in his own hand beyond six months. Cicero's Epistles to Atticus, concerning Cæsar, contain notable stuff to this purpose. The care of that people, in not permitting any man to bear the same office twice together," was all in character, because continuance in high office constantly exposed the state and constitution to the danger of being overturned and converted into an absolute

---

[45] [Adams makes this a direct rather than reported statement. The reference is Livy IV, xxiv, 4. Ed.]

[46] [Both selections are from Livy IX, xxxiv, 16. Ed.]

[47] [Livy III, xxxviii, 2. Ed.]

monarchy. In this constitution, too, in consequence of the checks between the senate, the tribunes, and the people, there was some chance for having this law observed. But an Æmilian law, in our author's "Right Constitution," would be made to no purpose; it would be set aside, without ceremony, when nothing but a vote of an all-powerful majority would be wanting to set it at defiance. But in a mixed constitution of three branches, such a law, if made, would be punctually executed, much more exactly and certainly than in the Roman constitution; but in such a constitution such a law would be unnecessary, as no danger can arise from the continuance of any general or admiral in command.

The same reasoning is applicable to the free states of Greece, where "Aristotle tells us this rule was observed. The speech of Cincinnatus to the people, to persuade them to let him lay down his command, now the time was come, though the enemy was almost at the gates, and never more need than at that time of his valor and prudence," is a terrible example against our author's system. For, though "no persuasion would serve the turn, resign he would, telling them there would be more danger to the state in prolonging his power than from the enemy, since it might prove a pernicious precedent to the Roman freedom;" yet, as no more than two or three such characters as Cincinnatus appeared in seven hundred years, a statesman would be mad who should place the existence of his form of government upon the presumption that a succession of characters so disinterested would appear to resist the people themselves in their desire to violate a law. If the people at that period could forget a rule so essential to their safety, what are we to expect when they and their idols too are more corrupt? "M. Rutilius Censorinus, although he too made a speech against it, gave way to the people, when they forced him to undergo the office of censor twice together, contrary to the intent and practice of their ancestors, and accepted it upon this condition, that a law might pass against the title in that and other officers, lest it should be drawn into precedent in time to come."

But our author all along mistakes the spirit of this rule; it was an aristocratical regulation altogether; it was the senate and patricians who procured it to be observed, from an aristocratical motive and principle; from a jealousy of the people on one side, and of kingly power on the other. It is the same spirit which precipitated Cassius and Manlius from the rock, and put Mælius to death without ceremony. The people, or their representatives, if uncontrolled, would not probably ever make such a law; if they did, they would never long observe it. The people would not suffer it to be much or long observed in Rome, notwithstanding all the exertions of the aristocracy. The times soon came when Cincinnatuses and Censorinuses were not found to refuse power and office offered them against law, any more than Horatii and Valerii were found to postpone their private fortune to plebeian liberty. Even the Grecian aristocracies could not observe this rule. It was a law of Sparta that no man should be twice admiral; but Lysander had address enough to persuade his countrymen to give the title to Aratus, but the real command to himself, under the title of vice-admiral. Even in that which was in appearance the most democratical state of Greece, Achaia, Aratus had the real power and command when he was out of place as much as when he was in. Our author mistakes, too, the spirit of the law, "that no tribune should be continued two years together." This law was a mere aristocratical artifice, to weaken the influence of the tribunes and their constituents, by preventing them from acquiring confidence, skill, and influence by experience. If the people had understood their own cause, they would have insisted upon the privilege of choosing the same tribune as long as they approved his conduct.

"*Fourth Rule*. Not to let two of one family to bear offices of high trust at one time, nor to permit a continuation of great powers in any one family." This rule is indispensable in aristocracies, where the sovereignty is in continual danger from individuals of great influence and powerful connections, where a jealousy of popular men and measures must be constantly kept up to its highest pitch. The Roman rule, "Ne duo vel plures ex unâ familiâ magnos magistratus gerant eodem tempore, let not two or more of one family bear great offices at the same time;" and the other, "Ne magna imperia ab unâ familiâ prescribantur, let not great commands be prescribed or continued in one family;" were necessary aristocratical rules, because, as the patricians were always afraid of the people, who were continually urging for more power, a very powerful family, by joining with the people, might have changed the constitution. It is a wise and useful rule in general in all governments; but in a simple democracy, though it may be more necessary than in any other form, it is always impracticable; the people will set it aside whenever they please, and will always be sure to depart from it in favor of a favorite man or family. But in a mixed constitution of three branches there is less necessity of observing the rule with strictness, and more facility of observing it when necessary. It is very doubtful whether the constitution of Rome could have been longer preserved, if Cicero had joined Antony instead of Octavius. The people were now uncontrolled and the senate had lost its authority; and the people behaved as they always do, when they pretend to exercise the whole executive and legislative power; that is, they set up immediately one man and one family for an emperor, in effect, sometimes respecting ancient forms at first, and sometimes rejecting them altogether.

But of all rules, this is the least possible to persuade them to observe in such a case. The Florentine family of the Medici were set up in this manner by the people, who, as Machiavel informs us, aimed at all power, and a simple democracy; and in such cases, "Cosimus is always easily admitted to succeed his cousin Alexander." It is not to be wondered at, that "Pompeius Columba stood up in the conclave, and showed them how dangerous and prejudicial it must of necessity prove to the liberties of Italy, that the popedom should be continued in one house, in the hands of two brothers, one after another;" but if the election of a pope had depended upon the people of Florence, Julian de Medici would have been chosen to succeed his brother, though Columba had harangued them with ever so much eloquence against it. A conclave of cardinals, and a body of people in a city, are very different electors. The continuation of power in the House of Orange, is another instance in point; that family have been continued in power by the will of the people, very often expressed in outrageous fury, and very often much against the inclination of the aristocracy.

In every nation, under every form of government, public affairs were always managed by a very small number of families, compared with the whole number. In a simple democracy they will ever be conducted by the smallest number of all; the people will confer all upon a very few families at first, and upon one alone at length. "The Roman senate carried all by families; so does the senate of Venice;" but the number is greater than will ever be intrusted by a people who exercise the whole executive and legislative power in one assembly. But the largest number of families that can be introduced into actual confidence and service, in any combination of the powers of society, is in the composition of three branches; because here as many families are employed to represent the people by numbers, as to represent property in the senate; and it is in such a form alone, that so many families may be employed without confusion and sedition. Here, then, this rule of policy may be best observed, not to let two or more, unnecessarily, bear high offices at once; or, if there are several of a family, whose merit is acknowledged, they may be employed without the smallest danger.

"*Fifth Rule.* To hold up the majesty and authority of their suffrages or votes, entire in their senators or supreme assemblies;" or, in other words, to maintain the free suffrages of senates or people, untainted with the influence or mixture of any commanding power; "for, if this were not secured from *control* or *influence* of any other power, then, *actum erat de libertate.*"[48]

To maintain the independence and integrity of suffrages, without corruption from flattery, artifice, bribes, or fear, is no doubt a good rule; but if the author here means that the power of the people should be absolute, and without control from a senate or a first executive magistrate, it is begging the question, and, what is more, it is notoriously false and destructive.

"So long," says our author, "as the Roman people kept up their credit and authority as sacred in their tribunes and supreme assemblies, so long they continued really free." But how long was this? While they were only defending themselves from the tyranny of the senate; while they were greatly inferior to the senate in power; while they were increasing their own power by obtaining the office of tribune, by obtaining liberty to marry into patrician families, to be appointed ædiles, consuls, censors, &c. In short, while their power was inferior to that of the senate, and

---

[48] ["liberty would have been at stake" Ed.]

controllable by it, they enjoyed as much liberty as ever was enjoyed under that government; but the moment they obtained an equality of power with the senate, they began to exercise more than their half, and to give it to their idols.

"When, by their own neglect, they gave Sylla, and his party in the senate, an opportunity of power to curb them, then their suffrages (once esteemed sacred) were trodden under foot; for immediately after, they came to debate and act but by courtesy, the authority being left by Sylla, after the expiration of his dictatorship, in the hands of the standing senate, so that it could never after be regained by the people. Cæsar, when he marched to Rome, deprived them also of the authority of their suffrages; only in a formal way made use of them; and so, under a shadow of legality, he assumed that power unto himself which they durst not deny him."

Our author is never weary of producing anecdotes and examples from history, which prove his own system to be infallibly destructive of liberty. It is a miserable consolation to a virtuous citizen who has lost his liberty, to tell him that he has lost it "by the neglect and fault of his fellow-citizens in general;" it is the most humiliating and desperate slavery of all. If he had lost it by the simple usurpation of a single man or senate, without the fault of the people (if that, indeed, is a possible or supposable case,) he might still entertain a hope of regaining it; but when we are told that a people lost their liberty by a neglect or fault that we know they will always commit when uncontrolled, is it not a conclusive argument for providing in the constitution for an effectual control? When the people exercise all powers in single assemblies, we know that the power of Sylla and Cæsar will always mix in, and influence and control; it is impossible, then, that in our author's form of government this fifth rule of policy ever should be observed, or the suffrages kept pure and upright. "Just in the same manner dealt Cosmus in the Florentine senate. He made use of their suffrages; but he had so played his cards beforehand, that they durst not but yield to his ambition. So, also, Tiberius first brought the suffrages of the senate at his own devotion, that they durst not but consent to his establishment; and then so ordered the matter, that he might seem to do nothing, not only without their consent, but to be forced to accept the empire by their intreaty; so that you see there was an empire in effect, long before it was declared in formality." Will duplicity be less practicable, or less common, in an assembly of the people than in a senate? May not an empire or despotism in effect, though democratical in form, be less difficult to accomplish than even under an aristocratical form? Empire of particular men will exist in effect under every simple form and every unequal mixture. An empire of laws in reality can be maintained only in an equal mixture of all three.

Sixth Rule. "That the people be continually trained up in the exercise of arms, and the militia lodged only in the people's hands, or that part of them which are most firm to the interest of liberty, that so the power may rest fully in the disposition of their supreme assemblies."

The limitation to "that part most firm to the interest of liberty" was inserted here, no doubt, to reserve the right of disarming all the friends of Charles Stuart, the nobles and bishops. Without stopping to inquire into the justice, policy, or necessity of this, the rule in general is excellent. All the consequences that our author draws from it, however, cannot be admitted. One consequence was, according to him,—

"That nothing could at any time be imposed upon the people but by their consent," that is, by the consent of themselves, or of such as were by them intrusted. "As Aristotle tells us, in his fourth book of Politics, the Grecian states ever had special care to place the use and exercise of arms in the people, because the commonwealth is theirs who held the arms. The sword and sovereignty ever walk hand in hand together." This is perfectly just. "Rome, and the territories about it, were trained up perpetually in arms, and the whole commonwealth, by this means, became one formal militia. There was no difference in order between the citizen, the husbandman, and the soldier." This was the "usual course, even before they had gained their tribunes and assemblies; that is, in the infancy of the senate, immediately after the expulsion of their kings."

But why does our author disguise that it was the same under the kings? This is the truth; and it is not honest to conceal it here. In the times of Tarquin, even, we find no standing army, "not any form of soldiery;" "nor do we find, that in after times they permitted a deposition of the arms of the commonwealth in any other way, till, their empire increasing, necessity constrained them to erect a continued stipendiary soldiery (abroad in foreign parts) either for the holding or winning of provinces."

Thus we have the truth from himself; the whole people were a militia under the kings, under the senate, and after the senate's authority was tempered by popular tribunes and assemblies; but after the people acquired power, equal, at least, if not superior to the senate, then "forces were kept up; the ambition of Cinna, the horrid tyranny of Sylla, the insolence of Marius, and the self ends of divers other leaders, both before and after them, filled all Italy with tragedies, and the world with wonder." Is not this an argument for the power of kings and senates, rather than the uncontrollable power of the people, when it is confessed that the two first used it wisely, and the last perniciously? The truth is, as he said before, "the sword and sovereignty go together." While the sovereignty was in the senate under kings, the militia obeyed the orders of the senate given out by the kings; while the sovereignty was in the senate, under the consuls, the militia obeyed the orders of the senate given out by consuls; but when the sovereignty was lost by the senate, and gained by the people, the militia was neglected, a standing army set up, and obeyed the orders of the popular idols.

"The people, seeing what misery they had brought on themselves by keeping their armies within the bowels of Italy, passed a law to prevent it, and to employ them abroad, or at a convenient distance. The law was, that if any general marched over the river of Rubicon, he should be declared a public enemy; and in the passage of that river this following inscription was erected, to put the men of arms in mind of their duty: 'Imperator, sive miles, sive tyrannus armatus quisquis, sistito vexillum, armaque deponito, nec citra hunc amnem trajicito;' general, or soldier, or tyrant in arms, whosoever thou be, stand, quit thy standard, and lay aside thy arms, or else cross not this river."[49]

---

[49] [An inscription now in the Archeological Museum at Cesena and generally considered a Medieval or Renaissance forgery. Ed.]

But to what purpose was the law? Cæsar knew the people now to be sovereign, without control of the senate, and that he had the confidence both of them and his army, and *cast the die*, and "erected a prætorian band, instead of a public militia; and was followed in it by his successors, by the Grand Signor, by Cosmus, the first great duke of Tuscany, by the Muscovite, the Russian, the Tartar, by the French," and, he might have added, by all Europe, "who by that means are all absolute, excepting England, because the late king Charles I., who attempted it, did not succeed;" and because our author's "Right Constitution of a Commonwealth" did not succeed. If it had, Oliver Cromwell and his descendants would have been emperors of Old England, as the Cæsars were of Old Rome. The militia and sovereignty are inseparable. In the English constitution, if the whole nation were a militia, there would be a militia to defend the crown, the lords, or the commons, if either were attacked. The crown, though it commands them, has no power to use them improperly, because it cannot pay or subsist them without the consent of the lords and commons; but if the militia are to obey a sovereignty in a single assembly, it is commanded, paid, and subsisted, and a standing army, too, may be raised, paid, and subsisted, by the vote of a majority; the militia, then, must all obey the sovereign majority, or divide, and part follow the majority, and part the minority. This last case is civil war; but, until it comes to this, the whole militia may be employed by the majority in any degree of tyranny and oppression over the minority. The constitution furnishes no resource or remedy; nothing affords a chance of relief but rebellion and civil war. If this terminates in favor of the minority, they will tyrannize in their turn, exasperated by revenge, in addition to ambition and avarice; if the majority prevail, their domination becomes more cruel, and soon ends in one despot. It must be made a sacred maxim, that the militia obey the executive power, which represents the whole people in the execution of laws. To suppose arms in the hands of citizens, to be used at individual discretion, except in private self-defence, or by partial orders of towns, counties, or districts of a state, is to demolish every constitution, and lay the laws prostrate, so that liberty can be enjoyed by no man; it is a dissolution of the government. The fundamental law of the militia is, that it be created, directed, and commanded by the laws, and ever for the support of the laws. This truth is acknowledged by our author, when he says: "The arms of the commonwealth should be lodged in the hands of that part of the people which are firm to its establishment."

"*Seventh Rule.* Children should be educated and instructed in the principles of freedom. Aristotle speaks plainly to this purpose, saying, 'that the institution of youth should be accommodated to that form of government under which they live; forasmuch as it makes exceedingly for the preservation of the present government, whatsoever it be.'"

It is unnecessary to take pains to show that the "impression men receive in youth are retained in full age, though never so bad, unless they happen, which is very rare, to quell the corrupt principles of education by an excellent reason and sound judgment;" nor is it necessary to cite the testimonies "of Plutarch or Isocrates," Plato or Solomon, or "Cæsar's Commentaries," nor the examples of "Greece or Gallia," and her "Druids." The example of the difficulty the Romans found to establish their aristocracy upon the ruins of monarchy, arising from the education of their youth (even the sons of Brutus) in different principles, and the obstructions experienced by the Cæsars in establishing despotism among a people educated under a commonwealth, are apposite enough. Education is more indispensable, and must be more general, under a free government than any other. In a monarchy, the few who are likely to govern must have some education, but the common people must be kept in ignorance; in an aristocracy, the nobles should be educated, but here it is even more necessary that the common people should be ignorant; but in a free government knowledge must be general, and ought to be universal. Yet such is the miserable blindness of mankind, that in our author's "Right Constitution" it is very doubtful whether the pitiful motive of saving the expense would not wholly extinguish public education. If there were not a senate, but the people in one assembly ruled all, it is a serious question, whether there is one people upon earth so generally generous and intelligent, as to maintain schools and universities at the public expense. The greater number of every people are still ignorant; and although their leaders might artfully persuade them to a thousand idle expenses, they would

286 THE POLITICAL WRITINGS OF JOHN ADAMS

not be able to persuade them to this. Education, then, must be supported by private munificence; and this source, although sufficient to maintain a few schools and a university in a great nation, can never be sufficient to maintain schools in sufficient numbers to educate a whole people. Where a senate is preserved, it is always a maxim with them to respect learning and educate their own families; their example is followed by all others, who are any way in easy circumstances. In a government of three branches, commoners as well as nobles are under a necessity of educating their children, because they hope to be called to public service, where it is necessary. In all the mixed governments of antiquity, education was necessary, and where the people had a share it was the most generally practised; but in a simple government it never was general. In Sparta it was far from being general; it was confined to youth of family; so it was under the aristocracy in Rome. And although we have no examples of simple democracy to recur to, we need only consider, that the majority must be ignorant and poor; and recollect the murmurs and opposition made by numbers of the lowest classes, who are often joined for sinister purposes by some men of consequence, to be convinced that a general public education never can long exist in a simple democracy; the stinginess, the envy, and malignity of the base and ignorant would be flattered by the artful and designing, and the education of every family left to its own expense, that the rich only might have their children educated.

"*Eighth Rule.* To use liberty with moderation, lest it turn to licentiousness; which, as it is a tyranny itself, so in the end it usually occasions the corruption and conversion of a free state into monarchical tyranny."

This is a caution to the people, and can do no harm; but will do little more good, than "be ye warned and be ye clothed," will relieve the wants of the poor. Lectures and sermons and admonitions will never be sufficient to make all men virtuous; political, as well as moral writers and exhorters will spend their ink and breath, not in vain, it is to be hoped, but without completely reforming the world and restoring innocence and purity to all mankind. How then is the tyranny of licentiousness to be avoided? By the energy of laws. And where will be the energy of law, when a majority may set it aside upon every question? Will not the licentious rich man, who has perhaps greater influence in elections for his licentiousness, be protected from punishment by his party in the house? Will not the continual prostitution of judgment in the executive courts, to the views of a political party, increase and propagate licentiousness? Will not the daily prostitution of the executive power, by bestowing offices, not for virtue or abilities, but merely for party merit, daily increase licentiousness? Will not the appropriation of the public money to elections increase the means of debauchery among the vicious? Will not the minor party be necessitated to imitate the majority in these practices as much as possible, in order to keep themselves in any hopes? When their hopes are gone, they must join the other side in worshipping the same idols, who then become complete despots. In our author's plan of government, then, his caution against licentiousness will be thrown away; but in a mixed government it will be extremely useful. The laws may be made to concur with sermons; and the scourge, the pillory, and the gallows may enforce the precepts of moral writers. The magistrate may be a terror to evil doers and a praise to them that do well, instead of being a terror only to the minority and a praise to those who oppress them. As cautions and admonitions, therefore, are undoubtedly useful in a government truly free, though idle and trifling in a simple democracy, let us proceed to consider those of our author.

His first caution under this eighth rule of policy is, "It is above all things necessary to avoid civil dissension;" and "the uttermost remedy is not to be used upon every distemper or default of those that shall be intrusted with the people's power and authority."

How charming it is for brothers to live in harmony! The smallest things increase by concord! How many beautiful sentiments, in heavenly numbers, from writers sacred and profane, might be said or sung in honor of peace, concord, harmony, and brotherly love! Repetitions of them from age to age have been made, no doubt, to the edification and comfort of many; but, alas! dissensions still exist and daily arise in every nation, city, village, and, I fear I may add, family, in the whole world. Something more efficacious, then, than moral song, ingenious fable, philosophic precept, or Christian ordinance, with reverence be it spoken, must be employed in society, or dissensions will still ravage and desolate the world.

In a simple democracy the citizens will not all think alike; various systems of policy will be approved by different persons; parties will be formed, even with the best intentions and from the purest motives; others will be formed from private views and from base motives. The majority must decide, and, to obtain this, the good will be obliged to unite with the bad, and probably there will be no circle or combination, no club or party in the house, but will be composed partly of disinterested men and partly of interested ones, partly by the virtuous and partly by the vicious; honest men and knaves, wise men and fools will be kneaded together in every mass. Out of the collisions of these, dissensions unavoidably grow, and, therefore, some provision must be made to decide them. An upright, independent tribunal, to judge of controversies, is indispensable; and an upright, independent, judiciary tribunal, in a simple democracy, is impossible. The judges cannot hold their commissions but *durante bene placito*[50] of the majority; if a law is made that their commissions shall be *quamdiu se bene gesserint*,[51] this may be repealed whenever the majority will, and, without repealing it, the majority only are to judge when the judges behave amiss, and, therefore, have them always at mercy. When disputes arise between the rich and poor, the higher and the lower classes, the majority in the house must decide them; there is no possibility, therefore, of having any fixed rule to settle disputes and compose contentions. But in a mixed government the judges cannot be displaced but by the concurrence of two branches, who are jealous of each other, and can agree in nothing but justice; the house must accuse and the senate condemn; this cannot be without a formal trial and a full defence. In the other, a judge may be removed or condemned to infamy without any defence or hearing or trial. This part of our author's caution, then, is vain, useless, and idle, in his own form of government, but wise, just, and excel-

[50] ["continuing good will." In other words, so long as the majority is satisfied—the same idea as the next item, in different words. Ed.]
[51] ["as long as they have acted (= behaved) well" Ed.]

lent, in a government properly mixed. Such cautions are provided by the constitution itself, that civil dissensions can scarcely ever arise; or, if they do, may be easily composed.

The other part of the caution, "that the uttermost remedy is not to be used upon every distemper or default of those that shall be intrusted with the people's power and authority," is, in a simple democracy, totally useless and impracticable. There is no other remedy but the uttermost for any distemper or default. The courts of justice, being tools of the majority, will give no remedy to any of the minority; petitions and remonstrances to the house itself, against its own proceedings, will be despised or resented; so that there can be absolutely no remedy but in arms or by the enormity of tumult, dissension, and sedition, which I suppose are meant by "the uttermost remedy."

It is very true, as our author says, "if one inconvenience happen in government, the correction or curing of it by violence introduceth a thousand; and for a man to think civil war or the sword is a way to be ordinarily used for the recovery of a sick state, it were as great a madness as to give strong waters in a high fever; or as if he shall let himself blood in the heart to cure the aching of his head." This is perfectly just, and expressed with great beauty, propriety, and force; yet it is certain, that a member of the minor party, in Nedham's and Turgot's government, has no chance for any other remedy; and even this is often as desperate as it is always dreadful, because the weaker must attack the stronger. If the only expedient to "confute the arguments" against such a collection of authority in one centre be, that such a people "give them the lie by a discreet and moderate behavior in all their proceedings, and a due reverence of such as they have once elected and made their superiors," these arguments will never be confuted, and the cause of liberty is desperate; because it is as desperate to expect that a majority uncontrolled should behave always discreetly and moderately, as to expect that all men will be wise and good.

Our author's criterion for determining the cases in which the people (in whom "all majesty and authority fundamentally resides, being only ministerially in their trustees or representatives) may use sharp and quick remedies for the cure of a commonwealth," is very judicious, and has been the rule in all English revolutions since; "in such cases only as appear to be manifest intrenchments, either in design or in being, by men of power, upon the fundamentals or essentials of their liberty, without which liberty cannot consist." This rule is common to him and Milton, and has been adopted by Sidney, Locke, Burnet, Hoadley; but this rule is useless in a simple democracy. The minority have no chance for justice in smaller cases, because every department is in the hands of their enemies; and when the tyranny arrives at this last extremity, they have no hope, for all the means, at least the most of the means, of quick and sharp remedies, are in the hands of their enemies too; so that the most desperate, irremediable, and forlorn condition of liberty, is in that very collection of all authority into one centre, that our author calls "a Right Constitution of a Commonwealth."

The instance brought by our author to illustrate his meaning, proves the same thing. In that contention of three hundred years in Rome, between the senate and people, about the division of the conquered lands, the people made a law that no citizen should possess above five hundred acres of land. The senators cried it was an abridgment of liberty; the people cried it was inconsistent with liberty, that the senators should engross too much wealth and power. Livy says, "the people were right, and the senators wrong, but that both did ill in making it a ground of civil dissension;" for the Gracchi, instead of finding out moderate expedients to reduce the senators to reason, proceeded with such heat and violence, that the senate was forced to choose Sylla for their general; which being observed by the people, they also raised an army, and made Marius their general, and herein came to a civil war, "which, through fines, banishment, inhuman cruelties acted on both sides, defeats in the open field, and massacres within the city, cost the best blood and estates of the nobility and commons, and in the end, cost them their liberty, for out of the root of this sprang that civil war between Pompey and Cæsar."

All this again, which is true and just, shows that our author had read the Roman history with discernment, and renders it more unaccountable that he should have perverted so much good sense and learning to support a fantastical image, that he must have seen could not endure. The example in question shows more than the impracticability of liberty in a simple democracy; it shows the imperfection of a mixture of two powers, a senate and people. In a simple democracy, whatever dispute arises, whether about a division of lands, or any thing else, must be decided by the majority; and if their decree is unjust, there is no remedy but to appoint Sylla and Marius generals. In the Roman mixture of two powers there is no remedy to decide the dispute, but to appoint Sylla and Marius, Pompey and Cæsar; but when there are three branches, after two have offered all possible arguments, and cannot agree, the third has only to consider which is nearest justice, and join with that, to decide the controversy and restore the peace. It shall readily be granted, that the civil war between Marius and Sylla was needless, and about an object which did not immediately affect the fundamentals of the constitution; yet indirectly it did; and the fact is, that the struggle now began to be serious which should be master. It was no longer a question, whether the senate should be restrained, but whether the people should be masters. The army under Pompey was necessary. Why? To prevent the people from being masters, and to defend the existence of the senate. The people indeed were already masters, and would have an idol. The instance of Charles I. may be equally applicable; but those times afford as melancholy an example of a *dominatio plebis,* as they do a successful one of resistance to a tyrant. But if any one thinks these examples and cautions, without a balance in the constitution, will instruct people how to demean themselves, and avoid licentiousness, tumult, and civil dissension, and in all the "necessary points of prudence and forbearance which ought to take place in respect of superiors, till it shall evidently appear unto a people, that there is a design on foot to surprise and seize their liberties," he will be miserably mistaken. In a simple democracy they will rise in arms, a thousand times, about common affairs of meum and tuum, between the major and minor party, before any fundamental attack shall be made on the constitution.

"*Second Caution.* That in all elections of magistrates, they have an especial eye upon the public, in making choice of such persons only as have appeared most eminent and active in the establishment and love of freedom."

But suppose any of the people should love their friends better than liberty, and themselves better than the public, as nine tenths of the people did in the purest moments of Grecian and Roman liberty, even when Aristides appeared as a rare phenomenon in one, and Cincinnatus in the other? In such case they will vote for their friends, though royalists, papists, malignants, or call them by what name you will. In our author's "Right Constitution" many will vote for a treat, many for a job, some for exemption from punishment for a crime, some for a monopoly, and some for the promise of an office. This will not be virtuous, but how can you help that?

"In the hands of those," says our author, "who have appeared most eminent and active in the establishment of freedom, may be safely placed the guardianship of liberty; because such men have made the public interest and their own all one, and therefore will neither betray nor desert it in prosperity or adversity."

This was modestly bespeaking unlimited confidence for Oliver Cromwell and his associates; and such blind, rash confidence has surrendered the liberties of all nations; but it is not the language nor the maxim of liberty; her universal precept should be, *trust not to human nature, without a control, the conduct of my cause.*

To lay it down "as a certain rule, that if any person be admitted into power that loves not the commonwealth above all other considerations, such a man is (as we say) every man's money; any state-merchant may have him for a factor; and for good consideration he will often make returns upon the public interest, have a stock going in every party, and with men of every opinion; and, if occasion serve, truck with the common enemy and commonwealth, both together," is perhaps to rely upon a patriotism that never existed in any whole nation. It is to be feared the commonwealth would suffer in most countries; but admitting so exalted an opinion of the patriotism of any given country, it will still remain true, that there will be differences of sentiment concerning the good of the commonwealth; and the parties formed by these divisions, if uncontrolled, will have all the ill consequences that have been pointed out. The more sincerely parties love the republic, with so much the more ardor will they pursue their own notions of its good. Aristotle's opinion, in the first book of his Politics, "Per negligentiam mutatur status reipublicæ, cum ad potestates assumuntur illi qui presentem statum non amant; the form of a commonwealth is then altered by negligence, when those men are taken into power who do not love the present establishment," may be well founded; and yet it may not follow that it is safe to trust omnipotence to those who are well affected, nay, even to those who really love the commonwealth above all other things, and prefer her good to their own, since that character may change, and those virtues, too, may not be accompanied with so many motives and so many advantages of information, in what the good of the public consists, as may be had in a division and mixture of powers.

It is a good rule "to avoid those who hate the commonwealth, and those who are neutral and indifferent about it;" and no doubt "most of the broils, tumults, and civil dissensions, in free states, have been occasioned by the ambitious, treacherous, and indirect practices of such persons admitted into power, as have not been firm in their hearts to the interests of liberty." But how shall the people know whose heart will stand the trial, when so many people have been disappointed before them? Rome is again quoted as an example; and the senate are said to have garbled, perplexed, and turmoiled the people's affairs, concernments, and understandings; but although this is true, it is equally so that the people perplexed their own affairs, and those of the senate too.

The reader, who has pardoned already so many digressions, will easily excuse another in this place. The words *virtue* and *patriotism* might have been enumerated among those of various and uncertain signification. Montesquieu's Spirit of Laws is a very useful collection of materials; but is it too irreverent to say that it is an unfinished work?★ He defines a republican

★ C'est le portefeuille d'un homme d'esprit, qui a été jeté par la fenêtre et ramassé par des sots, said Voltaire. ["It is the portfolio of a man of wit, which has been thrown out the window and gathered up by fools." Ed.]

government to be "that in which the body, or only a part of the people, is possessed of the supreme power."[†] This agrees with Johnson's definition, "a state in which the government is more than one." "When the body of the people," says Montesquieu,[‡] "in a republic, are possessed of the supreme power, this is called a democracy; when the supreme power is lodged in the hands of a part of the people, it is then an aristocracy." And again,[§] "it is the nature of a republican government, that either the collective body of the people, or particular families, should be possessed of the sovereign power." "In a popular state, virtue is the necessary spring of government. As virtue is necessary in a popular government, so it is necessary also under an aristocracy. True it is, that in the latter it is not so absolutely requisite."[‖]

Does this writer mean that honor and fear, the former of which he calls the principle of monarchy, and the latter of despotism, cannot exist in a republic? or that they are not necessary? Fear, surely, is necessary in a republican government; there can be no government without hopes and fears. Fear then, in truth, is at least one principle in every kind of government, in the simplest democracy as well as the simplest despotism. This arrangement, so exact and systematical in appearance, and which has been celebrated as a discovery of the principles of all government, is by no means satisfactory, since virtue and honor cannot be excluded from despotisms, nor fear nor virtue from monarchies, nor fear nor honor from republics; but at least it is apparent that in a republic, constituted as we propose, the three principles of fear, honor, and virtue, unite and produce more union among the citizens, and give greater energy to the laws.

But not to enlarge on this, let us proceed to the inquiry, what is virtue? It is not that classical virtue which we see personified in the choice of Hercules, and which the ancient philosophers summed up in four words,—prudence, justice, temperance, and fortitude. It is not Christian virtue, so much more sublime, which is summarily comprehended in

---

[†] *Spirit of Laws,* book ii. c. 1.
[‡] B. ii. c. 2.
[§] B. iii. c. 2.
[‖] B. iii. cc. 3 and 4.
[★] B. iii. c. 3.

universal benevolence. What is it then? According to Montesquieu,★ it should seem to be merely a negative quality; the absence only of ambition and avarice; and he thinks that what he thus advances is confirmed by the unanimous testimony of historians. But is this matter well considered? Look over the history of any republic, and can you find a period in it, in which ambition and avarice do not appear in very strong characters, and in which ambitious men were not the most popular? In Athens, Pisistratus and his successors were more popular, as well as ambitious, than Solon, Themistocles than Aristides, &c. In Rome, under the kings, the eternal plots of the nobles against the lives of the kings, to usurp their thrones, are proofs of an ardent and unbridled ambition. Nay, if we attentively examine the most virtuous characters, we shall find unequivocal marks of an ardent ambition. The elder Brutus, Camillus, Regulus, Curius, Æmilius, Cato, all discover an ambition, a thirst of glory, as strong as that of Cæsar; an honorable ambition, an ambition governed by justice, if you will; but an ambition still. But there is not a period in Athenian or Roman annals, when great characters did not appear actuated by ambition of another kind; an unjust and dishonorable ambition; such as Pisistratus, Themistocles, Appius Claudius, &c.; and these characters were always more popular than the others, and were supported chiefly by plebeians, not senates and patricians. If the absence of avarice is necessary to republican virtue, can you find any age or country in which republican virtue has existed? That single characters, or a few among the patricians, have existed, who were exempt from avarice, has been already admitted; but that a moment ever existed, in any country, where property was enjoyed, when the body of the people were universally or even generally exempted from avarice, is not easy to prove. Every page of the history of Rome appears equally marked with ambition and avarice; and the only difference appears in the means and objects. In some periods the nation was extremely poor, in others immensely rich; but the passions existed in all; and the Roman soldiers and common people were forever quarrelling with their most virtuous generals, for refusing to indulge their avarice, by

★Book v. cc. 2, 3.

distributing the spoils among them, and for loving the public too well, by putting the booty into the public treasury.

Shall we say then that republican virtue is nothing but simple poverty; and that poverty alone can support such a government? But Montesquieu tells us,★ virtue in a republic, is a love of the republic; virtue in a democracy, is a love of the democracy; and why might he not have said, that virtue in a monarchy is a love of the monarchy; in a despotism, of the despot; in a mixed government, of the mixture? Men in general love their country and its government. Can it be proved that Athenians loved Athens, or Romans, Rome, more than Frenchmen love France, or Englishmen their island?

There are two principal causes of discrimination; the first is, the greatness or smallness of the state. A citizen of a small republic, who knows every man and every house in it, appears generally to have the strongest attachment to it, because nothing can happen in it that does not interest and affect his feelings; but in a great nation, like France or England, a man is, as it were, lost in the crowd; there are very few persons that he knows, and few events that will much affect him; yet you will find him as much attached to his circle of friends and knowledge as the inhabitant of the small state. The second is, the goodness or badness of the constitution, the climate, soil, &c. Other things being equal, that constitution, whose blessings are the most felt, will be most beloved; and accordingly we find, that governments the best ordered and balanced have been most beloved, as Sparta, Athens, Carthage, Rome, and England, and we might add Holland, for there has been, in practice and effect, a balance of three powers in that country, though not sufficiently defined by law. Moral and Christian, and political virtue, cannot be too much beloved, practised, or rewarded; but to place liberty on that foundation only would not be safe; but it may be well questioned, whether love of the body politic is precisely moral or Christian virtue, which requires justice and benevolence to enemies as well as friends, and to other nations as well as our own. It is not true, in fact, that any people ever existed who loved the public better than themselves, their private friends, neighbors, &c., and therefore this

★ *Spirit of Laws*, book v. chap. 3.

kind of virtue, this sort of love, is as precarious a foundation for liberty as honor or fear; it is the laws alone that really love the country, the public, the whole better than any part; and that form of government which unites all the virtue, honor, and fear of the citizens, in a reverence and obedience to the laws, is the only one in which liberty can be secure, and all orders, and ranks, and parties, compelled to prefer the public good before their own; that is the government for which we plead.

The first magistrate may love himself, and family, and friends better than the public, but the laws, supported by the senate, commons, and judges, will not permit him to indulge it; the senate may love themselves, their families, and friends, more than the public, but the first magistrate, commons, and judges, uniting in support of public law, will defeat their projects; the common people, or their representatives, may love themselves and partial connections better than the whole, but the first magistrate, senate, and judges, can support the laws against their enterprises; the judges may be partial to men or factions, but the three branches of the legislature, united to the executive, will easily bring them back to their duty. In this way, and in no other, can our author's rule be always observed, "to avoid all who hate the commonwealth, and those who are neutral and indifferent about it."

Montesquieu adds,★ "a love of democracy is that of equality." But what passion is this? Every man hates to have a superior, but no man is willing to have an equal; every man desires to be superior to all others. If the meaning is, that every citizen loves to have every other brought down to a level with himself, this is so far true, but is not the whole truth. When every man is brought down to his level, he wishes them depressed below him; and no man will ever acknowledge himself to be upon a level or equality with others, till they are brought down lower than him.

Montesquieu subjoins, "a love of the democracy is likewise that of frugality." This is another passion not easily to be found in human nature. A passion for frugality, perhaps, never existed in a nation, if it ever did in an individual. It is a virtue; but reason and reflection prove the necessity and

298 THE POLITICAL WRITINGS OF JOHN ADAMS

utility of this virtue; and, after all, it is admired and esteemed more than beloved. But to prove that nations, as bodies, are never actuated by any such passion for frugality, it is sufficient to observe that no nation ever practised it but from necessity. Poor nations only are frugal, rich ones always profuse; excepting only some few instances, when the passion of avarice has been artfully cultivated, and has become the habitual national character; but the passion of avarice is not a love of frugality.

Is there, or is there not, any solid foundation for these doubts? Must we bow with reverence to this great master of laws, or may we venture to suspect that these doctrines of his are spun from his imagination? Before he delivered so many grave lessons upon democracies, he would have done well to have shown when or where such a government existed. Until some one shall attempt this, one may venture to suspect his love of equality, love of frugality, and love of the democracy, to be fantastical passions, feigned for the regulation and animation of a government that never had a more solid existence than the flying island of Lagado.

Suppose we should venture to advance the following propositions, for further examination and reflection:—

1. No democracy ever did or can exist.

2. If, however, it were admitted, for argument sake, that a democracy ever did or can exist, no such passion as a love of democracy, stronger than self-love, or superior to the love of private interest, ever did, or ever can prevail in the minds of the citizens in general, or of a majority of them, or in any party or individual of them.

3. That if the citizens, or a majority of them, or any party or individual of them, in action and practice, preferred the public to their private interest, as many undoubtedly would, it would not be from any such passion as love of the democracy, but from reason, conscience, a regard to justice, and a sense of duty and moral obligation; or else from a desire of fame, and the applause, gratitude, and rewards of the public.

4. That no love of equality, at least since Adam's fall, ever existed in human nature, any otherwise than as a desire of bringing others down to our own level, which implies a desire of raising ourselves above them, or depressing

them below us. That the real friends of equality are such from reflection, judgment, and a sense of duty, not from any passion, natural or artificial.

5. That no love of frugality ever existed as a passion; but always as a virtue, approved by deep and long reflection, as useful to individuals as well as the democracy.

6. That, therefore, the democracy of Montesquieu, and its principle of virtue, equality, frugality, &c., according to his definitions of them, are all mere figments of the brain, and delusive imaginations.

7. That his passion of love of the democracy would be, in the members of the majority, only a love of the majority; in those of the minority, only a love of the minority.

8. That his love of equality would not even be pretended towards the members of the minority; but the semblance of it would only be kept up among the members of the majority.

9. That the distinction between nature and philosophy is not enough attended to; that nations are actuated by their passions and prejudices; that very few in any nation, are enlightened by philosophy or religion enough to be at all times convinced that it is a duty to prefer the public to a private interest, and fewer still are moral, honorable, or religious enough to practise such self-denial.

10. Is not every one of these propositions proved beyond dispute, by all the histories in this and the preceding volumes, by all the other histories of the world, and by universal experience?

11. That, in reality, the word democracy signifies nothing more nor less than a nation of people without any government at all, and before any constitution is instituted.

12. That every attentive reader may perceive, that the notions of Montesquieu, concerning a democracy, are imaginations of his own, derived from the contemplation of the reveries of Xenophon and Plato, concerning equality of goods, and community of wives and children, in their delirious ideas of a perfect commonwealth.

13. That such reveries may well be called delirious, since, besides all the other arguments against them, they would not extinguish the family spirit, or produce the equality proposed; because, in such a state of things,

one man would have twenty wives, while another would have none, and one woman twenty lovers, while others would languish in obscurity, solitude, and celibacy.

...

CHAPTER FOURTH.

Conclusion.

IT should have been before observed, that the Western Empire fell in the fifth century, and the Eastern in the fifteenth.

Augustulus was compelled by Odoacer, King of the Heruli, in 475, to abdicate the Western Empire, and was the last Roman who possessed the imperial dignity at Rome. The dominion of Italy fell, soon afterwards, into the hands of Theodoric the Goth. The Eastern Empire lasted many centuries afterwards, till it was annihilated by Mahomet the Great, and Constantinople was taken in the year 1453. The *interval* between the fall of these two empires, making a period of about a thousand years, is called THE MIDDLE AGE.* During this term, republics without number arose in Italy; whirled upon their axes or single centres; foamed, raged, and burst, like so many waterspouts upon the ocean. They were all alike ill constituted; all alike miserable; and all ended in similar disgrace and despotism. It would be curious to pursue our subject through all of them whose records have survived the ravages of Goths, Saracens, and bigoted Christians; through those other republics of Castile, Arragon, Catalonia, Galicia, and all the others in Spain; through those in Portugal; through the several provinces that now compose the kingdom of France; through those in Germany, Sweden, Denmark, Holland, England, Scotland, Ireland, &c. But, if such a work should be sufficiently encouraged by the public, (which is not probable, for mankind, in general, dare not as yet read or think upon CONSTITUTIONS,) it is too extensive for my forces, and ought not to be done in so much haste. The preceding has been produced upon the spur of a particular occasion, which made it necessary to write and

---

* Barbeyrac's Preface to his *History of Ancient Treaties. Corps Dipl.* tom. xxii. Harris's *Philological Inquiries*, part iii, chap. 1.

publish with precipitation, or it might have been useless to have published at all. The whole has been done in the midst of other occupations, in so much hurry, that scarce a moment could be spared to correct the style, adjust the method, pare off excrescences, or even obliterate repetitions, in all which respects it stands in need of an apology. The investigation may be pursued to any length.

All nations, from the beginning, have been agitated by the same passions. The principles developed here will go a great way in explaining every phenomenon that occurs in the history of government. The vegetable and animal kingdoms, and those heavenly bodies whose existence and movements we are as yet only permitted faintly to perceive, do not appear to be governed by laws more uniform or certain than those which regulate the moral and political world. Nations move by unalterable rules; and education, discipline, and laws, make the greatest difference in their accomplishments, happiness, and perfection. It is the master artist alone who finishes his building, his picture, or his clock. The present actors on the stage have been too little prepared by their early views, and too much occupied with turbulent scenes, to do more than they have done. Impartial justice will confess that it is astonishing they have been able to do so much. It is for the young to make themselves masters of what their predecessors have been able to comprehend and accomplish but imperfectly.

A prospect into futurity in America, is like contemplating the heavens through the telescopes of Herschell. Objects stupendous in their magnitudes and motions strike us from all quarters, and fill us with amazement! When we recollect that the wisdom or the folly, the virtue or the vice, the liberty or servitude, of those millions now beheld by us, only as Columbus saw these times in vision,* are certainly to be influenced, perhaps decided, by the manners, examples, principles, and political institutions of the present generation, that mind must be hardened into stone that is not melted into reverence and awe. With such affecting scenes before his eyes, is there, can there be, a young American indolent and incurious; surrendered up to dissipation and frivolity; vain of imitating

---

* Barlow's *Vision of Columbus.*

the loosest manners of countries, which can never be made much better or much worse? A profligate American youth must be profligate indeed, and richly merits the scorn of all mankind.

The world has been too long abused with notions, that climate and soil decide the characters and political institutions of nations. The laws of Solon and the despotism of Mahomet have, at different times, prevailed at Athens; consuls, emperors, and pontiffs have ruled at Rome. Can there be desired a stronger proof, that policy and education are able to triumph over every disadvantage of climate? Mankind have been still more injured by insinuations, that a certain celestial virtue, more than human, has been necessary to preserve liberty. Happiness, whether in despotism or democracy, whether in slavery or liberty, can never be found without virtue. The best republics will be virtuous, and have been so; but we may hazard a conjecture, that the virtues have been the effect of the well ordered constitution, rather than the cause. And, perhaps, it would be impossible to prove that a republic cannot exist even among highwaymen, by setting one rogue to watch another; and the knaves themselves may in time be made honest men by the struggle.

It is now in our power to bring this work to a conclusion with unexpected dignity. In the course of the last summer, two authorities have appeared, greater than any that have been before quoted, in which the principles we have attempted to defend have been acknowledged.

The first is, an ORDINANCE of Congress, of the thirteenth of July, 1787, for the Government of the Territory of the United States, Northwest of the River Ohio.

The second is, the REPORT of the Convention at Philadelphia, of the seventeenth of September, 1787.

The former confederation of the United States was formed upon the model and example of all the confederacies, ancient and modern, in which the federal council was only a diplomatic body. Even the Lycian, which is thought to have been the best, was no more. The magnitude of territory, the population, the wealth and commerce, and especially the rapid growth of the United States, have shown such a government to be inadequate to their wants; and the new system, which seems admirably calculated to unite their interests and affections, and bring them to an uniformity of principles and sentiments, is equally well combined to unite their wills and forces as a single nation. A result of accommodation cannot be supposed to reach the ideas of perfection of any one; but the conception of such an idea, and the deliberate union of so great and various a people in such a plan, is, without all partiality or prejudice, if not the greatest exertion of human understanding, the greatest single effort of national deliberation that the world has ever seen. That it may be improved is not to be doubted, and provision is made for that purpose in the report itself. A people who could conceive, and can adopt it, we need not fear will be able to amend it, when, by experience, its inconveniences and imperfections shall be seen and felt.[52]

[52] Dr. Price, whose publication gave rise to this work, seems to have been convinced by it. In a letter addressed to the author, he says,—

"I cannot be sorry that I have given occasion for your book, by the publication of M. Turgot's *Letter*. At the time of this publication, I was entirely ignorant that you had delivered any opinion, with respect to the sentiment in the passage to which you have objected. I have lately written several letters to America, and in some of them I have taken occasion to mention your publication, and to say that you have convinced me of the main point which it is intended to prove; and that I wish I had inserted a note to signify the difference of opinion between M. Turgot and me on that point. The subject of civil government, next to religion, is of the highest importance to mankind. It is now, I believe, better understood than ever it was. Your book will furnish a help towards further improvement, and your country will, I hope, give such an example of this improvement as will be useful to the world."

Discourses on Davila
(1791)

U sing Henrico Caterino Davila's history of the French civil wars of the 16th century as a point of departure, Adams sets forth in some detail his views on human nature and motivation. Originally appearing as a series of essays in the *Gazette of the United States* in Philadelphia during his first year as vice president, they were published in 1805 as a single volume. Adams always considered the *Discourses* the fourth volume of his *Defence of the Constitutions of the United States*.

When they first appeared in the *Gazette*, these essays aroused considerable controversy because, on various grounds, they were so critical of the presumptions, goals, and beliefs closely associated with the French Revolution. His political opponents subsequently used these papers to brand him as a monarchist and an enemy of republican government—unwarranted charges that caused Adams considerable anguish. The series was abruptly discontinued when the dimensions of the intense controversy it had spawned were fully realized.

The notes that Adams jotted in the margins of his edition of the *Discourses* in 1813 are included in the text below. These selections from the *Discourses* are taken from *Works*, VI; 227-81.

DISCOURSES ON DAVILA.[1]
a Series of Papers on
Political History by an American Citizen.

THIS dull, heavy volume, still excites the wonder of its author,—first, that he could find, amidst the constant scenes of business and dissipation in which he was enveloped, time to write it; secondly, that he had the courage to oppose and publish his own opinions to the universal opinion of America, and, indeed, of all mankind. Not one man in America then believed him. He knew not one and has not heard of one since who then believed him. The work, however, powerfully operated to destroy his popularity. It was urged as full proof, that he was an advocate for monarchy, and laboring to introduce a hereditary president in America.
J.A. 1812.

I.

Felix, quem faciunt aliena pericula cautum.[2]

"THE French nation, known in antiquity under the appellation of the Franks, were originally from the heart of Germany. In the declension of

---

[1] Henrico Caterino Davila. *Dell' Istoria delle Guerre civili di Francia.*

This Italian writer, at one time so popular, has never been much known in America. He treats of a period of French history, perhaps more suggestive of reflection than any other, scarcely excepting the latest, and has the further merit of writing from personal observation of men and things. His work, of which fifteen thousand copies are said to have been sold in a single year, has been many times republished in the original, and has been repeatedly translated into French, Spanish, and English. The French translation in the library of Mr. Adams, which, judging from numerous marginal notes, he seems to have used in composing these Discourses, was made by the Abbé Mallet, and printed in three volumes, quarto, in 1757, nominally at Amsterdam, but really at Paris. An English translation, by W. Aylesbury, Esq., printed in folio, and published in London in the year 1647, is also in his library, but it does not seem to have been much consulted.

Davila is a courtly and catholic historian; but Lord Bolingbroke, in his fifth letter on the *Study of History*, recommends him very strongly as a writer equal in many respects to Livy, a recommendation which would have more authority, if it were not coupled with praise of Guicciardini, as superior to Thucydides; and Bayle, whilst finding fault with some of his statements, testifies to his substantial accuracy.

[2] ["Fortunate is he whom the dangers of others make careful." Ed.]

the Roman Empire, they inhabited a country in the north, along the river Rhine, situated between Bavaria and Saxony, which still preserves the name of Franconia. Having excessively multiplied, as it happens in cold climates, their country was found not sufficiently extensive to contain them, nor fertile enough to nourish them. Excited by the example of their neighbors, they resolved, by a common voice, to divide themselves into two nations; one of which should continue to inhabit their ancient country; and the other endeavor to procure elsewhere, by the force of arms, an establishment more vast, more commodious, and more fertile. This enterprise was resolved upon, and this division made by unanimous consent. Such as were destined by lot to essay their fortune, although trained to war, and incapable of terror at the apprehension of the dangers of such an enterprise, thought, however, that they ought not to abandon it to anarchy or hazard, but to conduct it with prudence and order. To concert the measures necessary for the execution of their project, they assembled in the plains, in the neighborhood of the river *Sala.* Accustomed for many ages to live in the obedience of a prince, and thinking the monarchical state the most convenient to a people who aspire to augment their power and extend their conquests, they resolved to choose a king who should unite in his single person *all the authority of the nation.*"★

Here, perhaps, Davila is incautious and incorrect; for the Franks, as well as Saxons and other German nations, though their governments were monarchical, had their grandees and people, who met and deliberated in national assemblies, whose results were often, to say the least, considered as laws. Their great misfortune was, that, while it never was sufficiently ascertained, whether the sovereignty resided in the king or in the *national assembly,* it was equally uncertain whether the king had a negative on the assembly; whether the grandees had a negative on the king or the people; and whether the people had a negative on both or either. This uncertainty will appear hereafter, in Davila himself, to mark its course in bloody characters; and the whole

---

★ Turgot's ideas were equally confused. His "all authority in one centre, the nation," is just as great nonsense. J. A. 1812.

history of France will show, that from the first migration of the Franks from Germany to this hour, it has never been sufficiently explained and decided.

"To this supreme degree of power in the king" (as Davila proceeds) "they added, that the *crown* should be *hereditary* in the family elected; foreseeing that if it were *elective* it would be a source of civil wars, which would prove destructive to all their enterprises. Mankind, in new establishments, generally act with sincerity and with a single view to the public good.* They listen neither to the ambition nor the interest of private persons. Pharamond was elected king by unanimous consent. He was a son of Marcomir, issue of the blood which had governed the nation for many ages; and, to an experienced valor, united a profound wisdom in the art of government. It was agreed that the same title and equal power should descend to his legitimate posterity of the male line, in default of which, the nation should return to their right of electing a new sovereign. But as unlimited authority may easily degenerate into tyranny, the Franks, at the time of the election of their king, demanded the establishment of certain perpetual and irrevocable laws, which should regulate the order of succession to the throne, and prescribe in a few words the form of government. These laws, proposed by their priests, whom they named *Saliens,* and instituted in the fields, which take their name from the river *Sala,* were originally called *Salique laws,* and have been considered, from the establishment of the monarchy, as the primitive regulations and fundamental constitutions of the kingdom.†

"Leaving their country to the old Prince Marcomir, and passing the Rhine, under the command of Pharamond, the Franks marched to the conquest of the Gauls, about the four hundred and nineteenth year of the Christian era. The Roman legions, united with the Gaulish troops, resisted Pharamond till his death. The sceptre was left to his son Clodion, an intrepid prince, in the flower of his age, who in several battles defeated the

---

* I wish this were true in any establishments, new or old. J. A.

† See the review of this work in the *Anthology.* The writer was "a young man; a forward young man." But he did not know that the first order of nobility among the Franks were priests. It is true, the Salique laws were made by the nobility; it is also true that they were made by their priests; because the nobility and the priests were the same persons. The writer's criticism, therefore, might have been spared. J. A. 1812.

nations of the country, dissipated the Roman armies, and established himself in Belgic Gaul. Meroveus, who succeeded him, made a rapid progress; penetrated into Celtic Gaul, and extended his empire to the gates of Paris. Judging that he had conquered country enough to contain his subjects and form a state of reasonable extent, he limited the course of his exploits, and turned all his cares to peace, after having united under the same laws and the same name, the conquerors and the vanquished, whom he governed peaceably. He died leaving the Franks solidly established in Gaul. Such is the origin of the French monarchy, and such are her fundamental laws.

"By the dispositions of the same laws, the work of the nation, are regulated the rights and prerogatives of the princes of the blood. As each of them, in default of direct heirs, may, according to his rank, be called to the crown, their interests are necessarily connected with those of the state. The people regard these privileges as inviolable. Neither length of time nor distance of degree has ever done them any injury. All these princes preserve the rank which nature has allotted them, to succeed to the throne. They have, indeed, in the course of time, taken different names, such as those of *Valois,* of *Bourbon,* of *Orléans,* of *Angoulême,* of *Vendôme,* of *Alençon,* of *Montpensier;* but they have not by these means lost the rights attached to the royal consanguinity, and that especially of succeeding to the crown. These different branches have from time to time asserted the preeminence due to their blood. To interest them the more forcibly in the preservation of a crown, to which, in succession, they may all be called, it has been commonly made a rule, in case of the minority or absence of the lawful king, to choose for the tutors or regents of the kingdom, the princes who were nearest related. It would not indeed be natural to intrust the administration to the hands of strangers, who might destroy, or at least dismember so beautiful a state; whereas princes born of the same blood, ought, for that reason, to watch over the conservation of an inheritance which belongs to them in some sort. This right is not simply founded upon usage. The *states general* of the kingdom, in whom resides the entire power of the whole nation whom they represent,★ have frequently confirmed it."

★ Here again is the French jargon of all authority in one centre, without one clear idea. 1812.

Here again we meet with another inaccuracy, if not a contradiction in Davila; or rather with another proof of that confusion of law, and that uncertainty of the sovereignty, which for fifteen hundred years has been to France the fatal source of so many calamities.* Here the sovereignty or whole power of the nation, is asserted to be in the *states general;* whereas only three pages before, he had asserted that the whole authority of the nation was united in the king.†

"These two prerogatives, of succeeding to the throne when a king dies without masculine posterity, and of governing the kingdom during the absence or minority of the legitimate sovereign, have at all times procured to the princes of the blood a great authority among the people and the best part in the government. They have applied themselves accordingly with remarkable vigilance to the administration of an empire which they regarded with justice as their patrimony. And the people, judging that they might have them one day for their first magistrates, have always shown them the more respect, as they have more than once known the younger branches to ascend the throne in default of the elder. Thus the crown has passed from the Merovingians to the Carlovingians, and finally to the Capetians; but always from male to male, in the princes of the blood of these three races. From the last of these descended the King Louis IX., whom the innocence of his life and the integrity of his manners have placed in the number of the saints. He left two sons, Philip III., surnamed the Hardy; and Robert, Earl of Clermont. Philip continued the elder branch, which reigned more than three hundred years, and took the surname of Valois. From Robert is descended the younger branch, or the House of Bourbon, so called from the province in which it possessed its settlement. This house, respectable not only by birth, which placed it near the throne, but also by the extent of its lands and riches, by the valor and number of its princes, almost all distinguished by their merit and a singular affability, arrived soon at a high degree of power. This elevation, joined

* Misera Servitus est, ubi jus est vagum aut incognitum. 1804. ["It is a wretched slavery, where the law is inconsistent or unknown." Ed.]

† Two authorities up, neither supreme. 1812.

to the favor of the people, excited against the Bourbons the jealousy and envy of the kings, whom this great credit and distinguished splendor displeased and alarmed. Every day brought fresh occasions of hatred, suspicion, and distrust, which several times broke out in arms. Thus in the war *for the public good,* John, Duke of Bourbon, declared himself against Louis XI., and Louis XII., before his accession to the throne, was at war with Peter of Bourbon. The jealousies which these princes inspired into kings, exposed them sometimes to secret vexations, and sometimes to declared enmities."

We may add to this reflection of Davila, that it is extremely probable that these princes, by frequently betraying symptoms of ambition, aspiring at the throne, might give to kings just grounds of jealousy and alarm.★

Before we proceed in our discourses on Davila, it will assist us, in comprehending his narration, as well as in making many useful reflections in morals and policy, to turn our thoughts for a few moments to the constitution of the human mind. This we shall endeavor to do in our next essay.

II.

C'est là le propre de l'esprit humain, que les exemples ne corrigent personne; les sottises des pères sont perdues pour leurs enfans; il faut que chaque génération fasse les siennes.†

MEN, in their primitive conditions, however savage, were undoubtedly gregarious; and they continue to be social, not only in every stage of civilization, but in every possible situation in which they can be placed. As nature intended them for society, she has furnished them with passions, appetites, and propensities, as well as a variety of faculties, calculated both for their individual enjoyment, and to render them useful to each other

---

★Thus the Prince de Conti was in opposition to Louis XV., and the Duke of Orleans to Louis XVI.

† Frederick borrowed this from Fontenelle. J. A. 1812. ["It is characteristic of the human mind that examples correct no one; the foolishness of fathers is wasted on their children; each generation must make its own mistakes." Ed.]

in their social connections. There is none among them more essential or remarkable, than the *passion for distinction*. A desire to be observed, considered, esteemed, praised, beloved, and admired by his fellows, is one of the earliest, as well as keenest dispositions discovered in the heart of man. If any one should doubt the existence of this propensity, let him go and attentively observe the journeymen and apprentices in the first workshop, or the oarsmen in a cockboat, a family or a neighborhood, the inhabitants of a house or the crew of a ship, a school or a college, a city or a village, a savage or civilized people, a hospital or a church, the bar or the exchange, a camp or a court. Wherever men, women, or children, are to be found, whether they be old or young, rich or poor, high or low, wise or foolish, ignorant or learned, every individual is seen to be strongly actuated by a desire to be seen, heard, talked of, approved and respected, by the people about him, and within his knowledge.

Moral writers have, by immemorial usage, a right to make a free use of the poets.

> The love of praise, howe'er conceal'd by art,
> Reigns, more or less, and glows, in every heart;
> The proud, to gain it, toils on toils endure,
> The modest shun it, but to make it sure.
> O'er globes and sceptres, now on thrones it swells,
> Now, trims the midnight lamp in college cells.
> 'T is tory, whig—it plots, prays, preaches, pleads,
> Harangues in Senates, squeaks in masquerades.
> It aids the dancer's heel, the writer's head,
> And heaps the plain with mountains of the dead;
> Nor ends with life; but nods in sable plumes,
> Adorns our hearse, and flatters on our tombs.

A regard to the sentiments of mankind concerning him, and to their dispositions towards him, every man feels within himself; and if he has reflected, and tried experiments, he has found, that no exertion of his reason, no effort of his will, can wholly divest him of it. In proportion to our affection for the notice of others is our aversion to their neglect; the stronger the desire of the esteem of the public, the more powerful the aversion to their disapprobation; the more exalted the wish for admiration, the more invincible the abhorrence of contempt. Every man not only desires the consideration of others, but he frequently compares himself with others, his friends or his enemies; and in proportion as he exults when he perceives that he has more of it than they, he feels a keener afflic- tion when he sees that one or more of them, are more respected than himself.

This passion, while it is simply a desire to excel another, by fair industry in the search of truth, and the practice of virtue, is properly called *Emula- tion*. When it aims at power, as a means of distinction, it is *Ambition*. When it is in a situation to suggest the sentiments of fear and apprehension, that another, who is now inferior, will become superior, it is denominated *Jeal- ousy*. When it is in a state of mortification, at the superiority of another, and desires to bring him down to our level, or to depress him below us, it is properly called *Envy*. When it deceives a man into a belief of false pro- fessions of esteem or admiration, or into a false opinion of his impor- tance in the judgment of the world, it is *Vanity*. These observations alone would be sufficient to show, that this propensity, in all its branches, is a principal source of the virtues and vices, the happiness and misery of human life; and that the history of mankind is little more than a simple narration of its operation and effects.

There is in human nature, it is true, simple *Benevolence,* or an affection for the good of others; but alone it is not a balance for the selfish affec- tions. Nature then has kindly added to benevolence, the desire of reputa- tion, in order to make us good members of society. *Spectemur agendo* expresses the great principle of activity for the good of others. Nature has sanctioned the law of self-preservation by rewards and punishments. The rewards of selfish activity are life and health; the punishments of negligence and indolence are want, disease, and death. Each individual, it is true, should consider, that nature has enjoined the same law on his neighbor, and therefore a respect for the authority of nature would oblige him to respect the rights of others as much as his own. But reasoning as abstruse, though as simple as this, would not occur to all men. The same nature therefore has imposed another law, that of promoting the good, as well as respecting the rights of mankind, and has sanctioned it by other rewards and punishments. The rewards in this case, in this life, are *esteem* and *admiration* of others; the punishments are *neglect* and *contempt;* nor may any one imagine that these are not as real as the others. The desire of the esteem of others is as real a want of nature as hunger; and the neglect and contempt of the world as severe a pain as the gout or stone. It sooner and oftener produces despair, and a detestation of existence; of equal importance to individuals, to families, and to nations. It is a principal end of government to regulate this passion, which in its turn becomes a principal means of government. It is the only adequate instrument of order and subordination in society, and alone commands effectual obedience to laws, since without it neither human reason, nor standing armies, would ever produce that great effect. Every personal quality, and every blessing of fortune, is cherished in proportion to its capacity of gratifying this universal affection for the esteem, the sympathy, admiration and congratulations of the public. Beauty in the face, elegance of figure, grace of attitude and motion, riches, honors, every thing is weighed in the scale, and desired, not so much for the pleasure they afford, as the attention they command. As this is a point of great importance, it may be pardonable to expatiate a little upon these particulars.

Why are the personal accomplishments of beauty, elegance, and grace, held in such high estimation by mankind? Is it merely for the pleasure which is received from the sight of these attributes? By no means. The taste for such delicacies is not universal; in those who feel the most lively sense of them, it is but a slight sensation, and of shortest continuance; but those attractions command the notice and attention of the public; they draw the eyes of spectators. This is the charm that makes them irresistible. Is it for such fading perfections that a husband or a wife is chosen? Alas, it is well known, that a very short familiarity totally destroys all sense and attention to such properties; and on the contrary, a very little time and habit destroy all the aversion to ugliness and deformity, when unattended with disease or ill temper. Yet beauty and address are courted and admired, very often, more than discretion, wit, sense, and many other accomplishments and virtues, of infinitely more importance to the happiness of private life, as well as to the utility and ornament of society. Is it for the momentous purpose of dancing and drawing, painting and music, riding or fencing, that men or women are destined in this life or any other? Yet those who have the best means of education, bestow more attention and expense on those, than on more solid acquisitions. Why? Because they attract more forcibly the attention of the world, and procure a better advancement in life. Notwithstanding all this, as soon as an establishment in life is made, they are found to have answered their end, are neglected and laid aside.

Is there any thing in birth, however illustrious or splendid, which should make a difference between one man and another? If, from a common ancestor, the whole human race is descended, they are all of the same family. How then can they distinguish families into the more or the less ancient? What advantage is there in an illustration of an hundred or a thousand years? Of what avail are all these histories, pedigrees, traditions? What foundation has the whole science of genealogy and heraldry? Are there differences in the breeds of men, as there are in those of horses? If there are not, these sciences have no foundation in reason; in prejudice they have a very solid one. All that philosophy can say is, that there is a general presumption, that a man has had some advantages of education, if he is of a family of note. But this advantage must be derived from his father and mother chiefly, if not wholly; of what importance is it then, in this view, whether the family is twenty generations upon record, or only two?

The mighty secret lies in this:—An illustrious descent attracts the notice of mankind. A single drop of royal blood, however illegitimately scattered, will make any man or woman proud or vain. Why? Because, although it excites the indignation of many, and the envy of more, it still attracts the *attention* of the world. Noble blood, whether the nobility be hereditary or elective, and, indeed, more in republican governments than in monarchies, least of all in despotisms, is held in estimation for the same reason. It is a name and a race that a nation has been interested in, and is in the habit of respecting. Benevolence, sympathy, congratulation, have been so long associated to those names in the minds of the people, that they are become national habits. National gratitude descends from the father to the son, and is often stronger to the latter than the former. It is often excited by remorse, upon reflection on the ingratitude and injustice with which the former has been treated. When the names of a certain family are read in all the gazettes, chronicles, records, and histories of a country for five hundred years, they become known, respected, and delighted in by every body. A youth, a child of this extraction, and bearing this name, attracts the eyes and ears of all companies long before it is known or inquired whether he be a wise man or a fool. His name is often a greater distinction than a title, a star, or a garter. This it is which makes so many men proud, and so many others envious of illustrious descent. The pride is as irrational and contemptible as the pride of riches, and no more. A wise man will lament that any other distinction than that of merit should be made. A good man will neither be proud nor vain of his birth, but will earnestly improve every advantage he has for the public good. A cunning man will carefully conceal his pride; but will indulge it in secret the more effectually, and improve his advantage to greater profit. But was any man ever known so wise, or so good, as really to despise birth or wealth? Did you ever read of a man rising to public notice, from obscure beginnings, who was not reflected on? Although, with every liberal mind, it is an honor and a proof of merit, yet it is a disgrace with mankind in general. What a load of sordid obloquy and envy has every such man to carry! The contempt that is thrown upon obscurity of ancestry, augments the eagerness for the stupid adoration that is paid to its illustration.

This desire of the consideration of our fellow-men, and their congratulations in our joys, is not less invincible than the desire of their sympathy in our sorrows. It is a determination of our nature, that lies at the foundation of our whole moral system in this world, and may be connected essentially with our destination in a future state.

III.

O fureur de se distinguer, que ne pouvez vous point!

VOLTAIRE.[3]

WHY do men pursue riches? What is the end of avarice?

The labor and anxiety, the enterprises and adventures, that are voluntarily undertaken in pursuit of gain, are out of all proportion to the utility, convenience, or pleasure of riches. A competence to satisfy the wants of nature, food and clothes, a shelter from the seasons, and the comforts of a family, may be had for very little. The daily toil of the million, and of millions of millions, is adequate to a complete supply of these necessities and conveniences. With such accommodations, thus obtained, the appetite is keener, the digestion more easy and perfect, and repose is more refreshing, than among the most abundant superfluities and the rarest luxuries. For what reason, then, are any mortals averse to the situation of the farmer, mechanic, or laborer? Why do we tempt the seas and encompass the globe? Why do any men affront heaven and earth to accumulate wealth, which will forever be useless to them? Why do we make an ostentatious display of riches? Why should any man be proud of his purse, houses, lands, or gardens? or, in better words, why should the rich man glory in his riches? What connection can there be between wealth and pride?

The answer to all these questions is, *because riches attract the attention, consideration, and congratulations of mankind;* it is not because the rich have really more of ease or pleasure than the poor. Riches force the opinion on a man that he is the object of the congratulations of others, and he feels that they attract the complaisance of the public. His senses all inform him, that his neighbors have a natural disposition to harmonize with all those pleasing emotions and agreeable sensations, which the elegant accommodations around him are supposed to excite.

His imagination expands, and his heart dilates at these charming illusions. His attachment to his possessions increases as fast as his desire to

[3]["O rage to distinguish oneself, what can you not lead to!" Ed.]

accumulate more; not for the purposes of beneficence or utility, but from the desire of illustration.

Why, on the other hand, should any man be ashamed to make known his poverty? Why should those who have been rich, or educated in the houses of the rich, entertain such an aversion, or be agitated with such terror, at the prospect of losing their property? or of being reduced to live at a humbler table? in a meaner house? to walk, instead of riding? or to ride without their accustomed equipage or retinue? Why do we hear of madness, melancholy, and suicides, upon bankruptcy, loss of ships, or any other sudden fall from opulence to indigence, or mediocrity? Ask your reason, what disgrace there can be in poverty? What moral sentiment of approbation, praise, or honor can there be in a palace? What dishonor in a cottage? What glory in a coach? What shame in a wagon? Is not the sense of propriety and sense of merit as much connected with an empty purse as a full one? May not a man be as estimable, amiable, and respectable, attended by his faithful dog, as if preceded and followed by a train of horses and servants? All these questions may be very wise, and the stoical philosophy has her answers ready. But if you ask the same questions of nature, experience, and mankind, the answers will be directly opposite to those of *Epictetus,* namely,—that there is more respectability, in the eyes of the greater part of mankind, in the gaudy trappings of wealth, than there is in genius or learning, wisdom or virtue.

The poor man's conscience is clear; yet he is ashamed. His character is irreproachable; yet he is neglected and despised. He feels himself out of the sight of others, groping in the dark. Mankind take no notice of him. He rambles and wanders unheeded. In the midst of a crowd, at church, in the market, at a play, at an execution, or coronation, he is in as much obscurity as he would be in a garret or a cellar. He is not disapproved, censured, or reproached; *he is only not seen.* This total inattention is to him mortifying, painful, and cruel. He suffers a misery from this consideration, which is sharpened by the consciousness that others have no fellow-feeling with him in this distress. If you follow these persons, however, into their scenes of life, you will find that there is a kind of figure which the meanest of them all endeavors to make; a kind of little grandeur and respect, which the most insignificant study and labor to procure in the small circle of their acquaintances. Not only the poorest mechanic, but the man who lives upon common charity, nay, the common beggars in the streets; and not only those who may be all innocent, but even those who have abandoned themselves to common infamy, as pirates, highwaymen, and common thieves, court a set of admirers, and plume themselves upon that superiority which they have, or fancy they have, over some others. There must be one, indeed, who is the last and lowest of the human species. But there is no risk in asserting, that there is no one who believes and will acknowledge himself to be the man. To be wholly overlooked, and to know it, are intolerable. Instances of this are not uncommon. When a wretch could no longer attract the notice of a man, woman, or child, he must be respectable in the eyes of his dog. "Who will love me then?" was the pathetic reply of one, who starved himself to feed his mastiff, to a charitable passenger, who advised him to kill or sell the animal. In this *"who will love me then?"* there is a key to the human heart; to the history of human life and manners; and to the rise and fall of empires. To feel ourselves unheeded, chills the most pleasing hope, damps the most fond desire, checks the most agreeable wish, disappoints the most ardent expectations of human nature.

Is there in science and letters a reward for the labor they require? Scholars learn the dead languages of antiquity, as well as the living tongues of modern nations; those of the east, as well as the west. They puzzle themselves and others with metaphysics and mathematics. They renounce their pleasures, neglect their exercises, and destroy their health, for what? Is curiosity so strong? Is the pleasure that accompanies the pursuit and acquisition of knowledge so exquisite? If *Crusoe,* on his island, had the library of *Alexandria,* and a certainty that he should never again see the face of man, would he ever open a volume? Perhaps he might; but it is very probable he would read but little. A sense of duty; a love of truth; a desire to alleviate the anxieties of ignorance, may, no doubt, have an influence on some minds. But the universal object and idol of men of letters is *reputation.* It is the *notoriety,* the *celebration,* which constitutes the charm that is to compensate the loss of appetite and sleep, and sometimes of riches and honors.

The same ardent desire of the *congratulations* of others in our joys, is the great incentive to the pursuit of honors. This might be exemplified in the career of civil and political life. That we may not be too tedious, let us instance in military glory.

Is it to be supposed that the regular standing armies of Europe engage in the service from pure motives of patriotism? Are their officers men of contemplation and devotion, who expect their reward in a future life? Is it from a sense of moral or religious duty that they risk their lives and reconcile themselves to wounds? Instances of all these kinds may be found. But if any one supposes that all or the greater part of these heroes are actuated by such principles, he will only prove that he is unacquainted with them. Can their pay be considered as an adequate encouragement? This, which is no more than a very simple and moderate subsistence, would never be a temptation to renounce the chances of fortune in other pursuits, together with the pleasures of domestic life, and submit to this most difficult and dangerous employment. No, it is the consideration and the chances of laurels which they acquire by the service.

The soldier compares himself with his fellows, and contends for promotion to be a corporal. The corporals vie with each other to be sergeants. The sergeants will mount breaches to be ensigns. And thus every man in an army is constantly aspiring to be something higher, as every citizen in the commonwealth is constantly struggling for a better rank, that he may draw the observation of more eyes.

IV.

Such bribes the rapid Greek o'er Asia hurled;
For such, the steady Romans shook the world.

In a city or a village, little employments and trifling distinctions are contended for with equal eagerness, as honors and offices in commonwealths and kingdoms.

What is it that bewitches mankind to marks and signs? A ribbon? a garter? a star? a golden key? a marshal's staff? or a white hickory stick?

Though there is in such frivolities as these neither profit nor pleasure, nor any thing amiable, estimable, or respectable, yet experience teaches us, in every country of the world, they attract the attention of mankind more than parts or learning, virtue or religion. They are, therefore, sought with ardor, very often, by men possessed in the most eminent degree, of all the more solid advantages of birth and fortune, merit and services, with the best faculties of the head, and the most engaging recommendations of the heart.

Fame has been divided into three species. *Glory,* which attends the great actions of lawgivers and heroes, and the management of the great commands and first offices of state. *Reputation,* which is cherished by every gentleman. And *Credit,* which is supported by merchants and tradesmen. But even this division is incomplete, because the desire and the object of it, though it may be considered in various lights and under different modifications, is not confined to gentlemen nor merchants, but is common to every human being. There are no men who are not ambitious of distinguishing themselves and growing considerable among those with whom they converse. This ambition is natural to the human soul. And as, when it receives a happy turn, it is the source of private felicity and public prosperity, and when it errs, produces private uneasiness and public calamities; it is the business and duty of private prudence, of private and public education, and of national policy, to direct it to right objects. For this purpose it should be considered, that to every man who is capable of a worthy conduct, the pleasure from the approbation of worthy men is exquisite and inexpressible.

It is curious to consider the final causes of things, when the physical are wholly unknown. The intellectual and moral qualities are most within our power, and undoubtedly the most essential to our happiness. The personal qualities of health, strength, and agility, are next in importance. Yet the qualities of fortune, such as birth, riches, and honors, though a man has less reason to esteem himself for these than for those of his mind or body, are everywhere acknowledged to glitter with the brightest lustre in the eyes of the world.

As virtue is the only rational source and eternal foundation of honor, the wisdom of nations, in the titles they have established as the marks of order and subordination, has generally given an intimation, not of personal qualities, nor of the qualities of fortune; but of some particular virtues, more especially becoming men in the high stations they possess. Reverence is attributed to the clergy; veneration to magistrates; honor to senators; serenity, clemency, or mildness of disposition to princes. The sovereign authority and supreme executive have commonly titles that designate power as well as virtue,—as *majesty* to kings; *magnificent, most honored*, and *sovereign lords* to the government of Geneva; *noble mightinesses* to the States of Friesland; *noble and mighty lords* to the States of Guelderland; *noble, great, and venerable lords* to the regency of Leyden; *noble and grand mightinesses* to the States of Holland; *noble, great, and venerable lords*, the regency of Amsterdam; *noble mightinesses*, the States of Utrecht; and *high mightinesses*, the States General.

A death bed, it is said, shows the emptiness of titles. That may be. But does it not equally show the futility of riches, power, liberty, and all earthly things? "The cloud-capt towers, the gorgeous palaces, the solemn temples, the great globe itself," appear "the baseless fabric of a vision," and "life itself, a tale, told by an idiot, full of sound and fury, signifying nothing." Shall it be inferred from this, that fame, liberty, property, and life, shall be always despised and neglected? Shall laws and government, which regulate sublunary things, be neglected because they appear baubles at the hour of death?

The wisdom and virtue of all nations have endeavored to regulate the passion for respect and distinction, and to reduce it to some order in society, by titles marking the gradations of magistracy, to prevent, as far as human power and policy can prevent, collisions among the passions of many pursuing the same objects, and the rivalries, animosities, envy, jealousy, and vengeance which always result from them.

Has there ever been a nation who understood the human heart better than the Romans, or made a better use of the passion for consideration, congratulation, and distinction? They considered that, as reason is the guide of life, the senses, the imagination and the affections are the springs of activity. Reason holds the helm, but passions are the gales. And as the direct road to these is through the senses, the language of signs was employed by Roman wisdom to excite the emulation and active virtue of the citizens. *Distinctions* of *conditions,* as well as of ages, were made by difference of clothing. The laticlave or large flowing robe, studded with broad spots of purple, the ancient distinction of their kings, was, after the establishment of the consulate, worn by the senators through the whole period of the republic and the empire. The tribunes of the people were, after their institution, admitted to wear the same venerable signal of sanctity and authority. The angusticlave, or the smaller robe, with narrower studs of purple, was the distinguishing habit of Roman knights. The golden ring was also peculiar to senators and knights, and was not permitted to be worn by any other citizens. The prætext, or long white robe, reaching down to the ancles, bordered with purple, which was worn by the principal magistrates, such as consuls, prætors, censors, and sometimes on solemn festivals by senators. The chairs of ivory; the lictors; the rods; the axes; the crowns of gold; of ivory; of flowers; of herbs; of laurel branches; and of oak leaves; the civil and the mural crowns; their ovations; and their triumphs; every thing in religion, government, and common life, among the Romans, was parade, representation, and ceremony. Every thing was addressed to the emulation of the citizens, and every thing was calculated to attract the attention, to allure the consideration and excite the congratulations of the people; to attach their hearts to individual citizens according to their merit; and to their lawgivers, magistrates, and judges, according to their rank, station, and importance in the state. And this was in the true spirit of republics, in which form of government there is no other consistent method of preserving order, or procuring submission to the laws. To such means as these, or to force and a standing army, recourse must be had for the guardianship of laws and the protection of the people. It is universally true, that in all the republics now remaining in Europe, there is, as there ever has been, a more constant and anxious attention to such forms and marks of distinctions than there is in the monarchies.*

The policy of Rome was exhibited in its highest perfection, in the triumph of Paulus Æmilius over Perseus. It was a striking exemplification of congratulation and sympathy, contrasted with each other. Congratulation with the conqueror; sympathy with the captive; both suddenly changed into sympathy with the conqueror. The description of this tri-

* Our mock funerals of Washington, Hamilton, and Ames, our processions, escorts, public dinners, balls, &c., are more expensive, more troublesome, and infinitely less ingenious. J.A. 1812.

umph is written with a pomp of language correspondent to its dazzling magnificence. The representation of the king and his children must excite the pity of every reader who is not animated with the ferocious sentiments of Roman insolence and pride. Never was there a more moving lesson of the melancholy lot of humanity, than the contrasted fortunes of the Macedonian and the Roman. The one divested of his crown and throne, led in chains, with his children before his chariot; the other, blazing in gold and purple, to the capitol. This instructive lesson is given us by the victor himself, in a speech to the people. "My triumph, Romans, as if it had been in derision of all human felicity, has been interposed between the funerals of my children, and both have been exhibited as spectacles before you. Perseus, who himself a captive, saw his children led with him in captivity, now enjoys them in safety. I, who triumphed over him, having ascended the capitol, from the funeral chariot of one of my sons, descended from that capitol to see another expire. In the house of Paulus none remains but himself.★ But your felicity, Romans, and the prosperous fortune of the public, is a consolation to me under this destruction of my family."

It is easy to see how such a scene must operate on the hearts of a nation; how it must affect the passion for distinction; and how it must excite the ardor and virtuous emulation of the citizens.

V.

The senate's thanks, the Gazette's pompous tale,
With force resistless o'er the brave prevail.
This power has praise, that virtue scarce can warm,
Till fame supplies the universal charm.

JOHNSON.

THE result of the preceding discourses is, that avarice and ambition, vanity and pride, jealousy and envy, hatred and revenge, as well as the love of knowledge and desire of fame, are very often nothing more than various

★ Logan. Not one drop of Logan's blood remains. *Jefferson's Notes.*

modifications of that desire of the attention, consideration, and congratulations of our fellow men, which is the great spring of social activity;
that all men compare themselves with others, especially those with whom
they most frequently converse, those who, by their employments or
amusements, professions or offices, present themselves most frequently at
the same time to the view and thoughts of that public, little or great, to
which every man is known; that emulations and rivalries naturally and
necessarily are excited by such comparisons; that the most heroic actions
in war, the sublimest virtues in peace, and the most useful industry in agriculture, arts, manufactures, and commerce, proceed from such emulations
on the one hand, and jealousies, envy, enmity, hatred, revenge, quarrels, factions, seditions, and wars on the other. The final cause of this constitution
of things is easy to discover. Nature has ordained it, as a constant incentive to activity and industry, that, to acquire the attention and complacency, the approbation and admiration of their fellows, men might be
urged to constant exertions of beneficence. By this destination of their
natures, men of all sorts, even those who have the least of reason, virtue
or benevolence, are chained down to an incessant servitude to their fellow
creatures; laboring without intermission to produce something which
shall contribute to the comfort, convenience, pleasure, profit, or utility of
some or other of the species, they are really thus constituted by their own
vanity, slaves to mankind. Slaves, I say again. For what a folly is it! On a selfish system, what are the thoughts, passions, and sentiments of mankind
to us?

"What's fame? A fancied life in others' breath."

What is it to us what shall be said of us after we are dead? Or in Asia,
Africa, or Europe, while we live? There is no greater possible or imaginable delusion. Yet the impulse is irresistible. The language of nature to
man in his constitution is this,—"I have given you reason, conscience, and
benevolence; and thereby made you accountable for your actions, and
capable of virtue, in which you will find your highest felicity. But I have
not confided wholly in your laudable improvement of these divine gifts.
To them I have superadded in your bosoms a passion for the notice and
regard of your fellow mortals, which, if you perversely violate your duty,

and wholly neglect the part assigned you in the system of the world and the society of mankind, shall torture you from the cradle to the grave."

Nature has taken effectual care of her own work. She has wrought the passions into the texture and essence of the soul, and has not left it in the power of art to destroy them. To regulate and not to eradicate them is the province of policy. It is of the highest importance to education, to life, and to society, not only that they should not be destroyed, but that they should be gratified, encouraged, and arranged on the side of virtue. To confine our observations at present to that great leading passion of the soul, which has been so long under our consideration. What discouragement, distress, and despair, have not been occasioned by its disappointment? To consider one instance, among many, which happen continually in schools and colleges. Put a supposition of a pair of twin brothers who have been nourished by the same nurse, equally encouraged by their parents and preceptors, with equal genius, health, and strength, pursuing their studies with equal ardor and success. One is at length overtaken by some sickness, and in a few days the other, who escapes the influenza, is advanced some pages before him. This alone will make the studies of the unfortunate child, when he recovers his health, disgustful. As soon as he loses the animating hope of preëminence, and is constrained to acknowledge a few others of his form or class, his superiors, he becomes incapable of industrious application. Even the fear of the ferule or the rod, will after this be ineffectual. The terror of punishment, by forcing attention, may compel a child to perform a task, but can never infuse that ardor for study, which alone can arrive at great attainments. Emulation really seems to produce genius, and the desire of superiority to create talents. Either this, or the reverse of it, must be true; and genius produces emulation, and natural talents, the desire of superiority; for they are always found together, and what God and nature have united, let no audacious legislator presume to put asunder.

When the love of glory enkindles in the heart, and influences the whole soul, then, and only then, may we depend on a rapid progression of the intellectual faculties. The awful feeling of a mortified emulation, is not peculiar to children. In an army, or a navy, sometimes the interest of the service requires, and oftener perhaps private interest and partial favor prevail, to promote officers over their superiors or seniors. But the consequence is, that those officers can never serve again together. They must be distributed in different corps, or sent on different commands. Nor is this the worst effect. It almost universally happens, that the superseded officer feels his heart broken by his disgrace. His mind is enfeebled by grief, or disturbed by resentment; and the instances have been very rare, of any brilliant action performed by such an officer. What a monument to this character of human nature is the long list of yellow admirals in the British service! Consider the effects of similar disappointments in civil affairs. Ministers of state are frequently displaced in all countries; and what is the consequence? Are they seen happy in a calm resignation to their fate? Do they turn their thoughts from their former employments, to private studies or business? Are they men of pleasant humor, and engaging conversation? Are their hearts at ease? Or is their conversation a constant effusion of complaints and murmurs, and their breast the residence of resentment and indignation, of grief and sorrow, of malice and revenge? Is it common to see a man get the better of his ambition, and despise the honors he once possessed; or is he commonly employed in projects upon projects, intrigues after intrigues, and manœuvres on manœuvres, to recover them? So sweet and delightful to the human heart is that complacency and admiration, which attends public offices, whether they are conferred by the favor of a prince, derived from hereditary descent, or obtained by election of the people, that a mind must be sunk below the feelings of humanity, or exalted by religion or philosophy far above the common character of men, to be insensible, or to conquer its sensibility. Pretensions to such conquests are not uncommon; but the sincerity of such pretenders is often rendered suspicious, by their constant conversation and conduct, and even by their countenances. The people are so sensible of this, that a man in this predicament is always on the compassionate list, and, except in cases of great resentment against him for some very unpopular principles or behavior, they are found to be always studying some other office for a disappointed man, to console him in his affliction. In short, the theory of education, and the science of government, may be reduced to the same simple principle, and be all comprehended in the knowledge of the means of actively conducting, controlling, and regulating the emulation and ambition of the citizens.

VI.

"Haud facile emergunt, quorum virtutibus obstat
Res angusta domi."

JUVENAL

"This mournful truth is everywhere confess'd,
Slow rises Worth, by Poverty depressed."

JOHNSON

IF we attempt to analyze our ideas still further upon this subject, we shall find, that the expressions we have hitherto used, *attention, consideration,* and *congratulation,* comprehend with sufficient accuracy the general object of the passion for distinction, in the greater part of mankind. There are not a few—from him who burned a temple, to the multitudes who plunge into low debauchery—who deliberately seek it by crimes and vices. The greater number, however, search for it, neither by vices nor virtues; but by the means which common sense and every day's experience show, are most sure to obtain it; by riches, by family records, by play, and other frivolous personal accomplishments. But there are a few, and God knows, but a few, who aim at something more. They aim at approbation as well as attention; at esteem as well as consideration; and at admiration and gratitude, as well as congratulation. Admiration is, indeed, the complete idea of approbation, congratulation, and wonder, united. This last description of persons is the tribe out of which proceed your patriots and heroes, and most of the great benefactors to mankind. But for our humiliation, we must still remember, that even in these esteemed, beloved, and adored characters, the passion, although refined by the purest moral sentiments, and intended to be governed by the best principles, is a passion still; and therefore, like all other human desires, unlimited and insatiable. No man was ever contented with any given share of this human adoration. When Cæsar declared that he had lived enough to glory, Cæsar might deceive himself, but he did not deceive the world, who saw his declaration contradicted by every action of his subsequent life. Man constantly craves for more, even when he has no rival. But when he sees another possessed of more, or drawing away from himself a part of what he had, he feels a mortification, arising from the loss of a good he thought his own. His desire is disappointed; the pain of a want unsatisfied, is increased by a resentment of an injustice, as he thinks it. He accuses his rival of a theft or robbery, and the public of taking away what was his property, and giving it to another. These feelings and resentments are but other names for jealousy and envy; and altogether, they produce some of the keenest and most tormenting of all sentiments. These fermentations of the passions are so common and so well known, that the people generally presume, that a person in such circumstances, is deprived of his judgment, if not of his veracity and reason. It is too generally a sufficient answer to any complaint, to any fact alleged, or argument advanced, to say that it comes from a disappointed man.

There is a voice within us, which seems to intimate, that real merit should govern the world; and that men ought to be respected only in proportion to their talents, virtues, and services. But the question always has been, how can this arrangement be accomplished? How shall the men of merit be discovered? How shall the proportions of merit be ascertained and graduated? Who shall be the judge? When the government of a great nation is in question, shall the whole nation choose? Will such a choice be better than chance? Shall the whole nation vote for senators? Thirty millions of votes, for example, for each senator in France! It is obvious that this would be a lottery of millions of blanks to one prize, and that the chance of having wisdom and integrity in a senator by hereditary descent would be far better. There is no individual personally known to an hundredth part of the nation. The voters, then, must be exposed to deception, from intrigues and manœuvres without number, that is to say, from all the chicanery, impostures, and falsehoods imaginable, with scarce a possibility of preferring real merit. Will you divide the nation into districts, and let each district choose a senator? This is giving up the idea of national merit, and annexing the honor and the trust to an accident, that of living on a particular spot. A hundred or a thousand men of the first merit in a nation, may live in one city, and none at all of this description in several whole provinces. Real merit is so remote from the knowledge of whole nations, that were magistrates to be chosen by that criterion alone, and by a universal suffrage, dissensions and venality would be endless. The difficulties, arising from this source, are so obvious and universal, that nations have tried all sorts of experiments to avoid them.

As no appetite in human nature is more universal than that for honor, and real merit is confined to a very few, the numbers who thirst for respect, are out of all proportion to those who seek it only by merit. The great majority trouble themselves little about merit, but apply themselves to seek for honor, by means which they see will more easily and certainly obtain it, by displaying their taste and address, their wealth and magnificence, their ancient parchments, pictures, and statues, and the virtues of their ancestors; and if these fail, as they seldom have done, they have recourse to artifice, dissimulation, hypocrisy, flattery, imposture, empiricism, quackery, and bribery. What chance has humble, modest, obscure, and poor merit in such a scramble? Nations, perceiving that the still small voice of merit was drowned in the insolent roar of such dupes of impudence and knavery in national elections, without a possibility of a remedy, have sought for something more permanent than the popular voice to designate honor. Many nations have attempted to annex it to land, presuming that a good estate would at least furnish means of a good education; and have resolved that those who should possess certain territories, should have certain legislative, executive, and judicial powers over the people. Other nations have endeavored to connect honor with offices; and the names and ideas at least of certain moral virtues and intellectual qualities have been by law annexed to certain offices, as veneration, grace, excellence, honor, serenity, majesty. Other nations have attempted to annex honor to families, without regard to lands or offices. The Romans allowed none, but those who had possessed curule offices, to have statues or portraits. He who had images or pictures of his ancestors, was called noble. He who had no statue or pictures but his own, was called a new man. Those who had none at all, were ignoble. Other nations have united all those institutions; connected lands, offices, and families; made them all descend together, and honor, public attention, consideration, and congratulation, along with them.

This has been the policy of Europe; and it is to this institution she owes her superiority in war and peace, in legislation and commerce, in agriculture, navigation, arts, sciences, and manufactures, to Asia and Africa.* These families, thus distinguished by property, honors, and privileges, by defending themselves, have been obliged to defend the people against the encroachments of despotism. They have been a civil and political militia, constantly watching the designs of the standing armies, and courts; and by defending their own rights, liberties, properties, and privileges, they have been obliged, in some degree, to defend those of the people, by making a common cause with them. But there were several essential defects in this policy; one was, that the people took no rational measures to defend themselves, either against these great families, or the courts. They had no adequate representation of themselves in the sovereignty. Another was, that it never was determined where the sovereignty resided. Generally it was claimed by kings; but not admitted by the nobles. Sometimes every baron pretended to be sovereign in his own territory; at other times, the sovereignty was claimed by an assembly of nobles, under the name of States or Cortes. Sometimes the united authority of the king and states was called the sovereignty. The common people had no adequate and independent share in the legislatures, and found themselves harassed to discover who was the sovereign, and whom they ought to obey, as much as they ever had been or could be to determine who had the most merit. A thousand years of barons' wars, causing universal darkness, ignorance, and barbarity, ended at last in simple monarchy, not by

* This is a truth; but by no means a justification of the system of nobility in France, nor in other parts of Europe. Not even in England without a more equitable representation of the Commons in the legislature. J. A. 1812.

express stipulation, but by tacit acquiescence, in almost all Europe; the people preferring a certain sovereignty in a single person, to endless disputes, about merit and sovereignty, which never did and never will produce any thing but aristocratical anarchy; and the nobles contenting themselves with a security of their property and privileges, by a government of fixed laws, registered and interpreted by a judicial power, which they called sovereign tribunals, though the legislation and execution were in a single person.

In this system to control the nobles, the church joined the kings and common people. The progress of reason, letters, and science, has weakened the church and strengthened the common people; who, if they are honestly and prudently conducted by those who have their confidence, will most infallibly obtain a share in every legislature. But if the common people are advised to aim at collecting the whole sovereignty in single national assemblies, as they are by the Duke de la *Rochefoucauld* and the Marquis of *Condorcet;* or at the abolition of the regal executive authority; or at a division of the executive power, as they are by a posthumous publication of the Abbé de *Mably,*★ they will fail of their desired liberty, as certainly as emulation and rivalry are founded in human nature, and inseparable from civil affairs. It is not to flatter the passions of the people, to be sure, nor is it the way to obtain a present enthusiastic popularity, to tell them that in a single assembly they will act as arbitrarily and tyrannically as any despot, but it is a sacred truth, and as demonstrable as any proposition whatever, that a sovereignty in a single assembly must necessarily, and will certainly be exercised by a majority, as tyrannically as any sovereignty was ever exercised by kings or nobles. And if a balance of passions and interests is not scientifically concerted, the present struggle in Europe will be little beneficial to mankind,† and produce nothing but another thousand years of feudal fanaticism, under new and strange names.

★Witness the quintuple directory and the triumvirate consulate. J. A.

† Witness France and Europe in 1813. J. A.

VII.

'Tis from high life high characters are drawn,
A saint in crape is twice a saint in lawn.

POPE.

PROVIDENCE, which has placed one thing over against another, in the moral as well as physical world, has surprisingly accommodated the qualities of men to answer one another. There is a remarkable disposition in mankind to congratulate with others in their joys and prosperity, more than to sympathize with them in their sorrows and adversity. We may appeal to experience. There is less disposition to congratulation with genius, talents, or virtue, than there is with beauty, strength, and elegance of person; and less with these than with the gifts of fortune and birth, wealth and fame. The homage of the world is devoted to these last in a remarkable manner. Experience concurs with religion in pronouncing, most decisively, that this world is not the region of virtue or happiness; both are here at school, and their struggles with ambition, avarice, and the desire of fame, appear to be their discipline and exercise. The gifts of fortune are more level to the capacities, and more obvious to the notice of mankind in general; and congratulation with the happiness or fancied happiness of others is agreeable; sympathy with their misery is disagreeable. From the former sources we derive pleasure, from the latter pain. The sorrow of the company at a funeral may be more profitable to moral purposes, by suggesting useful reflections, than the mirth at a wedding; but it is not so vivid nor so sincere. The acclamations of the populace, at an ovation or triumph, at a coronation or installation, are from the heart, and their joy is unfeigned. Their grief at a public execution is less violent at least. If their feelings at such spectacles were very distressing they would be less eager to attend them. What is the motive of that ardent curiosity to see sights and shows of exultation; the processions of princes; the ostentation of wealth; the magnificence of equipage, retinue, furniture, buildings, and entertainment? There is no other answer to be given to these questions than the gayety of heart, the joyous feelings of congratulation

with such appearances of felicity. And for the vindication of the ways of
God to man, and the perpetual consolation of the many who are spectators, it is certainly true that their pleasure is always as great, and commonly
much greater, than that of the few who are the actors.

National passions and habits are unwieldy, unmanageable, and formidable things. The number of persons in any country who are known even
by name or reputation to all the inhabitants is, and ever must be, very
small. Those whose characters have attracted the affections, as well as the
attention of a whole people, acquire an influence and ascendency that it
is difficult to resist. In proportion as men rise higher in the world, whether
by election, descent, or appointment, and are exposed to the observation
of greater numbers of people, the effects of their own passions and of the
affections of others for them become more serious, interesting, and dangerous. In elective governments, where first magistrates and senators are
at stated intervals to be chosen, these, if there are no parties, become at
every fresh election more known, considered, and beloved by the whole
nation. But if the nation is divided into two parties, those who vote for a
man, become the more attached to him for the opposition that is made by
his enemies. This national attachment to an elective first magistrate, where
there is no competition, is very great. But where there is a competition,
the passions of his party are inflamed by it into a more ardent enthusiasm. If there are two candidates, each at the head of a party, the nation
becomes divided into two nations, each of which is, in fact, a moral person, as much as any community can be so, and are soon bitterly enraged
against each other.

It has been already said, that in proportion as men rise higher in the
world, and are exposed to the observation of greater numbers, the effects
of these passions are more serious and alarming. Impressions on the feelings of the individual are deeper; and larger portions of mankind become
interested in them. When you rise to the first ranks and consider the first
men,—a nobility who are known and respected at least, perhaps habitually esteemed and beloved by a nation; princes and kings, on whom the
eyes of all men are fixed, and whose every motion is regarded,—the consequences of wounding their feelings are dreadful, because the feelings of

a whole nation, and sometimes of many nations, are wounded at the same time. If the smallest variation is made in their situation, relatively to each other; if one who was inferior is raised to be superior, unless it be by fixed laws, whose evident policy and necessity may take away disgrace, nothing but war, carnage, and vengeance has ever been the usual consequence of it. In the examples of the houses, Valois and Bourbon, Guise and Montmorenci, Guise and Bourbon, and Guise and Valois, we shall see very grave effects of these feelings; and the history of a hundred years, which followed, is nothing but a detail of other, and more tragical effects of similar causes.

To any one who has never considered the force of *national attention, consideration, and congratulation,* and the causes, natural and artificial, by which they have been excited, it will be curious to read, in Plato's *Alcibiades,* the manner in which these national attachments to their kings were created by the ancient Persians. The policy of the modern monarchies of Europe seems to be an exact imitation of that of the Persian court, as it is explained by the Grecian philosopher. In France, for example, the pregnancy of the queen is announced with great solemnity to the whole nation. Her majesty is scarcely afflicted with a pain which is not formally communicated to the public. To this embryo the minds of the whole nation are turned; and they follow him, day by day, in their thoughts, till he is born. The whole people have a right to be present at his birth; and as many as the chamber will hold, crowd in, till the queen and prince are almost suffocated with the loyal curiosity and affectionate solicitude of their subjects. In the cradle, the principal personages of the kingdom, as well as all the ambassadors, are from time to time presented to the royal infant. To thousands who press to see him, he is daily shown from the nursery. Of every step in his education, and of every gradation of his youthful growth, in body and mind, the public is informed in the gazettes. Not a stroke of wit, not a sprightly sally, not a trait of generous affection, can escape him, but the world is told of it, and, very often, pretty fictions are contrived for the same purpose, where the truth will not furnish materials. Thus it becomes the national fashion, it is the *tone* of the city and the court, to think and converse daily about the dauphin.

When he accedes to the throne, the same attention is continued till he dies.

In elective governments, something very like this always takes place towards the first character. His person, countenance, character, and actions, are made the daily contemplation and conversation of the whole people. Hence arises the danger of a division of this attention. Where there are rivals for the first place, the national attention and passions are divided, and thwart each other; the collision enkindles fires; the conflicting passions interest all ranks; they produce slanders and libels first, mobs and seditions next, and civil war, with all her hissing snakes, burning torches, and haggard horrors at last.

This is the true reason, why all civilized free nations have found, by experience, the necessity of separating from the body of the people, and even from the legislature, the distribution of honors, and conferring it on the executive authority of government. When the emulation of all the citizens looks up to one point, like the rays of a circle from all parts of the circumference, meeting and uniting in the centre, you may hope for uniformity, consistency, and subordination; but when they look up to different individuals, or assemblies, or councils, you may expect all the deformities, eccentricities, and confusion, of the Polemic system.

VIII.

Wise, if a minister, but if a king,
More wise, more learn'd, more just, more every thing.

POPE.

THERE is scarcely any truth more certain, or more evident, than that the *noblesse* of Europe are, in general, less happy than the common people. There is one irrefragable proof of it, which is, that they do not maintain their own population. Families, like stars or candles, which you will, are going out continually; and without fresh recruits from the plebeians, the nobility would in time be extinct. If you make allowances for the state, which they are condemned by themselves and the world to support, they are poorer than the poor; deeply in debt; and tributary to usurious capitalists, as greedy as the Jews. The kings of Europe, in the sight of a philosopher, are the greatest slaves on earth, how often soever we may call them despots, tyrants, and other rude names, in which our pride and vanity take a wonderful delight; they have the least exercise of their inclinations, the least personal liberty, and the least free indulgence of their passions, of any men alive. Yet how rare are the instances of resignations, and how universal is the ambition to be noble, and the wish to be royal.

Experience and philosophy are lost upon mankind. The attention of the world has a charm in it, which few minds can withstand. The people consider the condition of the great in all those delusive colors, in which imagination can paint and gild it, and reason can make little resistance to this impetuous propensity. To better their condition, to advance their fortunes, without limits, is the object of their constant desire, the employment of all their thoughts by day and by night. They feel a peculiar sympathy with that pleasure, which they presume those enjoy, who are already powerful, celebrated, and rich. "We favor," says a great writer, "all their inclinations, and forward all their wishes. What pity, we think, that any thing should spoil and corrupt so agreeable a situation; we could even wish them immortal; and it seems hard to us, that death should at last put an end to such perfect enjoyment. It is cruel, we think, in nature to compel them from their exalted stations to that humble, but hospitable home, which she has provided for all her children. Great king, live forever! is the compliment, which, after the manner of eastern adulation, we should readily make them, if experience did not teach us its absurdity. Every calamity that befalls them, every injury that is done them, excites in the breast of the spectator ten times more compassion and resentment than he would have felt, had the same things happened to other men. It is the misfortunes of kings only, which afford the proper subjects for tragedy; they resemble, in this respect, the misfortunes of lovers. Those two situations are the chief which interest us upon the theatre; because, in spite of all that reason and experience can tell us to the contrary, the prejudices of the imagination attach to these two states a happiness superior to any other. To disturb or to put an end to such perfect enjoyment, seems to be the most atrocious of all injuries. The traitor who conspires against the life of his monarch, is thought a greater monster than any other murderer. All the innocent blood that was shed in the civil wars, provoked less indignation than the death of Charles I. A stranger to human nature, who saw the indifference of men about the misery of their inferiors, and the regret and indignation which they feel for the misfortunes and sufferings of those above them, would be apt to imagine, that pain must be more agonizing, and the convulsions of death more terrible, to persons of higher rank than to those of meaner stations.

"Upon this disposition of mankind, to go along with all the passions of the rich and the powerful, is founded the distinction of ranks, and the order of society. Our obsequiousness to our superiors more frequently arises from our admiration for the advantages of their situation, than from any private expectations of benefit from their good will. Their benefits can extend but to a few; but their fortunes interest almost everybody. We are eager to assist them in completing a system of happiness that approaches so near to perfection; and we desire to serve them for their own sake, without any other recompense but the vanity or the honor of obliging them. Neither is our deference to their inclinations founded chiefly, or altogether, upon a regard to the utility of such submission, and to the order of society, which is best supported by it. Even when the order of society seems to require that we should oppose them, we can hardly bring ourselves to do it. That kings are the servants of the people, to be obeyed, resisted, deposed, or punished, as the public conveniency may require, is the doctrine of reason and philosophy; but it is not the doctrine of nature. Nature would teach us to submit to them, for their own sake, to tremble and bow down before their exalted station, to regard their smile as a reward sufficient to compensate any services, and to dread their displeasure, though no other evil were to follow from it, as the severest of all mortifications. To treat them in any respect as men, to reason and dispute with them upon ordinary occasions, requires such resolution, that there are few men whose magnanimity can support them in it, unless they are likewise assisted by familiarity and acquaintance. The strongest motives, the most furious passions, fear, hatred, and resentment, are scarce sufficient to balance this natural disposition to respect them; and their conduct must, either justly or unjustly, have excited the highest degree of all those passions, before the bulk of the people can be brought to oppose them with violence, or to desire to see them either punished or deposed. Even when the people have been brought to this length, they are apt to relent every moment, and easily relapse into their habitual state of deference. They cannot stand the mortification of their monarch. Compassion soon takes the place of resentment, they forget all past provocations, their old principles of loyalty revive, and they run to reestablish the ruined authority of their old masters, with the same violence with which they had opposed it. The death of Charles I. brought about the restoration of the royal family. Compassion for James II., when he was seized by the populace in making his escape on shipboard, had almost prevented the revolution, and made it go on more heavily than before.

"Do the great seem insensible of the easy price at which they may acquire the public admiration; or do they seem to imagine that to them, as to other men, it must be the purchase either of sweat or of blood? By what important accomplishments is the young nobleman instructed to support the dignity of his rank, and to render himself worthy of that superiority over his fellow-citizens, to which the virtue of his ancestors had raised them? Is it by knowledge, by industry, by patience, by self-denial, or by virtue of any kind? As all his words, as all his motions are attended to, he learns an habitual regard to every circumstance of ordinary behavior, and studies to perform all those small duties, with the most exact propriety. As he is conscious how much he is observed, and how much mankind are disposed to favor all his inclinations, he acts, upon the most indifferent occasions, with that freedom and elegance which the thought of this naturally inspires. His air, his manner, his deportment, all mark that elegant and graceful sense of his own superiority, which those who are born to inferior stations can hardly ever arrive at. These are the arts, by which he proposes to make mankind more easily submit to his authority, and to govern their inclinations according to his own pleasure; and in this he is seldom disappointed. These arts, supported by rank and preëminence, are, upon ordinary occasions, sufficient to govern the world.

"But it is not by accomplishments of this kind, that the man of inferior rank must hope to distinguish himself. Politeness is so much the virtue of the great, that it will do little honor to any body but themselves. The coxcomb, who imitates their manner, and affects to be eminent by the superior propriety of his ordinary behavior, is rewarded with a double share of contempt for his folly and presumption. Why should the man whom nobody thinks it worth while to look at, be very anxious about the manner in which he holds up his head, or disposes of his arms, while he walks through a room? He is occupied surely with a very superfluous attention, and with an attention, too, that marks a sense of his own importance, which no other mortal can go along with. The most perfect modesty and plainness, joined to as much negligence as is consistent with the respect due to the company, ought to be the chief characteristics of the behavior of a private man. If ever he hopes to distinguish himself, it must be by more important virtues; he must acquire dependents to balance the dependents of the great; and he has no other fund to pay them from, but the labor of his body, and the activity of his mind. He must cultivate these, therefore; he must acquire superior knowledge in his profession, and superior industry in the exercise of it; he must be patient in labor, resolute in danger, and firm in distress. These talents he must bring into public view, by the difficulty, importance, and at the same time, good judgment, of his undertakings, and by the severe and unrelenting application with which he pursues them. Probity and prudence, generosity and frankness, must characterize his behavior upon all ordinary occasions; and he must at the same time, be forward to engage in all those situations, in which it requires the greatest talents and virtues to act with propriety; but in which the greatest applause is to be acquired by those who can acquit themselves with honor. With what impatience does the man of spirit and ambition, who is depressed by his situation, look round for some great opportunity to distinguish himself? No circumstances, which can afford this appear to him undesirable; he even looks forward with satisfaction to the prospect of foreign war, or civil dissension; and with secret transport and delight, sees, through all the confusion and bloodshed which attend them, the probability of those wished-for occasions presenting

themselves, in which he may draw upon himself the attention and admiration of mankind. The man of rank and distinction, on the contrary,
whose whole glory consists in the propriety of his ordinary behavior; who
is contented with the humble renown which this can afford him, and has
no talents to acquire any other; is unwilling to embarrass himself with
what can be attended either with difficulty or distress. To figure at a ball
is his great triumph; he has an aversion to all public confusions, not from
want of courage, for in that he is seldom defective, but from a consciousness that he possesses none of the virtues which are required in such situations, and that the public attention will certainly be drawn away from
him by others; he may be willing to expose himself to some little danger,
and to make a campaign, when it happens to be the fashion; but he shud-
ders with horror at the thought of any situation which demands the continual and long exertion of patience, industry, fortitude, and application
of thought. These virtues are hardly ever to be met with in men who are
born to those high stations. In all governments, accordingly, even in
monarchies, the highest offices are generally possessed, and the whole
detail of the administration conducted, by men who were educated in
the middle and inferior ranks of life, who have been carried forward by
their own industry and abilities, though loaded with the jealousy, and
opposed by the resentment of all those who were born their superiors, and
to whom the great, after having regarded them, first with contempt, and
afterwards with envy, are at last contented to truckle with the same abject
meanness, with which they desire that the rest of mankind should behave
to themselves.

"It is the loss of this easy empire over the affections of mankind which
renders the fall from greatness so insupportable. When the family of the
King of Macedon was led in triumph by Paulus Æmilius, their misfortunes
made them divide with their conqueror the attention of the Roman
people. The sight of the royal children, whose tender age rendered them
insensible of their situation, struck the spectators, amidst the public rejoic-
ings and prosperity, with the tenderest sorrow and compassion. The King
appeared next in the procession, and seemed like one confounded and

astonished, and bereft of all sentiment, by the greatness of his calamities. His friends and ministers followed after him. As they moved along, they often cast their eyes upon their fallen sovereign, and always burst into tears at the sight; their whole behavior demonstrating that they thought not of their own misfortunes, but were occupied entirely by the superior greatness of his. The generous Romans, on the contrary, beheld him with disdain and indignation, and regarded as unworthy of all compassion the man who could be so mean-spirited as to bear to live under such calamities. Yet what did those calamities amount to? He was to spend the remainder of his days in a state which, in itself, should seem worthy of envy; a state of plenty, ease, leisure, and security, from which it was impossible for him, even by his own folly, to fall. But he was no longer to be surrounded by that admiring mob of fools, flatterers, and dependents, who had formerly been accustomed to attend upon all his motions; he was no longer to be gazed upon by multitudes, nor to have it in his power to render himself the object of their respect, their gratitude, their love, their admiration. The passions of nations were no longer to mould themselves upon his inclinations. This was that insupportable calamity which bereaved the King of all sentiment; which made his friends forget their own misfortunes; and which the Roman magnanimity could scarce conceive how any man could be so mean-spirited as to bear to survive.

"To those who have been accustomed to the possession, or even to the hope of public admiration, all other pleasures sicken and decay.

"Of such mighty importance does it appear to be, in the imaginations of men, to stand in that situation which sets them most in the view of general sympathy and attention; and thus, place, that great object which divides the wives of aldermen, is the end of half the labors of human life; and is the cause of all the tumult and bustle, all the rapine and injustice, which avarice and ambition have introduced into this world. People of sense, it is said, indeed, despise place; that is, they despise sitting at the head of the table, and are indifferent who it is that is pointed out to the company by that frivolous circumstance, which the smallest advantage is capable of overbalancing. But rank, distinction, preëminence, no man despises."[4]

IX.

Heroes, proceed! What bounds your pride shall hold?
What check restrain your thirst of power and gold?

JOHNSON.

The answer to the question in the motto can be none other than this, that, as nature has established in the bosoms of heroes no limits to those passions; and as the world, instead of restraining, encourages them, the check must be in the form of government.

The world encourages ambition and avarice, by taking the most decided part in their favor. The Roman world approved of the ambition of Cæsar; and, notwithstanding all the pains that have been taken, with so much reason, by moral and political writers to disgrace it, the world has approved it these seventeen hundred years, and still esteems his name an honor to the first empire in Europe. Consider the story of the ambition and the fall of Cardinal Wolsey and Archbishop Laud; the indignation of the world against their tyranny has been very faint; the sympathy with their fall has been very strong. Consider all the examples in history of successful ambition, you will find none generally condemned by mankind; on the other hand, think of the instances of ambition unsuccessful and dis-appointed, or of falls from great heights; you find the sympathy of the world universally affected. Cruelty and tyranny of the blackest kind must accompany the story, to destroy or sensibly diminish this pity. That world, for the regulation of whose prejudices, passions, imaginations, and inter-ests, governments are instituted, is so unjust, that neither religion, natural nor revealed, nor any thing, but a well-ordered and well-balanced gov-ernment, has ever been able to correct it, and that but imperfectly. It is true, in modern London, as it was in ancient Rome, that the sympathy of

---

[4] Adam Smith. *Theory of Moral Sentiments,* vol. i. pp. 125–141.

the world is less excited by the destruction of the house of a man of merit in obscurity, or even in middle life, though it be by the unjust violence of men, than by the same calamity befalling a rich man, by the righteous indignation of Heaven.

Nil habuit Codrus: quis enim negat? et tamen illud
Perdidit infelix totum nihil: ultimus autem
Ærumnæ cumulus, quad nudum et frusta rogantem
Nemo cibo, nemo hospitio tectoque juvabit.
Si magna Asturii cecidit domus, horrida mater,
Pullati proceres, differt vadimonia Prætor.
Tune gemimus casus urbis, tune odimus ignem.
Ardet adhuc, et jam occurrit, qui marmora donet,
Conferat impensas. Hic nuda et candida signa,
Hic aliquid præclarum Euphranoris et Polycleti,
Hæc Asianorum vetera ornamenta Deorum,
Hic libros dabit et forulos mediamque Minervam,
Hic modium argenti. Meliora et plura reponit
Persicus orborum lautissimus, ut merito jam
Suspectus, tanquam ipse suas incenderit ædes.

But, hark! th' affrighted crowd's tumultuous cries
Roll through the streets, and thunder to the skies;
Rais'd from some pleasing dream of wealth and power,
Some pompous palace, or some blissful bower,
Aghast you start, and scarce, with aching sight,
Sustain the approaching fire's tremendous light;
Swift from pursuing horrors take your way,
And leave your little all to flames a prey;
Then thro' the world a wretched vagrant roam,
For where can starving merit find a home?
In vain your mournful narrative disclose,
While all neglect, and most insult your woes.

But

> Should Heavn's just bolts Orgilio's wealth confound,
> And spread his flaming palace on the ground,
> Swift o'er the land the dismal rumor flies,
> And public mournings pacify the skies;
> The laureat tribe in venal verse relate,
> How virtue wars with persecuting fate;
> With well-feign'd gratitude, the pension'd band
> Refund the plunder of the beggar'd land.
> See! while he builds, the gaudy vassals come,
> And crowd with sudden wealth the rising dome;
> The price of boroughs and of souls restore;
> And raise his treasures higher than before.
> Now bless'd with all the baubles of the great,
> The polish'd marble, and the shining plate,
> Orgilio sees the golden pile aspire,
> And hopes from angry Heav'n another fire.

Although the verse, both of the Roman and Briton, is satire, its keenest severity consists in its truth.

X.

> *Order is Heaven's first law; and, this confess'd,*
> *Some are, and must be, greater than the rest;*
> *More rich, more wise; but who infers from hence,*
> *That such are happier, shocks all common sense.*

POPE.

THE world is sensible of the necessity of supporting their favorites under the first onsets of misfortunes, lest the fall should be dreadful and irrecoverable; for, according to the great Master of Nature,

Tis certain, greatness, once fallen out with fortune,

Must fall out with men too. What the declin'd is,
He shall as soon read in the eyes of others,
As feel in his own fall; for men, like butterflies,
Show not their mealy wings but to the summer;
And not a man, for being simply man,
Hath any honor; but's honor'd for those honors
That are without him,—as place, riches, favor,
Prizes of accident as oft as merit.

Mankind are so sensible of these things, that, by a kind of instinct or intuition, they generally follow the advice of the same author:—

Take the instant way,
For honor travels in a strait no narrow,
Where one but goes abreast. Keep, then, the path,
For emulation hath a thousand sons,
That one by one pursue; if you give way,
Or hedge aside from the direct forth-right,
Like to an enter'd tide, they all rush by,
And leave you hindmost;
Or like a gallant horse fall'n in first rank,
Lie there for pavement to the abject rear,
O'errun and trampled on.

The inference, from all the contemplations and experiments which have been made, by all nations, upon these dispositions to imitation, emulation, and rivalry, is expressed by the same great teacher of morality and politics:—

Degree being vizarded,
Th' unworthiest shows as fairly in the mask.
The heavens themselves, the planets, and this centre,
Observe degree, priority, and place,
Insisture, course, proportion, season, form,
Office, and custom, in all line of order;
And, therefore, is the glorious planet Sol,

In noble eminence, enthron'd and spher'd
Amidst the other; whose med'cinable eye
Corrects the ill aspects of planets evil,
And posts, like the commandment of a king,
Sans check, to good and bad; but when the planets
In evil mixture, to disorder wander,
What plagues and what portents! what mutiny!
What raging of the sea! Shaking of earth!
Commotion in the winds! Frights, changes, horrors,
Divert and crack, rend and deracinate,
The unity and married calm of states,
Quite from their fixture? O, when Degree is shak'd,
Which is the ladder to all high designs,
The enterprise is sick! How could communities,
Degrees in schools, and brotherhoods in cities,
The primogenitive and due of birth,
Prerogative of age, crowns, sceptres, laurels,
But by Degree, stand in authentic place?
Take but Degree away; untune that string
And hark! what discord follows! each thing meets
In mere oppugnancy. The bounded waters
Should lift their bosoms higher than the shores,
And make a sop of all this solid globe.
Strength should be lord of imbecility,
And the rude son should strike his father dead.
Force should be right; or rather, right and wrong
Should lose their names, and so should justice too.
Then every thing includes itself in power,
Power into will, will into appetite;
And appetite an universal wolf,
Must make perforce an universal prey,
And, last, eat up himself.
This chaos, when Degree is suffocate,
Follows the choking.

The General's disdain'd,
By him one step below. He, by the next;
That next, by him beneath. So every step,
Exampled by the first pace that is sick
Of his superior, grows to an envious fever
Of pale and bloodless emulation.
Troy in our weakness stands, not in her strength.
Most wisely hath Ulysses here discovered
The Fever whereof all our power is sick.★

CHAPTER THIRD.

Think we, like some weak prince, th' eternal cause
Prone, for his fav'rites, to reverse his laws?

MARCHAMONT NEDHAM.

EMULATION, which is imitation and something more—a desire not only
to equal or resemble, but to excel, is so natural a movement of the human
heart, that, wherever men are to be found, and in whatever manner associated or connected, we see its effects. They are not more affected by it,
as individuals, than they are in communities. There are rivalries between
every little society in the same city; between families and all the connections by consanguinity and affinity; between trades, faculties, and professions; between congregations, parishes, and churches; between schools,
colleges, and universities; between districts, villages, cities, provinces, and
nations.

National rivalries are more frequently the cause of wars than the ambition of ministers, or the pride of kings. As long as there is patriotism, there
will be national emulation, vanity, and pride. It is national pride which
commonly stimulates kings and ministers. National fear, apprehension of
danger, and the necessity of self-defence, is added to such rivalries for

★ The style in these quotations from Shakspeare has little of the fluency, and less of
that purity, which sometimes appear in his writings; but the sense is as immortal as human
nature. J. A. 1813.

wealth, consideration, and power. The safety, independence, and existence of a nation, depend upon keeping up a high sense of its own honor, dignity, and power, in the hearts of its individuals, and a lively jealousy of the growing power and aspiring ambition of a neighboring state. This is well illustrated in the Political Geography, published in our newspapers from London, within a few weeks. "The jealousies and enmities, the alliances and friendships, or rather the combinations of different states and princes, might almost be learned from a map, without attention to what has passed, or is now passing in the world. Next neighbors are political enemies. States between which a common neighbor, and, therefore, a common enemy intervenes, are good friends. In this respect, Europe may be compared to a chess-board marked with the black and with the white spots of political discord and concord. Before the union between England and Scotland, a friendship and alliance subsisted for centuries between the latter of these kingdoms and France, because they were both inimical to England. For a like reason, before a Prince of Bourbon, in the beginning of the present century, was raised to the Spanish throne, a good understanding subsisted for the most part between England and Spain; and before the late alliance, there was peace and kindness, with little interruption, for the space of centuries, between England and the Emperor. An alliance has long subsisted between the French and the Turks, on account of the intervening dominion of the Austrians. The Swedes were long the friends of France, on account of the intervention of Holland and Denmark; and because Sweden, the friend of France, was situated in the neighborhood of the Russian territories, a friendship and commercial intercourse were established, from the very first time that Muscovy appears on the political theatre of Europe, between England and Russia. It is superfluous to multiply instances of this kind. All past history and present observation will confirm the truth of our position,—which, though very simple, is like all other simple truths, of very great importance; for, however, the accidental caprices and passions of individual princes, or their ministers, may alter the relative dispositions and interests of nations for a time, there is a natural tendency to revert to the alteration already described. We have been led into these reflection by the treaty offensive and defensive, that has been formed between Sweden, Prussia, and the Sublime Porte; between Prussia and Holland; and the report, which is very probable, that a treaty offensive and defensive is on the point of being concluded between Turkey and Poland. In this chain of alliances we find the order of the chess-board adhered to, in some instances, but passed over in others. It is observed that there should be an alliance between Turkey and Sweden, and also that there should be an alliance between Poland and Turkey, because Russia intervenes between Turkey and Sweden, and Hungary between Turkey and Poland; but that there should be an alliance between Poland and Prussia is owing to particular and accidental circumstances. The two former alliances may, therefore, be expected to be lasting; the latter to be only temporary and precarious. In general, the chain of alliance, that is formed or forming among the Swedes, Prussians, Poles, Dutch, Turks, and we may say the English, is a most striking proof of the real or supposed strength and influence of the two imperial courts of Russia and Germany."

The writer of this paragraph might have added the alliance between England and Portugal, and that between the United States of America and France. The principle of all these examples is as natural as emulation, and as infallible as the sincerity of interest. On it turns the whole system of human affairs. The Congress of 1776 were fully aware of it. With no small degree of vehemence was it urged as an argument for the declaration of independence.* With the confidence and firmness was it foretold that France should not avoid accepting the propositions that should be made to her; that the Court of Versailles could not answer it to her own subjects, and that all Europe would pronounce her blind, lost, and undone, if she rejected so fair an opportunity of disembarrassing herself from the danger of so powerful and hostile a rival, whose naval superiority held all her foreign dominions, her maritime power, and commercial interest at mercy.†

But why all this of emulation and rivalry? Because, as the whole history of the civil wars of France, given us by Davila, is no more than a relation of

---

*By John Adams
† France has thrown away all advantages by her want of wisdom

rivalries succeeding each other in a rapid series, the reflections we have made
will assist us, both to understand that noble historian, and to form a right
judgment of the state of affairs in France at the present moment. They will
suggest also to Americans, especially to those who have been unfriendly, and
may be now lukewarm to their national constitution,★ some useful
inquiries, such as these, for example: Whether there are not emulations of a
serious complexion among ourselves? between cities and universities?
between north and south? the middle and the north? the middle and the
south? between one state and another? between the governments of states
and the national government? and between individual patriots and heroes in
all these? What is the natural remedy against the inconveniences and dangers
of these rivalries? Whether a well-balanced constitution, such as that of our
Union purports to be, ought not to be cordially supported by every good
citizen, as our only hope of peace and our ark of safety, till its defects, if it
has any, can be corrected? But it must be left to the contemplation of our
state physicians to discover the causes and the remedy of that "*fever, whereof
our power is sick.*" One question only shall be respectfully insinuated: Whether
equal laws, the result only of a balanced government, can ever be obtained
and preserved without some signs or other of distinction and degree?

We are told that our friends, the National Assembly of France, have
abolished all distinctions. But be not deceived, my dear countrymen.
Impossibilities cannot be performed. Have they levelled all fortunes and
equally divided all property? Have they made all men and women equally
wise, elegant, and beautiful? Have they annihilated the names of Bourbon and Montmorenci, Rochefoucauld and Noailles, Lafayette and La
Moignon, Necker and De Calonne, Mirabeau and Bailly? Have they committed to the flames all the records, annals, and histories of the nation?
All the copies of Mezerai, Daniel, De Thou, Velly, and a thousand others?
Have they burned all their pictures, and broken all their statues? Have they
blotted out of all memories, the names, places of abode, and illustrious
actions of all their ancestors? Have they not still princes of the first and
second order, nobles and knights? Have they no record nor memory who

★ The anti-federalists. J. A. 1813.

are the men who compose the present national assembly? Do they wish to have that distinction forgotten? Have the French officers who served in America melted their eagles and torn their ribbons?[†]

XII.

'Tis with our judgments as our watches—none
Go just alike, yet each believes his own.

POPE.

ALL the miracles enumerated in our last number, must be performed in France, before all distinctions can be annihilated, and distinctions in abundance would be found, after all, for French gentlemen, in the history of England, Holland, Spain, Germany, Italy, America, and all other countries on the globe.

The wisdom of nations has remarked the universal consideration paid to wealth; and that the passion of avarice excited by it, produced treachery, cowardice, and a selfish, unsocial meanness, but had no tendency to produce those virtues of patience, courage, fortitude, honor, or patriotism, which the service of the public required in their citizens in peace and war.

The wisdom of nations has observed that the general attention paid to birth produced a different kind of sentiments,—those of pride in the maxims and principles of religion, morals, and government, as well as in the talents and virtues, which first produced illustration to ancestors.

As the pride of wealth produced nothing but meanness of sentiment and a sordid scramble for money; and the pride of birth produced some degree of emulation in knowledge and virtue; the wisdom of nations has endeavored to employ one prejudice to counteract another; the prejudice in favor of birth, to moderate, correct, and restrain the prejudice in favor of wealth.

The national assembly of France is too enlightened a body to overlook the inquiry: What effect on the moral character of the nation would

[†] How are distinctions abolished now in 1813? J. A.

be produced, by destroying, if that were possible, all attention to families, and setting all the passions on the pursuit of gain? Whether universal venality and an incorrigible corruption in elections would not be the necessary consequence? It may be relied on, however, that the intentions of that august and magnanimous assembly are misunderstood and misrepresented. Time will develop their designs, will show them to be more judicious than to attempt impossibilities so obvious as that of the abolition of all distinctions.

ALPHONSUS X., the astronomical king of Castile, has been accused of impiety, for saying that "if, at the time of the creation, he had been called to the councils of the Divinity, he could have given some useful advice concerning the motions of the stars." It is not probable, that any thing was intended by him, more than a humorous sarcasm or a sneer of contempt at the Ptolemaic system, a projection of which he had before him. But if the national assembly should have seriously in contemplation, and should resolve in earnest the total abolition of all distinctions and orders, it would be much more difficult to vindicate them from an accusation of impiety. God, in the constitution of nature, has ordained that every man shall have a disposition to emulation, as well as imitation, and consequently a passion for distinction; and that all men shall not have equal means and opportunities of gratifying it. Shall we believe the national assembly capable of resolving that no man shall have any desire of distinction; or that all men shall have equal means of gratifying it? Or that no man shall have any means of gratifying it? What would this be better than saying, "if we had been called to the councils of the celestials, we could have given better advice in the constitution of human nature?" If nature and that assembly could be thus at variance, which however is not credible, the world would soon see which is the most powerful.

That there is already a scission in the national assembly, like all others, past, present, and to come, is most certain. There is an aristocratical party, an armed neutrality, and most probably a monarchical party; besides another division, who must finally prevail, or liberty will be lost; I mean a set of members, who are equal friends to monarchy, aristocracy, and democracy, and wish for an equal, independent mixture of all three in their constitution. Each of these parties has its chief, and these chiefs are, or will be, rivals. Religion will be both the object and the pretext of some; liberty, of others; submission and obedience of others; and levelling, downright levelling, of not a few. But the attention, consideration, and congratulations of the public will be the object of all. Situation and office will be aimed at by some of all parties. Contests and dissensions will arise between these runners in the same race. The natural and usual progress is, from debate in the assembly to discussions in print; from the search of truth and public utility in both, to sophistry and the spirit of party; evils so greatly dreaded by the ingenuous "Citizen of New Haven," to whom we have now the honor of paying our first respects, hoping that, hereafter, we may find an opportunity to make him our more particular compliments.★ From sophistry and party spirit, the transition is quick and easy to falsehood, imposture, and every species of artificial evolution and criminal intrigue. As unbalanced parties of every description can never tolerate a free inquiry of any kind, when employed against themselves, the license, and even the most temperate freedom of the press, soon excite resentment and revenge. A writer, unpopular with an opposite party, because he is too formidable in wit or argument, may first be burnt in effigy; or a printer may have his office assaulted. Cuffs and kicks, boxes and cudgels, are heard of among plebeian statesmen; challenges and single combats among the aristocratic legislators. Riots and seditions at length break men's bones, or flay off their skins. Lives are lost; and, when blood is once drawn, men, like other animals, become outrageous. If one party has not a superiority over the other, clear enough to decide every thing at its pleasure, a civil war ensues. When the nation arrives at this period of the progression, every leader, at the head of his votaries, even if you admit him to have the best intentions in the world, will find himself compelled to form them into some military

---

★ Condorcet. It was then my intention to have examined those letters at large; but the rage and fury of the Jacobinical journals against these discourses, increased as they proceeded, intimidated the printer, John Fenno, and convinced me, that to proceed would do more hurt than good. I therefore broke off abruptly. J. A. 1813.

(Condorcet's four letters are printed at the end of the first volume of M. Mazzei's *Recherches historiques et politiques sur les États Unis de l'Amérique septentrionale*.)

arrangement, both for offence and defence; to build castles and fortify eminences, like the feudal barons. For aristocratical rivalries, and democratical rivalries too, when unbalanced against each other by some third mediating power, naturally and unfailingly produce a feudal system. If this should be the course in France, the poor, deluded, and devoted partisans would soon be fond enough of decorating their leaders with the old titles of dukes, marquises and counts, or doing any thing else to increase the power of their commander over themselves, to unite their wills and forces for their own safety and defence, or to give him weight with their enemies.*

The men of letters in France are wisely reforming one feudal system; but may they not, unwisely, lay the foundation of another? A legislature, in one assembly, can have no other termination than in civil dissension, feudal anarchy, or simple monarchy. The best apology which can be made for their fresh attempt of a sovereignty in one assembly, an idea at least as ancient in France as *Stephen Boethius,* is, that it is only intended to be momentary. If a senate had been proposed, it must have been formed, most probably, of princes of the blood, cardinals, archbishops, dukes, and marquises; and all these together would have obstructed the progress of the reformation in religion and government, and procured an abortion to the regeneration of France. Pennsylvania established her single assembly, in 1776, upon the same principle. An apprehension, that the Proprietary and Quaker interests would prevail, to the election of characters disaffected to the American cause, finally preponderated against two legislative councils. Pennsylvania, and Georgia, who followed her example, have found by experience the necessity of a change; and France, by the same infallible progress of reasoning, will discover the same necessity; happy, indeed, if the experiment shall not cost her more dear. That the subject is considered in this light by the best friends of liberty in Europe, appears by the words of Dr. Price, lately published in this paper:—"Had not the aristocratical and clerical orders," says that sage and amiable writer, "been obliged to throw themselves into one chamber with the commons, no

---

* See Napoleon's speech, 20 December, 1812, at the close of these discourses.
He still proceeds to exemplify the effects and consequences of rivalries, in 1813. J. A.

reformation could have taken place, and the regeneration of the king-dom would have been impossible. And in future legislatures, were these two orders to make distinct and independent states, all that has been done would probably be soon undone. Hereafter, perhaps, when the new con-stitution, as now formed, has acquired strength by time, the national assembly may find it practicable, as well as expedient, to establish, by means of a third estate, such a check as now takes place in the American gov-ernment, and is indispensable in the British government."*

XIII.

First follow nature; and your judgment frame
By her just standard, which is still the same.

POPE.

THE world grows more enlightened. Knowledge is more equally diffused. Newspapers, magazines, and circulating libraries have made mankind wiser. Titles and distinctions, ranks and orders, parade and ceremony, are all going out of fashion. This is roundly and frequently asserted in the streets, and sometimes on theatres of higher *rank*.† Some truth there is in it; and if the opportunity were temperately improved, to the reformation of abuses, the rectification of errors, and the dissipation of pernicious prejudices, a great advantage it might be. But, on the other hand, false inferences may be drawn from it, which may make mankind wish for the age of dragons, giants, and fairies. If all decorum, discipline, and subordination are to be destroyed, and universal Pyrrhonism, anarchy, and insecurity of property are to be introduced, nations will soon wish their books in ashes, seek for dark-ness and ignorance, superstition and fanaticism, as blessings, and follow the standard of the first mad despot, who, with the enthusiasm of another Mahomet,‡ will endeavor to obtain them.

---

*Oh! that Dr. Price and Dr. Franklin had lived to read the addresses and answers, of 20 December, 1812, at the end of this volume. Jefferson has lived to see it. J. A. 1813.

† Read the history of the world, from 1790 to 1813, as a comment.

‡ Napoleon is not all this. J. A. 1813.

Are riches, honors, and beauty going out of fashion? Is not the rage for them, on the contrary, increased faster than improvement in knowledge? As long as either of these are in vogue, will there not be emulations and rivalries? Does not the increase of knowledge in any man increase his emulation; and the diffusion of knowledge among men multiply rivalries? Has the progress of science, arts, and letters yet discovered that there are no passions in human nature? no ambition, avarice, or desire of fame? Are these passions cooled, diminished, or extinguished? Is the rage for admiration less ardent in men or women? Have these propensities less a tendency to divisions, controversies, seditions, mutinies, and civil wars than formerly? On the contrary, the more knowledge is diffused, the more the passions are extended, and the more furious they grow. Had Cicero less vanity, or Cæsar less ambition, for their vast erudition? Had the King of Prussia less of one than the other? There is no connection in the mind between science and passion, by which the former can extinguish or diminish the latter. It, on the contrary, sometimes increases them, by giving them exercise. Were the passions of the Romans less vivid in the age of Pompey than in the time of Mummius. Are those of the Britons more moderate at this hour than in the reigns of the Tudors? Are the passions of monks the weaker for all their learning? Are not jealousy, envy, hatred, malice, and revenge, as well as emulation and ambition, as rancorous in the cells of Carmelites as in the courts of princes? Go to the Royal Society of London. Is there less emulation for the chair of Sir Isaac Newton than there was, and commonly will be, for all elective presidencies? Is there less animosity and rancor, arising from mutual emulations in that region of science, than there is among the most ignorant of mankind? Go to Paris. How do you find the men of letters? united, friendly, harmonious, meek, humble, modest, charitable? prompt to mutual forbearance? unassuming? ready to acknowledge superior merit? zealous to encourage the first symptoms of genius? Ask Voltaire and Rousseau, Marmontel and De Mably.

The increase and dissemination of knowledge, instead of rendering unnecessary the checks of emulation and the balances of rivalry in the orders of society and constitution of government, augment the necessity of both. It becomes the more indispensable that every man should know his place, and be made to keep it. Bad men increase in knowledge as fast as good men; and science, arts, taste, sense, and letters, are employed for the purposes of injustice and tyranny, as well as those of law and liberty; for corruption, as well as for virtue.

FRENCHMEN! Act and think like yourselves! confessing human nature, be magnanimous and wise. Acknowledging and boasting yourselves to be men, avow the feelings of men. The affectation of being exempted from passions is inhuman. The grave pretension to such singularity is solemn hypocrisy. Both are unworthy of your frank and generous natures. Consider that government is intended to set bounds to passions which nature has not limited; and to assist reason, conscience, justice, and truth, in controlling interests, which, without it, would be as unjust as uncontrollable.*

AMERICANS! Rejoice, that from experience you have learned wisdom; and instead of whimsical and fantastical projects, you have adopted a promising essay towards a well-ordered government. Instead of following any foreign example, to return to *the legislation of confusion,* contemplate the means of restoring decency, honesty, and order in society, by preserving and completing, if any thing should be found necessary to complete the balance of your government. In a well-balanced government, reason, conscience, truth, and virtue, must be respected by all parties, and exerted for the public good.[†] Advert to the principles on which you commenced that glorious self-defence, which, if you behave with steadiness and consistency, may ultimately loosen the chains of all mankind. If you will take the trouble to read over the memorable proceedings of the town of Boston, on the twenty-eighth day of October, 1772, when the Committee of Correspondence of twenty-one persons was appointed to state the rights of the colonists as men, as Christians, and as subjects, and to publish them to the world, with the infringements and violations of them,[‡]

---

* Frenchmen neither saw, heard, nor felt or understood this. J. A. 1813.

† Americans paid no attention or regard to this. And a blind, mad rivalry between the north and the south is destroying all morality and sound policy. God grant that division, civil war, murders, assassination, and massacres may not soon grow out of these rivalries of states, families, and individuals.

‡ This Boston pamphlet was drawn by the great James Otis. J. A. 1813.

you will find the great principles of civil and religious liberty for which you have contended so successfully, and which the world is contending for after your example. I could transcribe with pleasure the whole of this immortal pamphlet, which is a real picture of the sun of liberty rising on the human race; but shall select only a few words more directly to the present purpose.

"The first fundamental, positive law of all commonwealths or states is the establishment of the legislative power." Page 9.

"It is absolutely necessary in a mixed government like that of this province, that a *due proportion* or *balance* of power should be established among the several branches of the legislative. Our ancestors received from King William and Queen Mary a charter, by which it was understood by both parties in the contract, that such a proportion or balance was fixed; and, therefore, every thing which renders any one branch of the legislative more independent of the other two than it was originally designed, is an alteration of the constitution."

AMERICANS! in your Congress at Philadelphia, on Friday, the fourteenth day of October, 1774, you laid down the fundamental principles for which you were about to contend, and from which it is to be hoped you will never depart. For asserting and vindicating your rights and liberties, you declared, "That, by the immutable laws of nature, the principles of the English constitution and your several charters or compacts, you were entitled to life, liberty, and property; that your ancestors were entitled to all the rights, liberties, and immunities of free and natural born subjects in England; that you, their descendants, were entitled to the exercise and enjoyment of all such of them as your local and other circumstances enabled you to exercise and enjoy. That the foundation of English liberty and of all free governments, is a right in the people to participate in their legislative council. That you were entitled to the common law of England, and more especially to the great and inestimable privilege of being tried by your peers of the vicinage, according to the course of that law. *That it is indispensably necessary to good government, and rendered essential by the English constitution, that the constituent branches of the legislature be independent of each other.*"* These among others you then claimed, demanded, and insisted on, as your indubitable rights and liberties. These are the principles on which you first united and associated, and if you steadily and consistently maintain them, they will not only secure freedom and happiness to yourselves and your posterity, but your example will be imitated by all Europe, and in time, perhaps, by all mankind. The nations are in travail, and great events must have birth.

"The minds of men are in movement from the Boristhenes to the Atlantic. Agitated with new and strong emotions, they swell and heave beneath oppression, as the seas within the polar circle, at the approach of spring. The genius of philosophy, with the touch of Ithuriel's spear, is trying the establishments of the earth. The various forms of prejudice, superstition, and servility, start up in their true shapes, which had long imposed upon the world, under the revered semblances of honor, faith, and loyalty. Whatever is loose must be shaken; whatever is corrupted must be lopped away; whatever is not built on the broad basis of public utility must be thrown to the ground. Obscure murmurs gather and swell into a tempest; the spirit of inquiry, like a severe and searching wind, penetrates every part of the great body politic; and whatever is unsound, whatever is infirm, shrinks at the visitation. Liberty, led by philosophy, diffuses her blessings to every class of men; and even extends a smile of hope and promise to the poor African, the victim of hard, impenetrable avarice. Man, as man, becomes an object of respect. Tenets are transferred from theory to practice. The glowing sentiment, the lofty speculation, no longer serve 'but to adorn the pages of a book.' They are brought home to men's business and bosoms; and what, some centuries ago, it was daring but to think, and dangerous to express, is now realized and carried into effect. Systems

---

★ The declaration of independence of 4 July, 1776, contained nothing but the Boston declaration of 1772 and the congress declaration of 1774. Such are the caprices of fortune. This declaration of rights was drawn by the little John Adams. The mighty Jefferson, by the declaration of independence of 4 July, 1776, carried away the glory of the great and the little. J. A. 1813.

See for the congress declaration of 1774, vol. ii. pp. 375–377, and Appendix, C.

are analyzed into their first principles, and principles are fairly pursued to their legitimate consequences."★

This is all enchanting. But amidst our enthusiasm, there is great reason to pause and preserve our sobriety. It is true that the first empire of the world is breaking the fetters of human reason and exerting the energies of redeemed liberty. In the glowing ardor of her zeal, she condescends, Americans, to pay the most scrupulous attention to your maxims, principles, and example. There is reason to fear she has copied from you errors which have cost you very dear. Assist her, by your example, to rectify them before they involve her in calamities as much greater than yours, as her population is more unwieldy, and her situation more exposed to the baleful influence of rival neighbors. Amidst all their exultations, Americans and Frenchmen should remember that the perfectibility of man is only human and terrestrial perfectibility. Cold will still freeze, and fire will never cease to burn; disease and vice will continue to disorder, and death to terrify mankind. Emulation next to self-preservation will forever be the great spring of human actions, and the balance of a well-ordered government will alone be able to prevent that emulation from degenerating into dangerous ambition, irregular rivalries, destructive factions, wasting seditions, and bloody, civil wars.★

The great question will forever remain, *who shall work?* Our species cannot all be idle. Leisure for study must ever be the portion of a few. The number employed in government must forever be very small. Food, raiment, and habitations, the indispensable wants of all, are not to be obtained without the continual toil of ninety-nine in a hundred of mankind. As rest is rapture to the weary man, those who labor little will always be envied by those who labor much, though the latter in reality be probably the most enviable. With all the encouragements, public and private, which can

★ This was a summary of the language of the world in 1790, in newspapers, pamphlets, and conversation. In 1813 we can judge of it, as the author of these discourses judged of it then, to the destruction of all his popularity.

★ View France, Europe, and America, in 1813, and compare the state of them all with this paragraph written twenty-three years ago! J. A.

ever be given to general education, and it is scarcely possible they should be too many or too great, the laboring part of the people can never be learned. The controversy between the rich and the poor, the laborious and the idle, the learned and the ignorant, distinctions as old as the creation, and as extensive as the globe, distinctions which no art or policy, no degree of virtue or philosophy can ever wholly destroy, will continue, and rivalries will spring out of them. These parties will be represented in the legislature, and must be balanced, or one will oppress the other. There will never probably be found any other mode of establishing such an equilibrium, than by constituting the representation of each an independent branch of the legislature, and an independent executive authority, such as that in our government, to be a third branch and a mediator or an arbitrator between them. Property must be secured, or liberty cannot exist. But if unlimited or unbalanced power of disposing property, be put into the hands of those who have no property, France will find, as we have found, the lamb committed to the custody of the wolf. In such a case, all the pathetic exhortations and addresses of the national assembly to the people, to respect property, will be regarded no more than the warbles of the songsters of the forest. The great art of lawgiving consists in balancing the poor against the rich in the legislature, and in constituting the legislative a perfect balance against the executive power, at the same time that no individual or party can become its rival. The essence of a free government consists in an effectual control of rivalries. The executive and the legislative powers are natural rivals; and if each has not an effectual control over the other, the weaker will ever be the lamb in the paws of the wolf. The nation which will not adopt an equilibrium of power must adopt a despotism. There is no other alternative. Rivalries must be controlled, or they will throw all things into confusion; and there is nothing but despotism or a balance of power which can control them. Even in the simple monarchies, the nobility and the judicatures constitute a balance, though a very imperfect one, against the royalties.

Let us conclude with one reflection more which shall barely be hinted at, as delicacy, if not prudence, may require, in this place, some degree of reserve. Is there a possibility that the government of nations may fall into the hands of men who teach the most disconsolate of all creeds, that men are but fireflies, and that this *all* is without a father? Is this the way to make man, as man, an object of respect? Or is it to make murder itself as indifferent as shooting a plover, and the extermination of the Rohilla nation as innocent as the swallowing of mites on a morsel of cheese? If such a case should happen, would not one of these, the most credulous of all believers, have reason to pray to his eternal nature or his almighty chance (the more absurdity there is in this address the more in character) *give us again the gods of the Greeks; give us again the more intelligible as well as more comfortable systems of Athanasius and Calvin; nay, give us again our popes and hierarchies, Benedictines and Jesuits, with all their superstition and fanaticism, impostures and tyranny.* A certain duchess of venerable years and masculine understanding,★ said of some of the philosophers of the eighteenth century, admirably well,—"On ne croit pas dans le Christianisme, mais on croit toutes les sottises possibles."[5]

...

★ The Duchess d'Enville, the mother of the Duc de la Rochefoucauld. The author heard those words from that lady's own lips; with many other striking effusions of the strong and large mind of a great and excellent female character. J. A.

[5] ["They do not believe in Christianity, but they believe in every conceivable foolishness." Ed.]

II

Major Political Correspondence

Letters

to

John Taylor,

of

Caroline, Virginia

T he following letters were prompted by the publication of John
Taylor's An *Inquiry into the Principles and Policy of the Government of
the United States* (1814). In this work, Taylor provides extensive
commentary on Adams's *Defence* to which Adams felt compelled to
respond. These letters provided Adams the opportunity to amplify on
views expressed in *Defence*, as well as to deal at length with some of the
major distortions and misunderstandings of his positions.

Contrary to what one might expect from reading these letters, friendship and respect between Taylor and Adams developed over the years. In
a letter written in 1824, Taylor pays tribute to Adams:

"So early, I think, (for at this place I must speak merely from memory,)
as the year 1765, you braved the British lion, when his teeth and claws
were highly dangerous, in a series of essays [*Dissertation on the Canon and
Feudal Law*], containing principles which I have lately reperused with
delight; and, considering the early period at which they were written, with
admiration. And I believe that in the progress of the struggle for the liberty
of our country, your efforts in speaking and writing were a thousandfold
more efficacious than those of many individuals of great celebrity—of our
Henry, for instance. These designated you for a long series of the most
important negotiations, conducted with a diligence, integrity, and capacity, universally admired by your countrymen; and the hopes which your
early merits had inspired, being fulfilled, they placed you next to
Washington.

When your Presidency commenced, party spirit was highly inflamed,
and its capabilities may be conjectured by those who were not witnesses

of its effects then, by contemplating its effect now, in carrying men into unpremeditated excesses, even though it is invigorated by nothing but love of power. Yet during its bitterest prevalence, you soared above its prejudices, and saved your country from a ruinous war with France." [John Taylor to John Adams, April 8, 1824, *Works*, X, 412.] The following letters are taken from *Works*, VI, 447-521.

LETTERS

TO

JOHN TAYLOR

OF

CAROLINE.

I.

Quincy, 15 April, 1814.

SIR,—I have received your *Inquiry* in a large volume neatly bound. Though I have not read it in course, yet, upon an application to it of the *Sortes Virgilianæ*, scarce a page has been found in which my name is not mentioned, and some public sentiment or expression of mine examined. Revived as these subjects are, in this manner, in the recollection of the public, after an oblivion of so many years, by a gentleman of your high rank, ample fortune, learned education, and powerful connections, I flatter myself it will not be thought improper in me to solicit your attention to a few explanations and justifications of a book that has been misunderstood, misrepresented, and abused, more than any other, except the Bible, that I have ever read.

In the first words of the first section, you say, "Mr. Adams's political system deduces government from a *natural* fate; the policy of the United States deduces it from *moral* liberty."

This sentence, I must acknowledge, passes all my understanding. I know not what is meant by fate, nor what distinction there is, or may be made or conceived, between a natural and artificial, or unnatural fate. Nor do I well know what *"moral liberty"* signifies. I have read a great deal about the words *fate* and *chance;* but though I close my eyes to abstract my meditations, I never could conceive any idea of either. When an action or event happens or occurs without a cause, some say it happens by chance. This is equivalent to saying that chance is no cause at all; it is nothing. Fate, too, is no cause, no agent, no power; it has neither understanding, will, affections, liberty, nor choice; it has no existence; it is not even a figment of imagination; it is a mere invention of a word without a meaning; it is a nonentity; it is nothing. Mr. Adams most certainly never deduced any system from chance or fate, natural, artificial, or unnatural.

Liberty, according to my metaphysics, is an intellectual quality; an attribute that belongs not to fate nor chance. Neither possesses it, neither is capable of it. There is nothing moral or immoral in the idea of it. The definition of it is a self-determining power in an intellectual agent. It implies thought and choice and power; it can elect between objects, indifferent in point of morality, neither morally good nor morally evil. If the substance in which this quality, attribute, adjective, call it what you will, exists, has a moral sense, a conscience, a moral faculty; if it can distinguish between moral good and moral evil, and has power to choose the former and refuse the latter, it can, if it will, choose the evil and reject the good, as we see in experience it very often does.

"Mr. Adams's system," and "the policy of the United States," are drawn from the same sources, deduced from the same principles, wrought into the same frame; indeed, they are the same, and ought never to have been divided or separated; much less set in opposition to each other, as they have been.

That we may more clearly see how these hints apply, certain technical terms must be defined.

1. Despotism. A sovereignty unlimited, that is,—the *suprema lex,* the *summa potestatis* in one.[1] This has rarely, if ever, existed but in theory.

2. Monarchy. Sovereignty in one, variously limited.

3. Aristocracy. Sovereignty in a few.

---

[1] ["the highest law," "the highest power" Ed.]

4. Democracy. Sovereignty in the many, that is, in the whole nation, the whole body, assemblage, congregation, or if you are an Episcopalian, you may call it, if you please, *church,* of the whole people. This sovereignty must, in all cases, be exerted or exercised by the whole people assembled together. This form of government has seldom, if ever, existed but in theory; as rarely, at least, as an unlimited despotism in one individual.

5. The infinite variety of mixed governments are all so many different combinations, modifications, and intermixtures of the second, third, and fourth species or divisions.

Now, every one of these sovereigns possesses intellectual liberty to act for the public good or not. Being men, they have all what Dr. Rush calls a *moral faculty;* Dr. Hutcheson, a *moral sense;* and the Bible and the generality of the world, *a conscience.* They are all, therefore, under moral obligations to do to others as they would have others *do to them;* to consider themselves born, authorized, empowered for the good of society as well as their own good. Despots, monarchs, aristocrats, democrats, holding such high trusts, are under the most solemn and the most sacred moral obligations, to consider their trusts and their power to be instituted for the benefit and happiness of their nations, not their nations as servants to them or their friends or parties. In other words, to exert all their intellectual liberty to employ all their faculties, talents, and power for the public, general, universal good of their nations, not for their own separate good, or the interest of any party.

In this point of view, there is no difference in forms of government. All of them, and all men concerned in them,—all are under equal moral obligations. The intellectual liberty of aristocracies and democracies can be exerted only by votes, and ascertained only by ayes and noes. The sovereign judgment and will can be determined, known, and declared, only by majorities. This will, this decision, is sometimes determined by a single vote; often by two or three; very rarely by a large majority; scarcely ever by a unanimous suffrage. And from the impossibility of keeping together at all times the same number of voters, the majorities are apt to waver from day to day, and swing like a pendulum from side to side.

Nevertheless, the minorities have, in all cases, the same intellectual liberty, and are under the same moral obligations as the majorities.

In what manner these theoretical, intellectual liberties have been exercised, and these moral obligations fulfilled, by despots, monarchs, aristocrats, and democrats, is obvious enough in history and in experience. They have all in general conducted themselves alike.

But this investigation is not at present before us.

II.

IT is unnecessary to discuss the nice distinctions, which follow in the first page of your respectable volume, between mind, body, and morals. The essence and substance of mind and body, of soul and body, of spirit and matter, are wholly withheld as yet from our knowledge; from the penetration of our sharpest faculties; from the keenest of our incision knives, the most amplifying of our microscopes. With some of the attributes or qualities of each and of both we are well acquainted. We cannot pretend to improve the essence of either, till we know it. Mr. Adams has never thought "of limiting the improvements or amelioration" of the properties or qualities of either. The definition of matter is,—a dead, inactive, inert substance. That of spirit is,—a living, active substance, sometimes, if not always, intelligent. Morals are no qualities of matter; nor, as far as we know, of simple spirit or simple intelligence. Morals are attributes of spirits *only* when those spirits are *free* as well as intelligent agents, and have consciences or a moral sense, a faculty of discrimination not only between right and wrong, but between good and evil, happiness and misery, pleasure and pain. This freedom of choice and action, united with conscience, necessarily implies a responsibility to a lawgiver and to a law, and has a necessary relation to right and wrong, to happiness and misery.

It is unnecessary for Mr. Adams to allow or disallow the distinctions in this first page to be applicable to his theory. But if he speaks of natural political systems, he certainly comprehends not only all the intellectual and physical powers and qualities of man, but all his moral powers and faculties, all his duties and obligations as a man and a citizen of this world, as well as of the state in which he lives, and every interest, thing, or concern that belongs to him, from his cradle to his grave. This comprehension of all the perfections and imperfections, all the powers and wants of man, is certainly not for the purpose of *"circumscribing the powers of mind."* But it is to enlarge them, to give them free scope to run, expand, and be glorified.

If you should speak of a natural system of geography, would you not comprehend the whole globe, and even its relations to the sun, moon, and stars? of astronomy, all that the telescope has discovered? of chemistry or natural history, all that the microscope has found? of architecture, every thing that can make a building commodious, useful, elegant, graceful, and ornamental?

In the second page, Mr. Adams is totally misunderstood or misrepresented. He has never said, written, or thought, *"that the human mind is able to circumscribe its own powers."* Nor has he ever asserted or believed that, *"man can ascertain his own moral capacity."* Nor has he ever *"deduced any consequences from such postulata, or erected any scheme of government"* upon them or either of them.

If mankind have not "agreed upon any form of government," does it follow that there is no natural form of government? and that all forms are equally natural? It might as well be contended that all are equally good, and that the constitution of the Ottoman Empire is as natural, as free, and as good, as that of the United States. If men have not agreed in any system of architecture, will you infer that there are no natural principles of that noble art? If some prefer the Gothic, and others the Grecian models, will you say that both are equally natural, convenient, and elegant? If some prefer the Doric, and others the Corinthian pillars, are the five orders equally beautiful? If "human nature has been perpetually escaping from all forms," will it be inferred that all forms are equally natural? equal for the preservation of liberty?

There is no necessity of "confronting Mr. Adams's opinion, that aristocracy is natural, and therefore unavoidable, with the other, that it is artificial or factitious, and therefore avoidable," because the opinions are both true and perfectly consistent with each other.

By *natural aristocracy,* in general, may be understood those superiorities of influence in society which grow out of the constitution of human

nature. By *artificial aristocracy,* those inequalities of weight and superiorities of influence which are created and established by civil laws. Terms
must be defined before we can reason. By aristocracy, I understand all
those men who can command, influence, or procure more than an average of votes; by an aristocrat, every man who can and will influence one
man to vote besides himself. Few men will deny that there is a natural aristocracy of virtues and talents in every nation and in every party, in every
city and village. Inequalities are a part of the natural history of man.

III.

I believe that none but Helvetius will affirm, that all children are born
with equal genius.

None will pretend, that all are born of dispositions exactly alike,—of
equal weight; equal strength; equal length; equal delicacy of nerves; equal
elasticity of muscles; equal complexions; equal figure, grace, or beauty.

I have seen, in the Hospital of Foundlings, the *"Enfans Trouvés,"* at Paris,
fifty babes in one room;—all under four days old; all in cradles alike; all
nursed and attended alike; all dressed alike; all equally neat. I went from
one end to the other of the whole row, and attentively observed all their
countenances. And I never saw a greater variety, or more striking inequalities, in the streets of Paris or London. Some had every sign of grief, sorrow, and despair; others had joy and gayety in their faces. Some were
sinking in the arms of death; others looked as if they might live to
fourscore. Some were as ugly and others as beautiful, as children or adults
ever are; these were stupid; those sensible. These were all born to equal
rights, but to very different fortunes; to very different success and influence
in life.

The world would not contain the books, if one should produce all the
examples that reading and experience would furnish. One or two permit
me to hint.

Will any man say, would Helvetius say, that all men are born equal in
strength? Was Hercules no stronger than his neighbors? How many
nations, for how many ages, have been governed by his strength, and by

the reputation and renown of it by his posterity? If you have lately read Hume, Robertson or the Scottish Chiefs, let me ask you, if Sir William Wallace was no more than equal in strength to the average of Scotchmen? and whether Wallace could have done what he did without that extraordinary strength?

Will Helvetius or Roussean say that all men and women are born equal in beauty? Will any philosopher say, that beauty has no influence in human society? If he does, let him read the histories of Eve, Judith, Helen, the fair Gabrielle, Diana of Poitiers, Pompadour, Du Barry, Susanna, Abigail, Lady Hamilton, Mrs. Clark, and a million others. Are not despots, monarchs, aristocrats, and democrats, equally liable to be seduced by beauty to confer favors and influence suffrages?

Socrates calls beauty a short-lived tyranny; Plato, *the privilege of nature;* Theophrastus, a mute eloquence; Diogenes, the best letter of recommendation; Carneades, a queen without soldiers; Theocritus, a serpent covered with flowers; Bion, a good that does not belong to the possessor, because it is impossible to give ourselves beauty, or to preserve it. Madame du Barry expressed the philosophy of Carneades in more laconic language, when she said, *"La véritable royauté, c'est la beauté,"*—the genuine royalty is beauty. And she might have said with equal truth, that it is genuine aristocracy; for it has as much influence in one form of government as in any other; and produces aristocracy in the deepest democracy that ever was known or imagined, as infallibly as in any other form of government. What shall we say to all these philosophers, male and female? Is not beauty a privilege granted by nature, according to Plato and to truth, often more influential in society, and even upon laws and government, than stars, garters, crosses, eagles, golden fleeces, or any hereditary titles or other distinctions? The grave elders were not proof against the charms of Susanna. The Grecian sages wondered not at the Trojan war when they saw Helen. Holofernes's guards, when they saw Judith, said, "one such woman let go would deceive the whole earth."

Can you believe, Mr. Taylor, that the brother of such a sister, the father of such a daughter, the husband of such a wife, or even the gallant of such a mistress, would have but one vote in your moral republic?

Ingenious,—but not historical, philosophical, or political,—learned, classical, poetical Barlow! I mourn over thy life and thy death. Had truth, instead of popularity and party, been thy object, your pamphlet on privileged orders would have been a very different thing!

That all men are born to equal rights is true. Every being has a right to his own, as clear, as moral, as sacred, as any other being has. This is as indubitable as a moral government in the universe. But to teach that all men are born with equal powers and faculties, to equal influence in society, to equal property and advantages through life, is as gross a fraud, as glaring an imposition on the credulity of the people, as ever was practised by monks, by Druids, by Brahmins, by priests of the immortal Lama, or by the self-styled philosophers of the French revolution. For honor's sake, Mr. Taylor, for truth and virtue's sake, let American philosophers and politicians despise it.

Mr. Adams leaves to Homer and Virgil, to Tacitus and Quintilian, to Mahomet and Calvin, to Edwards and Priestley, or, if you will, to Milton's angels reasoning high in pandemonium, all their acute speculations about fate, destiny, foreknowledge absolute, necessity, and predestination. He thinks it problematical, whether there is, or ever will be, more than one Being capable of understanding this vast subject. In his principles of legislation, he has nothing to do with these interminable controversies. He considers men as free, moral, and accountable agents; and he takes men as God has made them. And will Mr. Taylor deny, that God has made some men deaf and some blind, or will he affirm that these will infallibly have as much influence in society, and be able to procure as many votes as any who can see and hear?

Honor the day,[2] and believe me no enemy.

IV.

THAT aristocracies, both ancient and modern, have been "variable and artificial," as well as natural and unchangeable, Mr. Adams knows as well

---

[2] 19 April. The anniversary of the action at Lexington.

as Mr. Taylor, and has never denied or doubted. That "they have all proceeded from moral causes," is not so clear, since many of them appear to proceed from physical causes, many from immoral causes, many from pharisaical, jesuitical, and Machiavelian villany; many from sacerdotal and despotic fraud, and as many as all the rest, from democratical dupery, credulity, adulation, corruption, adoration, superstition, and enthusiasm. If all these cannot be regulated by political laws, and controlled, checked, or balanced by constitutional energies, I am willing Mr. Taylor should say of them what Bishop Burnet said of the hierarchy, or the severest things he can express or imagine.

That nature makes king-bees or queen-bees, I have heard and read. But I never read in any philosopher or political writer, as I remember, that nature makes state-kings and lords of state. Though even this, for aught I know, might be sometimes pretended. I have read of hereditary rights from Adam to Noah; and the divine right of nobility derived from the Dukes of Edom; but those divine rights did not make kings, till holy oil was poured upon their heads from the vial brought down from heaven in her beak, by the Holy Ghost in the person of a dove. If we consult books, Mr. Taylor, we shall find that nonsense, absurdity, and impiety are infinite. Whether "the policy of the United States" has been wisdom or folly, is not the question at present. But it is confidently asserted, without fear of contradiction, that every page and every line Mr. Adams has ever written, was intended to illustrate, to prove, to exhibit, and to demonstrate its wisdom.

The association of "Mr. Adams with Filmer" in the third page, may excite a smile! I give you full credit, Mr. Taylor, for the wit and shrewdness of this remark. It is droll and good-humored. But if ever policy was in diametrical opposition to Filmer, it is that of the United States. If ever writings were opposed to his principles, Mr. Adams's are so opposed. They are as much so as those of Sidney or Locke.

Mr. Adams thanks Mr. Taylor for proposing in the third page to analyze and ascertain the ideas intended to be expressed by the word "aristocracy." This is one of those words which have been abused. It has been employed to signify any thing, every thing, and nothing. Mr. Taylor has read Mr. Locke's chapter "on the abuse of words," which, though it contains nothing but what daily experience exhibits to all mankind, ought, nevertheless, if he had never written any thing else, to secure him immortal gratitude and renown. Without the learning of Luzac, Vanderkemp, Jefferson, or Parsons, Mr. Adams recollects enough of Greek, to remember that "aristocracy" originally signified "the government of the best men."

But who are to be judges of the best men? Who is to make the selection of the best men from the second best? and the third? and the fourth? and so on *ad infinitum?* For good and bad are infinitely divisible, like matter. Ay! there's the rub! Despots, monarchs, aristocrats, and democrats have, in all ages hit, at times, upon the best men, in the best sense of the word. But, at other times, and much more frequently, they have all chosen the very worst men; the men who have the most devotedly and the most slavishly flattered their vanity, gratified their most extravagant passions, and promoted their selfish and private views. Without searching volumes, Mr. Taylor, I will tell you in a few words what I mean by an aristocrat, and, consequently, what I mean by aristocracy. By an aristocrat, I mean every man who can command or influence TWO VOTES; ONE BESIDES HIS OWN.

Take the first hundred men you meet in the streets of a city, or on a turnpike road in the country, and constitute them a democratical republic. In my next, you may have some conjectures of what will appear in your new democracy.

V.

WHEN your new democratical republic meets, you will find half a dozen men of independent fortunes; half a dozen, of more eloquence; half a dozen, with more learning; half a dozen, with eloquence, learning, and fortune.

Let me see. We have now four-and-twenty; to these we may add six more, who will have more art, cunning, and intrigue, than learning, eloquence, or fortune. These will infallibly soon unite with the twenty-four. Thus we make thirty. The remaining seventy are composed of farmers, shopkeepers, merchants, tradesmen, and laborers. Now, if each of these thirty can, by any means, influence one vote besides his own, the whole thirty can carry sixty votes,—a decided and uncontrolled majority of the hundred. These thirty I mean by aristocrats; and they will instantly convert your democracy of ONE HUNDRED into an aristocracy of THIRTY.

Take at random, or select with your utmost prudence, one hundred of your most faithful and capable domestics from your own numerous plantations, and make them a democratical republic. You will immediately perceive the same inequalities, and the same democratical republic, in a very few of the first sessions, transformed into an aristocratical republic; as complete and perfect an aristocracy as the senate of Rome, and much more so. Some will be beloved and followed, others hated and avoided by their fellows.

It would be easy to quote Greek and Latin, to produce a hundred authorities to show the original signification of the word *aristocracy* and its infinite variations and application in the history of ages. But this would be all waste water. Once for all, I give you notice, that whenever I use the word *aristocrat,* I mean a citizen who can command or govern two votes or more in society, whether by his virtues, his talents, his learning, his loquacity, his taciturnity, his frankness, his reserve, his face, figure, eloquence, grace, air, attitude, movements, wealth, birth, art, address, intrigue, good fellowship, drunkenness, debauchery, fraud, perjury, violence, treachery, pyrrhonism, deism, or atheism; for by every one of these instruments have votes been obtained and will be obtained. You seem to think aristocracy consists altogether in artificial titles, tinsel decorations of stars, garters, ribbons, golden eagles and golden fleeces, crosses and roses and lilies, exclusive privileges, hereditary descents, established by kings or by positive laws of society. No such thing! Aristocracy was, from the beginning, now is, and ever will be, world without end, independent of all these artificial regulations, as really and as efficaciously as with them!

Let me say a word more. Your democratical republic picked in the streets, and your democratical African republic, or your domestic republic, call it which you will, in its first session, will become an aristocratical republic. In the second session it will become an oligarchical republic;

because the seventy-four democrats and the twenty-six aristocrats will, by this time, discover that thirteen of the aristocrats can command four votes each; these thirteen will now command the majority, and, consequently, will be sovereign. The thirteen will then be an oligarchy. In the third session, it will be found that among these thirteen oligarchs there are seven, each of whom can command eight votes, equal in all to fifty-six, a decided majority. In the fourth session, it will be found that there are among these seven oligarchs four who can command thirteen votes apiece. The republic then becomes an oligarchy, whose sovereignty is in four individuals. In the fifth session, it will be discovered that two of the four can command six-and-twenty votes each. Then two will have the command of the sovereign oligarchy. In the sixth session, there will be a sharp contention between the two which shall have the command of the fifty-two votes. Here will commence the squabble of Danton and Robespierre, of Julius and Pompey, of Anthony and Augustus, of the white rose and the red rose, of Jefferson and Adams, of Burr and Jefferson, of Clinton and Madison, or, if you will, of Napoleon and Alexander.

This, my dear sir, is the history of mankind, past, present, and to come.

VI.

IN the third page of your "Inquiry," is an assertion which Mr. Adams has a right to regret, as a gross and egregious misrepresentation. He cannot believe it to have been intentional. He imputes it to haste; to ardor of temper; to defect of memory; to any thing rather than design. It is in these words,—"Mr. Adams asserts, 'that every society naturally produces an order of men, which it is impossible to confine to an equality of RIGHTS.'" This pretended quotation, marked as it is by inverted commas, is totally and absolutely unfounded. No such expression ever fell from his lips; no such language was ever written by his pen; no such principle was ever approved or credited by his understanding, no such sentiment was ever felt without abhorrence in his heart. On the contrary, he has through life asserted the moral equality of all mankind. His system of government, which is the system of Massachusetts, as well as the system of the United

States, which are the same as much as an original and a copy are the same, was calculated and framed for the express purpose of securing to all men equal laws and equal rights. Physical inequalities are proclaimed aloud by God Almighty through all his works. Mr. Adams must have been destitute of senses, not to have perceived them in men from their births to their deaths; and, at the same time, not to have perceived that they were incurable and inevitable, by human wisdom, goodness, or power. All that men can do, is to modify, organize, and arrange the powers of human society, that is to say, the physical strength and force of men, in the best manner to protect, secure, and cherish the moral, which are all the natural rights of mankind.

The French are very fond of the phrase "social order." The English commonly hear it, or read it with a broad grin. I am not Englishman enough to join in this ridicule. A "social order" there must be, unless we would return to the forests, and assert individual independence in a more absolute sense than Tartars or Arabs, African negroes, or North American Indians, or Samoyedes, or Hottentots have ever conceived.

A beggar said at my father's house, full seventy years ago, "The world is very unequally divided. But I do not wonder at it, nor think much of it. Because I know, that if it were equally divided to-day, in one month there would be as great odds as ever." The beggar's proverb contained as certain and as important truths as any that was ever uttered by the wise men of Greece.

Will Mr. Taylor profess himself a downright leveller? Will he vote for a community of property? or an equal division of property? and a community of wives and women? He must introduce and establish both, before he can reduce all men to an equality of influence. It is, indeed, questionable, whether such laws would not produce greater inequalities than ever were seen in the world. These are not new projects, Mr. Taylor. They are not original inventions, or discoveries of philosophers of the eighteenth century. They were as familiar to Plato as they were to Helvetius or Condorcet. If I were a young man, I should like to write a romance, and send a hero upon his travels through such a levelling community of wives and wealth. It would be very edifying to record his observations on the

opinions, principles, customs, institutions, and manners of this democratical republic and such a virtuous and happy age. But a gentleman whose
mind is so active, studious, and contemplative as Mr. Taylor's, must easily
foresee, that some men must take care of the property of others, or it
must perish with its owners; and that some men would have as many
wives as Solomon, and others none at all.

See, what is no uncommon sight, a family of six sons. Four of them
are prudent, discreet, frugal, and industrious men; the other two are idle
and profligate. The father leaves equal portions of his estate to all the six.
How long will it be before the two will request the four to purchase
their shares? and how long before the purchase money will be spent in
sports, gambled away at races, or cards, or dice, or billiards, or dissipated at
taverns or worse houses? When the two are thus reduced to beggars, will
they have as much influence in society as any one of the four?

VII.

Suppose another case, which is not without examples,—a family of six
daughters. Four of them are not only beautiful, but serious and discreet
women. Two of them are not only ugly, but ill tempered and immodest.
Will either of the two have an equal chance with any one of the four to
attract the attention of a suitor, and obtain a husband of worth, respectability, and consideration in the world?

Such, and many other natural and acquired and habitual inequalities are
visible, and palpable, and audible, every day, in every village, and in every
family, in the whole world. The imagination, therefore, of a government,
of a democratical republic, in which every man and every woman shall
have an equal weight in society, is a chimera. They have all equal rights; but
cannot, and ought not to have equal power.

Unhappily, the cases before stated are too often reversed, and four or
five out of six sons, are unwise, and only one or two praiseworthy; and four
or five out of six daughters, are mere triflers, and only one or two whose
"price is above rubies." And may I not ask, whether there are no instances,
in which the whole of six sons and daughters are found wanting; and

instead of maintaining their single vote, and their independence, become all dependent on others? Nay, there are examples of whole families wasted and totally lost by vice and folly. Can these, while any of them existed, have maintained an equality of consideration in Society, with other families of equal numbers, but of virtuous and considerate characters?

Matrimony, then, Mr. Taylor, I have a right to consider as another source of natural aristocracy.

Will you give me leave to ask you, Mr. Taylor, why you employ the phrase, "political power" in this third page, instead of sovereign power,— the *summa potestatis,* the supreme power, the legislative power, the power from which there is no appeal, but to Heaven, and the *ratio ultima regum et rerum-publicarum?*[3] This language would be understood by readers, by scientific people, and by the vulgar. But "political power" is so indefinite, that it belongs to every man who has a vote, and every woman who has a charm. What, Mr. Taylor, is the resemblance of a president or a governor to a monarch? It is the resemblance of Mount Vernon to the Andes; of the Tiber at Washington to the Ganges or Mississippi. A president has the executive power only, and that under severe restrictions, jealous restrictions; and as I am too old to court popularity, I will venture to say, in my opinion, very pernicious restrictions; restrictions that will destroy this constitution before its time. A president has no legislative power; a monarch has it all.

What resemblance has an American senate to a hereditary order? It has a negative upon the laws. In this, it resembles the house of lords in England; but in nothing else. It has no resemblance to any hereditary order. It has no resemblance even to the hereditary descent of lands, tenements, and hereditaments. There is nothing hereditary in it.

And here, Mr. Taylor, permit me to ask you, whether the descent of lands and goods and chattels does not constitute a hereditary order as decidedly as the descent of stars and garters? I will be still bolder. Has not this law of descents constituted the Honorable John Randolph one of a hereditary order, for a time, as clearly as any Montmorenci or Howard, any

[3] ["the ultimate justification of kings and republics" Ed.]

Julius, any of the Heraclides, or any of the blood of Mahomet, or any of his connections by marriage?

You must allow me twenty years to answer a book that cost you twenty years of meditation to compose.

You must allow me also to ask you a question still nearer home. You had the honor and felicity to marry the only child of my honest and sincere friend, the Honorable John Penn, of North Carolina. From this marriage, you derived, with an amiable consort, a handsome fortune.

If you complain that this is personal, I confess it, and intend it should be personal, that it might be more striking to you, and to all others who may ever see or hear of our controversy. In return, I give you full leave to ask me any questions relative to myself, my ancestors, my posterity, my natural or political friends. I will answer every question you can ask with the same frankness, candor, and sincerity.

I will be bolder still, Mr. Taylor. Would Washington have ever been commander of the revolutionary army or president of the United States, if he had not married the rich widow of Mr. Custis? Would Jefferson ever have been president of the United States if he had not married the daughter of Mr. Wales?

I am weary and so are you. Ceremonies avaunt.

VIII.

WHAT shall I say of the "resemblance of our house of representatives to a legislating nation?" It is perhaps a miniature which resembles the original as much as a larger picture would or could. But, sir, let me say, once for all, that as no picture, great or small, no statue, no bust in brass or marble, gold or silver, ever yet perfectly resembled the original, so no representative government ever perfectly represented or resembled the original nation or people.

Is not representation an essential and fundamental departure from democracy? Is not every representative government in the universe an aristocracy? Call it despotism; call it oligarchy; call it aristocracy; call it democracy; call it a mixture ever so complicated; still is it not an

aristocracy, in the strictest sense of the word, according to any rational definition of it that can be given? that is, a government OF A FEW, who have
the command of two votes, or more than two, over THE MANY, who
have only one?

Representation and democracy are a contradiction in terms. Pursue
your principles, then, sir; demolish all aristocratical and representative government; divide our continent from St. Croix to Mississippi, into districts
not of geographical miles, yards, or feet, but of voters of one hundred
men in each. I will not stay to make a mathematical calculation; but put a
certain for an uncertain number. Suppose the number of free, sovereign,
independent democracies to be eighty thousand. In these assemblies, all
questions of war and peace, commerce, &c. &c. &c. are to be discussed
and decided. And when and how, and what would be the national result?

I dare not comment upon your book, sir, without quoting your words.
You say, in this third page,—

"Upon this threefold resemblance Mr. Adams has seized, to bring the
political system of America within the *pale* of the English system of checks
and balances, by following the ANALYSIS OF ANTIQUITY; and, in obedience to THAT AUTHORITY, by modifying our temporary, elective, responsible governors, into monarchs; our senates into aristocratical orders; and
our representatives into a *nation* personally exercising the functions of
government."

I fear I shall fatigue you with my observations. But it is of no great
importance, since this correspondence is intended for your amusement
and mine. You are not obliged to read my letters any longer than they
amuse you; and I am confident that if my letters were printed, there would
not be found six people in the world who would read them with attention. We will then amuse ourselves a little with a few of my remarks.

1. Mr. Adams has seized "upon a threefold resemblance," to "bring the
political system of America within the pale of the English system." Figurative language is as dangerous in legislation and jurisprudence as in mathematics. This word PALE is a figure, a metaphor, an emblem, a hieroglyphic.
What is a pale? A slice of wood sunk in the ground at one end, to inclose
a plat. Here is another figure. A pale, or "the pale," is used to express many

pales; enough in number and measure to inclose a very spacious plat,—
"the English system of checks and balances." Now, sir, have I brought the
system of America within the pale of the English system? What, indeed,
had I to do with "the system of America?" America, when my three volumes were printed, had no system but the old confederation. My volumes had nothing in view but the state governments; and, in strict truth,
nothing in view, but the state constitution of Massachusetts,—a child, of
which I was, right or wrong, the putative father. How, then, is the system
of America brought within the English system? In the English system, the
executive power is universal, unlimited in all affairs, foreign and domestic,
and hereditary to all generations. In the system of America, the executive
power is limited, shackled in most matters, foreign and domestic, and so far
from being hereditary, it is limited to four years. The cereus, once in its
life, blooms at midnight, and for one, two, three, or four hours, glows,
with transcendent splendor, then fades and dies. A poet might bring this
flower within THE PALE of the sun, which shines with equal glory through
all ages, seen or unseen by the little animals whose sight is often obscured
by clouds, fogs, and vapors, or within the pale of American policy.

2. "BY FOLLOWING THE ANALYSIS OF ANTIQUITY." What is this analysis of antiquity? The one, the few, and the many. And why is this called
the "analysis of antiquity," rather than the analysis of modernity? Is there
a nation, at this hour of this sixteenth day of June, 1814, on this globe, in
which this analysis is not as obvious and undeniable as it ever was in any
age or any nation of antiquity? Is there a state in this union, is there a district, a parish, a party, a faction, a sedition, a rebellion, in the world, in
which this analysis is not glaring? Should you detect a conspiracy among
your domestics, which I hope you will, if it should exist, while I devoutly
pray it may never exist, you would find this analysis in its perfection. A *one,*
a *few,* and a *many.*

Why, then, sir, do you throw all the odium of this eternal, unchangeable
truth upon poor "antiquity?" An ancient might say to a modern, as Nathan
said unto David, Thou art the man.

3. "And in obedience to that authority!" What authority? "The authority of antiquity!" And why not the authority of St. Domingo? of the

Spanish colonies in America? of the British colonies in America before and since the revolution? of the French revolution and counter-revolutions, from Marat and Robespierre, nay, from Rochefoucauld, Condorcet, and Turgot, to Bonaparte, Talleyrand, and Sieyes, in the last scene of the last act of the tragedy? And why not the authority of every tribe of Indians in America? every nation or tribe of negroes in Africa? Why not in every horde of Arabs, Tartars, Hottentots, Icelanders, Samoyedes, or Kamtschatkans? These are all among my authorities, as well as all antiquity over the whole globe, where men have existed. These authorities are modern enough, and ancient enough, to prove the analysis of the one, the three, and the many, to be universal, and proceeding from natural causes. Which of these authorities, sir, will you deny, contradict, or explain away?

IX.

OBSERVATION fourth. "By modifying our temporary, elective, responsible governors into monarchs." How have I modified our governors into monarchs? My three volumes were written in defence of the constitution of Massachusetts, against a rude and insolent attack of M. Turgot. This constitution, which existed in my handwriting, made the governor ANNUALLY elective, gave him the executive power, shackled with a council, that I now wish was annihilated, and made him as responsible as any executive power in the United States, or any one of the separate states is to this day. How then are my annual governors modified into hereditary monarchs? my annual elective governors, limited and shackled, even in the exercise of the executive authority, and responsible for all things, modified into hereditary monarchs, possessed of unlimited legislative and executive power, or even only of unlimited executive power, and responsible for nothing?

Observation fifth. By modifying "our senates into aristocratical orders." What is meant by "our senates?" My books had not in contemplation any senate of the United States; for no such senate existed, or was expected by me. M. Turgot's attack was, in reality, on the senate of Massachusetts. That senate was annually elective; had no executive power, positive or negative; was merely an independent branch of the legislative power. How, then, did Mr. Adams modify "our senates into aristocratical orders?" What is the meaning, the definition, the analysis of "aristocratical orders?" My anomalistical friend, and friend of mankind, Horne Tooke, has said, "mankind are not sufficiently aware that words without meaning, or of equivocal meaning, are the everlasting engines of fraud and injustice." This wise saying of my learned friend, is no more than every attentive, thinking, and reflecting mind sees, feels, and laments every day. Yet "mankind are not sufficiently aware." You will charge me here with an aristocratical distinction; with erecting an aristocratical order of thinking men, in contradiction to the democratical order of unthinking men. Well! is there not such a distinction in nature? Are not some children thoughtful and others thoughtless from their earliest years? Among the thoughtful, indeed, there is a distinction. Some think for good and others for evil; and this distinction is manifest through life, and shows itself in all the prosperities and all the adversities of human life. Recollect the history of our own dear country for the last fifty years, and the principal, prominent characters in our political drama, and then tell me whether there has not been a very glaring distinction between thoughtful and thoughtless characters, both good and evil! Our governors resemble monarchs in nothing, but in holding, for short periods, the executive power of the laws, under shackles and trammels, that destroy the efficacy of the constitution. Our senates resemble "aristocratical orders" in nothing, but holding for short periods a negative upon the laws, with the addition of a participation in the executive power, in some instances, which mixes the legislative and executive power together, in such a manner as to destroy the efficacy of the constitution. Our national representatives have no more nor less power, that I recollect, than they ought to have.

X.

"WHETHER the terms 'monarchy, aristocracy, and democracy,' or the one, the few, and the many, are only numerical; or characteristic, like the calyx, petal, and stamina of plants; or complicated, with the idea of a balance;

they have never yet, singly or collectively, been used to describe a government deduced from good moral principles."

Linnæus is upon my shelf, very near me, but I will not take him down to consult him about calyx, petal, and stamina, because we are not now upon gardening, agriculture, or natural history. Politics and legislation are our present subjects.

I have no clear idea of your distinction between "numerical and characteristic." You say, if I understand you, that no simple or mixed or balanced form of government has ever yet singly or collectively been used to describe a government deduced from good moral principles.

What government, then, ever was deduced from good moral principles? Certainly none. For simple, or mixed, or complicated with a balance, surely comprehend every species of government that ever had a being, or that ever will exist. Because imagination cannot conceive of any government besides those of the one, the few, or the many, or such as are compounded of them, whether complicated with the idea of a balance or not. The whole is equal to all its parts, and all the parts are equal to the whole. In a right-angled triangle, the hypothenuse and the two legs comprehend the whole diagram.

Again, how are the United States distinguished from all other governments, or from any other government? What are the GOOD MORAL PRINCIPLES from which the governments of the United States are deduced, which are not common to many other governments? In all that great number and variety of constitutions which the last twenty-five years have produced in France, in Holland, in Geneva, in Spain, we find the most excellent moral principles, precepts, and maxims, and all of them *complicated with the idea of a balance.* We make ourselves popular, Mr. Taylor, by telling our fellow-citizens that we have made discoveries, conceived inventions, and made improvements. We may boast that *we* are the chosen people; we may even thank God that we are not like other men; but, after all, it will be but flattery, and the delusion, the self-deceit of the Pharisee.

Is not the constitution of the United States "complicated with the idea of a balance?" Is there a constitution upon record more complicated with balances than ours? In the first place, eighteen states and some territories are balanced against the national government, whether judiciously or injudiciously, I will not presume at present to conjecture. We have seen some effects of it in some of the middle and some of the southern and western states, under the two first administrations; and we now behold some similar effects of it under the two last. Some genius more prompt and fertile than mine, may infer from a little what a great deal means. In the second place, the house of representatives is balanced against the senate, and the senate against the house. In the third place, the executive authority is, in some degree, balanced against the legislative. In the fourth place, the judiciary power is balanced against the house, the senate, the executive power, and the state governments. In the fifth place, the senate is balanced against the president in all appointments to office, and in all treaties. This, in my opinion, is not merely a useless, but a very pernicious balance. In the sixth place, the people hold in their own hands the balance against their own representatives, by biennial, which I wish had been annual elections. In the seventh place, the legislatures of the several states are balanced against the senate by sextennial elections. In the eighth place, the electors are balanced against the people in the choice of the president. And here is a complication and refinement of balances, which, for any thing I recollect, is an invention of our own, and peculiar to us.

The state legislatures can direct the choice of electors by the people at large, or by the people in what districts they please, or by themselves, without consulting the people at all. However, all this complication of machinery, all these wheels within wheels, these *imperia* within *imperiis* have not been sufficient to satisfy the people. They have invented a balance to all balances in their caucuses. We have congressional caucuses, state caucuses, county caucuses, city caucuses, district caucuses, town caucuses, parish caucuses, and Sunday caucuses at church doors; and in these aristocratical caucuses *elections are decided*.

Do you not tremble, Mr. Taylor, with fear, that another balance to all these balances, an over balance of all "moral liberty," and to every moral principle and feeling, may soon be invented and introduced; I mean the balance of corruption? Corruption! Be not surprised, sir. If the spirit of party is corruption, have we not seen much of it already? If the spirit of faction is corruption, have we seen none of that evil spirit? If the spirit of banking is corruption, as you have uniformly proclaimed it to be, ever since I had the honor of your acquaintance, and as your "Arator" and your "Inquiry" everywhere sufficiently demonstrate, have you ever heard or read of any country in which this spirit prevailed to a greater degree than in this? Are you informed of any aristocratical institution by which the property of the many is more manifestly sacrificed to the profit of the few?

Are all these impure spirits "deduced from moral liberty," or are any of them reconcilable to moral principle?

XI.

IN your fourth page, you "are unable to discover in our form of government any resemblance of monarchy, aristocracy, or democracy, as defined by ancient writers, and by Mr. Adams himself."

As these words are technical terms, whose meaning is as well defined, both by ancients and moderns, as the words *point, line, surface,* or *solid,* in geometry, I shall not turn over volumes to quote authorities in a question of so easy a solution. To avoid misrepresentation, however, I shall explicitly premise that all intelligence, all power, all force, all authority, originally, inherently, necessarily, inseparably, and inalienably resides in the people.

In the language of civilians, the *summa potestatis,* the supreme, sovereign, absolute, and uncontrollable power, is placed by God and nature in the people, and they never can divest themselves of it. All this was truth, before the people themselves, by their own sagacity, or their moral sentiments, or, if you had rather say, by their own simplicity, credulity, and imbecility, began to distinguish the one and the few from their own average and level. For you may depend upon it, the people themselves, by their own observation and experience and feelings, their own sensations and reflections, made these distinctions before kingcraft, priestcraft, or noblecraft had any thing to do with them.

An inevitable consequence of this great truth is another, namely,—that all government, except the simplest and most perfect democracy, is REPRESENTATIVE GOVERNMENT. The simplest despotism, monarchy, or aristocracy, and all the most complicated mixtures of them that ever existed or can be imagined, are mere representatives of the people, and can exist no longer than the people will to support them.

À bas le tyran, à bas le gouvernement, bon ou mauvais,—good, bad, or indifferent, whenever the people decree and proclaim its downfall, it falls.

Is this explicit concession democratical enough? I beg your pardon. I had forgotten for a moment that you do not allow "democracy to be deduced from moral liberty." Let me vary my question then. Do you admit those two great truths to be consistent with "moral liberty" and "the constitution of the United States?"

But to return, and approach the question, if peradventure we can find it. Scientific definitions are commonly in the abstract merely ideal and intellectual and theoretical. For example,—"point has no parts;" "a line is longitude without latitude;" "a superficies is length and breadth without thickness;" yet, in practice, we can neither see nor feel these points, lines, or surfaces. Thus monarchy is defined to be "a sovereignty in one," that is to say, all the rights, powers, and authorities of a whole nation, committed in trust to a single man, without limitation or restriction. Aristocracy, the same ample and unlimited power, vested in a small number of men. Democracy reserves all these rights, prerogatives, and privileges to the whole nation, and every act of its volition must be determined by a vote.

Now it is manifest, that no such simple government as either of these, ever existed in any nation; no, nor in any city, town, village, nor scarcely in any private social club. To say, then, that a mixed, balanced government can be formed of monarchy, aristocracy, and democracy, in this sense of the words, would be as absurd, as for a Hindoo to say, that the best government would be that of three omniscient and almighty Brahmins, mixed or commixed together and reciprocally balancing each other. Thus far, for what I know, we may be pretty well agreed. But when you say, that, "in our form of government," no resemblance can be discovered of monarchy, aristocracy, or democracy, I beg leave to differ from you.

The Prince of Orange, William V., in a conversation with which he honored me in 1788, was pleased to say, that "he had read our new constitution," and he added, "Monsieur, vous allez avoir un roi, sous le titre de président," which may be translated, "Sir, you have given yourselves a king, under the title of president."

Turgot, Rochefoucauld and Condorcet, Brissot and Robespierre and Mazzei were all offended, that we had given too much eclat to our governors and presidents. It is true, and I rejoice in it, that our presidents, limited as they are, have more power, that is, more executive power, than the stadtholders, the doges, the podestàs, the avoyers, or the archons, or the kings of Lacedæmon or of Poland. To be brief, the general sense of mankind differs from you in opinion, and clearly sees, and fully believes, that our president's office has "some resemblance of monarchy," and God forbid that it should ever be diminished.

All these monarchical powers, however, "are deduced" in your judgment, "from moral liberty." I agree that they are "deduced" from morality and liberty; but if they had been more deliberately considered and better digested, the morality and liberty would have been better secured, and of longer duration, if the senatorial limitation of them had been omitted.

In my next, we will see if we can discover any resemblance of aristocracy in our form of government.

XII.

YOU "are unable to discover in our form of government any resemblance of aristocracy."

As every branch of executive authority committed or intrusted exclusively to one, resembles and is properly called a monarchical power, and a government, in proportion as its powers, legislative or executive, are lodged in one, resembles monarchy, so whatever authority or power of making or executing laws is exclusively vested in a few is properly called aristocratical; and a government, in proportion as it is constituted with such powers, resembles aristocracy.

Now, sir, let me ask you, whether you can discover no "resemblance of aristocracy in our form of government?" Are not great, very great, important, and essential powers intrusted to a few, a very few? Thirty-four senators, composed of two senators from each state, are an integral part of the legislature, which is the representative sovereignty of seven or eight millions of the people in the United States. These thirty-four men possess an absolute negative on all the laws of the nation. Nor is this all. These few, these very few, thirty-four citizens only in seven or eight millions, have an absolute negative upon the executive authority in the appointment of all officers in the diplomacy, in the navy, the army, the customs, excises, and revenues. They have, moreover, an absolute negative on all treaties with foreign powers, even with the aboriginal Indians. They are also an absolute judicature in all impeachments, even of the judges. Such are the powers in legislation, in execution, and in judicature, which in our form of government are committed to thirty-four men.

If in all these mighty powers and "exclusive privileges" you can "discover no resemblance of aristocracy," when and where did any resemblance of aristocracy exist? The Trigintivirs of Athens and the Decemvirs of Rome, I acknowledge, "resembled aristocracy" still more. But the lords of parliament in England do not resemble it so much. Nor did the nobility in Prussia, Germany, Russia, France, or Spain, possess such powers. The Palatines in Poland indeed!

How are these thirty-four senators appointed? Are they appointed by the people? Is the constitution of them democratical? They are chosen by the legislatures of the several states. And who are the legislatures of these separate states? Are they the people? No. They are a selection of the *best men* among the people, made by the people themselves. That is, they are the very ἄοιστοι of the Greeks.[4] Yet there is something more. These legislatures are composed of two bodies, a senate and a house of representatives, each assembly differently constituted, the senate more nearly "resembling aristocracy" than the house. Senators of the United States are chosen, in some states, by a convention of both houses; in others, by

---

[4] [*aristoi*—the "best men" Ed.]

separate, independent, but concurrent votes. The senates in the former have great influence, and often turn the vote; in the latter, they have an absolute negative in the choice.

Here are refinements upon refinements of "resemblances of aristocracy," a complication of checks and balances, evidently extended beyond any constitution of government that I can at present recollect. Whether an exact balance has been hit, or whether an exact balance will ever be hit, are different questions. But in this I am clear, that the nearer we approach to an exact balance, the nearer we shall approach to "moral liberty," if I understand the phrase.

We have agreed to be civil and free. In my number thirteen, I will very modestly hint to you my humble opinion of the point where your principal mistake lies.

XIII.

IN my last, I ventured to say, that I would hint in this at a principal misconception that had misled you or me. I shall submit the question to yourself and to the world, if you or I please, to be decided between us with candor.

You appear to me, in all your writings, to consider hereditary descent as essential to monarchy and aristocracy. When you mention monarchy, monarch, or king, you seem to understand an office and an officer, unlimited in authority, power, and duration. But is this correct in speculation or in language? Everybody knows that the word monarchy has its etymology in the Greek words μόνος and ἀογη, and signifies *single rule or authority in one.*[5] This authority may be limited or unlimited, of temporary or perpetual duration. It may be hereditary, or it may be for life, or it may be for years or only for one year, or for months or for one month, or for days or only for one day. Nevertheless, as far as it extends, and as long as it lasts, it may be called a monarchical authority with great propriety, by any man who is not afraid of a popular clamor and a scurrilous

[5] [*mónos* and *árkhe*—"single" and "rule" Ed.]

abuse of words. Monarchy, in this view of it, resembles property. A landed estate may be for years, a year, a half a year; or it may be for life, or for two, or three, or any number of lives; or it may be an inheritance to him, his heirs and assigns forever and ever. An estate in an office may be given by law for years, for life, or forever, as well as an estate in land. You or I may possess our houses for years, for life, or in tail, or in fee simple. And where is our title, our security for the possession of our firesides, but in the laws of society? And these laws of society have secured, and will secure to monarchs, to aristocrats, and to democrats such as you and I are, their estates in their offices, as well as in their houses, their lands, or their horses, in the same manner as they protect us asleep in our beds, or when at supper with our families. Mr. Madison has as clear a title to his estate in his office of president for four years, as you have to Hazelwood, to yourself, your heirs, and assigns forever, and by the same laws. Marshall has as good a right as either to his estate for life in his office of chief justice of the United States.

The Romans often conferred on the consuls, in very delicate terms, unlimited power to take care that the republic should suffer no injury. They conferred on Cincinnatus, on Sylla, and on Cæsar, the office of dictator, and the same power on many others, some for limited periods, some without limitation, and on Cæsar I believe for perpetuity. Were not the senates in such cases aristocrats or rather oligarchs for their several periods? Were not the dictators monarchs, some for years, some for life? Were they not made by law, in the strictest sense, monarchs, or if you will, despots? What were the kings of Crete or of Sparta? Monarchs, indeed, but how limited, though hereditary! What were the kings of Poland? How limited, and yet for life!

From these hints, I think it is clear, that the idea of hereditary descent is not an essential ingredient in the definition of monarchy or aristocracy; and that to employ those words in all cases, or in any case, as implying hereditary descent, is an abuse of words, and an imposition on vulgar popularity.

I know not how, when, or where, you discovered that Mr. Adams "supposed that monarchy, aristocracy, and democracy, or mixtures of them, constituted all the elements of government." This language is not mine. There is but one element of government, and that is, THE PEOPLE. From this element spring all governments. "For a nation to be free, it is only necessary that she wills it." For a nation to be slave, it is only necessary that she wills it. The governments of Hindostan and China, of Caffraria and Kamtschatka, the empires of Alexander the Macedonian, of Zingis Khan and Napoleon, of Tecumseh and Nimrod Hughes, all have grown out of this element,—THE PEOPLE. This fertile element, however, has never yet produced any other government than monarchy, aristocracy, democracy, and mixtures of them. And pray tell me *how* it can produce any other?

You say by "moral liberty." Will you be so good as to give me a logical, mathematical, or moral, or any other definition of this phrase, "moral liberty;" and to tell me who is to exercise this "liberty;" and by what principle or system of morality it is to be exercised? Is not this liberty and morality to reside in the great and universal element, "THE PEOPLE?" Have they not always resided there? And will they not always reside there?

This moral liberty resides in Hindoos and Mahometans, as well as in Christians; in Cappadocian monarchists, as well as in Athenian democrats; in Shaking Quakers, as well as in the General Assembly of the Presbyterian clergy; in Tartars and Arabs, Negroes and Indians, as well as in the people of the United States of America.

XIV.

IN your fourth page, you give us your opinion, that the moral "efforts of mankind towards political improvement have been restrained and disappointed by the erroneous opinion, that monarchy, aristocracy, and democracy, or mixtures of them, constitute all the elements of government." And you proceed to state, that "it will be an effort of your essay to prove, that the United States have refuted the ancient maxim, that monarchy, aristocracy, and democracy, are the only elements of government."

This phraseology is by no means familiar to me. I know not any writer or speaker who has asserted such a doctrine, or advanced such a maxim.

The words *monarchy, aristocracy,* and *democracy* are technical terms, invented by learned men, to express three different species of government. So they have invented many others,—*oligarchy, ochlocracy, mobocracy, anarchy, jacobinism, sans culottism, federalism, republicanism, quiddism,* or *gunarkism.* Any one of these hard words may be called an *element* of government, with as much propriety as any other.

The word *"element,"* as you employ it here, is a figure of rhetoric. Can you give—I acknowledge I have not ingenuity enough to invent—a logical or mathematical definition of it?

By *"elements,"* do you mean principles? If principles—physical or moral? If physical—I know of no physical principle of government but the bones and sinews, the timbers and ropes of the human body; that is, the mere strength, force, and power of constables, sheriffs, posse comitatus, armies and navies, soldiers and sailors. These elements or principles are applied in all the species of government that have been named, and must be the last resort of all that can be named or conceived. These elements or principles are not peculiar to the United States.

By *"elements,"* do you mean moral principles? If so, I know but one principle or element of government, and that is, "Constans et perpetua voluntas jus suum cuique tribuendi," that is, a constant and perpetual disposition and determination to render to every one his right; or, in other words, a constant and perpetual disposition and determination to do to others as we would have others do to us. This is a perfect principle, applicable at all times, in all places, among all persons, in all circumstances. Justice, therefore, is the only moral principle or element of government. But how shall justice be done in human society? It can be done only by general laws. These can never comprehend or foresee all the circumstances attending every particular case; and, therefore, it has been found necessary to introduce another principle or element, mercy. In strictness, perfect justice includes mercy, and perfect mercy includes justice. Both together make but one principle or moral element of government. Have you read, heard, or discovered any other moral principle or element of the government of God, angels, or men, than justice and benevolence united?

398 THE POLITICAL WRITINGS OF JOHN ADAMS

This principle has been professed by all governments, and all governors, throughout all time and space, with which we are acquainted. By King Theodore and the Emperor Napoleon, by the Prince Regent and Tecumseh.

How then is the government of the United States "planted in moral principles" more than other governments?

That we have conformed our practice to our principles as well, or better, upon the whole, than the majority, or, if you will, than any other nation hitherto, I will not dispute; because the question, decide it as you will, makes no alteration in the argument.

XV.

IN this fourth page you say, that "Mr. Adams's system tells us that the art of government can never change." I have said no such thing, Mr. Taylor! I know the art of government has changed, and probably will change, as often as the arts of architecture, painting, sculpture, music, poetry, agriculture, horticulture, medicine; and that is to say, almost as often as the weather or the fashion in dress.

But all these arts are founded in certain general principles of nature, which have never been known to change; and it is the duty of philosophers, legislators, and artists to study these principles; and the nearer they approach to them, the greater perfection will they attain in their arts. There may be principles in nature, not yet observed, that will improve all these arts; and nothing hinders any man from making experiments and pursuing researches, to investigate such principles and make such improvements. But America has made no discoveries of principles of government that have not been long known. Morality and liberty, and "moral liberty," too, whatever it may mean, have been known from the creation. Cain knew it when he killed Abel, and knew that he violated it.

You say, sir, that I have gravely counted up several victims "of popular rage, as proofs that democracy is more pernicious than monarchy or aristocracy." This is not my doctrine, Mr. Taylor. My opinion is, and always has been, that absolute power intoxicates alike despots, monarchs, aristocrats, and democrats, and jacobins, and *sans culottes.* I cannot say that democracy has been more pernicious, on the whole, than any of the others. Its atrocities have been more transient; those of the others have been more permanent. The history of all ages shows that the caprice, cruelties, and horrors of democracy have soon disgusted, alarmed, and terrified themselves. They soon cry, "this will not do; we have gone too far! We are all in the wrong! We are none of us safe! We must unite in some clever fellow, who can protect us all,—Cæsar, Bonaparte, who you will! Though we distrust, hate, and abhor them all; yet we must submit to one or another of them, stand by him, cry him up to the skies, and swear that he is the greatest, best, and finest man that ever lived!"

It has been my fortune, good or bad, to live in Europe ten years, from 1778 to 1788, in a public character. This destiny, singular in America, forced upon my attention the course of events in France, Holland, Geneva, and Switzerland, among many other nations; and this has irresistibly attracted my thoughts more than has been for my interest. The subject cannot have escaped you. What has been the conduct of the democratic parties in all those nations? How horribly bloody in some! Has it been steady, consistent, uniform, in any? Has it not leaped from democracy to aristocracy, to oligarchy, to military despotism, and back again to monarchy, as often, and as easily, as the birds fly to the lower, the middle, or the upper limbs of a tree, or leap from branch to branch, or hop from spray to spray?

Democracy, nevertheless, must not be disgraced; democracy must not be despised. Democracy must be respected; democracy must be honored; democracy must be cherished; democracy must be an essential, an integral part of the sovereignty, and have a control over the whole government, or moral liberty cannot exist, or any other liberty. I have been always grieved by the gross abuses of this respectable word. One party speak of it as the most amiable, venerable, indeed, as the sole object of its adoration; the other, as the sole object of its scorn, abhorrence, and execration. Neither party, in my opinion, know what they say. Some of them care not what they say, provided they can accomplish their own selfish purposes. These ought not to be forgiven.

You triumphantly demand: "What motives of preference between forms of government remain?" Is there no difference between a government of laws and a government of men? Between a government according to fixed laws, concerted by three branches of the legislature, composed of the most experienced men of a nation, established, recorded, promulgated to every individual, as the rule of his conduct, and a government according to the will of one man, or to a vote of a few men, or to a vote of a single assembly, whether of a nation or its representatives?

It is not Mr. Adams's system which can "arrest our efforts or appall our hopes in pursuit of political good." Other causes have obstructed and still embarrass the progress of the science of legislation.

XVI.

IN this number I have to hint at some causes which impede the course of investigation in civil and political knowledge. Religion, however, has been so universally associated with government, that it is impossible to separate them in this inquiry.

And where shall I begin, and where end? Shall I begin with the library at Alexandria, and finish with that at Washington, the latter Saracens more ferocious than the former, in proportion as they lived in a more civilized age? Where are the languages of antiquity? all the dialects of the Chaldean tongue? Where is Aristotle's history of eighteen hundred republics, that had existed before his time? Where are Cicero's writings upon government? What havoc has been made of books through every century of the Christian era? Where are fifty gospels, condemned as spurious by the bull of Pope Gelasius? Where are the forty wagon-loads of Hebrew manuscripts burned in France, by order of another pope, because suspected of heresy? Remember the *index expurgatorius*, the inquisition, the stake, the axe, the halter, and the guillotine; and, oh! horrible, the rack! This is as bad, if not worse, than a slow fire. Nor should the Lion's Mouth be forgotten.

Have you considered that system of holy lies and pious frauds that has raged and triumphed for fifteen hundred years; and which Chateaubriand appears at this day to believe as sincerely as St. Austin did? Upon this system depend the royalty, loyalty, and allegiance of Europe. The vial of holy oil, with which the Kings of France and England are anointed, is one of the most splendid and important events in all the legends. Do you think that Mr. Adams's system "arrests our efforts and appalls our hopes in pursuit of political good?" His maxim is, study government as you do astronomy, by facts, observations, and experiments; not by the dogmas of lying priests or knavish politicians.

The causes that impede political knowledge would fill a hundred volumes. How can I crowd a few hints at them in a single volume, much less, in a single letter?

Give me leave to select one attempt to improve civil, political, and ecclesiastical knowledge; or, at least, to arrest and retard the progress of ignorance, hypocrisy, and knavery; and the reception it met in the world, tending to "arrest our efforts and appall our hopes." Can you believe that Jesuits conceived this design? Yet true it is.

About the year 1643, Bollandus, a Jesuit, began the great work, the *"Acta Sanctorum."* Even Jesuits were convinced that impositions upon mankind had gone too far. Henschenius, another Jesuit, assisted him and Papebrock in the labor. The design was to give the lives of the saints, and to distinguish the miracles into the true, the false, and the dubious. They produced forty-seven volumes, in folio, an immense work, which, I believe, has never appeared in America. It was not, I am confident, in the library consumed by Ross, the savage, damned to everlasting fame,[6] and I fear it is not in the noble collection of Mr. Jefferson. I wish it was. This was a great effort in favor of truth, and to arrest imposture, though made by Jesuits. But what was their reward? Among the miracles, pronounced by these able men to be true, there are probably millions which you and I should believe no more than we do those related by Paulinus, Athanasius, Basil, Jerome, or Chrysostom, as of their own knowledge.

---

[6] The commander of the British troops, when the public buildings at Washington were burned.

Now, let us see how this generous effort in favor of truth was received and rewarded. Libels in abundance were printed against it. The authors were cited before the Inquisition in Spain, and the Pope in Italy, as authors of gross errors. The Inquisition pronounced its anathema in 1695. All Europe was in anxious suspense. The Pope, himself, was embarrassed by the interminable controversies excited, and, without deciding any thing, had no way to escape but by prohibiting all writings on the subject.

And what were the errors? They were only doubts.

1. Is it certain that the face of Jesus Christ was painted on the hand-kerchief of Saint Veronica?

2. Had the Carmelites the prophet Elias for their founder?

These questions set Europe in a flame, and might have roasted Pape-brock at an *auto-da-fé,* had he been in Spain.

Such dangers as these might "arrest efforts and appall hopes of political good;" but Mr. Adams's system cannot. That gaping, timid animal, man, dares not read or think. The prejudices, passions, habits, associations, and interests of his fellow-creatures surround him on every side; and if his reading or his thoughts interfere with any of these, he dares not acknowl-edge it. If he is hardy enough to venture even a hint, persecution, in some form or other, is his certain portion. *Party spirit,— l'esprit du corps,*—sects, factions, which threaten our existence in America at this moment, both in church and state, have "arrested all efforts, and appalled all hopes of political good." Have the Protestants accomplished a thorough reforma-tion? Is there a nation in Europe whose government is purified from monkish knavery? Even in England, is not the vial of holy oil still shown to travellers? How long will it be before the head of the Prince Regent, or the head of his daughter, will be anointed with this oil, and the right of impressing seamen from American ships deduced from it?

XVII

MR. ADAMS'S system is that of Pope, in his Essay on Criticism:—
"First follow Nature, and your judgment frame
By her just standard, which is still the same."

This rule, surely, cannot "arrest our efforts or appall our hopes." Study government as you build ships or construct steam-engines. The steam frigate will not defend New York, if Nature has not been studied, and her principles regarded. And how is the nature of man, and of society, and of government, to be studied or known, but in the history and by the experience of human nature in its terrestrial existence?

But to come nearer home, in search of causes which "arrest our efforts." Here I am, like the woodcutter on Mount Ida, who could not see wood for trees. Mariana wrote a book, *De Regno,* in which he had the temerity to insinuate that kings were instituted for good, and might be deposed if they did nothing but evil. Of course, the book was prohibited, and the writer prosecuted. Harrington wrote his *Oceana,* and other learned and ingenious works, for which he was committed to prison, where he became delirious and died. Sidney wrote discourses on government, for which he was beheaded, though they were only in manuscript, and robbed from his desk. Montesquieu was obliged to fly his country, and wander about Europe for many years; was compelled by the Sorbonne, after his return, to sign a recantation, as humiliating and as sincere as that of Galileo.[7] The chagrin produced by the criticisms and misrepresentations of his writings, and the persecutions he suffered, destroyed his health, and he died in 1755.

These instances, among others without number, are the discouragements which "arrest our efforts and appall our hopes." Nor are these all. Mankind do not love to read any thing upon any theory of government. Very few read any thing but libels. Theoretical books upon government will not sell. Booksellers and printers, far from purchasing the manuscript, will not accept it as a gift. For example, no printer would publish

---

[7] It is related of Montesquieu, that he suppressed some passages of his Persian Letters in a new edition, because they had been made by the king an obstacle to his admission to the French Academy. But he answered the Sorbonne without recanting; neither did he travel except from inclination. Voltaire says of him: "Montesquieu fut compté parmi les hommes les plus illustres du dixhuitième siècle, et cependant il ne fut pas persécuté, il ne fut au'un peu molesté pour ses *Lettres Persanes.* " ["Montesquieu was counted among the most distinguished men of the eighteenth century, and nevertheless he was not persecuted, only harassed a little on account of his *Persian Letters.*" Ed.]

these remarks at his own risk; and if I should print them at mine, they would fall dead from the press. I should never sell ten copies of them. I cannot learn that your Inquiry has had a rapid sale. I fear that you or your printer will be a loser, which I shall regret, because I really wish it could be read by every one who can read. To you, who are rich, this loss is of little moment; but to me, who am poor, such losses would be a dangerous "arrest of efforts," and a melancholy "appall of hopes." Writers, in general, are poor and hungry. Few write for fame. Even the great religionist, moralist, and literator, Johnson, could not compose a sermon for a priest from simple charity. He must have the pleasing hope, the animating contemplation of a guinea, before he could write. By all that I can learn, few rich men ever wrote any thing, from the beginning of the world to this day. You, sir, are a *rara avis in terris,* much to your honor.

But I have not yet enumerated all the discouragements which "arrest our efforts and appall our hopes."

I already feel all the ridicule of hinting at my poor four volumes of "Defence and Discourses on Davila," after quoting Mariana, Harrington, Sidney, and Montesquieu. But I must submit to the imputation of vanity, arrogance, presumption, dotage, or insanity, or what you will. How have my feeble "efforts been arrested, and faint hopes appalled?" Look back upon the pamphlets, the newspapers, the handbills, and above all, upon the circular letters of members of congress to their constituents for four-and-twenty years past, and consider in what manner my writings and myself have been treated. Has it not been enough to "arrest efforts and appall hopes?"

Is it not a damper to any ardor in search of truth, to read the absurd criticism, the stupid observations, the jesuitical subtleties, the studied lies that have been printed concerning my writings, in this my dear, native country, for five-and-twenty years? To read the ribaldry of Markoe and Brown, Paine and Callender, four vagabonds from Great Britain? and to see their most profligate effusions applauded and sanctioned by a nation?

In fine, is it not humiliating to see a volume of six or seven hundred pages written by a gentleman of your rank, fortune, learning, genius, and eloquence, in which my system, my sentiments, and my writings, from beginning to end, are totally misunderstood and misrepresented?

After all, I am not dead, like Harrington and Secondat. I have read in a Frenchman, "Je n'ai jamais trop bien compris ce que c'étoit que de mourir de chagrin." And I can say as confidently as he did, "I have never yet very well understood what it was to die of chagrin." Yet I am daily not out of danger of griefs that might put an end to me in a few hours! Nevertheless, I will wait, if I can, for distempers,—the messenger of NATURE, because I have still much curiosity to see what turn will be taken by public affairs in this country and others. Where can we rationally look for the theory or practice of government, but to nature and experiment, unless you appeal to revelation? If you do, I am ready and willing to follow you to that tribunal. I find nothing there inconsistent with my system.

XVIII.

IN your fifth page, you say, "Mr. Adams calls our attention to hundreds of wise and virtuous patricians, mangled and bleeding victims of popular fury, and gravely counts up several victims of democratic rage, as proofs that democracy is more pernicious than monarchy or aristocracy."

Is this fair, sir? Do you deny any one of my facts? I do not say that democracy has been more pernicious on the whole, and in the long run, than monarchy or aristocracy. Democracy has never been and never can be so durable as aristocracy or monarchy; but while it lasts, it is more bloody than either. I beseech you, sir, to recollect the time when my three volumes of "Defence" were written and printed, in 1786, 1787, and 1788. The history of the universe had not then furnished me with a document I have since seen,—an Alphabetical Dictionary of the Names and Qualities of Persons, "Mangled and Bleeding Victims of Democratic Rage and Popular Fury" in France, during the Despotism of Democracy in that Country, which Napoleon ought to be immortalized for calling IDEOLOGY. This work is in two printed volumes, in octavo, as large as Johnson's Dictionary, and is in the library of our late and excellent Vice-President, Elbridge Gerry, where I hope it will be preserved with anxious care. An

edition of it ought to be printed in America; otherwise it will be forever
suppressed. France will never dare look at it. The democrats themselves
could not bear the sight of it; they prohibited and suppressed it as far as
they could. It contains an immense number of as great and good men as
France ever produced. We curse the Inquisition and the Jesuits, and yet the
Inquisition and the Jesuits are restored. We curse religiously the memory
of Mary, for burning good men in Smithfield, when, if England had then
been democratical, she would have burned many more, and we murder
many more by the guillotine in the latter years of the eighteenth century.
We curse Guy Fawkes for thinking of blowing up Westminster Hall; yet
Ross blows up the capitol, the palace, and the library at Washington, and
would have done it with the same *sang froid* had congress and the president's family been within the walls. O! my soul! I am weary of these dis-
mal contemplations! When will mankind listen to reason, to *nature,* or to
revelation?

You say, I "might have exhibited millions of plebeians sacrificed to the
pride, folly, and ambition of monarchy and aristocracy." This is very true.
And I might have exhibited as many millions of plebeians sacrificed by the
pride, folly, and ambition of their fellow-plebeians and their own, in proportion to the extent and duration of their power. Remember, democracy
never lasts long. It soon wastes, exhausts, and murders itself. There never
was a democracy yet that did not commit suicide. It is in vain to say that
democracy is less vain, less proud, less selfish, less ambitious, or less avaricious than aristocracy or monarchy. It is not true, in fact, and nowhere
appears in history. Those passions are the same in all men, under all forms
of simple government, and when unchecked, produce the same effects of
fraud, violence, and cruelty. When clear prospects are opened before vanity, pride, avarice, or ambition, for their easy gratification, it is hard for the
most considerate philosophers and the most conscientious moralists to
resist the temptation. Individuals have conquered themselves. Nations
and large bodies of men, never.

When Solon's balance was destroyed by Aristides, and the preponderance given to the multitude, for which he was rewarded with the title of
JUST, when he ought to have been punished with the ostracism, the Athe-

nians grew more and more democratic. I need not enumerate to you the foolish wars into which the people forced their wisest men and ablest generals against their own judgments, by which the state was finally ruined, and Philip and Alexander became their masters.

In proportion as the balance, imperfect and unskilful as it was originally, here as in Athens, inclined more and more to the *dominatio plebis,*[8] the Carthaginians became more and more restless, impatient, enterprising, ambitions, avaricious, and rash, till Hannibal swore eternal hostility to the Romans, and the Romans were compelled to pronounce *delenda est Carthago.*[9]

What can I say of the democracy of France? I dare not write what I think and what I know. Were Brissot, Condorcet, Danton, Robespierre, and Monseigneur Egalité less ambitious than Cæsar, Alexander, or Napoleon? Were Dumouriez, Pichegru, Moreau, less generals, less conquerors, or, in the end, less fortunate than the last was? What was the ambition of this democracy? Nothing less than to propagate itself, its principles, its system, through the world; to decapitate all the kings, destroy all the nobles and priests in Europe. And who were the instruments employed by the mountebanks behind the scene, to accomplish these sublime purposes? The firewomen, the badauds, the stage players, the atheists, the deists, the scribblers for any cause at three livres a day, the Jews, and oh! that I could erase from my memory the learned divines,—profound students in the prophecies,—real philosophers and sincere Christians, in amazing numbers, over all Europe and America, who were hurried away by the torrent of contagious enthusiasm. Democracy is chargeable with all the blood that has been spilled for five-and-twenty years.

Napoleon and all his generals were but creatures of democracy, as really as Rienzi, Theodore, Massaniello, Jack Cade, or Wat Tyler. This democratical hurricane, inundation, earthquake, pestilence, call it which you will,

---

[8] ["the domination of the common people," i.e. the plebeians or lower classes, not just "the people" as opposed to the elected officials. Ed.]

[9] ["Carthage must be destroyed." The elder Cato always ended his speeches with these words. Ed.]

at last aroused and alarmed all the world, and produced a combination unexampled, to prevent its further progress.

XIX.

I HOPE my last convinced you that democracy is as restless, as ambitious, as warlike and bloody, as aristocracy or monarchy.

You proceed to say, that I "ought to have placed right before us the effects of these three principles, namely,—democracy, aristocracy, and monarchy, commixed in the wars, rebellions, persecutions, and oppressions of the English form."

Pray, sir, what was the object of my book? I was not writing a history of England, nor of the world. Inattention to this circumstance has been the cause of all the *honest* misapprehensions, misconstructions, and misrepresentations of the whole work. To see at one glance the design of the three volumes, you need only to look at the first page. M. Turgot "was not satisfied with the constitutions which had been formed for the different states of America. By most of them, the customs of England were imitated, without any particular motive. Instead of collecting all authority into one centre, that of the nation, they have established different bodies,—a body of representatives, a council, and a governor,—because there is in England a house of commons, a house of lords, and a king; they endeavor to balance these different powers."

This solemn opinion of M. Turgot, is the object of the whole of the three volumes. M. Turgot had seen only the constitutions of New York, Massachusetts, and Maryland, and the first constitution of Pennsylvania. His principal intention was to censure the three former. From these three the constitution of the United States was afterwards almost entirely drawn.

The drift of my whole work was, to vindicate these three constitutions against the reproaches of that great statesman, philosopher, and really excellent man, whom I well knew, and to defend them against his attacks, and only upon those points on which he had assaulted them. If this fact had been considered, it would have prevented a thousand witticisms and criticisms about the "misnomer," &c.

The points I had to illustrate and to prove, were,—

1. That the people of Massachusetts, New York, and Maryland were not to blame for instituting governors, councils, (or senates) and houses of representatives.

2. That they were not reprehensible for endeavoring to balance those different powers.

3. That they were to be applauded, not reproached, for not "collecting all authority into one centre, that of the nation," in whatever sense those dark, obscure, and incomprehensible words could be understood.

4. Construing these phrases, as it is believed they were intended, to recommend a sovereignty in a single assembly of representatives, that is, a representative of democracy, it was my duty to show that democracy was as unsteady, equally envious, ambitious, avaricious, vain, proud, cruel, and bloody, as aristocracy or monarchy.

5. That an equilibrium of those "different powers" was indispensably necessary to guard and defend the rights, liberties, and happiness of the people against the deleterious, contagious, and pestilential effects of those passions of vanity, pride, ambition, envy, revenge, lust, and cruelty, which domineer more or less in every government that has no BALANCE or an imperfect BALANCE.

6. That it was not an affected imitation of the English government, so much as an attachment to their old colonial forms, in every one of which there had been three branches,—a governor, a council, and a house of representatives,—which, added to the eternal reason and unalterable nature of things, induced the legislators of those three states to adopt their new constitutions.

The design of the three volumes, pursued from the first page of the first to the last page of the last, was to illustrate, elucidate, and demonstrate those six important truths. To illustrate and prove these truths, or to show them to be falsehoods, where can we look but into the heart of man and the history of his heart? In the heart were found those appetites, passions, prejudices, and selfish interests, which ought always to be controlled by reason, conscience, and social affections; but which are never perfectly so controlled, even by any individual, still less by nations and large bodies of men, and less and less, as communities grow larger and larger, more populous, more commercial, more wealthy, and more luxurious. In the history of his heart, a transient glance of the eye was cast over the most conspicuous, remarkable, and celebrated of those nations who had preserved any share of authority to the people, or who had approached the nearest to preserving all authority to the people, or who had mixed the authority of the people with that of patricians, or senates, or councils, or where the executive power had been separated from, or united with the legislative, or where the judicial power had been complicated with either, or separate from both. And it was endeavored to be shown, that those nations had been the happiest who had separated the legislative from the executive power, the judicial from both, and divided the legislative power itself into three branches, thereby producing a balance between the legislative and executive authority, a balance between the branches of the legislature, and a salutary check upon all these powers in the judicial, as had been done in the constitutions of Maryland, New York, and Massachusetts. I had nothing to do with despotisms or simple monarchies, unless it were incidentally, and by way of illustration.

I know not that any one of my FACTS has ever been denied or disputed or doubted. Do you deny any of them? Are they not a sufficient apology for the people of Massachusetts, New York, and Maryland, against the accusations of M. Turgot, as well as against Sharp and his followers, who taught the same dogmas?

XX.

IN my apology, if you like that word better than "defence," I passed over England for more reasons than one. I very well knew that there had been no nation that had produced so many materials for the illustration of my system and confirmation of my principles, as that in which I wrote. There was anciently no people but serfs; no house of commons. The struggle between kings, barons, and priests, from Thomas à Kempis to Cardinal Wolsey, and from him to Archbishop Laud, and from him to King William, would have been instructive enough; and it would not have been difficult to show that "the wars, rebellions, persecutions, and oppressions of the English form" arose (the frenzy of superstition apart) from the want of that limitation of power in the king, the lords, the commons, and the judges, and of the balances between them, for which I contended. I had nothing to do with the ecclesiastical establishment in England. My observations related exclusively to the civil and political arrangement of powers. These powers were never accurately defined, and, consequently, balanced, till the revolution, nor the judges completely independent, till the present reign.

Nor had I any thing to do with the hereditary quality, superadded to the monarchical and aristocratical powers in England. The three great powers may be separated for some purposes, united for others, as clearly defined, limited, and balanced, for one, two, or three years, as in the constitutions of Maryland, New York, and Massachusetts, as they can be for an age, or as they are in England for endless ages.

A large proportion of *"the wars, rebellions, persecutions, and oppressions,"* in England have arisen from ecclesiastical artifices, and the intoxication of religious enthusiasm. Are you sure that any form of government can at all times secure the people from fanaticism? Although this country has done much, are you confident that our moral, civil, or political liberties are perfectly safe on this quarter? Is a democracy less liable to this evil than a mixed government? It is true that, in my apology, I expressed in strong terms my admiration of the English constitution; but I meant no more of it than was to the purpose of my argument; that is, the division and union of powers in our American constitutions, which were, indeed, so far, imitations of it. My argument had no more to do with hereditary descent than it had with the Church or the Bank of England.

My mind, I acknowledge, was deeply impressed with apprehensions from the accounts of the dangerous and irregular proceedings in several counties in Massachusetts, and the alarming extent of similar discontents in all the other states. And more than all this. The fountains of the great deep were broken up in France, and the proud wave of democracy was spreading and swelling and rolling, not only through that kingdom, but into England, Holland, Geneva, and Switzerland, and, indeed, threatened an inundation all over Europe. Innovation was making bold and large strides in every direction. I had great doubts of the success of the leaders in any useful degree; but of one thing I was fully convinced,—that if they aimed at any constitution of civil government more popular than the English, they would ruin themselves, after setting Europe on fire and shedding oceans of blood. The rise, progress, and termination to this time need only be hinted. Are you now convinced that France must have a more permanent executive than she had in the time of Barrere? The constitutions in France, Spain, and Holland, have at last approached nearer to such a division and balance of powers as are contended for, than ever was attempted before; but these constitutions of 1814 are all essentially defective, and cannot endure. As to rebellions in England, there was one in 1715, another in 1745. I recollect no more, unless you claim for one Lord George Gordon's insanity, and that of his stupid, bigoted followers.

After all our "discoveries of new principles of moral liberty," we have had Shays's, Fries's, and I know not whose rebellion in the western counties of Pennsylvania. How near did Virginia and Kentucky approach in the last years of the last century? And how near is New England approaching at this hour in Hartford?

Must you and I humble ourselves in dust and ashes to acknowledge that the United States have had more rebellions and *quasi rebellions* in thirty years than England has had in one hundred and twenty?

John Wilkes said to a confidential friend, who broke in unexpectedly to his closet when he was writing his North-Briton, number fifty-five, "I have been studying these four hours to see how near I could come to treason without committing it." This study, Mr. Taylor, has become a fashionable study in the South, the Middle, and the North, of America.

You "admit that man is physically always the same, but deny that he is so morally." I have not admitted that he is physically always the same, nor have I asserted that he is so morally. On the contrary, some are born strong, others weak, some tall, others short, some agile, others clumsy, some handsome, others ugly, some black, others white. These physical qualities, too, may be, and are both improved and depraved by education, practice, exercise, and nourishment. They are all born alike morally innocent, but do not all remain so. They soon become as different and unlike, and unequal in morals as virtue and vice, merit and guilt. In their intellects they are never equal nor the same. Perception is more quick, memory more retentive, judgment more mature, reason more correct, thoughts better arranged, in some than in others. And these inequalities are the sources of the natural aristocracy among mankind, according to my express words quoted by you.

XXI.

The corporeal inequalities among mankind, from the cradle and from the womb to the age of Oglethorpe and Parr, the intellectual inequalities from Blackmore to Milton, from Crocker to Newton, and from Behmen to Locke, are so obvious and notorious, that I could not expect they would have been doubted. The moral equality, that is, the innocence, is only at the birth; as soon as they can walk or speak, you may discern a moral inequality. These inequalities, physical, intellectual, and moral, I have called sources of a natural aristocracy; and such they are, have been, and will be; and it would not be dangerous to say, they are sources of all the artificial aristocracies that have been, are, or will be.

Can you say that these physical, intellectual, and moral inequalities produce no inequalities of influence, consideration, and power in society?

You say, "upon the truth or error of this distinction, the truth or error of Mr. Adams's mode of reasoning, and of this essay, will somewhat depend." I know not whether I ought not to join issue with you upon this point. State the question or questions, then, fairly and candidly between us.

1. Are there, or are there not physical, corporeal, material inequalities among mankind, from the embryo to the tomb?

2. Are there, or are there not intellectual inequalities from the first opening of the senses, the sight, the hearing, the taste, the smell, and the touch, to the final loss of all sense?

3. Are there not moral inequalities, discernible almost, if not quite, from the original innocence to the last stage of guilt and depravity?

4. From these inequalities, physical, intellectual, and moral, does there or does there not arise a natural aristocracy among mankind? or, in other words, some men who have greater capacities and advantages to acquire the love, esteem, and respect of their fellow men, more wealth, fame, consideration, honor, influence, and power in society than other men?

When, where, have I said that men were always morally the same?

Never, in word or writing. I have said,—

1. There is an inequality of wealth.

2. There is an inequality of birth.

3. There are great inequalities of merit, talents, virtues, services, and reputations.

4. There are a few in whom all these advantages of birth, fortune, and fame, are united.

I then go on to say, "these sources of inequality, common to every people, founded in the constitution of nature a natural aristocracy, &c. &c."

Now, sir, let me modestly and civilly request of you a direct and simple answer to the three foregoing questions. Ay or no; yea or nay. You and I have been so drilled to such answers that we can have as little difficulty in promising them as in understanding them; at least, unless we have become greater proficients in pyrrhonism, than we were when we lived together. When I shall be honored with your yea or nay to those three questions, I hope I shall know the real questions between us, and be enabled to confess my error, express my doubts, or state my replication.

But, sir, let me ask you why you direct your artillery at me alone? at me, a simple individual *"in town obscure, of humble parents born?"* I had fortified myself behind the intrenchments of Aristotle, Livy, Sidney, Harrington, Dr. Price, Machiavel, Montesquieu, Swift, &c. You should have battered down these strong outworks before you could demolish me.

The word *"crown,"* which you have quoted from me in your eighth page, was used merely to signify *the executive authority.* You, sir, who are a lawyer, know that this figure signifies nothing more nor less. "The prince" is used by J. J. Rousseau, and by other writers on the social compact, for the same thing. Had I been blessed with time to revise a work which is full of errors of the press, I should have noted this as an erratum, especially if

I had thought of guarding against malevolent criticism in America. I now request a formal erratum; page 117, at the bottom, dele "crown," and insert "executive authority."

In your eighth page, you begin to consider my natural causes of aristocracy.

1. "Superior abilities." Let us keep to nature and experience. Is there no such thing as genius? Had Raphael no more genius than the common sign-post painters? Had Newton no more genius than even his great master, that learned, profound, and most excellent man, Dr. Barrow? Had Alexander no more genius than Darius? Had Cæsar no more than Catiline, or even than Pompey? Had Napoleon no more than Santerre? Has the Honorable John Randolph no more than Nimrod Hughes and Christopher Macpherson? Has every clerk in a counting-house as great a genius for numbers as Zerah Colburne, who, at six years of age, demonstrated faculties which Sanderson and Newton never possessed in their ripest days? Is there in the world a father of a family who has not perceived diversities in the natural capacities of his children?

These questions deserve direct answers. If you allow that there are natural inequalities of abilities, consider the effects that the genius of Alexander produced! They are visible to this day. And what effect has the genius of Napoleon produced? They will be felt for three thousand years to come. What effect have the genius of Washington and Franklin produced? Had these men no more influence in society than the ordinary average of other men? Genius is sometimes long lived; and it has accumulated fame, wealth, and power, greater than can be commanded by millions of ordinary citizens. These advantages are sometimes applied to good purposes, and sometimes to bad.

XXII.

WHEN superior genius gives greater influence in society than is possessed by inferior genius, or a mediocrity of genius, that is, than by the ordinary level of men, this superior influence I call natural aristocracy. This cause, you say, is "fluctuating." What then? it is aristocracy still, while it exists. And is not democracy "fluctuating" too? Are the waves of the sea, or the winds of the air, or the gossamer that idles in the wanton summer air, more fluctuating than democracy? While I admit the existence of democracy, notwithstanding its instability, you must acknowledge the existence of natural aristocracy, notwithstanding its fluctuations.

I find it difficult to understand you, when you say that "knowledge and ignorance are fluctuating." Knowledge is unchangeable; and ignorance cannot change, because it is nothing. It is a nonentity. Truth is one, uniform and eternal; knowledge of it cannot fluctuate any more than itself. Ignorance of truth, being a nonentity, cannot, surely, become entity and fluctuate and change like Proteus, or wind, or water. You sport away so merrily upon this topic, that I will have the pleasure of transcribing you. You say, "the aristocracy of superior abilities will be regulated by the extent of the space between knowledge and ignorance; as the space contracts or widens, it will be diminished or increased; and if aristocracy may be thus diminished, it follows that it may be thus destroyed."

What is the amount of this argument? Ignorance may be destroyed and knowledge increased *ad infinitum*. And do you expect that all men are to become omniscient, like the almighty and omniscient Hindoo, perfect Brahmins? Are your hopes founded upon an expectation that knowledge will one day be equally divided? Will women have as much knowledge as men? Will children have as much as their parents? If the time will never come when all men will have equal knowledge, it *seems* to follow, that some will know more than others; and that those who know most will have more influence than those who know least, or than those who know half way between the two extremes; and consequently will be aristocrats. "Superior abilities," comprehend abilities acquired by education and study, as well as genius and natural parts; and what a source of inequality and aristocracy is here! Suffer me to dilate a little in this place. Massachusetts has probably educated as many sons to letters, in proportion to her numbers, as any State in the Union, perhaps as any nation, ancient or modern. What proportion do the scholars bear to the whole number of people? I wish I had a catalogue of our Harvard University, that I might state exact numbers. Say that, in almost two hundred years, there have been three or four thousand educated, from perhaps two or three millions of people. Are not these aristocrats? or, in other words, have they not had more influence than any equal number of uneducated men? In fact, these men governed the province from its first settlement; these men have governed, and still govern, the state. These men, in schools, academies, colleges, and universities; these men, in the shape of ministers, lawyers, and physicians; these men, in academies of arts and sciences, in agricultural societies, in historical societies, in medical societies and in antiquarian societies, in banking institutions and in Washington benevolent societies, govern the state, at this twenty-sixth of December, 1814. The more you educate, without a balance in the government, the more aristocratical will the people and the government be. There never can be, in any nation, more than one fifth—no, not one tenth of the men, regularly educated to science and letters. I hope, then, you will acknowledge, that "abilities" form a DISTINCTION and confer a privilege, in fact, though they give no peculiar rights in society.

2. You appear, sir, to have overlooked or forgotten one great source of natural aristocracy, mentioned by me in my Apology, and dilated on in subsequent pages, I mean BIRTH. I should be obliged to you for your candid sentiments upon this important subject. Exceptions have been taken to the phrase *well born;* but I can see no more impropriety in it than in the epithets *well bred, well educated, well brought up, well taught, well informed, well read, well to live, well dressed, well fed, well clothed, well armed, well accoutred, well furnished, well made, well fought, well aimed, well meant, well mounted, well fortified, well tempered, well fatted, well spoken, well argued, well reasoned, well decked, well ducked, well trimmed, well wrought,* or any other *well* in common parlance.

And here, sir, permit me, by way of digression, to remark another discouragement to honest political literature, and the progress of real political science. If a *well-meant* publication appears, it is instantly searched for an unpopular word, or one that can be made so by misconstruction, misrepresentation, or by any credible and imposing deception. Some ambitions, popular demagogue gives the alarm,—"heresy?" Holy, democratical church has decreed that word to be "heresy!" Down with him! And, if there was no check to their passions, and no balance to their government, they would say, *à la lanterne! à la guillotine! roast him! bake him! boil him! fry him!* The Inquisition in Spain would not celebrate more joyfully an *auto-da-fé*.

Some years ago, more than forty, a writer unfortunately made use of the term *better sort*. Instantly, a popular clamor was raised, and an odium excited, which remains to this day, to such a degree, that no man dares to employ that expression at the bar, in conversation, in a newspaper, or pamphlet, no, nor in the pulpit; though the "baser sort" are sufficiently marked and distinguished in the New Testament, to prove that there is no wrong in believing a "better sort." And if there is any difference between virtue and vice, there is a "better sort" and a worse sort in every human society.

With sincere reverence, let me here quote one of the most profound philosophical, moral, and religious sentiments that ever was expressed:—
"We know not what spirit we are of."

XXIII.

I HAVE not yet finished what the poets call an episode, and prose-men a digression. Can you account for a caprice in the public opinion? Burke's *"swinish multitude"* has not been half so unpopular, nor excited half the irritation, odium, resentment, or indignation that "WELL BORN" and "better sort" have produced. Burke's phrase, nevertheless, must be allowed to be infinitely more unphilosophical, immoral, irreligious, uncivil, impolitic, inhuman, and insolent than either, or both the other. Impudent libeller of your species! Whom do you mean by your "multitude?" The multitude, in your country, means the people of England, Scotland, and Ireland, and all the rest of your dominions. The multitude, in this country, means the people of the United States. The multitude means mankind. Make your exceptions, and then say, after an attention, whether they are not, upon an average, as swinish as the rest. All the delicacy of your classical criticism, all the subtilty of your metaphysical discrimination, cannot devise a justifiable limitation of your words.

But, to return from this digression, till I meet another. Our present subject is BIRTH. It is acknowledged that we are all children of the same benevolent parent; all born under the same moral law of our nature; all equally free; and all entitled to the same equal rights. Thus far, I hope, we are agreed. But, not to repeat the physical inequalities and the intellectual inequalities of capacity, before enumerated, and perhaps more than once, is there not a distinction made in society between children of different parents? and is it not produced by natural causes? If you deny that such distinctions are made in fact and practice, how shall I prove it?

1. The general sense, and still more, the universal consent of mankind, is allowed to be a strong argument to prove the truth of any fact, or any opinion. Is there any practice, custom, or sentiment, in which mankind have more universally agreed, than in making distinctions of nativity, and manifesting more respect for the children of some parents than for those of others? Not only all civilized, cultivated, and polished societies, but all pastoral nations and savage hordes, the negroes of Africa and our Indian tribes, all concur in this usage. If, in all your reading, conversation, or experience, you have found an exception, I pray you to communicate it to me. I know none.

2. Look over our States, (which, I pray, may be sometime or other truly called United.) Is no distinction made here? It might be thought invidious to mention names, and indeed it would be endless. But are there not NAMES almost as much revered as those of patriarchs, prophets, or apostles? Have names no influence in governing men? Had the word "Gueux" no influence in the Dutch Revolution? Had the word *"sans culotte"* none in the French? Have the words "Jacobin," "democrat," no influence? Have the words "federalist" and "republican" no effect? If these transient, momentary, cant words of faction, or at best of party, have such effects, what must be the more permanent influence of names that have been revered for ages, and never heard but like music?

3. In this argument, I have a right to state cases as strong as any that occur in human life. Suppose ten thousand people assembled to see the execution of a man for burglary, robbery, arson, fratricide, patricide, or the meanest, most treacherous, perfidious, and cruel crime that can be committed or imagined. Suppose, the next day, the same ten thousand people should attend the funeral obsequies of Washington, Hamilton, or

Ames. Is it possible that these ten thousand people should have the same feelings for the children of the criminal that they have for the hero and the sages?

4. Is there not a presumption in favor of some children? At least a probable presumption, if not a violent presumption? Here, again, I have a right to put strong cases. Here are two families in the same neighborhood; the parents in one are ignorant, intemperate, idle, thievish, lying, and, consequently, destitute; in the other, they are sober, prudent, honest, decent, frugal, industrious, possessed of comfortable property, studious, inquisitive, well informed, and, if you will, literary and scientific. Is there not a violent presumption in favor of the children of the latter family, and against those of the former? Exceptions there are: but exceptions prove the general rule.

5. Is there not a prejudice in favor of some children, and against others? Prejudices, associations, habits, customs, usages, manners, must, in some cases and in some degree, be studied, respected, and indulged by legislators, even the most wise, virtuous, pious, learned, and profound. Here, sir, I will appeal to yourself. A young man appears. You ask of the bystanders who he is? The answer is, "I do not know." "No matter; let him go." Another appears,—"Who is he?" The answer is, "The son of A. B." "I do not know A. B." A third appears,—"Who is this?" "The son of C. D." "C. D.! my friend! He has been dead these fifty years; but I love his memory, and should be glad to be acquainted with any of his posterity. Please to walk in, sir, and favor me with your company for a few weeks or months; you will be always welcome to my house, and will always oblige me with your company."

6. Theognis, a Greek poet, twenty-four hundred years ago, complains that, although mankind were very anxious to purchase stallions, bulls, and rams of the best breed; yet, in some instances, men would marry wives of mean extraction for the sake of their fortunes, and ladies of high birth would marry men of low descent because they were rich.[4] And I believe

[10]Κριοὺς μεν καὶ ὄνους διζή,μεθα, Κύρνε, καὶ ἵππους
Εὐγενέας· καί τις βούλεται ἐξ ἀγαθῶν

there has not been a poet, orator, historian, or philosopher, from his age to this, who has not in his writings expressed or implied some distinction of nativities; nor has there been one of either sex who, in choosing a companion for life, between two rivals of equal youth, beauty, fortune, talents, and accomplishments, would not prefer the one of respectable parentage to the other of meaner and lower original.

XXIV.

I AM still upon birth, and my seventh argument is,—

7. It was a custom among the Greeks and Romans,—probably in all civilized nations,—to give names to the castles, palaces, and mansions of their consuls, dictators, and other magistrates, senators, &c. This practice is still followed in England, France, &c. Among the ancients, the distinctions of extraction were most constantly marked by the spots on which they were born. "Illustri loco natus," "claro loco natus," "clarissimo loco natus," "illustrissimo loco natus," were common expressions of conspicuous origin. On the contrary, "obscuro loco nati," "vili loco nati," designated low original, base extraction, sordid descent, and were expressions, however unjustly, of odium, or at least contempt.[11] I perceive, sir, that you gentlemen of Virginia, who are good classical scholars, have not suffered

Κτήσασθαι· γῆμαι δὲ κακὴν κακοῦ οὐ μελεδαίνει
Εσθλὸς ἀνὴρ, ἤν ο'ι χρήματα πολλὰ δισῷ.
Οὐδεμιά κακοῦ ἀνδρὸς ἀναίνεται εἰναι ἄκοιτις
Πλουσίου, ἀλλ' ἀφνεὸν βούλεται ἀντ' ἀγαθοῦ.
Χρήματα μὲν τιμῶσι, καὶ 'εκ κακοῦ 'εσθλος ἔγημε,
Καὶ κακὸς 'εξ ἀγαθοῦ· πλοῦτος ἔμιξε γένος.

["We all want the best-bred rams and asses and horses, Kyrnos, and one wishes to accumulate from good stock; yet a good man does not hesitate to marry the bad daughter of a bad man, if he gives him many possessions, nor does a woman refuse to be the wife of a bad man if he is wealthy, but wishes to be rich rather than good. For they honor possessions. A good man breeds from bad stock, and a bad man from good: wealth debases ancestry." Theognis 183-90. Ed.]

★ [*illustri loco natus*—"born in a distinguished position" (or "station" or "rank"); *claro loco natus*—"born in an eminent position"; *clarissimo loco natus*—"born in a most eminent position"; *illustrissimo loco natus*—"born in a most distinguished position"; *obscuro loco nati*—"born in an undistinguished position"; *vili loco nati*—"born in an ignoble position." Ed.]

this observation to escape you. You have taken the modest name of Hazlewood; my friend Richard Lee, the superb name, Chantilly; Mr. Madison, the beautiful name of Montpelier; and Mr. Jefferson, the lofty name of Monticello; and Mr. Washington, the very humble name of a British sea captain, Mount Vernon; the Hon. John Randolph, that of Roanoke. I would advise the present proprietor of Mount Vernon to change the name to Mount Talbot, Truxton, Decatur, Rodgers, Bainbridge, or Hull. And I would advise our Boston gentlemen, who have given this name of the British sea captain to the most beautiful hill on the globe, to change it to Mount Hancock, or Mount Perry, or Mount Macdonough.

8. I wish I could take a walk with you in all the churchyards and burying grounds in Virginia,—Episcopalian, Presbyterian, Methodist, or what you will. Are there not tombs, monuments, gravestones, and inscriptions, ancient and modern? Is there no distinction made among these memorials? Are they all seen with equal eyes, with equal indifference? Is there no peculiar attachment, no particular veneration for any of them? Are they all beheld by the whole people and by every individual with similar sensations and reflections? How many hundreds of thousands of men, women, and children have lived and died in Virginia, to whom no monument has been erected, whose posterity know not, and cannot conjecture, where their ancestors were deposited? Do all these cemeteries, which are found all over the world, exhibit no distinctions of names and families and persons? Are not these distinctions natural? produced by natural and inevitable causes?

9. I should be highly honored and vastly delighted to visit with you every great planter in Virginia. I should be pleased to look into their parlors, banqueting rooms, bedchambers, and great halls, as Mr. Jefferson and I once did together the most celebrated of the gentlemen's country seats in England. Should we there see no statues, no busts, no pictures, no portraits of their ancestors? no trinkets, no garments, no pieces of furniture carefully preserved, because they belonged to great grandfathers, and estimated at ten times the value of similar articles of superior quality, that might be bought at any shop or store? What are ancestors, or their little or great elegance or conveniences, to the present planter, more than those

of the fifty-acre man, his neighbor, who perhaps never knew the name of his grandfather or father? Are there no natural feelings, and, consequently, no natural distinctions here?

I think I have been impartial, and have suspected no vanity or weakness in Virginians, which I have not recognized in Massachusettensians; and I could enumerate many more. I will go farther. It seems to be generally agreed and settled among men, that John Adams is a weak and vain man. I fall down under the public opinion, the general sense, and frankly and penitently acknowledge, that I have been all my lifetime, and still am, a weak and vain man. One instance of my vanity and weakness I will distinguish. Within two or three years, I have followed to the tomb the nearest, the dearest, the tenderest connections, relations, and friends of my life, from almost ninety years of age to eighteen months. This has made me contemplate much among the tombs,—a gloomy region to which I had been much a stranger. In this churchyard, I found the monumental stones of my father and mother, my grandfather and grandmother, my great grandfather and great grandmother, and my great great grandfather. My great great grandmother died in England. If you will do me the favor, sir, to come to Quincy and spend a few weeks with me, I will take a walk with you, and show you all these monuments and inscriptions, and will confess to you, I would not exchange this line of ancestors for that of Guelphs, or Bowdoins, or Carters, or Winthrops. Such is my vanity, imbecility, and dotage! And I suspect that you are not a whit wiser than I am in this respect. Open your soul, sir, and disclose your natural feelings, and frankly say, whether you would exchange ancestors with any man living. I believe you would not. Is there a human being who would? If these feelings for ancestors are universal, how shall any legislator prevent the rich, the great, the powerful, the learned, the ingenious, from distinguishing by durable, costly, and permanent memorials, their own ancestors, and, consequently, their children and remote posterity, from the descendants of the vast, the immense majority, who lie mingled with the dust, totally forgotten? And how shall he prevent these names and families from being more noted and respected by nations, as well as smaller communities, than names never before heard?

XXV.

A WORD or two more upon birth.

10. Birth is naturally and necessarily and inevitably so connected and blended with property, fame, power, education, genius, strength, beauty, learning, science, taste, figure, air, attitudes, movements, &c. &c. &c., that it is often impossible, and always difficult to separate them. Two children are born on the same day, of equal genius,—one, the son of Mr. Jefferson; the other, of Nimrod Hughes. Which will meet with most favor in the world? Would a child of Anthony Benezet, good creature as he was, have an equal chance in life with a son of Robert Morris, when the wealth of nations was believed to be in his power? Would a son of the good Rutherford, the predecessor of General Morgan, have an equal favor in the world with a son of the great General and President Washington? Would a son of Sir Isaac Newton have no more favor in the sight of the whole human race than a son of Mr. Rittenhouse, the worthy President of the Philosophical Society of Philadelphia? Beau Nash meet no more complaisance than one of the Hercules du Roi, whom I have seen leap at Sadlers Wells, and turn his heels over his head, at a height of ten or twelve feet, and come down on the other side of the stage erect? I leave, sir, to your fertile genius, ample reading, and long experience, to pursue the inquiries. I could continue to enumerate examples through sheets of paper.

11. Have you not observed in life, and have you not remarked in history, that the common people,—and by *common people,* I here mean all mankind, despots, emperors, kings, princes, nobles, presidents, senators, representatives, lawyers, divines, physicians, merchants, farmers, shopkeepers, mechanics, tradesmen, day laborers, tavern haunters, dram-shop frequenters, mob, rabble, and canaille, that is to say, all human kind,—have you not observed that all these feel more respect, more real respect for birth than even for wealth; may I not say than for genius, fame, talents, or power? Though they follow and hosanna for the loaves and fishes, you will often hear them say, "proud as he is, I knew his father, who was only a blacksmith; his grandfather, who was only a carpenter; or his great grandfather, who was only a shoemaker; he need not be so topping."

12. Has not the experience of six thousand years shown that the common people submit more easily and quietly to birth than to wealth, genius, fame, or any other talents? Whence the prejudices against upstarts, parvenus, &c.? Whence the general respect, reverence, and submission in all ages and nations, of plebeians to patricians, of sieurs to monsieurs, of juffrouws to mevrouws? If a man of high birth is promoted, little or nothing is said by the plebeians. If one of their own level, the son of a tradesman or common farmer is advanced, all the envy and bile of his equals is excited. He is abused and belittled, if not reviled, by all his former equals, as they thought themselves, whatever may have been the superiority of his genius, education, services, experience, or other talents. There is nothing, Mr. Taylor, to which the vulgar, in general, so quietly and patiently and cordially submit as to birth.

13. What in all ages has been the source of the submission of nobility to royalty? Every nobleman envies his sovereign, and would pull him down, if he could get into his throne and wear his crown. But when nobles and ignobles have torn one another to pieces for years or ages in their eternal squabbles of jealousy, envy, rivalry, hatred, and revenge, and all are convinced that this anarchy will not do, that the world will be depopulated, that a head must be set up, and all the members must be guided by it, then, and not till then, will nobles submit to Kings as of superior birth. What subjects all the nobility of Europe to all the kings of Europe, but birth? though some of them cannot well make out their pretensions; particularly the proudest of them all,—the house of Austria.

14. What has excited a universal insurrection of all Europe against Bonaparte, (if we dive to the bottom of this awful gulf, and recollect the succession of coalitions against him and against republican France,) but because he was *obscuro loco natus,* the son of a simple gentillâtre of Corsica?

15. Such, and so universal are the manifest distinctions of birth in every village and every city, so tremendous are their effects on nations and governments, that one might almost pronounce them self-evident. I may justly be ridiculed for laboring to demonstrate *in re non dubià, testibus non*

necessariis.[12] Can you discern no good in this eternal ordinance of nature, the varieties of birth? If you cannot, as the facts are indisputable, you must assert that, so far as you can see, the world is ill made, and that the whole of mankind are miscreants. For there are no two of them born alike in any thing but divine right and moral liberty.

17. Please to remember that birth confers no right on one more than another! But birth naturally and unavoidably produces more influence in society, in some more than in others; and the superiority of influence in society, in some more than in others; and the superiority of influence is aristocracy.

18. When birth, genius, beauty, strength, wealth, education, fame, services, heroism, experience, unite in an individual, they produce inequality of influence, that is, aristocracy with a witness, so that one can chase a thousand, and two put ten thousand to flight in any political conflict; and without any hereditary descent, or any artificial marks, titles, or decorations, whatever.

XXVI.

In page 10, you say, "Mr. Adams has omitted a cause of aristocracy in the quotation, which he forgets not to urge in other places, namely,—exclusive wealth." This is your omission, sir, not mine. In page 109, vol. i. I expressly enumerated, "inequality of wealth" as one of the causes of aristocracy, and as having a natural and inevitable influence in society. I said nothing about "exclusive" wealth. The word "exclusive," is an interpolation of your own. This you acknowledge to be, "by much the most formidable with which mankind have to contend;" that is, as I understand you, superior wealth is the most formidable cause of aristocracy, or of superior influence in society. There may be some difficulty in determining the question, whether distinctions of birth, or distinctions of property, have the greatest influence in

---

[12] [In proving that no one can accomplish anything great without the help of others, the Stoic philosopher Panaetius calls upon "unnecessary witnesses in a matter that is not in doubt." Cicero, *On Duties* II, v, 16. Ed.]

the world? Both have very great influence, much too great, when not restrained by something besides the passions or the consciences of the possessors. Were I required to give an answer to the question, my answer would be, with some diffidence, that, in my opinion, taking into consideration history and experience, birth has had, and still has, most power and the greatest effects; because conspicuous birth is hereditary; it is derived from ancestors, descends to posterity, and is inalienable. Titles and ribbons, and stars and garters, and crosses and legal establishments, are by no means essential or necessary to the preservation of it. The evidences of it are in history and records, and in the memories and hearts they remain, and it never fails to descend to posterity as long as that posterity furnishes any one or more whose talents and virtues can support the reputation of the name. Birth and wealth are commonly so entangled together, from an emperor down to a constable or tithing-man, that it is difficult to separate them so distinctly as to place one in one scale, and the other in an opposite scale, to ascertain in grains and scruples the preponderance. The complaint of Theognis, that pelf is sometimes preferred to blood, was, and is true; and it is also true that beauty, wit, art, disposition, and "winning ways," are more successful than descent; yet, in general, I believe this prevails oftener than any of the others. I may be mistaken in this opinion; but of this I am certain; that it always has the same weight, when it is at all considered. You must recur, Mr. Taylor, to Plato's republic and the French republic, destroy all marriages, introduce a perfect community of women, render it impossible to know, or suspect, or conjecture one's own father or mother, son or daughter, brother or sister, uncle or aunt, before you can annihilate all distinctions of birth. I conclude, therefore, that birth has naturally and necessarily and unavoidably some influence, more or less, in human society. Will you say it has none? I have a right, sir, to an answer to this question, yea or nay. You have summoned me before the world and posterity, in my last hours, by your voluminous criticisms and ratiocinations, which gives me a right to demand fair play. On my part, I promise to answer any question you can state, by an affirmative, negative, or doubt, without equivocation. Property, wealth, riches, although you allow them to be a cause of aristocracy in your tenth page, yet you will not permit this cause to be "ascribed to nature." But why not? If, as I have heard, "the shortest road to men's hearts is down their throats," this is surely a natural route. Hunger and thirst are natural wants, and the supplies of them are natural. Nature has settled the point, that wood and stones shall not invigorate and enliven them like wine. Suppose one of your southern gentlemen to have only one hundred thousand acres of land. He settles one thousand tenants with families upon it. If he is a humane, easy, generous landlord, will not his tenants feel an attachment to him? will he not have influence among them? will they not naturally think and vote as he votes? If, on the contrary, he is an austere, griping, racking, rack-renting tyrant, will not his tenants be afraid to offend him? will not some, if not all of them, pretend to think with him, and vote as he would have them, upon the same principle as some nations have worshipped the devil, because they knew not into whose hands they might fall? Now, sir, my argument is this. If either the generous landlord or the selfish landlord can obtain by gratitude or fear only one vote more than his own from his tenants in general, he is an aristocrat, whether his vote and those of his dependents be beneficial or maleficial, salutary or pestilential, or fatal to the community.

I remember the time, Mr. Taylor, when one thousand families depended on Mr. Hancock for their daily bread; perhaps more. All men allowed him to be punctual, humane, generous. How many of the heads of these families would naturally be inclined to vote with and for Mr. Hancock? Could not Mr. Hancock command, or at least influence one vote, besides his own? If he could, he was an aristocrat, according to my definition and conscientious opinion. Let me appeal now to your own experience. Are there not in your own Caroline County, in Virginia, two or three, or four, five or six, eight or ten great planters, who, if united, can carry any point in your elections? These are every one of them aristocrats, and you, who are the first of them, are the most eminent aristocrat of them all.

XXVII.

GIVE me leave to add a few words on this topic. I remember the time when three gentlemen,—Thomas Hancock, Charles Apthorp, and

Thomas Green, the three most opulent merchants in Boston, all honorable, virtuous, and humane men,—if united, could have carried any election almost unanimously in the town of Boston.

Harrington, whom I read forty or fifty years ago, and shall quote from memory, being too old to hunt for books and fumble over the leaves of folios, has been called the Newton in politics, and is supposed to have made a great discovery, namely,—that mankind are governed by the teeth, and that dominion is founded on property in land. Mr. Locke and the French economists countenance this opinion. Landed gentlemen are generally not only aristocrats, but tories. What but commerce, manufactures, navigation, and naval power, supported by a moneyed interest, restrains them from establishing aristocracies or oligarchies, as absolute, arbitrary, oppressive, and cruel, as any monarchy ever was? What has annihilated the astonishing commerce and naval power of Holland, but the influence of the landed gentlemen in the inland provinces, overbearing and out-voting the maritime provinces? What is it that prevents France from reducing and restraining, if not annihilating, the commerce, manufactures, and naval power of Great Britain, but the landed gentry,—the proprietors of lands in France? Who never would suffer commerce, manufactures, or naval power to grow in that kingdom? Who would never permit Colbert or Necker to hold power, or even enjoy popularity, but with the moneyed interest? Yet these gentlemen could never be satisfied with the number of soldiers and land armies. No expense, no exertion to increase the number of officers and soldiers in the army could be too much. What has prevented our beloved country, to the astonishment of all Europe, from having at this hour a naval force amply sufficient to burn, sink, or destroy, or bring captive into our harbors, all the men of war that Britain has sent, or can send to our coasts, but the landed gentlemen, the great and little planters, the yeomen and farmers of the United States? Such it was in the beginning, is now, and, I fear, ever will be, world without end.

All these considerations prove the mighty influence of property in human affairs; they prove the influence of birth too; for landed property is hereditary generally all over the world. Truth, Mr. Taylor, cannot be ridiculed into error. Aristophanes could laugh Socrates out of his life, but not out of his merit or his fame. You seem to admit that "aristocracy is created by wealth," but you seem to think it is "artificially," not "naturally," so created. But if superior genius, birth, strength, and activity, naturally obtain superior wealth, and if superior wealth has naturally influence in society, where is the impropriety in calling the influence of wealth "natural?" I am not, however, bigoted to the epithet *natural;* and you may substitute the epithet "actual" in the place of it, if you think it worth while.

"Alienation," you say, "is the remedy for an aristocracy founded on landed wealth." But alienation only transfers the aristocracy from one hand to another. The aristocracy remains the same. If Brutus transfers to Cassius a villa or a principality purchased by the unrighteous profits of usury, Cassius becomes as influential an aristocrat as Brutus was before. If John Randolph should manumit one of his negroes and alienate to him his plantation, that negro would become as great an aristocrat as John Randolph. And the negro, John Randolph, Brutus, and Cassius, were, and are, and would be aristocrats of a scarlet color and a crimson dye, if they could. Alienation, therefore, is no remedy against an aristocracy founded on landed wealth.

You say, sir, that "inhibitions upon monopoly and incorporation are remedies for aristocracy founded on paper wealth." Here, sir, once for all, let me say, that you can write nothing too severe for me against "paper wealth." You may say, if you please, as Swift says of party, that it is the madness of the many for the profit of the few. You may call a swindler, a pickpocket, a pirate, a thief, or a robber, and I will not contradict you, nor dispute with you. But, sir, how will you obtain your "inhibitions upon monopoly and incorporation," when the few are craving and the many mad for the same thing? When democrats and aristocrats all unite, with perhaps only two or three exceptions, in urging these monopolies and incorporations to the last extremity, and when every man who opposes them is sure to be ruined? Paper wealth has been a source of aristocracy in this country, as well as landed wealth, with a vengeance. Witness the immense fortunes made *per saltum* by aristocratical speculations, both in land and paper. In human affairs, sir, we must consider what is practicable, as well as what is theoretical.

But, sir, land and paper are not the only sources of aristocracy. There are master shipwrights, housewrights, masons, &c. &c., who have each of them from twenty to a hundred families in their employment, and can carry a posse to the polls when they will. These are not only aristocrats, but a species of feudal barons. What are demagogues and popular orators, but aristocrats? John Cade and Wat Tyler were aristocrats. Callender and Paine were aristocrats. Shays and Fries were aristocrats. Mobs never follow any but aristocrats.

XXVIII.

KNOWLEDGE, you say, invented alienation, and became the natural enemy of aristocracy. This "invention" of knowledge was not very profound or ingenious. There are hundreds in the patent office more brilliant. The right, power, and authority of alienation are essential to property. If I own a snuffbox, I can burn it in the fire, cast it in a salt pond, crush it in atoms under a wagon wheel, or make a present of it to you,—which last alienation I should prefer to all the others,—or I could sell it to a peddler, or give it to a beggar. But, in either case, of gift or sale, would the aristocratical power of the snuffbox be lessened by alienation? Should a palatinate of Poland, or a prince of Russia, alienate his palatinate or his principality, with all the serfs attached to them, would not the buyer derive all the aristocratical influence from the purchase which the latter alienated by the sale? Should a planter in Virginia sell his *clarissimum el illustrissimum et celeberrimum locum*[13] with his thousand negroes, to a merchant, would not the merchant gain the aristocratical influence which the planter lost by his transfer? Run down, sir, through all the ranks of society, or, if you are shocked at the word *rank,* say all the classes, degrees, the ladder, the theatrical benches of society, from the first planter and the first merchant to the hog driver, the whiskey dramseller, or the Scottish peddler, and consider, whether the alienation of lands, wharves, stores, houses, funded stock, bank stock, bridge stock, canal stock, turnpike stock, or even lottery tick-

[13]["a most eminent and distinguished and glorious position" Ed.]

ets, does not transfer the aristocracy as well as the property. When the thirsty soul of a hundred acre man carries him to the whiskey shop till he has mortgaged all his acres, has he not transferred his aristocracy with them? I hope these hints, sir, have convinced you that alienation is not an adequate remedy against the aristocracy of property.

"Inhibitions upon monopoly and incorporation," you say, "are remedies for an aristocracy founded on paper wealth." And are such "inhibitions" your only hope against such an aristocracy? Have those principles of government which we have discovered, and those institutions which we have invented, which have established a "moral liberty" undiscovered and universal, uninvented by all nations before us, "inhibited monopolies and incorporations?" Is not every bank a monopoly? Are there not more banks in the United States than ever before existed in any nation under heaven? Are not these banks established by law upon a more aristocratical principle than any others under the sun? Are there not more legal corporations,—literary, scientifical, sacerdotal, medical, academical, scholastic, mercantile, manufactural, marine insurance, fire, bridge, canal, turnpike, &c. &c. &c.,—than are to be found in any known country of the whole world? Political conventions, caucuses, and Washington benevolent societies, biblical societies, and missionary societies, may be added,—and are not all these nurseries of aristocracy? If "alienations" and "inhibitions" fail us, where shall we look next for a remedy against aristocracy? Shall we have recourse, as you have done, page 9, to the art of printing? But this has not destroyed property or aristocracy or corporations or paper wealth in Europe or America, or diminished the influence of either; on the contrary, it has multiplied aristocracy and diminished democracy. I pray you, not to think this a paradox. You may hereafter be convinced, that it is a serious, a solemn, and melancholy truth. Admit that the press transferred the pontificate of Rome to Henry VIII. and to all the subsequent kings of England, even if you will, down to his present royal highness, the prince regent. Admit that the press demolished in some sort the feudal system, and set the serfs and villains free; admit that the press demolished the monasteries, nunneries, and religious houses; into whose hands did all these alienated baronies, monasteries, and religious houses and lands fall?

Into the hands of the democracy? into the hands of serfs and villains? Serfs and villains were the only real democracy in those times. No. They fell into the hands of other aristocrats, and there remain to this day, notwithstanding all the innumerable "alienations" and transfers from aristocrat to aristocrat to this hour. Admit, sir, that the press produced the reformation as well as the dissolution of the feudal system and the tenures in mortmain, what was the consequence? Two hundred years, at least, of thefts, larcenies, burglaries, robberies, murders, assassinations, such as no period of human history had before exhibited. The civil wars in England, the massacres in Ireland, the civil wars in France, and the massacre of Saint Bartholomew's day, all proceed from the same source, and so did the late French revolution; and the consequences are not ended, and cannot yet be foreseen. The real democracy of mankind has found very little alteration for the better or the worse through all these changes. The serfs of the barons or the church lands lived as well, and were as humanely treated, as the manufacturers or laborers are in England, France, Germany, or Spain, at this day. These are the real democracy of every nation and every age. These, who have either no vote at all, or at best but one vote, are the most numerous class in every society. Property in land, they have none; property in goods, besides their clothes, they have very little. When the national convention in France voted all the negroes in St. Domingo, Martinique, Guadaloupe, St. Lucia, &c., free, at a breath, did the poor democracy among the negroes gain any thing by the change? Did they not immediately fall into the power of aristocrats of their own color? Are they more free, from Toussaint to Petion and Christophe? Do they live better? Bananas and water they still enjoy, and a whole regiment would follow a leader who should hold a saltfish to their noses.

XXIX.

Suppose congress should, at one vote, or by one act, declare all the negroes in the United States free, in imitation of that great authority, the French sovereign legislature, what would follow? Would the democracy, nine in ten, among the negroes, be gainers? Would not the most shiftless among them be in danger of perishing for want? Would not nine in ten, perhaps ninety-nine in a hundred of the rest, petition their old aristocratical masters to receive them again, to protect them, to feed them, to clothe them, and to lodge and shelter them as usual? Would not some of the most thinking and philosophical among the aristocratical negroes ramble into distant states, seeking a poor and precarious subsistence by daily labor? Would not some of the most enterprising aristocrats allure a few followers into the wilderness, and become squatters? or, perhaps, incorporate with Indians? Would not others who have the courage of crimes,—"Le courage du crime,"—as well as of enterprise, collect little parties of followers, hide themselves in caves, behind rocks and mountains, in deep forests, or thick and boggy swamps, and commit inroads, depredations, and brigandages, as the villains did in Europe for ages, after the dissolution of fiefs and monasteries? Will the poor, simple, democratical part of the people gain any happiness by such a rash revolution?

I hope, sir, that all these considerations will convince you,—

1. That property has been, is, and everlastingly will be, a natural and unavoidable cause of aristocracy, and that God Almighty has made it such by the constitution of human nature and the globe, the land, the sea, the air, the water, and the fire, among which he has placed it.

2. That the advice which was given to me by a good deacon, in a quotation from an ancient divine, in the spring of 1774, after I was chosen to go to Congress,—"In all cases of difficulty and danger, when you know not what to do, be very careful that you do not do you know not what,"—was good advice. You and I have had to see the rise and progress, perfection, decline, and termination of hot, rash, blind, headlong, furious efforts to ameliorate the condition of society, to establish liberty, equality, fraternity, and the rights of man. And in what have they ended? *Festina lente! sobrius esto.*[14] Property makes a permanent distinction between aristocrats and democrats. There are many more persons in the world who have no property, than there are who have any; and, therefore, the democ-

---

[14] [The first two words are the emperor Augustus's motto, "make haste slowly." The last two words mean "be moderate." Ed.]

racy is, and will be, more numerous than the aristocracy. But we must remember that the art of printing, to which you appeal to level aristocracy, is almost entirely in the hands of the aristocracy. You resort to the press for the protection of democracy and the suppression of aristocracy! This, sir, in my humble opinion, is *"committere agnum lupo."*[15] It is to commit the lamb to the kind guardianship and protection of the wolf! a hungry wolf! a starving wolf! Emperors and kings and princes know the power of the press, at least as well, perhaps better, than you and I do. It is known to nobles and aristocrats of all shades, colors and denominations, much better than to democrats. It is known to domestic ministers and to foreign ambassadors, quite as well as to Duane, Benjamin Austin or John Randolph. Oxenstiern bid his son go among the ambassadors and ministers of state, to see by "what sort of men this world is governed." That sensible man might as sensibly have recommended to his son to go among the booksellers, the hireling scribblers, printers, and printers' devils. He might have more easily found how this lower world is governed. Half the expense would have let him into the secret. The gazettes, the journals, the newspapers, and fugitive pamphlets govern mankind at this day, and have governed, at least since the art of printing has become universal or even general. And what governors are these?

Here, Mr. Taylor, give me leave to relate an anecdote, which, upon honor, and, if you doubt, I will attest upon oath. There were times, when I had the honor to be in high favor with the Count de Vergennes, and to enjoy his confidence. I had found means to convey into English newspapers paragraphs and little essays, which he knew could come only from me. At his office, one morning, upon some particular business with him, he received me alone, and walked with me backwards and forwards in the most familiar conversation. "Mr. Adams," said the Count, "the gazettes, the journals govern the world. It is necessary that we should attend to them in all parts and in England; and I should be glad to communicate with you on this plan." You cannot conceive the impression these few

---

[15] ["To entrust a lamb to a wolf," an ancient proverb equivalent to the modern "setting a fox to guard the henhouse." Ed.]

words made upon me. I was dumb, but I said in my heart, "Monsieur le Comte, your spies have informed you, that I daily read the foreign gazettes, and that I have communicated some trifles in England; and I doubt not you know my channels of conveyance." The truth was, I daily read the foreign gazettes from Holland, Germany, England, and daily saw the hand of the Count de Vergennes and his office of interpreters of three hundred clerks, as I was told, skilled in the languages of all nations. I give you but a sketch, or rather a hint, of what would require volumes to explain at large. And I give you this hint merely, to convince you that ministers of state know the press as well as John Randolph or any other democrat, aristocrat, or mongrel.

XXX.

You remember I have reserved a right of employing twenty years to answer your book, because you consumed that number in writing it. I have now written you thirty letters, and have not advanced beyond a dozen pages of your work; at this rate, I must ask your indulgence for forty or fifty years more. You know that your amusement and my own are the principal objects that I have in view. My last was upon the power of the press and the influence of the art of printing; and I endeavored to convince you, that the great cause of democracy would not be exclusively promoted by that noble invention. It is certain that property is aristocracy, and that property commands the press. Think of this, sir! The types, the machinery, the office, the apprentices, the journeymen require a capital, and that capital is aristocracy. It does not appear that democracy has ever distinguished itself more than aristocracy, in zeal or exertion for the promotion of science, literature, the fine arts, or mechanic arts, not even the art of printing.

In ancient days, when all learning was in manuscript, it required a fortune to procure a small library. Books were in the hands of the rich. The Roman knights, with their gold rings, might have some knowledge; but the plebeians had none but such as they acquired from the actors on their theatres, and their popular orators in town meetings, all of whom were as proudly and vainly aristocratic, and nearly as flashy and as superficial, as your Baron of Roanoke. Will you call Terence and Epictetus and other Greek slaves, or the wandering sophists, the *Græci esurientes,* rambling about the world, like strolling players, to beg or earn a pitiful subsistence, democrats? Will you quote the rambling French dancing-masters, drawing-masters, fencing-masters, and grammarians, as democrats?

Have democrats been the promoters of science, arts, and literature? The aristocrat, monarchist, or tyrant, Pisistratus, his sons, &c., who assembled all the learned men of Greece to form a system of religion and government by the compilation of Homer, were not democrats. Alexander and Pericles, Themistocles and the Ptolemies, were not democrats. Augustus, nor Scipio, nor Lælius, were democrats. The Medici, who raised popes, emperors, queens, and kings, by the machinery of banks, were not democrats. Elizabeth, Anne, Louis XIV., Charles I., George III., Catherine, were not democrats. You may call Napoleon a democrat, if you will. These have been the great encouragers of arts and sciences and literature. But, perhaps, sir, I have rambled a little from the point. The question then is, concerning the influence of the art of printing, in diminishing aristocracy, and protecting, encouraging, supporting, increasing, and multiplying democracy. This subject will require volumes. My great misfortune, through a pretty long life, has been, that I have never had time to make my poor productions shorter. And I am more embarrassed now than ever, for I have neither eyes, nor fingers, nor clerks, nor secretaries, nor aids-de-camp, nor amanuenses, any more than time, at my command, to abridge and condense, or arrange and methodize any thing. Correction, revision,—*nonumque prematur in annum,*[16]—have all been forbidden fruit to me.

Has the art of printing increased democracy? It has humiliated kings; it has humiliated popes; it has demolished, in some degree, feudality and chivalry; it has promoted commerce and manufactures; agreed if you will, and sing *Io, triumphe,* if you will. But is democracy increased or bettered?

---

[16] [On an unfinished literary work: "Let it be locked up until the ninth year." Horace, *Art of Poetry* 388. Ed.]

Remember always, as we go along, that by democrats I mean exclusively those who are simple units, who have but one vote in society. How shall we decide this question? Have these simple units acquired property? Have they acquired knowledge? Do they live better? Are they become more temperate, more industrious, more frugal, more considerate? Run over all Europe, and see! In France, 24,500,000, who can neither read nor write; in England, Protestant as it is, not much less in proportion; nor in Holland, nor Germany, nor Russia, nor Italy, nor the peninsula of Spain and Portugal. Knowledge, in France, I may acknowledge, has been more spread and divided among the aristocracy of five hundred thousand aristocrats; but the democratical twenty-four million five hundred thousand have gained nothing. Bread and water, oatmeal and potatoes, are still their rations. The benevolence of Henry IV., and all his successors have never procured so much as a chicken in the pot once a week for the poor democrats. Depend upon it, unless you give a share in the sovereignty to the democrats, the more you increase knowledge in the nation, the more you will grind and gripe the democrats, till you reduce them to the calculations concerning West India negroes, Scottish and English coal-heavers, Dutch turf-lifters, and the street-walking girls of the night in Paris and London. For knowledge will forever be monopolized by the aristocracy. The moment you give knowledge to a democrat, you make him an aristocrat. If you give more than a share in the sovereignty to the democrats, that is, if you give them the command or preponderance in the sovereignty, that is, the legislature, they will vote all property out of the hands of you aristocrats, and if they let you escape with your lives, it will be more humanity, consideration, and generosity than any triumphant democracy ever displayed since the creation. And what will follow? The aristocracy among the democrats will take your places, and treat their fellows as severely and sternly as you have treated them. For every democracy and portion of democracy has an aristocracy in it as distinct as that of Rome, France, or England.

XXXI.

THAT the first want of man is his dinner, and the second his girl, were truths well known to every democrat and aristocrat, long before the great philosopher Malthus arose, to think he enlightened the world by the discovery.

It has been equally well known that the second want is frequently so impetuous as to make men and women forget the first, and rush into rash marriages, leaving both the first and second wants, their own as well as those of their children and grandchildren, to the chapter of accidents. The most religious very often leave the consideration of these wants to him who supplies the young ravens when they cry.

The natural, necessary, and unavoidable consequence of all this is, that the multiplication of the population so far transcends the multiplication of the means of subsistence, that the constant labor of nine tenths of our species will forever be necessary to prevent all of them from starving with hunger, cold, and pestilence. Make all men Newtons, or, if you will, Jeffersons, or Taylors, or Randolphs, and they would all perish in a heap!

Knowledge, therefore, sir, can never be equally divided among mankind, any more than property, real or personal, any more than wives or women.

> In pride, in reasoning pride, our error lies,
> All quit their sphere, and rush into the skies;
> Pride still is aiming at the blest abodes,
> Men would be angels, angels would be gods,
> Aspiring to be gods, if angels fell,
> Aspiring to be angels, men rebel.

The modern improvers of society,—ameliorators of the condition of mankind, instructors of the human species,—have assumed too much. They have not only condemned all the philosophy and policy of all ages of men, but they have undertaken to build a new universe, to ameliorate the system of eternal wisdom and benevolence. I wish, sir, that you would agree with me and my, and, I hope, your friends, Pope and Horace.

This vault of air, this congregated ball,
Self-centred sun, and stars that rise and fall,
There are, my friend, whose philosophic eyes
Look through, and trust the Ruler with his skies.
Hunc solem, et stellas, et decedentia certis
Tempora momentis, sunt qui formidine nullâ
Imbuti spectent.[17]

Turn our thoughts, in the next place, to the characters of learned men. The priesthood have, in all ancient nations, nearly monopolized learning. Read over again all the accounts we have of Hindoos, Chaldeans, Persians, Greeks, Romans, Celts, Teutons, we shall find that priests had all the knowledge, and really governed all mankind. Examine Mahometanism, trace Christianity from its first promulgation; knowledge has been almost exclusively confined to the clergy. And, even since the Reformation, when or where has existed a Protestant or dissenting sect who would tolerate A FREE INQUIRY? The blackest billingsgate, the most ungentlemanly insolence, the most yahooish brutality is patiently endured, countenanced, propagated, and applauded. But touch a solemn truth in collision with a dogma of a sect, though capable of the clearest proof, and you will soon find you have disturbed a nest, and the hornets will swarm about your legs and hands, and fly into your face and eyes.

When we are weary of looking at religion, we will, if you please, turn our eyes to government. Is there toleration in politics? Where shall we find it, if not in Virginia? The Honorable John Randolph informs us that, in consequence of the independence of his soul, he is on bad terms with the world; that his nerves are of too weak a fibre to bear the questions ordinary and extraordinary from our political inquisitors; talks of the rancorous hatred of the numerous enemies he has made in his course; and says, that the avenue to the public ear is shut against him in Virginia, where the press is under a virtual *imprimatur,* and where it would be easier to

---

[17] ["There are some who can look with no tinge of fear upon this sun, and the stars, and the seasons that pass in unvarying motion." Horace, *Epistles* I, vi, lines 3-5. Ed.]

force into circulation the treasurer's notes, than opinions militating against the administration, through the press. If these things are so in Virginia, sir, where Callender was applauded, nourished, cherished, and paid; where the great historian, Wood, who wrote and printed the elegant and classical History of the Administration of John Adams, was kindly received and employed; and where the sedition act, the gag law, was so unpopular; where can we look with any prospect or hope of finding a candid freedom of the press? The truth is, party opinions, interests, passions, and prejudices may be as decisive an *imprimatur* as that of a monarch; and the public opinion, which is not always right, until it is too late, is sometimes as arbitrary a prohibition as an *index expurgatorius*.[18] I hope it will be no offence to say, that public opinion is often formed upon imperfect, partial, and false information from the press. Public information cannot keep pace with facts. Knowledge cannot always accompany events. How many days intervene between a victory or a defeat, and the universal knowledge of it? How long do *we* wait for the result of a negotiation? How many erroneous public opinions are formed in the intervals? How long is a law enacted before the proclamation of it can reach the extremities of the nation?

XXXII.

A FEW words more concerning the characters of literary men. What sort of men have had the conduct of the presses in the United States for the last thirty years? In Germany, in England, in France, in Holland, the presses, even the newspapers, have been under the direction of learned men. How has it been in America? How many presses, how many newspapers have been directed by vagabonds, fugitives from a bailiff, a pillory, or a halter in Europe?

You know it is one of the sublimest and profoundest discoveries of the eighteenth century, that knowledge is corruption; that arts, sciences, and

---

[18] [The *Index Expurgatorius* of the Roman Catholic Church listed books that could not be read unless certain specified passages were omitted. Ed.]

taste have deformed the beauty and destroyed the felicity of human nature, which appears only in perfection in the savage state,—the children of nature. One writer gravely tells us that the first man who fenced a tobacco yard, and said, "this is mine," ought instantly to have been put to death; another as solemnly says, the first man who pronounced the word "dieu," ought to have been despatched on the spot; yet these are advocates of toleration and enemies of the Inquisition.[19]

I never had enough of the ethereal spirit to rise to these heights. My humble opinion is, that knowledge, upon the whole, promotes virtue and happiness. I therefore hope that you and all other gentlemen of property, education, and reputation will exert your utmost influence in establishing schools, colleges, academies, and universities, and employ every means and opportunity to spread information, even to the lowest dregs of the people, if any such there are, even among your own domestics and John Randolph's serfs. I fear not the propagation and dissemination of knowledge. The conditions of humanity will be improved and ameliorated by its expansion and diffusion in every direction. May every human being,—man, woman, and child,—be as well informed as possible! But, after all, did you ever see a rose without a briar, a convenience without an inconvenience, a good without an evil, in this mingled world? Knowledge is applied to bad purposes as well as to good ones. Knaves and hypocrites can acquire it, as well as honest, candid, and sincere men. It is employed as an engine and a vehicle to propagate error and falsehood, treason and vice, as well as truth, honor, virtue, and patriotism. It composes and pronounces, both panegyrics and philippics, with exquisite art, to confound all distinctions in society between right and wrong. And if I admit, as I do, that truth generally prevails, and virtue is, or will be triumphant in the end, you must allow that honesty has a hard struggle, and must prevail by many a well-fought and fortunate battle, and, after all, must often look to another world for justice, if not for pardon.

There is no necessary connection between knowledge and virtue. Simple intelligence has no association with morality. What connection is there

---

[19] *Vide* Rousseau and Diderot *passim.*

between the mechanism of a clock or watch and the feeling of moral good and evil, right or wrong? A faculty or a quality of distinguishing between moral good and evil, as well as physical happiness and misery, that is, pleasure and pain, or, in other words, a CONSCIENCE,—an old word almost out of fashion,—is essential to morality.

Now, how far does simple, theoretical knowledge quicken or sharpen conscience? La Harpe, in some part of his great work, his Course of Literature, has given us an account of a tribe of learned men and elegant writers, who kept a kind of office in Paris for selling at all prices, down to three livres, essays or paragraphs upon any subject, good or evil, for or against any party, any cause, or any person. One of the most conspicuous and popular booksellers in England, both with the courtiers and the citizens, who employed many printers and supported many writers, has said to me, "the men of learning in this country are stark mad. There are in this city a hundred men, gentlemen of liberal education, men of science, classical scholars, fine writers, whom I can hire at any time at a guinea a day, to write for me for or against any man, any party, or any cause." Can we wonder, then, at any thing we read in British journals, magazines, newspapers, or reviews?

Where are, and where have been, the greatest masses of science, of literature, or of taste? Shall we look for them in the church or the state, in the universities or the academies? among Greek or Roman philosophers, Hindoos, Brahmins, Chinese mandarins, Chaldean magi, British druids, Indian prophets, or Christian monks? Has it not been the invariable maxim of them all to deceive the people by any lies, however gross? "Bonus populus vult decipi; ergo decipiatur."[20]

And after all that can be done to disseminate knowledge, you never can equalize it. The number of laborers must, and will forever be so much more multitudinous than that of the students, that there will always be giants as well as pygmies, the former of which will have more influence than the latter; man for man, and head for head; and, therefore, the for-

---

[20] ["The worthy populace wants to be deceived; therefore let it be deceived." Ed.]

mer will be aristocrats, and the latter democrats, if not Jacobins or *sans culottes*.

These morsels, and a million others analogous to them, which will easily occur to you, if you will be pleased to give them a careful mastication and rumination, must, I think, convince you, that no practicable or possible advancement of learning can ever equalize knowledge among men to such a degree, that some will not have more influence in society than others; and, consequently, that some will always be aristocrats, and others democrats. You may read the history of all the universities, academies, monasteries of the world, and see whether learning extinguishes human passions or corrects human vices. You will find in them as many parties and factions, as much jealousy and envy, hatred and malice, revenge and intrigue, as you will in any legislative assembly or executive council, the most ignorant city or village. Are not the men of letters,—philosophers, divines, physicians, lawyers, orators, and poets,—all over the world, at perpetual strife with one another? Knowledge, therefore, as well as genius, strength, activity, industry, beauty, and twenty other things, will forever be a natural cause of aristocracy.

Three Letters
to
Roger Sherman
(1789)

By way of responding to Sherman's observations on the new Constitution, Adams sets forth his understanding of its nature and weaknesses. Sherman had been a staunch ally of Adams in pushing for independence, and he is the only Founding Father to have signed the Declaration of Independence, the Article of Confederation, and the Constitution.

Adams's response some twenty years later to a pamphlet urging constitutional amendments written by Mr. Hillhouse [see *Review*, pp 601-627] provides some interesting comparisons to the views expressed in these letters. These letters are taken from *Works*, VI, 427-36.

————

THREE LETTERS

TO

ROGER SHERMAN,

ON THE

CONSTITUTION OF THE UNITED STATES.

I.

Richmond Hill, (New York,) 17 July, 1789.

DEAR SIR,—I read over, with pleasure, your observations on the new federal constitution, and am glad to find an opportunity to communicate to you my opinion of some parts of them. It is by a free and amicable intercourse of sentiments, that the friends of our country may hope for such a unanimity of opinion and such a concert of exertions, as may sooner or later produce the blessings of good government.

You say, "it is by some objected that the executive is blended with the legislature, and that those powers ought to be entirely distinct and unconnected. But is not that a gross error in politics? The united wisdom and various interests of a nation should be combined in framing the laws by which all are to be governed and protected, though it should not be convenient to have them executed by the whole legislature. The supreme executive in Great Britain is one branch of the legislature, and has a negative on all the laws; perhaps that is an extreme not to be imitated by a republic; but the negative vested in the president by the new constitution on the acts of congress, and the consequent revision, may be very useful to prevent laws being passed without mature deliberation, and to preserve stability in the administration of government; and the concurrence of the senate in the appointment to office will strengthen the hands of the executive, and secure the confidence of the people much better than a select council, and will be less expensive."

Is it, then, "an extreme not to be imitated by a republic," to make the supreme executive a branch of the legislature, and give it a negative on all the laws? If you please, we will examine this position, and see whether it is well founded. In the first place, what is your definition of a republic? Mine is this: *A government whose sovereignty is vested in more than one person.* Governments are divided into *despotisms, monarchies,* and *republics.* A despotism is a government in which the three divisions of power, the legislative, executive and judicial, are all vested in one man. A monarchy is a government where the legislative and executive are vested in one man, but the judicial in other men. In all governments the sovereignty is vested in that man or body of men who have the legislative power. In despotisms and monarchies, therefore, the legislative authority being in one man, the sovereignty is in one man. In republics, as the sovereignty, that is, the legislative, is always vested in more than one, it may be vested in as many more as you please. In the United States it might be vested in two persons, or in three millions, or in any other intermediate number; and in every such supposable case the government would be a republic. In conformity to these ideas, republics have been divided into three species, monarchical, aristocratical, and democratical republics. England is a republic, a monarchical republic it is true, but a republic still; because the sovereignty, which is the legislative power, is vested in more than one man; it is equally divided, indeed, between the one, the few, and the many, or in other words, between the natural division of mankind in society,—the monarchical, the aristocratical, and democratical. It is essential to a monarchical republic, that the supreme executive should be a branch of the legislature, and have a negative on all the laws. I say essential, because if monarchy were not an essential part of the sovereignty, the government would not be a monarchical republic. Your position is therefore clearly and certainly an error, because the practice of Great Britain in making the supreme executive a branch of the legislature, and giving it a negative on all the laws, must be imitated by every monarchical republic.

I will pause here, if you please; but if you will give me leave, I will write another letter or two upon this subject. Meantime I am, with unalterable friendship, yours.

II.

DEAR SIR,—In my letter of yesterday I think it was demonstrated that the English government is a republic, and that the regal negative upon the laws is essential to that republic. Because, without it, that government would not be what it is, a monarchical republic; and, consequently, could not preserve the balance of power between the executive and legislative powers, nor that other balance which is in the legislature,—between the one, the few, and the many; in which two balances the excellence of that form of government must consist.

Let us now inquire, whether the new constitution of the United States is or is not a monarchical republic, like that of Great Britain. The monarchical and the aristocratical power in our constitution, it is true, are not hereditary; but this makes no difference in the nature of the power, in the nature of the balance, or in the name of the species of government. It would make no difference in the power of a judge or justice, or general or admiral, whether his commission were for life or years. His authority during the time it lasted, would be the same whether it were for one year or twenty, or for life, or descendible to his eldest son. The people, the nation, in whom all power resides originally, may delegate their power for one year or for ten years; for years, or for life; or may delegate it in fee simple or fee tail, if I may so express myself; or during good behavior, or at will, or till further orders.

A nation might unanimously create a dictator or a despot, for one year or more, or for life, or for perpetuity with hereditary descent. In such a case, the dictator for one year would as really be a dictator for the time his power lasted, as the other would be whose power was perpetual and descendible. A nation in the same manner might create a simple monarchy for years, life, or perpetuity, and in either case the creature would be equally a simple monarch during the continuance of his power. So the people of England might create king, lords, and commons, for a year, or for several years, or for life, and in any of these cases, their government would be a monarchical republic, or, if you will, a limited monarchy, during its continuance, as much as it is now, when the king and nobles are hereditary. They might make their house of commons hereditary too. What the consequence of this would be it is easy to foresee; but it would not in the first moment make any change in the legal power, nor in the name of the government.

Let us now consider what our constitution is, and see whether any other name can with propriety be given it, than that of a monarchical republic, or if you will, a limited monarchy. The duration of our president is neither perpetual nor for life; it is only for four years; but his power during those four years is much greater than that of an avoyer, a consul, a podestà, a doge, a stadtholder; nay, than a king of Poland; nay, than a king of Sparta. I know of no first magistrate in any republican government, excepting England and Neuchatel, who possesses a constitutional dignity, authority, and power comparable to his. The power of sending and receiving ambassadors, of raising and commanding armies and navies, of nominating and appointing and commissioning all officers, of managing the treasures, the internal and external affairs of the nation; nay, the whole executive power, coextensive with the legislative power, is vested in him, and he has the right, and his is the duty, to take care that the laws be faithfully executed. These rights and duties, these prerogatives and dignities, are so transcendent that they must naturally and necessarily excite in the nation all the jealousy, envy, fears, apprehensions, and opposition, that are so constantly observed in England against the crown.[1]

That these powers are necessary, I readily admit. That the laws cannot be executed without them; that the lives, liberties, properties and characters of the citizens cannot be secure without their protection, is most clear. But it is equally certain, I think, that they ought to have been still greater, or much less. The limitations upon them in the cases of war, treaties, and appointments to office, and especially the limitation on the president's independence as a branch of the legislative, will be the destruction of this constitution, and involve us in anarchy, if not amended. I shall pass over all particulars for the present, except the last; because that is now the point in dispute between you and me. Longitude, and the philosopher's stone, have not been sought with more earnestness by philosophers than a guardian of the laws has been studied by legislators from Plato to Montesquieu; but every project has been found to be no better than committing the lamb to the custody of the wolf, except that one which is called a *balance of power.* A simple sovereignty in one, a few, or many, has no balance, and therefore no laws. A divided sovereignty without a balance, or in other words, where the division is unequal, is always at war, and consequently has no laws. In our constitution the sovereignty,—that is, the legislative power,—is divided into three branches. The house and senate are equal, but the third branch, though essential, is not equal. The president

[1] M. de Tocqueville has taken a similar view of the President's powers:—

"Le président des États-Unis possède des prérogatives presque royales, dont il n'a pas l'occasion de se servir; et les droits dont jusqu'à présent il peut user sont très circonscrits; *les lois lui permettent d'être fort, les circonstances le maintiennent foible.*" *De la Démocratie en Amérique,* vol. i. chap. 8. ["The President of the United States has almost royal prerogatives, which he does not have the opportunity to exercise; and the rights that he can make use of are at present very limited; the law allows him to be strong, but circumstances keep him weak." Ed.]

must pass judgment upon every law; but in some cases his judgment may be overruled. These cases will be such as attack his constitutional power; it is, therefore, certain he has not equal power to defend himself, or the constitution, or the judicial power, as the senate and house have.

Power naturally grows. Why? Because human passions are insatiable. But that power alone can grow which already is too great; that which is unchecked; that which has no equal power to control it. The legislative power, in our constitution, is greater than the executive; it will, therefore, encroach, because both aristocratical and democratical passions are insatiable. The legislative power will increase, the executive will diminish. In the legislature, the monarchical power is not equal either to the aristocratical or democratical; it will, therefore, decrease, while the other will increase. Indeed, I think the aristocratical power is greater than either the monarchical or democratical. That will, therefore, swallow up the other two.

In my letter of yesterday, I think it was proved, that a republic might make the supreme executive an integral part of the legislature. In this, it is equally demonstrated, as I think, that our constitution ought to be amended by a decisive adoption of that expedient. If you do not forbid me, I shall write to you again.

III.

DEAR SIR,—There is a sense and degree in which the executive, in our constitution, is blended with the legislature. The president has the power of suspending a law; of giving the two houses an opportunity to pause, to think, to collect themselves, to reconsider a rash step of a majority. He has a right to urge all his reasons against it, by speech or message; which, becoming public, is an appeal to the nation. But the rational objection here is, not that the executive is blended with the legislature, but that it is not enough blended; that it is not incorporated with it, and made an essential part of it. If it were an integral part of it, it might negative a law without much noise, speculation, or confusion among the people. But as it now stands, I beg you to consider it is almost impossible, that a president should ever have the courage to make use of his partial negative. What a situation would a president be in to maintain a controversy against a majority of both houses before a tribunal of the public? To put a stop to a law that more than half the senate and house, and consequently, we may suppose more than half the nation, have set their hearts upon?[2] It is, moreover, possible, that more than two thirds of the nation, the senate, and house, may, in times of calamity, distress, misfortune, and ill success of the measures of government, from the momentary passion and enthusiasm, demand a law which will wholly subvert the constitution. The constitution of Athens was overturned in such a manner by Aristides himself. The constitution should guard against a possibility of its subversion; but we may take stronger ground, and assert that it is probable such cases will happen, and that the constitution will, in fact, be subverted in this way. Nay, I go further, and say, that from the constitution of human nature, and the constant course of human affairs, it is certain that our constitution will be subverted, if not amended, and that in a very short time, merely for want of a decisive negative in the executive.

There is another sense and another degree in which the executive is blended with the legislature, which is liable to great and just objection; which excites alarms, jealousies, and apprehensions, in a very great degree. I mean, 1st, the negative of the senate upon appointments to office; 2d. the negative of the senate upon treaties; and 3d. the negative of the two houses upon war. I shall confine myself, at present, to the first. The negative of the senate upon appointments is liable to the following objections:—

1. It takes away, or, at least, it lessens the responsibility of the executive. Our constitution obliges me to say, that it lessens the responsibility of the president. The blame of an injudicious, weak, or wicked appointment, is shared so much between him and the senate, that his part of it will be too small. Who can censure him, without censuring the senate, and the legislatures who appoint them? All their friends will be interested to vindicate the president, in order to screen them from censure. Besides, if an

---

[2] Thus far, this has not been found so difficult as was here predicted. But it must be admitted that the occasions in which the negative has been exercised, were not of a kind in which the popular passions are greatly excited.

impeachment against an officer is brought before them, are they not interested to acquit him, lest some part of the odium of his guilt should fall upon them, who advised to his appointment?

2. It turns the minds and attention of the people to the senate, a branch of the legislature, in executive matters. It interests another branch of the legislature in the management of the executive. It divides the people between the executive and the senate; whereas, all the people ought to be united to watch the executive, to oppose its encroachments, and resist its ambition. Senators and representatives, and their constituents, in short, the aristocratical and democratical divisions of society ought to be united on all occasions to oppose the executive or the monarchical branch, when it attempts to overleap its limits. But how can this union be effected, when the aristocratical branch has pledged its reputation to the executive, by consenting to an appointment?

3. It has a natural tendency to excite ambition in the senate. An active, ardent spirit, who is rich and able, and has a great reputation and influence, will be solicited by candidates for office. Not to introduce the idea of bribery, because, though it certainly would force itself in, in other countries, and will probably here, when we grow populous and rich, it is not yet to be dreaded, I hope, ambition must come in already. A senator of great influence will be naturally ambitious and desirous of increasing his influence. Will he not be under a temptation to use his influence with the president as well as his brother senators, to appoint persons to office in the several states, who will exert themselves in elections, to get out his enemies or opposers, both in senate and house of representatives, and to get in his friends, perhaps his instruments? Suppose a senator to aim at the treasury office for himself, his brother, father, or son. Suppose him to aim at the president's chair, or vice-president's, at the next election, or at the office of war, foreign, or domestic affairs. Will he not naturally be tempted to make use of his whole patronage, his whole influence, in advising to appointments, both with president and senators, to get such persons nominated as will exert themselves in elections of president, vice-president, senators, and house of representatives, to increase his interest and promote his views? In this point of view, I am very apprehensive that this

defect in our constitution will have an unhappy tendency to introduce corruption of the grossest kinds, both of ambition and avarice, into
all our elections, and this will be the worst of poisons to our constitution. It will not only destroy the present form of government, but render
it almost impossible to substitute in its place any free government, even a
better limited-monarchy, or any other than a despotism or a simple
monarchy.

4. To avoid the evil under the last head, it will be in danger of dividing
the continent into two or three nations, a case that presents no prospect
but of perpetual war.

5. This negative on appointments is in danger of involving the senate
in reproach, censure, obloquy, and suspicion, without doing any good. Will
the senate use their negative or not? If not, why should they have it? Many
will censure them for not using it; many will ridicule them, and call them
servile, &c. If they do use it, the very first instance of it will expose the senators to the resentment of not only the disappointed candidate and all his
friends, but of the president and all his friends, and these will be most of
the officers of government, through the nation.

6. We shall very soon have parties formed; a court and country party,
and these parties will have names given them. One party in the house of
representatives will support the president and his measures and ministers;
the other will oppose them. A similar party will be in the senate; these parties will study with all their arts, perhaps with intrigue, perhaps with corruption, at every election to increase their own friends and diminish their
opposers. Suppose such parties formed in the senate, and then consider
what factious divisions we shall have there upon every nomination.

7. The senate have not time. The convention and Indian treaties.[3]

You are of opinion "that the concurrence of the senate in the appointments to office, will strengthen the hands of the executive, and secure the
confidence of the people, much better than a select council, and will be
less expensive."

---

[3] This seems to be an imperfect sentence. The sense is explained at the close of the
letter.

But in every one of these ideas, I have the misfortune to differ from you.

It will weaken the hands of the executive, by lessening the obligation, gratitude, and attachment of the candidate to the president, by dividing his attachment between the executive and legislative, which are natural enemies. Officers of government, instead of having a single eye and undivided attachment to the executive branch, as they ought to have, consistent with law and the constitution, will be constantly tempted to be factious with their factious patrons in the senate. The president's own officers, in a thousand instances, will oppose his just and constitutional exertions, and screen themselves under the wings of their patrons and party in the legislature.[4] Nor will it secure the confidence of the people. The people will have more confidence in the executive, in executive matters, than in the senate. The people will be constantly jealous of factious schemes in the senators to unduly influence the executive, to serve each other's private views. The people will also be jealous that the influence of the senate will be employed to conceal, connive at, and defend guilt in executive officers, instead of being a guard and watch upon them, and a terror to them. A council, selected by the president himself, at his pleasure, from among the senators, representatives, and nation at large, would be purely responsible. In that case, the senate would be a terror to privy counsellors; its honor would never be pledged to support any measure or instrument of the executive beyond justice, law, and the constitution. Nor would a privy council be more expensive. The whole senate must now deliberate on every appointment, and if they ever find time for it, you will find that a great deal of time will be required and consumed in this service. Then, the president might have a constant executive council; now, he has none.

I said, under the seventh head, that the senate would not have time. You will find that the whole business of this government will be infinitely delayed by this negative of the senate on treaties and appointments. Indian treaties and consular conventions have been already waiting for months, and the senate have not been able to find a moment of time to

---

[4] A singular prediction of what actually happened, afterwards, to himself.

attend to them; and this evil must constantly increase. So that the senate must be constantly sitting, and must be paid as long as they sit....

But I have tired your patience. Is there any truth in these broken hints and crude surmises, or not? To me they appear well founded and very important.

I am, with usual affection, yours,
JOHN ADAMS.

III

Essays, Letters,
and
Other Works

Essays
(1763)

THE three Essays that follow, are the earliest printed productions known to have come from Mr. Adams. In a letter dated in 1819, he says, "There were many flickerings in the newspapers between Mr. Sewall and me, the precise dates of which I cannot recollect. Sewall wrote under the signature of Philanthropos sometimes, and at other times under the signature of a long J.; and I wrote under that of a great U., and, perhaps, other signatures that I do not remember. All these trifles of mine were printed in the Boston Gazette. There were several papers written by me on occasion of the assault of Colonel Murray upon General Brattle, on the council stairs of the old town house."

The first and third papers relate to this event, which caused some excitement at the moment, and led to a legal prosecution that continued it. All three bear the peculiar mental and moral characteristics of the author, and are therefore preserved.

Charles Francis Adams

The *Essays* are taken from *Works,* III, 427-44.

———

NO. I.[1]

On Private Revenge.

MAN is distinguished from other animals, his fellow inhabitants of this planet, by a capacity of acquiring knowledge and civility, more than by any excellency, corporeal, or mental, with which mere nature has furnished his species. His erect figure and sublime countenance would give him but little elevation above the bear or the tiger; nay, notwithstanding those advantages, he would hold an inferior rank in the scale of being, and would have a worse prospect of happiness than those creatures, were it not for the capacity of uniting with others, and availing himself of arts and inventions in social life. As he comes originally from the hands of his Creator, self-love or self-preservation is the only spring that moves within him; he might crop the leaves or berries with which his Creator had surrounded him, to satisfy his hunger; he might sip at the lake or rivulet to slake his thirst; he might screen himself behind a rock or mountain from the bleakest of the winds; or he might fly from the jaws of voracious beasts to preserve himself from immediate destruction. But would such an existence be worth preserving? Would not the first precipice or the first beast of prey that could put a period to the wants, the frights, and horrors of such a wretched being, be a friendly object and a real blessing?

When we take one remove from this forlorn condition, and find the species propagated, the banks of clams and oysters discovered, the bow and arrow invented, and the skins of beasts or the bark of trees employed for covering,—although the human creature has a little less anxiety and misery than before, yet each individual is independent of all others. There is no intercourse of friendship; no communication of food or clothing; no conversation or connection, unless the conjunction of sexes, prompted by instinct, like that of hares and foxes, may be called so. The ties of parent, son, and brother, are of little obligation. The relations of master and servant, the distinction of magistrate and subject, are totally unknown. Each individual is his own sovereign, accountable to no other upon earth, and pun-

[1] From the Boston Gazette, No. 435, 1 August, 1763.

ishable by none. In this savage state, courage, hardiness, activity, and strength, the virtues of their brother brutes, are the only excellencies to which men can aspire. The man who can run with the most celerity, or send the arrow with the greatest force, is the best qualified to procure a subsistence. Hence, to chase a deer over the most rugged mountain, or to pierce him at the greatest distance, will be held, of all accomplishments, in the highest estimation. Emulations and competitions for superiority in such qualities, will soon commence; and any action which may be taken for an insult, will be considered as a pretension to such superiority; it will raise resentment in proportion, and shame and grief will prompt the savage to claim satisfaction or to take revenge. To request the interposition of a third person to arbitrate between the contending parties, would be considered as an implicit acknowledgment of deficiency in those qualifications, without which, none in such a barbarous condition would choose to live. Each one, then, must be his own avenger. The offended parties must fall to fighting. Their teeth, their nails, their feet, or fists, or, perhaps, the first club or stone that can be grasped, must decide the contest, by finishing the life of one. The father, the brother, or the friend, begins then to espouse the cause of the deceased; not, indeed, so much from any love he bore him living, or from any grief he suffers for him dead, as from a principle of bravery and honor, to show himself able and willing to encounter the man who had just before vanquished another. Hence arises the idea of an avenger of blood, and thus the notions of revenge, and the appetite for it grow apace. Every one must avenge his own wrongs when living, or else lose his reputation, and his near relation must avenge them for him after he is dead, or forfeit his. Indeed, nature has implanted in the human heart a disposition to resent an injury when offered; and this disposition is so strong, that even the horse treading by accident on a gouty toe, or a brickbat falling on the shoulders, in the first twinges of pain, seems to excite the angry passions, and we feel an inclination to kill the horse and to break the brickbat. Consideration, however, that the horse and brick were without design, will cool us; whereas the thought that any mischief has been done on purpose to abuse, raises revenge in all its strength and terrors; and the man feels the sweetest, highest gratification, when he inflicts the punishment himself. From this source arises the ardent desire in men to judge for themselves, when, and to what degree they are injured, and to carve out their own remedies for themselves. From the same source arises that obstinate disposition in barbarous nations to continue barbarous, and the extreme difficulty of introducing civility and Christianity among them. For the great distinction between savage nations and polite ones, lies in this,—that among the former every individual is his own judge and his own executioner; but among the latter all pretensions to judgment and punishment are resigned to tribunals erected by the public; a resignation which savages are not, without infinite difficulty, persuaded to make, as it is of a right and privilege extremely dear and tender to an uncultivated nature.

To exterminate from among mankind such revengeful sentiments and tempers, is one of the highest and most important strains of civil and humane policy. Yet the qualities which contribute most to inspire and support them may, under certain regulations, be indulged and encouraged. Wrestling, running, leaping, lifting, and other exercises of strength, hardiness, courage, and activity, may be promoted among private soldiers, common sailors, laborers, manufacturers, and husbandmen, among whom they are most wanted, provided sufficient precautions are taken that no romantic, cavalier-like principles of honor intermix with them, and render a resignation of the right of judging, and the power of executing, to the public, shameful. But whenever such notions spread so inimical to the peace of society, that boxing, clubs, swords, or firearms, are resorted to for deciding every quarrel, about a girl, a game at cards, or any little accident that wine or folly or jealousy may suspect to be an affront,—the whole power of the government should be exerted to suppress them.

If a time should ever come when such notions shall prevail in this Province to a degree, that no privileges shall be able to exempt men from indignities and personal attacks, not the privilege of a counsellor, nor the privilege of a House of Representatives of "speaking freely in that assembly, without impeachment or question in any court or place," out of the General Court—when whole armed mobs shall assault a member of the House, when violent attacks shall be made upon counsellors, when no place shall be sacred, not the very walls of legislation, when no personages shall overawe, not the whole General Court added to all the other gentlemen on 'Change, when the broad noon-day shall be chosen to display before the world such high, heroic sentiments of gallantry and spirit, when such assailants shall live unexpelled from the legislature, when slight censures and no punishments shall be inflicted,—there will really be danger of our becoming universally ferocious, barbarous, and brutal, worse than our Gothic ancestors before the Christian era.

The doctrine, that the person assaulted "should act with spirit," "should defend himself by drawing his sword and killing, or by wringing noses, and boxing it out with the offender," is the tenet of a coxcomb and the sentiment of a brute. The fowl upon the dunghill, to be sure, feels a most gallant and heroic spirit at the crowing of another, and instantly spreads his cloak, and prepares for combat. The bull's wrath enkindles into a noble rage, and the stallion's immortal spirit can never forgive the pawings, neighings, and defiances of his rival. But are cocks and bulls and horses the proper exemplars for the imitation of men, especially of men of sense, and even of the highest personages in the government!

Such ideas of gallantry have been said to be derived from the army. But it was injuriously said, because not truly. For every gentleman, every man of sense and breeding in the army, has a more delicate and manly way of thinking, and from his heart despises all such little, narrow, sordid notions. It is true that a competition, and a mutual affectation of contempt, is apt to arise among the lower, more ignorant, and despicable, of every rank and order in society. This sort of men, (and some few such there are in every profession,) among divines, lawyers, physicians, as well as husbandmen, manufacturers, and laborers, are prone, from a certain littleness of mind, to imagine that their labors alone are of any consequence to the world, and to affect a contempt for all others. It is not unlikely, then, that the lowest and most despised sort of soldiers may have expressed a contempt for all other orders of mankind, may have indulged a disrespect to every personage in a civil character, and have acted upon such principles of revenge, rusticity, barbarity, and brutality, as have been above described. And, indeed, it has been observed by the great Montesquieu, that "From a manner of thinking that prevails among mankind," (the most ignorant and despicable of mankind, he means,) "they set a higher value upon courage than timorousness, on activity than prudence, on strength than counsel. Hence, the army will ever despise a senate, and respect their own officers; they will naturally slight the orders sent them by a body of men whom they look upon as cowards, and therefore unworthy to command them." This respect to their own officers, which produces a contempt of senates and councils, and of all laws, orders, and constitutions, but those of the army and their superior officers, though it may have prevailed among some soldiers of the illiberal character above described, is far from being universal. It is not found in one gentleman of sense and breeding in the whole service. All of this character know that the common law of England is superior to all other laws, martial or common, in every English government, and has often asserted triumphantly its own preëminence against the insults and encroachments of a giddy and unruly soldiery. They know, too, that civil officers in England hold a great superiority to military officers, and that a frightful despotism would be the speedy consequence of the least alteration in these particulars. And, knowing this, these gentlemen, who have so often exposed their lives in defence of the religion, the liberties, and rights of men and Englishmen, would feel the utmost indignation at the doctrine which should make the civil power give place to the military, which should make a respect to their superior officers destroy or diminish their obedience to civil magistrates, or which should give any man a right in conscience, honor, or even in punctilio and delicacy, to neglect the institutions of the public, and seek his own remedy for wrongs and injuries of any kind.

NO. II.

On Self-Delusion

TO THE PRINTERS.[2]

My worthy and ingenious friend, Mr. J., having strutted his hour upon the stage, and acquired as well as deserved a good reputation, as a man of sense and learning, some time since made his exit, and now is heard no more.

[2] From the Boston Gazette, No. 439, 29 August, 1763.

Soon after Mr. J.'s departure, your present correspondent made his appearance, but has not yet executed his intended plan. Mr. J. enlisted himself under the banners of a faction, and employed his agreeable pen in the propagation of the principles and prejudices of a party, and for this purpose he found himself obliged to exalt some characters, and depress others, equally beyond the truth. The greatest and best of all mankind deserve less admiration, and even the worst and vilest deserve more candor, than the world in general is willing to allow them. The favorites of parties, although they have always some virtues, have always many imperfections. Many of the ablest tongues and pens have, in every age, been employed in the foolish, deluded, and pernicious flattery of one set of partisans, and in furious, prostitute invectives against another; but such kinds of oratory never had any charms for me; and if I must do one or the other, I would quarrel with both parties and with every individual of each, before I would subjugate my understanding, or prostitute my tongue or pen to either.

To divert men's minds from subjects of vain curiosity, or unprofitable science, to the useful, as well as entertaining speculations of agriculture; to eradicate the Gothic and pernicious principles of private revenge that have been lately spread among my countrymen, to the debasement of their character, and to the frequent violation of the public peace, and to recommend a careful attention to political measures, and a candid manner of reasoning about them, instead of abusive insolence or uncharitable imputations upon men and characters, has, since I first undertook the employment of entertaining the public, been my constant and invariable view. The difficulty or impracticability of succeeding in my enterprise, has often been objected to me by my friends; but even this has not wholly disheartened me. I own it would be easier to depopulate a province, or subvert a monarchy, to transplant a nation, or enkindle a new war; and that I should have a fairer prospect of success in such designs as those. But my consolation is this,—that if I am unable by my writings to effect any good purpose, I never will subserve a bad one. If engagements to a party are necessary to make a fortune, I had rather make none at all; and spend the remainder of my days like my favorite author, that ancient and immortal husbandman, philosopher, politician, and general, Xenophon, in his retreat, considering kings and princes as shepherds, and their people and subjects like flocks and herds, or as mere objects of contemplation and parts of a curious machine in which I had no interest, than to wound my own mind by engaging in any party, and spreading prejudices, vices, or follies. Notwithstanding this, I remember the monkish maxim,—*fac officium taliter qualiter, sed sta bene cum priore;*[3] and it is impossible to stand well with the abbot without fighting for his cause through *fas* and *nefas.*[4]

Please to insert the foregoing and following, which is the last deviation I purpose to make from my principal and favorite views of writing on husbandry and mechanic arts.

THERE is nothing in the science of human nature more curious, or that deserves a critical attention from every order of men so much, as that principle which moral writers have distinguished by the name of self-deceit. This principle is the spurious offspring of self-love; and is, perhaps, the source of far the greatest and worst part of the vices and calamities among mankind.

The most abandoned minds are ingenious in contriving excuses for their crimes, from constraint, necessity, the strength or suddenness of temptation, or the violence of passion, which serve to soften the remordings of their own consciences, and to render them by degrees insensible equally to the charms of virtue and the turpitude of vice. What multitudes in older countries discover, even while they are suffering deservedly the most infamous and terrible of civil punishments, a tranquillity and even a magnanimity like that which we may suppose in a real patriot dying to preserve his country! Happy would it be for the world if the fruits of this pernicious principle were confined to such profligates. But, if we look abroad, shall we not see the most modest, sensible, and virtuous of the common people, almost every hour of their lives, warped and blinded by

---

[3] ["Do your duty as you should, but stand well (= stay on good terms) with the prior." Ed.]

[4] ["the permissible and the forbidden" Ed.]

the same disposition to flatter and deceive themselves? When they think themselves injured by any foible or vice in others, is not this injury always seen through the magnifying end of the perspective? When reminded of any such imperfection in themselves, by which their neighbors or fellow-citizens are sufferers, is not the perspective instantly reversed? Insensible of the beams in our own eyes, are we not quick in discerning motes in those of others? Nay, however melancholy it may be, and how humbling soever to the pride of the human heart, even the few favorites of nature, who have received from her clearer understandings and more happy tempers than other men, who seem designed, under Providence, to be the great conductors of the art and science, the war and peace, the laws and religion of this lower world, are often snared by this unhappy disposition in their minds, to their own destruction, and the injury, nay, often to the utter desolation of millions of their fellow-men. Since truth and virtue, as the means of present and future happiness, are confessed to be the only objects that deserve to be pursued, to what imperfection in our nature, or unaccountable folly in our conduct, excepting this of which we have been speaking, can mankind impute the multiplied diversity of opinions, customs, laws, and religions that have prevailed, and are still triumphant, in direct opposition to both? From what other source can such fierce disputations arise concerning the two things which seem the most consonant to the entire frame of human nature?

Indeed, it must be confessed, and it ought to be with much contrition lamented, that those eyes, which have been given us to see, are willingly suffered by us to be obscured, and those consciences, which by the commission of God Almighty have a rightful authority over us, to be deposed by prejudices, appetites, and passions, which ought to hold a much inferior rank in the intellectual and moral system. Such swarms of passions, avarice and ambition, servility and adulation, hopes, fears, jealousies, envy, revenge, malice, and cruelty, are continually buzzing in the world and we are so extremely prone to mistake the impulses of these for the dictates of our consciences,—that the greatest genius, united to the best disposition, will find it hard to hearken to the voice of reason, or even to be certain of the purity of his own intentions.

From this true, but deplorable condition of mankind, it happens that no improvements in science or literature, no reformation in religion or morals, nor any rectification of mistaken measures in government, can be made without opposition from numbers, who, flattering themselves that their own intentions are pure, (how sinister soever they may be in fact) will reproach impure designs to others, or, fearing a detriment to their interest or a mortification to their passions from the innovation, will even think it lawful directly and knowingly to falsify the motives and characters of the innocent.

Vain ambition and other vicious motives were charged by the sacred congregation upon Galileo, as the causes of his hypothesis concerning the motion of the earth, and charged so often and with so many terms, as to render the old man at last suspicious, if not satisfied, that the charge was true, though he had been led to this hypothesis by the light of a great genius and deep researches into astronomy. Sedition, rebellion, pedantry, desire of fame, turbulence, and malice, were always reproached to the great reformers, who delivered us from the worst chains that were ever forged by monks or devils for the human mind. Zosimus and Julian could easily discover or invent anecdotes to dishonor the conversion of Constantine, and his establishment of Christianity in the empire.

For these reasons we can never be secure in a resignation of our understandings, or in confiding enormous power either to the bramble or the cedar; no, nor to any mortal, however great or good; and for the same reasons we should always be upon our guard against the epithets and reflections of writers and declaimers, whose constant art it is to falsify and blacken the characters and measures they are determined to discredit.

These reflections have been occasioned by the late controversies in our newspapers about certain measures in the political world.[5] Controversies that have this in common with others of much greater figure and

---

[5] Hutchinson mentions the year 1765, as the time when parties in Massachusetts began to take their form. "Men took sides in New England upon mere speculative points in government, when there was nothing in practice which could give any grounds for forming parties." The next paragraph, however, betrays his sense of the connection these speculative points had with grounds for forming parties which all instinctively felt to be about to be furnished by the mother country. It was the ripple on the face of the still water, indicative of the storm that was soon to follow. *History of Massachusetts,* vol. iii. pp. 103–105.

importance, and, indeed, with all others, (in which numbers have been concerned,) from the first invention of letters to the present hour; that more pains have been employed in charging desire of popularity, restless turbulence of spirit, ambitious views, envy, revenge, malice, and jealousy on one side; and servility, adulation, tyranny, principles of arbitrary power, lust of dominion, avarice, desires of civil or military commissions on the other; or, in fewer words, in attempts to blacken and discredit the motives of the disputants on both sides, than in rational inquiries into the merits of the cause, the truth, and rectitude of the measures contested.

Let not writers nor statesmen deceive themselves. The springs of their own conduct and opinions are not always so clear and pure, nor are those of their antagonists in politics always so polluted and corrupted, as they believe, and would have the world believe too. Mere readers and private persons can see virtues and talents on each side; and to their sorrow they have not yet seen any side altogether free from atrocious vices, extreme ignorance, and most lamentable folly. Nor will mere readers and private persons be less excusable if they should suffer themselves to be imposed on by others, who first impose upon themselves. Every step in the public administration of government concerns us nearly. Life and fortune, our own and those of our posterity, are not trifles to be neglected or totally entrusted to other hands; and these, in the vicissitudes of human things, may be rendered in a few years either totally uncertain, or as secure as fixed laws and the British constitution well administered can make them, in consequence of measures that seem at present but trifles, and to many scarcely worth attention. Let us not be bubbled then out of our reverence and obedience to government on one hand; nor out of our right to think and act for ourselves in our own department on the other. The steady management of a good government is the most anxious, arduous, and hazardous vocation on this side the grave. Let us not encumber those, therefore, who have spirit enough to embark in such an enterprise, with any kind of opposition that the preservation or perfection of our mild, our happy, our most excellent constitution, does not soberly demand.

But, on the other hand, as we know that ignorance, vanity, excessive ambition and venality, will, in spite of all human precautions, creep into government, and will ever be aspiring at extravagant and unconstitutional emoluments to individuals, let us never relax our attention, or our resolution, to keep these unhappy imperfections in human nature, out of which material, frail as it is, all our rulers must be compounded, under a strict inspection and a just control. We electors have an important constitutional power placed in our hands; we have a check upon two branches of the legislature, as each branch has upon the other two; the power I mean of electing, at stated periods, one branch, which branch has the power of electing another. It becomes necessary to every subject then, to be in some degree a statesman, and to examine and judge for himself of the tendency of political principles and measures. Let us examine, then, with a sober, a manly, a British, and a Christian spirit; let us neglect all party virulence and advert to facts; let us believe no man to be infallible or impeccable in government, any more than in religion; take no man's word against evidence, nor implicitly adopt the sentiments of others, who may be deceived themselves, or may be interested in deceiving us.

NO. III.

On Private Revenge
Impiger, iracundus, inexorabilis, acer,
Jura neget sibi nata, nihil non arroget armis.
Hor.[6]
Rebuke the spearmen, and the troops
Of bulls that mighty be.
Novang.

TO THE PRINTERS.[7]

IT seems to be necessary for me, (notwithstanding the declaration in my last) once more to digress from the road of agriculture and mechanic arts, and to enter the list of disputation with a brace of writers in the Evening Post, one of whom has subscribed himself X, and the other W. I

---

[6] ["Impatient, wrathful, ruthless, and fierce, let him deny that the laws were made for him, and assign everything to arms." Horace, *Art of Poetry* 121-22. Ed.]

[7] From the Boston Gazette, 5 September, 1763.

shall agree with the first of these gentlemen, that "to preach up non-resistance with the zeal of a fanatic," would be as extraordinary as to employ a bastile in support of the freedom of speech or the press, or an inquisition in favor of liberty of conscience; but if he will leave his own imagination, and recur to what I have written, he will not find a syllable against resistance. Resistance to sudden violence, for the preservation not only of my person, my limbs and life, but of my property, is an indisputable right of nature which I never surrendered to the public by the compact of society, and which, perhaps, I could not surrender if I would. Nor is there any thing in the common law of England, (for which Mr. X supposes I have so great a fondness,) inconsistent with that right. On the contrary, the dogmas of Plato, the maxims of the law, and the precepts of Christianity, are precisely coincident in relation to this subject.

Plato taught that revenge was unlawful, although he allowed of self-defence. The divine Author of our religion has taught us that trivial provocations are to be overlooked; and that if a man should offer you an insult, by boxing one ear, rather than indulge a furious passion and return blow for blow, you ought even to turn the other also. This expression, however, though it inculcates strongly the duty of moderation and self-government upon sudden provocations, imports nothing against the right of resistance or of self-defense. The sense of it seems to be no more than this: that little injuries and insults ought to be borne patiently for the present, rather than run the risk of violent consequences by retaliation.

Now, the common law seems to me to be founded on the same great principle of philosophy and religion. It will allow of nothing as a justification of blows, but blows; nor will it justify a furious beating, bruising, and wounding, upon the provocation of a fillip of the finger, or a kick upon the shins; but if I am assaulted, I can justify nothing but laying my hands lightly upon the aggressor for my own defence; nothing but what was absolutely necessary for my preservation. I may parry or ward off any blow; but a blow received is no sufficient provocation for fifty times so severe a blow in return. When life, which is one of the three favorites of the law, comes into consideration, we find a wise and humane provision is made for its preservation. If I am assaulted by another, sword in hand,

and if I am even certain of his intention to murder me, the common law will not suffer me to defend myself, by killing him, if I can avoid it. Nay, my behavior must absolutely be what would be called cowardice, perhaps, by Mr. X and W, though it would be thought the truest bravery, not only by the greatest philosophers and legislators, but by the best generals of the world; I must run away from such an assailant, and avoid him if I have room, rather than stand my ground and defend myself; but if I have no room to escape, or if I run and am pursued to the wall or into a corner where I cannot elude his fury, and have no other way to preserve my own life from his violence, but by taking his there, I have an indisputable right to do it, and should be justified in wading through the blood of a whole army, if I had power to shed it and had no other way to make my escape.

What is said by Mr. W, that "if a gentleman should be hurried by his passions so far as to take the life of another, the common law will not adjudge it murder or manslaughter, but justifiable homicide only,"—by which he must mean, if in truth he had any meaning at all, that killing upon a sudden provocation is justifiable homicide,—is a position in comparison of which the observations of the grave-digger upon the death of the young lady, in Shakespeare's Hamlet, ought to be ranked among the *responsa prudentium.*[8]

Every catechumen in law, nay, every common man, and even every porter upon the dock, that ever attended a trial for murder, knows that a sudden provocation raising a violent passion, where there is no precedent malice, is, in consideration of human frailty, allowed to soften killing from murder down to manslaughter; but manslaughter is a heinous crime, and subjected to heavy punishments.

Such is the wisdom and humanity of English law; upon so thorough a knowledge of human nature is it founded, and so well is it calculated to preserve the lives and limbs of men and the interior tranquillity of societies! I shall not dispute with Mr. X my affection for this law, in preference to all other systems of law that have ever appeared in the world. I have

---

[8] ["the opinions of the wise" Ed.]

no connection with parishioners, nor patients, nor clients, nor any dependence upon either for business or bread; I study law as I do divinity and
physic; and all of them as I do husbandry and mechanic arts, or the
motions and revolutions of the heavenly bodies; or as I do magistracy
and legislation; namely, as means and instruments of human happiness. It
has been my amusement for many years past, as far as I have had leisure,
to examine the systems of all the legislators, ancient and modern, fantastical and real, and to trace their effects in history upon the felicity of
mankind; and the result of this long examination is a settled opinion that
the liberty, the unalienable, indefeasible rights of men, the honor and dignity of human nature, the grandeur and glory of the public, and the universal happiness of individuals, were never so skilfully and successfully
consulted as in that most excellent monument of human art, the common
law of England; a law that maintains a great superiority, not only to every
other system of laws, martial or canon, or civil and military, even to
majesty itself; it has a never-sleeping jealousy of the canon law, which in
many countries, Spain in particular, has subjected all officers and orders,
civil and military, to the avarice and ambition, the caprice and cruelty of
a clergy; and it is not less watchful over the martial law, which in many
cases and in many countries, France in particular, is able to rescue men
from the justice of the municipal laws of the kingdom; and I will own, that
to revive in the minds of my countrymen a reverence for this law, and to
prevent the growth of sentiments that seemed to me to be in their tendency destructive of it, especially to revive a jealousy of martial laws and
cavalier-like tempers, was the turn which I designed to serve for myself
and my friends in that piece which has given offence to X and W.

A certain set of sentiments have been lately so fashionable, that you
could go into few companies without hearing such smart sayings as
these,—"If a man should insult me, by kicking my shins, and I had a sword
by my side I would make the sun shine through him;"—"if any man, let
him be as big as Goliah, should take me by the nose, I would let his bowels out with my sword, if I had one, and if I had none, I would beat his
brains out with the first club I could find." And such tempers have been
animated by some inadvertent expressions that have fallen from persons of

higher rank and better sentiments. Some of these have been heard to say, that "should a man offer a sudden insult to them, they could not answer for themselves, but they should lay him prostrate at their feet in his own blood." Such expressions as these, which are to be supposed but modest expressions of the speaker's diffidence of his own presence of mind, and government of his passions, when suddenly assaulted, have been taken for a justification of such returns to an insult, and a determination to practise them upon occasion. But such persons as are watching the lips of others for wise speeches, in order to utter them afterwards as their own sentiments, have generally as little of understanding as they have of spirit, and most miserably spoil, in reporting, a good reflection. Now, what I have written upon this subject was intended to show the inhumanity of taking away the life of a man, only for pulling my nose or boxing my ear; and the folly of it too, because I should be guilty of a high crime, that of manslaughter at least, and forfeit all my goods, besides receiving a brand of infamy.

But I have not yet finished my history of sentiments. It has been said by others that "no man ought to receive a blow without returning it;" "a man ought to be despised that receives a cuff without giving another in return." This I have heard declared for a sober opinion by some men of figure and office and importance. But I beg leave to repeat it,—this is the tenet of a coxcomb and the sentiment of a brute; and the horse, the bull, and the cock, that I mentioned before, daily discover precisely the same temper and the same sense of honor and decency. If, in walking the streets of this town, I should be met by a negro, and that negro should lay me over the head with his cudgel, should I think myself bound in honor or regard to reputation to return the blow with another cudgel? to put myself on a level with that negro, and join with him in a competition which was most expert and skilful at cudgels? If a mad dog should meet me and bite me, should I think myself bound in honor, (I mean before the poison has worked upon me enough to make me as mad as the dog himself,) to fall upon that dog and bite him again? It is not possible for me to express that depth of contempt that I feel for such sentiments, and for every mortal that entertains them; and I should choose to be "the butt, the jest, and contempt" of all companies that entertain such opinions, rather than to be in their admiration or esteem. I would take some other way to preserve myself and other men from such insolence and violence for the future; but I would never place myself upon a level with such an animal for the present.

Far from aiming at a reputation for such qualities and accomplishments as those of boxing or cuffing, a man of sense would hold even the true martial qualities, courage, strength, and skill in war, in a much lower estimation than the attributes of wisdom and virtue, skill in arts and sciences, and a true taste to what is right, what is fit, what is true, generous, manly, and noble, in civil life. The competition between Ajax and Ulysses is well known.

"Tu vires sine mente geris, mihi cura futuri,

Tu pugnare potes:

Tu tantum corpore prodes,

Nos animo;

Pectora sunt potiora manu. Vigor omnis in illis."[9]

And we know in whose favor the prize was decreed.

I shall not be at the pains of remarking upon all the rodomontade in the two pieces under consideration, and Mr. X and Mr. W, and the whole alphabet of writers may scribble as many volumes as the twenty-four letters are capable of variations, without the least further notice from me, unless more reasoning and merit appear in proportion to the quantity of

[9] From the speech of Ulysses, in *Ovid. Metamorphos.* lib. iii. 1. 363–368.

["You wield strength without a mind, I take care for the future,

You are able to fight:

…You only benefit us with your body,

While I do so with my mind;

. . . .

Hearts are more powerful than hands. All our strength is in the former."

Ovid, *Metamorphoses* XIII, 363-69, with omissions.

Achilles has been killed at Troy, and his armor is to go to the best remaining warrior. In a debate, Ulysses explains why he, as the cleverest, should get the armor instead of Ajax, who is the strongest. Ed.]

lines than is to be found in those two pieces. But since I have made some remarks upon them, it will, perhaps, before I conclude, be worth my while to mention one thing more in each. Mr. X tells us "that cases frequently occur where a man's person or reputation suffer to the greatest degree, and yet it is impossible for the law to make him any satisfaction."

This is not strictly true; such cases but seldom occur, though it must be confessed they sometimes do; but it seldom happens, very seldom indeed, where you know the man who has done you the injury, that you can get no satisfaction by law; and if such a case should happen, nothing can be clearer than that you ought to sit down and bear it; and for this plain reason, because it is necessary, and you cannot get satisfaction in any way. The law, by the supposition, cannot redress you; and you cannot, if you consider it, by any means redress yourself. A flagellation in the dark would be no reparation of the injury, no example to others, nor have any tendency to reform the subject of it, but rather a provocation to him to contrive some other way to injure you again; and of consequence would be no satisfaction at all to a man even of that false honor and delicacy of which I have been speaking, unless he will avow an appetite for mere revenge, which is not only worse than brutal, but the attribute of devils; and to take satisfaction by a flagellation in public would be only, in other words, taking a severe revenge upon yourself; for this would be a trespass and a violation of the peace, for which you would expose yourself to the resentment of the magistrate and the action of the party, and would be like running your sword through your own body to revenge yourself on another for boxing your ears; or like the behavior of the rattle-snake that will snap and leap and bite at every stick that you put near him, and at last when provoked beyond all honorable bearing, will fix his sharp and poisonous teeth into his own body.

I have nothing more to add, excepting one word of advice to Mr. W and all his readers, to have a care how they believe or practise his rule about "passion and killing," lest the halter and the gibbet should become their portion; for a killing that should happen by the hurry of passion would be much more likely to be adjudged murder than justifiable homicide only. Let me conclude, by advising all men to look into their own hearts, which they will find to be deceitful above all things and desperately wicked. Let them consider how extremely addicted they are to magnify and exaggerate the injuries that are offered to themselves, and to diminish and extenuate the wrongs that they offer to others. They ought, therefore, to be too modest and diffident of their own judgment, when their own passions and prejudices and interests are concerned, to desire to judge for themselves in their own causes, and to take their own satisfactions for wrongs and injuries of any kind.

Instructions
of the
Town of Braintree
to their
Representative
(1765)

T**hese** instructions, drafted by Adams, were accepted by those assembled without amendment, testimony to the esteem in which he was held by his fellow citizens. The statement sets forth the grievances of the colonists within a framework that is to be employed throughout the pre-revolutionary period. The *Instructions* are taken from *Works*, III, 465-68.

INSTRUCTIONS

OF THE

TOWN OF BRAINTREE

TO THEIR

REPRESENTATIVE,

1765.

To Ebenezer Thayer, Esq.

SIR,—In all the calamities which have ever befallen this country, we have never felt so great a concern, or such alarming apprehensions, as on this occasion. Such is our loyalty to the King, our veneration for both houses of Parliament, and our affection for all our fellow-subjects in Britain, that measures which discover any unkindness in that country towards us are the more sensibly and intimately felt. And we can no longer forbear complaining, that many of the measures of the late ministry, and some of the late acts of Parliament, have a tendency, in our apprehension, to divest us of our most essential rights and liberties. We shall confine ourselves, how-

478

ever, chiefly to the act of Parliament, commonly called the Stamp Act, by which a very burthensome, and, in our opinion, unconstitutional tax, is to be laid upon us all; and we subjected to numerous and enormous penalties, to be prosecuted, sued for, and recovered, at the option of an informer, in a court of admiralty, without a jury.

We have called this a burthensome tax, because the duties are so numerous and so high, and the embarrassments to business in this infant, sparsely-settled country so great, that it would be totally impossible for the people to subsist under it, if we had no controversy at all about the right and authority of imposing it. Considering the present scarcity of money, we have reason to think, the execution of that act for a short space of time would drain the country of its cash, strip multitudes of all their property, and reduce them to absolute beggary. And what the consequence would be to the peace of the province, from so sudden a shock and such a convulsive change in the whole course of our business and subsistence, we tremble to consider. We further apprehend this tax to be unconstitutional. We have always understood it to be a grand and fundamental principle of the constitution, that no freeman should be subject to any tax to which he has not given his own consent, in person or by proxy. And the maxims of the law, as we have constantly received them, are to the same effect, that no freeman can be separated from his property but by his own act or fault. We take it clearly, therefore, to be inconsistent with the spirit of the common law, and of the essential fundamental principles of the British constitution, that we should be subject to any tax imposed by the British Parliament; because we are not represented in that assembly in any sense, unless it be by a fiction of law, as insensible in theory as it would be injurious in practice, if such a taxation should be grounded on it.

But the most grievous innovation of all, is the alarming extension of the power of courts of admiralty. In these courts, one judge presides alone! No juries have any concern there! The law and the fact are both to be decided by the same single judge, whose commission is only during pleasure, and with whom, as we are told, the most mischievous of all customs has become established, that of taking commissions on all condemnations; so that he is under a pecuniary temptation always against the subject. Now, if the wisdom of the mother country has thought the independency of the judges so essential to an impartial administration of justice, as to render them independent of every power on earth,—independent of the King, the Lords, the Commons, the people, nay, independent in hope and expectation of the heir-apparent, by continuing their commissions after a demise of the crown, what justice and impartiality are we, at three thousand miles distance from the fountain, to expect from such a judge of admiralty? We have all along thought the acts of trade in this respect a grievance; but the Stamp Act has opened a vast number of sources of new crimes, which may be committed by any man, and cannot but be committed by multitudes, and prodigious penalties are annexed, and all these are to be tried by such a judge of such a court! What can be wanting, after this, but a weak or wicked man for a judge, to render us the most sordid and forlorn of slaves?—we mean the slaves of a slave of the servants of a minister of state. We cannot help asserting, therefore, that this part of the act will make an essential change in the constitution of juries, and it is directly repugnant to the Great Charter itself; for, by that charter, "no amerciament shall be assessed, but by the oath of honest and lawful men of the vicinage;" and, "no freeman shall be taken, or imprisoned, or disseized of his freehold, or liberties of free customs, nor passed upon, nor condemned, but by lawful judgment of his peers, or by the law of the land." So that this act will "make such a distinction, and create such a difference between" the subjects in Great Britain and those in America, as we could not have expected from the guardians of liberty in "both."

As these, sir, are our sentiments of this act, we, the freeholders and other inhabitants, legally assembled for this purpose, must enjoin it upon you, to comply with no measures or proposals for countenancing the same, or assisting in the execution of it, but by all lawful means, consistent with our allegiance to the King, and relation to Great Britain, to oppose the execution of it, till we can hear the success of the cries and petitions of America for relief.

We further recommend the most clear and explicit assertion and vindication of our rights and liberties to be entered on the public records, that the world may know, in the present and all future generations, that we have a clear knowledge and a just sense of them, and, with submission to Divine Providence, that we never can be slaves.[1]

Nor can we think it advisable to agree to any steps for the protection of stamped papers or stamp-officers. Good and wholesome laws we have already for the preservation of the peace; and we apprehend there is no further danger of tumult and disorder, to which we have a well-grounded aversion; and that any extraordinary and expensive exertions would tend to exasperate the people and endanger the public tranquillity, rather than the contrary. Indeed, we cannot too often inculcate upon you our desires, that all extraordinary grants and expensive measures may, upon all occasions, as much as possible, be avoided. The public money of this country is the toil and labor of the people, who are under many uncommon difficulties and distresses at this time, so that all reasonable frugality ought to be observed. And we would recommend particularly, the strictest care and the utmost firmness to prevent all unconstitutional draughts upon the public treasury.

---

[1] A Cambridge correspondent of the Evening Post, in October, 1765, enters into a comparison of these instructions with some of an opposite nature, coming from Marblehead, and published at the same time, and picks out this paragraph, as "worthy to be wrote in letters of gold."

Thoughts on Government
(1776)
and
Letter to John Penn
(January 1776)

Anticipating that the colonies would declare their independence, Adams took the lead in setting forth the nature and forms that their new governments should take. "Thoughts on Government" was originally a letter to George Wythe of Virginia, who had asked Adams for his views on this matter. Wythe showed the letter to Richard Henry Lee, who asked Adams for permission to print it. Adams agreed so long as his authorship was not revealed.

His "Thoughts on Government" presents in succinct form major elements of his political thought, particularly those contained in his *Defense of the Constitutions of the United States of America* that appeared some ten years later. *Thoughts* is taken from *Works*, IV, 193-200.

The letter to John Penn was a response to an inquiry by the North Carolina delegation to the Continental Congress directed to Adams concerning the most suitable form of government to establish. He repeats much of what is set forth in "Thoughts," but he also amplifies certain aspects of his thinking. The letter to John Penn is taken from *Works*, IV, 203-209.

THOUGHTS ON GOVERNMENT

MY DEAR SIR,—If I was equal to the task of forming a plan for the government of a colony, I should be flattered with your request, and very happy to comply with it; because, as the divine science of politics is the science of social happiness, and the blessings of society depend entirely on the constitutions of government, which are generally institutions that last for many generations, there can be no employment more agreeable to a benevolent mind than a research after the best.

> Pope flattered tyrants too much when he said,
> "For forms of government let fools contest,
> That which is best administered is best."

Nothing can be more fallacious than this. But poets read history to collect flowers, not fruits; they attend to fanciful images, not the effects of social institutions. Nothing is more certain, from the history of nations and nature of man, than that some forms of government are better fitted for being well administered than others.

We ought to consider what is the end of government, before we determine which is the best form. Upon this point all speculative politicians will agree, that the happiness of society is the end of government, as all divines and moral philosophers will agree that the happiness of the individual is the end of man. From this principle it will follow, that the form of government which communicates ease, comfort, security, or, in one word, happiness, to the greatest number of persons, and in the greatest degree, is the best.

All sober inquirers after truth, ancient and modern, pagan and Christian, have declared that the happiness of man, as well as his dignity, consists in virtue. Confucius, Zoroaster, Socrates, Mahomet, not to mention authorities really sacred, have agreed in this.

If there is a form of government, then, whose principle and foundation is virtue, will not every sober man acknowledge it better calculated to promote the general happiness than any other form?

Fear is the foundation of most governments; but it is so sordid and brutal a passion, and renders men in whose breasts it predominates so stupid and miserable, that Americans will not be likely to approve of any political institution which is founded on it.

Honor is truly sacred, but holds a lower rank in the scale of moral excellence than virtue. Indeed, the former is but a part of the latter, and consequently has not equal pretensions to support a frame of government productive of human happiness.

The foundation of every government is some principle or passion in the minds of the people. The noblest principles and most generous affections in our nature, then, have the fairest chance to support the noblest and most generous models of government.

A man must be indifferent to the sneers of modern Englishmen, to mention in their company the names of Sidney, Harrington, Locke, Milton, Nedham, Neville, Burnet, and Hoadly. No small fortitude is necessary to confess that one has read them. The wretched condition of this country, however, for ten or fifteen years past, has frequently reminded me of their principles and reasonings. They will convince any candid mind, that there is no good government but what is republican. That the only valuable part of the British constitution is so; because the very definition of a republic is "an empire of laws, and not of men." That, as a republic is the best of governments, so that particular arrangement of the powers of society, or, in other words, that form of government which is best contrived to secure an impartial and exact execution of the laws, is the best of republics.

Of republics there is an inexhaustible variety, because the possible combinations of the powers of society are capable of innumerable variations.

As good government is an empire of laws, how shall your laws be made? In a large society, inhabiting an extensive country, it is impossible that the whole should assemble to make laws. The first necessary step, then, is to depute power from the many to a few of the most wise and good. But by what rules shall you choose your representatives? Agree upon the number and qualifications of persons who shall have the benefit of choosing, or annex this privilege to the inhabitants of a certain extent of ground.

The principal difficulty lies, and the greatest care should be employed, in constituting this representative assembly. It should be in miniature an exact portrait of the people at large. It should think, feel, reason, and act like them. That it may be the interest of this assembly to do strict justice at all times, it should be an equal representation, or, in other words, equal interests among the people should have equal interests in it. Great care should be taken to effect this, and to prevent unfair, partial, and corrupt elections. Such regulations, however, may be better made in times of greater tranquillity than the present; and they will spring up themselves naturally, when all the powers of government come to be in the hands of the people's friends. At present, it will be safest to proceed in all established modes, to which the people have been familiarized by habit.

A representation of the people in one assembly being obtained, a question arises, whether all the powers of government, legislative, executive, and judicial, shall be left in this body? I think a people cannot be long free, nor ever happy, whose government is in one assembly. My reasons for this opinion are as follow:—

1. A single assembly is liable to all the vices, follies, and frailties of an individual; subject to fits of humor, starts of passion, flights of enthusiasm, partialities, or prejudice, and consequently productive of hasty results and absurd judgments. And all these errors ought to be corrected and defects supplied by some controlling power.

2. A single assembly is apt to be avaricious, and in time will not scruple to exempt itself from burdens, which it will lay, without compunction, on its constituents.

3. A single assembly is apt to grow ambitious, and after a time will not hesitate to vote itself perpetual. This was one fault of the Long Parliament; but more remarkably of Holland, whose assembly first voted themselves from annual to septennial, then for life, and after a course of years, that all vacancies happening by death or otherwise, should be filled by themselves, without any application to constituents at all.

4. A representative assembly, although extremely well qualified, and absolutely necessary, as a branch of the legislative, is unfit to exercise the executive power, for want of two essential properties, secrecy and despatch.

5. A representative assembly is still less qualified for the judicial power, because it is too numerous, too slow, and too little skilled in the laws.

6. Because a single assembly, possessed of all the powers of government, would make arbitrary laws for their own interest, execute all laws arbitrarily for their own interest, and adjudge all controversies in their own favor.

But shall the whole power of legislation rest in one assembly? Most of the foregoing reasons apply equally to prove that the legislative power ought to be more complex; to which we may add, that if the legislative power is wholly in one assembly, and the executive in another, or in a single person, these two powers will oppose and encroach upon each other, until the contest shall end in war, and the whole power, legislative and executive, be usurped by the strongest.

The judicial power, in such case, could not mediate, or hold the balance between the two contending powers, because the legislative would undermine it. And this shows the necessity, too, of giving the executive power a negative upon the legislative, otherwise this will be continually encroaching upon that.

To avoid these dangers, let a distinct assembly be constituted, as a mediator between the two extreme branches of the legislature, that which represents the people, and that which is vested with the executive power.

Let the representative assembly then elect by ballot, from among themselves or their constituents, or both, a distinct assembly, which, for the sake of perspicuity, we will call a council. It may consist of any number you please, say twenty or thirty, and should have a free and independent exercise of its judgment, and consequently a negative voice in the legislature.

These two bodies, thus constituted, and made integral parts of the legislature, let them unite, and by joint ballot choose a governor, who, after being stripped of most of those badges of domination, called prerogatives, should have a free and independent exercise of his judgment, and be made also an integral part of the legislature. This, I know, is liable to objections; and, if you please, you may make him only president of the council, as in Connecticut. But as the governor is to be invested with the executive power, with consent of council, I think he ought to have a negative upon the legislative. If he is annually elective, as he ought to be, he will always have so much reverence and affection for the people, their representatives and counsellors, that, although you give him an independent exercise of his judgment, he will seldom use it in opposition to the two houses, except in cases the public utility of which would be conspicuous; and some such cases would happen.

In the present exigency of American affairs, when, by an act of Parliament, we are put out of the royal protection, and consequently discharged from our allegiance, and it has become necessary to assume government for our immediate security, the governor, lieutenant-governor, secretary, treasurer, commissary, attorney-general, should be chosen by joint ballot of both houses. And these and all other elections, especially of representatives and counsellors, should be annual, there not being in the whole circle of the sciences a maxim more infallible than this, "where annual elections end, there slavery begins."

> These great men, in this respect, should be, once a year,
> "Like bubbles on the sea of matter borne,
> They rise, they break, and to that sea return."

This will teach them the great political virtues of humility, patience, and moderation, without which every man in power becomes a ravenous beast of prey.

This mode of constituting the great offices of state will answer very well for the present; but if by experiment it should be found inconvenient, the legislature may, at its leisure, devise other methods of creating them, by elections of the people at large, as in Connecticut, or it may enlarge the term for which they shall be chosen to seven years, or three years, or for life, or make any other alterations which the society shall find productive of its ease, its safety, its freedom, or, in one word, its happiness.

A rotation of all offices, as well as of representatives and counsellors, has many advocates, and is contended for with many plausible arguments. It would be attended, no doubt, with many advantages; and if the society has a sufficient number of suitable characters to supply the great number of vacancies which would be made by such a rotation, I can see no objection to it. These persons may be allowed to serve for three years, and then be excluded three years, or for any longer or shorter term.

Any seven or nine of the legislative council may be made a quorum, for doing business as a privy council, to advise the governor in the exercise of the executive branch of power, and in all acts of state.

The governor should have the command of the militia and of all your armies. The power of pardons should be with the governor and council.

Judges, justices, and all other officers, civil and military, should be nominated and appointed by the governor, with the advice and consent of council, unless you choose to have a government more popular; if you do, all officers, civil and military, may be chosen by joint ballot of both houses; or, in order to preserve the independence and importance of each house, by ballot of one house, concurred in by the other. Sheriffs should be chosen by the freeholders of counties; so should registers of deeds and clerks of counties.

All officers should have commissions, under the hand of the governor and seal of the colony.

The dignity and stability of government in all its branches, the morals of the people, and every blessing of society depend so much upon an upright and skilful administration of justice, that the judicial power ought to be distinct from both the legislative and executive, and independent upon both, that so it may be a check upon both, as both should be checks upon that. The judges, therefore, should be always men of learning and experience in the laws, of exemplary morals, great patience, calmness, coolness, and attention. Their minds should not be distracted with jarring interests; they should not be dependent upon any man, or body of men. To these ends, they should hold estates for life in their offices; or, in other words, their commissions should be during good behavior, and their salaries ascertained and established by law. For misbehavior, the grand inquest of the colony, the house of representatives, should impeach them before the governor and council, where they should have time and opportunity to make their defence; but, if convicted, should be removed from their offices, and subjected to such other punishment as shall be thought proper.

A militia law, requiring all men, or with very few exceptions besides cases of conscience, to be provided with arms and ammunition, to be trained at certain seasons; and requiring counties, towns, or other small districts, to be provided with public stocks of ammunition and intrenching utensils, and with some settled plans for transporting provisions after the militia, when marched to defend their country against sudden invasions; and requiring certain districts to be provided with field-pieces, companies of matrosses, and perhaps some regiments of light-horse, is always a wise institution, and, in the present circumstances of our country, indispensable.

Laws for the liberal education of youth, especially of the lower class of people, are so extremely wise and useful, that, to a humane and generous mind, no expense for this purpose would be thought extravagant.

The very mention of sumptuary laws will excite a smile. Whether our countrymen have wisdom and virtue enough to submit to them, I know not; but the happiness of the people might be greatly promoted by them, and a revenue saved sufficient to carry on this war forever. Frugality is a great revenue, besides curing us of vanities, levities, and fopperies, which are real antidotes to all great, manly, and warlike virtues.

But must not all commissions run in the name of a king? No. Why may they not as well run thus, "The colony of   to A. B. greeting," and be tested by the governor?

Why may not writs, instead of running in the name of the king, run thus, "The colony of   to the sheriff," &c., and be tested by the chief justice?

Why may not indictments conclude, "against the peace of the colony of   and the dignity of the same?"

A constitution founded on these principles introduces knowledge among the people, and inspires them with a conscious dignity becoming freemen; a general emulation takes place, which causes good humor, sociability, good manners, and good morals to be general. That elevation of sentiment inspired by such a government, makes the common people brave and enterprising. That ambition which is inspired by it makes them sober, industrious, and frugal. You will find among them some elegance, perhaps, but more solidity; a little pleasure, but a great deal of business; some politeness, but more civility. If you compare such a country with the regions of domination, whether monarchical or aristocratical, you will fancy yourself in Arcadia or Elysium.

If the colonies should assume governments separately, they should be left entirely to their own choice of the forms; and if a continental constitution should be formed, it should be a congress, containing a fair and adequate representation of the colonies, and its authority should sacredly be confined to these cases, namely, war, trade, disputes between colony and colony, the post-office, and the unappropriated lands of the crown, as they used to be called.

These colonies, under such forms of government, and in such a union, would be unconquerable by all the monarchies of Europe.

You and I, my dear friend, have been sent into life at a time when the greatest lawgivers of antiquity would have wished to live. How few of the human race have ever enjoyed an opportunity of making an election of government, more than of air, soil, or climate, for themselves or their children! When, before the present epocha, had three millions of people full power and a fair opportunity to form and establish the wisest and happiest government that human wisdom can contrive? I hope you will avail yourself and your country of that extensive learning and indefatigable industry which you possess, to assist her in the formation of the happiest governments and the best character of a great people. For myself, I must beg you to keep my name out of sight; for this feeble attempt, if it should be known to be mine, would oblige me to apply to myself those lines of the immortal John Milton, in one of his sonnets:—

"I did but prompt the age to quit their clogs
By the known rules of ancient liberty,

When straight a barbarous noise environs me
Of owls and cuckoos, asses, apes, and dogs."

LETTER TO JOHN PENN
(JANUARY 1776).

IF I was possessed of abilities equal to the great task you have imposed upon me, which is to sketch out the outlines of a constitution for a colony, I should think myself the happiest of men in complying with your desire. Because, as politics is the art of securing human happiness, and the prosperity of societies depends upon the constitution of government under which they live, there cannot be a more agreeable employment to a benevolent mind than the study of the best kinds of government.

It has been the will of Heaven that we should be thrown into existence at a period when the greatest philosophers and lawgivers of antiquity would have wished to live. A period when a coincidence of circumstances without example, has afforded to thirteen Colonies, at once, an opportunity of beginning government anew from the foundation, and building as they choose. How few of the human race have ever had any opportunity of choosing a system of government for themselves and their children! How few have ever had any thing more of choice in government than in climate! These Colonies have now their election; and it is much to be wished that it may not prove to be like a prize in the hands of a man who has no heart to improve it.

In order to determine which is the best form of government, it is necessary to determine what is the end of government. And I suppose, that in this enlightened age, there will be no dispute, in speculation, that the happiness of the people, the great end of man, is the end of government; and, therefore, that form of government which will produce the greatest quantity of happiness is the best.

All sober inquirers after truth, ancient and modern, divines, moralists, and philosophers, have agreed that the happiness of mankind, as well as the real dignity of human nature, consists in virtue; if there is a form of government whose principle and foundation is virtue, will not every wise man acknowledge it more likely to promote the general happiness than any other?

Fear, which is said, by Montesquieu and other political writers, to be the foundation of some governments, is so sordid and brutal a passion, that it cannot possibly be called a principle, and will hardly be thought in America a proper basis of government.

Honor is a principle which ought to be sacred; but the Grecians and Romans, pagan as well as Christian, will inform us that honor, at most, is but a part of virtue, and therefore a feeble basis of government.

A man must be indifferent to sneer and ridicule, in some companies, to mention the names of Sidney, Harrington, Locke, Milton, Nedham, Neville, Burnet, Hoadly; for the lines of John Milton, in one of his sonnets, will bear an application, even in this country, upon some occasions:—

"I did but prompt the age to quit their clogs
By the known rules of ancient liberty,
When straight a barbarous noise environs me,
Of owls and cuckoos, asses, apes, and dogs."

These great writers, however, will convince any man who has the fortitude to read them, that all good government is republican; that the only valuable part of the British constitution is so; for the true idea of a republic is an empire of laws, and not of men; and, therefore, as a republic is the best of governments, so that particular combination of power which is best contrived for a faithful execution of the laws, is the best of republics.

There is a great variety of republics, because the arrangements of the forms of society are capable of many variations.

As a good government is an empire of laws, the first question is, how shall the laws be made?

In a community consisting of large numbers, inhabiting an extensive country, it is not possible that the whole should assemble to make laws. The most natural substitute for an assembly of the whole, is a delegation of power from the many to a few of the most wise and virtuous. In the first place, then, establish rules for the choice of representatives; agree upon the number of persons who shall have the privilege of choosing one. As the representative assembly should be an exact portrait, in miniature, of the people at large, as it should think, feel, reason, and act like them, great care should be taken in the formation of it, to prevent unfair, partial, and corrupt elections. That it may be the interest of this assembly to do equal right and strict justice, upon all occasions, it should be an equal representation of their constituents; or, in other words, equal interests among the people should have equal interests in the representative body.

That the representatives may often mix with their constituents, and frequently render them an account of their stewardship, elections ought to be frequent:—

"Like bubbles on the sea of matter borne,
They rise, they break, and to that sea, return."

These elections may be septennial or triennial; but, for my own part, I think they ought to be annual; *for there is not in all science a maxim more infallible than this, where annual elections end, there slavery begins.*

But all necessary regulations for the method of constituting this assembly may be better made in times of more quiet than the present, and they will suggest themselves naturally, *when the powers of government shall be in the hands of the people's friends.* For the present, it will be safest to go on in the usual way.

But we have as yet advanced only one step in the formation of a government. Having obtained a representative assembly, what is to be done next? Shall we leave all the powers of government to this assembly? Shall they make, and execute, and interpret laws too? I answer, No; a people cannot be long free, and never can be happy, whose laws are made, executed, and interpreted by one assembly. My reasons for this opinion are these:—

A single assembly is liable to all the vices, follies, and frailties of an individual; subject to fits of humor, transports of passion, partialities of prejudice; and, from these and other causes, apt to make hasty results and absurd judgments; all which errors ought to be corrected, and inconveniences guarded against, by some controlling power.

A single assembly is apt to grow avaricious, and in time would not scruple to exempt itself from burdens, which it would lay upon its constituents without sympathy.

A single assembly will become ambitious, and after some time will vote itself perpetual. This was found in the case of the Long Parliament; but more remarkably in the case of Holland, whose assembly first voted that they should hold their seats for seven years, then for life, and after some time, that they would fill up vacancies as they should happen, without applying to their constituents at all.

The executive power cannot be well managed by a representative assembly for want of two essential qualities, secrecy and despatch.

Such an assembly is still less qualified to exercise the judicial power; because it is too numerous, too slow, and generally too little skilled in the laws.

But shall the whole legislative power be left in the hands of such an assembly? The three first, at least, of the foregoing reasons will show that the legislative power ought not to be wholly entrusted to one assembly.

Let the representative body, then, elect from among themselves, or their constituents, or both, a distinct assembly, which we will call a council. It may consist of any number you please, say, twenty or thirty. To this assembly should be given a free and independent exercise of its judgment upon all acts of legislation, that it may be able to check and arrest the errors of the other.

But there ought to be a third branch of the legislature; and wherever the executive power of the state is placed, there the third branch of the legislature ought to be found.

Let the two houses, then, by joint ballot, choose a governor. *Let him be chosen annually. Divest him of most of those badges of slavery called preroga-*

tives, and give him a negative upon the legislature. This, I know, is liable to some objections, to obviate which, you may make him in a legislative capacity only president of the council. But if he is annually elective, you need not scruple to give him a free and independent exercise of his judgment; for he will have so great an affection for the people, the representatives and council, that he would seldom exercise this right, except in cases the public utility of which would soon be manifest, and some such cases would happen.

In the present exigency of American affairs, when, by an Act of Parliament, we are put out of the royal protection, and consequently discharged from all obligations of allegiance; and when it has become necessary to assume governments for immediate security, the governor, lieutenant-governor, secretary, treasurer, and attorney-general, should be chosen by joint ballot of both houses.

The governor, by and with, and not without, the advice and consent of council, should appoint all judges, justices, and all other officers, civil and military, who should have commissions signed by the governor, and under the seal of the colony.

Sheriffs should be chosen by the freeholders of the counties. If you choose to have a government more popular, all officers may be chosen by one house of assembly, subject to the negative of the other.

The stability of government, in all its branches, the morals of the people, and every other blessing of society and social institutions, depend so much upon an able and impartial administration of justice, *that the judicial power* should be separated from the legislative and executive, and independent upon both; the judges should be men of experience in the laws, of exemplary morals, invincible patience, unruffled calmness, and indefatigable application; their minds should not be distracted with complicated, jarring interests; they should not be dependent on any man or body of men; they should lean to none, be subservient to none, nor more complaisant to one than another. To this end, they should hold estates for life in their offices; or, in other words, their commissions should be during good behavior, and their salaries ascertained and established by law.

If accused of misbehavior by the representative body before the governor and council, and if found guilty after having an opportunity to make their defence, they should be removed from their offices, and subjected to such other punishment as their offences deserve.

A rotation of offices in the legislative and executive departments has many advocates, and, if practicable, might have many good effects. A law may be made, that no man shall be governor, lieutenant-governor, secretary, treasurer, counsellor, or representative, more than three years at a time, nor be again eligible until after an interval of three years.

A constitution like this, of which the foregoing is a very imperfect plan, naturally introduces general knowledge into the community, and inspires the people with a conscious dignity becoming freemen. A general desire of reputation and importance among their neighbors, which cannot be obtained without some government of their passions, some good humor, good manners, and good morals, takes place in the minds of men, and naturally causes general virtue and civility. That pride which is introduced by such a government among the people, makes them brave and enterprising. That ambition which is introduced into every rank, makes them sober, industrious, and frugal. You will find among them some elegance, but more solidity; a little politeness, but a great deal of civility; some pleasure, but more business.

Let commissions run thus: "Colony of North Carolina to A. B. greeting," &c., and be tested by the governor.

Let writs run: "The Colony of, &c., to the sheriff," &c.

Let indictments conclude: "against the peace of the Colony of North Carolina, and the dignity of the same;" or if you please: "against the peace of the Thirteen United Colonies."

We have heard much of a continental constitution; I see no occasion for any but a congress. Let that be made an equal and fair representative of the Colonies; and let its authority be confined to three cases,—war, trade, and controversies between colony and colony. If a confederation was formed, agreed on in Congress, and ratified by the assemblies, these Colonies, *under such forms of government and such a confederation, would be unconquerable by all the monarchies of Europe.*

This plan of a government for a colony, you see, is intended as a temporary expedient under the present pressure of affairs. The government once formed, and having settled its authority, will have leisure enough to make any alterations that time and experience may dictate. Particularly, a plan may be devised perhaps, and be thought expedient, *for giving the choice of the governor to the people at large, and of the counsellors to the freeholders of the counties.* But, be these things as they may, two things are indispensably to be adhered to,—one is, some regulation for securing forever an equitable choice of representatives; another is, the education of youth, both in literature and morals.

I wish, my dear sir, that I had time to think of these things more at leisure, and to write more correctly; but you must take these hints, rough as they run. Your own reflections, *assisted by the patriots of North Carolina,* will improve upon every part of them.

As you brought upon yourself the trouble of reading these crude thoughts, you can't blame your friend[1],

JOHN ADAMS.

---

[1] A letter of the same description was addressed to Jonathan Dickinson Sergeant, of New Jersey, in answer to a similar application, made at the time of the formation of the constitution in that State; but no copy has been found.

The
Report of a Constitution,
or
Form of Government,
for the
Commonwealth of Massachusetts
(1780)

The Massachusetts Constitution enjoyed a special status among the State constitutions adopted after the Declaration of Independence because it was not the product of the state legislature, but of the a convention elected directly by the people for the specific purpose of drafting a constitution. The product of the convention was, in turn, subject to approval or rejection by the people.

Adams assumed a leading role in drafting the Massachusetts Constitution. The convention initially designated thirty individuals to draft a declaration of rights and frame of government. This committee then appointed three individuals, James Bowdoin, Samuel Adams, and John Adams, to perform this task. In turn, Bowdoin and Samuel Adams delegated this responsibility to John Adams. The Constitution, thus, embodies many of his principles and ideas concerning sound government that had previously been set forth in his writings. In fact, though he would have preferred greater independence for the governor, he was highly pleased with the final product.

The only political activity Adams engaged in after leaving the presidency was to serve as a delegate to the Massachusetts Constitutional Convention of 1820. This Convention significantly revised the Constitution of 1780, though keeping its basic framework of divided powers.

The introductory explanation of Charles Francis Adams—John Adams's grandson and editor of the ten volume compilation of his works from which this selection is taken—on the form in which the following materials are presented is most helpful for their understanding: "the text is that of the Report made by the committee of the convention, and prepared for them by Mr. Adams. The passages inclosed within brackets are those which were entirely erased by the convention. Those marked with Italic letters are such as underwent changes; the exact substitutes are supplied in notes to the respective places. Wherever a blank occurs, the note will indicate the words inserted in the form as finally adopted. The amendment engrafted by the later convention of 1820, as well as subsequently, under the authority created by that assembly, are appended to those sections and articles which they respectively affect." The *Report* is taken from *Works*, IV, 219-67.

<hr />

THE

REPORT OF A CONSTITUTION,

OR

FORM OF GOVERNEMENT,

FOR THE

COMMONWEALTH OF MASSACHUSETTS

Agreed upon by the Committee,—to be laid before the CONVENTION OF DEL-EGATES, *assembled at* CAMBRIDGE, *on the first day of September, 1779; and continued by adjournment to the twenty-eighth day of October following.*

<hr />

PREAMBLE.

THE end of the institution, maintenance, and administration of government is to secure the existence of the body politic; to protect it, and to furnish the individuals who compose it with the power of enjoying, in safety and tranquillity, their natural rights and the blessings of life; and whenever these great objects are not obtained, the people have a right to alter the government, and to take measures necessary for their safety, happiness, and prosperity.

The body politic is formed by a voluntary association of individuals. It is a social compact, by which the whole people covenants with each citizen, and each citizen with the whole people, that all shall be governed by certain laws for the common good. It is the duty of the people, therefore, in framing a Constitution of Government, to provide for an equitable mode of making laws, as well as for an impartial interpretation and a faithful execution of them, that every man may, at all times, find his security in them.

We, therefore, [the delegates of] the people of Massachusetts, [in general convention assembled, for the express and sole purpose of framing a constitution, or form of government, to be laid before our constituents, according to their instructions,] acknowledging, with grateful hearts, the goodness of the great Legislator of the universe, in affording *to this people,*[1] in the course of His providence, an opportunity *of entering into an original, explicit, and solemn compact with each other, deliberately and peaceably, without fraud, violence, or surprise;*[2] and of forming a new constitution of civil government for *themselves*[3] and [their] posterity; and devoutly imploring His direction in *a design so interesting*[4] [to them and their posterity,]— do, [by virtue of the authority vested in us by our constituents,] agree upon   [5]the following DECLARATION OF RIGHTS, AND FRAME OF GOVERNMENT, AS THE CONSTITUTION OF THE COMMONWEALTH OF MASSACHUSETTS.

[CHAPTER I.][6]

A DECLARATION OF THE RIGHTS OF THE INHABITANTS OF THE COMMONWEALTH OF MASSACHUSETTS.

ART. I. All men are born [equally] free and *independent,*[7] and have certain natural, essential, and unalienable rights, among which may be

[1] "us,"

[2] The two clauses in Italics transposed.

[3] "ourselves"

[4] "so interesting a design,"

[5] "ordain and establish"

[6] PART THE FIRST.

[7] "equal." The language of this article, as reported, is nearly the same with that of the first article of the Bill of Rights of Virginia.

reckoned the right of enjoying and defending their lives and liberties; that of acquiring, possessing, and protecting [their] property; in fine, that of seeking and obtaining their safety and happiness.

II. It is the   [8]duty of all men in society, publicly, and at stated seasons, to worship the SUPREME BEING, the great Creator and Preserver of the universe. And no subject shall be hurt, molested, or restrained, in his person, liberty, or estate, for worshipping GOD in the manner   [9]most agreeable to the dictates of his own conscience; or, for his religious profession or sentiments; provided he doth not disturb the public peace, or obstruct others in their religious worship.

III. [Good morals being necessary to the preservation of civil society; and the knowledge and belief of the being of GOD, His providential government of the world, and of a future state of rewards and punishment, being the only true foundation of morality, the legislature hath, there-fore, a right, and ought to provide, at the expense of the subject, if neces-sary, a suitable support for the public worship of GOD, and of the teachers of religion and morals; and to enjoin upon all the subjects an attendance upon their instructions at stated times and seasons; provided there be any such teacher on whose ministry they can conscientiously and conve-niently attend.][10]

---

[8] "right as well as the"

[9] "and season"

[10] This clause was not at all satisfactory to the convention. After several days spent in discussion, and the proposal of various amendments, the subject was recommitted to a committee of seven persons, with the Reverend Mr. Alden as the chairman, who reported this substitute, which was finally adopted, in an amended form, and after long debates:—

"III. As the happiness of a people, and the good order and preservation of a civil gov-ernment, essentially depend upon piety, religion, and morality; and as these cannot be generally diffused through a community, but by the institution of the public worship of GOD, and of public instruction in piety, religion, and morality,—therefore, to pro-mote their happiness, and to secure the good order and preservation of their government, the people of this commonwealth have a right to invest their legislature with power to authorize and require, and the legislature shall, from time to time, authorize and require the several towns, parishes, precincts, and other bodies politic or religious societies, to make suitable provision, at their own expense, for the institution of the public worship of God, and for the support and maintenance of public Protestant teachers

All moneys paid by the subject to the support of public worship, and of the *instructors in religion and morals*,[11] shall, if he require it, be uniformly applied to the support of the   [12]teacher or teachers of his own religious   [13]denomination, *if there be such whose ministry he attends upon;*[14] otherwise it may be paid *to*[15] the teacher or teachers of the parish or precinct *where he usually resides.*[16] [17]

of piety, religion, and morality, in all cases where such provision shall not be made v-oluntarily.

"And the people of this commonwealth have also a right to, and do, invest their legislature with authority to enjoin upon all the subjects, an attendance upon the instructions of the public teachers aforesaid, at stated times and seasons, if there be any on whose instructions they can conscientiously and conveniently attend.

"Provided, notwithstanding, that the several towns, parishes, precincts, and other bodies politic, or religious societies, shall, at all times, have the exclusive right of electing their public teachers, and of contracting with them for their support and maintenance."

[11] "public teachers aforesaid,"

[12] "public"

[13] "sect or"

[14] "provided there be any on whose instruction he attends;"

[15] "towards the support of"

[16] "in which the said moneys are raised."

[17] A new clause was appended to this article by the convention, as follows:—

"And every denomination of Christians, demeaning themselves peaceably and as good subjects of the commonwealth, shall be equally under the protection of the law; and no subordination of any one sect or denomination to another shall ever be established by law."

It has already been remarked, that the third article, as it appears in the original report, was not made by Mr. Adams. In a letter written long afterwards, to Mr. Williamson, the historian of Maine, he gives, as a reason, "that he could not satisfy his own judgment with any article that he thought would be accepted; and, further, that some of the clergy, and graver persons than himself, would be more likely to hit the taste of the public."

The amended form of the article is said, in the address of the convention to the people, to have been "finally agreed upon, with much more unanimity than usually takes place in disquisitions of this nature." It was not, however, adopted without strong and vehement remonstrance, which was again manifested at the time of the popular ratification, and it never was quietly acquiesced in afterwards. Indeed, it may truly be said to be the only portion of the constitution which furnished a constant topic of dispute, until finally abandoned in 1833. The reason is obvious enough. Professing carefully to secure an equality among Christians of all denominations, it did yet, in practice, give a decided advantage to one sect over the rest. In this respect, a marked difference is perceptible between the original and the amended form of the article. The former broadly embraces men of all classes of religious belief, including the Catholic on one side, and the

IV. The people of this commonwealth have the sole and exclusive right of governing themselves, as a free, sovereign, and independent state; and do, and forever hereafter shall, exercise and enjoy every power, jurisdiction,

Deist on the other; and, doubtless, this was one of the most serious grounds of objection to it. For, even in the meagre journal that remains, it appears that, not content with the amended form, limiting the authority of the legislature to require provision to be made by the towns to the maintenance of public *Protestant* teachers, and confining the moneys to be raised to the support of such teachers, amendments were pressed, specifically excepting "Papists," and "Christians whose principles are repugnant to the constitution," or, "whose avowed principles are inconsistent with the peace and safety of society," from "the protection of the law." These amendments did not prevail, it is true; but the steadiness with which they were urged, is one among many indications here visible, how gradually the old puritan feeling was receding before the modern movement of religious equality.

The grievance to which this article gave rise was that, in addition to compulsory taxation, there were many cases in which the property of persons became liable to be used, against their will, for the benefit of forms of religious faith which they most disapproved; and latterly, by the construction of the courts, a limitation was made upon the power of selection, even among the churches of the denomination to which the contributor himself belonged. This occasioned so great uneasiness, as at last to require from the legislature of 1811 the passage of a law, designed partially to remedy the evil. The call of a new convention to revise the constitution, made necessary by the separation of Maine in 1819, furnished an opportunity for the revival of the controversy. All the abilities of that somewhat remarkable assembly became enlisted upon one or the other side, until the dispute finally settled into the ordinary form of a question between the old and the new, between conservatism and reform.

Mr. Adams, although at the time infirm, by reason of his great age, he being eighty-five years old, was a member of this convention. Yet on this subject he showed more interest than upon any other. The tendency of his mind will appear most clearly from the following extracts taken from the Report of the Debates:—

"Mr. Parker, of Boston, rose, at the request of the gentleman from Quincy, who was unavoidably absent, to propose that, in the third article of the Declaration of Rights, the words, 'all men, of all religions, demeaning themselves as good subjects, shall enjoy the equal protection of the laws,' should be inserted instead of the words, 'men of every denomination of Christians.'

"Mr. Williams had no special objection to this proposition; but did not think it would meet the wishes of the people of this commonwealth.

"Mr. Parker withdrew the proposition."

Unable, from physical debility, to attend regularly, and still less to take an active part in the debates, Mr. Adams yet had this point so much at heart, that he made a new effort to get it before the body, at a later moment, as appears from the Journal.

"Mr. Boylston, of Princeton, at the suggestion of Mr. Adams, of Quincy, who was absent, offered a resolution proposing to alter the constitution, so that instead of 'every denomination of Christians,' &c, it should read, 'all men of all religions, demeaning themselves peaceably, and as good subjects of the commonwealth, shall be equally under the protection of the law.'

"Referred to the committee of the whole on the Declaration of Rights."

On the 28th the resolution was taken up, and the following discussion took place:—

"Mr. Boylston, of Princeton, said, that his object was entirely in a commercial relation. It was intended to invite foreigners to come to our shores, by the offer of equal protection to men of all religious opinions. As the constitution now stands, the offer of protection was confined to persons of the Christian religion.

"Mr. Hubbard read the second article of the Bill of Rights, which he thought made the most ample provision for the object.

"Mr. J. Davis, of Boston, opposed the resolution. He thought it would be better to leave it to legislative discretion. Persons of all religions have, in fact, full and equal protection.

"Mr. Quincy objected to the resolution, because it seemed to imply that persons of all religions were not now under the protection of the law. He showed on what ground he thought the object was fully provided for.

"The resolution was negatived."

It seems scarcely necessary, at this day, to show how entirely the reasoning of the objectors evaded the question at issue. In all probability the remark of Mr. Williams was correct,—that the popular sentiment was not then ready to carry out the abstract principle, of total separation between church and state, even though it underlies the whole theory of republican government. Yet the very same amendment had been proposed by Dr. Price, in his Observations, published thirty-six years before!

In the convention of 1820, the conservative section, constituted, as it was, of a large proportion of the ability, learning, and weight of character in the commonwealth, prevailed so far as to retain the feature of compulsory taxation for the support of religious worship. But the article which, after great labor and contention, had been shaped in a form to meet the assent of a majority of that assembly, was decisively rejected by the people, when submitted for ratification. The matter remained unsettled from that period until the year 1833, when, through the power of amendment vested by the revised constitution in the action of two successive legislative assemblies, the following article received the assent of the requisite numbers, and was approved by the popular vote. Although it has worked some inconvenient change in the structure of religious societies, it cannot thus far be said to have been attended with those serious evils to the habits of worship which were predicted as about to flow from it:—

"Art 11. As the public worship of God, and instructions in piety, religion, and morality promote the happiness and prosperity of a people, and the security of a republican government,—therefore, the several religious societies of this commonwealth, whether corporate or unincorporate, at any meeting legally warned and holden for that purpose, shall ever have the right to elect their pastors or religious teachers; to contract with them for their support; to raise money for erecting and repairing houses for public worship, for the maintenance of religious instruction, and for the payment of necessary expenses. And all persons belonging to any religious society shall be taken and held to be members, until they shall file with the clerk of such society a written notice, declaring the dissolution of their membership, and thenceforth shall not be liable for any grant and right, which *are*[18] not, or may not hereafter be by them expressly delegated to the United States of America, in congress assembled.

V. All power residing originally in the people, and being derived from them, the several magistrates and officers of government, vested with authority, whether legislative, executive, or judicial, are their substitutes and agents, and are at all times accountable to them.[19]

VI. No man, nor corporation or association of men, have any other title to obtain advantages, or particular and exclusive privileges, distinct from those of the community, than what arises from the consideration of services rendered to the public; and this title, being in nature neither hereditary nor transmissible to children, or descendants, or relations by blood, the idea of a man born a magistrate, lawgiver, or judge, is absurd and unnatural.[20]

VII. Government is instituted for the common good; for the protection, safety, prosperity, and happiness of the people; and not for the profit, honor, or private interest of any one man, family, or class of men; therefore, the people alone have an incontestable, unalienable, and indefeasible right to institute government; and to reform, alter, or totally change the same, when their protection, safety, prosperity, and happiness require it.[21]

VIII. In order to prevent those who are vested with authority from becoming oppressors, the people have a right, at such periods and in such manner as *may be delineated in*[22] their frame of government, to cause their public officers to return to private life, and to fill up vacant places by certain and regular elections.   [23]

---

or contract which may be thereafter made or entered into by such society. And all religious sects and denominations, demeaning themselves peaceably, and as good citizens of the commonwealth, shall be equally under the protection of the law; and no subordination of any one sect or denomination to another shall ever be established by law."

[18] ";is"

[19] This is an amplification of the second article of the Virginia Bill of Rights.

[20] The fourth article of the Virginia Bill amplified.

[21] The third article of Virginia expanded.

[22] "they shall establish by"

[23] "and appointments."

IX. All elections ought to be free; and all the [male] inhabitants of this commonwealth, having *sufficient qualifications,*[24] have an equal right to elect officers, and to be elected, for public employments.

X. Each individual of the society has a right to be protected by it in the enjoyment of his life, liberty, and property, according to standing laws. He is obliged, consequently, to contribute his share to the expense of this protection; and to give his personal service, or an equivalent, when necessary. But no part of the property of any individual can, with justice, be taken from him, or applied to public uses, without his own consent, or that of the representative body of the people. In fine, the people of this commonwealth are not controllable by any other laws than those to which their constitutional representative body have given their consent. [25]

XI. Every subject of the commonwealth ought to find a certain remedy, by having recourse to the laws, for all injuries or wrongs which he may receive in his person, property, or character. He ought to obtain right and justice freely, and without being obliged to purchase it; completely, and without any denial; promptly, and without delay, conformably to the laws.

XII. No subject shall be held to answer for any crime or offence, until the same is fully and plainly, substantially and formally described to him. *He cannot*[26] be compelled to accuse [himself,] or [to] furnish evidence against himself; and every subject shall have a right *to be fully heard in his defence, by himself or his counsel at his election; to meet the witnesses against him face to face; to produce all proofs that may be favorable to him;*[27] [to require a speedy and public trial by an impartial jury of the country, without whose unanimous consent, or his own voluntary confession, he cannot

---

[24] "such qualifications as they shall establish by their frame of government,"

[25] "And whenever the public exigencies require that the property of any individual should be appropriated to public uses, he shall receive a reasonable compensation therefor."

[26] "; or"

[27] The last three parts of this sentence were placed by the convention in an order exactly reversed.

finally be declared guilty, or sentenced to loss of life, liberty, or property.][28]

XIII. In criminal prosecutions, the verification of facts in the vicinity where they happen, is one of the greatest securities of the life, liberty, and property of the citizen.

[XIV.][29] No subject [of the commonwealth] shall be arrested, imprisoned, despoiled, or deprived of his property, immunities, or privileges, put out of the protection of the law, exiled, or deprived of his life, liberty, or estate, but by the judgment of his peers, or the law of the land.

XIV. [XV.] Every *man*[30] has a right to be secure from all unreasonable searches and seizures of his person, his houses, his papers, and all his possessions. All warrants, therefore, are contrary to this right, if the cause or foundation of them be not previously supported by oath or affirmation, and if the order in the warrant to a civil officer, to make search in suspected places, or to arrest one or more suspected persons, or to seize their property, be not accompanied with a special designation of the persons or objects of search, arrest, or seizure; and no warrant ought to be issued but in cases and with the formalities prescribed by the laws.

XV. [XVI.] In all controversies concerning property, and in all suits between two or more persons,   [30]the parties have a right to a trial by [a] jury; and this method of procedure shall be held sacred; unless in causes arising on the high seas, and such as relate to mariners' wages, the legislature shall hereafter find it necessary to alter it.

---

[28] That which makes the fourteenth article in the report now follows, and is incorporated into the twelfth, with a single amendment, above noted.

The following addition, in lieu of the portion stricken out, completes the article as it appears in the constitution:—

"And the legislature shall not make any law, that shall subject any person to a capital or infamous punishment, excepting for the government of the army and navy, without trial by jury."

[29] "subject"

[30] "except in cases in which it has heretofore been otherways used and practised,"

XVI. [XVII.] *The people have a right to the freedom of speaking, writing, and publishing their sentiments. The liberty of the press, therefore, ought not to be restrained.*[31]

XVII. [XVIII.] The people have a right to keep and to bear arms for the common defence. And as in time of peace [standing] armies are dangerous to liberty, they ought not to be maintained without the consent of the legislature; and the military power shall always be held in an exact subordination to the civil authority, and be governed by it.

XVIII. [XIX.] A frequent recurrence to the fundamental principles of the constitution, and a constant adherence to those of piety, justice, moderation, temperance, industry, and frugality, are absolutely necessary to preserve the advantages of liberty, and to maintain a free government. The people ought, consequently, to have a particular attention to all those principles, in the choice of their officers and representatives. And they have a right to require of their lawgivers and magistrates an exact and constant observance of them, in the formation and execution of the laws necessary for the good administration of the commonwealth.

XIX. [XX.] The people have a right, in an orderly and peaceable manner, to assemble to consult upon the common good, give instructions to their representatives, and to request of the legislative body, by the way of addresses, petitions, or remonstrances, redress of the wrongs done them, and the grievances they suffer.

XX. [XXI.] The power of suspending the laws, or the execution of the laws, ought never to be exercised but by the legislature, or by author-

---

[31] This article was recommitted by the convention, when the following substitute was reported and adopted. Much objection was made to it, among the people, as insufficient:—

"XVI. The liberty of the press is essential to the security of freedom in a state; it ought not, therefore, to be restrained in this commonwealth."

ity derived from it, to be exercised in such particular cases only as the legislature shall expressly provide for; [and there shall be no suspension of any law for the private interest, advantage, or emolument, of any one man, or class of men.]

XXI. [XXII.] The freedom of deliberation, speech, and debate, in either house of the legislature, is so essential to the rights of the people, that it cannot be the foundation of any accusation or prosecution, action or complaint, in any other court or place whatsoever.

XXII. [XXIII.] The legislature ought frequently to assemble for the redress of grievances, for correcting, strengthening, and confirming the laws, and for making new laws as the common good may require.

XXIII. [XXIV.] No subsidy, charge, tax, impost, or duties ought to be established, fixed, laid, or levied, under any pretext whatsoever, without the consent of the people, or their representatives in the legislature.

XXIV. [XXV.] Laws made to punish for actions done before the existence of such laws, and which have not been declared crimes by preceding laws, are unjust, oppressive, and inconsistent with the fundamental principles of a free government.

XXV. [XXVI.] No *man*[32] ought in any case, or in any time, to be declared guilty of treason or felony by [any act of] the legislature.

XXVI. [XXVII.] No magistrate or court of law shall demand excessive bail, or sureties, impose excessive fines, or inflict cruel or unusual punishments.

XXVII. [XXVIII.] In time of peace, no soldier ought to be quartered in any house without the consent of the owner; and in time of war, such quarters ought not to be made, but by the civil magistrate in a manner ordained by the legislature.

---

[32] "subject"

XXVIII. [XXIX.] No person can in any case be subjected to law martial, or to any penalties or pains by virtue of that law, except those employed in the army or navy, and except the militia in actual service, but by authority of the legislature.

XXIX. [XXX.] It is essential to the preservation of the rights of every individual, his life, liberty, property, and character, that there be an impartial interpretation of the laws, and administration of justice. It is the right of every citizen to be tried by judges as free, impartial, and independent as the lot of humanity will admit. It is, therefore, not only the best policy, but for the security of the rights of the people and of every citizen, that the judges[33] should hold their offices as long as they behave themselves well, and that they should have honorable salaries ascertained and established by standing laws.

XXX. [XXXI.] *The judicial department of the state ought to be separate from, and independent of, the legislative and executive powers.*[34]

---

[33] "of the supreme judicial court"
Extract from the Journal of the Convention.
"After long debate, it was moved and seconded, that the sense of the convention be taken upon the word 'judges,' in said article; in order to which a question was moved and seconded, namely,—'whether it be the sense of this convention, that the judges of the supreme judicial court of this commonwealth, ought to be appointed to hold their office during good behavior;' which, being put, passed in the affirmative, by seventy-eight out of one hundred and thirteen, (ayes 78, noes 35.)

"It was then moved and seconded, that a question be put: whether it is the opinion of this convention, that the judges of the courts of common pleas, in this commonwealth, ought to be appointed to hold their offices during good behavior; which was accordingly put, and passed in the negative, by fifty-seven out of one hundred and nineteen, (ayes 57, noes 62.)"

This decision was reversed on a subsequent day, by sixty-two out of eighty-six, (ayes 62, nays 24.)

[34] XXX. In the government of this commonwealth, the legislative department shall never exercise the executive and judicial powers, or either of them; the executive shall never exercise the legislative and judicial powers, or either of them; the judicial shall never exercise the legislative and executive powers, or either of them, to the end it may be a government of laws and not of men.

[CHAPTER II.[35]]

THE FRAME OF GOVERNMENT.

THE people inhabiting the territory *heretofore*[36] called the Province of Massachusetts Bay, do hereby solemnly and mutually agree with each other to form themselves into a free, sovereign, and independent body politic, or State, by the name of THE COMMONWEALTH OF MASSACHUSETTS.

In the government of the Commonwealth of Massachusetts, the legislative, executive, and judicial power shall be placed in separate departments, to the end that it might be a government of laws, and not of men.[37]

[38]

SECTION I.

[39]

ART. I. THE department of legislation shall be formed by two branches, A SENATE and HOUSE OF REPRESENTATIVES; each of which shall have a negative on the other.

They [40]shall assemble *once,*[41] on the last Wednesday in May, and at such other times as they shall judge necessary, [every year,] [42]   and shall be styled THE GENERAL COURT OF MASSACHUSETTS.

---

[35] "PART THE SECOND."

[36] "formerly"

[37] XXX. In the government of this commonwealth, the legislative department shall never exercise the executive and judicial powers, or either of them; the executive shall never exercise the legislative and judicial powers, or either of them; the judicial shall never exercise the legislative and executive powers, or either of them, to the end it may be a government of laws and not of men.

Extract from the Journal.

"On a motion, made and seconded, that the word 'Massachusetts' be expunged, and that the word 'Oceana' be substituted, the same was put, and passed in the negative."

[38] "CHAPTER I. THE LEGISLATIVE POWER."

[39] *The General Court.*

[40] "The legislative body"

[41] "every year"

[42] "and shall dissolve and be dissolved on the day next preceding the said last Wednesday in May,"

[And the first magistrate shall have a negative upon all the laws, that he may have power to preserve the independence of the executive and judicial departments.][43]

The convention of 1820 changed the beginning of the legislative year to January, as will be seen by the following, which is the tenth amendment adopted by the people:—
Amendment.

ART. 10. The political year shall begin on the first Wednesday of January, instead of the last Wednesday of May; and the general court shall assemble every year on the said first Wednesday of January, and shall proceed, at that session, to make all the elections, and do all the other acts, which are by the constitution required to be made and done at the session which has heretofore commenced on the last Wednesday of May. And the general court shall be dissolved on the day next preceding the first Wednesday of January, without any proclamation or other act of the governor. But nothing herein contained shall prevent the general court from assembling at such other times as they shall judge necessary, or when called together by the governor. The governor, lieutenant-governor, and counsellors, shall also hold their respective offices for one year next following the first Wednesday of January, and until others are chosen and qualified in their stead.

The meeting for the choice of governor, lieutenant-governor, senators, and representatives, shall be held on the second Monday of November in every year; but meetings may be adjourned, if necessary, for the choice of representatives, to the next day, and again to the next succeeding day, but no further. But in case a second meeting shall be necessary for the choice of representatives, such meetings shall be held on the fourth Monday of the same month of November.

All the other provisions of the constitution respecting the elections and proceedings of the members of the general court, or any other officers or persons whatever, that have reference to the last Wednesday of May as the commencement of the political year, shall be so far altered as to have like reference to the first Wednesday of January.

This article shall go into operation on the first day of October next following the day when the same shall be duly ratified and adopted as an amendment of the constitution; and the governor, lieutenant-governor, counsellors, senators, representatives, and all other state officers who are annually chosen, and who shall be chosen for the current year, when the same shall go into operation, shall hold their respective offices until the first Wednesday of January then next following, and until others are chosen and qualified in their stead, and no longer; and the first election of the governor, lieutenant-governor, senators, and representatives, to be had in virtue of this article, shall be had conformably thereunto, in the month of November following the day on which the same shall be in force and go into operation, pursuant to the foregoing provision.

[43] In lieu of this absolute negative, which, in the opinion of Mr. Adams, was an essential part of the plan, the convention adopted the following, as a separate article:—

II. No bill or resolve of the senate or house of representatives, shall become a law, and have force as such, until it shall have been laid before the governor for his revisal. And if he, upon such revision, approve thereof, he shall signify his approbation by signing the same. But if he have any objection to the passing of such bill or resolve, he shall return the

same, together with his objections thereto, in writing, to the senate or house of representatives, in which soever the same shall have originated, who shall enter the objections sent down by the governor, at large on their records, and proceed to reconsider
the said bill or resolve. But if, after such reconsideration, two thirds of the said senate or
house of representatives shall, notwithstanding the said objections, agree to pass the
same, it shall, together with the objections, be sent to the other branch of the legislature,
where it shall also be reconsidered, and, if approved by two thirds of the members present,
shall have the force of a law. But in all such cases the votes of both houses shall be determined by yeas and nays, and the names of the persons voting for or against the said bill
or resolve, shall be entered upon the public records of the commonwealth.

And in order to prevent unnecessary delays, if any bill or resolve shall not be returned
by the governor within five days after it shall have been presented, the same shall have the
force of a law.

Extract from the Journal of the Convention.

"The paragraph from the report of the general committee,—namely, 'That the first
magistrate shall have a negative upon all laws, that he may have power to preserve the
independence of the executive and judicial departments,'—on a motion made and seconded, was then put, and passed in the negative; thirty-two in seventy-six. (Ayes 32,
nays 44.)"

At a subsequent period, the subject came up again, on the report of a commitee to
whom the article had been referred,—

"When it was moved and seconded, that the report be amended by introducing the
following words; namely,—

" 'That the governor of this commonwealth have a negative upon all the laws, except
those which shall be made and passed for the military defence of the State; and that he
have a revision on those, to be conducted by the rules hereafter prescribed.'

"Which being largely debated, when the question was put, the same was determined
in the negative; twenty in seventy-three."

The decline in importance of the State governments, by the subsequent withdrawal of
the power over the most material of the public interests into the national sphere, has
rendered this question one of inferior interest in Massachusetts. But it is yet agitated in
the federal system, and bids fair to continue unsolved for some time to come. Although
cheerfully acquiescing in the alteration at the time, the abstract opinion of Mr. Adams,
of the absolute necessity of this power to the maintenance of the executive independence,
remained unchanged to the last.

In order that the period of five days conceded to the governor for consideration
should not be cut off by the delay of the legislature to pass a measure until just before its
adjournment, the convention of 1820 proposed, and the people ratified, the following
amendment, which now stands as part of the constitution:—

ART. I. If any bill or resolve shall be objected to, and not approved by the governor,
and if the general court shall adjourn within five days after the same shall have been laid
before the governor for his approbation, and thereby prevent his returning it, with his
objections, as provided by the constitution, such bill or resolve shall not become a law, nor
have force as such.

III. [II.] The general court shall forever have full power and authority to erect and constitute judicatories and courts of record, or other courts, to be held in the name of the commonwealth, for the hearing, trying, and determining of all manner of crimes, offences, pleas, processes, plaints, actions, matters, causes, and things, whatsoever, arising or happening within the commonwealth, or between or concerning persons inhabiting, or residing, or brought within the same; whether the same be criminal or civil, or whether the said crimes be capital or not capital, and whether the said pleas be real, personal or mixt; and for the awarding and making out of execution thereupon. To which courts and judicatories are hereby given and granted full power and authority, from time to time, to administer oaths or affirmations, for the better discovery of truth in any matter in controversy, or depending before them.

IV. [III.] And further, full power and authority are hereby given and granted to the said general court, from time to time, to make, ordain, and establish all manner of wholesome and reasonable orders, laws, statutes, and ordinances, directions, and instructions, either with penalties or without; so as the same be not repugnant or contrary to this constitution, as they shall judge to be for the good and welfare of this commonwealth, and for the government and ordering thereof, and of the subjects of the same, and for the necessary support and defence of the government thereof; and to name and settle annually, or provide by fixed laws, for the naming and settling all civil officers within the said commonwealth, [such officers excepted] the election and constitution of whom are not hereafter in this Form of Government otherwise provided for; and to set forth the several duties, powers, and limits, of the several civil and military officers of this commonwealth, and the forms of such oaths [44]as shall be respectively administered unto them for the execution of their several offices and places, so as the same be not repugnant or contrary to this constitution; [and also to impose fines, mulets, imprisonments, and other punishments;] and to impose and levy proportional and reasonable

---

[44] "or affirmations"

assessments, rates, and taxes, upon [the persons of] all the inhabitants of, and   [45]within the said commonwealth, [and upon all estates within the same,]   [46]to be issued and disposed of by warrant, under the hand of the governor of this commonwealth for the time being, with the advice and consent of the council, for the public service, in the necessary defence and support of the government of the said commonwealth, and the protection and preservation of the subjects thereof, according to such acts as are or shall be in force within the same [and to dispose of matters and things whereby they may be religiously, peaceably, and civilly governed, protected, and defended.]

And *that public*[47] assessments may be made with equality, there shall be a valuation of estates within the commonwealth taken anew once in every ten years at [the] least,[48]   [49]

---

[45] "persons resident, and estates lying,"

[46] "and also to impose and levy reasonable duties and excises upon any produce, goods, wares, merchandise, and commodities whatsoever, brought into, produced, manufactured, or being within the same;"

[47] "while the public charges of government, or any part thereof, shall be assessed on polls and estates, in the manner that has hitherto been practised, in order that such"

[48] " and as much oftener as the general court shall order."

[49] The convention of 1820 further enlarged the powers of the general court by the following article, which was ratified, and now stands as the second article of amendment:—

"ART. 2. The general court shall have full power and authority to erect and constitute municipal or city governments in any corporate town or towns in this commonwealth, and to grant to the inhabitants thereof such powers, privileges, and immunities, not repugnant to the constitution, as the general court shall deem necessary or expedient for the regulation and government thereof, and to prescribe the manner of calling and holding public meetings of the inhabitants, in wards or otherwise, for the election of officers under the constitution, and the manner of returning the votes given at such meetings. Provided, that no such government shall be erected or constituted in any town not containing twelve thousand inhabitants; nor unless it be with the consent and on the application of a majority of the inhabitants of such town, present and voting thereon, pursuant to a vote at a meeting duly warned and holden for that purpose. And provided also, that all by-laws made by such municipal or city government, shall be subject, at all times, to be annulled by the general court."

SECTION II.

Senate.

I. THERE shall be annually elected by the freeholders and other inhabitants of this commonwealth, qualified as in this constitution is provided,
forty persons, to be counsellors and senators for the year ensuing their
election, to be chosen [in and] by the inhabitants of the districts into
which the commonwealth may from time to time be divided by the general court, for that purpose. And the general court, in assigning the numbers, to be elected by the respective districts, shall govern themselves by
the proportion of the public taxes paid by the said districts;[50] and timely
make known to the inhabitants of the commonwealth, the limits of each
district, and the number of counsellors and senators to be chosen therein;
provided that the number of such districts shall *be never more than sixteen,
nor less than ten.*[51]

And the several counties in this commonwealth shall, until the general
court shall determine it necessary to alter said districts, be districts for the
choice of counsellors and senators (except that the counties of Dukes
County and Nantucket shall form one district for that purpose,) and shall
elect the following number for counsellors and senators, namely,—

Suffolk	6	[York,	2]
Essex,	6	[Dukes County and	
Middlesex,	5	Nantucket	2]
Hampshire,	4	Worcester,	5
Plymouth,	3	[Cumberland,	1]

[50] By the latest or thirteenth article of amendment adopted under the new power in
the legislature, granted in 1820, the basis of the senate has been changed as follows:—

"The several senatorial districts now existing shall be permanent. The senate shall consist of forty members; and, in the year one thousand eight hundred and forty, and every
tenth year thereafter, the governor and council shall assign the number of senators to be
chosen in each district, according to the number of inhabitants in the same. But, in all
cases, at least one senator shall be assigned to each district."

[51] "never be less than thirteen; and that no district be so large as to entitle the same
to choose more than six senators."

Barnstable, ... 1   [Lincoln,. . . . . 1]⁵²

Bristol, ... 3   Berkshire, ... 2

II. The senate shall be the first branch of the legislature; and the senators shall be chosen in the following manner, namely,—There shall be a meeting on the first Monday in April, annually, forever, of the inhabitants of *all the towns*⁵³ in the several counties of this commonwealth, to be called by the selectmen, and warned in due course of law, at least seven days before the first Monday in April, for the purpose of electing persons to be senators and counsellors. And at such meetings every male *person*⁵⁴ of twenty-one years of age and upwards, *resident in such towns one year next preceding the annual election of senators, having a freehold estate within the commonwealth of the annual income of three pounds, or other real or personal estate of the value of sixty pounds, shall have a right to give in his vote for the senators for the district.*

The selectmen of the several towns shall preside at such meetings, and shall be under oath, as well as the town-clerk, to preside impartially, according to their best skill and judgment; and to make a just and true return.

*The selectmen shall receive the votes of all the inhabitants of such towns,*⁵⁵ qualified to vote for senators, and shall sort and count them in open town meeting, and in presence of the town-clerk, who shall make a fair record, in

---

⁵² This provision was made to include that portion of the territory which has since been separated, and now constitutes the state of Maine. The county of Hampshire has since been subdivided into three countries, and the number now apportioned on the basis of population has not been reduced.

⁵³ "each town"

⁵⁴ "inhabitant"

⁵⁵ "having a freehold estate within the commonwealth, of the annual income of three pounds, or any estate of the value of sixty pounds, shall have a right to give in his vote for the senators for the district of which he is an inhabitant. And, to remove all doubts concerning the meaning of the word 'inhabitant' in this constitution, every person shall be considered as an inhabitant, for the purpose of electing and being elected into any office or place within this state, in that town, district, or plantation, where he dwelleth or hath his home.

"The selectmen of the several towns shall preside at such meetings inpartially; and shall receive the votes of all the inhabitants of such towns present, and"

The qualification of voters was altered by the convention of 1820, in the manner pointed out in the note to the fourth article of the third section.

presence of the selectmen, and in open town meeting, of the name of every person voted for, and of the number of votes against his name; and a fair copy of this record shall be attested by the selectmen and the town-clerk, and shall be sealed up, directed to the secretary of the commonwealth, for the time being, with a superscription, expressing the purport of the contents thereof, and delivered by the town-clerk of such towns to the sheriff of the county in which such town lies, thirty days at least before the last Wednesday in May, annually; or it shall be delivered into the secretary's office seventeen days at least before the said last Wednesday in May; and the sheriff of each county shall deliver all such certificates by him received into the secretary's office, seventeen days before the said last Wednesday in May.

And the inhabitants of plantations unincorporated, qualified as this constitution provides, who are or shall be empowered and required to assess taxes upon themselves toward the support of government, shall have the same privilege of voting for counsellors and senators in the plantations where they reside, as town inhabitants have in their respective towns; and the plantation meetings for that purpose shall be held annually, on the same first Monday in April, at such place in the plantations respectively, as the assessors thereof shall direct; which assessors shall have like authority for notifying the electors, collecting and returning the votes, as the selectmen and town-clerks have in their several towns by this constitution. And all other persons living in places unincorporated (qualified as aforesaid) who shall be assessed to the support of government by the assessors of an adjacent town, shall have the privilege of giving in their votes for counsellors and senators, in the town where they shall be assessed, and be notified of the place of meeting by the selectmen of the town where they shall be assessed for that purpose accordingly.

III. And that there may be a due convention of senators on the last Wednesday in May, annually, the governor, with five of the council, for the time being, shall, as soon as may be, examine the returned copies of such records; and fourteen days before the said day he shall issue his summons to such persons as shall appear to be chosen by a majority of voters, to attend on that day, and take their seats accordingly; provided, nevertheless, that, for the first year, the said returned copies shall be examined by the president and five of the council of the former constitution of government; and the said president shall, in like manner, issue his summons to the persons so elected, that they may take their seats, as aforesaid.

IV. The senate [however] shall be the final judge of the elections, returns, and qualifications of their own members,   [56] and shall, on the said last Wednesday in May, annually, determine and declare who are elected by each district to be senators, by a majority of votes. And, in case there shall not appear to be the full number of senators returned, elected by a majority of votes for any district, the deficiency shall be supplied in the following[57] manner, namely:—The members of the house of representatives, and such senators as shall be declared elected, shall take the names of *twice the number of senators wanting, from those who shall be found to have the highest number of votes in such district, and not elected;*[58] and out of these shall elect, by ballot, a number of senators sufficient to fill up the vacancies in such district. And in this manner all such vacancies shall be filled up in every district of the commonwealth; and in like manner all vacancies in the senate, arising by death, removal out of the state, or otherwise, shall be supplied as soon as may be after such vacancies shall happen.

[56] "as pointed out in the constitution;"

[57] The mode of electing the senate was very much debated in the convention, and not decided upon without great difference of opinion. But it was acquiesced in, and has remained substantially unchanged to this day. Yet it may be justly objected to as defective in simplicity, and ill adapted to the equal representation as well of property as of public opinion in the commonwealth. The mode now generally pursued in the other states, of apportioning the members into separate districts, and doing away with the contingency of a vacancy, to be filled by a body other than the immediate constituents of the person elected, and often not in political sympathy with them, seems to recommend itself as more direct and consonant with the spirit of republican institutions.

[58] "such persons as shall be found to have the highest number of votes in such district, and not elected, amounting to twice the number of senators wanting, if there be so many voted for;"

V. Provided, nevertheless, that no person shall be capable of being elected as a senator, who is not [of the Christian religion, and][59] seised in his own right of a freehold within this commonwealth, of the value of three hundred pounds at least,   [60] and who has not been an inhabitant of this commonwealth for the space of *seven*[61] years, [three of which] immediately preceding his election, and   [62]in the district for which he shall be chosen.

VI. The senate shall have power to adjourn themselves, provided such adjournments do not exceed two days at a time.

VII. The senate shall choose its own president, appoint its own officers, and determine its own rules of proceeding[s].

VIII. The senate shall be a court, with full authority to hear and determine all impeachments made by the house of representatives, against any officer or officers of the commonwealth, for misconduct and maladministration in their offices. But previous to the trial of every impeachment, the members of the senate shall respectively be sworn, truly and impartially to try and determine the charge in question, according to evidence. Their judgment, however, shall not extend farther than to removal from office, and disqualification to hold or enjoy any place of honor, trust, or profit under this commonwealth. But the party so convicted shall be, nevertheless, liable to indictment, trial, judgment, and punishment, according to the laws of the land.[63]

---

[59] *Extract from the Journal.* "Moved and seconded, That the word 'Protestant' be inserted in lieu of the word 'Christian,' which, being put, passed in the negative.

"The question was then put upon the paragraph, so far as it takes up the qualification of religion. The same was rejected, and the words 'of the Christian religion and' voted to be expunged."

[60] "or possessed of personal estate to the value of six hundred pounds at least, or of both to the amount of the same sum,"

[61] "five"

[62] "at the time of his election he shall be an inhabitant"

[63] The following article was added by the convention:—

"IX. Not less than sixteen members of the senate shall constitute a quorum for doing business."

SECTION III.

House of Representatives.

I. THERE shall be in the legislature of this commonwealth a representation of the people annually elected, and founded *in*[64] equality.

II. And, in order to provide for a representation of the citizens of this commonwealth, founded upon the principle of equality, every corporate town, containing one hundred and fifty ratable polls, may elect one representative. Every corporate town, containing three hundred and seventy-five ratable polls, may elect two representatives. Every corporate town, containing six hundred ratable polls, may elect three representatives; and proceeding in that manner, making two hundred and twenty-five ratable polls the mean increasing number for every additional representative.

[And forever, hereafter, the least number of ratable polls necessary to entitle a corporate town to elect one representative, when increased by the addition of a number equal to half the said least number, shall be the mean increasing number of ratable polls for every additional representative any corporate town may elect.

And, to prevent hereafter the house of representatives from becoming unwieldy, and incapable of debating and deliberating, by the great additions it would continually receive from the increasing settlement and population of this commonwealth, no corporate town shall, from and after the year of our Lord, one thousand seven hundred and ninety, be entitled to elect one representative, unless it shall contain two hundred ratable polls; nor to elect two representatives, unless it shall contain five hundred ratable polls; nor to elect three representatives, unless it shall contain eight hundred ratable polls; and so proceeding in that manner, making, by the aforesaid rule, three hundred ratable polls the mean increasing number for every additional representative. And every tenth year, from and after the said year of our Lord, one thousand seven hundred and ninety, and until such time as the number of representatives which may be elected for this commonwealth shall not exceed the number of two hundred, the least

---

[64] "upon the principle of"

number of ratable polls which, at that time, any corporate town must contain to entitle it to elect one representative, shall be increased by the addition of fifty; and the least number aforesaid, thus increased by the said addition, shall be the number of ratable polls any corporate town must contain to entitle it to elect one representative; and the number of representatives any corporate town may elect shall be regulated accordingly, by the rules aforesaid.

The freeholders and other inhabitants of this commonwealth, qualified to vote for representatives, living in corporate towns, which, severally, shall contain a less number of ratable polls than is necessary to entitle them, respectively, to elect one representative, shall, nevertheless, have a right to associate with some town or towns adjoining, for the election of representatives; and, in such cases, the voters thus united, shall have a right to elect the same number of representatives as they would have done were they inhabitants of one corporate town; which representatives may be elected out of either of the associated towns, indifferently. And the legislature shall, from time to time, determine what towns shall thus associate, the manner of the association, and the method and manner of calling and conducting the meetings of the associated towns for the election of representatives.][65]

---

[65] The subject of representation seems to have exercised the skill of the convention more than any other portion of the instrument, and it has remained a difficulty from the beginning to this time. The problem has been to unite with the popular and just principle of the representation of townships, a ratio of tolerable equality, and a limitation of numbers sufficient for practical legislation.

Instead of the passage inclosed within brackets, the convention of 1780 adopted the following proviso:—

"Provided, nevertheless, that each town now incorporated, not having one hundred and fifty ratable polls, may elect one representative; but no place shall hereafter be incorporated, with the privilege of electing a representative, unless there are within the same one hundred and fifty ratable polls.

"And the house of representatives shall have power, from time to time to impose fines upon such towns as shall neglect to choose and return members to the same, agreeably to this constitution.

"The expenses of travelling to the general assembly, and returning home, once in every session, and no more, shall be paid by the government out of the public treasury, to every member who shall attend, as seasonably as he can, in the judgment of the house, and does not depart without leave."

The check here imposed upon an excess of members, consisted in the necessity laid upon the respective towns to pay their own representatives. This answered very well in all but high party times, when the evil was sure to be felt. But dissatisfaction with it existed on other grounds. It was found so much more easy and convenient to draw the means of payment from the common treasury of the state, that most persons of influence favored the inclination of the towns to shift the burden. Yet the desire to make this change was counteracted by the difficulty of finding a good substitute. The convention of 1820 attempted the experiment, and recommended an article to the people, but it was rejected. The legislatures of 1835 and 1836 proposed another, which received their assent, and now makes the twelfth article of amendments:—

"Art. 12. In order to provide for a representation of the citizens of this commonwealth, founded upon the principles of equality, a census of the ratable polls in each city, town, and district of the commonwealth, on the first day of May, shall be taken, and returned into the secretary's office, in such manner as the legislature shall provide, within the month of May, in the year of our Lord, one thousand eight hundred and thirty-seven, and in every tenth year thereafter, in the month of May, in manner aforesaid; and each town or city, having three hundred ratable polls at the last preceding decennial census of polls, may elect one representative; and for every four hundred and fifty ratable polls, in addition to the first three hundred, one representative more.

"Any town having less than three hundred ratable polls shall be represented thus,—the whole number of ratable polls, at the last preceding decennial census of polls, shall be multiplied by ten, and the product divided by three hundred, and such town may elect one representative as many years within ten years as three hundred is contained in the product aforesaid.

"Any city or town having ratable polls enough to elect one or more representatives, with any number of polls beyond the necessary number, may be represented as to that surplus number, by multiplying such surplus number by ten, and dividing the product by four hundred and fifty; and such city or town may elect one additional representative as many years within ten years as four hundred and fifty is contained in the product aforesaid.

"Any two or more of the several towns and districts may, by consent of a majority of the legal voters, present at a legal meeting in each of said towns and districts, respectively, called for that purpose, and held previous to the first day of July, in the year in which the decennial census of polls shall be taken, form themselves into a representative district, to continue until the next decennial census of polls, for the election of a representative or representatives; and such district shall have all the rights, in regard to representation, which would belong to a town containing the same number of ratable polls.

"The governor and council shall ascertain and determine, within the months of July and August, in the year of our Lord, one thousand eight hundred and thirty-seven, according to the foregoing principles, the number of representatives which each city, town, and representative district is entitled to elect, and the number of years within the period of ten years, then next ensuing, that each city, town, and representative district may elect an additional representative; and where any town has not a sufficient number of polls to elect a representative each year, then, how many years within the ten years such town may elect a representative; and the same shall be done once in ten years thereafter, by the governor and council, and the number of ratable polls in each decennial census of polls shall determine the number of representatives which each city, town, and representative district may elect, as aforesaid; and when the number of representatives, to be elected by each city, town, or representative district, is ascertained and determined, as aforesaid, the governor shall cause the same to be published forthwith for the information of the people, and that number shall remain fixed and unalterable for the period of ten years.

"All the provisions of the existing constitutions, inconsistent with the provisions herein contained, are hereby wholly annulled."

This amendment had not been in operation a year, before it was discovered to be open to serious objections. Whilst it did not effectively remedy the serious evil of excess in the representation, the apportionment of it among the fractions created an extraordinary practical inequality. A new effort was made to remedy this, in connection with a radical change of the basis upon which the whole system originally rested, from polls or taxation, to population or numbers. This resulted, in 1840, in the modification of the basis of the senate, which has already been noticed under the proper head, and in the following article, which now constitutes the rule of representation in the lower house:—

"Art. 13. A census of the inhabitants of each city and town, on the first day of May, shall be taken, and returned into the secretary's office, on or before the last day of June of the year one thousand eight hundred and forty, and of every tenth year thereafter, which census shall determine the apportionment of senators and representatives for the term of ten years.

"The members of the house of representatives shall be apportioned in the following manner:—Every town or city, containing twelve hundred inhabitants, may elect one representative; and two thousand four hundred inhabitants shall be the mean increasing number which shall entitle it to an additional representative.

"Every town containing less than twelve hundred inhabitants, shall be entitled to elect a representative as many times within ten years, as the number one hundred and sixty is contained in the number of the inhabitants of said town. Such towns may also elect one representative for the year in which the valuation of estates within the commonwealth shall be settled.

"Any two or more of the several towns may, by consent of a majority of the legal voters, present at a legal meeting in each of said towns, respectively, called for that purpose, and held before the first day of August, in the year one thousand eight hundred and forty, and every tenth year thereafter, form themselves into a representative district, to continue for the term of ten years; and such district shall have all the rights, in regard to representation, which would belong to a town containing the same number of inhabitants.

"The number of inhabitants which shall entitle a town to elect one representative, and the mean increasing number, which shall entitle a town or city to elect more than one, and also the number by which the population of towns, not entitled to a representative every year, is to be divided, shall be increased respectively, by one tenth of the numbers above-mentioned, whenever the population of the commonwealth shall have increased to seven hundred and seventy thousand; and for every additional increase of seventy thou-

III. *The members*[66] of the house of representatives shall be chosen by written votes; [and no person shall be qualified or eligible to be a member of the said house, unless he be of the Christian religion,] and, for one year at least, next preceding his election, shall have been an inhabitant of, and have been seised in his own right of a freehold of the value of one hundred pounds, within the town [or towns] he shall be chosen to represent;   [67]and he shall cease to represent the said town [or towns] immediately on his ceasing to be *a freeholder within the same.*[68]

IV. Every male person, being twenty-one years of age, and resident in any particular town in this commonwealth for the space of one year next preceding, having a freehold estate within the same town, of the annual income of three pounds, or *other*[69] estate [real or personal or mixt] of the

---

sand inhabitants, the same addition of one tenth shall be made respectively to the said numbers above mentioned.

"In the year of each decennial census, the governor and council shall, before the first day of September, apportion the number of representatives which each city, town, and representative district is entitled to elect, and ascertain how many years within ten years, any town may elect a representative, which is not entitled to elect one every year; and the governor shall cause the same to be published forthwith."

The practical effect of the last amendment is to give a great preponderance to the power of the large towns, whilst the right of representation of the small ones is liable to be cut off at moments when it might be most for their interest that they should enjoy it. These disadvantages are not balanced by the slight relative inequality in their favor of the ratio of representation. This is one of the instances that can be quoted in modern times, (the Reform Bill in Great Britain is another,) in which an apparent concession to the popular principle has shown a practical movement in an opposite direction. The change of the basis, from property to population, has really promoted the influence of property. It may reasonably be doubted, whether any change yet made from the article as it originally stood in the constitution has been an improvement, although some change was made indispensable by the progress of the population.

[66] "Every member"

[67] "or any ratable estate to the value of two hundred pounds;"

[68] "qualified as aforesaid."

By the last or thirteenth amendment of the constitution, adopted in 1840, it is provided: "That no possession of a freehold, or of any other estate, shall be required as a qualification for holding a seat in either branch of the general court, or in the executive council."

[69] "any"

value of sixty pounds, shall have a right to vote in the choice of a representative or representatives for the said town, [or for the towns united as aforesaid.][70]

V. The members of the house of representatives shall be chosen annually in the month of May, ten days at least before the last Wednesday of that month, [from among the wisest, most prudent, and virtuous of the freeholders.]

VI. The house of representatives shall be the grand inquest of this commonwealth; and all impeachments made by them shall be heard and tried by the senate.

VII. All money-bills shall originate in the house of representatives; but the senate may propose or concur with amendments, as on other bills.

VIII. The house of representatives shall have power to adjourn themselves; provided such adjournment shall not exceed two days at a time.

IX. Not less than sixty members of the house of representatives shall constitute a quorum for doing business.

X. The house of representatives shall   [71]choose their own speaker, appoint their own officers, and settle the rules and orders of proceeding in

---

[70] The convention of 1820 proposed the following substitute for this article, which was adopted by the people, and now stands as the third article of amendments:—

"ART. 3. Every male citizen of twenty-one years of age, and upwards, (excepting paupers and persons under guardianship,) who shall have resided within the commonwealth one year, and within the town or district in which he may claim a right to vote, six calendar months next preceding any election of governor, lieutenant-governor, senators, or representatives, and who shall have paid, by himself or his parent, master, or guardian, any state or county tax, which shall, within two years next preceding such election, have been assessed upon him in any town or district of this commonwealth, and also every citizen who shall be by law exempted from taxation, and who shall be in all other respects qualified as above-mentioned, shall have a right to vote in such election of governor, lieutenant-governor, senators, and representatives; and no other person shall be entitled to vote in such election."

[71] "be the judge of the returns, elections, and qualifications of its own members, as pointed out in the constitution; shall"

their own house. They shall have authority to punish, by imprisonment, every person   [72]who shall be guilty of disrespect to the house, in its presence, by any disorderly or contemptuous behavior; *or by threatening or ill-treating any of its members; or, in a word, by obstructing its deliberations; every person guilty of a breach of its privileges, in making arrests for debts, or by assaulting one of its members during his attendance at any session, or on the road, whether he be going to the house or returning home; in assaulting any one of its officers, or in disturbing him in the execution of any order or procedure of the house; in assaulting or troubling any witness or other person ordered to attend the house, in his way in going or returning, or in rescuing any person arrested by order of the house.*[73]

XI. The senate shall have the same powers in the like cases; and the governor and council shall have the same authority to punish in like cases. Provided, that no imprisonment on the warrant or order of the governor, council, senate, or house of representatives, for either of the above described offences, be for a term exceeding thirty days.[74]

———————

[72] "not a member"

[73] "or who, in the town where the general court is sitting, and during the time of its sitting, shall threaten harm to the body or estate of any of its members, for any thing said or done in the house; or who shall assault any of them therefor; or who shall assault or arrest any witness or other person ordered to attend the house, in his way in going or returning; or who shall rescue any person arrested by the order of the house.

"And no member of the house of representatives shall be arrested, or held to bail on mean process, during his going unto, returning from, or his attending, the general assembly."

[74] Addition:—

"And the senate and house of representatives may try and determine all cases where their rights and privileges are concerned, and which, by the constitution, they have authority to try and determine, by committees of their own members, or in such other way as they may respectively think best."

CHAPTER II. [III.]

Executive Power.

SECTION I.

Governor.

ART. I. THERE shall be a supreme executive magistrate, who shall be styled, THE GOVERNOR OF THE COMMONWEALTH OF MASSACHUSETTS, and whose title shall be, HIS EXCELLENCY.

II. The governor shall be chosen annually; and no person shall be eligible to this office unless, at the time of his election, he shall have been an inhabitant of this commonwealth for seven years next preceding; and unless he shall at the same time be seised in his own right of a freehold within the commonwealth, of the value of one thousand pounds; and unless he shall[75] be of the Christian religion.

III. Those persons who shall be qualified to vote for senators and representatives within the several towns of this commonwealth, shall, at a meeting to be called for that purpose, on the first Monday of April annually, give in their votes for a governor, to the selectmen, who shall preside at such meetings; and the town clerk, in the presence and with the assistance of the selectmen, shall in open town meeting sort and count the votes, and form a list of the persons voted for, with the number of votes for each person against his name, and shall make a fair record of the same in the town books, and a public declaration thereof in the said meeting; and shall, in the presence of the inhabitants, seal up copies of the said list, attested by him and the selectmen, and transmit the same to the sheriff of the county, thirty days at least before the last Wednesday in May; *or shall*[76] cause returns of the same to be made to the office of the secretary of the

---

[75] "declare himself to"

This declaration was annulled by the convention of 1820, in the seventh amendment which appears in the note to the fourth article.

[76] "and the sheriff shall transmit the same to the secretary's office, seventeen days at least before the said last Wednesday in May; or the selectmen may"

commonwealth, seventeen days at least before the said day, *who*[77] shall lay the same before the senate and the house of representatives, on the last Wednesday in May, to be by them examined; and, in case of an election by a majority of *votes through the commonwealth,*[78] the choice shall be by them declared and published. But if no person shall have a majority of votes, the house of representatives shall, by ballot, elect two out of four persons who had the highest number of votes, if so many shall have been voted for, but if otherwise, out of the number voted for; and make return to the senate of the two persons so elected, on which the senate shall proceed, by ballot, to elect one, who shall be declared governor.

[IV.] [79] (*Transposed.*)

IV. [V.] The governor shall have authority, from time to time, at his discretion, to assemble and call together the counsellors of this commonwealth, for the time being; and the governor, with the said counsellors, or five of them at least, shall and may, from time to time, hold and keep a council for the ordering and directing the affairs of the commonwealth *according to law.*[80]

V. [VI.] The governor, with advice of council, shall have full power and authority, in the recess of the general court, to prorogue the same from time to time, not exceeding ninety days in any one recess of the said court; and during the session of the said court, to adjourn or prorogue it to any time the two houses shall desire, and to dissolve the same, at their request,

---

[77] "and the secretary"

[78] "all the votes returned,"

[79] Here follows in this draught a form of oath for the governor. But this, with several other articles, was transposed by the convention, as appears by the subjoined extract from the journal, February 25, 1780:—"It was then moved and seconded, that there be a distinct chapter in the constitution for the several oaths and tests which have been, or shall be, prescribed to be taken and subscribed by the officers of government, and the two houses of assembly, and also for the list of persons excluded from a seat in either house, and such miscellaneous matters as the convention shall direct to stand in the same." See under the head of Chapter VI.

[80] "agreeably to the constitution and the laws of the land."

or on the Wednesday next preceding the last Wednesday in May; and to call it together sooner than the time to which it may be adjourned or prorogued, if the welfare of the commonwealth shall require the same.[81]

VI. [VII.] In cases of disagreement between the two houses, with regard to the   [82]time of adjournment or prorogation, the governor, with advice of the council, shall have a right to adjourn or prorogue the general court,   [83]as he shall determine the public good shall require.

VII. [VIII.] The governor of this commonwealth, for the time being, shall be the commander-in-chief of the army and navy, and of all the military forces of the state by sea and land; and shall have full power, by himself or by any [chief] commander, or other officer or officers, [to be appointed by him,] from time to time to train, instruct, exercise, and govern the militia and navy; and for the special defence and safety of the commonwealth, to assemble in martial array and put in warlike posture, the inhabitants thereof; and to lead and conduct them, and with them to encounter, [expulse,] repel, resist,   [84]and pursue, by force of arms, as well by sea as by land, within or without the limits of this commonwealth, and also to kill, slay, destroy, [85]and conquer, by all fitting ways, enterprises, and means whatsoever, all and every such person and persons as shall at any time hereafter, in a hostile manner, attempt or enterprise the destruction, invasion, detriment, or annoyance of this commonwealth; and to use and exercise over the army and navy, and over the militia in actual service, the law martial in time of war,

---

[81] The several clauses of this article are transposed in the constitution as adopted; but, as the language is not changed, it is not deemed important to note the variations.

The following clauses were added:—

"And in case of any infectious distemper prevailing in the place where the said court is next, at any time, to convene, or any other cause happening, whereby danger may arise to the health or lives of the members from their attendance, he may direct the session to be held at some other, the most convenient, place within the state.

"And the governor shall dissolve the said general court, on the day next preceding the last Wednesday in May."

[82] "necessity, expediency, or"

[83] "not exceeding ninety days,"

[84] "expel"

[85] "if necessary,"

invasion, or rebellion,   [86]as occasion shall necessarily require; [and also from time to time to erect forts, and to fortify any place or places within the said commonwealth, and the same to furnish with all necessary ammunition, provisions, and stores of war, for offence or defence, and to commit from time to time the custody and government of the same to such person or persons as to him shall seem meet; and in times of emergency the said forts and fortifications to demolish at his discretion;] and to take and surprise, by all ways and means whatsoever, all and every such person or persons, with their ships, arms, ammunition, and other goods, as shall in a hostile manner invade, or attempt the invading, conquering, or annoying this commonwealth, and [in fine] that the governor be intrusted with all [87]other powers, incident to the offices of captain-general and commander-in-chief and admiral, to be exercised agreeably to the rules and regulations of the constitution and the laws of the land   [88]

Provided, that the said governor shall not at any time hereafter, by virtue of any power by this constitution granted, or hereafter to be granted to him by the legislature, transport any of the inhabitants of this commonwealth, or oblige them to march, out of the limits of the same, without their free and voluntary consent, or the consent of the general court,

[89][nor grant commissions for exercising the law martial upon any of the inhabitants of this commonwealth, without the advice and consent of the council of the same.]

VIII. [IX.] The power of pardoning offences, except such as persons may be convicted of before the senate by an impeachment of the house, shall be in the governor, by and with the advice of council. But no charter of pardon granted by the governor, with advice of the council, before conviction, shall avail the party pleading the same, notwithstanding any

---

[86] "or invasion, and also in time of rebellion declared by the legislature to exist,"
[87] "these and."
[88] "and not otherwise."
[89] "except so far as may be necessary to march or transport them by land or water, for the defence of such part of the state to which they cannot otherwise conveniently have access"

general or particular expressions contained therein, descriptive of the offence or offences intended to be pardoned.

IX. [X.] All judicial officers, the attorney-general, the solicitor-general, all sheriffs, coroners, registers of probate, [and registers of maritime courts,] shall be nominated and appointed by the governor, by and with the advice and consent of the council; and every such nomination shall be made by the governor, and made at least seven days prior to such appointment.

[XI.] [All officers of the militia shall be appointed by the governor, with the advice and consent of the council; he first nominating them seven days at least before the appointment.][90]

[90] The convention, in adopting the following substitute, made what, in the opinion of Mr. Adams, was the second material alteration of the executive power:—

"X. The captains and subalterns of the militia shall be elected by the written votes of the train-band and alarm list of their respective companies, of twenty-one years of age and upwards. The field-officers of regiments shall be elected by the written votes of the captains and subalterns of their respective regiments. The brigadiers shall be elected, in like manner, by the field-officers of their respective brigades. And such officers, so elected, shall be commissioned by the governor, who shall determine their rank.

"The legislature shall, by standing laws, direct the time and manner of convening the electors, and of collecting votes, and of certifying to the governor the officers elected.

"The major-generals shall be appointed by the senate and house of representatives, each having a negative upon the other; and be commissioned by the governor.

"And if the electors of brigadiers, field-officers, captains, or subalterns shall neglect or refuse to make such elections, after being duly notified, according to the laws for the time being, then the governor, with advice of council, shall appoint suitable persons to fill such offices.

"And no officer duly commissioned to command in the militia, shall be removed from his office, but by the address of both houses to the governor, or by fair trial in court-martial, pursuant to the laws of the commonwealth for the time being.

"The commanding officers of regiments shall appoint their adjutants and quarter-masters; the brigadiers their brigade-majors; and the major-generals their aids; and the governor shall appoint the adjutant-general.

"The governor, with advice of council, shall appoint all officers of the continental army, whom, by the confederation of the United States, it is provided that this commonwealth shall appoint; as, also, all officers of forts and garrisons.

"The divisions of the militia into brigades, regiments, and companies, made in pursuance of the militia laws now in force, shall be considered as the proper divisions of the militia of this commonwealth, until the same shall be altered in pursuance of some future law."

XI. [XII.] *All*[91] moneys shall be issued out of the treasury of this commonwealth, and disposed of [92]by warrant, under the hand of the governor for the time being, with the advice and consent of the council, for the necessary defence and support of the commonwealth; and for the protection and preservation of the inhabitants thereof, agreeably to the acts and resolves of the general court.

XII. [XIII.] All public boards, the commissary-general, all superintending officers of public magazines and stores, belonging to this commonwealth, and all commanding officers of forts and garrisons within the same, shall, once in every three months officially, and without requisition, and at other times, when required by the governor, deliver to him an account of all goods, stores, provisions, ammunition, cannon with their appendages, and small arms with their accoutrements, and of all other public property whatever under their care respectively; distinguishing the quantity, number, quality, and kind of each, as particularly as may be; together with the condition of such forts and garrisons. And the said commanding officers shall exhibit to the governor, when required by him, true and exact plans of such forts, and of the land and sea, or harbor or harbors, adjacent.

And the said boards, and all public officers, shall communicate to the governor, as soon as may be after receiving the same, all letters, despatches, and intelligences, of a public nature, which shall be directed to them respectively.

The convention of 1820 once more revised this section by adopting the following article, which was ratified by the people:—

"Article 5. In the elections of captains and subalterns of the militia, all the members of their respective companies, as well those under as those above the age of twenty-one years, shall have a right to vote."

And, with regard to removals, at the close of the fourth article of amendments:—

"All officers commissioned to command in the militia, may be removed from office in such manner as the legislature may, by law, prescribe."

[91] "No"

[92] "(except such sums as may be appropriated for the redemption of bills of credit or treasurer's notes, or for the payment of interest arising thereon) but"

[XIV. And to prevent an undue influence in this commonwealth, which the first magistrate thereof may acquire, by the long possession of the important powers and trusts of that office; as also to stimulate others to qualify themselves for the service of the public in the highest stations, no man shall be eligible as governor of this commonwealth, more than five years in any seven years.][93]

XIII. [XV.] As the public good requires that the governor should not be under the undue influence of any of the members of the general court, by a dependence on them for his support; that he should, in all cases, act with freedom for the benefit of the public; that he should not have his attention necessarily diverted from that object to his private concerns; and that he should maintain the dignity of the commonwealth, in the character of its chief magistrate, it is necessary that he should have an honorable stated salary, of a fixed and permanent value, amply sufficient for those purposes, and established by standing laws; and it shall be among the first acts of the general court, after the commencement of this constitution, to establish such salary by law accordingly.

Permanent and honorable salaries shall also be established by law for the justices of the *superior*[94] court.

And if it shall be found that any of the salaries aforesaid, so established, are insufficient, they shall from time to time be enlarged, as the general court shall judge proper.

---

[93] This provision, establishing a principle of rotation in office, was stricken out by the convention. The practice under the constitution shows that, without any express limitation, but a single case has occurred exceeding seven years, as the longest period that any individual remains governor.

The transfer to the general government of the most important attributes to executive power, has materially lessened the consequence of this post as an object of ambition. But in analyzing the theory upon which this plan is based, it is obvious that this section was incorporated for the purpose of counterbalancing the effect of the gift in other sections of such extensive powers as might make the chief magistrate's place the object of great contention. The convention preferred to take away the powers, on the one hand, and withdraw the limitation, on the other.

[94] "supreme judicial"

SECTION II.

Lieutenant-Governor, [and the ascertaining the Value of the Money mentioned in this Constitution, as Qualifications to Office, &c.]

I. THERE shall be annually elected a lieutenant-governor of the Commonwealth of Massachusetts, whose title shall be HIS HONOR, and who shall be qualified, in point of religion, property, and residence in the commonwealth, in the same manner with the governor. *He shall be chosen on the same day, in the same manner, and by the same persons.*[95] The return of the votes for this officer, and the declaration of his election shall be in the same manner. And if no one person shall be found to have a majority of *votes,*[96] the vacancy shall be filled by the senate and house of representatives, in the same manner as the governor is to be elected, in case no one person *has*[97] a majority of *votes*[98] to be governor.

II. *The lieutenant-governor shall always be, ex-officio, a member, and, in the absence of the governor, president, of the council.*[99]

III. Whenever the chair of the governor shall be vacant, by reason of his death, or absence from the commonwealth, or otherwise, the lieutenant-governor, for the time being, shall, during such vacancy, [100]have and exercise all the powers and authorities which, by this constitution, the governor is vested with, when personally present.

[IV. and V.] (*Transposed. See Chapter VI..*)

[95] "And the day and manner of his election, and the qualifications of the electors shall be the same as are required in the election of a governor."

[96] "all the votes returned"

[97] "shall have"

[98] "the votes of the people"

[99] Substitute:—

"The governor, and, in his absence, the lieutenant-governor, shall be president of the council, but shall have no vote in council. And the lieutenant-governor shall always be a member of the council, except when the chair of the governor shall be vacant."

[100] "perform all the duties incumbent upon the governor, and shall"

SECTION III.

Council, and the Manner of settling Elections by the Legislature; [Oaths to be taken, &c.]

I. THERE shall be a council for advising the governor in the executive part of government, to consist of nine persons besides the lieutenant-governor, whom the governor, for the time being, shall have full power and authority, from time to time, at his discretion, to assemble and call together. And the governor, with the said counsellors, or five of them at least, shall and may, from time to time, hold and keep a council, for the ordering and directing the affairs of the commonwealth, according to the laws of the land.

II. Nine counsellors shall *out of*[101] the persons returned for counsellors and senators, [be annually chosen,] on the last Wednesday in May, by the joint ballot of the senators and representatives assembled in one room [102] The seats of the persons thus elected *into the council*[103] and accepting the trust, shall be vacated in the senate, [and, in this manner, the number of senators shall be reduced to thirty-one.][104]

III. The counsellors, in the civil arrangements of the commonwealth, shall have rank next after the lieutenant-governor.

---

[101] "be annually chosen from among"

[102] "And in case there shall not be found, upon the first choice, the whole number of nine persons who will accept a seat in the council, the deficiency shall be made up by the electors aforesaid, from among the people at large; and the number of senators left shall constitute the senate for the year."

[103] "from the senate."

[104] The last or thirteenth amendment of the constitution, adopted in 1840, contains the following modification of the provisions respecting the council:—

"Nine counsellors shall be annually chosen from among the people at large, on the first Wednesday of January, or as soon thereafter as may be, by the joint ballot of the senators and representatives, assembled in one room, who shall, as soon as may be, in like manner, fill up any vacancies that may happen in the council, by death, resignation, or otherwise. No person shall be elected a counsellor who has not been an inhabitant of this commonwealth for the term of five years, immediately preceding his election; and not more than one counsellor shall be chosen from any one senatorial district in the commonwealth."

IV. Not more than two counsellors shall be chosen out of any one *county*[105] of this commonwealth.

V. The resolutions and advice of the council shall be recorded in a register, and signed by the members present; and this record may be called for at any time by either house of the legislature; and any member of the council may insert his opinion contrary to the resolution of the majority.

VI. Whenever the office of the governor and lieutenant-governor shall be vacant, by reason of death, absence, or otherwise, then the council, or the major part of them, shall, during such vacancy, have full power and authority to do and execute all and every such acts, matters, and things, as the governor or the lieutenant-governor might or could, by virtue of this constitution, do or execute, if they, or either of them, were personally present.

VII. And whereas, the elections appointed to be made by this constitution, on the last Wednesday in May, annually, by the two houses of the legislature, may not be completed on that day, the said elections may be adjourned from day to day, until the same shall be completed. And the order of elections shall be as follows,—the vacancies in the senate, if any, shall first be filled up; the governor and lieutenant-governor shall then be elected, provided there should be no choice of them by the people; and afterwards the two houses shall proceed to the election of the council.

[VIII.] (*Transposed. See Chapter VI.*)

SECTION IV.

Secretary, Treasurer, Commissary, & c.

I. THE secretary, treasurer, and receiver-general, and the commissary-general, notaries-public, and naval officers shall be chosen annually, by joint ballot of the senators and representatives, in one room. And that the citizens of this commonwealth may be assured, from time to time, that the moneys remaining in the public treasury, upon the settlement and

---

[105] "district"

liquidation of the public accounts, are their property, no man shall be eligible as treasurer and receiver-general more than five years successively.[106]

II. The records of the commonwealth shall be kept in the office of the secretary, who   [107]shall attend the governor and council, the senate, and house of representatives in person, or by his deputies, as they shall respectively require.

CHAPTER III. [IV.]

Judiciary Power.

ART. I. THE tenure, that all commission officers *by law hold*[108] in their offices, shall be expressed in their respective commissions. All judicial officers, duly appointed, commissioned, and sworn, shall hold their offices during good behavior   [109]provided, nevertheless, the governor, with consent of the council, may remove them upon the address of both houses of the legislature. [And all other officers, appointed by the governor and council, shall hold their offices during pleasure.]

---

[106] The convention of 1820 framed an article somewhat changing these modes of appointment, which was approved by the people, and is now the fourth of the amendments:—

"Art 4. Notaries-public shall be appointed by the governor, in the same manner as judicial officers are appointed, and shall hold their offices during seven years, unless sooner removed by the governor, with the consent of the council, upon the address of both houses of the legislature.

"In case the office of secretary or treasurer of the commonwealth shall become vacant from any cause, during the recess of the general court, the governor, with the advice and consent of the council, shall nominate and appoint, under such regulations as may be prescribed by law, a competent and suitable person to such vacant office, who shall hold the same until a successor shall be appointed by the general court.

"Whenever the exigencies of the commonwealth shall require the appointment of a commissary-general, he shall be nominated, appointed, and commissioned in such manner as the legislature may, by law, prescribe."

[107] "may appoint his deputies, for whose conduct he shall be accountable; and he"

[108] "shall by law have"

[109] "excepting such concerning whom there is different provision made in this constitution;"

[II.] (*Transposed. See Chapter VI.*)

II. [III.] *The senate, nevertheless,*[110] as well as the governor and council, shall have authority to require the opinions of the *judges*[111] upon important questions of law, and upon solemn occasions.

III. [IV.] In order that the people may not suffer from the long continuance in place of any justice of the peace, who shall fail of discharging the important duties of his office with ability or fidelity, all commissions of justices of the peace shall expire and become void, in the term of seven years from their respective dates; and, upon the expiration of any commission, the *governor and council may, if necessary, renew such commissions, or appoint another person,*[112] as shall most conduce to the well-being of the commonwealth.

IV. [V.] The judges of probate of wills and for granting letters of administration, shall hold their courts at such place or places, on fixed days, as the convenience of the people shall require. And the legislature shall, from time to time, hereafter, appoint such times and places; until which appointments, the said courts shall be holden at the times and places which the respective judges shall direct.

V. [VI.] All causes of marriage, divorce, and alimony, [shall be determined by the senate;] and all appeals from the judges of probate shall be heard and determined by the governor and council, until the legislature shall, by law, make other provision.[113]

———————

[110] "Each branch of the legislature"
[111] "justices of the supreme judicial court"
[112] "same may, if necessary, be renewed, or another person appointed,"
[113] This power was early transferred by statute to the supreme judicial court of the state.

CHAPTER IV. [V.]

Delegates to Congress, [Commissions, Writs, Indictments, &c.; Confirmation of Laws, Habeas Corpus, and enacting Style.]

ART. I. The delegates of this commonwealth to the Congress of the United States [of America,] shall, *on the second Wednesday of November, if the general court be then sitting, or on the second Wednesday of the session next after,*[114] be elected annually, by the joint ballot of the senate and house of representatives, assembled together in one room.   [115] They shall have commissions under the hand of the governor, and under the great seal of the commonwealth; but may be recalled at any time within the year, and others chosen and commissioned, in the same manner in their stead.[116]

CHAPTER V. [VI.]

The University at Cambridge, and Encouragement of Literature, &c.

SECTION I.

The University.

ART. I. WHEREAS our wise and pious ancestors, so early as the year one thousand six hundred and thirty-six, laid the foundation of Harvard College, in which university many persons of great eminence have by the blessing of God been initiated in those arts and sciences which qualified them for public employments, both in church and state. And whereas the encouragement of arts and sciences, and all good literature, tends to the honor of God, the advantage of the Christian religion, and the great benefit of this and the other United States of America,—it is declared, That the PRESIDENT AND FELLOWS OF HARVARD COLLEGE,

[114] "sometime in the month of June,"

[115] "to serve in congress for one year, to commence on the first Monday in November, then next ensuing."

[116] This article was annulled by the adoption of the federal constitution. Six other articles contained in this chapter were transposed to the sixth chapter, by vote of the convention.

in their corporate capacity, and their successors in that capacity, their officers and servants, shall have, hold, use, exercise, and enjoy, all the powers, authorities, rights, liberties, privileges, immunities, and franchises, which they now have, or are entitled to have, hold, use, exercise, and enjoy; and the same are hereby ratified and confirmed unto them, the said President and Fellows of Harvard College, and to their successors, and to their officers and servants, respectively, forever.

II. And whereas there have been at sundry times, by divers persons, gifts, grants, devises, of houses, lands, tenements, goods, chattels, legacies, and conveyances, heretofore made, either to Harvard College, in Cambridge, in New England, or to the President and Fellows of Harvard College, or to the said College, by some other description, under several charters successively;—IT IS DECLARED, That all the said gifts, grants, devises, legacies, and conveyances, are hereby forever confirmed unto the President and Fellows of Harvard College, and to their successors, in the capacity aforesaid, according to the true intent and meaning of the donor or donors, grantor or grantors, devisor or devisors.

III. And whereas, by an act of the general court of the colony of Massachusetts Bay, passed in the year one thousand six hundred and forty-two, the governor and deputy governor for the time being, and all the magistrates of that jurisdiction, were, with the president, and a number of the clergy, in the said act described, constituted the overseers of Harvard College. And it being necessary, in this new constitution of government, to ascertain who shall be deemed successors to the said governor, deputy-governor, and magistrates;—IT IS DECLARED, That the Governor, Lieutenant-Governor, Council, and Senate of this Commonwealth, are, and shall be deemed, their successors; who, with the President of Harvard College for the time being, together with the Ministers of the Congregational Churches in the towns of Cambridge, Watertown, Charlestown, Boston, Roxbury, and Dorchester, mentioned in the said act, shall be and hereby are, vested with all the powers and authority belonging, or in any way appertaining to the overseers of Harvard College. PROVIDED, that nothing herein shall be construed to prevent the legislature of this

542 THE POLITICAL WRITINGS OF JOHN ADAMS

commonwealth from making such alterations in the government of the said university as shall be conducive to its advantage, and the interest of the republic of letters, in as full a manner as might have been done by the legislature of the province of the Massachusetts Bay.[117]

SECTION II.

The Encouragement of Literature, &c.

WISDOM and knowledge, as well as virtue, diffused generally among the body of the people, being necessary for the preservation of their rights and liberties, and as these depend on spreading the opportunities and advantages of education in the various parts of the country, and among the

---

[117] In Quincy's *History of Harvard University,* the following account of the origin of these three articles is given:—

"In September, 1779, the convention assembled to frame a constitution for the State of Massachusetts, being in session, a committee was raised in relation to the college, and was instructed 'to prepare an article to be inserted in the new constitution, for confirming its privileges, and for such other purposes as they shall think proper, after consulting with the corporation of the college.' James Bowdoin, President of the Convention, communicated these proceedings to the corporation; and a committee of the board was raised to take the subject into consideration. On the seventh of the ensuing October, this committee made a report, recapitulating all the leading facts of the constitutional history of the college, and submitting two proposals to be laid before the convention, containing articles to be inserted into the constitution of the commonwealth, on the interests of the college. These proposals, being accepted by the corporation and approved by the overseers, were subsequently adopted by the state convention, and now constitute distinct articles in the constitution of Massachusetts.... The new organization of the state government also rendered it necessary to insert a third article in the same section of the constitution, declarative of the branches of the government which should succeed to the office of overseers, in place of those which were abrogated."

It should be remarked, that from the journal of the convention, it is clear there was no special committee raised in relation to the college. This unimportant error grows out of the confounding of the convention with the grand committee of thirty, of which Mr. Bowdoin, the president, was chairman. It was by this committee that a vote was adopted, instructing the sub-committee of three, which was to have the general draught in its charge, to prepare the article, in conjunction with the corporation, as above described. The first and second articles were drawn up by a committee of the latter body, and entitled "Proposals to be laid before the Committee of the Convention." They were, with only one or two verbal alterations, incorporated into the general report. The third article seems to have emanated from the sub-committee of the convention.

different orders of the people, it shall be the duty of legislators and magistrates, in all future periods of this commonwealth, to cherish the interests
of literature and the sciences, and all seminaries of them; especially the
university at Cambridge, public schools and grammar schools in the
towns; to encourage private societies and public institutions, rewards and
immunities for the promotion of agriculture, arts, sciences, commerce,
trades, manufactures, and a natural history of the country; to countenance and inculcate the principles of humanity and general benevolence,
public and private charity, industry and frugality, honesty and punctuality
in their dealings, sincerity, good humor, and all social affections and generous sentiments among the people.[118]

---

[118] This feature of the constitution of Massachusetts is peculiar, and in one sense
original with Mr. Adams. The recognition of the obligation of a state to promote a higher
and more extended policy than is embraced in the protection of the temporal interests
and political rights of the individual, however understood among enlightened minds,
had not at that time been formally made a part of the organic law. Those clauses, since
inserted in other state constitutions, which, with more or less of fulness, acknowledge
the same principle, are all manifestly taken from this source. The following history of the
origin of it is taken from an account given by the author in 1809:—

"In travelling from Boston to Philadelphia, in 1774, 5, 6, and 7, I had several times
amused myself, at Norwalk in Connecticut, with the very curious collection of birds
and insects of American production made by Mr. Arnold; a collection which he afterwards sold to Governor Tryon, who sold it to Sir Ashton Lever, in whose apartments in
London I afterwards viewed it again. This collection was so singular a thing that it made
a deep impression upon me, and I could not but consider it a reproach to my country, that
so little was known, even to herself, of her natural history.

"When I was in Europe, in the years 1778 and 1779, in the commission to the King
of France, with Dr. Franklin and Mr. Arthur Lee, I had opportunities to see the king's collections and many others, which increased my wishes that nature might be examined and
studied in my own country, as it was in others.

"In France, among the academicians, and other men of science and letters, I was frequently entertained with inquiries concerning the Philosophical Society of Philadelphia,
and with enlogiums on the wisdom of the institution, and encomiums on some publications in their transactions. These conversations suggested to me the idea of such an
establishment at Boston, where I knew there was as much love of science, and as many
gentlemen who were capable of pursuing it, as in any other city of its size.

"In 1779, I returned to Boston in the French frigate La Sensible, with the Chevalier de
la Luzerne and M. Marbois. The corporation of Harvard College gave a public dinner in
honor of the French ambassador and his suite, and did me the honor of an invitation to dine

CHAPTER VI.[119]

Oaths and Subscriptions; Incompatibility of and Exclusion from Offices; Pecuniary Qualifications; Commissions; Writs; Confirmation of Laws; Habeas Corpus; the Enacting Style; Continuance of Officers; Provision for a future Revisal of the Constitution, &c.

I. (*From Chapter III. sect. I. art. 4.*) The[120] person chosen governor, [121]and accepting the trust, shall, [in the presence of the two houses, and]

with them. At table, in the Philosophy Chamber, I chanced to sit next to Dr. Cooper. I entertained him during the whole of the time we were together, with an account of Arnold's collections, the collections I had seen in Europe, the compliments I had heard in France upon the Philosophical Society at Philadelphia, and concluded with proposing that the future legislature of Massachusetts should institute an academy of arts and sciences.

"The doctor at first hesitated, thought it would be difficult to find members who would attend to it; but his principal objection was, that it would injure Harvard College, by setting up a rival to it that might draw the attention and affections of the public in some degree from it. To this I answered,—first, that there were certainly men of learning enough that might compose a society sufficiently numerous; and secondly, that instead of being a rival to the university, it would be an honor and advantage to it. That the president and principal professors would no doubt be always members of it; and the meetings might be ordered, wholly or in part, at the college and in that room. The doctor at length appeared better satisfied; and I entreated him to propagate the idea and the plan, as far and as soon as his discretion would justify. The doctor accordingly did diffuse the project so judiciously and effectually, that the first legislature under the new constitution adopted and established it by law.

"Afterwards, when attending the convention for forming the constitution, I mentioned the subject to several of the members, and when I was appointed by the sub-committee to make a draught of a project of a constitution, to be laid before the convention, my mind and heart were so full of this subject, that I inserted the chapter fifth, section second.

"I was somewhat apprehensive that criticism and objections would be made to the section, and particularly that the 'natural history,' and the 'good humor,' would be stricken out; but the whole was received very kindly, and passed the convention unanimously, without amendment."

It is a singularity, perhaps worthy of note in connection with these injunctions, that the individuals who have since been elevated by the popular voice to the chief offices of the state, with a single exception, have not been noted among their fellow-citizens for any superior acquisitions of learning or intellectual culture. A considerable number have not gone through the higher grades of education in Massachusetts at all.

[119] The articles contained in this chapter, as it stands in the constitution, were scattered among the preceding ones, and from them transposed to here.
[120] "Any"
[121] "lieutenant-governor, counsellor, senator, or representative,"

before he proceed to execute the duties of his   [122]office, make and subscribe the following declaration, [and take the following oaths, to be administered by the president of the senate,] namely,—

I, A B, [being declared duly elected governor of the commonwealth of Massachusetts,] do [now] declare, that I believe [and profess] the Christian religion, *from*[123] a firm persuasion of its truth; and that I am seised and possessed, in my own right, of the property required by *law*,[124] as one qualification for *that office*.[125]

[126]I, A B, do solemnly swear,   [127][that I bear faith and true allegiance to the commonwealth of Massachusetts;] that I will faithfully and

---

[122] "place or"

[123] "and have"

[124] "the constitution,"

[125] "the office or place to which I am elected."

[126] Previous to this second oath, the following is here inserted as a substitute for the greater part of the other forms:—

"And the governor, lieutenant-governor, and counsellors shall make and subscribe the said declaration, in the presence of the two houses of assembly; and the senators and representatives first elected under this constitution, before the president and five of the council of the former constitution, and forever afterwards, before the governor and council for the time being.

"And every person chosen to either of the places or offices aforesaid, as also any person appointed or commissioned to any judicial, executive, military, or other office under the government, shall, before he enters on the discharge of the business of his place or office, take and subscribe the following declaration and oaths or affirmations, namely,—

" 'I, A B, do truly and sincerely acknowledge, profess, testify, and declare, that the commonwealth of Massachusetts is, and of right ought to be, a free, sovereign, and independent state; and I do swear, that I will bear true faith and allegiance to the said commonwealth, and that I will defend the same against traitorous conspiracies and all hostile attempts whatsoever. And that I do renounce and abjure all allegiance, subjection, and obedience to the king, queen, or government of Great Britain, (as the case may be,) and every other foreign power, whatsoever. And that no foreign prince, person, prelate, state or potentate, hath, or ought to have, any jurisdiction, superiority, preëminence, authority, dispensing, or other power, in any matter, civil, ecclesiastical, or spiritual, within this commonwealth; except the authority and power which is or may be vested by their constituents in the congress of the United States. And I do further testify and declare, that no man or body of men hath, or can have, any right to absolve or discharge me from the obligation of this oath, declaration, or affirmation; and that I do make this acknowledgment, profession, testimony, declaration, denial, renunciation, and abjuration, heartily and truly, according to the common meaning and acceptation of the foregoing words, without any equivocation, mental evasion, or secret reservation, whatsoever. So help me GOD.' "

[127] "and affirm,"

impartially discharge and perform all the duties incumbent on me, as [a governor of this commonwealth,] according to the best of my abilities and understanding, agreeably to the rules and regulations of the constitution, and   [128]*that I will not attempt or consent to a violation thereof.* So help me God.

(*From Chapter III. sect. III. art.* 8.) [The lieutenant-governor, counsellors, senators, and members of the house of representatives shall, before they enter on the execution of their respective offices, make and subscribe the same declaration, and take the same oath, (*mutatis mutandis,*) which the governor is directed by this constitution to make, subscribe, and take.]

[And every person appointed to any civil or military office of this commonwealth shall, previous to his entering on the execution of his office, make and subscribe the following declaration, (*mulatis mutandis,*) namely,—

I, A B, being appointed   , do now declare, that I believe and profess the Christian religion, from a firm persuasion of the truth thereof.]

[And he shall likewise take an oath of the form following, (*mudatis mutandis,*)] namely,—

[I, A B, do solemnly swear, that I will bear faith and true allegiance to the commonwealth of Massachusetts; that I will faithfully and impartially discharge and perform all the duties incumbent on me, as   , according to the best of my abilities and understanding, agreeably to the rules and regulations of the constitution; and that I will not attempt or consent to a violation thereof. So help me God.]

[Provided, notwithstanding, that any person so appointed, who has conscientious scruples relative to taking oaths, may be admitted to make solemn affirmation, under the pains and penalties of perjury, to the truth of the matters contained in the form of the said oath, instead of taking the same.][129]

---

[128] "the laws of the commonwealth."

[129] "Provided, always, that when any person, chosen or appointed as aforesaid, shall be of the denomination of the people called Quakers, and shall decline taking the said oaths, he shall make his affirmation in the foregoing form, and subscribe the same, omit-

II. (*From Chapter IV. art.* 2.) [No justice of the superior court of judicature, court of assize, and general jail delivery, shall have a seat in the senate or house of representatives.][130]

III. (*From Chapter III. sect. II. art.* 4.) ["The respective values assigned by the several articles of this constitution to the property necessary to qualify the subjects of this commonwealth to be electors, and also to be elected into the several offices, for the holding of which such qualifications

---

ting the words *'I do swear,' 'and abjure,' 'oath or,' 'and abjuration,'* in the first oath; and in the second oath, the words *'swear and;'* and in each of them the words *'So help me God;'* subjoining instead thereof, 'This I do under the pains and penalties of perjury.'

"And the said oaths or affirmations shall be taken and subscribed by the governor, lieutenant-governor, and counsellors, before the president of the senate, in the presence of the two houses of assembly; and by the senators and representatives first elected under this constitution, before the president and five of the council of the former constitution; and forever afterwards, before the governor and council for the time being; and by the residue of the officers aforesaid, before such persons, and in such manner as, from time to time, shall be prescribed by the legislature."

The convention of 1820 recommended, and the people adopted, the following, which make the sixth and seventh articles of amendment:—

"Art. 6. Instead of the oath of allegiance prescribed by the constitution, the following oath shall be taken and subscribed by every person chosen or appointed to any office, civil or military, under the government of this commonwealth, before he shall enter on the duties of his office, to wit:—

" 'I, A B, do solemnly swear, that I will bear true faith and allegiance to the commonwealth of Massachusetts, and will support the constitution thereof. So help me God.'

"*Provided,* That when any person shall be of the denomination called Quakers, and shall decline taking said oath, he shall make his affirmation in the foregoing form, omitting the word 'swear,' and inserting, instead thereof, the word 'affirm;' and omitting the words 'so help me God,' and subjoining, instead thereof, the words, 'This I do, under the pains and penalties of perjury.'

"Art. 7. No oath, declaration, or subscription, excepting the oath prescribed in the preceding article, and the oath of office, shall be required of the governor, lieutenant-governor, counsellors, senators, or representatives, to qualify them to perform the duties of their respective offices."

[130] This article was much discussed in the convention, and gradually enlarged and extended, until it embraced the following restrictions:—

"II. No governor, lieutenant-governor, or judge of the supreme judicial court shall hold any other office or place, under the authority of this commonwealth, except such as by this constitution they are admitted to hold, saving that the judges of the said court may hold the offices of justices of the peace through the state; nor shall they hold any

are required, shall always be computed in silver, at the rate of six shillings and eight pence per ounce."][131]

other place or office, or receive any pension or salary from any other state, or government, or power, whatever.

"No person shall be capable of holding or exercising, at the same time, within this state, more than one of the following offices, namely,—judge of probate, sheriff, register of probate, or register of deeds; and never more than any two offices which are to be held by appointment of the governor, or the governor and council, or the senate, or the house of representatives, or by the election of the people of the state at large, or of the people of any county, military offices and the offices of justice of the peace excepted, shall be held by one person.

"No person holding the office of judge of the supreme judicial court, secretary, attorney-general, solicitor-general, treasurer or receiver-general, judge of probate, commissary-general, president, professor or instructor of Harvard College, sheriff, clerk of the house of representatives, register of probate, register of deeds, clerk of the supreme judicial court, clerk of the inferior court of common pleas, or officer of the customs, including in this description naval officers, shall at the same time have a seat in the senate or house of representatives; but their being chosen or appointed to, and accepting the same, shall operate as a resignation of their seat in the senate or house of representatives; and the place so vacated shall be filled up.

"And the same rule shall take place in case any judge of the said supreme judicial court, or judge of probate, shall accept a seat in council; or any counsellor shall accept of either of those offices or places.

"And no person shall ever be admitted to hold a seat in the legislature, or any office of trust or importance under the government of this commonwealth, who shall, in the due course of law, have been convicted of bribery or corruption in obtaining an election or appointment."

This was again modified by the convention of 1820, which prepared the following article of amendment, and the people approved it:—

Amendment.

"Art. 8. No judge of any court of this commonwealth, (except the court of sessions,) and no person holding any office under the authority of the United States, (postmasters excepted,) shall, at the same time, hold the office of governor, lieutenant-governor, or counsellor, or have a seat in the senate or house of representatives of this commonwealth; and no judge of any court in this commonwealth, (except the court of sessions,) nor the attorney-general, solicitor-general, county attorney, clerk of any court, sheriff, treasurer and receiver-general, register of probate, nor register of deeds, shall continue to hold his said office, after being elected a member of the Congress of the United States, and accepting that trust; but the acceptance of such trust, by any of the officers aforesaid, shall be deemed and taken to be a resignation of his said office; and judges of the courts of common pleas shall hold no other office under the government of this commonwealth, the office of justice of the peace and militia offices excepted."

[131] "III. In all cases where sums of money are mentioned in this constitution, the value thereof shall be computed in silver, at six shillings and eight pence per ounce."

(*From Chapter III. sect. II. art.* 5.) And it shall be in the power of the legislature, from time to time, to increase such qualifications, [132]of the persons to be elected to offices, as the circumstances of the commonwealth shall require.

IV. (*From Chapter V. art.* 2.) All commissions shall be in the name of the commonwealth of Massachusetts, signed by the governor, and attested by the secretary or his deputy, and have the great seal of the commonwealth affixed thereto.

V. (*From Chapter V. art.* 3.) All writs issuing out of the clerk's office in any of the courts of law, shall be in the name of the commonwealth of Massachusetts. They shall be under the seal of the court from whence they issue. They shall bear test of the [chief justice, or] first [or senior] justice of the court, to which they shall be returnable,   [133]and be signed by the clerk of such court."

VI. (*From Chapter V. art.* 5.) All the [statute] laws [of the province, colony, or state of Massachusetts Bay, *the common law, and all such parts of the English or British statutes as*] *have*[134] been adopted, used, and approved in the [said] province, colony, or state,   [135]and usually practised on in the courts of law, shall still remain and be in full force, until altered or repealed by the legislature; such parts only excepted as are repugnant to the rights and liberties contained in this constitution.

VII. (*From Chapter V. art.* 6.) The privilege and benefit of the writ of *habeas corpus* shall be enjoyed in this commonwealth in the most free, easy, cheap, expeditious, and ample manner; and shall not be suspended by the legislature, except upon the most urgent and pressing occasions, and for a [short and] limited time,   [136]

---

[132] "as to property,"
This article, with the amendment, is joined to and makes a part of the third or preceding one in the constitution.
[133] "who is not a party,"
[134] "which have heretofore"
[135] "of Massachusetts Bay,"
[136] "not exceeding twelve months."

VIII. (*From Chapter V. art.* 7.) The enacting style, in making and passing all acts, statutes, and laws, shall be: "Be it enacted, by [his excellency the governor,] the senate, and house of representatives, in general court assembled, and by the authority of the same;" [or "By his honor the lieutenant-governor," &c.; or "The honorable the council," &c., as the case may be.]

[CHAPTER VII. AND LAST.][137]

[Continuance of Officers, &c.]

IX. To the end there may be no failure of justice, or danger arise to the commonwealth from a change of the form of government, all officers,

[137] This caption was stricken out by the convention, and the article was inserted as the ninth in the sixth chapter. The following wholly new articles were added as the tenth and eleventh:—

"X. In order the more effectually to adhere to the principles of the constitution, and to correct those violations which by any means shall be made herein, as well as to form such alterations as from experience shall be found necessary, the general court, which shall be in the year of our Lord, one thousand seven hundred and ninety-five, shall issue precepts to the selectmen of the several towns, and to the assessors of the unincorporated plantations, directing them to convene the qualified voters of their respective towns and plantations, for the purpose of collecting their sentiments on the necessity or expediency of revising the constitution, in order to amendments.

"And if it shall appear, by the returns made, that two thirds of the qualified voters throughout the state, who shall assemble and vote in consequence of the said precepts, are in favor of such revision or amendment, the general court shall issue precepts, or direct them to be issued from the secretary's office to the several towns, to elect delegates to meet in convention, for the purpose aforesaid.

"The said delegates to be chosen in the same manner and proportion as their representatives in the second branch of the legislature are by this constitution to be chosen.

"XI. This form of government shall be enrolled on parchment, and deposited in the secretary's office, and be a part of the laws of the land; and printed copies thereof shall be prefixed to the book containing the laws of this commonwealth, in all future editions of the said laws."

One other article was adopted, at the recommendation of the convention of 1820, intended to open the way to further changes, without the necessity of resorting to a special assembly and a general revision. Thus far, in thirty years, under the operation of this rule, only three amendments have been adopted; but each of them has worked more fundamental alterations of the original instrument than were made by all the civil and military, holding commissions under the government and people of Massachusetts Bay in New England, and all other officers of the said government and people, at the time this constitution shall take effect, shall have, hold, use, exercise, and enjoy all the powers and authority to them granted or committed, until other persons shall be appointed in their stead. And all courts of law shall proceed in the execution of the business of their respective departments; and all the executive and legislative officers, bodies, and powers, shall continue in full force, in the enjoyment and exercise of all their trusts, employments, and authority, until the general court, and the supreme and executive officers, under this constitution, are designated, and invested with their respective trusts, powers, and authority.

recommendations of the convention; and it is not unreasonable to infer, that an avenue has been opened by which many more will be hereafter introduced:—

"Art. 9. If at any time hereafter any specific and particular amendment or amendments to the constitution be proposed in the general court, and agreed to by a majority of the senators and two thirds of the members of the house of representatives present, and voting thereon, such proposed amendment or amendments shall be entered on the journals of the two houses, with the yeas and nays taken thereon, and referred to the general court then next to be chosen, and shall be published; and if in the general court next chosen, as aforesaid, such proposed amendment or amendments shall be agreed to by a majority of the senators and two thirds of the members of the house of representatives present and voting thereon; then it shall be the duty of the general court to submit such proposed amendment or amendments to the people; and if they shall be approved and ratified by a majority of the qualified voters voting thereon, at meetings legally warned and holden for that purpose, they shall become part of the constitution of this commonwealth."

Letters
Upon
Interesting Subjects
Respecting the
Revolution of America

The following is the account of the composition of these letters, as given by Mr. Adams.

'At dinner one day, with a large company, at the house of a great capitalist, I met the giant of the law in Amsterdam, Mr. Calkoen. He was very inquisitive concerning the affairs of America, and asked me many ingenious questions. But he had spent his life in such ardent study of his institutes, codes, novelles, and pandects, with his immensely voluminous comments upon them, that he had neglected entirely the English language, and was very inexpert in the French. Interpreters were, therefore, necessary; but conversation that requires interpreters on both sides, is a very dull amusement. Though his questions were always ready, and my answers not less so, yet the interpretation was very slow and confused. After some time, one of the gentlemen asked me if I had any objection to answering Mr. Calkoen's questions in writing. I answered, none at all. It was soon agreed, that the questions and answers should be written. Accordingly, in a few days, Mr. Calkoen sent me his questions in Dutch, Mr. Le Roy, now of New York, was obliging enough to translate them for me into English, and I wrote an answer to each question in a separate letter. They gave so much satisfaction to Mr. Calkoen, that he composed, from the information contained in them, a comparison between the revolt of the low countries from Spain, and the Revolution of the United States of America, in which his conclusion was, that as it was a kind of miracle that the former succeeded, it would be a greater miracle still if the latter should not. This composition was read by him to a society of gentlemen of letters, about forty in number, who met at stated times in Amsterdam;

and by that means, just sentiments of American affairs began to spread, and prevail over the continual misrepresentations of English and Stadtholderian gazettes, pamphlets, and newspapers.

'The publications of General Howe and General Burgoyne, in vindication of themselves, were procured to be translated into French, and propagated, together with many other pamphlets, which assisted in the same design, and contributed to excite the citizens to those applications, by petition to the regencies of the several cities, which finally procured the acknowledgment of American independency, the treaty of commerce, and a loan of money.'

These letters were collected and printed in London, in 1786, by Mr. Adams, but not published. They were reprinted in 1789, in New York, and published with the title here prefixed, by John Fenno, and they also make a part of the volume published in Boston, in 1809, under the title, *Correspondence of the late President Adams.*"

Charles Francis Adams

These *Letters* are taken from *Works*, VII, 265-312.

TWENTY-SIX

LETTERS

UPON

INTERESTING SUBJECTS

RESECTING THE

REVOLUTION OF AMERICA

WRITTEN IN HOLLAND, IN THE YEAR MCCCLXXX

To Mr. Calkoen

AMSTERDAM, 4 OCTOBER, 1780.

SIR,—You desire an exact and authentic information of the present situation of American affairs, with a previous concise account of their course before, during, and after the commencement of hostilities.

To give a stranger an adequate idea of the rise and progress of the dispute between Great Britain and America would require much time and many volumes; it comprises the history of England and the United States of America for twenty years; that of France and Spain for five or six; and that of all the maritime powers of Europe for two or three. Suffice it to say, that immediately upon the conquest of Canada from the French in the year 1759, Great Britain seemed to be seized with a jealousy against the Colonies, and then concerted the plan of changing their forms of government, of restraining their trade within narrower bounds, and raising a revenue within them by authority of parliament, for the avowed or pretended purpose of protecting, securing, and defending them. Accordingly, in the year 1760, orders were sent from the board of trade in England to the custom-house officers in America, to apply to the supreme courts of justice for writs of assistance to enable them to carry into a more rigorous execution certain acts of parliament called the acts of trade (among which the famous act of navigation was one, the fruit of the ancient English jealousy of Holland) by breaking open houses, ships, or cellars, chests, stores, and magazines, to search for uncustomed goods. In most of the Colonies these writs were refused. In the Massachusetts Bay the question, whether such writs were legal and constitutional, was solemnly and repeatedly argued before the supreme court by the most learned counsel in the Province.

The judges of this court held their commissions during the pleasure of the governor and council; and the chief justice dying at this time, the famous Mr. Hutchinson was appointed, probably with a view of deciding this cause in favor of the crown, which was accordingly done. But the arguments advanced upon that occasion by the bar and the bench, opened to the people such a view of the designs of the British government against their liberties and of the danger they were in, as made a deep impression upon the public, which never wore out.

From this moment, every measure of the British court and parliament and of the king's governors and other servants confirmed the people in an opinion of a settled design to overturn those constitutions under which their ancestors had emigrated from the old world, and with infinite toil, danger, and expense, planted a new one. It would be endless to enumerate all the acts of parliament and measures of government; but, in 1764, Mr. George Grenville moved a number of resolutions in parliament, which passed, for laying a vast number of heavy duties upon stamped paper; and, in 1765, the act of parliament was made, called the stamp act. Upon this, there was a universal rising of the people in every Colony, compelling the stamp-officers by force to resign, and preventing the stamped papers from being used, and, indeed, compelling the courts of justice to proceed in business without them. My Lord Rockingham perceiving the impossibility of executing this statute, moved, by the help of Mr. Pitt, for the repeal of it, and obtained it, which restored peace, order, and harmony to America; which would have continued to this hour, if the evil genius of Great Britain had not prompted her to revive the resistance of the people by fresh attempts upon their liberties and new acts of parliament imposing taxes upon them.

In 1767 they passed another act of parliament laying duties upon glass, paper, and painters' colors, and tea. This revived the discontents in America; but government sent over a board of commissioners to oversee the execution of this act of parliament and all others imposing duties, with a multitude of new officers for the same purpose; and, in 1768, for the first time, it sent four thousand regular troops to Boston, to protect the revenue officers in the collection of the duties.

Loth to commence hostilities, the people had recourse to non-importation agreements and a variety of other measures, which, in 1770, induced parliament to repeal all the duties upon glass, paper, and painters' colors, but left the duty upon tea unrepealed. This produced an association not to drink tea. In 1770, the animosity between the inhabitants of Boston and the king's troops grew so high, that a party of the troops fired upon a crowd of people in the streets, killing five or six and wounding some others. This raised such a spirit among the inhabitants, that, in a body, they demanded the instant removal of the troops; which was done, the governor ordering them down to Castle Island, some miles from the town.

In 1773, the British government, determined to carry into execution the duty upon tea, empowered the East India Company to export it to

America. They sent some cargoes to Boston, some to New York, some to Philadelphia, and some to Charleston. The inhabitants of New York and Philadelphia sent the ships back to London, and they sailed up the Thames, to proclaim to all the nation, that New York and Pennsylvania would not be enslaved. The inhabitants of Charleston unloaded it and stored it in cellars where it could not be used, and where it finally perished. The inhabitants of Boston tried every measure to send the ships back, like New York and Philadelphia; but not being permitted to pass the castle, the tea was all thrown into the sea.

This produced several vindictive acts of parliament,—one for starving the town of Boston by shutting up the port; another for abolishing the constitution of the Province by destroying their charter; another for sending persons to England to be tried for treason, &c.

These acts produced the congress of 1774, who stated the rights and grievances of the Colonies, and petitioned for redress. Their petitions and remonstrances were all neglected, and treated with contempt. General Gage had been sent over with an army to enforce the Boston port bill and the act for destroying the charter. This army, on the 19th of April, 1775, commenced hostilities at Lexington, which have been continued to this day.

You see, sir, by this most imperfect and hasty sketch, that this war is already twenty years old. And I can truly say, that the people, through the whole course of this long period, have been growing constantly every year more and more unanimous and determined to resist the designs of Great Britain.

I should be ashamed to lay before a gentleman of Mr. Calkoen's abilities so rude a sketch, if I had not an equal confidence in his candor and discretion, which will induce me, as I may have leisure, to continue to sketch a few observations upon your questions.

5 OCTOBER.

YOUR first proposition is, "to prove, by striking facts, that an implacable hatred and aversion reigns throughout America."

In answer to this, I beg leave to say, that the Americans are animated by higher principles, and better and stronger motives, than hatred and aversion. They universally aspire after a free trade with all the commercial world, instead of that mean monopoly, in which they were shackled by Great Britain, to the disgrace and mortification of America, and to the injury of all the rest of Europe; to whom it seems as if God and nature intended that so great a magazine of productions, the raw materials of manufactures, so great a source of commerce, and so rich a nursery of seamen, as America is, should be open. They despise, sir, they disdain the idea of being again monopolized by any one nation whatsoever; and this contempt is at least as powerful a motive of action as any hatred whatsoever.

Moreover, sir, they consider themselves contending for the purest principles of liberty, civil and religious; for those forms of government, under the faith of which their country was planted; and for those great improvements of them, which have been made by their new constitutions. They consider themselves not only as contending for these great blessings, but against the greatest evils that any country ever suffered; for they know, if they were to be deceived by England, to break their union among themselves, and their faith with their allies, they would ever after be in the power of England, who would bring them into the most abject submission to the government of a parliament the most corrupted in the world, in which they would have no voice nor influence, at three thousand miles distance from them.

But if hatred must come into consideration, I know not how to prove their hatred better, than by showing the provocations they have had to hatred.

If tearing up from the foundation those forms of government under which they were born and educated, and thrived and prospered, to the infinite emolument of England; if imposing taxes upon them, or endeavoring to do it, for twenty years, without their consent; if commencing hostilities upon them, burning their towns, butchering their people, deliberately starving prisoners, ravishing their women, exciting hosts of Indians to butcher and scalp them, and purchasing Germans to destroy them, and hiring negro servants to murder their masters;—if all these, and many other things as bad, are not provocations enough to hatred, I would request Mr. Calkoen to tell me what is or can be. All these horrors the English have practised in every part of America, from Boston to Savannah.

2. Your second proposition is "to show that this is general, at least so general, that the tories are in so small a number, and of such little force, that they are counted as nothing."

If Mr. Calkoen would believe me, I could testify as a witness; I could describe all the sources, all the grounds, springs, principles, and motives to toryism through the continent. This would lead me into great length; and the result of all would be, my sincere opinion, that the tories throughout the whole continent do not amount to the twentieth part of the people. I will not, however, obtrude my testimony, nor my opinion; I will appeal to witnesses who cannot be suspected, General Burgoyne and General Howe. Burgoyne has published a Narrative of his Proceedings, in which he speaks of the tories. I left the pamphlet at Paris, but it may easily be had from London.

General Howe has also published a Narrative relative to his Conduct in America, to which the reader is referred.[1]

I have quoted to you General Howe's words; and one would think this was sufficient to show how much or how little zeal there is for the British cause in North America. When we consider that, in the period here mentioned, the English army had been in possession of the cities of Boston, Newport, New York, and Philadelphia, and that they had marched through the Jersies, part of Maryland, and Pennsylvania, and with all their arts, bribes, threats, and flatteries, which General Howe calls their efforts and exertions, they were able to obtain so few recruits, and very few of these Americans, I think that any impartial man must be convinced that the aversion and antipathy to the British cause is very general; so general, that the tories are to be accounted but a very little thing.

The addresses which they have obtained to the King and his generals, when their army was in Boston, Newport, New York, Philadelphia, Savannah, and Charleston, show the same thing. It is well known that every art of flattery and of terror was always used to obtain subscribers to these

---

[1] Here follow, in the original copy, several extracts from General Howe's *Narrative,* showing his disappointments in the performance of the promises of aid given by the royalists in America. These extracts were omitted in the republication in 1809, and are therefore omitted here.

addresses. Yet the miserable numbers they have obtained, and the still more despicable character of most of these small numbers, show that the British cause is held in very low esteem. Even in Charleston, the capital of a Province which contains two hundred thousand whites, they were able to obtain only two hundred and ten subscribers, and among these there is not one name that I ever remember to have heard before.

I am sorry I have not Burgoyne's Narrative, which shows in the same point of light the resources the English are likely to find in the tories to be nothing more than a sure means of getting rid of a great number of their guineas.

To learn the present state of America, it is sufficient to read the public papers. The present state of Great Britain and its dependencies may be learned the same way. The omnipotence of the British parliament, and the omnipotence of the British navy, are like to go the same way.

6 OCTOBER.

YOUR third proposition is "to show that America, notwithstanding the war, daily increases in strength and force."

It is an undoubted fact that America daily increases in strength and force; but it may not be so easy to prove this to the satisfaction of a European who has never been across the Atlantic; however, some things may be brought into consideration, which may convince, if properly attended to.

1. It may be argued from the experience of former wars, during all which the population of that country was so far from being diminished or even kept at a stand, that it was always found at the end of a war that the numbers of people had increased during the course of it, nearly in the same ratio as in time of peace. Even in the last French war, which lasted from 1755 to 1763 (during which time the then American Colonies made as great exertions, had in the field as great a number of men, and put themselves to as great an expense in proportion to the numbers of people, as the United States have done during this war) it was found that the population had increased nearly as fast as in times of peace.

2. If you make inquiry into the circumstances of the different parts of America at this day, you find the people in all the States pushing their

settlements out into the wilderness upon the frontiers, cutting down the woods, and subduing new lands with as much eagerness and rapidity as they used to do in former times of war or peace. This spreading of the people into the wilderness is a decisive proof of the increasing population.

3. The only certain way of determining the ratio of the increase of population is, by authentic numerations of the people and regular official returns. This has, I believe, never been done generally in former wars, and has been generally omitted in this. Yet some States have made these returns. The Massachusetts Bay, for example, had a valuation about the year 1773 or 1774, and again the last year, 1779, they had another. In this period of five years, that State was found to have increased, both in number of people and in value of property, more than it ever had grown before in the same period of time. Now the Massachusetts Bay has had a greater number of men employed in the war, both by land and sea, in proportion to the number of her inhabitants, than any other State of the thirteen. She has had more men killed, taken prisoners, and died of sickness, than any other State; yet her growth has been as rapid as ever, from whence it may be fairly argued that all the other States have grown in the same or a greater proportion.

4. It has been found by calculations, that America has doubled her numbers, even by natural generation alone, upon an average, about once in eighteen years. This war has now lasted near six years; in the course of it, we commonly compute in America that we have lost by sickness and the sword and captivity about five-and-thirty thousand men. But the numbers of people have not increased less than seven hundred and fifty thousand souls, which give at least an hundred thousand fighting men. We have not less, probably, than seventy thousand fighting men in America more than we had on the day that hostilities were first commenced, on the 19th of April, 1775. There are near twenty thousand fighting men added to the numbers in America every year. Is this the case with our enemy, Great Britain? Which then can maintain the war the longest?

5. If America increases in numbers, she certainly increases in strength. But her strength increases in other respects,—the discipline of her armies increases; the skill of her officers increases by sea and land; her skill in military manufactures, such as those of saltpetre, powder, firearms, cannon,

increases; her skill in manufactures of flax and wool for the first necessity increases; her manufactures of salt also increase; and all these are augmentations of strength and force to maintain her independence. Further, her commerce increases every year,—the number of vessels she has had this year in the trade to the West Indies; the number of vessels arrived in Spain, France, Holland, and Sweden, show that her trade is greatly increased this year.

But, above all, her activity, skill, bravery, and success in privateering increase every year; the prizes she has made from the English this year will defray more than one half of the whole expense of this year's war. I only submit to your consideration a few hints which will enable you to satisfy yourself by reflection how fast the strength and force of America increase.

7 OCTOBER.

YOUR fourth question is,—"Whether America, in and of itself, by means of purchasing or exchanging the productions of the several provinces, would be able to continue the war for six, eight, or ten years, even if they were entirely deprived of the trade with Europe; or their allies, exhausted by the war, and forced to make a separate peace, were to leave them?"

This is an extreme case. And where is the necessity of putting such a supposition? Is there the least appearance of France or Spain being exhausted by the war? Are not their resources much greater than those of England, separated as she is from America? Why should a suspicion be entertained that France or Spain will make a separate peace? Are not these powers sufficiently interested in separating America from England? All the world knows that their maritime power and the possession of their Colonies depend upon separating them. Such chimeras as these are artfully propagated by the English to terrify stockjobbers; but thinking men and well-informed men know that France and Spain have the most pressing motives to persevere in the war. Besides, infractions so infamous of solemn treaties made and avowed to all mankind are not committed by any nation. In short, no man who knows any thing of the real wealth and power of England on one hand, and of the power and resources of France, Spain, and America on the other, can believe it possible, in the ordinary course of human events, and without the interposition of miracles, that

France and Spain should be so exhausted by the war as to be forced to make a separate peace.

The other supposition here made is equally extreme. It is in the nature of things impossible that America should ever be deprived entirely of the trade of Europe. In opposition to one extreme, I have a right to advance another. And I say, that if all the maritime powers of Europe were to unite their navies to block up the American ports and prevent the trade of Europe, they could not wholly prevent it. All the men-of-war in Europe would not be sufficient to block up a seacoast of two thousand miles in extent, varied as that of America is by such an innumerable multitude of ports, bays, harbors, rivers, creeks, inlets, and islands; with a coast so tempestuous, that there are many occasions in the course of the year when merchant vessels can push out and in, although men-of-war cannot cruise. It should be remembered that this war was maintained by America for three years before France took any part in it. During all that time, the English had fifty men-of-war upon that coast, which is a greater number than they ever will have again; yet all their vigilance was not sufficient to prevent American trade with Europe. At the worst time we ever saw, one vessel in three went and came safe. At present, there is not one in four taken. It should also be remembered, that the French navy have never, until this year, been many days together upon the American coast. So that we have in a sense maintained the trade of the continent five years against all that the English navy could do, and it has been growing every year.

Why then should we put cases that we know can never happen? However, I can inform you that the case was often put before this war broke out; and I have heard the common farmers in America reasoning upon these cases seven years ago. I have heard them say, if Great Britain could build a wall of brass a thousand feet high all along the seacoast, at low-water mark, we can live and be happy. America is, most undoubtedly, capable of being the most independent country upon earth. It produces every thing for the necessity, comfort, and conveniency of life, and many of the luxuries too. So that, if there were an eternal separation between Europe and America, the inhabitants of America would not only live but multiply, and, for what I know, be wiser, better, and happier than they will be as it is.

That it would be unpleasant and burthensome to America to continue the war for eight or ten years is certain. But will it not be unpleasant and burthensome to Great Britain too? There are between three and four millions of people in America. The kingdom of Sweden, that of Denmark, and even the republic of the United Provinces, have not each of them many more than that number; yet these States can maintain large standing armies even in time of peace, and maintain the expenses of courts and governments much more costly than the government of America. What then should hinder America from maintaining an army sufficient to defend her altars and her firesides? The Americans are as active, as industrious, and as capable as other men.

America could undoubtedly maintain a regular army of twenty thousand men forever. And a regular army of twenty thousand men would be sufficient to keep all the land forces, that Great Britain can send there, confined to the seaport towns, under cover of the guns of their men-of-war. Whenever the British army shall attempt to penetrate far into the country, the regular American army will be joined by such reinforcements from the militia, as will ruin the British force. By desertions, by fatigue, by sickness, and by the sword, in occasional skirmishes, their numbers will be wasted, and the miserable remains of them Burgoyned.

V.

9 OCTOBER.

THE fifth inquiry is, "Whether a voluntary revolt of any one or more of the States in the American confederation is to be apprehended: and if one or more were to revolt, whether the others would not be able to defend themselves?"

This is a very judicious and material question. I conceive that the answer to it is easy and decisive. There is not the least danger of a voluntary revolt of any one State in the Union. It is difficult to prove a negative, however; and still more difficult to prove a future negative. Let us, however, consider the subject a little.

Which State is the most likely to revolt, or submit? Is it the most ancient Colony, as Virginia, or the Massachusetts? Is it the most numerous and powerful, as Virginia, Massachusetts, or Pennsylvania? I believe nobody will say, that any one of these great States will take the lead in a revolt or a voluntary submission.

Will it be the smallest and weakest States that will be most likely to give up voluntarily? In order to satisfy ourselves of this, let us consider what has happened; and by the knowledge of what is passed, we may judge of what is to come.

The three smallest States are Rhode Island, Georgia, and Delaware.

The English have plainly had it in view to bring one of these States to a submission, and have accordingly directed very great forces against them.

Let us begin with Rhode Island. In the latter end of the year 1776, General Howe sent a large army of near seven thousand men, by sea, under a strong convoy of men-of-war, detached by Lord Howe, to take possession of Newport, the capital of Rhode Island. Newport stands upon an island. It was neither fortified nor garrisoned sufficiently to defend itself against so powerful a fleet and army, and, therefore, the English made themselves masters of the place. But what advantage did they derive from it? Did the Colony of Rhode Island, small as it is, submit? So far from it, that they were rendered the more eager to resist; and an army was assembled at Providence, which confined the English to the prison of Rhode Island, until the fall of the year 1779, when they were obliged to evacuate it, and our army entered it in triumph.

The next little State which the English attempted, was Delaware. This State consists of three counties only, situated upon the river Delaware, below Philadelphia, and is the most exposed to the English men-of-war of any of the States, because they are open to invasion not only upon the ocean, but all along the river Delaware. It contains not more than thirty thousand souls. When the English got possession of Philadelphia, and had the command of the whole navigation of the Delaware, these people were more in the power of the English than any part of America ever was, and the English generals, admirals, commissioners, and all the tories, used all their arts to seduce this little State, but they could not succeed; they never could get the appearance of a government erected under the King's authority. The people continued their delegation in congress, and continued to elect their governors, senate, and assemblies, under their new constitution, and to furnish their quota to the continental army, and their proportion to the militia, until the English were obliged to evacuate Philadelphia. There are besides, in this little State, from various causes, more tories, in proportion, than in any other. And as this State stood immovable, I think we have no reason to fear a voluntary submission of any other.

The next small State that was attempted was Georgia. This State is situated at the southern extremity of all, and at such a distance from all the rest, and such difficulties of communication, being above an hundred miles from Charleston, in South Carolina, that it was impossible for the neighboring States to afford them any assistance. The English invaded this little State, and took the capital, Savannah, and have held it to this day; but this acquisition has not been followed by any submission of the province; on the contrary, they continue their delegation in congress, and their new officers of government. This Province, moreover, was more immediately the child of England than any other; the settlement of it cost England more than all the rest, from whence one might expect they would have more friends here than any where.

New Jersey is one of the middling-sized States. New Jersey had a large British army in Philadelphia, which is on one side, and another in New York, which is on the other side, and the British army has marched quite through it; and the English have used every policy of flattery, of terror, and severity, but all in vain, and worse than in vain; all has conspired to make the people of New Jersey some of the most determined against the English, and some of the most brave and skilful to resist them.

New York, before the commencement of hostilities, was supposed to be the most lukewarm of the middling States, in the opposition to the designs of the English. The English armies have invaded it from Canada and from the ocean, and have long been in possession of three islands, New York Island, Long Island, and Staten Island; yet the rest of that Province has stood immovable, through all the varieties of the fortune of war, for four years, and increases in zeal and unanimity every year.

I think, therefore, there is not even a possibility, that any one of the thirteen States should ever voluntarily revolt or submit.

The efforts and exertions of General Howe in New York, Long Island, Staten Island, New Jersey, Pennsylvania, Delaware, and Maryland, to obtain recruits; the vast expense that he put his master to in appointing new corps of officers, even general officers; the pains they took to enlist men, among all the stragglers in those countries, and among many thousands of prisoners which they then had in their hands; all these measures obtaining but three thousand six hundred men, and very few of these Americans, according to General Howe's own account, shows, I think, to a demonstration, that no voluntary revolt or submission is ever to be apprehended.

But even supposing that Rhode Island should submit, what could this small colony of fifty thousand souls do, in the midst of Massachusetts, Connecticut, and New Hampshire?

Supposing Delaware, thirty thousand souls, should submit, what influence could it have upon the great States of New Jersey, Pennsylvania, Maryland, and Virginia, among which it lies?

If Georgia, at the extremity of all, should submit, what influence could this little society of thirty thousand souls have upon the two Carolinas and Virginia? The Colonies are at such vast distances from one another, and the country is so fortified every where, by rivers, mountains, and forests, that the conquest or submission of one part has no influence upon the rest.

10 OCTOBER.

THE sixth task is to show, "that no person in America is of so much influence, power, or credit, that his death, or corruption by English money, could be of any namable consequence."

This question is very natural for a stranger to ask; but it would not occur to a native American, who had passed all his life in his own country; and upon hearing it proposed, he could only smile.

It should be considered, that there are in America no kings, princes, or nobles; no popes, cardinals, patriachs, archbishops, bishops, or other ecclesiastical dignitaries. They are these, and such like lofty subordinations, which place great bodies of men in a state of dependence upon one, which enable one or a few individuals, in Europe, to carry away after them large numbers, wherever they may think fit to go. There are no hereditary offices, or titles, in families; nor even any great estates that descend in a right line to the eldest sons. All estates of intestates are distributed among all the children; so that there are no individuals nor families who have, either from office, title, or fortune, any extensive power or influence. We are all equal in America, in a political view, and as much alike as Lycurgus's haycocks. All public offices and employments are bestowed by the free choice of the people, and at present, through the whole continent, are in the hands of those gentlemen who have distinguished themselves the most by their counsels, exertions, and sufferings, in the contest with Great Britain. If there ever was a war, that could be called *the people's war,* it is this of America against Great Britain; it having been determined on by the people, and pursued by the people in every step of its progress.

But who is it in America that has credit to carry over to the side of Great Britain any numbers of men? General Howe tells us that he employed Mr. Delancey, Mr. Cortland Skinner, Mr. Chalmers, and Mr. Galloway, the most influential men they could find; and he tells you their ridiculous success.

Are they members of congress who, by being corrupted, would carry votes in congress in favor of the English? I can tell you of a truth there has not been one motion made in congress, since the declaration of independency, on the fourth of July, 1776, for a reconciliation with Great Britain; and there is not one man in America of sufficient authority or credit to make a motion in congress for a peace with Great Britain, upon any terms short of independence, without ruining his character forever. If a delegate from any one of the thirteen States were to make a motion for peace upon any conditions short of independency, that delegate would be recalled with indignation by his constituents as soon as they should know it. The English have artfully represented in Europe that congress have been governed by particular gentlemen; but you may depend upon it it is false. At one time the English would have made it believed that Mr. Randolph, the first President of Congress, was its soul. Mr. Randolph died, and congress proceeded as well as ever. At another time, Mr. Hancock was all and all.

Mr. Hancock left the congress, and has scarcely been there for three years; yet congress has proceeded with as much wisdom, honor, and fortitude as ever. At another time, the English represented that Mr. Dickinson was the ruler of America. Mr. Dickinson opposed openly, and upon principle, the declaration of independency; but, instead of carrying his point, his constituents differed with him so materially that they recalled him from congress, and he was absent for some years; yet congress proceeded with no less constancy; and Mr. Dickinson lately, finding all America unalterably fixed in the system of independency, has fallen in like a good citizen, and now supports it in congress with as much zeal as others. At another time, the English have been known to believe that Dr. Franklin was the essential member of congress; but Dr. Franklin was sent to France in 1776, and has been there ever since; yet congress has been as active and as capable as before. At another time, Mr. Samuel Adams was represented as the man who did every thing; yet Mr. Samuel Adams has been absent for the greatest part of three years, attending his duty as Secretary of State in the Massachusetts Bay; yet it does not appear that Mr. Adams's absence has weakened the deliberations of congress in the least. Nay, they have sometimes been silly enough to represent your humble servant, Mr. John Adams, as an essential member of congress; it is now, however, three years since congress did him the honor to send him to Europe, as a Minister Plenipotentiary to the Court of Versailles, and he has never been in congress since; yet congress have done better since he came away than they ever did before.

In short, sir, all these pretences are the most ridiculous imaginable. The American cause stands upon the essential, unalterable character of the whole body of the people; upon their prejudices, passions, habits, and principles, which they derived from their ancestors, their education, drew in with their mothers' milk, and have been confirmed in by the whole course of their lives; and the characters whom they have made conspicuous, by placing them in their public employments,

Are but bubbles on the sea of matter borne;

They rise, they break, and to that sea return.

The same reasoning is applicable to all the governors, lieutenant-governors, secretaries of state, judges, senators, and representatives of particular states. They are all eligible, and elected every year by the body of the people; and would lose their characters and influence the instant they should depart, in their public conduct, from the political system that the people are determined to support.

But are there any officers of the army who could carry over large numbers of people? The influence of these officers is confined to the army; they have very little among the citizens. But if we consider the constitution of that army, we shall see that it is impossible that any officer could carry with him any numbers, even of soldiers. These officers are not appointed by a king, or a prince, nor by General Washington; they can hardly be said to be appointed by congress. They have all commissions from congress, it is true; but they are named and recommended, and are generally appointed, by the executive branch of government in the particular State to which they belong, except the general officers, who are appointed by congress. The continental army consists of the quotas of officers and troops furnished by thirteen different States. If an officer of the Massachusetts Bay forces, for example, should go over to the enemy, he might, possibly, carry with him half a dozen soldiers belonging to that State; yet I even doubt, whether any officer whatever, who should desert from that State, could persuade so many as half a dozen soldiers to go with him.

Is it necessary to put the supposition, that General Washington should be corrupted? Is it possible, that so fair a fame as Washington's should be exchanged for gold or for crowns? A character so false, so cruel, so bloodthirsty, so detestable as that of Monk might betray a trust; but a character so just, so humane, so fair, so open, honorable, and amiable as Washington's, never can be stained with so foul a reproach.

Yet I am fully of opinion, that even if Mr. Washington should go over to the English, which I know to be impossible, he would find none or very few officers or soldiers to go with him. He would become the contempt and execration of his own army as well as of all the rest of mankind.

No, sir! the American cause is in no danger from the defection of any individual. Nothing short of an entire alteration in the sentiments of the whole body of the people can make any material change in the councils or in the conduct of the arms of the United States; and I am very sure that

Great Britain has not power or art sufficient to change essentially the temper, the feelings, and the opinions of between three and four millions of people at three thousand miles distance, supported as they are by powerful allies.

If such a change could ever have been made, it would have been seven years ago, when offices, employments, and power in America were in the hands of the King. But every ray of royal authority has been extinguished now between four and five years, and all civil and military authority is in hands determined to resist Great Britain to the last.

VII.

YOUR seventh inquiry is,—"Whether the common people in America are not inclined, nor would be able to find sufficient means to frustrate by force the good intentions of the skilful politicians?"

In answer to this, it is sufficient to say, that the commonalty have no need to have recourse to force to oppose the intentions of the skilful; because the law and the constitution authorize the common people to choose governors and magistrates every year; so that they have it constantly in their power to leave out any politician, however skilful, whose principles, opinions, or systems they do not approve.

The difference, however, in that country, is not so great as it is in some others, between the common people and the gentlemen; for noblemen they have none. There is no country where the common people, I mean the tradesmen, the husbandmen, and the laboring people, have such advantages of education as in that; and it may be truly said, that their education, their understanding, and their knowledge are as nearly equal as their birth, fortune, dignities, and titles.

It is therefore certain, that whenever the common people shall determine upon peace or submission, it will be done. But of this there is no danger. The common people are the most unanimously determined against Great Britain of any; it is the war of the common people; it was undertaken by them, and has been, and will be supported by them.

The people of that country often rose in large bodies against the measures of government while it was in the hands of the King. But there has been no example of this sort under the new constitutions, excepting one, which is mentioned in General Howe's Narrative, in the back part of North Carolina. This was owing to causes so particular, that it rather serves to show the strength of the American cause in that State than the contrary.

About the year 1772, under the government of Tryon, who has since made himself so obnoxious to all America, there were some warm disputes in North Carolina concerning some of the internal regulations of that Province; and a small number of people in the back parts rose in arms, under the name of Regulators, against the government. Governor Tryon marched at the head of some troops drawn from the militia, gave battle to the regulators, defeated them, hanged some of their ringleaders, and published proclamations against many others. These people were all treated as having been in rebellion, and they were left to solicit pardon of the Crown. This established in the minds of those regulators such a hatred towards the rest of their fellow-citizens, that in 1775, when the war broke out, they would not join with them. The King has since promised them pardon for their former treasons, upon condition that they commit fresh ones against their country. In 1777, in conjunction with a number of Scotch Highlanders, they rose; and Governor Caswell marched against them, gave them battle, and defeated them. This year they have risen again, and been again defeated. But these people are so few in number, there is so much apparent malice and revenge, instead of any principle, in their disaffection, that any one who knows any thing of the human heart will see that, instead of finally weakening the American cause in North Carolina, it will only serve to give a keenness and an obstinacy to those who support it.

Nothing, indeed, can show the unanimity of the people throughout America in a stronger light than this,—that the British army has been able to procure so few recruits, to excite so few insurrections and disturbances. Nay, although the freedom of the press and the freedom of speech are carried to as great lengths in that country as in any under the sun, there has never been a hint in a newspaper, or even in a handbill, nor a single speech or vote in any assembly, that I have heard of, for submission, or even for reconciliation.

VIII.

16 OCTOBER.

THE eighth inquiry is,—"What England properly ought to do to force America to submission, and preserve her in it? How much time, money, and how many vessels would be wanted for that purpose?"

I assure you, sir, I am as much at a loss to inform you in this particular as Lord George Germaine would be. I can fix upon no number of men, nor any sum of money, nor any number of ships that I think would be sufficient. But most certainly no number of ships or men which Great Britain now has, or ever can have, nor any sum of money that she will ever be able to command, will be sufficient.

If it were in the power of Great Britain to send a hundred thousand men to America, and they had men-of-war and transports enough to convey them there in safety amidst the dangers that await them from French, Spanish, and American men-of-war, they might possibly get possession of two or three provinces, and place so many garrisons in various parts as to prevent the people from exercising the functions of government under their new constitutions; and they might set up a sham appearance of a civil government under the King; but I do not believe that a hundred thousand men could gain and preserve them the civil government of any three States in the Confederation. The States are at such distances from one another, there are such difficulties in passing from one to another by land, and such a multitude of posts are necessary to be garrisoned and provided in order to command any one Colony, that an army of a hundred thousand men would soon find itself consumed in getting and keeping possession of one or two States. But it would require the armies of Semiramis to command and preserve them all.

Such is the nature of that country, and such the character of the people, that if the English were to send ever so many ships, and ever so many troops, they never would subdue all the Americans. Numbers, in every State, would fly to the mountains, and beyond the mountains, and there maintain a constant war against the English. In short, if the English could conquer America, which they never can, nor any one State in it, it would cost them a standing army of an hundred thousand men to preserve their conquest; for it is in vain for them ever to think of any other government's taking place again under the King of England, but a military government.

As to the number of ships, it must be in proportion to the number of troops; they must have transports enough to carry their troops, and men-of-war enough to convoy them through their numerous French, Spanish, and American enemies upon the seas.

As to the sums of money, you will easily see, that adding two hundred millions more to the two hundred millions they already owe, would not procure and maintain so many ships and troops.

It is very certain the English can never send any great numbers more of troops to America. The men are not to be had; the money is not to be had; the seamen, and even the transports, are not to be had.

I give this to Mr. Calkoen as my private opinion concerning the question he asks. As Mr. Calkoen observes, this is a question that had better not be publicly answered; but time will show the answer here given is right. It would, at present, be thought extravagance or enthusiasm. Mr. Adams only requests Mr. Calkoen to look over this letter a few years hence, and then say what his opinion of it is. Victories gained by the English, in taking seaport towns, or in open field fighting, will make no difference in my answer to this question. Victories gained by the English will conquer themselves sooner than the Americans. Fighting will not fail, in the end, to turn to the advantage of America, although the English may gain an advantage in this or that particular engagement.

IX.

THE ninth question is, "how strong the English land force is in America? How strong it was at the beginning? And whether it increases or diminishes?"

According to the estimates laid before parliament, the army under General Howe, General Carleton, and General Burgoyne, amounts to fifty-five thousand men, besides volunteers, refugees, tories, in short, all the recruits raised in Canada, and all other parts of America, under whatever denomination. If we suppose that all these, in Canada and elsewhere, amounted to five thousand men, the whole, according to this computation, amounted to sixty thousand land forces.

This estimate, however, must have been made from the number of regiments, and must have supposed them all to be full.

General Howe, himself, however, in his Narrative, page 45, tells us, that his whole force, at the time when he landed on Long Island, in 1776, amounted to twenty thousand one hundred and twenty-one rank and file, of which one thousand six hundred and seventy-seven were sick.

By a regular return of General Burgoyne's army, after its captivity in 1777, it amounted, in Canadians, Provincials, British and German troops, to upwards of ten thousand men. We may suppose, that four thousand men were left in Canada for the garrison of Quebec, Montreal, and the great number of other posts in that Province. To these numbers if we add the officers, we may fairly allow the whole land force at that time to be forty thousand combatants.

This is all the answer that I am able to give from memory to the question "How strong the British army was?"

In order to give an answer to the other,—"How strong it is?"—let us consider—

1. There has been no large reinforcement ever sent to America since that time. They have sent some troops every year; but these never amounted to more than recruits, and, probably, rather fall short of filling up the vacancies which were made in the course of the year by desertion and death, by sickness and by the sword; so that, upon the whole, I think it may be safely said, that the army never has been greater than it was in 1776.

But we must deduct from this ten thousand men taken with Burgoyne, one thousand Hessians taken at Trenton and Princeton, and indeed many more, taken by two or three hundred at a time, upon other occasions.

In the next place, we must deduct, I suppose, about ten thousand more sent since the French war to Jamaica, St. Lucia, Barbadoes, and the other West India Islands.

So that, upon the whole, I think we make an ample allowance, if we state the whole number now in New York, Carolina, and Georgia, including all refugees, &c., at twenty thousand men, officers included.

This is, in part, an answer to the question, "Whether their force increases or diminishes?" But it should be further considered that there is a constant and rapid consumption of their men. Many die of sickness, numbers desert, there have been frequent skirmishes, in which they have ever had more men killed and wounded than the Americans; and now, so many of their troops are in Carolina and Georgia, where the climate is unhealthy, that there is great reason to expect the greatest part of that army will die of disease. And whoever considers the efforts the English have made in Germany, Ireland, Scotland, and England, as well as America, for seven years successively, to raise men, the vast bounties they have offered, and the few they have obtained; whoever considers the numbers they must lose this year by the severity of duty and by sickness, in New York, Carolina, Georgia, and the West India Islands, and the numbers that have been taken going to Quebec, North America, the East and West Indies, will be convinced that all the efforts they can make, will not enable them for the future to keep their numbers good.

X.

THE tenth head of inquiry is, "How great is the force of America? The number of men? Their discipline, &c., from the commencement of the troubles? Is there a good supply of warlike stores? Are these to be found partly or entirely in America? Or must they be imported?"

The force of America consists of a regular army, and of a militia; the regular army has been various at different times. The first regular army, which was formed in April, 1775, was enlisted for six months only; the next was enlisted for one year; the next for three years; the last period expired last February. At each of these periods, between the expiration of a term of enlistment, and the formation of a new army, the English have given themselves airs of triumph, and have done some brilliant exploits. In the winter of 1775–6, indeed, they were in Boston; and although our army, after the expiration of the first period of enlistment for six months, was reduced to a small number, yet the English were not in a condition to attempt any thing. In the winter of 1776–7, after the expiration of the second term of enlistment, and before the new army was brought together, the English marched through the Jersies. After the expiration of the last term of enlistment, which was for three years, and ended last January or February, the English went to their old exultations again, and undertook the expedition to Charleston. In the course of the last spring and summer, however, it seems the army has been renewed; and they are now enlisted, in general, during the war.

To state the numbers of the regular army according to the establishment, that is, according to the number of regiments at their full complement, I suppose the continental army has sometimes amounted to fourscore thousand men. But the American regiments have not often been full, any more than the English. There are in the war office, at Philadelphia, regular monthly returns of the army, from 1775 to this day, but I am not able, from memory, to give any accurate account of them; it is sufficient to say, that the American regular army has been generally superior to that of the English; and it would not be good policy to keep a larger army, unless we had a prospect of putting an end to the British power in America by it. But this, without a naval superiority, is very difficult, if not impracticable; the English take possession of a seaport town, fortify it in the strongest manner, and cover it with the guns of their men-of-war, so that our army cannot come at it. If France and Spain should coöperate with us so far as to send ships enough to maintain the superiority at sea, it would not require many years, perhaps not many months, to exterminate the English from the United States. But this policy those courts have not adopted, which is a little surprising, because it is obvious that by captivating the British fleet and army in America, the most decisive blow would be given to their power, which can possibly be given in any quarter of the globe.

What number of regular troops General Washington has at this time under his immediate command, I am not able precisely to say; I presume, however, that he has not less than twenty thousand men, besides the

French troops under the Comte de Rochambeau. Nor am I able to say, how many General Gates has to the southward.

But besides the regular army, we are to consider the militia. Several of the Colonies were formed into a militia, from the beginning of their settlement. After the commencement of this war, all the others followed their example, and made laws, by which all the inhabitants of America are now enrolled in a militia, which may be computed at five hundred thousand men. But these are scattered over a territory of one hundred and fifty miles in breadth, and at least fifteen hundred miles in length, lying all along upon the sea-coast. This gives the English the advantage, by means of their superiority at sea, to remove suddenly and easily from one part of the continent to another, as from Boston to New York, from New York to Rhode Island, from New York to Chesapeake or Delaware Bay, or to Savannah or Charleston; and the Americans the disadvantage, of not being able to march either the regular troops or the militia to such vast distances, without immense expense of money and of time. This puts it in the power of the English to take so many of our seaport towns, but not to make any long and successful marches into the interior country, or make any permanent establishment there.

As to discipline, in the beginning of the war there was very little, either among the militia or the regular troops. The American officers have, however, been industrious; they have had the advantage of reading all the books which have any reputation concerning military science; they have had the example of their enemies, the British officers, before their eyes a long time, indeed, from the year 1768; and they have had the honor of being joined by British, German, French, Prussian, and Polish officers, of infantry and cavalry, of artillery and engineering; so that the art of war is now as well understood in the American army, and military discipline is now carried to as great perfection, as in any country whatever.

As to a supply of warlike stores: at the commencement of hostilities, the Americans had neither cannon, arms, or ammunition, but in such contemptible quantities as distressed them beyond description; and they have all along been straitened, at times, by a scarcity of these articles, and are to this day.

They have, however, at present, an ample field artillery; they have arms and powder; and they can never be again absolutely destitute, because the manufactures of all sorts of arms, of cannon of all sorts, of saltpetre and powder, have been introduced and established. These manufactures, although very good, are very dear, and it is difficult to make enough for so constant and so great a consumption. Quantities of these articles are imported every year; and it is certain they can be imported and paid for by American produce, cheaper than they can be made.

But the Americans, to make their system perfect, want five hundred thousand stands of arms, that is,—one at least for every militia man, with powder, ball, and accoutrements in proportion. This, however, is rather to be wished for than expected. The French fleet carried arms to America; and if the communication between America and France and Spain should become more frequent by frigates and men-of-war, and, especially, if this republic should be compelled into a war with England, America will probably never again suffer much for want of arms or ammunition.

The English began the war against the northern Colonies; here they found the effects of ancient militia laws; they found a numerous and hardy militia, who fought and defeated them upon many occasions. They then thought it necessary to abandon these, and fall upon the middle Colonies, whose militia had not been so long formed; however, after several years' experience, they found they were not able to do any thing to the purpose against them. They have lastly conceived the design of attacking the southern Colonies; here, the white people, and consequently the militia, are not so numerous, and have not yet been used to war. Here, therefore, they have had some apparent successes; but they will find in the end their own destruction in these very successes. The climate will devour their men; their first successes will embolden them to rash enterprises; the people there will become inured to war, and will finally totally destroy them; for, as to the silly gasconade of bringing the southern Colonies to submission, there is not even a possibility of it. The people of those States are as firm in principle, and as determined in their tempers against the designs of the English, as the middle or the northern States.

XI.

17 OCTOBER.

YOUR eleventh question will give an opportunity of making some observations upon a subject that is quite misunderstood in every part of Europe. I shall answer it with great pleasure, according to the best of my information, and with the utmost candor.

The question is,—

"How great is the present debt of America? What has she occasion for yearly to act defensively? Are those wants supplied by the inhabitants themselves, or by other nations? If in the latter case, what does America lose of her strength by it? Are they not, in one manner or other, recompensed again by some equivalent advantage? If so, in what manner? What would be required to act offensively, and by that means shorten the war?"

All Europe has a mistaken apprehension of the present debt of America. This debt is of two sorts,—that which is due from the thirteen United States, in congress assembled; and that which is owing from each of the thirteen States in its separate capacity. I am not able to say, with precision, what the debt of each separate State is; but all these added together, fall far short of the debt of the United States.

The debt of the United States consists of three branches:—

1. The sums which have been lent them by France and Spain, and by M. Beaumarchais & Co. These have been for purchasing some supplies of cannon, arms, ammunition, and clothing for the troops; for assisting prisoners escaped from England, and for some other purposes. But the whole sum amounts to no great thing.

2. The loan-office certificates, which are promissory notes given to individuals in America who have lent paper money to the congress, and are their securities for the payment of the principal and interest. These the congress have equitably determined shall be paid, according to the value of the paper bills, in proportion to silver, at the time of their dates.

3. The paper bills which are now in circulation, or which were in circulation on the 18th day of March last. These bills amounted to the nominal sum of two hundred millions of dollars; but the real value of them

to the possessors is estimated at forty for one, amounting to five millions of Spanish dollars, or one million and a quarter sterling. This is the full value of them, perhaps more; but this estimation of them has given satisfaction in America to the possessors of them, who certainly obtained them in general at a cheaper rate.

These three branches of debt, which are the whole (according to a calculation made last May, and sent me by a member of congress who has been four years a member of their treasury board, and is perfect master of the subject) amount in the whole to five millions sterling and no more. The national debt of America then is five millions sterling.

In order to judge of the burden of this debt, we may compare it with the numbers of people. They are three millions. The national debt of Great Britain is two hundred millions. The number of people in England and Scotland is not more than six millions. Why should not America, with three millions of people, be able to bear a debt of one hundred millions as well as Great Britain, with six millions of people, a debt of two hundred millions?

We may compare it with the exports of America. In 1774, the exports of America were six millions sterling. In the same year the exports of Great Britain were twelve millions. Why would not the exports of America, of six millions, bear a national debt of one hundred millions, as well as the twelve millions of British exports bear a debt of two hundred millions?

We may compare it in this manner with the national debt of France, Spain, the United Provinces, Russia, Sweden, Denmark, Portugal, and you will find that it is but small in comparison.

We may compare it in another point of view. Great Britain has already spent in this war sixty millions sterling; America, five millions. Great Britain has annually added to her national debt more than the whole amount of her annual exports; America has not added to hers in the whole course of five years' war a sum equal to one year's exports.

The debt of Great Britain is, in a large proportion of it, due to foreigners, for which they must annually pay the interest by sending cash abroad. A very trifle of the American debt is yet due to foreigners.

Lord North borrowed last year twelve millions; and every future year of the war must borrow the same or a larger sum. America could carry on this war a hundred years by borrowing only one million sterling a year.

The annual expense of America has not hitherto exceeded one million a year; that of Great Britain has exceeded twenty millions some years. America may therefore carry on this war a hundred years, and at the end of it will be no more in debt, in proportion to her present numbers of people and her exports in 1774, than Great Britain is now.

There is another consideration of some weight; the landed interest in America is vastly greater, in proportion to the mercantile interest than it is in Great Britain. The exports of America are the productions of the soil *annually,* which increase every year. The exports of Great Britain are manufactures, which will decrease every year while this war with America lasts.

The only objection to this reasoning is this,—that America is not used to great taxes, and the people there are not yet disciplined to such enormous taxation as in England. This is true; and this makes all their perplexity at present; but they are capable of bearing as great taxes in proportion as the English; and if the English force them to it, by continuing the war, they will reconcile themselves to it; and they are in fact now taxing themselves more and more every year, and to an amount, that a man who knew America only twenty years ago would think incredible.

Her wants have hitherto been supplied by the inhabitants themselves, and they have been very little indebted to foreign nations. But, on account of the depreciation of her paper, and in order to introduce a more stable currency, she has now occasion to borrow a sum of money abroad, which would enable her to support her credit at home, to exert herself more vigorously against the English, both by sea and land, and greatly assist her in extending her commerce with foreign nations, especially the Dutch. America would not lose of her strength by borrowing money; but, on the contrary, would gain vastly. It would enable her to exert herself more by privateering, which is a mine of gold to her. She would make remittances in bills of exchange to foreign merchants for their commodities; and it would enable many persons to follow their true interest in cultivating the land, instead of attending to manufactures, which, being indispensable, they are now obliged more or less to follow, though less profitable. The true profit of America is the continual augmentation of the price and value of land. Improvement in land is her principal employment, her best policy, and the principal source of her growing wealth.

The last question is easily answered. It is,—"What would be required to act offensively, and by that means shorten the war?"

To this I answer, nothing is wanted but a loan of money and a fleet of ships.

A fleet of ships, only sufficient to maintain a superiority over the English, would enable the infant Hercules to strangle all the serpents that environ his cradle. It is impossible to express in too strong terms the importance of a few ships of the line to the Americans. Two or three French, or Dutch, or Spanish ships of the line, stationed at Rhode Island, Boston, Delaware River, or Chesapeake Bay, would have prevented the dreadful sacrifice at Penobscot. Three or four ships of the line would have prevented the whole expedition to Charleston. Three or four ships of the line more, added to the squadron of the Chevalier de Ternay, would have enabled the Americans to have taken New York.

A loan of money is now wanted, to give stability to the currency of America; to give vigor to the enlistments for the army; to add alacrity to the fitting out privateers; and to give an ample extension to their trade.

The Americans will labor through, without a fleet, and without a loan. But it is ungenerous and cruel to put them to such difficulties, and to keep mankind embroiled in all the horrors of war, for want of such trifles, which so many of the powers of Europe wish they had, and could so easily furnish. But if mankind must be embroiled, and the blood of thousands must be shed, for want of a little magnanimity in some, the Americans must not be blamed; it is not their fault.

XII.

WE are now come to your twelfth head of inquiry, which is, "What countenance have the finances? How much does the expense exceed the yearly income? Does the annual revenue, deriving from the taxes, increase or diminish, in the whole, or in any particulars? and what are the reasons to be given for it?"

Here I am apprehensive I shall find a difficulty to make myself understood, as the American finances, and mode of taxation, differ so materially from any that I know of in Europe.

In the month of May, 1775, when the congress came together, for the first time, after the battles of Lexington and Concord, they found it necessary to raise an army, or, rather, to adopt an army already raised, at Cambridge, in order to oppose the British troops, and shut them up in the prison of Boston. But they found that the Colonies were but just got out of debt, had just paid off the debts contracted in the last French war. In the several treasuries of the Colonies they found only a few thousand pounds. They had before them a prospect of a stagnation, or interruption of their trade, pretty universally, by the British men-of-war. They had a thousand perplexities before them, in the prospect of passing through thirteen revolutions of government, from the royal authority to that under the people. They had armies and navies to form; they had new constitutions of government to attend to; they had twenty tribes of Indians to negotiate with; they had vast numbers of negroes to take care of; they had all sorts of arms, ammunition, artillery, to procure, as well as blankets and clothing and subsistence for the army; they had negotiations to think of in Europe, and treaties to form, of alliance and commerce; and they had even salt to procure, for the subsistence of the inhabitants, and even of their cattle, as well as their armies.

In this situation, with so many wants and demands, and no money or revenues to recur to, they had recourse to an expedient, which had been often practised in America, but nowhere else; they determined to emit paper money.

The American paper money is nothing but bills of credit, by which the public, the community, promises to pay the possessor a certain sum in a limited time. In a country where there is no coin, or not enough, in circulation, these bills may be emitted to a certain amount, and they will pass at par; but as soon as the quantity exceeds the value of the ordinary business of the people, it will depreciate, and continue to fall in its value, in proportion to the augmentation of the quantity.

The congress, on the 18th of March last, stated this depreciation at forty for one. This may be nearly the average, but it often passes much lower. By this resolution, all the bills in circulation on that day (and none have been emitted since) amount to about one million and a quarter sterling. To this if you add the money borrowed upon loan certificates, and the debt contracted abroad in France and Spain, the whole does not amount to but little more than five millions.

Yearly income we have none, properly speaking. We have no imposts or duties laid upon any articles of importation, exportation, or consumption. The revenue consists entirely in grants annually made by the legislatures, of sums of money for the current service of the year, and appropriated to certain uses. These grants are proportioned upon all the polls and estates, real and personal, in the community; and they are levied and paid into the public treasury with great punctuality, from whence they are issued in payments of the demands upon the public.

You see then that it is in the power of the legislatures to raise what sums are wanted, at least as much as the people can bear; and they are usually proportioned to the public wants, and the people's abilities. They are now constantly laying on and paying very heavy taxes, although for the first three or four years of the war the obstructions of trade, &c., made it difficult to raise any taxes at all. The yearly taxes, annually laid on, have increased every year for these three years past, and will continue to be increased in proportion to the abilities of the people. This ability, no doubt, increases in proportion as population increases, as new lands are cultivated, and as property is in any way added to the common stock; it will also increase as our commerce increases, and as the success in privateering increases.

But by the method of taxing, you see that it is in the power of the legislature to increase the taxes every year, as the public exigencies may require; and they have no other restraint or limit than the people's ability.

XIII.

26 OCTOBER.

YOUR thirteenth inquiry is, "What resources might America hereafter still make use of?"

There are many resources, yet untried, which would certainly be explored, if America should be driven to the necessity of them.

1. Luxury prevails in that young country, notwithstanding all the confident assertions of the English concerning their distress, to a degree, that retrenching this alone would enable them to carry on the war. There are expenses in wheel carriages, horses, equipage, furniture, dress, and the table, which might be spared, and would amount to enough to carry on the war.

2. The Americans might, and, rather than the English should prevail against them, they would, be brought to impose duties upon articles of luxury and convenience, and even of necessity, as has been done by all the nations of Europe. I am not able at present, and upon memory, to entertain you with accurate calculations; but in general it may be said, with certainty, that, if as heavy duties were laid upon articles of consumption and importation as are laid in England, or even in Holland, they would produce a revenue sufficient to carry on this war without borrowing at all. I hope, however, they will never come to this. I am clear they need not. Such systematical and established revenues are dangerous to liberty; which is safe, while the revenue depends upon annual grants of the people, because this secures public economy.

3. If there should be hereafter any accession to the population of America, by migrations from Europe, this will be a fresh resource; because, in that country of agriculture, the ability to raise a revenue will bear a constant proportion to the numbers of people.

4. There are immense tracts of uncultivated lands. These lands are all claimed by particular States; but if these States should cede these claims to the congress, which they would do in case of necessity, the congress might sell these lands, and they would become a great resource; no man can say how great, or how lasting.

5. There is a great deal of plate in America; and if she were driven to extremities, the ladies, I assure you, have patriotism enough to give up their plate to the public, rather than lose their liberties, or run any great hazard of it.

6. There is another resource still. The war may be carried on by means of a fluctuating medium of paper money. The war has been carried on in this manner hitherto; and I firmly believe, if the people could not find a better way, they would agree to call in all the paper, and let it lie as a demand upon the public, to be hereafter equitably paid, according to its fluctuating value, in silver; and emit new bills to depreciate, and carry on the war in the same way. This, however, would occasion many perplexities and much unhappiness; it would do injustice to many individuals, and will and ought to be avoided, if possible.

7. A loan in Europe, however, would be the best resource, as it would necessarily extend our trade, and relieve the people from too great a present burden. Very heavy taxes are hurtful, because they lessen the increase of population, by making the means of subsistence more difficult.

8. There are resources of agriculture, manufactures, and labor, that would produce much, if explored and attempted.

9. The resources of trade and privateering ought to be mentioned again. The real cause of our doing so little hitherto, is this:—The congress, in 1774, agreed upon a non-exportation, to begin in September, 1775. This induced the merchants in every part of America to send their ships and sailors to England, from whence the most of them never returned. The consequence of which was, that the Americans have been distressed for want of ships and seamen ever since. But the number of both has increased every year, in spite of all that the English have taken and destroyed. The vast number of ships and seamen taken this year will repair those losses; and no man can say to what an extent trade and privateering will be carried the next and the succeeding years.

XIV.

THE fourteenth question is,—"What is the quantity of paper money in circulation? What credit the inhabitants have for it in their daily business? What designs the inhabitants have, by maintaining its credit? What by preventing its increase? And in what manner do they realize it?"

The quantity of paper bills in circulation on the 18th of March last, was two hundred millions of paper dollars.

The congress then stated the value of it, upon an average, at forty for one; amounting in the whole to five millions of silver dollars, or one million and a quarter sterling. This they did, by resolving to receive one silver dollar in lieu of forty paper ones, in the payment of taxes. This was probably allowing more than the full value for the paper; because, by all accounts, the bills passed from hand to hand, in private transactions, at sixty or seventy for one.

The designs of the inhabitants, in preserving its credit as much as they can, are very good and laudable. The designs are, that they may have a fixed and certain medium, both for external and internal commerce; that every man may have an equal profit from his industry and for his commodities; that private and public debts may be justly paid; and that every man may pay an equal and proportional share of the public expenses. And this is their design in preventing its increase; because it is impossible, if the quantity is increased, to prevent the depreciation of the whole in circulation.

They realize it in various ways. Some have lent it to the public, and received loan-office certificates for it, upon interest, which are to be paid in proportion to their value in silver at the time of their dates. Some purchase with it the produce of the country, which they export to the West Indies and to Europe; and, by this means, supply the French and Spanish fleets and armies, both upon the continent of America and in the West India Islands. Others purchase merchandises imported with it; others purchase bills of exchange upon France, Spain, &c.; others purchase silver and gold with it; and others purchase houses and lands. Others have paid their debts with it, to such a degree, that the people of America were never so little in debt, in their private capacities, as at present.

XV.

YOUR fifteenth quære is, "Does not the English army lay out its pay in America? At how much can the yearly benefit be calculated? Are not the prisoners provided for in America? Who has the care of their maintenance? How was Burgoyne's army supplied?"

When the English army was in Boston, they bought all that they could, and left considerable sums there in silver and gold. So they did at Rhode Island. Since they have been in New York, they have purchased every thing they could, of provisions and fuel, on Long Island, Staten Island, New York Island, and in those parts of the States of New York and New Jersey where they have been able to carry on any clandestine traffic. When they were in Philadelphia, they did the same; and General Howe tells you, that he suspects that General Washington, from political motives, connived at the people's supplying Philadelphia, in order essentially to serve his country, by insinuating it into large sums of silver and gold. They are doing the same now, more or less, in South Carolina and Georgia; and they cannot go into any part of America, without doing the same.

The British prisoners, in the hands of the Americans, receive their clothing chiefly from the English; and flags of truce are permitted to come out from their lines, for this purpose. They receive their pay, also, from their master, and spend the most of it where they are; they also purchase provisions in the country, and pay for them in hard money.

I am not able to ascertain exactly the yearly benefit; but it must be considerable; and the addition now of a French fleet and army to supply, will make a great addition of cash and bills of exchange, which will facilitate commerce and privateering. And the more troops and ships Great Britain and France send to America, the greater will this resource necessarily be to the Americans.

XVI.

THE sixteenth inquiry is, "Who loses most by desertion? Do the English and German deserters serve voluntarily and well in the American army? How can those who do not enter into the army subsist?"

These questions I answer with great pleasure. There has been, from the beginning of the war to this day, scarcely an example of a native American's deserting from the army to the English. There have been, in the American army, some scattering Scotch, Irish, and German soldiers; some of these have deserted, but never in great numbers; and among the prisoners they have taken, it is astonishing how few they have ever been able to persuade, by all their flatteries, threatenings, promises, and even cruelties, to enlist into their service.

The number of deserters from them has been all along considerably more. Congress have generally prohibited their officers from enlisting deserters; for some particular services permission has been given, and they have served well.

Those who do not enlist into the army have no difficulty to subsist. Those of them who have any trades, as weavers, tailors, smiths, shoemakers, tanners, curriers, carpenters, bricklayers, in short, any trade whatsoever, enter immediately into better business than they ever had in Europe, where they gain a better subsistence and more money; because tradesmen of all denominations are now much wanted; those who have no trade, if they are capable of any kind of labor, are immediately employed in agriculture, &c., labor being much wanted, and very dear.

I am not able to tell the precise numbers that have deserted; but if an hundred thousand were to desert, they would find no difficulty in point of subsistence or employment, if they can and will work.

XVII.

THE seventeenth inquiry is, "Whether we have any information that we can rely on, concerning the population? Has it increased or diminished, since the war?"

In some former letters, I have made some observations upon the subject of the increase of mankind in America.

In the year 1774 there was much private conversation among the members of congress, concerning the number of souls in every Colony. The delegates of each were consulted, and the estimates made by them were taken down as follows:—

In New Hampshire	150,000	Pennsylvania and Delaware	350,000
Massachusetts	400,000	Maryland	320,000
Rhode Island	59,678	Virginia	640,000
Connecticut	192,000	North Carolina	300,000
New York	250,000	South Carolina	225,000
New Jersey	130,000	Total	3,016,678

This, however, was but an estimate, and some persons have thought there was too much speculation in it. It will be observed, that Georgia was not represented in the first congress, and, therefore, is not included in the estimate.

In a pamphlet published in England about a year ago, entitled, "A Memorial to the Sovereigns of Europe, on the present State of Affairs, between the Old and New World," written by Mr. Pownall, a member of parliament, and formerly Governor of Massachusetts, and Lieutenant-Governor of New Jersey, we are told, that "The Massachusetts had, in the year 1722, ninety-four thousand inhabitants; in 1742, one hundred and sixty-four thousand; in 1751, when there was a great depopulation, both by war and the smallpox, one hundred and sixty-four thousand four hundred and eighty-four; in 1761, two hundred and sixteen thousand; in 1765, two hundred and fifty-five thousand five hundred; in 1771, two hundred and ninety-two thousand; in 1773, three hundred thousand.

In Connecticut, in 1756, one hundred and twenty-nine thousand nine hundred and ninety-four; in 1774, two hundred and fifty-seven thousand three hundred and fifty-six. These numbers are not increased by strangers, but decreased by wars and emigrations to the westward and to other States; yet they have nearly doubled in eighteen years.

In New York, in 1756, ninety-six thousand seven hundred and seventy-six; in 1771, one hundred and sixty-eight thousand and seven; in 1774, one hundred and eighty-two thousand two hundred and fifty-one.

In Virginia, in 1756, one hundred and seventy-three thousand three hundred and sixteen; in 1764, two hundred thousand; in 1774, three hundred thousand.

In South Carolina, in 1750, sixty-four thousand; in 1770, one hundred and fifteen thousand.

In Rhode Island, in 1738, fifteen thousand; in 1748, twenty-eight thousand four hundred and thirty-nine.

As there never was a militia in Pennsylvania before this war, with authentic lists of the population, it has been variously estimated on speculation. There was a continual importation for many years of Irish and German emigrants, yet many of these settled in other provinces; but the progress of population, in the ordinary course, advanced in a ratio between that of Virginia and that of Massachusetts. The city of Philadelphia advanced more rapidly,—it had, in 1749, two thousand and seventy-six houses; in 1753, two thousand three hundred; in 1760, two thousand nine hundred and sixty-nine; in 1769, four thousand four hundred and seventy-four; from 1749 to 1753, from sixteen to eighteen thousand inhabitants; from 1760 to 1769, from thirty-one thousand three hundred and eighteen to thirty-five thousand.

There were, in 1754, various calculations and estimates made of the numbers on the continent. The sanguine made the numbers one million and a half; those who admitted less speculation into the calculation, but adhered closer to facts and lists as they were made out, stated them at one million two hundred and fifty thousand. Governor Pownall thinks that two million one hundred and forty-one thousand three hundred and seven would turn out nearest to the real amount in 1774. But what an amazing progress, which in eighteen years has added a million to a million two hundred and fifty thousand, although a war was maintained in that country for seven years of the term! In this view, one sees a community unfolding itself, beyond any example in Europe.

Thus, you have the estimates made by the gentlemen in congress, in 1774, and that of Governor Pownall for the same epocha. That made in congress is most likely to be right. If, in their estimate, some States were rated too high, it has been since made certain that others were too low.

But, admitting Mr. Pownall's estimate to be just, the numbers have grown since 1774 so much, notwithstanding the war and the interruption of migrations from Europe, that they must be wellnigh three millions. If the calculation made by the members of congress was right, the numbers now must be nearer four millions than three millions and a half.

I have observed to you, in a former letter, that the Massachusetts Bay has been lately numbered, and found to have increased in numbers as much as in former periods, very nearly.

I now add, that in Delaware, which in 1774 was estimated at thirty thousand, upon numbering the people since, they appeared to be forty thousand.

Pennsylvania is undoubtedly set too low in both estimates.

XVIII.

QUESTION eighteenth. "Do sufficient tranquillity, contentment, and prosperity reign in those places where the war does not rage? Can one sufficiently subsist there without feeling the oppression of the taxes? Does plenty abound there? Is there more than is necessary for consumption? Are the people well affected and encouraged to pursue the war and endure its calamities? or is there poverty and dejection?"

There has been more of this tranquillity and contentment, and fewer riots, insurrections, and seditions throughout the whole war, and in the periods of its greatest distress, than there was for seven years before the war broke out, in those parts that I am best acquainted with. As to subsistence, there never was or will be any difficulty. There never was any real want of any thing but warlike stores and clothing for the army, and salt and rum both for the army and the people; but they have such plentiful importations of these articles now, that there is no want, excepting of blankets, clothing, and warlike stores for the army.

The taxes are rising very high, but there never will be more laid on than the people can bear, because the representatives who lay them tax themselves and their neighbors in exact proportion. The taxes indeed fall heaviest upon the rich and the higher classes of people.

The earth produces grain and meat in abundance for the consumption of the people, for the support of the army, and for exportation.

The people are more universally well affected and encouraged to pursue the war than are the people of England, France, or Spain, as far as I can judge.

As to poverty, there is hardly a beggar in the country. As to dejection, I never saw, even at the time of our greatest danger and perplexity, so much of it as appears in England or France upon every intelligence of a disastrous event.

The greatest source of grief and affliction is the fluctuation of the paper money; but this, although it occasions unhappiness, has no violent or fatal effects.

XIX.

QUESTION nineteenth. "Is not peace very much longed for in America? Might not this desire of peace induce the people to hearken to proposals, appearing very fair, but which really are not so, which the people might be too quick in listening to, and the government forced to accept?"

The people, in all ages and countries, wish for peace; human nature does not love war; yet this does not hinder nations from going to war, when it is necessary, and often indeed for frivolous purposes of avarice, ambition, vanity, resentment, and revenge. I have never been informed of more desire of peace in America than is common to all nations at war. They in general know that they cannot obtain it, without submitting to conditions infinitely more dreadful than all the horrors of this war.

If they are ever deceived, it is by holding out to them false hopes of independence, and Great Britain's acknowledging it.

The people of America are too enlightened to be deceived in any great plan of policy. They understand the principles and nature of government too well to be imposed on by any proposals short of their own object.

Great Britain has tried so many experiments to deceive them, without effect, that I think it is scarcely worth her while to try again. The history of these ministerial and parliamentary tricks would fill a volume. I have not records nor papers to recur to; but if Mr. Calkoen desires it, I could give him a sketch from memory of these artifices and their success, which, I think, would convince him there is no danger from that quarter.

XX.

QUESTION twentieth. "Have there not been different opinions in congress, with regard to this (that is,—to proposals appearing fair which were not so,) from whence animosities have arisen?"

There has never been any difference of sentiment in congress since the declaration of independency, concerning any proposals of reconciliation. There have been no proposals of reconciliation made since the 4th of July, 1776, excepting twice.

The first was made by Lord Howe, who, together with his brother, the General, were appointed by the King commissioners for some purpose or other. The public has never been informed what powers they had. Lord Howe sent a message by General Sullivan to congress, desiring a conference with some of its members. There were different sentiments concerning the propriety of sending any members until we knew his Lordship's powers. A majority decided to send. Dr. Franklin, Mr. John Adams, and Mr. Rutledge were sent. Upon their report, there was a perfect unanimity of sentiment in congress.

The second was the mission of Lord Carlisle, Governor Johnstone, and Mr. Eden, in 1778. Upon this occasion again there was a perfect unanimity in congress.

Before the declaration of independency, Lord North moved several conciliatory propositions in parliament, in which a good deal of art was employed to seduce, deceive, and divide. But there was always an unanimity in congress upon all these plans.

There were different opinions concerning the petition to the King, in the year 1775; and before that, concerning the non-exportation agreement. There have been different opinions concerning articles of the confederation; concerning the best plans for the conduct of the war; concerning the best officers to conduct them; concerning territorial controversies between particular States, &c.; but these differences of opinion, which are essential to all assemblies, have never caused greater animosities than those which arise in all assemblies where there is freedom of debate.

XXI.

27 OCTOBER.

QUESTION twenty-first. "Are there no malcontents in America against the government, who are otherwise much inclined for the American cause, who may force the nation, or congress, against their resolutions and interests, to conclude a peace?"

There is no party formed in any of the thirteen States against the new constitution, nor any opposition against the government, that I have ever heard of, excepting in Pennsylvania, and in North Carolina. These by no means deserve to be compared together.

In Pennsylvania there is a respectable body of people, who are zealous against Great Britain, but yet wish for some alteration in their new form of government; yet this does not appear to weaken their exertions; it seems rather to excite an emulation in the two parties, and to increase their efforts.

I have before explained the history of the rise and progress of the party, in North Carolina, consisting of regulators and Scotch Highlanders; and General Howe has informed you of their fate. This party has ever appeared to make North Carolina more stanch and decided, instead of weakening it.

The party in Pennsylvania will never have an inclination to force the congress, against their interests, to make peace; nor would they have the power, if they had the will.

The party in North Carolina, whose inclination cannot be doubted, is too inconsiderable to do any thing.

XXII.

QUESTIONS twenty-second and twenty-third. "General Monk repaired the King's government in England: Might not one American general or another be able, by discontent or corruption, to do the same? Would the army follow his orders on such an occasion? Could one or more politicians, through intrigues, undertake the same with any hopes of success, should even the army assist him in such a case?"

I have before observed, that no politicians, or general officers, in America, have any such influence. Neither the people nor the soldiers would follow them. It was not attachment to men, but to a cause, which first produced, and has supported, the revolution; it was not attachment to officers, but to liberty, which made the soldiers enlist. Politicians in America can only intrigue with the people; these are so numerous, and so scattered, that no statesman has any great influence but in his own small circle. In courts, sometimes, gaining two or three individuals may produce a revolution; no revolution in America can be accomplished without gaining the majority of the people; and this not all the wealth of Great Britain is able to do, at the expense of their liberties.

Question twenty-fourth. "The revolution must have made a great change in affairs, so that many people, though at present free of the enemy's incursions, have lost their daily subsistence. Have the occupations, which come instead of their old ones, been sufficient to supply their wants?"

All the difficulties which were ever apprehended, of this sort, are long since past. In 1774, some were apprehensive that the fishermen, sailors, and shipwrights would be idle; but some went into the army, some into the navy, and some went to agriculture; and if there had been twice as many, they would all have found employment. The building of frigates and privateers has employed all the carpenters. Manufactories, besides, have been set up, of cannon, arms, powder, saltpetre, salt. Flax and wool have been raised in greater quantities, and coarse manufactures of cloth a nd linen been increased. In short, the greatest difficulty is, that there are not hands enough. Agriculture alone, in that country, would find employment enough for millions, and privateering for thousands, more than there are.

XXIII.

QUESTION twenty-fifth. "Do they who have lost their possessions and fortunes by the war, endure it patiently, as compatriots, so that nothing can be
feared from them?"

Losing fortunes in America has not such dreadful consequences, to
individuals or families, as it has in Europe. The reason is obvious; because
the means of subsistence are easier to be obtained, so that nobody suffers
for want. As far as I am acquainted with the sufferers, they have borne their
losses, both of property and relations, with great fortitude; and, so far
from producing in their minds a desire of submission, they have only
served to irritate them, to convince them more fully of the precarious and
deplorable situation they would be in under the government of the English, and to make them more eager to resist it.

Question twenty-sixth. "How has it gone with the cultivation of the
land before the troubles, at their commencement, and at present? What
change has taken place?"

Agriculture ever was, and ever will be, the dominant interest in America. Nevertheless, before this war, perhaps, she ran more into commerce
than was for her interest. She depended too much, perhaps, upon importations for her clothing, utensils, &c., and indulged in too many luxuries.
When the prospect opened, in 1775, of an interruption of her commerce,
she applied herself more to agriculture; and many places that depended
upon the lumber trade, the fishery, &c., for the importation of even their
bread, have turned their labor and attention to raising corn, wool, flax, and
cattle, and have lived better, and advanced in wealth and independence
faster, than ever they did. For example, the towns in the neighborhood of
the sea, in the Massachusetts Bay, used to depend upon the fishery and
commerce to import them their wheat and flour from Philadelphia,
Maryland, and Virginia, and rice from South Carolina and Georgia; the
communication being interrupted by sea since the war, they have planted
their own corn.

The eastern parts of the Massachusetts Bay, before the war, depended on
the commerce of lumber for the West India market, and of masts, yards,

and bowsprits for the royal navy of Great Britain, to procure them clothes, meat, and strong liquors. Since the war, they have cultivated their lands, raised their own corn, wool, flax, and planted the apple tree instead of drinking rum, in consequence of which, they are more temperate, wealthy, and independent than ever.

North Carolina depended upon the commerce of pitch, tar, and turpentine and tobacco, for the importation of many things. Since the war, they have turned their labor to raise more of the things which they wanted.

Maryland, Virginia, and North Carolina depended upon the trade of tobacco to import coarse cloths for their negroes. Since the war, they have raised less tobacco, and more wheat, wool, and cotton, and made the coarse cloths themselves.

So that, upon the whole, the lessening of commerce, and the increase of agriculture, have rendered America more independent than she ever was.

XXIV.

QUESTION twenty-seventh. "How was the situation of manufactures, manual art, and trade in general, at the beginning of this war? What change have they suffered?"

Manufactures in general never flourished in America. They were never attended only by women and children who could not work in the field, and by men at certain seasons of the year, and at certain intervals of time, when they could not be employed in the cultivation of the lands; because that labor upon land, in that country, is more profitable than in manufactures. These they could import and purchase, with the produce of their soil, cheaper than they could make them. The cause of this is the plenty of wild land. A day's work, worth two shillings, upon wild land, not only produced two shillings in the crop, but made the land worth two shillings more. Whereas, a day's work of the same price, applied to manufactures, produced only the two shillings.

Since the war, however, freight and insurance have been so high, that manufactures have been more attended to. Manufactures of saltpetre, salt, powder, cannon, arms, have been introduced; clothing, in wool and flax, has been made, and many other necessary things; but these, for the reason before given, will last no longer than the war or than the hazard of their trade.

America is the country of raw materials, and of commerce enough to carry them to a good market; but Europe is the country for manufactures and commerce. Thus Europe and America will be blessings to each other, if some malevolent policy does not frustrate the purposes of nature.

XXV.

QUESTION twenty-eight. "Has America gained, or lost, by the mutual capture of ships? How much is the benefit or prejudice of it, by calculation?"

America has gained. She took early, from the English, ordnance and ammunition ships, and supplied herself in that way with those articles when she had them not, and could not otherwise obtain them; she has taken, in this way, a great number of British and German soldiers; she has taken a vast number of seamen, who have generally enlisted on board our privateers; she has taken great quantities of provisions, clothing, arms, and warlike stores; she has taken every year more and more, since 1775, and will probably continue to take more and more every year, while the war lasts. I have certain intelligence, that there have been this year carried into Boston and Philadelphia only, ninety-nine vessels, in the months of July and August. On board of these vessels there were not less than eight hundred seamen; many of the ships were very rich. The vessels the English have taken from the Americans were of small value; this year they have been few in number.

I am not able to give you an exact calculation. The Quebec ships were worth from thirty to forty thousand pounds sterling each, and there were two-and-twenty of them in number.

Privateering is a great nursery of seamen; and if the Americans had not imprudently sacrificed such a number of their frigates and privateers in the attack and defence of places, these alone would, by this time, wellnigh have ruined the British commerce, navy, and army.

XXVI.

I BELIEVE you will be pleased, when I tell you, that we are now come to the twenty-ninth, and last question, which is, "What are the real damages sustained, or still to be suffered, by the loss of Charleston? And what influence has it had upon the minds of the people?"

An interruption of the commerce of indigo and rice; the loss of many negroes, which the English will steal from the plantations, and send to the West India islands for sale; a great deal of plunder of every sort; much unhappiness among the people; and several lives of very worthy men will be lost; but the climate will be death to European troops; and, at an immense expense of men and money, they will ravage for a while, and then disappear.

The effect of the surrender of Charleston, and the defeat of Gates, has only been to awaken the people from their dreams of peace.

The artifices of the English, holding out ideas of peace, seem to have deceived both the Americans and their allies, while they were only contriving means to succor Gibraltar, and invade Carolina. The people are now convinced of their mistake, and generally roused. But these disasters will have no more effect towards subduing America, than if they had taken place in the East Indies. I have the honor to be, sir,

Your humble servant,
JOHN ADAMS.

Review
of the Hillhouse Proposal

A mong the manuscripts of Mr. Adams was found the following review of a pamphlet published in 1808, entitled "Propositions for Amending the Constitution of the United States, submitted by Mr. Hillhouse to the Senate, on the twelfth day of April, 1808, with his Explanatory Remarks." It seems to have been prepared for publication, though no trace of it has been found in print. For the better understanding of the strictures, it is necessary to give, in the first place, the amendments as they were proposed by Mr. Hillhouse.

Charles Francis Adams

The *Review* is taken from *Works*, VI, 525–50.

REVIEW.

Article the First.

After the third day of March, one thousand eight hundred and thirteen, the house of representatives shall be composed of members chosen every year by the people of the several states; their electors in each state shall have the qualifications requisite for electors of the most numerous branch of the state legislature; and their term of service shall expire on the first Tuesday of April in each year.

Article the Second.

After the third day of March, 1813, the senators of the United States shall be chosen for three years; and their term of service shall expire on the first Tuesday of April.

Immediately after they shall be assembled in consequence of the first election, they shall be divided as equally as may be, into three classes. The seats of the first class shall be vacated at the expiration of the first year; of the second class, at the expiration of the second year; and of the third class, at the expiration of the third year; so that one third may be chosen every year. Vacancies to be filled as already provided.

Article the Third.

On the third day of March, 1813, the president of the United States shall be appointed, and shall hold his office until the expiration of the first Tuesday of April, 1814. And on the first Tuesday of April, 1814, and on the first Tuesday of April in each succeeding year, the president shall be appointed to hold his office during the term of one year. The mode of appointment shall be as follows:—

In presence of the senate and house of representatives, each senator belonging to the class whose term of service will first expire, and constitutionally eligible to the office of president, of which the house of representatives shall be the sole judges, and shall decide without debate, shall, beginning with the first on the alphabet, and in their alphabetical order, draw a ball out of a box containing the same number of uniform balls as there shall be senators present and eligible, one of which balls shall be colored, the others white. The senator who shall draw the colored ball shall be president. A committee of the house of representatives, to consist of a member from each state, to be appointed in such manner as the house shall direct, shall place the balls in the box, shall shake the same so as to intermix them, and shall superintend the drawing thereof.

In case of the removal of the president from office, or of his death, resignation, or inability to discharge the powers and duties thereof, if congress be then in session, or if not, as soon as they shall be in session, the president shall, in the manner beforementioned, be appointed for the residue of the term. And, until the disability be removed, or a president be appointed, the speaker of the senate shall act as president. And congress may, by law, provide for the case of removal by death, resignation, or inability of the president, and vacancy in the office, or inability of the speaker of the senate; and such officer shall act accordingly, until the disability of the president be removed, or another be appointed.

The seat of a senator who shall be appointed as president, shall thereby be vacated.

Article the Fourth.

After the third day of March, 1813, the compensation of the president shall not exceed fifteen thousand dollars a year.

Article the Fifth.

After the third day of March, 1813, the office of vice-president shall cease. And the senate, on the same day in each year, when the president shall be annually appointed, shall choose a speaker; and, in the absence of the speaker, or when he shall exercise the office of president, the senate shall choose a speaker *pro tempore*.

Article the Sixth.

After the third day of March, 1813, the president shall nominate, and by and with the advice and consent of the senate and of the house of representatives, shall appoint ambassadors, other public ministers and consuls, judges of the supreme court, and all other officers of the United States, whose appointments are not herein otherwise provided for, and which shall be established by law. But congress may, by law, vest the appointment of such officers as they think proper, in the president, by and with the advice and consent of the senate; and of the inferior officers in the president alone, in the courts of law, or in the heads of departments. But no law, vesting the power of appointment, shall be for a longer term than two years. All proceedings on nominations shall be with closed doors and without debate; but information of the character and qualifications of the person nominated, shall be received.

Article the Seventh.

After the third day of March, 1813, the president shall have power to fill all vacancies that may happen during the recess of congress, by granting commissions which shall expire at the end of their next session. No removal from office shall take place without the consent of the senate and of the house of representatives. But congress may, by law, authorize the removal by the same power, as may by law be authorized to make the appointment. But in every case of misconduct in office, where the consent of the senate, or of the senate and house of representatives, shall be necessary to a removal, the president, during the recess of congress, may suspend the officer, and make a temporary appointment of a person to exercise the office, until the next meeting of congress, and until a decision can be had by the senate, or by the senate and house of representatives, as the case may be, on a question for the removal of the officer suspended. All proceedings respecting removal from office shall be had, without debate, upon the information and reasons which shall be communicated by the president, and with closed doors.

These radical propositions, coming as they did from a leading member of the party originally formed for the purpose of sustaining the federal constitution, and supported by him in an elaborate speech, were well calculated to fix the attention of Mr. Adams. It is not unlikely that he gave to the plan more importance, as a political movement, than it merited; for it does not appear to have been followed up, either by the originator or any one else. This may be the reason why the review was never published. The general argument is, however, of a permanent nature, and deserves to be placed among the memorials of the author.

WHEN a speech or a pamphlet appears in public from the press, the most rational course would be to read it and judge of its merits, without prejudice. But republican jealousy is so much the spirit of the times, that the first question is, who is the author? of what party is he? What are his motives? and whose election is he aiming to promote? This inquisitive temper has been sufficiently alive concerning the publication of Mr. Hill-house. Some have conjectured that his design was, to throw the nation into confusion, in hopes that a better order than prevails at present, might arise out of it. Others have suggested that this work is a burlesque on the crude projects of amendment which appear in such numbers. One set of men have suspected that this gentleman has been so long in public business, and has been so much disappointed, becoming yearly of less and less influence, and, at present, finding himself in a minority, consisting at most of three or four in the senate, that he is grown impatient, and determined, at any rate, to make himself a name, and increase his importance. I shall leave these uncandid insinuations to those who delight in them; and take it for granted, that Mr. Hillhouse is sincere, that he honestly believes what he says, and proposes his amendments for the public good. It shall be my endeavor to be as concise as possible, in a few observations which, I hope, may show in a clear light, the merit of his work.

In pages five and six, Mr. Hillhouse defines his terms,—*monarchy, aristocracy,* and *democracy, federalists* and *republicans.* I shall make no objection to any thing here, but his idea of aristocracy. But before I come to that, I must take notice of what he says at the bottom of page six.

"Some of the important features of our constitution were borrowed from a model which did not very well suit our condition. I mean the constitution and government of England,—a mixed monarchy,—in which monarchy, aristocracy, and democracy are so combined, as to form a check on each other. One important and indispensable requisite of such a government is, that the first two branches should be hereditary."

Would it not have been more conformable to the fact to have said, that those important features of our constitution were borrowed from our colonial constitutions? Every colony on the continent, except Pennsylvania, had a governor, a council or senate, and a house of representatives.

The governors were not hereditary; the counsellors were not hereditary. Some of the governors were chosen by the people, and so were some of the councils. Some were appointed by the king, but commonly changed upon an average of less than seven years. There is little difference between our present governments and those under which our ancestors emigrated, lived, and, after having founded a respectable and flourishing nation, died; excepting that their governors were appointed from abroad, and our presidents and governors are chosen by ourselves. I am sorry to add, that we show the executives of our own choice and own blood infinitely less respect than our ancestors did those who were foreigners and appointed by a king. Governments, therefore, may be mixed and compounded of monarchical, aristocratical, and democratical ingredients, without one particle of hereditary power or privilege in them, except the common privileges of the people, such as their hereditary lands, goods, and liberties. Say, if you will, that in such an empire as the British, it is necessary that the executive and senate should be hereditary, because elections to these powers would totally corrupt the nation, produce a civil war, and raise a military despotism at the first trial. But, in an experiment of twenty years, we have not yet found such dangers among us.

Mr. Hillhouse further observes, that "to form an aristocracy, hereditary succession is indispensable." But Mr. Hillhouse is mistaken. Holland was an aristocracy; but the burgomasters, pensionaries, counsellors, and schepens, in whom the sovereignty resided, were not hereditary. There is a small number of nobles in the legislature of each state, but this body has but one vote. Every city has an equal vote with the whole body of nobles, and, in critical times, they have no influence. Bern was an aristocracy; but the members of the grand council were not hereditary, but elective. There were six noble families; but they had no prerogatives, but mere precedency; and these were not counsellors, unless elected into a legislature of two hundred and ninety-nine members,—counsellors and assessors.

In short, hereditary powers and peculiar privileges enter in no degree into the definition of aristocracy. There may be an aristocracy for life, or for years, or for half a year, or a month, or a day. Infinite art and chicanery have been employed in this country to deceive the people in their understanding of this term *aristocracy,* as well as of that of *well-born,* as if aristocracy could not exist without hereditary power and exclusive privileges; and as if a man could not be well-born, without being a hereditary nobleman and a peer of the realm.

Chancellor Livingston inherited a name, numerous and wealthy family connections, and a fine manor. These are all hereditary privileges, and have given him more influence in this country than all the titles and immense landed estates of the Duke of Norfolk, with all the hereditary rank and seat in the house of lords, have given him in England. Mr. John Randolph inherited his name, family connections, his fine plantations and thousand negroes, which have given him more power in this country than the Duke of Bedford has in England, and more than he would have, if he possessed all the brilliant wit, fine imagination, and flowing eloquence of that celebrated Virginian. Were not, then, Mr. Livingston and Mr. Randolph well-born? The state of Connecticut has always been governed by an aristocracy, more decisively than the empire of Great Britain is. Half a dozen, or, at most, a dozen families, have controlled that country when a colony, as well as since it has been a state. An aristocracy can govern the elections of the people without hereditary legal dignities, privileges, and powers, better than with them. In the Massachusetts, many of our prime quality were banished in the Revolution. Most of our present rulers are new men. But these have been promoted by an aristocracy.

Mr. Hillhouse says, "the United States do not possess the materials for forming an aristocracy." But we do possess one material which actually constitutes an aristocracy that governs the nation. That material is wealth. Talents, birth, virtues, services, sacrifices, are of little consideration with us. The greatest talents, the highest virtues, the most important services are thrown aside as useless, unless they are supported by riches or parties, and the object of both parties is chiefly wealth. When the rich observe a young man, and see he has talents to serve their party, they court and employ him; but if he deviates from their line, let him have a care. He will soon be discarded. In the Roman history we see a constant struggle between the rich and the poor, from Romulus to Cæsar. The great division was not so much between patricians and plebeians, as between debtor and creditor.

Speculation and usury kept the state in perpetual broils. The patricians usurped the lands, and the plebeians demanded agrarian laws. The patricians lent money at exorbitant interest, and the plebeians were sometimes unable and always unwilling to pay it. These were the causes of dividing the people into two parties, as distinct and jealous, and almost as hostile to each other, as two nations. Let Mr. Hillhouse say, whether we have not two parties in this country springing from the same sources? Whether a spirit for speculation in land has not always existed in this country, from the days of William Penn, and even long before? Whether this spirit has not become a rage, from Georgia to New Hampshire, within the last thirty years? Whether foundations have not been laid for immense fortunes in a few families, for their posterity? Whether the variations of a fluctuating medium and an unsteady public faith have not raised vast fortunes in personal property, in banks, in commerce, in roads, bridges, &c.? Whether there are not distinctions arising from corporations and societies of all kinds, even those of religion, science, and literature, and whether the professions of law, physic, and divinity are not distinctions? Whether all these are not materials for forming an aristocracy? Whether they do not in fact constitute an aristocracy that governs the country?

On the other side, the common people, by which appellation I designate the farmers, tradesmen, and laborers, many of the smaller merchants and shopkeepers, and even the unfortunate and necessitous who are obliged to fly into the wilderness for a subsistence, and all the debtors, cannot see these inequalities without grief and jealousy and resentment. A farmer or a tradesman, who cannot, by his utmost industry and frugality, in a life of seventy years, do more than support a moderate family, and lay up four or five thousand dollars, must think it very hard when he sees these vast fortunes made *per saltum,* these mushrooms growing up in a night; and they throw themselves naturally into the arms of a party whose professed object is to oppose the other party.

Two such parties, therefore, always will exist, as they always have existed, in all nations, especially in such as have property, and, most of all, in commercial countries. Each of these parties must be represented in the legislature, and the two must be checks on each other. But, without a mediator between them, they will oppose each other in all things, and go to war till one subjugates the other. The executive authority is the only mediator that can maintain peace between them.

Mr. Hillhouse thinks, "we have not the means of making an aristocratical branch to our government." I think we have the means, and that we have in fact, an aristocratical branch to our government, and that is, the senate; and a very useful, honorable, and necessary branch it is; but it would be more useful and more safe, if every particle of executive power was taken away from it. There are materials in great plenty, out of which to form this aristocratical branch. Mercuries ought not, indeed, to be sculptured out of every kind of wood; but there are gentlemen of fortune, talents, experience, and integrity, in every state, out of whom the legislatures may select the most eminent, and so they might, if the number of senators were doubled, as I wish it was, and hope it will be. These would compose an aristocratical branch, as respectable as any in the world. Our senate for twenty years has been very well chosen, and has abounded with able and excellent men. How Mr. Hillhouse can be at a loss for means of making an aristocratical branch, I know not. Our senators are not hereditary, nor have they any exclusive privileges, nor are these necessary, so long as we have not a hereditary executive; nor is a hereditary executive necessary, so long as we have not a hereditary senate. When one is so, the other must be, or it will be no check.

It is to no purpose to declaim against "demagogues." There are as many and as dangerous aristocratical demagogues as there are democratical. Neither party will get any thing by such invectives. Sylla and Pompey were as arrant, aristocratical demagogues as Marius and Cæsar, or even Catiline, were democratical ones. Sylla was more cruel than Marius, and Pompey had less humanity than Cæsar. Even Cicero and Brutus, the honestest men in Rome, were but aristocratical demagogues; and Milo was as much an agitator for the patricians as Clodius for the plebeians; and Hamilton was as much a demagogue as Burr. An independent executive, to mediate between the two parties, was wanting, and this defect was the ruin of the Roman republic, and will be ours, if Mr. Hillhouse's motion prevails. When Mr. Hillhouse declares that, "when a citizen claims to be an exclusive patriot, and is very officious in proclaiming his own merit, it is time for the people to be alarmed," I agree with him. But, I must add, when a senator declaims against executive influence under our constitution, it is time for the people to be upon their guard against an aristocratical spirit and preponderance.

Further, Mr. Hillhouse says, "there is always such a spirit of jealousy existing between aristocracy and democracy, and between monarchy and democracy, they cannot long exist together without a third balancing power." Mr. Hillhouse should have added, an equal jealousy between aristocracy and monarchy, and then I should have agreed with him. But this last jealousy it was not convenient for Mr. H. to acknowledge. He says, "as well might a man take up his abode in a tiger's den, as aristocracy with democracy, unless protected by the strong arm of monarchy." And I say, as well might a man take up his abode with Shadrach, Meshech, and Abednego, in the fiery furnace, as democracy with aristocracy, without the strong arm of monarchy to protect it. Witness the thirty tyrants of Athens and the decemvirs at Rome, and every other instance since the creation, in which democracy has been in the power of aristocracy. I say further, that as well might a man take up his abode with Daniel in the lion's den as monarchy with aristocracy, without the million arms of democracy to defend it. All these jealousies exist in some degree; but the greatest jealousy of all, is that of aristocracy against monarchy. Aristocracy is the natural enemy of monarchy; and monarchy and democracy are the natural allies against it, and they have always felt the necessity of uniting against it, sooner or later. Hence the ultimate destruction of all republics. The aristocracy would not suffer the executive to have power to defend the constitution, to defend itself, or to defend the people. The aristocracy has oppressed the people and the executive, till the people, out of all patience, have given the aristocracy, and themselves, too, a master. As to "surrounding the throne by a powerful aristocracy," they have always proved to be prætorian guards, and cut off the head of their general, when the discipline of the laws has, by any calamity, been weakened. It is true, when the people have been seditious and rebellious against them, their property, privileges, and distinctions, they have united with the executive to defend themselves. Like fire, they are good servants, but all-consuming masters.

Little need be said on shortening the period of the elections of the two houses. This, instead of diminishing the spirit of party, will only increase and inflame it. There will be no time for it to cool. The causes of the two parties I have already shown to be permanent and unchangeable. Both must be represented in the legislature, and there must be a mediator between them in the executive. This mediator must have power for the purpose. He must calm and restrain the ardor of both, and be more impartial between them than any president ever yet has been.[1] And the senators themselves must not constrain him to be partial, as they so often have done. Their power to do so, instead of being increased, as Mr. Hillhouse proposes, ought to be wholly taken from them. They ought to have nothing to do with executive power. If Mr. Hillhouse, however, should carry this point, and the people, instead of being glutted and satiated with elections, should wish to double the number, I hope he will introduce that admirable aristocratical invention of Connecticut,—a nomination list,—that every thing may not depend upon the election fever,—the *ictus febrilis*[2] of one election day.

The sixth article of Mr. Hillhouse's amendments reduces the president's office to that of a mere Doge of Venice, a mere head of wood, a mere tool of the aristocracy of the country. He is to be appointed by chance from the most aristocratic branch,—the senate. Although the senators in general have been respectable men, and some of them illustrious for virtues, talents, experience, and services, yet it must be confessed, that there have been very weak men in that body. These will have as good a chance as the best. A Blount, or a Burr, as good a chance as an Ellsworth, or a Strong, or a Richard Henry Lee. But this is of less importance than the proposal to submit all nominations and removals to the senate and house of representatives. There never was, and never can be, a project more perfectly aristocratical than this.

[1] It is difficult to suppose any president will be impartial between two parties, to one of which he must owe his own elevation, and see in the other all his enemies.

[2] ["feverish stroke" Ed.]

Mr. Hillhouse informs us, that "man is fond of power." True. But is not man, in the shape of a senator or a representative, as fond of power as a president? Mr. H. also admonishes us, that "ambition and favoritism," (and he should have added, avarice, jealousy, envy, hatred, love, and lust,) "are evils to be guarded against in a republican government." True, again; but are not ambition and favoritism, and all other vicious passions and sinister interests, as strong and active in a senator or a representative as in a president? Cannot, indeed, the members of the legislature conceal their private views and improper motives more easily than a president? Every senator and every representative has in his own district friends and favorites, to whose esteem, affection, activity, and influence, he has been indebted for his election. Is it not natural, that his mutual esteem, affection, and gratitude to these friends, should excite him to exert himself in obtaining favors, offices, and employments for them? Mr. Hillhouse probably knows, that great pains have sometimes been taken by senators, and representatives, too, to obtain nominations to offices, sometimes for themselves, and sometimes for their favorites; sometimes with success, and sometimes without.

Again, has Mr. Hillhouse never known combinations and consultations between general officers, heads of department, leading members of the senate and house of representatives, I will not say to overawe, but to influence the president in favor of some appointments, and against others? Has he never known such combinations resisted, and nominations made in opposition to them all? I say, such instances have been; and such nominations have proved the most fortunate, important, and successful of any that were ever made under the constitution. Has Mr. Hillhouse never known combinations and committees of senators sent to the president, to remonstrate privately against nominations? and when they could not prevail, have they not obtained majorities in senate to negative such nominations? Mr. Hillhouse has known favoritisms and anti-favoritisms enough in both houses, I should think, to be convinced that favoritism would be increased by his project, at least one hundred and fifty-fold.

Let us now consider how Mr. Hillhouse's project would operate. The president sends a nomination to the senate. Probably the person named has been selected by the president out of twenty candidates, who have been previously recommended to him by some senator and some representative. Nineteen senators are of course disappointed, because their favorites have been set aside. These nineteen will then combine together to negative the present nomination, in hopes that their favorites will have a better chance at the next time. There is to be no debate. How is this possible? Members are to give information, and information may be sent in from abroad, by petition or remonstrance. Vices, follies, crimes, incapacity, may be alleged and contradicted. How can these questions be determined but by witnesses, and how can false witnesses be counteracted but by confrontation? And, after all, the favorite member of the senate, by intrigue, artifice, or eloquence out of doors, will carry his candidate. After this, it must go down to the house of representatives; and what will happen there? The member who has previously recommended him to the president will rise and give him a character. Twenty other members, perhaps a hundred, who have recommended another man, or other men, will be disappointed. Sins and crimes and disqualifications may be alleged against the nomination. The subject will be postponed for days or weeks. In the mean time, caucuses will be held of evenings, combinations will be formed, and the favorite members of the house will carry their favorites.

But removals from office, too, must be laid before both houses. The mischiefs and inconveniences of this would be greater, if possible, than of the other. The officers of the army, navy, and revenue are necessarily numerous. Complaints and accusations often occur; these must be laid before congress. Witnesses must be summoned, examined, and cross-examined. Counsel would be humbly requested; it would be inhumanity to refuse it. Parties, cabals, and caucuses would be formed, and corruption introduced in a thousand shapes. Those who had favorites gaping for the place, would be tempted too slightly to vote for removal; and those who had no such favorites to gratify, would be too tender. The year would be too short for both houses to go through with all these appointments and removals. Again, how is military discipline to be maintained in your army and navy? How is the subordination of the military to the civil power to be supported? Give your general an estate for life in his office, defeasible only on the vote of the two houses, and he will soon be master of your president; he will soon have ten times as much influence in the nation.

To illustrate this subject still further, recollect the instances already recorded. In the case of Blount, a conspiracy was fully proved,—to dismember the empire, and carry off an immense portion of it to a foreign dominion; yet how much time was consumed, and how much debate excited, before that important subject could be decided! and the accused person, with all his guilt upon his head, was finally suffered to escape with impunity. In the case of Judge Pickering,—although his incapacity to discharge the functions of his office was indisputable, and although incapacity and non-user are a legal forfeiture of a judicial office; yet, it is well remembered how much time was necessarily employed in the investigation of the law and the evidence, and how much the house and the senate were divided in opinions on the final decision. In the case of Judge Chase,—the time, the expense, and the public anxiety of his impeachment and trial are well known, and how much exertion of the ablest and best men in the legislature, as well as of the counsel, were requisite to save a great and upright judge from unmerited ignominy, disgrace, and ruin. In the more recent case of Mr. John Smith, of Ohio,—what a vast expense of time and money and travel, what numbers of witnesses, what intricate questions of law, as well as collisions of testimony, occurred, and how critical was the final determination upon his innocence! In the case of General Wilkinson,—the complication of law and facts, the length of time through the whole of which his conduct is to be examined, the number of witnesses, the various parts of the Union from whence they must be collected, the conflicts of parties, the great legal and political questions which arise, and the vast importance to the public as well as the individual, are all to be taken into consideration. The time already passed in this inquiry is very great; and how much longer it will continue to irritate and inflame the public and divide the nation, no man can conjecture. The case of Colonel Burr is the most remarkable of all. If this was to be tried, first in the senate, and then in the house of representatives, when would it have an end? and who can pretend to divine what would be the decision?

Now every custom-house officer, every judge, and every marshal, every attorney-general and district-attorney, every secretary of state, treasury, war, or navy, and every officer of the army or navy, every postmaster, general or particular, would have as fair a right to a public and impartial trial, as a judge of the supreme court, upon an impeachment. In trials at law the jurors cannot be solicited; but the solicitations of members of congress, from culprits and their friends, would be infinite; and, where guilt or innocence is to be determined by a single vote in one hundred and fifty, as would often happen, if a corrupt member could be found, a bribe would not seldom be offered. Especially in cases where foreign interests and intrigues could intervene.

This is the system Mr. Hillhouse would introduce. It may without scruple be pronounced, though Mr. Hillhouse certainly did not see it in that light, the most corrupt project that ever was conceived by a man of sense and virtue. The endless confusion and distraction that would arise from it, would be as certain as its injustice, inhumanity, and corruption.

The appointment and removal of ambassadors and foreign ministers and consuls, as well as judges and general officers and admirals, would take the whole year, and convulse the continent. Take away from the president the nominations to those offices, and give it to every member of the senate and house, and how many nominations would there be to every vacancy? The disputes would be endless between the North and the South, the East and the West. One state would have more than its proportion, and others less. The question would be more concerning the abode of the candidate, and less concerning the talents, qualifications, and merits, than ever it has been yet; and it has already, and always been, more so than it ought to have been for the public good. The members of the house of representatives are so numerous, and often so young and inexperienced, that they must vote for men, nine times in ten, of whom they know nothing, not even by common fame; and as often will be incompetent to judge of the appropriate qualifications for the office.

The old congress was a small body of men, in comparison of the present two branches, and their deliberations were always in secret; yet, if there is anybody living who was present, and knew the contests on the appointments of general officers and foreign ministers, let him recollect the disputes about Dr. Franklin, Silas Deane, and Arthur and William Lee; Mr. Izard, Mr. Williams, Mr. Morris, Commodore Jones, Captain Landais, and Lieutenant Simpson; General Lincoln, General Arnold, General Wooster, Commodore Hopkins, and many others; nay, even concerning General Washington, General Ward, General Lee, General Schuyler, and General Gates, &c.; and he must remember that congress was torn to pieces by these disputes, and that days and months and years were wasted in such controversies, to the inexpressible injury of the service. To these causes are to be attributed the wants of the army, the distresses of General Washington, the loss of Canada, after we had conquered all but Quebec, the loss of the Penobscot enterprise, and almost all the disasters of the war. The complaints against general officers, the financier and his agents, and especially against foreign ministers, were as perpetual and endless as the debates in congress, not to say intrigues, to the delay and neglect of the most essential measures for the support and supply of the army and navy.

No! the real fault is, that the president has not influence enough, and is not independent enough. Parties will not allow him to act himself. For twelve years one party prevailed, and that party would not allow their presidents to be impartial. The other party has now prevailed eight years, and they have not permitted their president, in many instances, to act his own judgment. The power of removal was never abused in the first twelve years, except, perhaps, in two instances, and those removals were made at the earnest and repeated solicitations of all the members of the house, and one of the members of the senate, from New Hampshire, much against the inclination of the president. Representations of misconduct in office were made to the president, and probably credited by those members of congress; but there is now reason to suspect, that they were dictated by too much of a party spirit.

In short, presidents must break asunder their leading strings, and the people must support them in it. They must unite the two parties, instead of inflaming their divisions. They must look out for merit, wherever they can find it; and talent and integrity must be a recommendation to office, wherever they are seen, though differing in sentiments from the president, and in an opposite party to that whose little predominance brought him into power.

People of the United States!—you know not half the solicitude of your presidents for your happiness and welfare, nor a hundredth part of the obstructions and embarrassments they endure from intrigues of individuals of both parties. You must support them in their independence, and turn a deaf ear to all the false charges against them. But, if you suffer them to be overawed and shackled in the exercise of their constitutional powers, either by aristocratical or democratical manœuvres, you will soon repent of it in bitter anguish. Anarchy and civil war cannot be far off. Whereas, by a steady support of the independence of the president's office, your liberties and happiness will be safe, in defiance of all foreign influence, French or English, and of all popular commotion and aristocratical intrigue.

The proposal of diminishing the president's salary to fifteen thousand dollars, is so mean a thought that it scarcely deserves to be mentioned. If the present compensation is too high for seven or eight millions of industrious people, possessing a very fertile and productive agricultural country, and the second commerce in the universe, to support a president who represents their majesty, and must support their dignity in the eyes of all nations and people, let it be diminished by an amendment of the constitution, as it is, without making the president a mere painted head of a ship, made of wood, and incapable of being helmsman or pilot.

In several passages, Mr. Hillhouse is very anxious, and with great reason, about party spirit. He calls it a demon and a fiend, by a figure which is natural enough, for indeed it is

A monster of so frightful mien

As, to be hated, needs but to be seen.

But how shall this monster be chained? How shall this foul fiend be exorcised? Sermons, orations, speeches, pamphlets, odes, hymns, and heroic poems, have been long enough tried, to no purpose. Homer, Milton, and Spenser, whose immortal poems were all written expressly to show the dreadful effects of party spirit and discord among aristocratic *chiefs,* and the passions of envy, jealousy, ambition, and revenge, from whence they sprung, have been as little heeded as Mr. Hillhouse and his humble reviewer will be. It is a devil, I believe, that will not be cast out even by fasting and prayer. It was turned out of paradise with the first pair, immediately made a division in their family, and produced a duel or an assassination between their first two sons. From that family it has descended through all successive generations to the present most enlightened and virtuous age, and still produces assassinations and duels as frequently as ever. It inhabits all climes, and is found under all forms of government. It prevails in Turkey and Persia, Morocco and Tripoli, as well as in France and England; and in every tribe of savages in Africa and America, as well as among the most enlightened people on earth. There never existed three men together, two of whom did not love one another better than either of them loved the third, and better than the third loved either of the other two. If this fact be indubitable, as I believe it is, it will necessarily follow, that three men never lived together without a party spirit among them.

In despotisms and simple monarchies it is well known by what means the monster is quelled; but in limited monarchies and free republics the conquest is attended with more difficulty. If Mr. Hillhouse will run over in his thoughts all his researches into history and the science of government, he will oblige the public by pointing out one instance, in which party spirit has been confined within any bounds compatible with public good and national happiness, but by a counterpoise of interests, passions, and parties. Party spirit confounds the distinctions between truth and falsehood, right and wrong, and it corrupts the moral sense. There can be, therefore, no ultimate remedy in any moral principle or political maxim, against its final and fatal excesses. Nothing but power lodged somewhere in impartial hands can ever moderate, soften, or control it.

When Mr. Hillhouse says, that "state or local parties will have but a feeble influence on the general government," I cannot comprehend him. Will not a state party avail itself of the influence of the general government, to increase its own influence at home, and to diminish that of its rival? Will not a local party request Mr. Pickering, Mr. Hillhouse, and Mr. Ely, to write public and private letters to stimulate their own friends and disgrace their antagonists? And will not the opposite party avail themselves of even a letter from a man of no party, whose conscience is not yet seared with the red hot iron of faction, to support itself if it can? Will not both parties cut off at a blow at present, and after some time, perhaps by a proscription or a guillotine, or a banishment to Cayenne or to Botany Bay, every man who dares to vote or speak or write from his conscience and his honor? "Curse ye Meroz, curse ye bitterly the inhabitants thereof, because they came not up to the help of the Lord, to the help of the Lord against the mighty," is the language of all parties; and when it is infallibly known to be the cause of the Lord, it is just; but when it is the cause of mere faction, the language should be changed to "cursed be their anger, for it was fierce; and their wrath, for it was cruel." The time is well remembered when Mr. Madison, Mr. Giles, and several other members of congress, finding themselves unable to elevate their party in the great council of the nation, resigned their seats, and became members of their state legislatures, in order to revolutionize the primary assemblies, influence the elections to the general government, and overawe the national measures. Mr. Hillhouse, no doubt, remembered the great efforts, and, among many others, the representations and legislative pamphlets against the alien law and sedition law. He must clearly see, and readily acknowledge, that his amendments will be no remedy against such party spirit and party contrivances. Senators and representatives of the national government, and ministers of state, too, will continue to resign, in order to increase their fame, to be made governors at home, and promote the views of their party; and, on the other hand, governors, &c., of states will resign to be made senators, vice-presidents, secretaries of state, judges, and presidents. As long as the state governments retain their sovereignty, that is, their legislatures, or, in other words, as long as the national government is, in any sense, a federative republic, mutual sympathies or mutual antipathies will subsist between them and the national government; and there can never exist the smallest spirit of party in one, without producing a similar spirit of party in the other.

That there are "regular, organized parties, extending from the northern to the southern extremity, and from the Atlantic to the western limits of the United States," is very true. And it is equally certain, that there ever have been such, and that there ever will be such, unless you lay an embargo on all printing presses, private letters, private clubs, and on all travelling from one state to another. A standing army of a hundred thousand infantry and another hundred thousand cavalry, and twenty thousand gun-boats, will not effect it. Caucuses of patricians and caucuses of plebeians always prevailed in Rome and in all other free countries. Our revolution was effected by caucuses. The federal constitution was formed by caucuses, and the federal administrations, for twenty years, have been supported or subverted by caucuses. There is little more of the kind now, than there was twenty years ago. Alexander Hamilton was the greatest organist that ever played upon this instrument. He made all the use he could of these bodies of Cincinnati and others, to prevent Mr. Adams from being chosen vice-president. The reason of his antipathy, I know not; for he had never seen him. He caused it to be propagated in the Northern States, that Virginia would not vote for Washington, and in the Southern States, that New England would not vote for Washington, or, at least, that their votes would not be unanimous; at the same time, that there was a great probability there would be a unanimous vote for Adams; that, therefore, the electors must throw away so many of their votes that Adams could not have a majority, and, consequently, could not be president. If he believed one word of the apprehensions he propagated, it is very unaccountable; for there was a very great certainty in the public opinion, that Washington would have a unanimous vote.[3]

At the second election, he was pleased to permit Mr. Adams to have a considerable majority as vice-president.[4]

At the third election, he intrigued with all his might to get Major Thomas Pinckney chosen president. He dared not attempt to exclude Mr.

---

[3] "You know the constitution has not provided the means of distinguishing in certain cases, and it would be disagreeable even to have a man treading close upon the person we wish as president. May not the malignity of the opposition be, in some instances, exhibited even against him? Of all this we shall best judge, when we know who are our electors; and *we must, in our different circles, take our measures accordingly.*" Hamilton to Madison. *Works of A. Hamilton,* edited by J. C. Hamilton, vol. i. p. 489.

[4] In a letter to C. C. Pinckney of 10 October, 1792, upon this subject, Mr. Hamilton says,—"Mr. Adams, whatever objections may lie against some of his theoretic opinions, is a firm, honest, and independent politician." *Works of A. Hamilton,* vol. v. p. 533.

Adams, because he knew that such a project would defeat his plan; but his scheme was to get a vote or two more for Pinckney than for Adams, or, at least, an equal number for each, in hopes that his intrigues in the house might prevail to have Pinckney preferred to Adams.[5]

At the fourth election, his caucuses were more bold, open, and decided. Not only a caucus of members of Congress was assembled at Philadelphia, to exclude Mr. Jefferson, and turn him out, but to bring in General Pinckney with an equal vote with Mr. Adams. This was given out as a point determined, and the whole continent pledged to it upon their sacred honor. In the mean time, Hamilton prepared his famous pamphlet, intending to keep it secret till the election was passed, and then put it into the hands of the members of the house, to decide the election there in favor of Pinckney. Besides all this, a caucus of the Cincinnati was called at New York, in which he was chosen president of that society; but it was determined to sacrifice Adams; and even the two clergymen, President Dwight and Dr. Hitchcock, were found explicit in the pious opinion of sacrificing Adams. Not satisfied with all this, he made a journey through New England to Boston and to Providence, in prosecution of this patriotic design. In Boston, I doubt not, he found some as patriotic as himself. In Rhode Island he was less successful. He labored with Governor Fenner to no purpose. Fenner would not sacrifice Adams.[6]

The opposite party had their caucuses, too, and Burr made as many journeys, and reasoned to greater effect than Hamilton. The republican party had a caucus in Boston, in 1793, and wrote to Mr. Jefferson, upon his resignation of the office of secretary of state, that if he would place himself at their head, they would choose him at the next election; and they organized their party by their correspondences through the states.

---

[5] See the letter of Stephen Higginson to Mr. Hamilton of 9 December, 1796, in the *Works of A. Hamilton,* vol. vi. pp. 185–187. Mr. Hamilton's own letter of the 28 November, to which it is in answer, is not given, but the tenor of it may be clearly gathered from the reply.

[6] See the letter of Mr. Hamilton to C. Carroll, dated 1 July, 1800, which gives the result of his efforts on this journey. *Works of A. Hamilton,* vol. vi. pp. 445, 446.

This detail sufficiently shows, that caucuses have been from the beginning. There is, no doubt, some regard to public good, in the prosecution of these measures. They are considered as necessary. There is, also, ambition, avarice, envy, jealousy, and revenge. As these causes, good and bad, have hitherto produced such combinations, and as these causes will continue to the end of the world, we may presume the combinations will continue too. They have been, perhaps, too openly avowed, and published in too dictatorial a style; but they will continue with more or less reserve. You cannot prevent them any more than you can prevent gentlemen from conversing at their lodgings.

The question now is, whether Mr. Hillhouse's amendments of the constitution will remedy or qualify the evil. I think not. On the contrary, they will aggravate the distemper, and make it mortal. As the government vibrates at present between parties about once in twelve years, if you make the elections annual, there will be a chance of its vibrating every year, and you will have no stability in government at all. If that "prince of the power of the air," that "fiend, party spirit," can now "invade every sphere;" if that demon can "pass the bounds of every state," will he be

> Hurl'd headlong, flaming from the ethereal sky,
> To bottomless perdition; there to dwell
> In adamantine chains,

when elections become annual? Will Hamilton be prohibited from visiting Boston and Rhode Island, and Burr from travelling in New Jersey and Pennsylvania? The communication by letters in the post offices, and by private hands, will be as easy as ever, and mercenary emissaries from the British and French courts may write, speak, and hold caucuses, as well as federalists and republicans, when elections are annual, as well as at this time, when they are for two years, for six years, and for four years. The monster who now *fremit ore cruento,*[7] but cannot gorge himself more than once in six years, will then have his appetite increased by being annually feasted. He will then be monthly and daily employed all the year round, in "sowing dis-

---

[7][A lion "roars with bloody mouth." Virgil, *Aeneid* IX, 341. Ed.]

cord and divisions, destroying social harmony, overturning the most valuable institutions, and endangering the liberties of our country."

It is true, that parties have commenced in this country; but that they are progressing with more gigantic strides than usual, I know not. At every election of representatives, senators, and presidents, they have appeared; and the nation was as much divided in 1787, 1788, and 1789, as it is now. It was united in nothing but in the choice of Washington. When Mr. Benson moved that the blank in the bill, directing what officer should hold the office of president, in case of the death of the president and vice-president, should be filled with the chief justice, meaning Mr. Jay, Mr. Madison instantly moved that it should be filled with the secretary of state, meaning Mr. Jefferson. So fierce a spirit of party between the friends of the two rivals appeared all at once, that neither side had the courage to engage in the debate; the blank was never filled, and the bill was dropped. And both parties have ever had a successor in view from that time to this. Notwithstanding all the ardor of popular affection for Washington, and the great, I will not say unlimited confidence in him, congress and the nation were more divided, during the eight years of his administration, than they ever have been since. The senate, in constitutional questions and subjects of foreign relations, were, in most instances, divided half and half. The federal majority in the house of representatives was very small. During the administration of his immediate successor, the federalists had a majority of two thirds in the senate, and a larger majority in the house than at any period of the first eight years. This appearance of strength made them, or, at least, their great leader, Hamilton, presumptuous, and proved their ruin.

During the whole administration of Mr. Jefferson, the nation has been more united, and the majorities in both houses have been uniformly much greater, than under either of his predecessors. How, then, can it be said, that parties are progressing with gigantic strides? It should rather seem that the nation is advancing towards greater unanimity. The next election, however, of president, will show whether party spirit or unanimity is increasing. The belligerent powers have, indeed, driven us, by their intemperate measures, into circumstances of danger and distress, which have increased the anxiety of all men of all parties; but it does not yet appear, that the parties are more dangerous or alarming than they have been. A little time may decide. But, however this may be, the question still remains, whether Mr. Hillhouse's amendment will quell one monster, or propagate more and fiercer? Mr. H. is for "cutting off the head of the demon." I think he will find it the head of a hydra, and that a hundred heads will sprout from the blood of the one exscinded. "Without a head, no dangerous party can be formed; no such party can exist," says Mr. H. Indeed! Is it so? Perhaps it is. But parties will find heads enough; an oligarchy of heads, an aristocracy of heads, a democracy of heads; for the deepest democracies always have heads. One would think that the ancient experiment of cutting off the heads of the tallest poppies, had been tried often enough. Go into your field, and strike off the heads of all the tallest, and when you have gone over the whole, turn round and survey the whole ground. You will find as many taller than others as ever; and you must cut off every plant but one, before you can say there is no poppy taller than another. One would think that the recent example of France could not be so soon forgotten. Mirabeau, Marat, Brissot, Danton, Robespierre, were all heads cut off in succession, and all succeeding heads were saved only by having recourse to one head and one arm, in the Emperor Napoleon. The common sense and common feeling of mankind operated in France, after beholding the horrible massacres of aristocracy and democracy, as they have done in all other nations where these frantic parties have not been balanced. If you cut off one head, three other heads, at least, will spring up in its stead. The aristocratical party will have one head; the democratic party another; and the quids a third; but the last will always be a small, feeble, and insignificant party. They will be men of candor, impartiality, and equity, who will have no view but the public good; and this party has, unhappily, in all times, been very small and feeble, in comparison with the other two parties. That I may be more clearly understood,—the federal party will have their head, their leader, their aristocracy and democracy; the republican party will have their head and leader, their aristocracy and democracy; the quids will probably be too feeble and timid, finding themselves unsupported by either of the other great parties, and discountenanced by both, to fix upon any head. But if they should ever become a numerous party, as has seldom, if ever, happened, they must have a head, an aristocracy, and democracy, too; for no party ever can exist without these three divisions.

We will suppose, then, Mr. Hillhouse's amendment adopted. The divisions of rich and poor, debtor and creditor, will still continue, and produce a federal and a republican party in every state. All appointments to office, and removals from it, will be in the senate and house of the United States. These two parties, then, in every state, will live in a constant struggle, which shall send the representatives to the senate and house of the United States; and each will strive to send its head, that he may have the greatest influence in determining national measures, and especially in appointing officers and bestowing favors to favorites. The senate and house of the United States will thus be divided into federal and republican parties as much as they are now; and, as all offices will be in their gift, their whole time will be consumed in eternal intrigues and furious conflicts for the loaves and fishes. Each party will have its head in each house; and even the quids, once in an age, may have their leader too. Mr. Hillhouse will find two or three heads in the senate, as many in the house, and thus have six heads to cut off after he has cut off one; and then, he will instantly find six more shoot up in their stead, in the persons next esteemed in their respective parties. The caucuses in each state, and correspondences between different states, will not be lessened. There will still be central committees and committees of correspondence, from the north to the south, and from the east to the west. So long as education, talents, property, or even beauty, stature, or color, shall make inequalities among mankind, there will be an aristocratical and a democratical party in every country, especially in opulent commercial countries. Mr. Hillhouse's amendment, instead of diminishing, will increase them; instead of moderating, will inflame them; instead of reducing them to order, will throw them into greater confusion, exasperate their passions, and multiply their intrigues without end.

For example,—an eminent judge or a learned lawyer, in Connecticut or Massachusetts, or any other state, may wish to be a judge or a chief justice of the United States, or his friends and admirers may desire to

626 THE POLITICAL WRITINGS OF JOHN ADAMS

promote him. If he is of the federal party, the leading members of the senate and house of the United States will be solicited by letters, throughout the Union, to exert their influence to obtain his election. If he is of the republican party, the heads of that party in congress will be instigated, in the same manner, to obtain his election; and there will be always a federal judge and a republican judge, and perhaps such a pair, in every state, contending, intriguing, and lying, perhaps, in the newspapers; and how shall congress judge? If federalism has a majority in the senate and house, a federalist will be chosen. If republicanism predominates, a republican will undoubtedly be elected. But what if republicanism should prevail in the house, and federalism in the senate? a case that may often happen. What is to be done then? Why, no appointment can be made.

Again,—a gentleman of talents, education, fortune, family, aspires to visit foreign countries, in the capacity of an ambassador. He will certainly have one name or another. He must be either federalist, republican, or quid. If the first, he will have all the federalists in his state for him; if the second, all the republicans; if the third, he must stay at home at his farm, merchandise, or books. Central committees and organized correspondences will be at work in recommending him to their respective parties through the Union. When the choice comes before congress, perhaps, a candidate or two of each party in each state will be nominated, and after weeks of debate in public, and intrigues and caucuses in private, an ambassador may be chosen; unless either house should be equally divided, as they were between Jefferson and Burr, and then no ambassador can be sent, though peace or war may depend upon the mission. But, in every case, the ambassador will be of the party that outnumbers the other in congress.

But, of all party contentions, the choice of a commander-in-chief of the army will be the sharpest; because a commander-in-chief of the army, in time of war, will be a more popular and powerful man than a president is now. What will become of your come-by-chance president, if he presumes to dispute any point with your general, who has ten thousand officers and twenty thousand soldiers under him, drawn from all parts, attached to his person, and trumpeting his fame through the Union, and all espousing his opinions and reputation against the president?

When such an office is to be filled, all the militia officers, all the old soldiers, all the societies of the Cincinnati will be set in motion; and, for what I know, all the religious sects,—the Catholics, the Protestant Episcopalians, the Anabaptists, the Presbyterian assemblies and conventions, and even the Quaker meetings,—may interest themselves in the choice; and, after all, it must be a federalist or a republican who will carry the day. As one party will always rather lean to France, and the other to England, foreign emissaries will certainly not be idle; and if a hand can be found to receive a bribe, we certainly know that both courts are in the habit of employing money in other countries.

We might go through the list of all offices under the general government, and all elections would be made upon the same general principle.

Anarchy, confusion, and every evil work, besides a total depravation of moral and honest public principles, would be the undeniable effect.

Entries
from the
Diary
of
John Adams

...

MARCH 14, 1759.

Reputation ought to be the perpetual subject of my thoughts, and aim of my behavior. How shall I gain a reputation? how shall I spread an opinion of myself as a lawyer of distinguished genius, learning, and virtue? Shall I make frequent visits in the neighborhood, and converse familiarly with men, women, and children, in their own style, on the common tittletattle of the town and the ordinary concerns of a family, and so take every fair opportunity of showing my knowledge in the law? But this will require much thought and time, and a very particular knowledge of the province law and common matters, of which I know much less than I do of the Roman law. Shall I endeavor to renew my acquaintance with those young gentlemen in Boston who were at college with me, and to extend my acquaintance among merchants, shopkeepers, tradesmen, &c., and mingle with the crowd upon Change, and traipse the town-house floor with one and another, in order to get a character in town! But this, too, will be a lingering method and will require more art, and address, and patience, too, than I am master of. Shall I, by making remarks and proposing questions to the lawyers at the bar, endeavor to get a great character for understanding and learning with them? But this is slow and tedious, and will be ineffectual; for envy, jealousy, and self-interest, will not suffer them to give a young fellow a free, generous character, especially me. Neither of these projects will bear examination, will avail. Shall I look out for a cause to speak to, and exort all the soul and all the body I own, to cut a flash, strike amazement, to catch the vulgar; in short, shall I walk a lingering, heavy pace, or shall I take one bold determined leap into the midst of fame, cash, and business? That is the question;—a bold push, a resolute attempt, a determined enterprise, or a slow, silent, imperceptible creeping; shall I creep or fly?

I feel vexed, fretted, chafed; the thought of no business mortifies, stings me. But let me banish these fears; let me assume a fortitude, a greatness of mind.

…

December 22, 1770

The good of the governed is the end, and rewards and punishments are the means, of all government. The government of the supreme and all-perfect Mind, over all his intellectual creation, is by proportioning rewards to piety and virtue, and punishments to disobedience and vice. Virtue, by the constitution of nature, carries in general its own reward, and vies its own punishment, even in this world. But, as many exceptions to this rule take place upon earth, the joys of heaven are prepared, and the horrors of hell in a future state, to render the moral government of the universe perfect and complete. Human government is more or less perfect, as it approaches nearer or diverges further from an imitation of this perfect plan of divine and moral government.

In times of simplicity and innocence, ability and integrity will be the principal recommendations to the public service, and the sole title to those honors and emoluments which are in the power of the public to bestow. But when elegance, luxury, and effeminacy begin to be established, these rewards will begin to be distributed to vanity and folly; but when a government becomes totally corrupted, the system of God Almighty in the government of the world, and the rules of all good government upon earth, will be reversed, and virtue, integrity, and ability, will become the objects of the malice, hatred, and revenge of the men in power, and folly, vice, and villany will be cherished and supported. In such times you will see a Governor of a Province, for unwearied industry in his endeavors to ruin and destroy the people, whose welfare he was under every moral obligation to study and promote, knighted and ennobled.[1] You will see a "Philanthrop," for propagating as many lies and slanders against his country as ever fell from the pen of a sycophant, rewarded with the places of Solicitor-General,[2] Attorney-General, Advocate-General, and Judge of Admiralty, with six thousands a year.

You will see seventeen rescinders,[3] wretches without sense or sentiment, rewarded with commissions to be justices of peace, justices of the common pleas, and presently justices of the King's Bench. The consequence of this will be that the iron rod of power will be stretched out against the poor people in every....[4]

...

FEBRUARY 9, 1772

"If I would but go to hell, for an eternal moment or so, I might be knighted."

Shakespeare.

Shakespeare, that great master of every affection of the heart and every sentiment of the mind, as well as of all the powers of expression, is sometimes fond of a certain pointed oddity of language, a certain quaintness of style that is an imperfection in his character. The motto prefixed to this paper may be considered as an example to illustrate this observation.

Abstracted from the point and conceit in the style, there is sentiment enough in these few words to fill a volume. It is a striking representation of that struggle which I believe always happens between virtue and ambition, when a man first commences a courtier. By a courtier, I mean one who applies himself to the passions and prejudices, the follies and vices of great men, in order to obtain their smiles, esteem, and patronage, and

---

[1] Sir Francis Bernard.

[2] Jonathan Sewall, author of certain articles in the newspapers, signed Philanthropos, defending Governor Bernard.

[3] See page 243, note.

[4] This article remains imperfect.

consequently their favors and preferment. Human nature, depraved as it is, has interwoven in its very frame a love of truth, sincerity, and integrity, which must be overcome by art, education, and habit, before the man can become entirely ductile to the will of a dishonest master. When such a master requires of all who seek his favor an implicit resignation to his will and humor, and these require that he be soothed, flattered, and assisted in his vices and follies, perhaps the blackest crimes that men can commit, the first thought of this will produce in a mind not yet entirely debauched, a soliloquy something like my motto, as if he should say,—

"The Minister of State or the Governor would promote my interest, would advance me to places of honor and profit, would raise me to titles and dignities that will be perpetuated in my family; in a word, would make the fortune of me and my posterity forever, if I would but comply with his desires, and become his instrument to promote his measures. But still I dread the consequences. He requires of me such compliances, such horrid crimes, such a sacrifice of my honor, my conscience, my friends, my country, my God, as the Scriptures inform us must be punished with nothing less than hell-fire, eternal torment; and this is so unequal a price to pay for the honors and emoluments in the power of a Minister or Governor, that I cannot prevail upon myself to think of it. The duration of future punishment terrifies me. If I could but deceive myself so far as to think eternity a moment only, I could comply and be promoted."

Such as these are probably the sentiments of a mind as yet pure and undefiled in its morals; and many and severe are the pangs and agonies it must undergo, before it will be brought to yield entirely to temptation.

Notwithstanding this, we see every day that our imaginations are so strong, and our reason so weak, the charms of wealth and power are so enchanting, and the belief of future punishment so faint, that men find ways to persuade themselves to believe any absurdity, to submit to any prostitution, rather than forego their wishes and desires. Their reason becomes at last an eloquent advocate on the side of their passions, and they bring themselves to believe that black is white, that vice is virtue, that folly is wisdom, and eternity a moment.

Selections
from the
Autobiography
of
John Adams

...

On Wednesday, October 18th, the delegates from New Hampshire laid before the Congress a part of the instructions delivered to them by their Colony, in these words:—

"We would have you immediately use your utmost endeavors to obtain the advice and direction of the Congress, with respect to a method for our administering justice, and regulating our civil police. We press you not to delay this matter, as its being done speedily will probably prevent the greatest confusion among us."

This instruction might have been obtained by Mr. Langdon, or Mr. Whipple, but I always supposed it was General Sullivan who suggested the measure, because he left Congress with a stronger impression upon his mind of the importance of it, than I ever observed in either of the others. Be this, however, as it may have been, I embraced with joy the opportunity of haranguing on the subject at large, and of urging Congress to resolve on a general recommendation to all the States to call conventions and institute regular governments. I reasoned from various topics, many of which, perhaps, I could not now recollect. Some I remember; as,

1. The danger to the morals of the people from the present loose state of things, and general relaxation of laws and government through the Union.

2. The danger of insurrections in some of the most disaffected parts of the Colonies, in favor of the enemy, or as they called them, the mother country, an expression that I thought it high time to erase out of our language.

3. Communications and intercourse with the enemy, from various parts of the continent could not be wholly prevented, while any of the powers of government remained in the hands of the King's servants.

4. It could not well be considered as a crime to communicate intelligence, or to act as spies or guides to the enemy, without assuming all the powers of government.

5. The people of America would never consider our Union as complete, but our friends would always suspect divisions among us, and our enemies who were scattered in larger or smaller numbers, not only in every State and city, but in every village through the whole Union, would forever represent Congress as divided and ready to break to pieces, and in this way would intimidate and discourage multitudes of our people who wished us well.

6. The absurdity of carrying on war against a king, when so many persons were daily taking oaths and affirmations of allegiance to him.

7. We could not expect that our friends in Great Britain would believe us united and in earnest, or exert themselves very strenuously in our favor, while we acted such a wavering, hesitating part.

8. Foreign nations, particularly France and Spain, would not think us worthy of their attention while we appeared to be deceived by such fallacious hopes of redress of grievances, of pardon for our offences, and of reconciliation with our enemies.

9. We could not command the natural resources of our own country. We could not establish manufactories of arms, cannon, saltpetre, powder, ships, &c., without the powers of government; and all these and many other preparations ought to be going on in every State or Colony, if you will, in the country.

Although the opposition was still inveterate, many members of Congress began to hear me with more patience, and some began to ask me civil questions. "How can the people institute governments?" My answer was, "By conventions of representatives, freely, fairly, and proportionably chosen." "When the convention has fabricated a government, or a constitution rather, how do we know the people will submit to it?" "If there is any doubt of that, the convention may send out their project of a constitution, to the people in their several towns, counties, or districts, and the people may make the acceptance of it their own act." "But the people know nothing about constitutions." "I believe you are much mis-

taken in that supposition; if you are not, they will not oppose a plan prepared by their own chosen friends; but I believe that in every considerable portion of the people, there will be found some men, who will
understand the subject as well as their representatives, and these will assist
in enlightening the rest." "But what plan of a government would you
advise?" "A plan as nearly resembling the government under which we
were born, and have lived, as the circumstances of the country will admit.
Kings we never bad among us. Nobles we never had. Nothing hereditary
ever existed in the country; nor will the country require or admit of any
such thing. But governors and councils we have always had, as well as
representatives. A legislature in three branches ought to be preserved, and
independent judges." "Where and how will you get your governors and
councils?" "By elections." "How,—who shall elect?" "The representatives
of the people in a convention will be the best qualified to contrive a
mode."

...

Inaugural Speech
to
Both Houses
of
Congress

When it was first perceived, in early times, that no middle course for America remained between unlimited submission to a foreign legislature and a total independence of its claims, men of reflection were less apprehensive of danger from the formidable power of fleets and armies they must determine to resist, than from those contests and dissensions, which would certainly arise, concerning the forms of government to be instituted, over the whole, and over the parts of this extensive country. Relying, however, on the purity of their intentions, the justice of their cause, and the integrity and intelligence of the people, under an overruling Providence, which had so signally protected this country from the first, the representatives of this nation, then consisting of little more than half its present numbers, not only broke to pieces the chains which were forging, and the rod of iron that was lifted up, but frankly cut asunder the ties which had bound them, and launched into an ocean of uncertainty.

The zeal and ardor of the people during the revolutionary war, supplying the place of government, commanded a degree of order, sufficient at least for the temporary preservation of society. The confederation, which was early felt to be necessary, was prepared from the models of the Batavian and Helvetic confederacies, the only examples which remain, with any detail and precision, in history, and certainly the only ones which the people at large had ever considered. But, reflecting on the striking difference in so many particulars between this country and those where a courier may go from the seat of government to the frontier in a single day, it was then certainly foreseen by some, who assisted in Congress at the formation of it, that it could not be durable.

Negligence of its regulations, inattention to its recommendations, if not disobedience to its authority, not only in individuals but in States, soon appeared, with their melancholy consequences; universal languor, jealousies, rivalries of States; decline of navigation and commerce; discouragement of necessary manufactures; universal fall in the value of lands and their produce; contempt of public and private faith; loss of consideration and credit with foreign nations; and, at length, in discontents, animosities, combinations, partial conventions, and insurrection; threatening some great national calamity.

In this dangerous crisis the people of America were not abandoned by their usual good sense, presence of mind, resolution, or integrity. Measures were pursued to concert a plan to form a more perfect union, establish justice, ensure domestic tranquillity, provide for the common defence, promote the general welfare, and secure the blessings of liberty. The public disquisitions, discussions, and deliberations, issued in the present happy constitution of government.

Employed in the service of my country abroad, during the whole course of these transactions, I first saw the Constitution of the United States in a foreign country. Irritated by no literary altercation, animated by no public debate, heated by no party animosity, I read it with great satisfaction, as a result of good heads, prompted by good hearts; as an experiment better adapted to the genius, character, situation, and relations of this nation and country, than any which had ever been proposed or suggested. In its general principles and great outlines, it was conformable to such a system of government as I had ever most esteemed, and in some States, my own native State in particular, had contributed to establish. Claiming a right of suffrage in common with my fellow-citizens, in the adoption or rejection of a constitution, which was to rule me and my posterity as well as them and theirs, I did not hesitate to express my approbation of it on all occasions, in public and in private. It was not then nor has been since any objection to it, in my mind, that the Executive and

Senate were not more permanent. Nor have I entertained a thought of promoting any alteration in it, but such as the people themselves, in the course of their experience, should see and feel to be necessary or expedient, and by their representatives in Congress and the State legislatures, according to the Constitution itself, adopt and ordain.

Returning to the bosom of my country, after a painful separation from it for ten years, I had the honor to be elected to a station under the new order of things, and I have repeatedly laid myself under the most serious obligations to support the Constitution. The operation of it has equalled the most sanguine expectations of its friends; and, from an habitual attention to it, satisfaction in its administration, and delight in its effect upon the peace, order, prosperity, and happiness of the nation, I have acquired an habitual attachment to it, and veneration for it.

What other form of government, indeed, can so well deserve our esteem and love?

There may be little solidity in an ancient idea, that congregations of men into cities and nations, are the most pleasing objects in the sight of superior intelligences; but this is very certain, that, to a benevolent human mind, there can be no spectacle presented by any nation, more pleasing, more noble, majestic, or august, than an assembly like that which has so often been seen in this and the other chamber of Congress; of a government, in which the executive authority, as well as that of all the branches of the legislature, are exercised by citizens selected at regular periods by their neighbors, to make and execute laws for the general good. Can any thing essential, any thing more than mere ornament and decoration, be added to this by robes or diamonds? Can authority be more amiable or respectable, when it descends from accidents or institutions established in remote antiquity, than when it springs fresh from the hearts and judgments of an honest and enlightened people? For it is the people only that are represented; it is their power and majesty that is reflected, and only for their good, in every legitimate government, under whatever form it may appear. The existence of such a government as ours, for any length of time, is a full proof of a general dissemination of knowledge and virtue throughout the whole body of the people. And what object of consideration, more pleasing than this, can be presented to the human mind? If national pride is ever justifiable or excusable, it is when it springs, not from power or riches, grandeur or glory, but from conviction of national innocence, information, and benevolence.

In the midst of these pleasing ideas, we should be unfaithful to ourselves, if we should ever lose sight of the danger to our liberties, if any thing partial or extraneous should infect the purity of our free, fair, virtuous, and independent elections. If an election is to be determined by a majority of a single vote, and that can be procured by a party, through artifice or corruption, the government may be the choice of a party, for its own ends, not of the nation, for the national good. If that solitary suffrage can be obtained by foreign nations, by flattery or menaces; by fraud or violence; by terror, intrigue, or venality; the government may not be the choice of the American people, but of foreign nations. It may be foreign nations who govern us, and not we, the people, who govern ourselves. And candid men will acknowledge, that, in such cases, choice would have little advantage to boast of over lot or chance.

Such is the amiable and interesting system of government (and such are some of the abuses to which it may be exposed), which the people of America have exhibited, to the admiration and anxiety of the wise and virtuous of all nations, for eight years; under the administration of a citizen, who, by a long course of great actions regulated by prudence, justice, temperance, and fortitude, conducting a people, inspired with the same virtues, and animated with the same ardent patriotism and love of liberty, to independence and peace, to increasing wealth and unexampled prosperity, has merited the gratitude of his fellow-citizens, commanded the highest praises of foreign nations, and secured immortal glory with posterity.

In that retirement which is his voluntary choice, may he long live to enjoy the delicious recollection of his services, the gratitude of mankind, the happy fruits of them to himself and the world, which are daily increasing, and that splendid prospect of the future fortunes of his country, which is opening from year to year! His name may be still a rampart, and the knowledge that he lives, a bulwark against all open or secret enemies of his country's peace.

This example has been recommended to the imitation of his successors, by both Houses of Congress, and by the voice of the legislatures and the people throughout the nation.

On this subject it might become me better to be silent, or to speak with diffidence; but, as something may be expected, the occasion, I hope, will be admitted as an apology, if I venture to say, that, if a preference upon principle of a free republican government, formed upon long and serious reflection, after a diligent and impartial inquiry after truth; if an attachment to the Constitution of the United States, and a conscientious determination to support it, until it shall be altered by the judgments and the wishes of the people, expressed in the mode prescribed in it; if a respectful attention to the constitutions of the individual States, and a constant caution and delicacy towards the State governments; if an equal and impartial regard to the rights, interests, honor, and happiness of all the States in the Union, without preference or regard to a northern or southern, eastern or western position, their various political opinions on essential points, or their personal attachments; if a love of virtuous men of all parties and denominations; if a love of science and letters, and a wish to patronize every rational effort to encourage schools, colleges, universities, academies, and every institution for propagating knowledge, virtue, and religion among all classes of the people, not only for their benign influence on the happiness of life in all its stages and classes and of society in all its forms, but as the only means of preserving our constitution from its natural enemies, the spirit of sophistry, the spirit of party, the spirit of intrigue, profligacy, and corruption, and the pestilence of foreign influence, which is the angel of destruction to elective governments; if a love of equal laws, of justice and humanity, in the interior administration; if an inclination to improve agriculture, commerce, and manufactures for necessity, convenience, and defence; if a spirit of equity and humanity towards the aboriginal nations of America, and a disposition to meliorate their condition by inclining them to be more friendly to us, and our citizens to be more friendly to them; if an inflexible determination to maintain peace and inviolable faith with all nations, and that system of neutrality and impartiality among the belligerent powers of Europe, which has been adopted by the government, and so solemnly sanctioned by both Houses of Congress, and applauded by the legislatures of the States and the public opinion, until it shall be otherwise ordained by Congress; if a personal esteem for the French nation, formed in a residence of seven years chiefly among them, and a sincere desire to preserve the friendship which has been so much for the honor and interest of both nations; if, while the conscious honor and integrity of the people of America, and the internal sentiment of their own power and energies must be preserved, an earnest endeavor to investigate every just cause, and remove every colorable pretence of complaint; if an intention to pursue, by amicable negotiation, a reparation for the injuries that have been committed on the commerce of our fellow-citizens by whatever nation, and (if success cannot be obtained) to lay the facts before the legislature, that they may consider what further measures the honor and interest of the government and its constituents demand; if a resolution to do justice, as far as may depend upon me, at all times, and to all nations, and maintain peace, friendship, and benevolence with all the world; if an unshaken confidence in the honor, spirit, and resources of the American people, on which I have so often hazarded my all, and never been deceived; if elevated ideas of the high destinies of this country, and of my own duties towards it, founded on a knowledge of the moral principles and intellectual improvements of the people, deeply engraven on my mind in early life, and not obscured, but exalted by experience and age; and with humble reverence I feel it my duty to add, if a veneration for the religion of a people, who profess and call themselves Christians, and a fixed resolution to consider a decent respect for Christianity among the best recommendations for the public service;—can enable me in any degree to comply with your wishes, it shall be my strenuous endeavor that this sagacious injunction of the two Houses shall not be without effect.

With this great example before me, with the sense and spirit, the faith and honor, the duty and interest of the same American people, pledged to support the Constitution of the United States, I entertain no doubt of its continuance in all its energy; and my mind is prepared without hesitation, to lay myself under the most solemn obligations to support it to the utmost of my power.

And may that Being, who is supreme over all, the patron of order, the fountain of justice, and the protector, in all ages of the world, of virtuous liberty, continue his blessing upon this nation and its government, and give it all possible success and duration, consistent with the ends of his providence!

Various
Letters

The letters that follow cover a variety of subjects and concerns. Some are of interest because they provide Adams's recollections of and insights into the revolutionary movement, as well as his assessment of the political actors in different eras. Others supplement his thinking on basic questions concerning government. Most reveal aspects of Adams's thought and personality that are not so readily apparent from reading his major works in political theory.

VARIOUS LETTERS

To Richard Henry Lee

PHILADELPHIA, 15 NOVEMBER, 1775.

DEAR SIR,—The course of events naturally turns the thoughts of gentlemen to the subjects of legislation and jurisprudence; and it is a curious problem, what form of government is most readily and easily adopted by a colony upon a sudden emergency. Nature and experience have already pointed out the solution of this problem, in the choice of conventions and committees of safety. Nothing is wanting, in addition to these, to make a complete government, but the appointment of magistrates for the due administration of justice.

Taking nature and experience for my guide, I have made the following sketch, which may be varied in any one particular an infinite number of ways, so as to accommodate it to the different genius, temper, principles, and even prejudices, of different people.

A legislative, an executive, and a judicial power comprehend the whole of what is meant and understood by government. It is by balancing each of these powers against the other two, that the efforts in human nature towards tyranny can alone be checked and restrained, and any degree of freedom preserved in the constitution.

Let a full and free representation of the people be chosen for a house of commons.

Let the house choose, by ballot, twelve, sixteen, twenty-four, or twenty-eight persons, either members of the house, or from the people at large, as the electors please, for a council.

Let the house and council, by joint ballot, choose a governor, annually, triennially, or septennially, as you will.

Let the governor, council, and house, be each a distinct and independent branch of the legislature, and have a negative on all laws.

Let the governor, secretary, treasurer, commissary, attorney-general, and solicitor-general, be chosen annually, by joint ballot of both houses.

Let the governor, with seven counsellors, be a quorum.

Let all officers and magistrates, civil and military, be nominated and appointed by the governor, by and with the advice and consent of his council.

Let no officer be appointed but at a general council; and let notice be given to all the counsellors seven days, at least, before a general council.

Let the judges, at least of the supreme court, be incapacitated by law from holding any share in the legislative or executive power; let their commissions be during good behavior, and their salaries ascertained and established by law.

Let the governor have the command of the army, the militia, forts, &c.

Let the Colony have a seal, and affix it to all commissions.

In this way, a single month is sufficient, without the least convulsion, or even animosity, to accomplish a total revolution in the government of a colony. If it is thought more beneficial, a law may be made, by their new legislature, leaving to the people at large the privilege of choosing their governor and counsellors annually, as soon as affairs get into a more quiet course.

In adopting a plan in some respects similar to this, human nature would appear in its proper glory, asserting its own real dignity, pulling down tyrannies at a single exertion, and erecting such new fabrics as it thinks best calculated to promote its happiness.

As you were last evening polite enough to ask me for this model, if such a trifle will be of any service to you, or any gratification of curiosity, here you have it from, Sir,

Your friend and humble servant,
JOHN ADAMS.

The Earl of Clarendon to William Pym.

ON the 20th of August, 1765, there appeared in the London Evening Post an article, under the somewhat singularly-chosen signature of PYM, the purport of which seems to have been to avow to the people of the Colonies a settled design in Great Britain to overthrow whatever they had been in the habit of regarding as safeguards to their liberties. The writer of this article is not known; but his style, which is clear and forcible, indicates confidence and connection with the sources of power. The drift of his argument may be gathered from the statement of his position in these words: 'Let me inform my fellow-subjects in America, that a resolution of the British Parliament can at any time set aside all the charters that have ever been granted by our monarchs.' Starting in this manner, it is not surprising his consequences should be, that the rights of the colonists were wholly at the mercy of Great Britain.

This article was deemed of such importance as to gain immediate admittance into the columns of the Boston Evening Post, in which it appeared on the 25th of November following. It at once roused a host of writers on the Colonial side, among whom the most conspicuous were James Otis, as HAMPDEN, and John Adams, as CLARENDON [Earl of Clarendon, 1609-1674]. However singular the assumption of this last title may appear in the latter, his letters clearly show how much he had studied the character of the man to whom the name had belonged, and of the age in which he lived.

Charles Francis Adams

NO. III.[1]

SIR,—You are pleased to charge the colonists with ignorance of the British constitution; but let me tell you there is not ever a son of liberty among them who has not manifested a deeper knowledge of it, and a warmer attachment to it, than appears in any of your late writings; they know the true constitution and all the resources of liberty in it, as well as in the law of nature, which is one principal foundation of it, and in the temper and character of the people much better than you, if we judge by your late impudent pieces, or than your patron and master, if we judge by his late conduct.

The people in America have discovered the most accurate judgment about the real constitution, I say, by their whole behavior, excepting the excesses of a few, who took advantage of the general enthusiasm to perpetrate their ill designs; though there has been great inquiry and some apparent puzzle among them about a formal, logical, technical definition of it. Some have defined it to be the practice of parliament; others, the judgments and precedents of the king's courts; but either of these definitions would make it a constitution of wind and weather, because the parliaments have sometimes voted the king absolute, and the judges have sometimes adjudged him to be so. Some have called it custom, but this is as fluctuating and variable as the other. Some have called it the most perfect combination of human powers in society which finite wisdom has yet contrived and reduced to practice for the preservation of liberty and the production of happiness. This is rather a character of the constitution and a just observation concerning it, than a regular definition of it, and leaves

[1]From the Boston Gazette, 27 January, 1766.

us still to dispute what it is. Some have said that the whole body of the laws, others that king, lords, and commons, make the constitution. There has also been much inquiry and dispute about the essentials and fundamentals of the constitution, and many definitions and descriptions have been attempted; but there seems to be nothing satisfactory to a rational mind in any of these definitions; yet I cannot say that I am at a loss about any man's meaning when he speaks of the British constitution or the essentials and fundamentals of it.

What do we mean when we talk of the constitution of the human body? what by a strong and robust, or a weak and feeble constitution? Do we not mean certain contextures of the nerves, fibres, and muscles, or certain qualities of the blood and juices, as sizy or watery, phlegmatic or fiery, acid or alkaline? We can never judge of any constitution without considering the end of it; and no judgment can be formed of the human constitution without considering it as productive of life or health or strength. The physician shall tell one man that certain kinds of exercise or diet or medicine are not adapted to his constitution, that is, not compatible with his health, which he would readily agree are the most productive of health in another. The patient's habit abounds with acid and acrimonious juices. Will the doctor order vinegar, lemon juice, barberries, and cranberries, to work a cure? These would be unconstitutional remedies, calculated to increase the evil which arose from the want of a balance between the acid and alkaline ingredients in his composition. If the patient's nerves are overbraced, will the doctor advise to jesuits'-bark? There is a certain quantity of exercise, diet, and medicine, best adapted to every man's constitution, which will keep him in the best health and spirits, and contribute the most to the prolongation of his life. These determinate quantities are not perhaps known to him or any other person; but here lies the proper province of the physician, to study his constitution and give him the best advice what and how much he may eat and drink; when and how long he shall sleep; how far he may walk or ride in a day; what air and weather he may improve for this purpose; when he shall take physic, and of what sort it shall be, in order to preserve and perfect his health and prolong his life.

But there are certain other parts of the body which the physician can, in no case, have any authority to destroy or deprave; which may properly be called *stamina vitæ,*[2] or essentials and fundamentals of the constitution; parts, without which, life itself cannot be preserved a moment. Annihilate the heart, lungs, brain, animal spirits, blood, any one of these, and life will depart at once. These may be strictly called fundamentals of the human constitution. Though the limbs may be all amputated, the eyes put out, and many other mutilations practised to impair the strength, activity, and other attributes of the man, and yet the essentials of life may remain unimpaired many years.

Similar observations may be made, with equal propriety, concerning every kind of machinery. A clock has also a constitution, that is a certain combination of weights, wheels, and levers, calculated for a certain use and end, the mensuration of time. Now, the constitution of a clock does not imply such a perfect constructure of movement as shall never go too fast or too slow, as shall never gain nor lose a second of time in a year or century. This is the proper business of Quare, Tomlinson, and Graham, to execute the workmanship like artists, and come as near to perfection, that is, as near to a perfect mensuration of time, as the human eye and finger will allow. But yet there are certain parts of a clock, without which it will not go at all, and you can have from it no better account of the time of day than from the ore of gold, silver, brass, and iron, out of which it was wrought. These parts, therefore, are the essentials and fundamentals of a clock. Let us now inquire whether the same reasoning is not applicable in all its parts to government. For government is a frame, a scheme, a system, a combination of powers for a certain end, namely,—the good of the whole community. The public good, the *salus populi,* is the professed end of all government, the most despotic as well as the most free. I shall enter into no examination which kind of government, whether either of the forms of the schools, or any mixture of them, is best calculated for this end. This is the proper inquiry of the founders of empires. I shall take for granted, what I am sure no Briton will controvert, namely,—that

[2]["the fabric of life" Ed.]

liberty is essential to the public good, the *salus populi*. And here lies the difference between the British constitution and other forms of government, namely, that liberty is its end, its use, its designation, drift, and scope, as much as grinding corn is the use of a mill, the transportation of burdens the end of a ship, the mensuration of time the scope of a watch, or life and health the designation of the human body.

Were I to define the British constitution, therefore, I should say, it is a limited monarchy, or a mixture of the three forms of government commonly known in the schools, reserving as much of the monarchical splendor, the aristocratical independency, and the democratical freedom, as are necessary that each of these powers may have a control, both in legislation and execution, over the other two, for the preservation of the subject's liberty.

According to this definition, the first grand division of constitutional powers is into those of legislation and those of execution. In the power of legislation, the king, lords, commons, and people are to be considered as essential and fundamental parts of the constitution. I distinguish between the house of commons and the people who depute them; because there is in nature and fact a real difference, and these last have as important a department in the constitution as the former—I mean the power of election. The constitution is not grounded on "the enormous faith of millions made for one." It stands not on the supposition, that kings are the favorites of heaven, that their power is more divine than the power of the people, and unlimited but by their own will and discretion. It is not built on the doctrine, that a few nobles or rich commons have a right to inherit the earth, and all the blessings and pleasures of it; and that the multitude, the million, the populace, the vulgar, the mob, the herd, and the rabble, as the great always delight to call them, have no rights at all, and were made only for their use, to be robbed and butchered at their pleasure. No, it stands upon this principle, that the meanest and lowest of the people are by the unalterable, indefeasible laws of God and nature, as well entitled to the benefit of the air to breathe, light to see, food to eat, and clothes to wear, as the nobles or the king. All men are born equal; and the drift of the British constitution is to preserve as much of this equality as is compatible with the people's security against foreign invasions and domestic usurpation. It is upon these fundamental principles that popular power was placed, as essential, in the constitution of the legislature; and the constitution would be as complete without a kingly as without a popular power. This popular power, however, when the numbers grew large, became impracticable to be exercised by the universal and immediate suffrage of the people; and this impracticability has introduced from the feudal system an expedient which we call represen-tation. This expedient is only an equivalent for the suffrage of the whole people in the common management of public concerns. It is in reality nothing more than this, the people choose attorneys to vote for them in the great council of the nation, reserving always the fundamentals of the gov-ernment, reserving also a right to give their attorneys instructions how to vote, and a right at certain, stated intervals, of choosing a-new; discarding an old attorney, and choosing a wiser and better. And it is this reservation of fundamentals, of the right of giving instructions, and of new elections, which creates a popular check upon the whole government which alone secures the constitution from becoming an aristocracy, or a mixture of monarchy and aristocracy only.

The other grand division of power is that of execution. And here the king is, by the constitution, supreme executor of the laws, and is always present, in person or by his judges, in his courts, distributing justice among the people. But the executive branch of the constitution, as far as respects the administration of justice, has in it a mixture of popular power too. The judges answer to questions of fact as well as law; being few, they might be easily corrupted; being commonly rich and great, they might learn to despise the common people, and forget the feelings of humanity, and then the subject's liberty and security would be lost. But by the British constitution, *ad quæstionem facti respondent juratores,*—the jurors answer to the question of fact. In this manner, the subject is guarded in the execution of the laws. The people choose a grand jury, to make inquiry and pre-sentment of crimes. Twelve of these must agree in finding the bill. And the petit jury must try the same fact over again, and find the person guilty, before he can be punished. Innocence, therefore, is so well protected in this wise constitution, that no man can be punished till twenty-four of his neighbors have said upon oath that he is guilty. So it is also in the trial of causes between party and party. No man's property or liberty can be taken from him till twelve men in his neighborhood have said upon oath, that by laws of his own making it ought to be taken away, that is, that the facts are such as to fall within such laws.

Thus, it seems to appear, that two branches of popular power, voting for members of the house of commons, and trials by juries, the one in the legislative and the other in the executive part of the constitution, are as essential and fundamental to the great end of it, the preservation of the subject's liberty, to preserve the balance and mixture of the government, and to prevent its running into an oligarchy or aristocracy, as the lords and commons are to prevent its becoming an absolute monarchy. These two popular powers, therefore, are the heart and lungs, the mainspring and the centre wheel, and without them the body must die, the watch must run down, the government must become arbitrary, and this our law books have settled to be the death of the laws and constitution. In these two powers consist wholly the liberty and security of the people. They have no other fortification against wanton, cruel power; no other indemnification against being ridden like horses, fleeced like sheep, worked like cattle, and fed and clothed like swine and hounds; no other defence against fines, imprisonments, whipping-posts, gibbets, bastinadoes, and racks. This is that constitution which has prevailed in Britain from an immense antiquity. It prevailed, and the house of commons and trials by jury made a part of it, in Saxon times, as may be abundantly proved by many monuments still remaining in the Saxon language. That constitution which has been for so long a time the envy and admiration of surrounding nations; which has been no less than five and fifty times since the Norman conquest, attacked in parliament, and attempted to be altered, but without success; which has been so often defended by the people of England, at the expense of oceans of their blood; and which, coöperating with the invincible spirit of liberty inspired by it into the people, has never failed to work the ruin of the authors of all settled attempts to destroy it.

What a fine reflection and consolation is it for a man, that he can be subjected to no laws which he does not make himself, or constitute some of his friends to make for him,—his father, brother, neighbor, friend, a man of his own rank, nearly of his own education, fortune, habits, passions, prejudices, one whose life and fortune and liberty are to be affected, like those of his constituents, by the laws he shall consent to for himself and them! What a satisfaction is it to reflect, that he can lie under the imputation of no guilt, be subjected to no punishment, lose none of his property, or the necessaries, conveniencies, or ornaments of life, which indulgent Providence has showered around him, but by the judgment of his peers, his equals, his neighbors, men who know him and to whom he is known, who have no end to serve by punishing him, who wish to find him innocent, if charged with a crime, and are indifferent on which side the truth lies, if he disputes with his neighbor!

Your writings, Mr. Pym, have lately furnished abundant proofs that the infernal regions have taken from you all your shame, sense, conscience, and humanity; otherwise I would appeal to them, who has discovered the most ignorance of the British constitution,—you who are for exploding the whole system of popular power with regard to the Americans, or they who are determined to stand by it, in both its branches, with their lives and fortunes.

CLARENDON.

To Abigail Adams

PHILADELPHIA, 3 JULY, 1776.

...

Yesterday, the greatest question was decided, which ever was debated in America, and a greater, perhaps, never was nor will be decided among men. A resolution was passed without one dissenting colony, "that these United Colonies are, and of right ought to be, free and independent States, and as such they have, and of right ought to have, full power to make war, conclude peace, establish commerce, and to do all other acts and things which other States may rightfully do." You will see in a few days a Declaration setting forth the causes which have impelled us to this mighty revolution, and the reasons which will justify it in the sight of God and man. A plan of confederation will be taken up in a few days.

When I look back to the year 1761, and recollect the argument concerning writs of assistance in the superior court, which I have hitherto considered as the commencement of this controversy between Great Britain and America, and run through the whole period, from that time to this, and recollect the series of political events, the chain of causes and effects, I am surprised at the suddenness as well as greatness of this revolution. Britain has been filled with folly, and America with wisdom. At least, this is my judgment. Time must determine. It is the will of Heaven that the two countries should be sundered forever. It may be the will of Heaven that America shall suffer calamities still more wasting, and distresses yet more dreadful. If this is to be the case, it will have this good effect at least. It will inspire us with many virtues, which we have not, and correct many errors, follies and vices which threaten to disturb, dishonor, and destroy us. The furnace of affliction produces refinement, in States as well as individuals. And the new governments we are assuming in every part will require a purification from our vices, and an augmentation of our virtues, or they will be no blessings. The people will have unbounded power, and the people are extremely addicted to corruption and venality, as well as the great. But I must submit all my hopes and fears to an overruling Providence, in which, unfashionable as the faith may be, I firmly believe.

3 JULY.

Had a Declaration of Independency been made seven months ago, it would have been attended with many great and glorious effects. We might, before this hour, have formed alliances with foreign States. We should have mastered Quebec, and been in possession of Canada. You will perhaps wonder how such a declaration would have influenced our affairs in Canada, but if I could write with freedom, I could easily convince you that it would, and explain to you the manner how. Many gentlemen in high stations and of great influence have been duped by the ministerial bubble of commissioners to treat. And in real, sincere expectation of this event, which they so fondly wished, they have been slow and languid in promoting measures for the reduction of that province. Others there are in the colonies who really wished that our enterprise in Canada would be defeated, that the colonies might be brought into danger and distress between two fires, and be thus induced to submit. Others really wished to defeat the expedition to Canada, lest the conquest of it should elevate the minds of the people too much to hearken to those terms of reconciliation, which, they believed, would be offered us. These jarring views, wishes, and designs, occasioned an opposition to many salutary measures, which were proposed for the support of that expedition, and caused obstructions, embarrassments, and studied delays, which have finally lost us the province.

All these causes, however, in conjunction, would not have disappointed us, if it had not been for a misfortune which could not be foreseen, and, perhaps, could not have been prevented—I mean the prevalence of the smallpox among our troops. This fatal pestilence completed our destruction. It is a frown of providence upon us, which we ought to lay to heart.

But, on the other hand, the delay of this declaration to this time has many great advantages attending it. The hopes of reconciliation, which were fondly entertained by multitudes of honest and well-meaning, though weak and mistaken people, have been gradually and, at last, totally extinguished. Time has been given for the whole people maturely to consider the great question of independence, and to ripen their judgment, dissipate their fears, and allure their hopes, by discussing it in newspapers and pamphlets, by debating it in assemblies, conventions, committees of safety and inspection, in town and county meetings, as well as in private conversations, so that the whole people, in every colony of the thirteen, have now adopted it as their own act. This will cement the union, and avoid those heats, and perhaps convulsions, which might have been occasioned by such a declaration six months ago.

But the day is past. The second day of July, 1776, will be the most memorable epocha in the history of America. I am apt to believe that it will be celebrated by succeeding generations as the great anniversary festival. It ought to be commemorated, as the day of deliverance, by solemn acts of devotion to God Almighty. It ought to be solemnized with pomp and parade, with shows, games, sports, guns, bells, bonfires, and illuminations, from one end of this continent to the other, from this time forward, forevermore.

You will think me transported with enthusiasm, but I am not. I am well aware of the toil, and blood, and treasure, that it will cost us to maintain this declaration, and support and defend these States. Yet, through all the gloom, I can see the rays of ravishing light and glory. I can see that the end is more than worth all the means, and that posterity will triumph in that day's transaction, even although we should rue it, which I trust in God we shall not.

To Joseph Hawley

PHILADELPHIA, 25 AUGUST, 1776.

...

We have been apt to flatter ourselves with gay prospects of happiness to the people, prosperity to the State, and glory to our arms, from those free kinds of governments which are to be created in America. And it is very true that no people ever had a finer opportunity to settle things upon the best foundations. But yet I fear that human nature will be found to be the same in America as it has been in Europe, and that the true principles of liberty will not be sufficiently attended to.

Knowledge is among the most essential foundations of liberty. But is there not a jealousy or an envy taking place among the multitude, of men of learning, and a wish to exclude them from the public councils and from military command? I could mention many phenomena in various parts of these States which indicate such a growing disposition. To what cause shall I attribute the surprising conduct of the Massachusetts Bay? How has it happened that such an illiterate group of general and field-officers have been thrust into public view by that commonwealth, which, as it has an indisputable superiority of power to every other in America, as well as of experience and skill in war, ought to have set an example to her sisters, by sending into the field her best men, men of the most genius, learning, reflection, and address? Instead of this, every man you send into the army, as a General or a Colonel, exhibits a character which nobody ever heard of before, as an awkward, illiterate, illbred man. Who is General Fellows? And who is General Brickett? Who is Colonel Holman, Cary, Smith? This conduct is sinking the character of the province into the lowest contempt, and is injuring the service beyond description. Able officers are the soul of an army. Good officers will make good soldiers, if you give them human nature as a material to work upon. But ignorant, unambitious, unfeeling, unprincipled officers will make bad soldiers of the best men in the world.

I am ashamed and grieved to my inmost soul for the disgrace brought upon the Massachusetts in not having half its proportions of general officers. But there is not a single man among all our Colonels that I dare to recommend for a general officer, except Knox and Porter, and these are so low down in the list, that it is dangerous promoting them over the heads of so many. If this is the effect of popular elections, it is but a poor panegyric upon such elections. I fear we shall find that popular elections are not oftener determined upon pure principles of merit, virtue, and public spirit than the nominations of a Court, if we do not take care. I fear there is an infinity of corruption in our elections already crept in. All kinds of favor, intrigue, and partiality in elections are as real corruption, in my mind, as threats and bribes. A popular government is the worst curse to which human nature can be devoted, when it is thoroughly corrupted. Despotism is better. A sober, conscientious habit of electing for the public good alone must be introduced, and every appearance of interest, favor, and partiality reprobated, or you will very soon make wise and honest men wish for monarchy again; nay, you will make them introduce it into America.

There is another particular in which it is manifest that the principles of liberty have not sufficient weight in men's minds, or are not well understood.

Equality of representation in the legislature is a first principle of liberty, and the moment the least departure from such equality takes place, that moment an inroad is made upon liberty. Yet, this essential principle is disregarded in many places in several of these republics. Every county is to have an equal voice, although some counties are six times more numerous and twelve times more wealthy. The same iniquity will be established in Congress. Rhode Island will have an equal weight with the Massachusetts, the Delaware government with Pennsylvania, and Georgia with Virginia. Thus we are sowing the seeds of ignorance, corruption, and injustice in the fairest field of liberty that ever appeared upon earth, even in the first attempts to cultivate it. You and I have very little to hope or expect for ourselves. But it is a poor consolation, under the cares of a whole life spent in the vindication of the principles of liberty, to see them violated in the first formation of governments, erected by the people themselves on their own authority, without the poisonous interposition of kings or priests.

To Samuel Adams

PHILADELPHIA, 17 SEPTEMBER, 1776.

In a few lines of the 8th instant I promised you a more particular account of the conference. On Monday, the committee set off from Philadelphia, and reached Brunswick on Tuesday night. Wednesday morning, they proceeded to Amboy, and from thence to Staten Island, where they met the Lord Howe, by whom they were politely received and entertained. His lordship opened the conference by giving us an account of the motive which first induced him to attend to the dispute with America, which he said was the honor which had been done to his family by the Massachusetts Bay, which he prized very highly. From whence I concluded, in my own mind, that his lordship had not attended to the controversy earlier than the Port Bill and the Charter Bill, and consequently must have a very inadequate idea of the nature as well as of the rise and progress of the contest.

His lordship then observed, that he had requested this interview, that he might satisfy himself whether there was any probability that America would return to her allegiance; but he must observe to us, that he could not acknowledge us as members of Congress, or a committee of that body, but that he only desired this conversation with us as private gentlemen, in hopes that it might prepare the way for the people's returning to their allegiance and to an accommodation of the disputes between the two countries; that he had no power to treat with us as independent States, or in any other character than as British subjects and private gentlemen; but that upon our acknowledging ourselves to be British subjects, he had power to *consult* with us; that the act of parliament had given power to the king, upon certain conditions, of declaring the colonies to be at peace; and his commission gave him power to *confer, advise,* and *consult* with any number or description of persons concerning the complaints of the people in America; that the king and ministry had very good dispositions to redress the grievances of the people, and reform the errors of administration in America; that his commission gave him power to converse with any persons whatever in America concerning the former instructions to governors, and the acts of parliament complained of; that the king and ministry were very willing to have all these revised and reconsidered, and if any errors had crept in, if they could be pointed out, were very willing that they should be rectified.

Mr. Rutledge mentioned to his Lordship what General Sullivan had said, that his Lordship told him he would set the acts of parliament wholly aside, and that parliament had no right to tax America, or meddle with her internal polity. His Lordship answered Mr. Rutledge that General Sullivan had mis-understood him, and extended his words much beyond their import.

His Lordship gave us a long account of his negotiations in order to obtain powers sufficiently ample for his purpose. He said he told them (the ministry, I suppose he meant) that those persons whom you call rebels, are the most proper to confer with of any, because they are the persons who complain of grievances. The others, those who are not in arms, and are not, according to your ideas, in rebellion, have no complaints or grievances; they are satisfied, and therefore it would be to no purpose to converse with them. To that his Lordship said, he would not accept the command or commission until he had full power to confer with any persons whom he should think proper, who had the most abilities and influence. But, having obtained these powers, he intended to have gone directly to Philadelphia, not to have treated with Congress as such, or to have acknowledged that body, but to have consulted with gentlemen of that body in their private capacities upon the subjects in his commission.

His Lordship did not incline to give us any further account of his pow-ers, or to make any other propositions to us, in one capacity or another, than those which are contained in substance in the foregoing lines.

I have the pleasure to assure you, that there was no disagreement in opinion among the members of the committee upon any one point. They were perfectly united in sentiment and in language, as they are in the result of the whole, which is, that his Lordship's powers are fully expressed in the late act of parliament, and that his commission contains no other authority than that of granting pardons, with such exceptions as the commissioners shall think proper to make, and of declaring America, or any part of it, to be at peace, upon submission, and of inquiring into the state of America of any persons with whom they might think proper to confer, advise, converse, and consult, even although they should be officers of the army or members of Congress, and then representing the result of their inquiries to the ministry, who, after all, might or might not, at their pleasure, make any alterations in the former instructions to governors, or propose, in parliament, any alterations in the acts complained of.

The whole affair of the commission appears to me, as it ever did, to be a bubble, an ambuscade, a mere insidious manœuvre, calculated only to decoy and deceive, and it is so gross, that they must have a wretched opinion of our generalship to suppose that we can fall into it.

The committee assured his Lordship, that they had no authority to wait upon him, or to treat or converse with him, in any other character but that of a committee of Congress, and as members of independent States; that the vote which was their commission, clearly ascertained their character; that the declaration which had been made of independence, was the result of long and cool deliberation; that it was made by Congress, after long and great reluctance, in obedience to the positive instructions of their constituents, every Assembly upon the continent having instructed their delegates to this purpose, and since the declaration has been made and published, it has been solemnly ratified and confirmed by the Assemblies, so that neither this committee nor that Congress which sent it here, have authority to treat in any other character than as independent States. One of the committee, Dr. Franklin, assured his Lordship that, in his private opinion, America would not again come under the domination of Great Britain, and therefore that it was the duty of every good man, on both sides of the water, to promote peace, and an acknowledgment of American independency, and a treaty of friendship and alliance between the two countries. Another of the committee, Mr. J. A., assured his Lordship, that, in his private opinion, America would never treat in any other character than as independent States. The other member, Mr. Rutledge, concurred in the same opinion.

His Lordship said he had no powers nor instructions upon that subject; it was entirely new. Mr. Rutledge observed to his Lordship that most of the colonies had submitted for two years to live without governments, and to all the inconveniences of anarchy, in hopes of reconciliation; but now they had instituted governments. Mr. J. A. observed that all the colonies had gone completely through a revolution; that they had taken all authority from the officers of the Crown, and had appointed officers of their own, which his Lordship might easily conceive had cost great struggles, and that they could not easily go back; and that Americans had too much understanding not to know that, after such a declaration as they had made, the government of Great Britain never would have any confidence in them, or could govern them again but by force of arms.

To John Jebb

LONDON, 21 AUGUST, 1785.

As I had the misfortune, the other day, not to agree fully with you in opinion concerning the 36th article of the Constitution of Pennsylvania,[3] I beg leave to state to you my objections against it, and then to ask you if there is not some weight in them.

My first objection is, that it is not intelligible. It is impossible to discover what is meant by "offices of profit." Does it mean that there can be no necessity for, nor use in, annexing either salary, fees, or perquisites, to public offices? and that all who serve the public should have no pay from the public, but should subsist themselves and families out of their own

---

[3]This was the first Constitution of that State. The article is in these words: "As every freeman, to preserve his own independence, (if without a sufficient estate), ought to have some profession, calling, trade, or farm, whereby he may honestly subsist, there can be no necessity for, nor use in, establishing offices of profit, the usual effects of which are dependence and servility unbecoming freemen in the possessors and expectants, faction, contention, corruption, and disorder among the people. But if any man is called into public service to the prejudice of his private affairs, he has a right to expect a reasonable compensation for his services; and whenever an office, through increase of fees, or otherwise, becomes so profitable as to occasion many to apply for it, the profits ought to be, and shall be lessened by the legislature.

private fortunes, or their own labor in their private profession, calling, trade, or farm? This seems to be the sense of it, and in this sense it may make its court to the Quakers and Moravians, Dunkers, Mennonites, or other worthy people in Pennsylvania, that is to say, to their prejudices, and it will recommend itself to whatever there is of popular malignity and envy, and of vulgar avarice, in every country. But it is founded in error and mischief. For public offices in general require the whole time, and all the attention of those who hold them. They can have no time nor strength of body or mind for their private professions, trades, or farms. They must then starve with their families unless they have ample fortunes. But would you make it a law that no man should hold an office who had not a private income sufficient for the subsistence and prospects of himself and family? What would be the consequence of this? All offices would be monopolized by the rich; the poor and the middling ranks would be excluded, and an aristocratic despotism would immediately follow, which would take by fraud and intrigue at first, and by open avowed usurpation soon, whatever they pleased for their compensation.

My second objection to the article is, that it is inconsistent. After seeming to require that offices should have no emoluments, it stumbles at its own absurdity, and adds: "But if any man is called into public service to the prejudice of his private affairs, he has a right to a reasonable compensation." Is not this contrary to the doctrine that there can be no use in offices of profit? Are not the profits of offices intended as a reasonable compensation for time, labor, and neglect and prejudice of private affairs? If you look into the salaries and fees of offices in general, that is, into the legal profits, you will find them, not only in America, but in France, Holland, nay in England, far from being extravagant. You will find them but a moderate and reasonable compensation for their unavoidable expenses and the prejudice to their private affairs. It is not the legal profit, but the secret perquisites, the patronage, and the abuse, which is the evil. And this is what I complain of in the article, that it diverts the attention, jealousy, and hatred of the people from the perquisites, patronage, and abuse, which is the evil, to the legal, honest profit of the office, which is a blessing.

3. The dependence and servility in the possessors and expectants, and the faction, contention, corruption, and disorder among the people, do not proceed from the legal profits of offices, which are known to all, but from the perquisites, patronage, and abuses, which are known only to a few.

4. Nor is it by any means a good rule, that whenever an office, through increase of fees or otherwise, becomes so profitable as to occasion many to apply for it, the profit ought to be lessened by the legislature.

We are so fond of being seen and talked of, we have such a passion for the esteem and confidence of our fellow-men, that wherever applications for office are permitted by the laws and manners, there will be many to apply, whether the profits are large or small, or none at all. If the profits are none, all the rich will apply, that is to say, all who can live upon their own incomes; all others will be excluded, because, if they labor for the public, themselves and families must starve. By this means an aristocracy or oligarchy of the rich will be formed, which will soon put an end by their arts and craft to this self-denying system. If many apply, all applications should be forbidden, or, if they are permitted, a choice should be made of such out of the multitude as will be contented with legal profits, without making advantage of patronage and perquisites.

I do not mean by this, that the legal profits should be very great. They should afford a decent support, and should enable a man to educate and provide for his family as decent and moderate men do in private life; but it would be unjust as well as impolitic in the public, to call men of the best talents and characters from professions and occupations where they might provide for their families plentifully, and let them spend their lives in the service of the public, to the impoverishment and beggary of their posterity.

I have given you this trouble, because I think these to be fundamental errors in society. Mankind will never be happy nor their liberties secure, until the people shall lay it down as a fundamental rule to make the support and reward of public offices a matter of justice and not gratitude. Every public man should be honestly paid for his services; then justice is done to him. But he should be restrained from every perquisite not known to the laws, and he should make no claims upon the gratitude of the public, nor ever confer an office within his patronage, upon a son, a brother, a friend, upon pretence that he is not paid for his services by the profits of his office. Members of parliament should be paid, as well as soldiers and sailors.

I know very well that the word "disinterested" turns the heads of the people by exciting their enthusiasm. But although there are disinterested men, they are not enough in any age or any country to fill all the necessary offices, and therefore the people may depend upon it, that the hypocritical pretence of disinterestedness will be set up to deceive them, much oftener than the virtue will be practised for their good. It is worth while to read the lives of the Roman Catholic saints; your St. Ignatius Loyolas, your St. Bernards, and hundreds of others. It was always disinterestedness, which enabled them to excite enthusiasm among the people, and to command their purses to any amount, in order to establish their wild and pernicious institutions. The cry of gratitude has made more men mad, and established more despotism in the world, than all other causes put together. Every throne has been erected on it, and every mitre has sprung out of it; so has every coronet; and whenever any man serves the public without pay, a cry of gratitude is always set up, which pays him, or his cousins or sons, ten times as much as he ever deserved. Let government, then, be founded in justice; and let all claims upon popular gratitude be watched with a jealous eye. Hang well and pay well, conveys to my understanding infinitely more sense and more virtue than this whole article of the Pennsylvania Constitution.

I have long wanted to communicate with some of the enlightened friends of liberty here upon some parts of our constitutions, and I know of none who merits the character better. If you are willing, I will take some future opportunity to write you a few thoughts upon some other things. Meantime, let this remain between ourselves, if you please.

To Richard Price

NEW YORK, 19 APRIL, 1790.

MY DEAR FRIEND,—Accept of my best thanks for your favor of February 1st, and the excellent discourse[4] that came with it. I love the zeal and the spirit which dictated this discourse, and admire the general sentiments of it. From the year 1760 to this hour, the whole scope of my life has been to support such principles and propagate such sentiments. No sacrifices of myself or my family, no dangers, no labors, have been too much for me in this great cause. The revolution in France could not therefore be indifferent to me; but I have learned by awful experience to rejoice with trembling. I know that encyclopedists and economists, Diderot and D'Alembert, Voltaire and Rousseau, have contributed to this great event more than Sidney, Locke, or Hoadley, perhaps more than the American revolution; and I own to you, I know not what to make of a republic of thirty million atheists. The Constitution is but an experiment, and must and will be altered. I know it to be impossible that France should be long governed by it. If the sovereignty is to reside in one assembly, the king, princes of the blood, and principal quality, will govern it at their pleasure as long as they can agree; when they differ, they will go to war, and act over again all the tragedies of Valois, Bourbons, Lorraines, Guises, and Colignis, two hundred years ago. The Greeks sung the praises of Harmodius and Aristogiton for restoring equal laws. Too many Frenchmen, after the example of too many Americans, pant for equality of persons and property. The impracticability of this, God Almighty has decreed, and the advocates for liberty, who attempt it, will surely suffer for it.

I thank you, Sir, for your kind compliment. As it has been the great aim of my life to be useful, if I had any reason to think I was so, as you seem to suppose, it would make me happy. For "eminence" I care nothing; for though I pretend not to be exempt from ambition, or any other human passion, I have been convinced from my infancy and have been confirmed every year

[4] On the Love of Country. This sermon was the occasion of Burke's Reflections on the French Revolution.

and day of my life, that the mechanic and peasant are happier than any noble-man, or magistrate, or king, and that the higher a man rises, if he has any sense of duty, the more anxious he must be. Our new government is an attempt to divide a sovereignty; a fresh essay at imperium in imperio.[5] It cannot, therefore, be expected to be very stable or very firm. It will prevent us for a time from drawing our swords upon each other, and when it will do that no longer, we must call a new Convention to reform it. The difficulty of bringing millions to agree in any measures, to act by any rule, can never be conceived by him who has not tried it. It is incredible how small is the num-ber, in any nation, of those who comprehend any system of constitution or administration, and those few it is wholly impossible to unite. I am a sincere inquirer after truth, but I find very few who discover the same truths. The king of Prussia has found one which has also fallen in my way. "That it is the peculiar quality of the human understanding, that example should cor-rect no man. The blunders of the father are lost to his children, and every gen-eration must commit its own." I have never sacrificed my judgment to kings, ministers, nor people, and I never will. When either shall see as I do, I shall rejoice in their protection, aid, and honor; but I see no prospect that either will ever think as I do, and therefore I shall never be a favorite with either. I do not desire to be; but I sincerely wish and devoutly pray, that a hundred years of civil wars may not be the portion of all Europe for want of a little attention to the true elements of the science of government. With sentiments, moral sentiments, which are and must be eternal, I am your friend, &c.

To Samuel Adams

NEW YORK, 18 OCTOBER, 1790.

DEAR SIR,—I am thankful to our common friend, as well as to you, for your favor of the fourth, which I received last night. My fears are in uni-son with yours, that hay, wood, and stubble, will be the materials of the new political buildings in Europe, till men shall be more enlightened and friendly to each other.

[5]["a sovereign power in a sovereign power" Ed.]

You agree, that there are undoubtedly principles of political architecture. But, instead of particularizing any of them, you seem to place all your hopes in the universal, or at least more general, prevalence of knowledge and benevolence. I think with you, that knowledge and benevolence ought to be promoted as much as possible; but, despairing of ever seeing them sufficiently general for the security of society, I am for seeking institutions which may supply in some degree the defect. If there were no ignorance, error, or vice, there would be neither principles nor systems of civil or political government.

I am not often satisfied with the opinions of Hume; but in this he seems well founded, that all projects of government, founded in the supposition or expectation of extraordinary degrees of virtue, are evidently chimerical. Nor do I believe it possible, humanly speaking, that men should ever be greatly improved in knowledge or benevolence, without assistance from the principles and system of government.

I am very willing to agree with you in fancying, that in the greatest improvements of society, government will be in the republican form. It is a fixed principle with me, that all good government is and must be republican. But, at the same time, your candor will agree with me, that there is not in lexicography a more fraudulent word. Whenever I use the word *republic* with approbation, I mean a government in which the people have collectively, or by representation, an essential share in the sovereignty. The republican forms of Poland and Venice are much worse, and those of Holland and Bern very little better, than the monarchical form in France before the late revolution. By the republican form, I know you do not mean the plan of Milton, Nedham, or Turgot. For, after a fair trial of its miseries, the simple monarchical form will ever be, as it has ever been, preferred to it by mankind. Are we not, my friend, in danger of rendering the word *republican* unpopular in this country by an indiscreet, indeterminate, and equivocal use of it? The people of England have been obliged to wean themselves from the use of it, by making it unpopular and unfashionable, because they found it was artfully used by some, and simply understood by others, to mean the government of their interregnum parliament. They found they could not wean themselves from that destructive form of government so entirely, as that a mischievous party would not still remain in favor of it, by any other means than by making the words *republic* and *republican* unpopular. They have succeeded to such a degree, that, with a vast majority of that nation, a republican is as unamiable as a witch, a blasphemer, a rebel, or a tyrant. If, in this country, the word *republic* should be generally understood, as it is by some, to mean a form of government inconsistent with a mixture of three powers, forming a mutual balance, we may depend upon it that such mischievous effects will be produced by the use of it as will compel the people of America to renounce, detest, and execrate it as the English do. With these explanations, restrictions, and limitations, I agree with you in your love of republican governments, but in no other sense.

With you, I have also the honor most perfectly to harmonize in your sentiments of the humanity and wisdom of promoting education in knowledge, virtue, and benevolence. But I think that these will confirm mankind in the opinion of the necessity of preserving and strengthening the dikes against the ocean, its tides and storms. Human appetites, passions, prejudices, and self-love will never be conquered by benevolence and knowledge alone, introduced by human means. The millennium itself neither supposes nor implies it. All civil government is then to cease, and the Messiah is to reign. That happy and holy state is therefore wholly out of this question. You and I agree in the utility of universal education; but will nations agree in it as fully and extensively as we do, and be at the expense of it? We know, with as much certainty as attends any human knowledge, that they will not. We cannot, therefore, advise the people to depend for their safety, liberty, and security, upon hopes and blessings which we know will not fall to their lot. If we do our duty then to the people, we shall not deceive them, but advise them to depend upon what is in their power and will relieve them.

Philosophers, ancient and modern, do not appear to me to have studied nature, the whole of nature, and nothing but nature. Lycurgus's principle was war and family pride; Solon's was what the people would bear, &c. The best writings of antiquity upon government, those, I mean, of Aristotle, Zeno, and Cicero, are lost. We have human nature, society, and universal history to observe and study, and from these we may draw all the real principles which ought to be regarded. Disciples will follow their masters, and interested partisans their chieftains; let us like it or not, we cannot help it. But if the true principles can be discovered, and fairly, fully, and impartially laid before the people, the more light increases, the more the reason of them will be seen, and the more disciples they will have. Prejudice, passion, and private interest, which will always mingle in human inquiries, one would think might be enlisted on the side of truth, at least in the greatest number; for certainly the majority are interested in the truth, if they could see to the end of all its consequences. "Kings have been deposed by aspiring nobles." True, and never by any other. "These" (the nobles, I suppose,) "have waged everlasting war against the common rights of men." True, when they have been possessed of the *summa imperii* in one body, without a check. So have the plebeians; so have the people; so have kings; so has human nature, in every shape and combination, and so it ever will. But, on the other hand, the nobles have been essential parties in the preservation of liberty, whenever and wherever it has existed. In Europe, they alone have preserved it against kings and people, wherever it has been preserved; or, at least, with very little assistance from the people. One hideous despotism, as horrid as that of Turkey, would have been the lot of every nation of Europe, if the nobles had not made stands. By nobles, I mean not peculiarly an hereditary nobility, or any particular modification, but the natural and actual aristocracy among mankind. The existence of this you will not deny. You and I have seen four noble families rise up in Boston,—the CRAFTS, GORES, DAWES, and AUSTINS. These are as really a nobility in our town, as the Howards, Somersets, Berties, &c., in England. Blind, undistinguishing reproaches against the aristocratical part of mankind, a division which nature has made, and we cannot abolish, are neither pious nor benevolent. They are as pernicious as they are false. They serve only to foment prejudice, jealousy, envy, animosity, and malevolence. They serve no ends but those of sophistry, fraud, and the spirit of party. It would not be true, but it would not be more egregiously false, to say that the people have waged everlasting war against the rights of men.

"The love of liberty," you say, "is interwoven in the soul of man." So it is, according to La Fontaine, in that of a wolf; and I doubt whether it be much more rational, generous, or social, in one than in the other, until in man it is enlightened by experience, reflection, education, and civil and political institutions, which are at first produced, and constantly supported and improved by a few; that is, by the nobility. The wolf, in the fable, who preferred running in the forest, lean and hungry, to the sleek, plump, and round sides of the dog, because he found the latter was sometimes restrained, had more love of liberty than most men. The numbers of men in all ages have preferred ease, slumber, and good cheer to liberty, when they have been in competition. We must not then depend alone upon the love of liberty in the soul of man for its preservation. Some political institutions must be prepared, to assist this love against its enemies. Without these, the struggle will ever end only in a change of impostors. When the people, who have no property, feel the power in their own hands to determine all questions by a majority, they ever attack those who have property, till the injured men of property lose all patience, and recur to finesse, trick, and stratagem, to outwit those who have too much strength, because they have too many hands to be resisted any other way. Let us be impartial, then, and speak the whole truth. Till we do, we shall never discover all the true principles that are necessary. The multitude, therefore, as well as the nobles, must have a check. This is one principle.

"Were the people of England free, after they had obliged King John to concede to them their ancient rights?" The people never did this. There was no people who pretended to any thing. It was the nobles alone. The people pretended to nothing but to be villains, vassals, and retainers to the king or the nobles. The nobles, I agree, were not free, because all was determined by a majority of their votes, or by arms, not by law. Their feuds deposed their "Henrys, Edwards, and Richards," to gratify lordly ambition, patrician rivalry, and "family pride." But, if they had not been deposed, those kings would have become despots, because the people would not and could not join the nobles in any regular and constitutional opposition to them. They would have become despots, I repeat it, and that by means of the villains, vassals, and retainers aforesaid. It is not family pride, my friend, but family popularity, that does the great mischief, as well as the great good. Pride, in the heart of man, is an evil fruit and concomitant of every advantage; of riches, of knowledge, of genius, of talents, of beauty, of strength, of virtue, and even of piety. It is sometimes ridiculous, and often pernicious. But it is even sometimes, and in some degree, useful. But the pride of families would be always and only ridiculous, if it had not family popularity to work with. The attachment and devotion of the people to some families inspires them with pride. As long as gratitude or interest, ambition or avarice, love, hope, or fear, shall be human motives of action, so long will numbers attach themselves to particular families. When the people will, in spite of all that can be said or done, cry a man or a family up to the skies, exaggerate all his talents and virtues, not hear a word of his weakness or faults, follow implicitly his advice, detest every man he hates, adore every man he loves, and knock down all who will not swim down the stream with them, where is your remedy? When a man or family are thus popular, how can you prevent them from being proud? You and I know of instances in which popularity has been a wind, a tide, a whirlwind. The history of all ages and nations is full of such examples.

Popularity, that has great fortune to dazzle; splendid largesses, to excite warm gratitude; sublime, beautiful, and uncommon genius or talents, to produce deep admiration; or any thing to support high hopes and strong fears, will be proud; and its power will be employed to mortify enemies, gratify friends, procure votes, emoluments, and power. Such family popularity ever did, and ever will govern in every nation, in every climate, hot and cold, wet and dry, among civilized and savage people, Christians and Mahometans, Jews and Heathens. Declamation against family pride is a pretty, juvenile exercise, but unworthy of statesmen. They know the evil and danger is too serious to be sported with. The only way, God knows, is to put these families into a hole by themselves, and set two watches upon them; a superior to them all on one side, and the people on the other.

There are a few popular men in the Massachusetts, my friend, who have, I fear, less honor, sincerity, and virtue, than they ought to have. These, if they are not guarded against, may do another mischief. They may excite a party spirit and a mobbish spirit, instead of the spirit of liberty, and produce another Wat Tyler's rebellion. They can do no more. But I really think their party language ought not to be countenanced, nor their shibboleths pronounced. The miserable stuff that they utter about the *well-born* is as despicable as themselves. The ἐυγενεῖς of the Greeks, the *bien nées* of the French, the *welgebohren* of the Germans and Dutch, the *beloved families* of the Creeks, are but a few samples of national expressions of the same thing, for which every nation on earth has a similar expression. One would think that our scribblers were all the sons of redemptioners or transported convicts. They think with Tarquin, *"In novo populo, ubi omnis repentina atque ex virtute nobilitas fit, futurum locum forti ac strenuo viro."*[6]

Let us be impartial. There is not more of family pride on one side, than of vulgar malignity and popular envy on the other. Popularity in one family raises envy in others. But the popularity of the least deserving will triumph over envy and malignity; while that which is acquired by real merit, will very often be overborne and oppressed by it.

Let us do justice to the people and to the nobles; for nobles there are, as I have before proved, in Boston as well as in Madrid. But to do justice to both, you must establish an arbitrator between them. This is another principle.

It is time that you and I should have some sweet communion together. I do not believe, that we, who have preserved for more than thirty years an uninterrupted friendship, and have so long thought and acted harmoniously together in the worst of times, are now so far asunder in sentiment as some people pretend; in full confidence of which, I have used this freedom, being ever your warm friend.

JOHN ADAMS.

His Honor, SAMUEL ADAMS, Esq.,

Lieut.-Governor of Mass.

---

[6]["In a young people, where all nobility is produced quickly and by merit, there will be room for a strong and active man." Livy I, xxxiv, 6. Ed.]

To Skelton Jones

QUINCY, 11 MARCH, 1809.

I received yesterday your favor of the month of August, 1808, and if the following answers to your questions will be any gratification to your curiosity, or any aid to your work, they are at your service.

1. My father was John Adams, the son of Joseph Adams, the son of another Joseph Adams, the son of Henry Adams, who all lived independent New England farmers, and died and lie buried in this town of Quincy, formerly called Braintree, and more anciently still, Mount Wollaston. My mother was Susanna Boylston, daughter of Peter Boylston, of Brookline, the oldest son of Thomas Boylston, a physician who came from England in 1656, and purchased a farm in that town near Boston.

2. I was born in Quincy, on the 19th of October, 1735.

3. My early life and education were, first at the public latin school in the then town of Braintree; then at a private academy under Mr. Joseph Marsh, within three doors of my father's house; then at Harvard College, in Cambridge, where, after four years' studies, I received a degree as bachelor of arts in 1755, and, after three years more, that of master of arts.

4. Among these accidents,[7] the principal that I recollect were certain theological controversies, which were conducted, as I thought, with an uncharitable spirit of intolerance that convinced me I should be forever unfit for the profession of divinity, and determined me to the profession of the law. To this cause were added many compliments from my academical companions, who endeavored to make me believe that I had a voice and a tongue, as well as a face and front, for a public speaker, and that I was better fitted for the bar than the pulpit. For the faculty of medicine I never had any inclination, having an aversion to sick rooms and no fondness for rising at all hours of the night to visit patients.

5. Mr. Maccarty, a clergyman of Worcester, authorized by the selectmen, at the commencement at college, in 1755, happening to be pleased

---

[7] Mr. Jones's inquiry was, respecting "those accidents which decided your destiny, and gave a color and complexion to all your future prospects and conduct."

with the performance of my part in the public exhibition, engaged me to take the charge of the latin school in that town, where in a few months I entered as a clerk in the office of Colonel James Putnam, a counsellor at law in very large practice and of very respectable talents and information. Here, as I boarded in his family, I had opportunities of conversing with all the judges, lawyers, and many others of the principal characters of the province, and heard their speculations upon public affairs. This was highly delightful to me, because my father, who had a public soul, had drawn my attention to public affairs. From my earliest infancy I had listened with eagerness to his conversation with his friends during the whole expedition to Cape Breton, in 1745, and I had received very grievous impressions of the injustice and ingratitude of Great Britain towards New England in that whole transaction, as well as many others before and after it, during the years 1754, 1755, 1756, and 1757. The conduct of Generals Shirley, Braddock, Abercrombie, Webb, and above all Lord London, which were daily discussed in Mr. Putnam's family, gave me such an opinion and such a disgust of the British government, that I heartily wished the two countries were separated for ever. I was convinced we could defend ourselves against the French, and manage our affairs better without, than with, the English. In 1758 and 1759, Mr. Pitt coming into power, sent Wolfe, and Amherst, whom I saw with his army, as they passed through Worcester, and these conquered Cape Breton and Quebec. I then rejoiced that I was an Englishman, and gloried in the name of Briton. But, alas! how short was my triumph in British wisdom and justice! In February, 1761, I heard the argument in the council chamber in Boston upon writs of assistance, and there saw that Britain was determined to let nothing divert me from my fidelity to my country.

6.[8] An inflexible course of studies and labors, to promote, preserve, and secure that independence of my country, which I so early saw to be inevitable, against all parties, factions, and nations that have shown themselves unfriendly to it.

---

[8] Mr. Jones's sixth question was as to "the part you acted during the time in which you were in a public station."

7. The 4th of March, 1801. The causes of my retirement are to be found in the writings of Freneau, Markoe, Ned Church, Andrew Brown, Paine, Callender, Hamilton, Cobbet, and John Ward Fenno and many others, but more especially in the circular letters of members of Congress from the southern and middle States. Without a complete collection of all these libels, no faithful history of the last twenty years can ever be written, nor any adequate account given of the causes of my retirement from public life.

8. My life for the last eight years has been spent in the bosom of my family, surrounded by my children and grandchildren; on my farm, in my garden and library. But in all this there is nothing interesting to the public.

9. Five feet, seven or nine inches, I really know not which.

10. I have one head, four limbs, and five senses, like any other man, and nothing peculiar in any of them.

11. I have been married forty-four years.

12. To Miss Abigail Smith, on the 25th of October, 1764, in her father's house at Weymonth, the next town to this, and by her father, who was a clergyman.

13. Three sons and a daughter.

14. This would require twenty volumes.[9]

15. My temper in general has been tranquil, except when any instance of extraordinary madness, deceit, hypocrisy, ingratitude, treachery or perfidy, has suddenly struck me. Then I have always been irascible enough, and in three or four instances, very extraordinary ones, too much so. The storm, however, never lasted for half an hour, and anger never rested in the bosom.

16. Very little, I believe.[10]

17. Under my first latin master, who was a churl, I spent my time in shooting, skating, swimming, flying kites, and every other boyish exercise and diversion I could invent. Never mischievous. Under my second master, who was kind, I began to love my books and neglect my sports.

---

[9] 14. "Anecdotes relative to yourself or any of your acquaintances who have borne public offices."

[10] 16. "Has it (your temper) undergone any change?" *Mr. Jones's queries.*

18. From that time I have been too studious. At college, next to the ordinary routine of classical studies, mathematics and natural philosophy were my favorite pursuits. When I began to study law, I found ethics, the law of nations, the civil law, the common law, a field too vast to admit of many other inquiries. Classics, history, and philosophy have, however, never been wholly neglected to this day.

19. Such persons are all dead, or so old as to be incapable of writing any long details.

20. I have no miniature, and have been too much abused by painters ever to sit to any one again.

To Samuel Perley

QUINCY, 19 JUNE, 1809.

I received your favor of the 12th. You propose to me an abridgment of my works. Some fifty-five years ago, I learned from Lord Coke, that abridgments were chiefly useful to the makers of them. It would be of no use to me to abridge my poor productions; besides, I had rather write as many new ones than undertake to abridge the old ones.

You say that our ungovernable newspapers have published something concerning my works, to my disadvantage. I thank you for this epithet "ungovernable." It is so fine an expression, and at the same time so simple, natural, and exact, that I wonder it has never occurred before. A great minister of State, in the estimation of the world, the Comte de Vergennes, once said to me, "Mr. Adams, the newspapers govern the world!" Let me ask you, Mr. Perley, whether this apothegem has not been verified in our own country, sometimes to her profit, and sometimes to her loss. Let me ask you again, if the world is governed by ungovernable newspapers, whether it does not follow by necessary logical consequence that the world is ungovernable.

The newspapers have represented my writings as monarchical, as having a monarchical tendency; as aristocratical, and having an aristocratical tendency. In answer to these charges, I only ask that they may be read.

I have represented the British Constitution as the most perfect model that has as yet been discovered or invented by human genius and experience, for the government of the great nations of Europe. It is a masterpiece. It is the only system that has preserved or can preserve the shadow, the color, the semblance of liberty to the people in any of the great nations of Europe. Consider the republics, Venice, Holland, Switzerland; not a particle of liberty to the people was preserved in any of them more than there was in France, nor so much either. Our own Constitutions I have represented as the best for us in our peculiar situation, and while we preserve ourselves independent and unallied to any of the great powers of Europe. An alliance with either France or England would, in my humble opinion, put an end to our fine system of liberty.

Let me give you a few hints of the history of my "Defence of the Constitutions of Government of the United States."

In 1775 and 1776 there had been great disputes, in Congress and in the several States, concerning a proper constitution for the several States to adopt for their government. A Convention in Pennsylvania had adopted a government in one representative assembly, and Dr. Franklin was the President of that Convention. The Doctor, when he went to France in 1776, carried with him the printed copy of that Constitution, and it was immediately propagated through France that this was the plan of government of Mr. Franklin. In truth, it was not Franklin, but Timothy Matlack, James Cannon, Thomas Young, and Thomas Paine, who were the authors of it. Mr. Turgot, the Duke de la Rochefoucauld, Mr. Condorcet, and many others, became enamored with the Constitution of Mr. Franklin. And in my opinion, the two last owed their final and fatal catastrophe to this blind love.

In 1780, when I arrived in France, I carried a printed copy of the report of the Grand Committee of the Massachusetts Convention, which I had drawn up; and this became an object of speculation. Mr. Turgot, the Duke de la Rochefoucauld, and Mr. Condorcet and others, admired Mr. Franklin's Constitution and reprobated mine. Mr. Turgot, in a letter to Dr. Price, printed in London, censured the American Constitution as adopting three branches, in imitation of the Constitution of Great Britain. The intention was to celebrate Franklin's Constitution and condemn mine. I understood it, and undertook to defend my Constitution, and it cost me three volumes.

In justice to myself, however, I ought to say, that it was not the miserable vanity of justifying my own work, or eclipsing the glory of Mr. Franklin's, that induced me to write. I never thought of writing till the Assembly of Notables in France had commenced a revolution, with the Duke de la Rochefoucauld and Mr. Condorcet at their head, who I knew would establish a government in one assembly, and that I knew would involve France and all Europe in all the horrors we have seen; carnage and desolation, for fifty, perhaps for a hundred years.

At the same time, every western wind brought us news of town and county meetings in Massachusetts, adopting Mr. Turgot's ideas, condemning my Constitution, reprobating the office of governor and the assembly of the Senate as expensive, useless, and pernicious, and not only proposing to toss them off, but rising in rebellion against them.

In this situation I was determined to wash my hands of the blood that was about to be shed in France, Europe, and America, and show to the world that neither my sentiments nor actions should have any share in countenancing or encouraging any such pernicious, destructive, and fatal schemes. In this view I wrote my defence of the American Constitutions. I had only the Massachusetts Constitution in view, and such others as agreed with it in the distribution of the legislative power into three branches, in separating the executive from the legislative power, and the judiciary power from both. These three volumes had no relation to the Constitution of the United States. That was not in existence, and I scarcely knew that such a thing was in contemplation till I received it at the moment my third volume was about to issue from the press. I had hardly time to annex it at the end.

I was personally acquainted with Mr. Turgot, the Duke de la Rochefoucauld, and Mr. Condorcet. They were as amiable, as learned, and as honest men as any in France. But such was their inexperience in all that relates to free government, so superficial their reading in the science of government, and so obstinate their confidence in their own great characters for science and literature, that I should trust the most ignorant of our honest town meeting orators to make a Constitution sooner than any or all of them.

And now, Sir, give my compliments to Mr. Simon Greenleaf, your lawyer, and tell him that he is welcome to publish this letter, if he pleases, provided he publishes yours before it, not otherwise.

To Josiah Quincy

QUINCY, 9 FEBRUARY, 1811.

I have received with much pleasure your favor of the 29th of January. Before I proceed, let me premise a few preliminaries.

1. I disclaim all pretensions and thoughts of authority, superiority, or influence, arising from age, experience, or any thing else; and expect and desire and insist that you give no more attention or respect to any opinion of mine than if it were the opinion of the celebrated sexton of our church, Caleb Hayden.

2. That difference of opinion make no unnecessary alteration in private friendship. In the course of my life I have differed in sentiments, in religion and politics, from my master Putnam, and my master Gridley, and fifty others of my friends, without any diminution of esteem or regard. I have differed for many years in political sentiments from your grandfather, your uncle Samuel, your cousin Jonathan Sewall, Daniel Leonard, and some others, the most intimate friends I ever enjoyed, without the smallest personal altercation, and, I am bold to say, without a diminution of esteem on either side. I might enumerate a long catalogue of others in subsequent periods, but you will think you already have enough of my gossiping garrulity.

Now for your letter. When I applied the epithet "glorious" to the uncertainty of politics, I meant it ironically, as we say the "glorious uncertainty of the law." Those who smarted under the lash of the law probably applied it sarcastically to the lawyers, as the frogs said to the boys who pelted them, "It is sport to you, but death to us."

I ought not to object to your reverence for your fathers, as you call them, meaning, I presume, the government, and those concerned in the direction of public affairs; much less can I be displeased at your numbering me among them. But, to tell you a very great secret, as far as I am capable of comparing the merit of different periods, I have no reason to believe that we were better than you are. We had as many poor creatures and selfish beings, in proportion, among us as you have among you; nor were there then more enlightened men, or in greater number, in proportion, than there are now.

"Heaven from all creatures hides the book of fate." "Le grand rouleau en haut,"[11] cannot be read by our telegraphic telescopes.

Should I let loose my imagination into futurity, I could imagine that I foresee changes and revolutions, such as eye hath not seen nor ear heard; changes in forms of government, changes in religion, changes in ecclesiastical establishments, changes in armies and navies, changes in alliances and foreign relations, changes in commerce, &c., &c., &c., without end. I cannot see any better principle at present than to make as little innovation as possible; keep things going as well as we can in the present train.

The Union appears to me to be the rock of our salvation, and every reasonable measure for its preservation is expedient. Upon this principle, I own, I was pleased with the purchase of Louisiana, because, without it, we could never have secured and commanded the navigation of the Mississippi. The western country would infallibly have revolted from the Union. Those States would have united with England, or Spain, or France, or set up an independence, or done any thing else to obtain the free use of that river. I wish the Constitution had been more explicit, or that the States had been consulted; but it seems Congress have not entertained any doubts of their authority, and I cannot say that they are destitute of plausible arguments to support their opinion.

Your eloquence and oratory upon this question are worthy of your father, your grandfather, and your great grandfather. You spoke your own sentiments, I doubt not, with integrity, and the sense of a majority of your immediate constituents, and will not only increase your popularity

[11]["the great roll on high." The allusion is biblical, specifically to the Book of Revelation. Ed.]

with them, but extend your fame as a statesman and an orator; but will not influence at present the great body of the people in the nation.

Prophecies of division have been familiar in my ears for six-and-thirty years. They have been incessant, but have had no other effect than to increase the attachment of the people to the Union. However lightly we may think of the voice of the people sometimes, they not unfrequently see farther than you or I, in many great fundamental questions; and you may depend upon it, they see, in a partition of the Union, more danger to American liberty than poor Ames's distempered imagination conceived, and a total loss of independence for both fragments, or all the fragments, of the Union.

But I was about saying a word upon the Constitution. You appear to be fully convinced that the Convention had it not in contemplation to admit any State or States into our confederation, then situated without the limits of the thirteen States. In this point I am not so clear. The Constitution, it is true, must speak for itself, and be interpreted by its own phraseology; yet the history and state of things at the time may be consulted to elucidate the meaning of words, and determine the *bonâ fide* intention of the Convention. Suppose we should admit, for argument's sake, that no member of the Convention foresaw the purchase of Louisiana! It will not follow that many of them did not foresee the necessity of conquering, some time or other, the Floridas, and other territories on this side of the Mississippi. The state of things between this country and Spain in 1787, was such as to render the apprehensions of a war with that power by no means improbable. The boundaries were not settled, the navigation of the river was threatened, and Spain was known to be tampering, and England too.

You think it impossible the Convention could have a thought of war with Great Britain, and the conquest of Canada. In this point I differ from you very widely. The conduct of Great Britain, and the conduct of our States, too, was such as to keep up very serious apprehensions between the two powers. The treaty of peace was not fulfilled on either side. The English had carried away the negroes, in direct violation of a most express stipulation; they held possession by strong garrisons of a long chain of posts within our territory, commanding many nations of Indians, among whom they excited dispositions hostile to us; the limits were not settled against Nova Scotia, and many turbulences between the inhabitants arose. On the other side the old debts were not paid, and positive laws existed in many, if not most, of the States, against their recovery. I therefore think it highly probable that the Convention meant to authorize Congress in future to admit Canada and Nova Scotia into the Union, in case we should have a war, and be obliged to conquer them by kindness or force.

As I love a freedom and boldness in debate, I was sorry to see the personalities against you and your constituents; yet I think Mr. Poindexter and others have offered arguments in answer to you of great weight. The precedent in the admission of Vermont I have not seen answered.

To William Plumer

QUINCY, 28 MARCH, 1813.

You inquire, in your kind letter of the 19th, whether "every member of Congress did, on the 4th of July, 1776, in fact, cordially approve of the declaration of independence."

They who were then members, all signed it, and, as I could not see their hearts, it would be hard for me to say that they did not approve it; but, as far as I could penetrate the intricate, internal foldings of their souls, I then believed, and have not since altered my opinion, that there were several who signed with regret, and several others, with many doubts and much lukewarmness. The measure had been upon the carpet for months, and obstinately opposed from day to day. Majorities were constantly against it. For many days the majority depended on Mr. Hewes, of North Carolina. While a member, one day, was speaking, and reading documents from all the colonies, to prove that the public opinion, the general sense of all, was in favor of the measure, when he came to North Carolina, and produced letters and public proceedings which demonstrated that the majority of that colony were in favor of it, Mr. Hewes, who had hitherto constantly voted against it, started suddenly upright, and lifting up both his hands to Heaven, as if he had been in a trance, cried out, "It is done! and I will abide by it." I would give more for a perfect painting of the terror and horror upon the faces of the old majority, at that critical moment, than for the best piece of Raphael. The question, however, was eluded by an immediate motion for adjournment.

The struggle in Congress was long known abroad. Some members, who foresaw that the point would be carried, left the house and went home, to avoid voting in the affirmative or negative. Pennsylvania and New Jersey recalled all their delegates who had voted against independence, and sent new ones expressly to vote for it. The last debate but one was the most copious and the most animated; but the question was now evaded by a motion to postpone it to another day; some members, however, declaring that, if the question should be now demanded, they should vote for it, but they wished for a day or two more to consider of it. When that day arrived, some of the new members desired to hear the arguments for and against the measure. When these were summarily recapitulated, the question was put and carried. There were no yeas and nays in those times. A committee was appointed to draw a declaration; when reported, it underwent abundance of criticism and alteration; but, when finally accepted, all those members who had voted against independence, now declared they would sign and support it.

The appointment of General Washington to the command, in 1775, of an army in Cambridge, consisting altogether of New England men, over the head of officers of their own flesh and choice, a most hazardous step, was another instance of apparent unanimity, and real regret in nearly one half. But this history is too long for this letter.

The taxes must be laid, and the war supported.

I have nothing from my son since 28th October. I know not how we shall ever get him home, though that is the most anxious wish of my heart. Pray write him as often as you can. I regret the change of hands in New Hampshire at this juncture very much.

To Thomas McKean

QUINCY, 31 AUGUST, 1813.

Your friendly letter of the 20th, with the authentic account of the proceedings of the Congress held at New York, A. D. 1765, on the subject of the American stamp act, though they found me in the deepest affliction for the loss of my daughter, were very acceptable, and deserve my thanks.

There was a prior Congress held at Albany in 1754 or 1755, in which Franklin, Hutchinson, Wells, and Brattle, with others, assisted. Where is any account of that to be found?

Can you account for the apathy, the antipathy of this nation to their own history? Is there not a repugnance to the thought of looking back? While thousands of frivolous novels are read with eagerness and got by heart, the history of our own native country is not only neglected, but despised and abhorred.

You may conjecture my suspicious from what follows. Were I a man of fortune, I would offer a gold medal to the man who should produce the most instances of the friendship of Great Britain toward this country from 1600 to 1813.

I have had knowledge enough of the Marquis de Casa Yrujo and his lady, your lovely daughter, and notwithstanding all political flickerings, to esteem them both, and wish them all the felicity that you can desire for them. They live, as you and I have lived, in times of confusion and uncertainty more distressing than the ordinary lot of humanity.

In times like those in which you and I have lived, we are not masters, we can scarcely be said to be fathers, of our own families. I have three children born in Quincy, one in Boston. I have one grandson born in London, another on Long Island, another in Berlin, several in Quincy, several in New York, several in Boston, one born and died in St. Petersburg. Is this a desirable history of a family? I trow not.

I will not tell you what I would prefer. You would think me a dunce or an hypocrite.

Your history of Otis and Ruggles is familiar to me. I knew them both. Ruggles was my cousin; Otis, my friend and one of my patrons. I could not have drawn the character of either with more precision than you have done. Both high-minded men, exalted souls, acting in scenes they could not comprehend, and acting parts, whose effects and consequences will last longer than their names will be remembered.

You say that at the time of the Congress, in 1765, "The great mass of the people were zealous in the cause of America." "The great mass of the people" is an expression that deserves analysis. New York and Pennsylvania were so nearly divided, if their propensity was not against us, that if New England on one side and Virginia on the other had not kept them in awe, they would have joined the British. Marshall, in his life of Washington, tells us, that the southern States were nearly equally divided. Look into the Journals of Congress, and you will see how seditious, how near rebellion were several counties of New York, and how much trouble we had to compose them. The last contest, in the town of Boston, in 1775, between whig and tory, was decided by five against two. Upon the whole, if we allow two thirds of the people to have been with us in the revolution, is not the allowance ample? Are not two thirds of the nation now with the administration? Divided we ever have been, and ever must be. Two thirds always had and will have more difficulty to struggle with the one third than with all our foreign enemies.

A letter from you will always console your old friend.

To James Lloyd

QUINCY, JANUARY, 1815.

Although I have no recollection that I ever met you more than once in society, and that, I presume, was the instance you have recorded, yet I feel as if I was intimately acquainted with you. The want of familiarity between us, I regret, not only because I have known, esteemed, and I may say, loved your family, from an early age, but, especially, because whatever I have heard or read of your character in life, has given me a respect for your talents and a high esteem for your character.

Having read Mr. Randolph's letter to you, and your answer to him, I shall not question the propriety of your taking so much notice of him.[12] It would give me pleasure to dilate on the various parts of your letter, and mark the many points in which I fully agree with you, as well as the few which are not so clear to me; but I shall confine myself at present to those things which personally relate to myself and my administration. You say, Sir, that "I built upon the sand." And so, indeed, I did. I had no material for a foundation, but a rope of it. The union of the States was at that time nothing better. In this respect I was in a worse situation than Mr. Madison is at this hour.

You are pleased to say, Sir, that "upon the earlier part of my administration you could dilate *con amore*." I believe you, Sir. The addresses, of which Mr. Randolph "defies you to think without a bitter smile," will remain immortal monuments, in proof that one third at least of the people of the United States thought and felt as you did. But, Sir, did you then consider, or have you since considered, that this Mr. Randolph, with two thirds of the people of the United States, then "dilated on that earlier part of my administration," *con odio?*

There is not, Sir, in your masterly letter a more correct or important observation than that of "the unhappy ignorance which exists among the members of this great family, but resident in different sections of it, with regard to the objects and qualities of each other. This ignorance, the offspring of narrow prejudice and illiberality, is now presenting brimful the chalice of envy and hatred, where it should offer nothing but the cup of conciliation and confidence. It sprang from the little intercourse and less knowledge which the people of the then British Provinces possessed of each other antecedently to the American revolution, and instead of being dissipated by an event so honorable to them all, has been cherished and perpetuated for political party purposes, and for the promotion of the sinister views and ambitious projects of a few restless and unprincipled individuals, until the present period."

[12] Mr. John Randolph had addressed a letter, dated Philadelphia, 15th December, 1814, through the newspapers, to Mr. James Lloyd, of Massachusetts, deprecating a resort to extreme measures by the federalists of New England. He was answered by Mr. Lloyd in a letter published in the Boston Daily Advertiser, of January 1815.

Of this ignorance, when I went to Congress in 1774, I can assure you, Sir, I had a most painful consciousness in my own bosom. There I had the disappointment to find, that almost every gentleman in that assembly was, in this kind of information, nearly as ignorant as myself; and what was a more cruel mortification than all the rest, the greatest part even of the most intelligent, full of prejudices and jealousies, which I had never before even suspected. Between 1774 and 1797, an interval of twenty-three years, this ignorance was in some measure removed from some minds. But some had retired in disgust, some had gone into the army, some had been turned out for timidity, some had deserted to the enemy, and all the old, steadfast patriots, weary of the service, always irksome in Congress, had retired to their families and States, to be made governors, judges, marshals, collectors, &c., &c. So that in 1797, there was not an individual in the House of Representatives, in the Senate, or in either of the executive departments of government, who had been in the national controversy from the beginning. Mr. Jefferson himself, the Vice-President, the oldest in service of them all, was but a young and a new man in comparison with the earliest conductors of the cause of the country, the real founders and legitimate fathers of the American republic. The most of them had been but a very few years in public business, and a large proportion of these were of a party which had been opposed to the revolution, at least in the beginning of it. If I were called to calculate the divisions among the people of America, as Mr. Burke did those of the people of England, I should say that full one third were averse to the revolution. These, retaining that overweening fondness, in which they had been educated, for the English, could not cordially like the French; indeed, they most heartily detested them. An opposite third conceived a hatred of the English, and gave themselves up to an enthusiastic gratitude to France. The middle third, composed principally of the yeomanry, the soundest part of the nation, and always averse to war, were rather lukewarm both to England and France; and sometimes stragglers from them, and sometimes the whole body, united with the first or the last third, according to circumstances.

The depredations of France upon our commerce, and her insolence to our ambassadors, and even to the government, united, though for a short time, with infinite reluctance, the second third with the first, and produced that burst of applause to the administration, in which you concurred, though it gave much offence to Mr. Randolph. Nor to him alone, I assure you. It appeared to me then, and has appeared ever since, that a great majority of the people of the United States, and even in New England, in their hearts disapproved of those addresses as much as they did of those pompous escorts, public dinners, and childish festivals, which tormented me much more than they did them. They thought, that such things led to monarchy and aristocracy as well as to a long and interminable war, a war with France, our sister republic; and a war with any body, must bring expenses and taxes. Those hosannas, moreover, excited envy and bitter jealousy in many breasts in the first class, whose names I will not mention at present.

National defence is one of the cardinal duties of a statesman. On this head I recollect nothing with which to reproach myself. The subject has always been near my heart. The delightful imaginations of universal and perpetual peace have often amused, but have never been credited by me. From the year 1755 to this day, almost three score years, I have thought a naval force the most natural, safe, efficacious, and economical bulwark for this country. In 1775, I labored day and night to lay the foundation of a navy, and in the four last years of the last century I hesitated at no expense to purchase navy yards, to collect timber to build ships, and spared no pains to select officers. And what was the effect? No part of my administration was so unpopular, not only in the western, the southern, and middle States, but in all New England, and, strange to tell, even in Marblehead, Salem, Newburyport, and Boston. The little army, the fortifications, the manufactures of arms and ammunition, were all unpopular. They were the reign of terror. They were to introduce monarchy and aristocracy. John Adams and John Jay were sold to Great Britain.

In this critical state of things, when Virginia and Kentucky, too nearly in unison with the other southern and western States, were menacing a separation; when insurrection was flaming in Pennsylvania; when Baltimore, at the head of one half of Maryland, was glowing with opposition; when the two great interests in New York, headed by the Clintons and

Livingstons, were united with Colonel Burr, General Gates, and their little band, in open opposition to the administration and the contest with
France; when the administration was threatened, even in the town of
Boston, I will not say at present by whom, nor with what; there was not
one man in either house of Congress of the then majority, nor in any
executive department of government, who was not chargeable with the
grossest ignorance of the nation, which you impute to the north and south
before and since the revolution, nor one who had any experience of foreign affairs. Never was any majority more grossly deceived in their opinion of their own importance and influence. No! not Napoleon, when he
undertook the conquest of Russia. Had the administration persevered in
the war against France, it would have been turned out at the election of
1800 by two votes to one. Had Washington himself, with his transcendent popularity and all the fascination of his name, been a candidate, he
would have undergone the same fate.

The democratic societies, affiliated without number and concate-
nated to an unknown extent, had long been laying their trains to explode
Washington, to sacrifice Adams, and bring in Jefferson. The population in
the southern and western States had increased, and their votes with it to
an astonishing degree. Yet, all these things were unknown to the ruling
majority; or, if partially known, they were not sufficiently considered.
Their self-love deluded them to believe what they wished to be true.
Washington was aware of this, and prudently retreated. But what had he
done before he left the chair? Ellsworth, the firmest pillar of his whole
administration in the Senate, he had promoted to the high office of Chief
Justice of the United States; King, he had sent ambassador to London;
Strong was pleased to resign, as well as Cabot; Hamilton had fled from his
unpopularity to the bar in New York; Ames, to that in Boston; and Murray was ordered by Washington to Holland. The utmost efforts of
Ellsworth, King, and Strong in the Senate had scarcely been sufficient to
hold the head of Washington's administration above water, during the
whole of his eight years.

And how was I elected? By a majority of one, or at most two votes. And
was this a majority strong enough to support a war, especially against

France? Mr. Madison can now scarcely support a war against England, a much more atrocious offender, elected as he was, and supported as he is, by two thirds of the votes. And what was my support in the Senate? Mr. Goodhue, from Massachusetts. Of this man I will say nothing; let the world speak. Mr. Sedgwick, without dignity, never able to win the complacency, or command the attention of his hearers in either house, but ever ready to meet in private caucuses and secret intrigues to oppose me. Mr. Langdon, of New Hampshire, was constant in opposition, as was one from Rhode Island. Had Ellsworth, Strong, and King been there, the world would never have heard of the disgraceful cabals and unconstitutional proceedings of that body.

You say, Sir, that my missions to France, "the great shade in my Presidential escutcheon, paralyzed the public feeling and weakened the foundations of the goodly edifice." I agree, Sir, that they did with that third part of the people, who had been averse to the revolution, and who were then, and always, before and since, governed by English prejudices; and who then, and always, before and since, constantly sighed for a war with France and an alliance with Great Britain; but with none others. The house would have fallen with a much more violent explosion, if those missions to France had not been instituted.

I wish not to fatigue you with too long a letter at once; but, Sir, I will defend my missions to France, as long as I have an eye to direct my hand, or a finger to hold my pen. They were the most disinterested and meritorious actions of my life. I reflect upon them with so much satisfaction, that I desire no other inscription over my gravestone than: "Here lies John Adams, who took upon himself the responsibility of the peace with France in the year 1800."

In the mean time, I recommend to you, Sir, to inquire into the state of the nation at that time, and into the state of Europe, especially France and Great Britain, and the state of our relations with both, and to consider, at the same time, the important question, whether it is our interest to enlist under the banners of either against the other, or to support at all hazards, and at every sacrifice, our independence of all. I am, Sir, with great esteem and sincere affection, your friend.

To James Lloyd

QUINCY, 11 FEBRUARY, 1815.

We are ignorant, as you intimate, of one another. We are ignorant of our own nation; we are ignorant of the geography, the laws, customs, and manners and habits of our own country. Massachusetts, as knowing as any State in the Union, is deplorably ignorant of her sister States, and, what is more to be lamented still, she is ignorant of herself. She is composed of two nations, if not three. One party reads the newspapers and pamphlets of its own church, and interdicts all writings of the opposite complexion. The other party condemns all such as heresy, and will not read or suffer to be read, as far as its influence extends, any thing but its own libels. "The avenue to the public ear is shut" in Massachusetts, as Mr. Randolph says it is in Virginia. With us, the press is under a virtual imprimatur, to such a degree, that I do not believe I could get these letters to you printed in a newspaper in Boston. Each party is deliberately and studiously kept in ignorance of the other. Have naked truth and honest candor a fair hearing or impartial reading in this or any other country? Have not narrow bigotry, the most envious malignity, the most base, vulgar, sordid, fishwoman scurrility, and the most palpable lies, a plenary indulgence, and an unbounded licentiousness? If there is ever to be an amelioration of the condition of mankind, philosophers, theologians, legislators, politicians and moralists will find that the regulation of the press is the most difficult, dangerous, and important problem they have to resolve. Mankind cannot now be governed without it, nor at present with it. Instead of a consolation, it is an aggravation to know that this kind of ignorance is not peculiar to Massachusetts. It is universal. It runs through every State in the Union. It is at least as prevalent in New York, Pennsylvania, and Virginia, as in Massachusetts. Parties in politics, like sects in religion, will not read, indeed they are not permitted by their leaders to read, any thing against their own creed, nor indeed to converse with any but their own club. The Bible is forbidden to the vulgar by all parties.

Let me give an example. Coming down from the Senate chamber, when I was Vice-President, a hawker, at the bottom of the stairs presented to me an octavo volume. Turning to the title-page, I found it was the "American Remembrancer," written by Callender. I knew nothing of the book or its author, gave the pedlar his price, and pocketed the book. Turning over the leaves at home, I found it full of the grossest lies and calumnies against Washington, against myself, and the whole government. I pointed to passages, but the gentlemen of the ruling party would take no notice of them. "They were below contempt." New England is ignorant of this book, but it was circulated in the middle and southern States, and believed as an oracle. No measures were taken to counteract an engine that contributed so essentially to the final prevalence of the southern over the northern interests. "The Prospect before Us" appeared afterwards, but no measures were taken as an antidote to that poison. Not only was ignorance permitted to remain, but error and falsehood to run and be glorified.

If we turn our attention to another subject, we shall see the same ignorance, inadvertency, nonchalance, or apathy in the leaders of the faction, who were for continuing the war. The utmost exertions of all their recruiting officers, with all the influence of Hamilton and Pinckney, reënforced by the magical name of Washington, had not been able to raise one half of their favorite little army. That army was as unpopular, as if it had been a ferocióus wild beast let loose upon the nation to devour it. In newspapers, in pamphlets, and in common conversation they were called cannibals. A thousand anecdotes, true or false, of their licentiousness, were propagated and believed. There was not in the house of representatives a more unbridled tongue or a more licentious vituperatory orator against war, the army, the navy, the administration, and all their measures and men, than Mr. Randolph. He called the army ragamuffins, and was not even called to order. Yet all these things did not remove from the minds of those leaders the ignorance of the faintness of their own influence and the imbecility of their power. No proper measures were taken by means of the press to counteract abuses. Indiscreet and injudicious prosecutions were instituted by some of the law officers of the United States, which did more harm than good; yet these were thought sufficient to suppress all opposition. I pray you to remark, Sir, that I speak of the leaders, of the advocates for continuing the war. The soundest statesmen of the ruling party in both houses approved of my missions to France, and were highly pleased with them, as I will show you hereafter.

Another demonstration of the inattention and inconsideration, if not of the ignorance of those leaders, arose from an unfashionable source of mischief, which I fear *labitur et labetur in omne volubilis ævum*.[13] I mean that stream of misrepresentations of the men and measures of the administration in circular letters from members of Congress to their constituents in the middle and especially in the southern States, which began as early as 1789, when Congress was held in New York, and continued through the eight years of Washington's administration, flowing all the time in peculiarly copious abundance against me, and which, in the electioneering parliamentary campaign of 1796, and from thence to 1801, swelled, raged, foamed in all the fury of a tempest at sea against me. A collection of those circular letters would make many volumes, and contain more lies in proportion to the time than the *Acta Sanctorum*. Yet no measures were taken to raise dikes against this inundation!

Another proof of ignorance may surprise you; I hope it will not offend you. Washington, Hamilton, and Pinckney were assembled at Philadelphia to advise in the selection of officers for the army. The history of the formation of this triumvirate would be as curious as that of Pompey, Cæsar, and Crassus, or that of Antony, Octavius, and Lepidus, and the effects of it have been and may be, for any thing I know, as prosperous or adverse to mankind. One thing I know, that Cicero was not sacrificed to the vengeance of Antony by the unfeeling selfishness of the latter triumvirate more egregiously than John Adams was to the unbridled and unbounded ambition of Alexander Hamilton in the American triumvirate.

Washington, Hamilton, and Pinckney depended for the support of their power and the system of their politics entirely on New York and Penn-

---

[13]["It glides along and will glide along, rolling for all eternity." Horace, *Epistles* I, 2, 43. Ed.]

sylvania. The northern and the southern States were immovably fixed in opposition to each other. If this triumvirate did not know this, they were as ignorant as you and I know, and acknowledge, we all are of each other. Pennsylvania was compounded of Germans, Irish, Quakers, and a few ancient English families, who had been generally attached to the proprietary government. These were the great capital classes. The subdivisions of Roman Catholics, Episcopalians, Presbyterians, Methodists, Anabaptists, Moravians, &c., &c., &c., were infinite. The Quakers were all in principle hostile to war.

To William Tudor

QUINCY, I JUNE, 1817.

That Mr. Hutchinson repented as sincerely as Mr. Hamilton did, I doubt not. I hope the repentance of both has been accepted, and their faults pardoned. And I hope I have repented, do repent, and shall ever repent of mine, and meet them both in another world, where there will need no repentance. Such vicissitudes of fortune command compassion; I pity even Napoleon.

You "never profoundly admired Mr. Hancock. He had vanity and caprice." I can say, with truth, that I profoundly admired him, and more profoundly loved him. If he had vanity and caprice, so had I. And if his vanity and caprice made me sometimes sputter, as you know they often did, mine, I well know, had often a similar effect upon him. But these little flickerings of little passions determine nothing concerning essential characters. I knew Mr. Hancock from his cradle to his grave. He was radically generous and benevolent. He was born in this town, half way between this house and our congregational temple, son of a clergyman of this parish, and grandson of a clergyman of Lexington, both of excellent characters. We were at the same school together, as soon as we were out of petticoats. His father died when he was very young. His uncle, the most opulent merchant in Boston, who had no children, adopted him, placed him in Mr. Lovell's school, educated him at Harvard college, and then took him into his store. And what a school was this! Four large ships constantly plying between

Boston and London, and other business in proportion. This was in 1755. He became an example to all the young men of the town. Wholly devoted to business, he was as regular and punctual at his store as the sun in his course. His uncle sent him to London, from whence, after a residence of about a year, he returned to his store, with the same habits of business, unaltered in manners or deportment, and pursued his employments with the same punctuality and assiduity, till the death of his uncle, who left him his business, his credit, his capital, and his fortune; who did more—he left him the protector of his widow. This lady, though her husband left her a handsome independence, would have sunk into oblivion, like so many other most excellent widows, had not the public attention been fastened upon her by the fame of her nephew. Never was a nephew to an aunt more affectionate, dutiful, or respectful. No alteration appeared in Mr. Hancock, either from his travels in England, or from his accession to the fortune of his uncle. The same steady, regular, punctual, industrious, indefatigable man of business; and, to complete his character with the ladies, always genteelly dressed, according to the fashions of those days.

What shall I say of his fortune, his ships? His commerce was a great one. Your honored father told me, at that time, that not less than a thousand families were, every day in the year, dependent on Mr. Hancock for their daily bread. Consider his real estate in Boston, in the country, in Connecticut, and the rest of New England. Had Mr. Hancock fallen asleep to this day, he would now awake one of the richest men. Had he persevered in business as a private merchant, he might have erected a house of Medicis. Providence, however, did not intend or permit, in this instance, such a calamity to mankind. Mr. Hancock was the delight of the eyes of the whole town. There can be no doubt that he might have had his choice, and he had his choice of a companion; and that choice was very natural, a granddaughter of the great patron and most revered friend of his father. Beauty, politeness, and every domestic virtue justified his predilection.

At the time of this prosperity, I was one day walking in the mall, and, accidentally, met Samuel Adams. In taking a few turns together, we came in full view of Mr. Hancock's house. Mr. Adams, pointing to the stone building, said, "This town has done a wise thing to-day." "What?" "They have made that young man's fortune their own." His prophecy was literally fulfilled; for no man's property was ever more entirely devoted to the public. The town had, that day, chosen Mr. Hancock into the legislature of the province. The quivering anxiety of the public, under the fearful looking for of the vengeance of king, ministry, and parliament, compelled him to a constant attendance in the House; his mind was soon engrossed by public cares, alarms, and terrors; his business was left to subalterns; his private affairs neglected, and continued to be so to the end of his life. If his fortune had not been very large, he must have died as poor as Mr. S. Adams or Mr. Gerry.

I am not writing the life of Mr. Hancock; his biography would fill as many volumes as Marshall's Washington, and be quite as instructive and entertaining. Though I never injured or justly offended him, and though I spent much of my time, and suffered unknown anxiety, in defending his property, reputation, and liberty from persecution, I cannot but reflect upon myself for not paying him more respect than I did in his lifetime. His life will, however, not ever be written. But if statues, obelisks, pyramids, or divine honors were ever merited by men, of cities or nations, James Otis, Samuel Adams, and John Hancock, deserved these from the town of Boston and the United States. Such adulations, however, are monopolized by profligate libellers, by cringing flatterers, by unprincipled ambition, by sordid avarice, by griping usurers, by scheming speculators, by plundering bankers, by blind enthusiasts, by superstitions bigots, by puppies and butterflies, and by every thing but honor and virtue. Hence the universal slavery of the human species. Hence a commentary on the well known and most expressive figure of rhetoric, "It grieved the Almighty, at his heart, that he had made man." Nevertheless, this is a good world, and I thank the Almighty that he has made man.

Mr. Hancock had a delicate constitution. He was very infirm; a great part of his life was passed in acute pain. He inherited from his father, though one of the most amiable and beloved of men, a certain sensibility, a keenness of feeling, or, in more familiar language, a peevishness of temper, that sometimes disgusted and afflicted his friends. Yet it was astonishing with what patience, perseverance, and punctuality he attended to business to the last. Nor were his talents or attainments inconsiderable.

They were far superior to many who have been much more celebrated. He had a great deal of political sagacity and penetration into men. He was by no means a contemptible scholar or orator. Compared with Washington, Lincoln, or Knox, he was learned. So much, for the present, of Mr. Hancock.

When, in the beginning of this letter, I agreed with you in your opinion of Mr. Hutchinson's repentance, I should have added, he had great reason for repentance. Fled, in his old age, from the detestation of a country, where he had been beloved, esteemed, and admired, and applauded with exaggeration—in short, where he had been every thing, from his infancy—to a country where he was nothing; pinched by a pension, which, though ample in Boston, would barely keep a house in London; throwing round his baleful eyes on the exiled companions of his folly; hearing daily of the slaughter of his countrymen and conflagration of their cities; abhorred by the greatest men, and soundest part of the nation, and neglected, if not despised, by the rest, hardened as had been my heart against him, I assure you I was melted at the accounts I heard of his condition. Lord Townsend told me that he put an end to his own life. Though I did not believe this, I know he was ridiculed by the courtiers. They laughed at his manners at the levee, at his perpetual quotation of his brother Foster, searching his pockets for letters to read to the king, and the king turning away from him with his head up, &c.

A few words concerning S. Adams in my next.

To William Tudor.

QUINCY, 5 JUNE, 1817.

You "never profoundly admired Mr. Hancock." I have suggested some hints in his favor. You "never profoundly admired Mr. Samuel Adams." I have promised you an apology for him. You may think it a weak one, for I have no talent at panegyric or apology. "There are all sorts of men in the world." This observation, you may say, is self-evident and futile; yet Mr. Locke thought it not unworthy of him to make it, and, if we reflect upon it, there is more meaning in it than meets the eye at the first blush.

You say, Mr. S. Adams "had too much sternness and pious bigotry." A man in his situation and circumstances must possess a large fund of sternness of stuff, or he will soon be annihilated. His piety ought not to be objected to him, or any other man. His bigotry, if he had any, was a fault; but he certainly had not more than Governor Hutchinson and Secretary Oliver, who, I know from personal conversation, were as stanch Trinitarians and Calvinists as he was, and treated all Arians and Arminians with more contempt and scorn than he ever did. Mr. Adams lived and conversed freely with all sectarians, in philosophy and divinity. He never imposed his creed on any one, or endeavored to make proselytes to his religious opinions. He was as far from sentencing any man to perdition, who differed from him, as Mr. Holley, Dr. Kirkland, or Dr. Freeman. If he was a Calvinist, a Calvinist he had been educated, and so had been all his ancestors for two hundred years. He had been, from his childhood, too much devoted to politics to be a profound student in metaphysics and theology, or to make extensive researches or deep investigations into such subjects. Nor had any other man attempted it, in this nation, in that age, if any one has attempted it since. Mr. Adams was an original—*sui generis, sui juris.* The variety of human characters is infinite. Nature seems to delight in showing the inexhaustibility of her resources. There never were two men alike, from the first man to the last, any more than two pebbles or two peas.

Mr. Adams was born and tempered a wedge of steel to split the knot of *lignum vitæ,* which tied North America to Great Britain. Blunderheaded as were the British ministry, they had sagacity enough to discriminate from all others, for inexorable vengeance, the two men most to be dreaded by them, Samuel Adams and John Hancock; and had not James Otis been then dead, or worse than dead, his name would have been at the head of the TRIUMVIRATE.

...

James Otis, Samuel Adams, and John Hancock were the three most essential characters; and Great Britain knew it, though America does not. Great and important and excellent characters, aroused and excited by these, arose in Pennsylvania, Virginia, New York, South Carolina, and in all the other States; but these three were the first movers, the most

constant, steady, persevering springs, agents, and most disinterested sufferers and firmest pillars of the whole Revolution. I shall not attempt even to
draw the outlines of the biography of Mr. Samuel Adams. Who can
attempt it?

*"Quæ ante conditam condendamve urbem, poëticis magis decora fabulis, quam
incorruptis rerum gestarum monumentis traduntur, ea"*[14] *nec possum refellere. Quia
non tempus, nec oculos, nec manus habeo.* But, if I had time, eyes, and fingers at
my command, where should I find documents and memorials? Without
the character of Samuel Adams, the true history of the American Revolution can never be written. For fifty years, his pen, his tongue, his activity,
were constantly exerted for his country without fee or reward. During
that time, he was an almost incessant writer. But where are his writings?
Who can collect them? And, if collected, who will ever read them? The letters he wrote and received, where are they? I have seen him, at Mrs. Yard's
in Philadelphia, when he was about to leave Congress, cut up with his
scissors whole bundles of letters into atoms that could never be reunited,
and throw them out of the window, to be scattered by the winds. This was
in summer, when he had no fire; in winter he threw whole handfuls into
the fire. As we were on terms of perfect intimacy, I have joked him, perhaps rudely, upon his anxious caution. His answer was, "Whatever becomes
of me, my friends shall never suffer by my negligence." This may be thought
a less significant anecdote than another. Mr. Adams left the letters he had
received and preserved in possession of his widow. This lady, as was natural, lent them to a confidential friend of her husband, Mr. Avery, who then
was, and had been secretary of the commonwealth under the administration of Mr. Adams and Mr. Hancock. Mr. Avery informed me, that he "had
them, and that they were a complete history of the Revolution." I will

---

[14]Livy finishes the sentence thus, *nec affirmare nec refellere, in animo est.* The addition in
the text is by the writer. [Livy I, Pref. vi. ends, therefore, as follows: "I intend neither to
affirm nor to refute." Adams's whole passage may be rendered: "The pretty stories about
what happened before the city was founded, or was near to be being founded, have
been handed down more by the fables of the poets than by the uncorrupted records of
history, nor can I refute them. Because I have neither the time, nor the eyes, nor the
hands." The idea is that he would need his eyes to read and his hands to write. Ed.]

not say into whose hands they fell, after Mr. Avery's death, and I cannot say where they are now; but I have heard that a gentleman in Charlestown, Mr. Austin, undertook to write the life of Mr. Adams; but, finding his papers had been so garbled that the truth could not be discovered, he abandoned his design. Never will those letters, which Secretary Avery possessed, be brought together again; nor will they ever be found. So much for Mr. Adams, at present. Now for Mr. Otis.

I write no biographies or biographical sketches; I give only hints. James Otis was descended from our most ancient families. His education was the best his country afforded. He was bred to the bar under Mr. Gridley, the greatest lawyer and the greatest classic scholar I ever knew at any bar. His application was incessant and indefatigable. Justice Richard Dana has often told me, that the apartment in which Otis studied, when a pupil and a clerk of Mr. Gridley, was near his house; that he had watched him from day to day, and that he had never known a student in law so punctual, so steady, so constant and persevering. Accordingly, as soon as he was admitted to the bar, he became a conspicuous figure. And among whom? Gridley, Pratt, Trowbridge; and he was much admired, and as much celebrated as any of them. His generous, manly, noble character, as a private gentleman, his uncommon attainments in literature, especially in the law, and his nervous, commanding eloquence at the bar, were everywhere spoken of. The government soon discerned his superiority, and commissioned him Advocate-General. He married a lady, who, in that day, was esteemed a fortune. From 1755 to 1758, I heard my master, Colonel James Putnam, of Worcester, who was a critical judge, and Mr. Trowbridge, the then Attorney-General, and his lady, constantly speaking of Otis as the greatest, the most learned, the most manly, and most honest young man of his age. All this was before I had ever seen Mr. Otis. I never saw him till late in the autumn of 1758, nor Mr. Samuel Adams till after that year.

To sum up in a few words, the two young men, whom I have known to enter the stage of life with the most luminous, unclouded prospects, and the best founded hopes, were James Otis and John Hancock. They were both essential to the Revolution, and both fell sacrifices to it. Mr. Otis, from 1760 to 1770, had correspondences in this province, in New

England, in the middle and southern colonies, in England, and in Scotland. What has become of these letters and answers?

Mr. Otis, soon after my earliest acquaintance with him, lent me a summary of Greek Prosody of his own collection and composition, a work
of profound learning and great labor. I had it six months in my possession,
before I returned it. Since my return from Europe, I asked his daughter
whether she had found that work among her father's manuscripts. She
answered me with a countenance of woe that you may more easily imagine than I can describe, that she "had not a line from her father's pen; that
he had spent much time, and taken great pains, to collect together all his
letters and other papers, and, in one of his unhappy moments, committed
them all to the flames." I have used her own expressions.

Such has been the fate of the memorials of Mr. James Otis and Mr.
Samuel Adams. It was not without reason, then, that I wrote to Mr. Niles,
of Baltimore, that the true history of the American Revolution is lost
forever. I could write volumes of other proofs of the same truth, before,
during, and since the Revolution. But *cui bono?* They would be read by
very few, and by very few of those few would be credited, and, by this
minimum of a few, would be imputed to the vanity, egotism, ill humor,
envy, jealousy, and disappointed ambition of your sincere friend, John
Adams; for the character of this nation is strangely altered.

To James Madison

QUINCY, 17 JUNE, 1817.

Accept my thanks for your favor of last month. The safe arrival of your
books has quieted my conscience.

There is nothing within the narrow compass of human knowledge
more interesting than the subject of your letter. If the idea of a government in one centre seems to be everywhere "exploded," perhaps something remains undefined, as dangerous, as plausible, and pernicious as that
idea. Half a million of people in England have petitioned Parliament for
annual parliaments and universal suffrage. Parliament is unanimous against
them. What is this state of things short of a declaration of war between

the government and people? And is not this the picture of all Europe? Sovereigns, who modestly call themselves legitimate, are conspiring, in holy and unhallowed leagues, against the progress of human knowledge and human liberty.

War seems on the point of breaking out between government and people. Were the latter united, the question would be soon decided; but they are everywhere divided into innumerable sects, whereas the former are united, and have all the artillery and bayonets in their hands; and what is most melancholy of all, an appeal to arms almost always results in an exchange of one military tyranny for another.

The questions concerning universal suffrage, and those concerning the necessary limitations of the power of suffrage, are among the most difficult. It is hard to say that every man has not an equal right; but, admit this equal right and equal power, and an immediate revolution would ensue. In all the nations of Europe, the number of persons, who have not a penny, is double those who have a groat; admit all these to an equality of power, and you would soon see how the groats would be divided. Yet, in a few days, the party of the pennies and the party of the groats would be found to exist again, and a new revolution and a new division must ensue.

If there is anywhere an exception from this reasoning, it is in America; nevertheless, there is in these United States a majority of persons, who have no property, over those who have any. I know of nothing more desirable in society than the abolition of all hereditary distinctions. But is not distinction among voters as arbitrary and aristocratical as hereditary distinctions? You will remember that, between thirty and forty years ago, the Irish patriots asked advice of the Duke of Richmond, Dr. Price, Dr. Jebb, &c. These three great statesmen, divines, and philosophers, solemnly advised a universal suffrage. Tracy, in his review of Montesquieu, adopts this principle in its largest extent. A party among mankind, countenanced, at this day, by such numbers and such names, is not to be despised, neglected, nor easily overborne.

There is nothing more irrational, absurd, or ridiculous in the sight of philosophy than the idea of hereditary kings and nobles; yet all the nations of the earth, civilized, savage, and brutal, have adopted them. Whence this universal and irresistible propensity? How shall it be controlled, restrained, corrected, modified, or managed? A government, a mixed government, may be so organized, I hope, as to preserve the liberty, equality, and fraternity of the people without any hereditary ingredient in its composition. Our nation has attempted it, and, if any people can accomplish it, it must be this; and may God Almighty prosper and bless them!

I have seen the efforts of the people in France, Holland, and England. You have read them in all Europe. We both know the result. What is to come, we know not.

My personal interest in such disquisitions can last but a few hours; but, still, *homo sum,* and *homo* I shall be.[15]

May you live to a greater age than mine, and be able to die with brighter prospects for your species than can fall to the lot of your friend.

To H. Niles

QUINCY, 13 FEBRUARY, 1816.

The American Revolution was not a common event. Its effects and consequences have already been awful over a great part of the globe. And when and where are they to cease?

But what do we mean by the American Revolution? Do we mean the American war? The Revolution was effected before the war commenced. The Revolution was in the minds and hearts of the people; a change in their religious sentiments of their duties and obligations. While the king, and all in authority under him, were believed to govern in justice and mercy, according to the laws and constitution derived to them from the God of nature and transmitted to them by their ancestors, they thought themselves bound to pray for the king and queen and all the royal family, and all in authority under them, as ministers ordained of God for their

[15]["I am a human being." The full quotation is *homo sum: humani nihil a me alienum puto:* "I am a human being, and consider nothing human (to be) alien to me." Terence, *The Self-Tormentor* 77. Ed.]

good; but when they saw those powers renouncing all the principles of authority, and bent upon the destruction of all the securities of their lives, liberties, and properties, they thought it their duty to pray for the continental congress and all the thirteen State congresses, &c.

There might be, and there were others who thought less about religion and conscience, but had certain habitual sentiments of allegiance and loyalty derived from their education; but believing allegiance and protection to be reciprocal, when protection was withdrawn, they thought allegiance was dissolved.

Another alteration was common to all. The people of America had been educated in an habitual affection for England, as their mother country; and while they thought her a kind and tender parent, (erroneously enough, however, for she never was such a mother,) no affection could be more sincere. But when they found her a cruel beldam, willing like Lady Macbeth, to "dash their brains out," it is no wonder if their filial affections ceased, and were changed into indignation and horror.

This radical change in the principles, opinions, sentiments, and affections of the people, was the real American Revolution.

By what means this great and important alteration in the religious, moral, political, and social character of the people of thirteen colonies, all distinct, unconnected, and independent of each other, was begun, pursued, and accomplished, it is surely interesting to humanity to investigate, and perpetuate to posterity.

To this end, it is greatly to be desired, that young men of letters in all the States, especially in the thirteen original States, would undertake the laborious, but certainly interesting and amusing task, of searching and collecting all the records, pamphlets, newspapers, and even handbills, which in any way contributed to change the temper and views of the people, and compose them into an independent nation.

The colonies had grown up under constitutions of government so different, there was so great a variety of religions, they were composed of so many different nations, their customs, manners, and habits had so little resemblance, and their intercourse had been so rare, and their knowledge of each other so imperfect, that to unite them in the same principles in theory and the same system of action, was certainly a very difficult enterprise. The complete accomplishment of it, in so short a time and by such simple means, was perhaps a singular example in the history of mankind. Thirteen clocks were made to strike together—a perfection of mechanism, which no artist had ever before effected.

In this research, the gloriole of individual gentlemen, and of separate States, is of little consequence. The *means and the measures* are the proper objects of investigation. These may be of use to posterity, not only in this nation, but in South America and all other countries. They may teach mankind that revolutions are no trifles; that they ought never to be undertaken rashly; nor without deliberate consideration and sober reflection; nor without a solid, immutable, eternal foundation of justice and humanity; nor without a people possessed of intelligence, fortitude, and integrity sufficient to carry them with steadiness, patience, and perseverance, through all the vicissitudes of fortune, the fiery trials and melancholy disasters they may have to encounter.

The town of Boston early instituted an annual oration on the 4th of July, in commemoration of the principles and feelings which contributed to produce the revolution. Many of those orations I have heard, and all that I could obtain, I have read. Much ingenuity and eloquence appears upon every subject, except those principles and feelings. That of my honest and amiable neighbor, Josiah Quincy, appeared to me the most directly to the purpose of the institution. Those principles and feelings ought to be traced back for two hundred years, and sought in the history of the country from the first plantations in America. Nor should the principles and feelings of the English and Scotch towards the colonies, through that whole period, ever be forgotten. The perpetual discordance between British principles and feelings and of those of America, the next year after the suppression of the French power in America, came to a crisis, and produced an explosion.

It was not until after the annihilation of the French dominion in America that any British ministry had dared to gratify their own wishes, and the desire of the nation, by projecting a formal plan for raising a national revenue from America, by parliamentary taxation. The first great mani-

704   THE POLITICAL WRITINGS OF JOHN ADAMS

festation of this design was by the order to carry into strict executions those acts of parliament, which were well known by the appellation of the *acts of trade,* which had lain a dead letter, unexecuted for half a century, and some of them, I believe, for nearly a whole one.

This produced, in 1760 and 1761, an awakening and a revival of American principles and feelings, with an enthusiasm which went on increasing till, in 1775, it burst out in open violence, hostility, and fury.

The characters the most conspicuous, the most ardent and influential in this revival, from 1760 to 1766, were, first and foremost, before all and above all, James Otis; next to him was Oxenbridge Thacher; next to him, Samuel Adams; next to him, John Hancock; then Dr. Mayhew; then Dr. Cooper and his brother. Of Mr. Hancock's life, character, generous nature, great and disinterested sacrifices, and important services, if I had forces, I should be glad to write a volume. But this, I hope, will be done by some younger and abler hand. Mr. Thacher, because his name and merits are less known, must not be wholly omitted. This gentleman was an eminent barrister at law, in as large practice as any one in Boston. There was not a citizen of that town more universally beloved for his learning, ingenuity, every domestic and social virtue, and conscientious conduct in every relation of life. His patriotism was as ardent as his progenitors had been ancient and illustrious in this country. Hutchinson often said, "Thacher was not born a plebeian, but he was determined to die one." In May, 1763, I believe, he was chosen by the town of Boston one of their representatives in the legislature, a colleague with Mr. Otis, who had been a member from May, 1761, and he continued to be reëlected annually till his death in 1765, when Mr. Samuel Adams was elected to fill his place, in the absence of Mr. Otis, then attending the Congress at New York. Thacher had long been jealous of the unbounded ambition of Mr. Hutchinson, but when he found him not content with the office of Lieutenant-Governor, the command of the castle and its emoluments, of Judge of Probate for the county of Suffolk, a seat in his Majesty's Council in the Legislature, his brother-in-law Secretary of State by the king's commission, a brother of that Secretary of State, a Judge of the Supreme Court and a member of Council, now in 1760 and 1761, soliciting and accepting the office of Chief Justice of the Superior Court of Judicature, he concluded, as Mr. Otis did, and as every other enlightened friend of his country did, that he sought that office with the determined purpose of determining all causes in favor of the ministry at St. James's, and their servile parliament.

His indignation against him henceforward, to 1765, when he died, knew no bounds but truth. I speak from personal knowledge. For, from 1758 to 1765, I attended every superior and inferior court in Boston, and recollect not one, in which he did not invite me home to spend evenings with him, when he made me converse with him as well as I could, on all subjects of religion, morals, law, politics, history, philosophy, belles lettres, theology, mythology, cosmogony, metaphysics,—Locke, Clark, Leibnitz, Bolingbroke, Berkeley,—the preëstablished harmony of the universe, the nature of matter and of spirit, and the eternal establishment of coincidences between their operations; fate, foreknowledge absolute; and we reasoned on such unfathomable subjects as high as Milton's gentry in pandemonium; and we understood them as well as they did, and no better. To such mighty mysteries he added the news of the day, and the tittle-tattle of the town. But his favorite subject was politics, and the impending, threatening system of parliamentary taxation and universal government over the colonies. On this subject he was so anxious and agitated that I have no doubt it occasioned his premature death. From the time when he argued the question of writs of assistance to his death, he considered the king, ministry, parliament, and nation of Great Britain as determined to new-model the colonies from the foundation, to annul all their charters, to constitute them all royal governments, to raise a revenue in America by parliamentary taxation, to apply that revenue to pay the salaries of governors, judges, and all other crown officers; and, after all this, to raise as large a revenue as they pleased, to be applied to national purposes at the exchequer in England; and further, to establish bishops and the whole system of the Church of England, tithes and all, throughout all British America. This system, he said, if it was suffered to prevail, would extinguish the flame of liberty all over the world; that America would be employed as an engine to batter down all the miserable remains of liberty in Great Britain and Ireland, where only any semblance of it was left in the world. To this system he considered Hutchinson, the Olivers, and all their

connections, dependents, adherents, shoelickers, &c., entirely devoted. He
asserted that they were all engaged with all the crown officers in America
and the understrappers of the ministry in England, in a deep and treasonable
conspiracy to betray the liberties of their country, for their own private,
personal, and family aggrandizement. His philippics against the unprincipled
ambition and avarice of all of them, but especially of Hutchinson, were
unbridled; not only in private, confidential conversations, but in all companies and on all occasions. He gave Hutchinson the sobriquet of "Summa
Potestatis,"[16] and rarely mentioned him but by the name of "Summa." His
liberties of speech were no secrets to his enemies. I have sometimes wondered that they did not throw him over the bar, as they did soon afterwards
Major Hawley. For they hated him worse than they did James Otis or
Samuel Adams, and they feared him more, because they had no revenge for
a father's disappointment of a seat on the superior bench to impute to him,
as they did to Otis; and Thacher's character through life had been so modest, decent, unassuming; his morals so pure, and his religion so venerated, that
they dared not attack him. In his office were educated to the bar two eminent characters, the late Judge Lowell and Josiah Quincy, aptly called the
Boston Cicero. Mr. Thacher's frame was slender, his constitution delicate;
whether his physicians overstrained his vessels with mercury, when he had
the smallpox by inoculation at the castle, or whether he was overplied by
public anxieties and exertions, the smallpox left him in a decline from which
he never recovered. Not long before his death he sent for me to commit to
my care some of his business at the bar. I asked him whether he had seen the
Virginia resolves: "Oh yes—they are men! they are noble spirits! It kills me
to think of the lethargy and stupidity that prevails here. I long to be out. I
will go out. I will go out. I will go into court, and make a speech, which shall
be read after my death, as my dying testimony against this infernal tyranny
which they are bringing upon us." Seeing the violent agitation into which
it threw him, I changed the subject as soon as possible, and retired. He had
been confined for some time. Had he been abroad among the people, he
would not have complained so pathetically of the "lethargy and stupidity

[16]["the height of power" Ed.]

that prevailed;" for town and country were all alive, and in August became active enough; and some of the people proceeded to unwarrantable excesses, which were more lamented by the patriots than by their enemies. Mr. Thacher soon died, deeply lamented by all the friends of their country.

Another gentleman, who had great influence in the commencement of the Revolution, was Doctor Jonathan Mayhew, a descendant of the ancient governor of Martha's Vineyard. This divine had raised a great reputation both in Europe and America, by the publication of a volume of seven sermons in the reign of King George the Second, 1749, and by many other writings, particularly a sermon in 1750, on the 30th of January, on the subject of passive obedience and non-resistance, in which the saintship and martyrdom of King Charles the First are considered, seasoned with wit and satire superior to any in Swift or Franklin. It was read by everybody; celebrated by friends, and abused by enemies. During the reigns of King George the First and King George the Second, the reigns of the Stuarts, the two Jameses and the two Charleses were in general disgrace in England. In America they had always been held in abhorrence. The persecutions and cruelties suffered by their ancestors under those reigns, had been transmitted by history and tradition, and Mayhew seemed to be raised up to revive all their animosities against tyranny, in church and state, and at the same time to destroy their bigotry, fanaticism, and inconsistency. David Hume's plausible, elegant, fascinating, and fallacious apology, in which he varnished over the crimes of the Stuarts, had not then appeared. To draw the character of Mayhew, would be to transcribe a dozen volumes. This transcendent genius threw all the weight of his great fame into the scale of his country in 1761, and maintained it there with zeal and ardor till his death, in 1766. In 1763 appeared the controversy between him and Mr. Apthorp, Mr. Caner, Dr. Johnson, and Archbishop Secker, on the charter and conduct of the Society for Propagating the Gospel in Foreign Parts. To form a judgment of this debate, I beg leave to refer to a review of the whole, printed at the time and written by Samuel Adams, though by some, very absurdly and erroneously, ascribed to Mr. Apthorp. If I am not mistaken, it will be found a model of candor, sagacity, impartiality, and close, correct reasoning.

If any gentleman supposes this controversy to be nothing to the present purpose, he is grossly mistaken. It spread an universal alarm against the authority of Parliament. It excited a general and just apprehension, that bishops, and dioceses, and churches, and priests, and tithes, were to be imposed on us by Parliament. It was known that neither king, nor ministry, nor archbishops, could appoint bishops in America, without an act of Parliament; and if Parliament could tax us, they could establish the Church of England, with all its creeds, articles, tests, ceremonies, and tithes, and prohibit all other churches, as conventicles and schism shops.

Nor must Mr. Cushing be forgotten. His good sense and sound judgment, the urbanity of his manners, his universal good character, his numerous friends and connections, and his continual intercourse with all sorts of people, added to his constant attachment to the liberties of his country, gave him a great and salutary influence from the beginning in 1760.

Let me recommend these hints to the consideration of Mr. Wirt, whose Life of Mr. Henry I have read with great delight. I think that, after mature investigation, he will be convinced that Mr. Henry did not "give the first impulse to the ball of independence," and that Otis, Thacher, Samuel Adams, Mayhew, Hancock, Cushing, and thousands of others, were laboring for several years at the wheel before the name of Henry was heard beyond the limits of Virginia.

To William Tudor

QUINCY, 23 SEPTEMBER, 1818.

If, in our search of principles, we have not been able to investigate any moral, philosophical, or rational foundation for any claim of dominion or property in America, in the English nation, their Parliament, or even in their king; if the whole appears a mere usurpation of fiction, fancy, and superstition, what was the right to dominion or property in the native Indians?

Shall we say that a few handfuls of scattering tribes of savages have a right of dominion and property over a quarter of this globe capable of nourishing hundreds of millions of happy human beings? Why had not Europeans a right to come and hunt and fish with them?

The Indians had a right to life, liberty, and property in common with all men; but what right to dominion or property beyond these? Every Indian had a right to his wigwam, his armor, his utensils; when he had burned the woods about him, and planted his corn and beans, his squashes and pompions, all these were his undoubted right; but will you infer from this, that he had right of exclusive dominion and property over immense regions of uncultivated wilderness that he never saw, that he might have the exclusive privilege of hunting and fishing in them, which he himself never expected or hoped to enjoy?

These reflections appear to have occurred to our ancestors, and their general conduct was regulated by them. They do not seem to have had any confidence in their charter, as conveying any right, except against the king who signed it. They considered the right to be in the native Indians. And, in truth, all the right there was in the case lay there. They accordingly respected the Indian wigwams and poor plantations, their clam-banks and muscle-banks and oyster-banks, and all their property.

Property in land, antecedent to civil society, or the social compact, seems to have been confined to actual possession and power of commanding it. It is the creature of convention, of social laws and artificial order. Our ancestors, however, did not amuse, nor puzzle themselves with these refinements. They considered the Indians as having rights; and they entered into negotiations with them, purchased and paid for their rights and claims, whatever they were, and procured deeds, grants, and quitclaims of all their lands, leaving them their habitations, arms, utensils, fishings, huntings, and plantations. There is scarcely a litigation at law concerning a title to land that may not be traced to an Indian deed. I have in my possession, somewhere, a parchment copy of a deed of Massasoit,[17] of the township of Braintree incorporated by the legislature in one thousand six hundred and thirty-nine. And this was the general practice through the country, and has been to this day through

[17] Slight inaccuracies occur here. The deed is a deed of release, in 1665, from Wampatuck, the son of Chickatabut, deceased, of all lands in Braintree, with certain exceptions therein named, granted by his predecessors. The township was incorporated in 1640.

the continent. In short, I see not how the Indians could have been treated with more equity or humanity than they have been in general in North America. The histories of Indian wars have not been sufficiently regarded.

When Mr. Hutchinson's History of Massachusetts Bay first appeared, one of the most common criticisms upon it was the slight, cold, and unfeeling manner in which he passed over the Indian wars. I have heard gentlemen the best informed in the history of the country say, "he had no sympathy for the sufferings of his ancestors. Otherwise he could not have winked out of sight one of the most important, most affecting, afflicting, and distressing branches of the history of his country."

There is somewhere in existence, as I hope and believe, a manuscript history of Indian wars, written by the Reverend Samuel Niles, of Braintree. Almost sixty years ago, I was an humble acquaintance of this venerable clergyman, then, as I believe, more than fourscore years of age. He asked me many questions, and informed me, in his own house, that he was endeavoring to recollect and commit to writing a history of Indian wars, in his own time, and before it, as far as he could collect information. This history he completed and prepared for the press; but no printer would undertake it, or venture to propose a subscription for its publication. Since my return from Europe, I inquired of his oldest son, the Honorable Samuel Niles, of Braintree, on a visit he made me at my own house, what was become of that manuscript. He laughed, and said it was still safe in the till of a certain trunk; but no encouragement had ever appeared for its publication. Ye liberal Christians! Laugh not at me, nor frown upon me, for thus reviving the memory of your once formidable enemy. I was then no more of a disciple of his theological science than ye are now. But I then revered and still revere the honest, virtuous, and pious man. *Fas est et ab hoste doceri.*[18] And his memorial of facts might be of great value to this country.[19]

What infinite pains have been taken and expenses incurred in treaties, presents, stipulated sums of money, instruments of agriculture, education,

---

[18]["It is permissible to learn even from an enemy." Ovid, *Metamorphoses* IV, 428. Ed.]

[19] A part of this history has been published by the Historical Society of Massachusetts, in their Transactions, vol. vi. of the third series.

what dangerous and unwearied labors, to convert these poor, ignorant savages to Christianity! And, alas! with how little success! The Indians are as bigoted to their religion as the Mahometans are to their Koran, the Hindoos to their Shaster, the Chinese to Confucius, the Romans to their saints and angels, or the Jews to Moses and the Prophets. It is a principle of religion, at bottom, which inspires the Indians with such an invincible aversion both to civilization and Christianity. The same principle has excited their perpetual hostilities against the colonists and the independent Americans.

If the English nation, their Parliaments, and all their kings, have appeared to be totally ignorant of all these things, or at least to have vouchsafed no consideration upon them; if we, good, patriotic Americans, have forgotten them, Mr. Otis had not. He enlarged on the merits of our ancestors in undertaking so perilous, arduous, and almost desperate an enterprise, in disforesting bare creation, in conciliating and necessarily contending with Indian natives, in purchasing rather than conquering a quarter of the globe at their own expense, at the sweat of their own brows, at the hazard and sacrifice of their own lives, without the smallest aid, assistance, or comfort from the government of England, or from England itself as a nation; on the contrary, constant jealousy, envy, intrigue against their charter, their religion, and all their privileges. Land, the pious tyrant, dreaded them, as if he foresaw they would overthrow his religion.

Mr. Otis reproached the nation, parliaments, and kings, with injustice, ungenerosity, ingratitude, cruelty, and perfidy in all their conduct towards this country, in a style of oratory that I never heard equalled in this or any other country.

Note
on the
Editors

GEORGE W. CAREY

GEORGE W. CAREY is professor of government at Georgetown University, where he has taught American political theory for over thirty years. His major works include *The Basic Symbols of the American Political Tradition* (with Willmoore Kendall), recently reissued by Catholic University Press with a new introduction; *The Federalist: Design for a Constitutional Republic*; and *In Defense of the Constitution*. For the past twenty-seven years he has edited *The Political Science Reviewer*, an annual journal devoted to article length reviews of leading classic and contemporary works in politics.

CHRISTOPHER B. BRIGGS

Conservative Leadership Series editor Christopher B. Briggs holds degrees from Bowdoin College and The Catholic University of America. Currently senior book editor at the Intercollegiate Studies Institute, he is also assistant editor of *Humanitas*, a journal of the humanities published in Washington, D.C.